Business Communication Essentials

CANADIAN EDITION

Courtland L. Bovée
Professor of Business Communication
C. Allen Paul Distinguished Chair
Grossmont College

John V. Thill
Chief Executive Officer
Communication Specialists of America

Barbara E. Schatzman
Keller Graduate School of Management
President
Summit One Global Business Solutions

Jean A. Scribner
British Columbia Institute of Technology
Partner
The Communication Works

Toronto

National Library of Canada Cataloguing in Publication

Business communication essentials / Courtland L. Bovée ... [et al.]. — Canadian ed.

ISBN 0-13-123277-0
Business communication. I. Bovée, Courtland L.
HF5718.B96 2005 651.7 C2003-905954-5

Canadian Edition, adapted by Jean Scribner
Original edition published by Pearson Education, Inc.
Upper Saddle River, New Jersey, USA. This edition is authorized for sale in Canada only.

ISBN 0-13-123277-0

Vice President, Editorial Director: Michael J. Young
Executive Editor: Dave Ward
Developmental Editor: Jennifer Murray
Director of Marketing: Bill Todd
Production Editor: Judith Scott
Copy Editor: Susan Broadhurst
Production Manager: Wendy Moran
Page Layout: Janet Zanette
Creative Director: Julia Hall
Cover and Interior Design: The Art Plus Group
Cover Image: The Stock Illustration Source/Chad J. Shaffer

Statistics Canada information is used with the permission of the Minister of Industry, as Minister responsible for Statistics Canada. Information on the availability of the wide range of data from Statistics Canada can be obtained from Statistics Canada's Regional Offices, its World Wide Web site at http://www.statcan.ca, and its toll-free access number 1-800-263-1136.

Credits and acknowledgements borrowed from other sources and reproduced, with permission, in this textbook appear on page R-1 and AC-1.

2 3 4 5 09 08 07 06 05

Printed and bound in the United States of America.

Contents in Brief

Unit 1: Business Communication Foundations

Chapter 1 Understanding Business Communication in Today's Workplace 1
Chapter 2 Communicating in Teams: Listening, Nonverbal, and Meeting Skills 21

Unit 2: The Three-Step Writing Process

Chapter 3 Planning Business Messages 42
Chapter 4 Writing Business Messages 67
Chapter 5 Completing Business Messages 93

Unit 3: Brief Business Correspondence

Chapter 6 Working with Letters, Memos, and E-mail Messages 121
Chapter 7 Writing Routine, Good-News, and Goodwill Messages 148
Chapter 8 Writing Bad-News Messages 181
Chapter 9 Writing Persuasive Messages 217

Unit 4: Composing Business Reports, Proposals, and Presentations

Chapter 10 Understanding and Planning Business Reports and Proposals 245
Chapter 11 Writing and Completing Business Reports and Proposals 276
Chapter 12 Planning, Writing, and Delivering Oral Presentations 324

Unit 5: Employment Messages

Chapter 13 Searching for Employment and Preparing Employment Messages 352
Chapter 14 Interviewing for Employment and Following Up 392

Appendix A Format and Layout of Business Documents A-1
Appendix B Documentation of Report Sources A-19
Appendix C Correction Symbols A-25

Handbook of Grammar, Mechanics, and Usage H-1
Answer Key to the Level 1 Self-Assessment Exercises AK-1
References R-1
Acknowledgements AC-1
Index I-1

Contents

Unit 1: Business Communication Foundations 1

Chapter 1 Understanding Business Communication in Today's Workplace 1

Succeeding Through Effective Communication 2
Adapting to the Changing Workplace 2
Understanding the Communication Process 3
Improving Business Communication 3
Committing to Ethical Communication 4
Adopting an Audience-Centred Approach 5
Improving Your Intercultural Sensitivity 6
Improving Your Workplace Sensitivity 10
Reviewing Key Points 11
Test Your Knowledge 11
Apply Your Knowledge 12
Practise Your Knowledge 13
Expand Your Knowledge 15
Learn Interactively 16
Improve Your Grammar, Mechanics, and Usage 16
Business Communication Notebook 20

Chapter 2 Communicating in Teams: Listening, Nonverbal, and Meeting Skills 21

Working in Teams 21
Preparing, Conducting, and Attending Meetings 22
Preparing for Team Meetings 22
Conducting and Attending Meetings 24
Following Up 24
Listening to Others 25
The Listening Process 25
Obstacles to Effective Listening 25
Strategies for Effective Listening 26
Using Telephones and Voice Mail 27
Receiving Telephone Calls Effectively 27
Making Effective Telephone Calls 28
Using Voice Mail Effectively 28
Understanding Nonverbal Communication 30
The Importance of Nonverbal Communication 30
The Types of Nonverbal Communication 30
Ways to Improve Your Nonverbal Communication 31
Reviewing Key Points 32
Test Your Knowledge 32
Apply Your Knowledge 33
Practise Your Knowledge 34

Expand Your Knowledge 36
Learn Interactively 37
Improve Your Grammar, Mechanics, and Usage 37
Business Communication Notebook 41

Unit 2: The Three-Step Writing Process 42

Chapter 3 Planning Business Messages 42

Creating Audience-Centred Messages 42
What Is the Three-Step Process? 43
How Does the Three-Step Process Work? 43
Analyzing the Situation and Identifying Your Audience 43
Define Your Purpose 44
Develop an Audience Profile 44
Investigating the Topic 46
Adapting Your Message to Your Audience and Purpose 46
Select the Best Channel and Medium 46
Establish a Good Relationship with Your Audience 48
Reviewing Key Points 52
Test Your Knowledge 52
Apply Your Knowledge 54
Practise Your Knowledge 54
Expand Your Knowledge 61
Learn Interactively 61
Improve Your Grammar, Mechanics, and Usage 62
Business Communication Notebook 66

Chapter 4 Writing Business Messages 67

Organizing Your Message 67
Define the Main Idea 69
Limit the Scope 69
Group Your Points in an Outline 69
Choose Between the Direct and Indirect Approaches 70
Composing Your Message 71
Control Your Style and Tone 72
Select the Best Words 73
Create Effective Sentences 75
Develop Coherent Paragraphs 77
Reviewing Key Points 79
Test Your Knowledge 80
Apply Your Knowledge 81
Practise Your Knowledge 82
Expand Your Knowledge 87
Learn Interactively 88
Improve Your Grammar, Mechanics, and Usage 88
Business Communication Notebook 92

Chapter 5 Completing Business Messages 93

Revising Your Message 93
Rewrite and Edit for Clarity 93
Rewrite and Edit for Conciseness 97

Producing Your Message 99
Select the Right Design Elements 100
Make Design Elements Effective 102
Use Computers to Improve Your Documents 102
Proofreading Your Message 103
What to Look for When Proofreading 104
How to Adapt the Proofreading Process 104
Reviewing Key Points 104
Test Your Knowledge 105
Apply Your Knowledge 106
Practise Your Knowledge 107
Expand Your Knowledge 113
Learn Interactively 113
Improve Your Grammar, Mechanics, and Usage 114
Business Communication Notebook 119

Unit 3: Brief Business Correspondence 121

Chapter 6 Working with Letters, Memos, and E-mail Messages 121

Sending Memos, E-mail, and Letters 121
Internal or External Communication 121
Format Differences 122
Improving Readability in Short Business Messages 123
Vary Sentence Length 124
Keep Paragraphs Short 124
Use Lists and Bullets 125
Use Headings and Subheadings 126
Improving Readability in E-mail Messages 127
Make Subject Lines Informative 127
Make Your E-mail Messages Easy to Follow 127
Personalize E-mail Messages 127
Observe Basic E-mail Etiquette 128
Reviewing Key Points 129
Test Your Knowledge 130
Apply Your Knowledge 131
Practise Your Knowledge 132
Expand Your Knowledge 138
Learn Interactively 138
Cases 139
Improve Your Grammar, Mechanics, and Usage 141
Business Communication Notebook 146

Chapter 7 Writing Routine, Good-News, and Goodwill Messages 148

Using the Three-Step Writing Process for Routine Messages 148
Making Routine Requests 149
Strategy for Routine Requests 149
Types of Routine Requests 150
Sending Routine Replies and Positive Messages 154
Strategy for Routine Replies and Positive Messages 154
Types of Routine Replies and Positive Messages 156
Reviewing Key Points 163
Test Your Knowledge 164

Apply Your Knowledge 165
Practise Your Knowledge 166
Expand Your Knowledge 172
Learn Interactively 172
Cases 173
Improve Your Grammar, Mechanics, and Usage 175
Business Communication Notebook 180

Chapter 8 Writing Bad-News Messages 181

Using the Three-Step Writing Process for Bad-News Messages 181
Step 1: Planning Your Bad-News Messages 181
Step 2: Writing Your Bad-News Messages 182
Step 3: Completing Your Bad-News Messages 182
Strategies for Bad-News Messages 182
Creating Audience-Centred Tone 182
Using the Direct Approach 183
Using the Indirect Approach 184
Types of Bad-News Messages 188
Sending Negative Answers to Routine Requests 188
Sending Negative Organizational News 189
Reviewing Key Points 195
Test Your Knowledge 195
Apply Your Knowledge 196
Practise Your Knowledge 197
Expand Your Knowledge 201
Learn Interactively 202
Cases 203
Improve Your Grammar, Mechanics, and Usage 206
Business Communication Notebook 210

Chapter 9 Writing Persuasive Messages 211

Using the Three-Step Writing Process for Persuasive Messages 211
Step 1: Planning Persuasive Messages 212
Step 2: Writing Persuasive Messages 214
Step 3: Completing Persuasive Messages 215
Strategies for Persuasive Messages 215
Balancing Emotional and Logical Appeals 216
Using AIDA for Indirect Plans 216
Types of Persuasive Requests 218
Persuasive Requests for Action 218
Persuasive Claims and Requests for Adjustments 219
Sending Sales and Fundraising Messages 220
Strategies for Sales Messages 222
Strategies for Fundraising Messages 222
Reviewing Key Points 226
Test Your Knowledge 226
Apply Your Knowledge 227
Practise Your Knowledge 228
Expand Your Knowledge 235
Learn Interactively 235
Cases 236
Improve Your Grammar, Mechanics, and Usage 240
Business Communication Notebook 244

Unit 4: Composing Business Reports, Proposals, and Presentations 245

Chapter 10 Understanding and Planning Business Reports and Proposals 245

Working with Business Reports and Proposals 245
Informational Reports 246
Analytical Reports 246
Applying the Three-Step Writing Process to Business Reports and Proposals 250
Step 1: Planning Business Reports and Proposals 250
Analysis for Reports and Proposals 250
Investigation for Reports and Proposals 256
Reviewing Key Points 262
Test Your Knowledge 262
Apply Your Knowledge 263
Practise Your Knowledge 264
Expand Your Knowledge 266
Learn Interactively 266
Cases 267
Improve Your Grammar, Mechanics, and Usage 269
Business Communication Notebook 274

Chapter 11 Writing and Completing Business Reports and Proposals 276

Step 2: Writing Business Reports and Proposals 276
Organizing Reports and Proposals 277
Organizing Graphics 279
Composing Reports and Proposals 284
Step 3: Completing Business Reports and Proposals 288
Components of a Formal Report 288
Components of a Formal Proposal 304
Reviewing Key Points 310
Test Your Knowledge 311
Apply Your Knowledge 311
Practise Your Knowledge 312
Expand Your Knowledge 315
Learn Interactively 315
Cases 316
Improve Your Grammar, Mechanics, and Usage 318
Business Communication Notebook 323

Chapter 12 Planning, Writing, and Delivering Oral Presentations 324

The Three-Step Oral Presentation Process 324
Step 1: Planning Speeches and Presentations 325
Clarify Your Purpose 325
Analyze Your Audience 325
Step 2: Writing Speeches and Presentations 325
Organize Your Speech or Presentation 325
Compose Your Speech or Presentation 328

Step 3: Revising and Rehearsing Speeches and Presentations 331
Using Visual Aids in Your Speech or Presentation 331
Mastering the Art of Delivery 337
Reviewing Key Points 341
Test Your Knowledge 342
Apply Your Knowledge 343
Practise Your Knowledge 344
Expand Your Knowledge 346
Learn Interactively 347
Improve Your Grammar, Mechanics, and Usage 347
Business Communication Notebook 351

Unit 5: Employment Messages 352

Chapter 13 Searching for Employment and Preparing Employment Messages 352

Building Toward a Career 352
Understanding Today's Changing Workplace 352
Adapting to the Changing Workplace 353
Seeking Employment in the Changing Workplace 355
Preparing Resumés 357
Planning Your Resumé 357
Writing Your Resumé 358
Completing Your Resumé 367
Preparing Other Types of Employment Messages 373
Application Letters 373
Application Forms 378
Application Follow-Ups 378
Reviewing Key Points 378
Test Your Knowledge 379
Apply Your Knowledge 380
Practise Your Knowledge 381
Expand Your Knowledge 384
Learn Interactively 384
Cases 385
Improve Your Grammar, Mechanics, and Usage 386
Business Communication Notebook 391

Chapter 14 Interviewing for Employment and Following Up 392

Understanding the Interviewing Process 392
The Typical Sequence of Interviews 393
Types of Interviews 393
Preparing for a Job Interview 394
Do Some Additional Research 394
Think Ahead About Questions 395
Bolster Your Confidence 398
Polish Your Interview Style 398
Plan to Look Good 398
Be Ready When You Arrive 398
Interviewing for Success 399
The Warm-Up 399

The Question-and-Answer Stage 400
The Close 401
Interview Notes 402
Following up After the Interview 402
Thank-You Message 402
Letter of Inquiry 403
Reviewing Key Points 404
Test Your Knowledge 404
Apply Your Knowledge 405
Practise Your Knowledge 406
Expand Your Knowledge 407
Learn Interactively 408
Cases 409
Improve Your Grammar, Mechanics, and Usage 410
Business Communication Notebook 414

Appendix A Format and Layout of Business Documents A-1
Appendix B Documentation of Report Sources A-19
Appendix C Correction Symbols A-25

Handbook of Grammar, Mechanics, and Usage H-1
Answer Key to the Level 1 Self-Assessment Exercises AK-1
References R-1
Acknowledgements AC-1
Index I-1

A Guided Tour of

Business Communication Essentials

An All-in-One Text-Workbook with Business English Exercises

This new book is a textbook, a workbook, and a Handbook of Grammar, Mechanics, and Usage, providing an all-in-one package for a course covering the essentials of business communication.

The book includes numerous real-world examples and document critiques and features the most extensive end-of-chapter activities available, including questions, extensive worksheet exercises, assignments, and cases.

A unique three-level approach for learning grammar and mechanics identifies students' weaknesses and helps strengthen their skills using a variety of print and electronic resources.

The Canadian Edition

The Canadian edition builds on the excellent work of authors John V. Thill, Courtland L. Bovée, and Barbara E. Schatzman. Professionals from business and academic communities have reviewed the materials, and the book has been tested in Canadian college and polytechnic classrooms. Students liked the direct style of the advice, the relevant and current examples from "the real world," the language support exercises, and the extensive range of activities.

Each chapter features successful Canadian companies and business leaders from across the country and from different sectors. The selection reflects the diversity of Canadian businesses such as non-profit agencies, high-tech successes, large corporations, and aboriginal businesses, including

- Creo
- Bell Canada
- RBC Royal Bank
- VanCity Community Foundation
- Province of Nova Scotia
- Ernst & Young Canada
- Xerox Canada
- Inuvialuit Regional Corporation.

In addition to the Canadian content, the examples and cases also give students the context of doing business in the international marketplace.

Some of the content changes in the Canadian edition include more emphasis on

- planning documents—focusing on an "action" purpose
- using the direct pattern—adding more examples of direct-plan persuasive requests and bad-news messages
- using document design features—reinforcing key parts of messages to make documents easy to skim for busy readers
- adding subject lines and headings to all documents—improving "access" to key ideas
- using e-mail—reflecting the increasingly preferred method for written communication in business

On the suggestion of students who used the book, each chapter now ends with a checklist for the review summary.

An Integrated Learning System

Business Communication Essentials' integrated learning system is designed to help students develop employment skills more quickly and more effectively than with any other book. Each of the 14 chapters implements this learning system in four important ways:

1. Previewing

Each chapter's learning objectives provide a clear overview of the key concepts students are expected to master.

THE THREE-STEP WRITING PROCESS — *Unit 2*

Writing Business Messages — **4**

After studying this chapter, you will be able to

1. Explain why good organization is important to both you and your audience
2. List the four activities required to organize business messages effectively
3. Summarize five features of an effective outline
4. Identify three factors you must consider before choosing a direct or an indirect approach
5. Explain four things you should avoid to achieve a conversational tone in business messages
6. Describe five techniques for selecting the best words when writing business messages
7. Discuss three measures you can take to help you create more effective sentences
8. List four methods of establishing transitions to make paragraphs coherent

From the Real World

"My college professor said to take what you know, close your eyes, and pretend you're running home and opening the door and saying, 'Hey, Mom, guess what?' The next words will be your first line."

—Julie Galle
Writer/Producer
weather.com

Julie Galle is writer/producer for the official Web site of The Weather Channel, weather.com. Whether writing a short news item about a snowstorm on the prairies or a lengthy report on the effects of global warming, Galle must organize and compose her messages so that members of her audience can easily understand the information, believe it, and quickly apply it to their own lives. Galle limits the scope of her articles and carefully organizes them. Although short news stories may require only the briefest notes of a few facts, Galle prepares outlines for long pieces. For non-news items and long reports, she usually writes three drafts: for style, for covering meteorological points, and for proofing grammar and punctuation.[1]

Organizing Your Message

Misinterpreted messages waste time, lead to poor decision making, and shatter business relationships. So you can see how valuable clear writing and good organization can be.[2] Successful communicators like Julie Galle rely on good organization to make their messages meaningful.[3]

Poor organization costs time, efficiency, and relationships.

What exactly makes a particular organization "good"? Although the definition of good organization varies from country to country, in Canada and the United States it generally means creating a linear message that proceeds point by point and delivers the main message near the beginning. Consider Figure 4.1. The poorly written draft displays weak organization, but the organization is much improved in the revised version. Before you begin to write, think about what you're going to say and how you're going to say it.

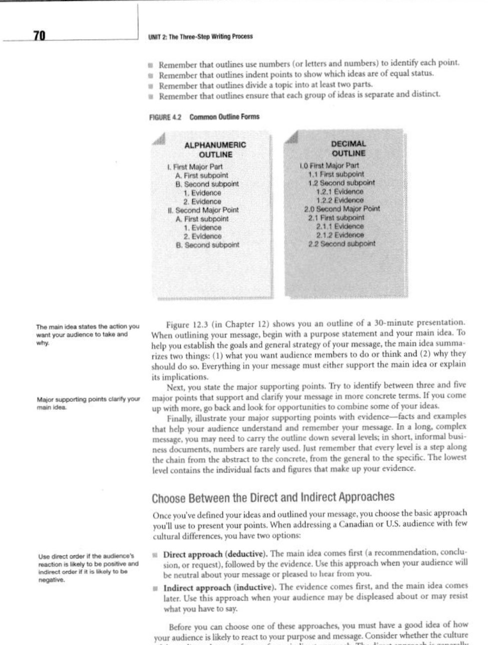

70 UNIT 2: The Three-Step Writing Process

- Remember that outlines use numbers (or letters and numbers) to identify each point.
- Remember that outlines indent points to show which ideas are of equal status.
- Remember that outlines divide a topic into at least two parts.
- Remember that outlines ensure that each group of ideas is separate and distinct.

FIGURE 4.2 Common Outline Forms

The main idea states the action you want your audience to take and why.

Figure 12.3 (in Chapter 12) shows you an outline of a 30-minute presentation. When outlining your message, begin with a purpose statement and your main idea. To help you establish the goals and general strategy of your message, the main idea summarizes two things: (1) what you want audience members to do or think and (2) why they should do so. Everything in your message must either support the main idea or explain its implications.

Major supporting points clarify your main idea.

Next, you state the major supporting points. Try to identify between three and five major points that support and clarify your message in more concrete terms. If you come up with more, go back and look for opportunities to combine some of your ideas.

Finally, illustrate your major supporting points with evidence—facts and examples that help your audience understand and remember your message. In a long, complex message, you may need to carry the outline down several levels; in short, informal business documents, numbers are rarely used. Just remember that every level is a step along the chain from the abstract to the concrete, from the general to the specific. The lowest level contains the individual facts and figures that make up your evidence.

Choose Between the Direct and Indirect Approaches

Once you've defined your ideas and outlined your message, you choose the basic approach you'll use to present your points. When addressing a Canadian or U.S. audience with few cultural differences, you have two options:

Use direct order if the audience's reaction is likely to be positive and indirect order if it is likely to be negative.

- **Direct approach (deductive).** The main idea comes first (a recommendation, conclusion, or request), followed by the evidence. Use this approach when your audience will be neutral about your message or pleased to hear from you.
- **Indirect approach (inductive).** The evidence comes first, and the main idea comes later. Use this approach when your audience may be displeased about or may resist what you have to say.

Before you can choose one of these approaches, you must have a good idea of how your audience is likely to react to your purpose and message. Consider whether the culture of the audience has a preference for an indirect approach. The direct approach is generally

2. Developing

The chapters' textual material develops, explains, and elaborates on concepts with a highly organized, concise presentation that enables students to grasp concepts quickly and easily.

3. Enhancing

Student learning is enhanced and strengthened by the chapters' real-life examples and annotated model documents. A writing process appears throughout the book to give students a method for writing business messages. Plus, student interest is piqued and maintained by a striking selection of exhibits and by a state-of-the-art design in a full-colour book.

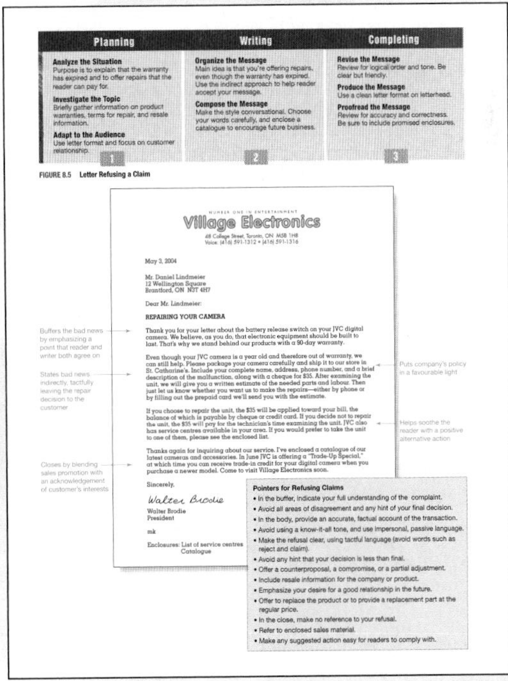

FIGURE 8.5 Letter Refusing a Claim

NUMBER ONE IN ENTERTAINMENT
Village Electronics
48 College Street, Toronto, ON M5B 1H8
Voice: (416) 591-1312 • (416) 591-1316

May 3, 2004

Mr. Daniel Lindmeier
12 Wellington Square
Brantford, ON N3T 4H7

Dear Mr. Lindmeier:

REPAIRING YOUR CAMERA

Thank you for your letter about the battery release switch on your JVC digital camera. We believe, as you do, that electronic equipment should be built to last. That's why we stand behind our products with a 90-day warranty.

Even though your JVC camera is a year old and therefore out of warranty, we can still help. Please package your camera carefully and ship it to our store in St. Catharine's. Include your complete name, address, phone number, and a brief description of the malfunction, along with a cheque for $35. After examining the unit, we will give you a written estimate of the needed parts and labour. Then just let us know whether you want us to make the repairs—either by phone or by filling out the prepaid card we'll send you with the estimate.

If you choose to repair the unit, the $35 will be applied toward your bill, the balance of which is payable by cheque or credit card. If you decide not to repair the unit, the $35 will pay for the technician's time examining the unit. JVC also has service centres available in your area. If you would prefer to take the unit to one of them, please see the enclosed list.

Thanks again for inquiring about our service. I've enclosed a catalogue of our latest cameras and accessories. In June JVC is offering a "Trade-Up Special," at which time you can receive trade-in credit for your digital camera when you purchase a newer model. Come to visit Village Electronics soon.

Sincerely,

Walter Brodie

Walter Brodie
President

mk

Enclosures: List of service centres
Catalogue

Pointers for Refusing Claims

- In the buffer, indicate your full understanding of the complaint.
- Avoid all areas of disagreement and any hint of your final decision.
- In the body, provide an accurate, factual account of the transaction.
- Avoid using a know-it-all tone, and use impersonal, passive language.
- Make the refusal clear, using tactful language (avoid words such as reject and claim).
- Avoid any hint that your decision is less than final.
- Offer a counterproposal, a compromise, or a partial adjustment.
- Include resale information for the company or product.
- Emphasize your desire for a good relationship in the future.
- Offer to replace the product or to provide a replacement part at the regular price.
- In the close, make no reference to your refusal.
- Refer to enclosed sales material.
- Make any suggested action easy for readers to comply with.

4. Reinforcing Essentials

Chapter material is reinforced not only with margin notes and a chapter summary checklist but also with end-of-chapter exercises, assignments, and cases that have been logically sorted into categories such as "Test Your Knowledge," "Apply Your Knowledge," "Practise Your Knowledge," and "Expand Your Knowledge." In addition, the extensive "Improve Your Grammar, Mechanics, and Usage" section in each chapter helps students polish their English skills.

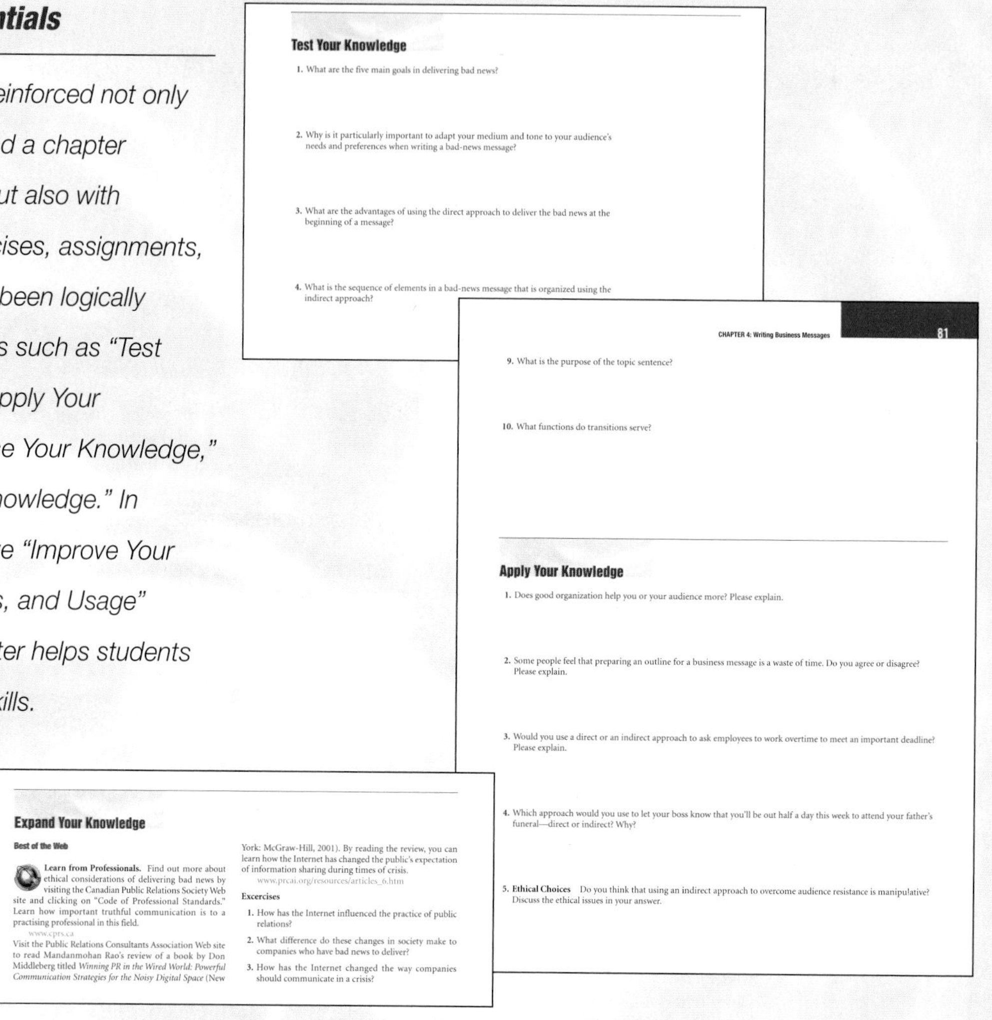

Test Your Knowledge

1. What are the five main goals in delivering bad news?
2. Why is it particularly important to adapt your medium and tone to your audience's needs and preferences when writing a bad-news message?
3. What are the advantages of using the direct approach to deliver the bad news at the beginning of a message?
4. What is the sequence of elements in a bad-news message that is organized using the indirect approach?

CHAPTER 4: Writing Business Messages 81

9. What is the purpose of the topic sentence?
10. What functions do transitions serve?

Apply Your Knowledge

1. Does good organization help you or your audience more? Please explain.
2. Some people feel that preparing an outline for a business message is a waste of time. Do you agree or disagree? Please explain.
3. Would you use a direct or an indirect approach to ask employees to work overtime to meet an important deadline? Please explain.
4. Which approach would you use to let your boss know that you'll be out half a day this week to attend your father's funeral—direct or indirect? Why?
5. **Ethical Choices** Do you think that using an indirect approach to overcome audience resistance is manipulative? Discuss the ethical issues in your answer.

Expand Your Knowledge

Best of the Web

Learn from Professionals. Find out more about ethical considerations of delivering bad news by visiting the Canadian Public Relations Society Web site and clicking on "Code of Professional Standards." Learn how important truthful communication is to a practising professional in this field.

www.cprs.ca

Visit the Public Relations Consultants Association Web site to read Mandanmohan Rao's review of a book by Don Middleberg titled *Winning PR in the Wired World: Powerful Communication Strategies for the Noisy Digital Space* (New York: McGraw-Hill, 2001). By reading the review, you can learn how the Internet has changed the public's expectation of information sharing during times of crisis.

www.prcai.org/resources/articles_6.htm

Excercises

1. How has the Internet influenced the practice of public relations?
2. What difference do these changes in society make to companies who have bad news to deliver?
3. How has the Internet changed the way companies should communicate in a crisis?

Business Communication Essentials is the centrepiece of a comprehensive package that includes a remarkable assembly of resources to support teaching and promote learning. With its heavy emphasis on exercises to improve grammar, punctuation, style, usage, and writing skills, this text offers students—especially those who lack proficiency in business English—the tools they need to succeed in today's workplace.

Explore This Text's Exciting Features

Emphasis on Writing Process and Model Documents

The authors have organized the text into a process of three easy-to-follow steps, offering students a practical strategy for writing business messages. The three-step process comprises

- planning business messages
- writing business messages
- completing business messages

This process is applied not only to memos, e-mails, and letters but also to reports, presentations, and employment messages.

To complement the text's focus on process, the authors have provided numerous sample documents throughout the book so that students can refer to a variety of effective messages—including e-mails, memos, letters, business reports, and even resumés.

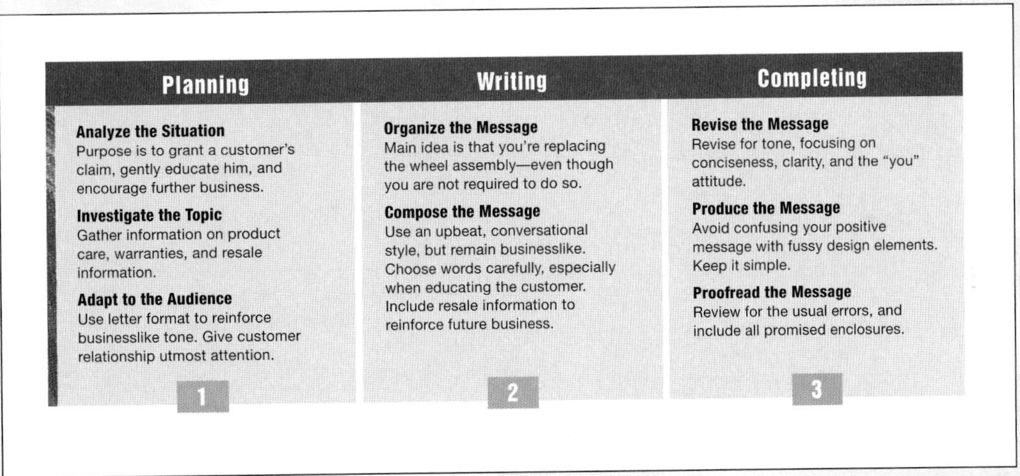

Sample Documents and Critiques

Students can examine sample documents, many collected by the authors in their consulting work at well-known companies. "Document Critiques" include marginal annotations to help students understand how to apply the principles being discussed. Many documents are also accompanied by a three-step-writing-process graphic that gives students important insights into the issues the writer considered when planning, writing, and completing the document. In addition, pairs of poor and improved drafts help students recognize the best writing practices.

Documents to Analyze

This text-workbook provides a wide selection of documents that students can critique and revise. Documents include memos, e-mails, letters, graphic aids, a letter of application, and resumés. Hands-on experience in analyzing and improving sample documents will help students revise their own business messages. "Document Critiques" are also part of the activities in the "Improve Your Grammar, Mechanics, and Usage" section, providing students with even more opportunities for analyzing and revising actual business messages.

CHAPTER 1: Understanding Business Communication in Today's Workplace 13

3. Your company has relocated to Vancouver, where a Vietnamese subculture is strongly established. Many employees will be from this subculture. As a member of the human resources department, what suggestions can you make to improve communication between management and the Vietnamese Canadians your company is hiring?

4. Do you think that written or spoken messages would be more susceptible to cultural misunderstanding? Why?

5. **Ethical Choices** Because of your excellent communication skills, your boss always asks you to write his reports for him. But when the CEO compliments him on his logical organization and clear writing style, your boss responds as if he'd written all those reports himself. What kind of ethical choice does this represent? What can you do in this situation? Briefly explain your solution and your reasoning.

Practise Your Knowledge

Activities

For live links to all Web sites discussed in this chapter, visit this text's Web site at www.pearsoned.ca/bovee. Just log on, select Chapter 1, and click on "Student Resources." Locate the page or the URL related to the material in the text. For the "Best of the Web" exercises, you'll also find navigational directions. Click on the live link to the site.

1. **Analyze This Document** Your boss wants to send a brief e-mail message welcoming employees recently transferred to your department from your Hong Kong branch. They all speak English, but your boss asks you to review her message for clarity. What would you suggest your boss change in the following e-mail message—and why? Would you consider this message to be audience centred? Why or why not?

   I wanted to welcome you ASAP to our little family here in B.C. It's high time we shook hands in person and not just across the sea. I'm pleased as punch about getting to know you, and I for one will do my level best to sell you on Canada.

2. **Ethical Choices** In less than a page, explain why you think each of the following is or is not ethical.

   a. De-emphasizing negative test results in a report on your product idea
   b. Taking a computer home to finish a work-related assignment
   c. Telling an associate and close friend that she'd better pay more attention to her work responsibilities or management will fire her
   d. Recommending the purchase of excess equipment to use up your allocated funds before the end of the fiscal year so that your budget won't be cut next year

3. **The Changing Workplace: Always in Touch** Technological devices such as faxes, cellular phones, electronic mail, and voice mail are making business people easily accessible at any time of day or night, at work and at home. What kind of impact might frequent intrusions have on their professional and personal lives? Please explain your answer in less than a page.

Questions and Exercises

The end-of-chapter questions are divided into two types:

- Test Your Knowledge (10 review questions)
- Apply Your Knowledge (5 application questions)

These questions are designed to get students thinking about the concepts explained in the chapter and may prompt students to stretch their learning beyond the chapter content. Instructors can use these questions for class discussion, in-class assignments, student teamwork, homework, or extra-credit assignments.

Dozens of exercises give students practical assignments like those they will most often face at work. Each exercise is labelled by type, such as "Analyze This Document," "Team," "Ethical Choices," "Internet," and so on.

Test Your Knowledge

1. What are the three main tasks involved in completing a business message?

2. What is a hedging sentence, and how can you correct one?

3. What is parallel construction, and why is it important?

4. Why is it a good idea to use verbs instead of noun phrases?

5. What are some ways you can make your message more concise?

6. What are design elements?

Cases

Nearly all companies featured in this text's cases are real. Both interesting and functional, these cases give students a chance to flex their communication muscles while learning about all types and sizes of organizations, both domestic and international. Labels indicate those cases that focus on team, e-mail, or Web skills.

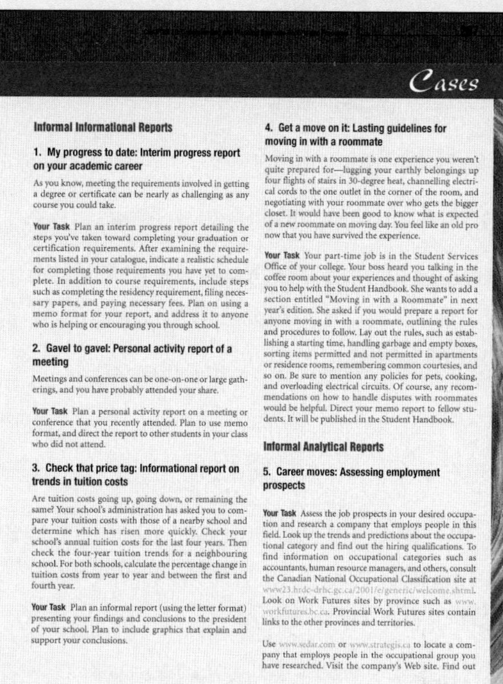

Cases

Informal Informational Reports

1. My progress to date: Interim progress report on your academic career

As you know, meeting the requirements involved in getting a degree or certificate can be nearly as challenging as any course you could take.

Your Task Plan an interim progress report detailing the steps you've taken toward completing your graduation or certification requirements. After examining the requirements listed in your catalogue, indicate a realistic schedule for completing those requirements you have yet to complete. In addition to course requirements, include steps such as completing the residency requirement, filing necessary papers, and paying necessary fees. Plan on using a memo format for your report, and address it to anyone who is helping or encouraging you through school.

2. Gavel to gavel: Personal activity report of a meeting

Meetings and conferences can be one-on-one or large gatherings, and you have probably attended your share.

Your Task Plan a personal activity report on a meeting or conference that you recently attended. Plan to use memo format, and direct the report to other students in your class who did not attend.

3. Check that price tag: Informational report on trends in tuition costs

Are tuition costs going up, going down, or remaining the same? Your school's administration has asked you to compare your tuition costs with those of a nearby school and determine which has risen more quickly. Check your school's annual tuition costs for the last four years. Then check the four-year tuition trends for a neighbouring school. For both schools, calculate the percentage change in tuition costs from year to year and between the first and fourth year.

Your Task Plan an informal report (using the letter format) presenting your findings and conclusions to the president of your school. Plan to include graphics that explain and support your conclusions.

4. Get a move on it: Lasting guidelines for moving in with a roommate

Moving in with a roommate is one experience you weren't quite prepared for—lugging your earthly belongings up four flights of stairs in 30-degree heat, channelling electrical cords to the one outlet in the corner of the room, and negotiating with your roommate over who gets the bigger closet. It would have been good to know what is expected of a new roommate on moving day. You feel like an old pro now that you have survived the experience.

Your Task Your part-time job is in the Student Services Office of your college. Your boss heard you talking in the coffee room about your experiences and thought of asking you to help with the Student Handbook. She wants to add a section entitled "Moving in with a Roommate" in next year's edition. She asked if you would prepare a report for anyone moving in with a roommate, outlining the rules and procedures to follow. Lay out the rules, such as establishing a starting time, handling garbage and empty boxes, sorting items permitted and not permitted in apartments or residence rooms, remembering common courtesies, and so on. Be sure to mention any policies for pets, cooking, and overloading electrical circuits. Of course, any recommendations on how to handle disputes with roommates would be helpful. Direct your memo report to fellow students. It will be published in the Student Handbook.

Informal Analytical Reports

5. Career moves: Assessing employment prospects

Your Task Assess the job prospects in your desired occupation and research a company that employs people in this field. Look up the trends and predictions about the occupational category and find out the hiring qualifications. To find information on occupational categories such as accountants, human resource managers, and others, consult the Canadian National Occupational Classification site at www23.hrdc-drhc.gc.ca/2001/e/generic/welcome.shtml. Look on Work Futures sites by province such as www.workfutures.bc.ca. Provincial Work Futures sites contain links to the other provinces and territories.

Use www.sedar.com or www.strategis.ca to locate a company that employs people in the occupational group you have researched. Visit the company's Web site. Find out

Technology **Business Communication Notebook**

Communicating Through the Internet

Understanding the Internet

The *Internet* is the world's largest computer network. Started in 1969 by the U.S. Department of Defense, it is a voluntary, cooperative undertaking; no one individual, organization, or government owns it. The Internet is accessible to individuals, companies, colleges and universities, government agencies, and other institutions all over the world.

Accessing the Net
To use the Internet, you need a computer (with a modem) and an *Internet service provider (ISP)*—a company that connects you to the Internet. For a fee, you can dial into one of the ISP's host computers, which will link you to one of the Internet's networked computers. Although many people use a standard phone line, others pay a bit more for the speed and convenience of a cable connection or a *digital subscriber line (DSL)*, a high-speed phone line that carries both voice and data. You can also connect "on the go," using either a handheld computer or a cellphone that is set up for wireless access.

The most widely used part of the Internet is the World Wide Web. Developed in 1990, the Web enables users to search for, display, and save multimedia resources such as graphics, text, audio, and video files. This information is stored on a *Web site*—a series of *Web pages* that contain related files of multimedia data. To read Web pages, you need a Web *browser*—software such as Netscape Navigator or Microsoft's Internet Explorer.

Navigating the Net
The *home page* of a Web site is the primary screen that users first access when visiting a site. Each page in a Web site is identified by a unique address known as a *uniform resource locator (URL)*. An example is http://www.yahoo.ca. The address begins with *http* (the abbreviation for *hypertext transfer protocol*, the protocol that allows you to navigate the Web). The address continues with *www*, indicating that the site is located on the World Wide Web. The next part of the address is the registered *domain name* (in this case yahoo), a name unique to that site. The abbreviation following the period is the *top-level domain (TLD)*. The TLDs now available include com (company), biz (business), info (general information), pro (professional), museum (museum), aero (aviation), name (individual), coop (cooperative), edu (educational), gov (government), int (international), mil (military), net (network resources), org (nonprofit organizations), and numerous country codes such as fr (France), ca (Canada), or jp (Japan).

A convenient way to navigate the Web is through hyperlinks or *hotlinks*. To automatically jump to another Web page or Web site, just use your mouse to click on words in *hypertext markup language (HTML)*—coloured, underlined, or highlighted words. Once you get to your new destination, you can *bookmark* the site by using a browser feature that places the site's URL in a file on your computer for future use. You can also navigate your trail backward or forward at any time by using the Back and Forward buttons or menus on your browser.

How Businesses Are Using the Internet

The Internet helps businesses make closer connections with other organizations and customers all over the planet. They use the Internet to

- Share text, photos, slides, videos, and other data within the organization
- Permit employees to *telecommute*, or work away from a conventional office, whether at home, on the road, or across the country
- Recruit employees cost-effectively
- Locate information from external sources
- Find new business partners and attract new customers
- Locate and buy parts and materials from domestic and international suppliers
- Promote and sell goods and services to customers in any location
- Provide customers with service, technical support, and product information
- Collaborate with local, national, and international business partners
- Inform investors, industry analysts, and government regulators about business developments

In addition, companies can set up special employee-only Web sites using an *intranet*, a private internal corporate network. Intranets use the same technology as the Internet but restrict the information and access to members of the organization (regardless of a member's actual location). Once a company has an intranet, it can add an *extranet* that allows people to communicate and exchange data within a secure network of qualified people outside the organization—such as suppliers, contractors, and customers who use a password to access the system.

274

Business Communication Notebook

This feature, placed near the end of each chapter, centres on one of four themes: ethics, technology, intercultural communication, and workplace skills. To enrich their learning, students are referred to a Website related to the subject of the feature. In addition, "Applications for Success" discussion questions are included.

Real-World Chapter Openers

Each chapter opens with a quote, "From the Real World," that gives a Canadian business leader or communication expert's insights into an important aspect of business communication. Diverse Canadian businesses are profiled.

Focus on Teams

Communicating effectively through teamwork is covered extensively in Chapter 2. Also, teamwork activities are identified and labelled in the end-of-chapter "Practise Your Knowledge" section. Students can complete exercises, solve cases, and work on other assignments that help them prepare for the widespread use of teams in business today.

Workplace Skills

This text emphasizes the skills and competencies necessary for students to make the transition from academia to the workplace. As described in the *Employability Skills 2000+* report of the Conference Board of Canada, communication skills topped the list of skills sought by employers.

Employment Interviewing

This text has a chapter dedicated to interviewing for employment and following up. The text describes the types and stages of interviews and advises students on how to prepare for an interview, ways to bolster their confidence, and how to polish their interview style.

Model Employment-Related Documents

This text explains how to prepare electronic and HTML resumés as well as resumés in traditional formats, and how to write letters of application and other employment documents. The text helps students master the skills needed to conduct a successful job search, including exploring electronic sources for job openings.

Learning Objectives

Chapter-opening learning objectives are clearly stated to signal important concepts that students are expected to master.

Margin Notes and Chapter Summaries

To reinforce learning, the book's margins contain short summary statements that highlight key points in the text. At the end of each chapter, a checklist sums up key content. These notes are no substitute for reading the chapters, but they can help students quickly get the gist of a section, review a chapter, and locate areas of greatest concern.

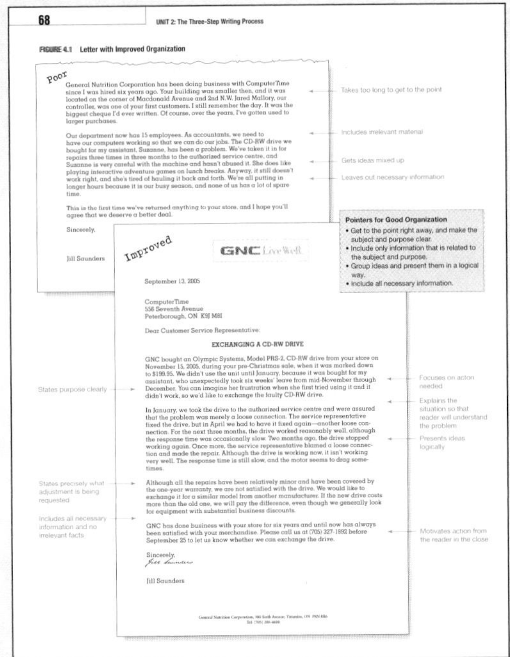

68 UNIT 2: The Three-Step Writing Process

FIGURE 4.1 Letter with Improved Organization

Poor

General Nutrition Corporation has been doing business with ComputerTime since I was hired six years ago. Your building was smaller then, and it was located on the corner of Macdonald Avenue and 2nd N.W. Jared Mallory, our controller, was one of your first customers. I still remember the day. It was the biggest cheque I'd ever written. Of course, over the years, I've gotten used to larger purchases. ← Takes too long to get to the point

Our department now has 15 employees. As accountants, we need to have our computers working so that we can do our jobs. The CD-RW drive we bought for my assistant, Suzanne, has been a problem. We've taken it in for repairs three times in three months to the authorized service centre, and Suzanne is very careful with the machine and hasn't abused it. She does like playing interactive adventure games on lunch breaks. Anyway, it still doesn't work right, and she's tired of hauling it back and forth. We're all putting in longer hours because it is our busy season, and none of us has a lot of spare time. ← Includes irrelevant material ← Gets ideas mixed up ← Leaves out necessary information

This is the first time we've returned anything to your store, and I hope you'll agree that we deserve a better deal.

Sincerely,

Jill Saunders

Pointers for Good Organization

- Get to the point right away, and make the subject and purpose clear.
- Include only information that is related to the subject and purpose.
- Group ideas and present them in a logical way.
- Include all necessary information.

Improved

GNC Live Well

September 13, 2005

ComputerTime
556 Seventh Avenue
Peterborough, ON K9J M8I

Dear Customer Service Representative:

EXCHANGING A CD-RW DRIVE

States purpose clearly → GNC bought an Olympic Systems, Model PRS-2, CD-RW drive from your store on November 15, 2005, during your pre-Christmas sale, when it was marked down to $199.95. We didn't use the unit until January, because it was bought for my assistant, who unexpectedly took six weeks' leave from mid-November through December. You can imagine her frustration when she first tried using it and it didn't work, so we'd like to exchange the faulty CD-RW drive. ← Focuses on acton needed

In January, we took the drive to the authorized service centre and were assured that the problem was merely a loose connection. The service representative fixed the drive, but in April we had to have it fixed again—another loose connection. For the next three months, the drive worked reasonably well, although the response time was occasionally slow. Two months ago, the drive stopped working again. Once more, the service representative blamed a loose connection and made the repair. Although the drive is working now, it isn't working very well. The response time is still slow, and the motor seems to drag sometimes. ← Explains the situation so that reader will understand the problem ← Presents ideas logically

States precisely what adjustment is being requested → Although all the repairs have been relatively minor and have been covered by the one-year warranty, we are not satisfied with the drive. We would like to exchange it for a similar model from another manufacturer. If the new drive costs more than the old one, we will pay the difference, even though we generally look for equipment with substantial business discounts.

Includes all necessary information and no irrelevant facts → GNC has done business with your store for six years and until now has always been satisfied with your merchandise. Please call us at (705) 327-1892 before September 25 to let us know whether we can exchange the drive. ← Motivates action from the reader in the close

Sincerely,

Jill Saunders

Pointers

A boxed insert appears near many sample documents, giving students a concise list of writing pointers. Students will also find these pointers handy when they are on the job and need to refresh their memory about effective writing techniques.

Video Cases

These entirely new, professionally produced videos on topics such as ethics, technology, and intercultural communication feature real-world examples and are designed to bring life and a deeper understanding to the concepts and issues covered in the text. Available on the companion Website (**www.pearsoned.ca/bovee**), the video cases are introduced with a list of learning objectives followed by a short paragraph of background information. Exercises ask students to react to the videos by responding to questions, making decisions, and taking the initiative to solve real business communication problems. Exercises conclude with a follow-up assignment and further exploration exercises on the Web.

Get Excellent Results with Business English Exercises

In each of this book's 14 chapters, students are taken step by step through the essential elements of English grammar, mechanics, and usage. Space is allocated for students to write their answers, and instructors can have students submit their answers if they choose. The "Improve Your Grammar, Mechanics, and Usage" section includes activities on three levels of difficulty:

Level 1. Self-Assessment. *These 15 self-assessment exercises help students identify specific areas of weakness and overcome them by studying the basics presented in the Handbook of Grammar, Mechanics, and Usage that appears near the end of the book.*

Level 2. Workplace Applications. *These 15 real-world exercises contain common errors in grammar, punctuation, capitalization, abbreviation, number style, word division, and vocabulary that students learn to recognize and correct.*

Level 3. Document Critique. *Students are given a document that contains numerous errors, and they're asked to correct the errors by using standard proofreading marks, which are listed in Appendix C.*

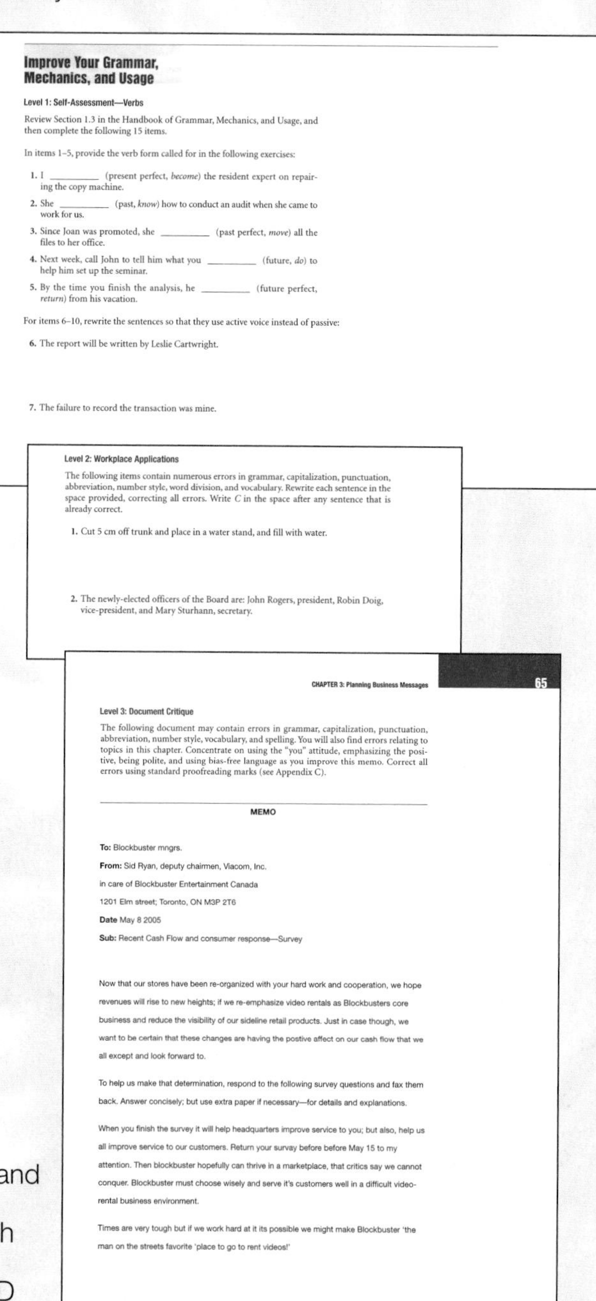

Improve Your Grammar, Mechanics, and Usage

Level 1: Self-Assessment—Verbs

Review Section 1.3 in the Handbook of Grammar, Mechanics, and Usage, and then complete the following 15 items.

In items 1–5, provide the verb form called for in the following exercises:

1. I __________ (present perfect, *become*) the resident expert on repairing the copy machine.
2. She __________ (past, *know*) how to conduct an audit when she came to work for us.
3. Since Joan was promoted, she __________ (past perfect, *move*) all the files to her office.
4. Next week, call John to tell him what you __________ (future, *do*) to help him set up the seminar.
5. By the time you finish the analysis, he __________ (future perfect, *return*) from his vacation.

For items 6–10, rewrite the sentences so that they use active voice instead of passive:

6. The report will be written by Leslie Cartwright.
7. The failure to record the transaction was mine.

Level 2: Workplace Applications

The following items contain numerous errors in grammar, capitalization, punctuation, abbreviation, number style, word division, and vocabulary. Rewrite each sentence in the space provided, correcting all errors. Write *C* in the space after any sentence that is already correct.

1. Cut 5 cm off trunk and place in a water stand, and fill with water.
2. The newly-elected officers of the Board are: John Rogers, president, Robin Doig, vice-president, and Mary Sturhann, secretary.

CHAPTER 3: Planning Business Messages 65

Level 3: Document Critique

The following document may contain errors in grammar, capitalization, punctuation, abbreviation, number style, vocabulary, and spelling. You will also find errors relating to topics in this chapter. Concentrate on using the "you" attitude, emphasizing the positive, being polite, and using bias-free language as you improve this memo. Correct all errors using standard proofreading marks (see Appendix C).

MEMO

To: Blockbuster mngrs.

From: Sid Ryan, deputy chairmen, Viacom, Inc.

in care of Blockbuster Entertainment Canada

1201 Elm street; Toronto, ON M3P 2T6

Date May 8 2005

Sub: Recent Cash Flow and consumer response—Survey

Now that our stores have been re-organized with your hard work and cooperation, we hope revenues will rise to new heights; if we re-emphasize video rentals as Blockbusters core business and reduce the visibility of our sideline retail products. Just in case though, we want to be certain that these changes are having the postive affect on our cash flow that we all except and look forward to.

To help us make that determination, respond to the following survey questions and fax them back. Answer concisely; but use extra paper if necessary—for details and explanations.

When you finish the survey it will help headquarters improve service to you; but also, help us all improve service to our customers. Return your survay before before May 15 to my attention. Then blockbuster hopefully can thrive in a marketplace, that critics say we cannot conquer. Blockbuster must choose wisely and serve it's customers well in a difficult video-rental business environment.

Times are very tough but if we work hard at it its possible we might make Blockbuster 'the man on the streets favorite 'place to go to rent videos!'

Peak Performance Grammar and Mechanics CD

Students can get extensive additional practice and reinforcement of their business English skills with the free Peak Performance Grammar and Mechanics CD that comes with the book.

Develop Cutting-Edge Skills with the Text's Six-Way Approach to Technology

Business Communication Essentials reinforces the importance of using technology effectively in business communication. Throughout the text, the authors' six-way approach to technology adds a dimension to student learning not found in other books.

1. **In-text discussion.** Chapter text covers communicating through the Internet and effective use of e-mail, voice mail, faxes, software, electronic slides, and more.
2. **Business Communication Notebook.** One of the themes of this special end-of-chapter feature is technology and how to use it to one's advantage in business communication. The feature includes discussion questions. In addition, students are referred to a Website related to the topic.
3. **Focus on e-business.** Critiques and document-writing cases feature communication challenges that students are likely to encounter in the world of e-business.
4. **Internet exercises.** Students become acquainted with the wealth of business communication information on the Web by participating in the end-of-chapter "Expand Your Knowledge" activities. Students are encouraged to visit the "Best of the Web" sites and complete the "Best of the Web" exercises. Plus, they are encouraged to explore the Web on their own by visiting other chapter-related Websites.
5. PEAK **Peak Performance Grammar and Mechanics CD.** Students can get extensive additional practice and reinforcement of their business English skills with this free CD that is easy to navigate, graphically appealing, self-paced, and keyed to the book. The CD offers a wealth of grammar, punctuation, mechanics, word usage, and spelling exercises that use the latest technology to provide immediate feedback so that students will be able to understand and correct their errors. The exercises are different from those in the text but cover the same concepts and more.
6. **Companion Website.** This powerful site (at **www.pearsoned.ca/bovee**) is for students and faculty. For students it offers an interactive study guide that includes multiple-choice and true/false items, as well as essay questions and Internet exercises drawn directly from the book's end-of-chapter material. For faculty, downloadable supplements are available.

Teach with an Unparalleled Supplements Package

The instructional resource package accompanying this text is specially designed to simplify the task of teaching and learning.

Instructor's Resource Manual

This comprehensive supplement is an instructor's tool kit. Among its many teaching aids, this manual provides a section about collaborative writing, suggested solutions to exercises, and suggested solutions in the form of fully formatted documents for *every* case in the letter-writing chapters. This comprehensive manual contains a set of completely integrated support materials. It is designed to assist instructors in quickly finding and assembling the resources available for each chapter of the text and includes the following material:

- Course planning guide
- Sample syllabuses
- Collaborative writing guide
- Diagnostic tests of English skills
- Chapter outline
- Lecture notes
- Outline of difficulties students often face with suggestions for overcoming them
- Answers to all end-of-chapter questions and assignments
- Solutions to all cases and exercises
- One pop quiz consisting of 10–15 questions for each chapter

Test Item File

The Test Item File contains 14 chapters of 100+ questions per chapter, all of which have been carefully checked for accuracy and quality. This comprehensive set consists of multiple-choice, true/false, fill-in-the-blank, and essay questions. Each test question is ranked by level of difficulty (easy, moderate, or difficult) and type of question (concept or application) and includes page and learning objective references to allow the instructor a quick and easy way to balance the level of exams or quizzes.

Pearson Education Canada's TestGen

Our user-friendly software allows you to generate error-free tests quickly and easily by previewing questions individually on the screen and then selecting items randomly by query or by number. The TestGen allows you to generate random tests with an extensive bank of questions. You can also edit the questions/answers and even add some of your own. You can create an exam, administer it traditionally or online, and analyze your success with a simple click of the mouse.

All-New Videos

A series of thematically driven business communication videos include "Communicating Effectively in the Global Workplace," "Technology and the Tools of Communication," and "Communicating Ethically in Today's Workplace."

PowerPoint Presentation

Enhance your classroom presentations with this well-developed PowerPoint presentation set. It comes in two versions:

1. Instructor version: an enhanced PowerPoint package for instructors to use for class, with colourful text-specific electronic slides that highlight and reinforce important concepts in the text. Free to adopters, these PowerPoint presentation slides are available on CD or can be downloaded from the instructor's resource section of the Companion Website at **www.pearsoned.ca/bovee**.
2. Student version: a special PowerPoint version for students to use for review purposes; it can also be conveniently printed three to a page for in-class note taking. These slides can be accessed in the student's resource section of this text's Website.

Instructor's Resource CD-ROM

This CD includes the Instructor's Resource Manual, PowerPoint presentations, and Computerized Test Item File, among other items. Instructors can easily adapt materials for their classroom preferences.

Electronic Newsletter

Delivered exclusively by e-mail six months a year, *Business Communication Update* provides helpful reminders, tips, and teaching ideas directly from the authors to keep your course exciting and current. To receive a complimentary subscription, send an e-mail to bovee@leadingtexts.com with "BCU" in the subject line and your name and institutional affiliation in the message area. You can also subscribe at the authors' Website at www.leadingtexts.com.

PREVIEW THE COMPANION WEBSITE FOR *BUSINESS COMMUNICATION ESSENTIALS*

The Companion Web site is your personal tool to the free online resources for this book, located at **www.pearsoned.ca/bovee**.

The Web site features one-click access to a wide array of resources created by an award-winning team of educators. Here is a preview of its exciting features:

For the Student

- **Companion Website Home Page.** Unite all your texts with this personal access page.
- **Study Guide.** Test your knowledge with this interactive study guide that offers a wide variety of self-assessment questions for every chapter. Results from the automatically graded questions for every chapter provide immediate feedback that can serve as practice or can be e-mailed to the instructor for extra credit.
- **Internet Exercises.** Drawn directly from the book's end-of-chapter material. Students can link to a variety of Websites and answer question based on both Website and content.
- **Student Resources.** Access the Websites featured in this text by using the hotlinks provided and updated by the authors, review chapter content by viewing the PowerPoint slides, or use the special materials developed for this course.
- **Research Area.** Let the Website save you time finding the most valuable and relevant material available on the Web. With a compilation of the best search tools currently available, plus links to virtual libraries, students and instructors can quickly and efficiently search the Web for just the right piece of information.
- **Study Hall.** Includes information on personal finance, time management, study skills, and academic majors. Get career information, view sample resumés, even apply for jobs online.

For the Instructor

- **Online Faculty Support.** In this password-protected area, get the most current and advanced support materials available, including downloadable supplements such as the Instructor's Manual, PowerPoints, articles, links, and suggested answers to current activities on the Website.

- **Syllabus Editor.** Follow the easy steps for creating and revising a syllabus, with direct links to companion Websites and other online content. Changes you make to your syllabus are immediately available to your students at their next log-in.
- **Messages.** Send messages to individual students or to all students linked to a course.

Personal Acknowledgements

My thanks go to Courtland Bovée, John Thill, and Barbara Schatzman, who made *Business Communication Essentials* an excellent and successful book in the United States. Together we are indebted to our friends, colleagues, and business associates who have assisted us in writing and adapting this book.

We thank Creo, RBC Royal Bank, Bell Canada, Xerox Canada, Inuvialuit Regional Corporation, the Province of Nova Scotia, VanCity Credit Union, Ernst & Young Canada, Ferguson Walker, BC Lotteries Corporation, Ace Hardware, Swiss Army Brands, Office Depot, Qantas, Petsmart, General Nutrition, Host Marriot Services, Carnival Cruise Lines, National Geographic Society, Greyhound Lines, and Kelly Services for granting permission to use material from their companies. The model memos, letters, and e-mails that are shown in this textbook on company stationery have been included to provide realistic examples of company documents for educational purposes. They do not always represent actual business documents created by these companies.

A heartfelt thanks to Christopher Wilson of Kwantlen University College, for his insightful comments, research assistance, and support during the course of adapting this book for the Canadian market. I am also grateful to Linda Matsuba, Business Librarian at BC Institute of Technology, for her expertise, ideas, and research assistance, and to Caroline Jellinck of Ray & Berndtsen, Tanton Mitchell, for her excellent advice and extensive contacts in Canadian business. Thanks goes to Bonnie Benoit, SAIT; Martha Finnigan, Durham College; Paula Harris, Southern Alberta Institute of Technology; Linda Large, Canadore College of Applied Arts and Technology; Doug McLean, Sprott-Shaw Community College; Kate Sangha, Douglas College; Alberta Smith, Algonquin College; Tom Swankey; Vancouver Community College; Vaska Tumir, Conestoga College; George Tripp, Fanshawe College for their many helpful suggestions during the review process.

I also deeply appreciate the support and suggestions of my Communication Department colleagues at the British Columbia Institute of Technology and the dedicated professionals at Pearson Education. They include acquisitions editor David Ward, developmental editor Jennifer Murray, production editor Judith Scott, and copy editor Susan Broadhurst. A final thanks goes to my two daughters, Casey and Anna, for their encouragement.

Understanding Business Communication in Today's Workplace

1

After studying this chapter, you will be able to

1 Explain what effective communication is
2 Discuss four developments in the workplace that are intensifying the need to communicate effectively
3 List and briefly define the six phases of the communication process
4 Identify four ways to improve business communication
5 Differentiate between an ethical dilemma and an ethical lapse
6 Define and briefly discuss four types of cultural differences that can affect communication

From the Real World

"Creo passionately believes in being open with information and communicating everything possible to all employees. To connect with staff around the world, we use many different channels to communicate as effectively as we can."

–Judi Hess
President, Creo

After acquiring the prepress assets of Scitex in 2002, Vancouver's Creo more than doubled its size overnight in revenue and employees, and it instantly became a global company of 4300 employees with operations in Asia, Europe, the U.S., the Middle East, Australia, and Africa. The leadership team at Creo ensures that communication within this worldwide company not only keeps employees informed but also empowers them as decision makers.[1]

Succeeding Through Effective Communication

Communication enables organizations to function.

Organizations such as Creo understand that achieving success in today's workplace is closely tied to the ability of employees and managers to communicate effectively with each other and with people outside the organization. **Communication** is the process of sending and receiving messages. However, communication is *effective* only when the message is understood and when it stimulates action or encourages the receiver to think in new ways.

Your ability to communicate effectively gives both you and your organization tangible benefits:

Effective communication offers real benefits.

- Quicker problem solving
- Stronger decision making
- Increased productivity
- Steadier workflow
- Stronger business relationships
- Clearer promotional materials
- Enhanced professional image
- Improved response from colleagues, employees, supervisors, investors, customers, and other stakeholders

Canadian employers acknowledge the role of strong communication skills in business. Communication skills ranked highest on the list of employability skills noted in the Conference Board of Canada report *Employability Skills 2000+*.[2]

In this course, you will learn how to create effective business messages.

People aren't "born" writers or speakers. The more they write and speak, the more their skills improve. This course teaches you how to create effective messages and helps you improve your communication skills through practice in an environment that provides honest, constructive criticism. Working hard in this course will not only improve your writing skills, but it will also help you avoid making costly mistakes on the job.

No matter what career you pursue, this course will help you discover how to collaborate in teams, listen well, master nonverbal communication, and participate in productive meetings. You'll learn about communicating across cultures and through the Internet. You'll learn a three-step process for writing business messages, and you'll get specific tips for writing letters, memos, e-mail messages, and reports and making oral presentations. You'll learn how to write effective resumés and job application letters and how to handle employment interviews. Plus, this text offers a superb collection of communication examples.

Before we get to all these topics, consider some of the communication challenges you'll be facing in today's workplace as you communicate in an organizational setting.

Adapting to the Changing Workplace

Effective communication helps us adapt to change.

Good communication skills are more vital today than ever before because people need to adapt to a workplace that is constantly changing. Effective communication will help you meet challenges such as advances in technology, the need to access vast amounts of information, the growth of globalization and workforce diversity, and the increasing use of teams in the workplace.

- **Communicating amid advancing technology.** The Internet, e-mail, voice mail, faxes, pagers, and other wireless devices have revolutionized the way people communicate. These tools increase the speed, frequency, and reach of our communication. People from opposite ends of the world can work together seamlessly, 24 hours a day, whether they are at the office, in a car, in an airport, in a hotel, or at home. Technology reveals your communication skill with every e-mail, phone conversation, or videoconference.[3] Today, you have to think not only about what you're going to say and how you're going to say it but also about which technological tools you will use.
- **Communicating in the age of information.** In today's workplace, you must know how to find, evaluate, process, and communicate information effectively and efficiently. Plus, you must be able to use what information you receive to make strong, speedy decisions. Unfortunately, people are so inundated with information, they tend to ignore messages they see as less important. Your challenge is to get your audience's attention and to make your messages easy to skim or "scannable" so that your audience will read and act on them.

Scannable messages help readers cope with information overload.

- **Communicating globally and within a culturally diverse workforce.** More and more businesses are crossing national boundaries to compete on a global scale. More than two million North Americans now work for multi-national employers, and the number of foreign companies with plants in Canada is increasing.[4] Plus, the Canadian workforce includes growing numbers of people with diverse ethnic backgrounds. To communicate effectively, you must understand other backgrounds, personalities, and perceptions. Creo keeps in touch with staff in many different countries by using video calls and teleconferences, live Webcasts, and globally linked internal voice mail and e-mail systems. Cultural and language barriers among staff from many different language groups are overcome through careful planning and management of communication.

- **Communicating in team-based organizations.** Traditional management style is changing in today's fast-paced, e-commerce environment.[5] Successful companies no longer limit decisions to a few managers at the top of a formal hierarchy. Instead, organizations use teams and work groups to collaborate and make fast decisions. "At Creo," says Hess, "information is shared with all employees to enable decentralized decision making." As Chapter 2 discusses in detail, before you can function in a team-based organization, you must understand how groups interact. You must be a good listener and correctly interpret all the nonverbal cues you receive from others. Such interaction requires a basic understanding of the communication process in organizational settings.

Understanding the Communication Process

Effective communication doesn't occur haphazardly in organizations. Nor does it happen all at once. Communication is a dynamic, two-way process that can be broken down into six phases (see Figure 1.1 on page 4):

The communication process has six steps.

1. **The sender has an idea.** You conceive an idea and want to share it.
2. **The sender encodes the idea.** You decide on the message's form (word, facial expression, gesture), length, organization, tone, and style—all of which depend on your idea, your audience, and your personal style or mood.
3. **The sender transmits the message.** You select a **communication channel** (verbal or nonverbal, spoken or written) and a **medium** (telephone, letter, memo, e-mail, report, face-to-face exchange). This choice depends on your message, your audience's location, your need for speed, and the formality required.
4. **The receiver gets the message.** Your audience must receive the message. If you send a letter, your receiver has to read it before understanding it. If you're giving a speech, your audience has to be able to hear you, and they have to be paying attention.
5. **The receiver decodes the message.** Your receiver must absorb, understand, and mentally store your message. If all goes well, the receiver interprets your message correctly, assigning the same meaning to your words as you intended.
6. **The receiver sends feedback.** After decoding your message, the receiver responds in some way and signals that response to you. This **feedback** enables you to evaluate the effectiveness of your message: If your audience doesn't understand what you mean, you can tell by the response and refine your message.

As Figure 1.1 illustrates, the communication process is repeated until both parties have finished expressing themselves.[6] To communicate effectively, don't cram too much information into one message. Instead, limit the content of your message to a specific subject, and use this repeated back-and-forth exchange to provide additional information or details in subsequent messages.

Improving Business Communication

You can improve your business communication by

- Committing to ethical communication
- Adopting an audience-centred approach
- Improving your intercultural sensitivity
- Improving your workplace sensitivity.

In the coming chapters, you'll find real-life examples of both good and bad communication, with explanations of what's good or bad about them. After a while you'll begin to see a pattern. You'll notice that four themes keep surfacing: (1) committing to ethical communication, (2) adopting an audience-centred approach, (3) improving your intercultural sensitivity, and (4) improving your workplace sensitivity. Close attention to these themes will help you improve your business communication.

FIGURE 1.1 The Communication Process

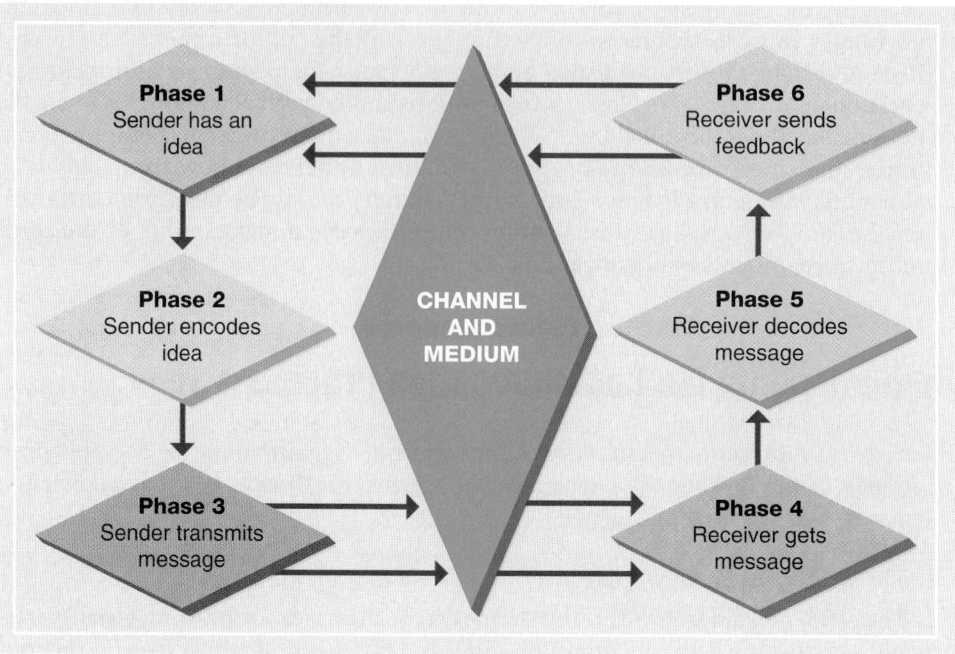

Committing to Ethical Communication

Ethics refers to the principles of conduct that govern a person or a group. Unethical people say or do whatever it takes to achieve an end. Ethical people are generally trustworthy, fair, impartial, respectful of the rights of others, and concerned about the impact of their actions on society. Ethics is "knowing the difference between what you have a right to do and what is the right thing to do."[7]

For business communication to be effective, it must be ethical.

Ethical communication includes all relevant information, is true in every sense, and is not deceptive in any way. By contrast, unethical communication can include falsehoods and misleading information (or exclude important information). Some examples of unethical communication include[8]

Avoid unethical practices when preparing your business messages.

- **Plagiarism.** Stealing someone else's words or work and claiming it as your own
- **Selective misquoting.** Deliberately omitting damaging or unflattering comments to paint a better (but untruthful) picture of you or your company
- **Misrepresenting numbers.** Increasing or decreasing numbers, exaggerating, altering statistics, or omitting numerical data
- **Distorting visuals.** Making a product look bigger or changing the scale of graphs and charts to exaggerate or conceal differences

An ethical message is accurate and sincere. It avoids language that manipulates, discriminates, or exaggerates. To communicate ethically, do not hide negative information behind an optimistic attitude, don't state opinions as facts, and be sure to portray graphic data fairly. Be honest with employers, co-workers, and clients, and never seek personal gain by making others look better or worse than they are. Don't allow personal preferences to influence your perception or the perception of others. In short, act in good faith.

On the surface, such ethical practices appear fairly easy to recognize. But deciding what is ethical can be quite complex.

Recognizing Ethical Choices

Every company has responsibilities to various groups: customers, employees, shareholders, suppliers, neighbours, the community, and the country. Unfortunately, what's right for one group may be wrong for another.[9] Moreover, as you attempt to satisfy the needs of one group, you may be presented with an option that seems right on the surface but that somehow feels wrong. When people must choose between conflicting loyalties and weigh difficult trade-offs, they are facing a dilemma.

An **ethical dilemma** involves choosing between alternatives that aren't clear-cut (perhaps two conflicting alternatives are both ethical and valid, or perhaps the alternatives lie somewhere in the vast grey area between right and wrong). Suppose you are president of a company that's losing money. You have a duty to your shareholders to try to cut your losses and a duty to your employees to be fair and honest. After looking at various options, you conclude that you'll have to lay off 500 people immediately. You suspect you may have to lay off another 100 people later on, but right now you need those 100 workers to finish a project. What do you tell them? If you confess that their jobs are shaky, many of them may quit just when you need them most. However, if you tell them that the future is rosy, you'll be stretching the truth.

When choosing between two ethical alternatives, you are facing an ethical dilemma.

Unlike a dilemma, an **ethical lapse** is making a clearly unethical or illegal choice. Suppose you have decided to change jobs and have discreetly landed an interview with your boss's largest competitor. You get along well with the interviewer, who is impressed enough with you to offer you a position on the spot. Not only is the new position a step up from your current job, but the pay is also double what you're getting now. You accept the job and agree to start next month. Then as you're shaking hands with the interviewer, she asks you to bring along profiles of your current company's 10 largest customers when you report for work. Do you comply with her request? How do you decide between what's ethical and what is not?

When choosing an alternative that is unethical or illegal, you are experiencing an ethical lapse.

Making Ethical Choices

One place to look for guidance is the law. If saying or writing something is clearly illegal, you have no dilemma: You obey the law. However, even though legal considerations will resolve some ethical questions, you'll often have to rely on your own judgment and principles. One guideline: If your intent is honest, your message is ethical, even though it may be factually incorrect. However, if your intent is to mislead or manipulate your audience, the message is unethical, regardless of whether it is true. You might look at the consequences of your message and opt for the solution that provides the greatest good to the greatest number of people—a solution that you can live with.[10] You might ask yourself[11]

For ethical guidance, first look to the law.

- **Is this message legal?** Does it violate civil law or company policy?
- **Is this message balanced?** Does it do the most good and the least harm? Is it fair to all concerned in the short term as well as the long term? Does it promote positive, win-win relationships? Did you weigh all sides before drawing a conclusion?
- **Is it a message you can live with?** Does it make you feel good about yourself? Does it make you proud? Would you feel good about your message if a newspaper published it? If your family knew about it?
- **Is this message feasible?** Can it work in the real world? Have you considered your position in the company? Your company's competition? Its financial and political strength? The likely costs or risks of your message? The time available?

To help make an ethical decision, you can ask yourself four questions.

One way to help you make your messages ethical is to consider your audience: What does your audience need? What will help your audience the most?

Adopting an Audience-Centred Approach

Adopting an **audience-centred approach** means focusing on and caring about the members of your audience, making every effort to get your message across in a way that is meaningful to them. To create an effective message, you need to learn as much as possible about the biases, education, age, status, and background of your audience. When you address strangers, try to find out more about them; if that's impossible, try to project yourself into their position by using your common sense and imagination. By writing and speaking from your audience's point of view, you can help them understand and

An effective business message focuses on its audience.

accept your message—an approach that is discussed in more detail in Chapter 3, "Planning Business Messages." Audience focus takes on special importance when you're communicating with someone from another culture. You will improve your business communication tremendously by becoming more sensitive to the differences that exist among people from various cultures.

Improving Your Intercultural Sensitivity

Effective business communicators take cultural differences into account.

To communicate more effectively, be aware of and sensitive to cultural differences. **Culture** is a shared system of symbols, beliefs, attitudes, values, expectations, and norms for behaviour. Members of a culture have similar assumptions about how people should think, behave, and communicate, and they all tend to act on those assumptions in much the same way.

Yet, from group to group, cultures differ widely. When you write to or speak with someone from another culture, you encode your message using the assumptions of your own culture. However, the members of your audience decode your message using the assumptions of their culture, so your intended meaning may be misunderstood.[12]

For example, when Japanese auto manufacturer Mazda opened a plant in North America, officials passed out company baseball caps and told employees that they could wear the caps at work, along with their mandatory company uniform (blue pants and khaki shirts). The employees assumed that the caps were a *voluntary* accessory, and many decided not to wear them. This decision upset Japanese managers, who regarded this behaviour as a sign of disrespect. Managers believed that employees who really cared about the company would *want* to wear the caps. However, the North American employees resented being told what they should *want* to do.[13]

Improve your cultural sensitivity by

- Recognizing cultural differences
- Overcoming the tendency to stereotype
- Polishing your written intercultural communication skills
- Polishing your oral intercultural communication skills

You can improve your ability to communicate effectively across cultures by recognizing such cultural differences, by overcoming your tendency to judge others based on your own standards, by polishing your written intercultural skills, and by polishing your oral intercultural skills.

Recognizing Cultural Differences

Problems arise when we assume, wrongly, that other people's attitudes and lives are like ours. A graduate of one intercultural training program said, "I used to think it was enough to treat people the way I wanted to be treated. But [after taking the course] . . . I realized you have to treat people the way *they* want to be treated."[14] You can improve intercultural sensitivity by recognizing and accommodating cultural differences in such areas as context, ethics, social customs, and nonverbal communication.

Cultural differences exist in areas such as context, ethics, social custom, and nonverbal communication.

To communicate with one another, members of different cultures rely on the context of physical cues, environmental stimuli, and implicit understanding to different degrees.

Context **Cultural context** is the pattern of physical cues, environmental stimuli, and implicit understanding that conveys meaning between two members of the same culture (see Table 1.1). In a **high-context culture** such as South Korea or Taiwan, people rely less on verbal communication and more on the context of nonverbal actions and environmental setting to convey meaning. A Chinese speaker expects the audience to *discover* the essence of a message and uses indirectness and metaphor to provide a web of meaning.[15] In high-context cultures, the rules of everyday life are rarely explicit; instead, as individuals grow up, they learn how to recognize situational cues (such as gestures and tone of voice) and how to respond as expected.[16]

To communicate in high-context cultures, members rely less on words and more on context.

To communicate in low-context cultures, members rely more on words and less on context.

On the other hand, in a **low-context culture** such as Canada, Germany or the United States, people rely more on verbal communication and less on circumstances and cues to convey meaning. An English speaker feels responsible for transmitting the meaning of the message and often places sentences in chronological sequence to establish a cause-and-effect pattern.[17] In low-context cultures, rules and expectations are usually spelled out through explicit statements such as "Please wait until I'm finished" or "You're welcome to browse."[18]

Contextual differences are apparent in the way cultures approach problem solving, negotiations, and decision making. For example, in lower-context cultures such as

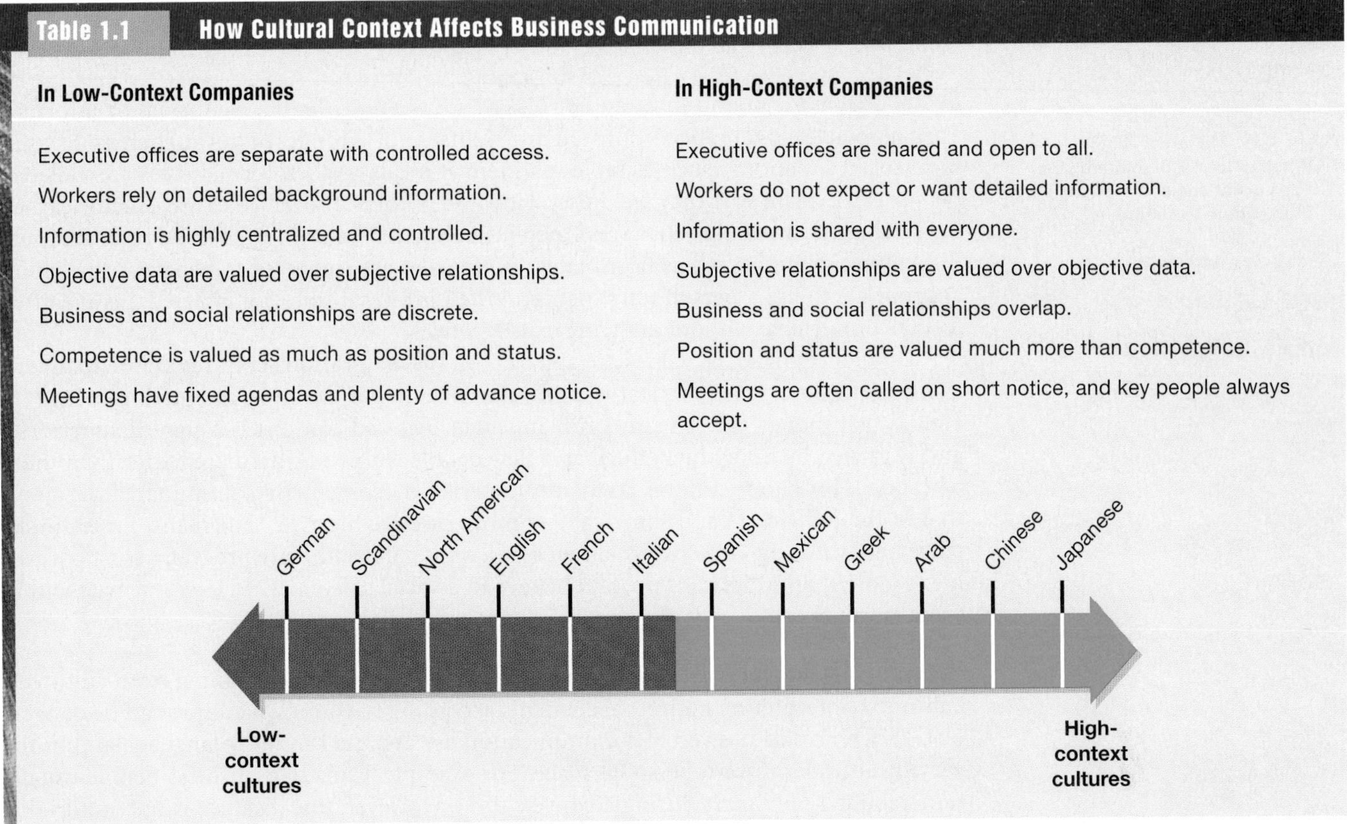

Table 1.1 How Cultural Context Affects Business Communication

In Low-Context Companies	In High-Context Companies
Executive offices are separate with controlled access.	Executive offices are shared and open to all.
Workers rely on detailed background information.	Workers do not expect or want detailed information.
Information is highly centralized and controlled.	Information is shared with everyone.
Objective data are valued over subjective relationships.	Subjective relationships are valued over objective data.
Business and social relationships are discrete.	Business and social relationships overlap.
Competence is valued as much as position and status.	Position and status are valued much more than competence.
Meetings have fixed agendas and plenty of advance notice.	Meetings are often called on short notice, and key people always accept.

Germany, business people want to make decisions as quickly and efficiently as possible. However, in higher-context cultures such as Greece, business people consider it a mark of good faith to spend time on each little point before reaching a decision. Even in Canada, contextual differences between French and English Canada influence styles of negotiation and decision making. The French, the English, and the Americans are ranked as low-context cultures, with English falling in the middle of the three.[19]

Ethics Legal and ethical behaviours are also affected by cultural context. For example, because members of low-context cultures value the written word, they consider written agreements binding. They also tend to view laws with flexibility. However, members of high-context cultures put less emphasis on the written word and consider personal pledges more important than contracts. Plus, they tend to adhere more strictly to the law.[20]

Members of different cultures have different views of what is ethical and even legal.

Legal systems differ from culture to culture. In the United Kingdom and Canada, someone is presumed innocent until proved guilty, a principle rooted in English common law. However, in Mexico and Turkey, someone is presumed guilty until proved innocent, a principle rooted in the Napoleonic code.[21] These distinctions are particularly important if your firm must communicate about a legal dispute in another country.

Making ethical choices can be difficult within your own culture. But trying to make these choices across cultures can seem incredibly complicated. When communicating across cultures, keep your messages ethical by applying four basic principles:[22]

Four principles will help you keep your intercultural messages ethical.

- **Actively seek mutual ground.** Both parties must be flexible and avoid insisting that an interaction take place strictly in terms of one culture or another.
- **Send and receive messages without judgment.** Both parties must recognize that values vary from culture to culture, and they must find a way to trust each other.
- **Send messages that are honest.** Both parties must see a situation as it is—not as they would like it to be. They must be fully aware of their personal and cultural biases.

- **Show respect for cultural differences.** Both parties must understand and acknowledge the other's needs and preserve each other's dignity by communicating without deception.

Whether formal or informal, the rules governing social custom differ from culture to culture.

Social Customs In any culture, the rules of social etiquette may be formal or informal. Formal social rules are specifically taught "rights" and "wrongs" of how to behave in common social situations (such as table manners at meals). When formal rules are violated, people can explain why they feel upset. However, informal social rules are usually learned by watching how people behave and then imitating that behaviour, so these rules are more difficult to identify (such as how males and females are supposed to behave, or when it's appropriate to use a person's first name). When informal rules are violated, people often feel uncomfortable without knowing exactly why.[23]

Differences in social values are apparent in the way various cultures define manners, think about time, recognize status, and value wealth. For example, the predominant U.S. view is that money solves many problems, that material comfort is a sign of superiority and is earned by individual effort, and that people who work hard are better than those who don't. But other cultures condemn materialism, some prize communal effort above that of the individual, and some value a more carefree lifestyle. Canadians, for example, place high value on collective goals such as a national health-care program, trust government more than Americans do, and believe in a social safety net.[24] However, even within Canada values can differ by region.

Nonverbal Communication The simplest hand gestures change meaning from culture to culture, so interpreting nonverbal elements according to your own culture can be dangerous. Differences in nonverbal communication are apparent in body language and in the varying attitudes toward personal space. For example, Canadian business people usually stand about 1.6 m apart during a conversation. However, this distance is uncomfortably close for people from Germany or Japan and uncomfortably far for Arabs and Latin Americans. (See more on nonverbal communication in Chapter 2.)

Overcoming Ethnocentrism

Being aware of cultural differences is only the first step in improving your intercultural communication. To communicate across cultures successfully, you must be able to overcome our human tendency to judge others by our own standards. When communicating across cultures, your effectiveness depends on maintaining an open mind. Unfortunately, many people lapse into **ethnocentrism,** the belief that their own cultural background is superior to all others. They lose sight of the possibility that their words and actions can be misunderstood, and they forget that they are likely to misinterpret the actions of others.

Ethnocentrism blocks effective communication because it closes the mind to new information.

When you first begin to investigate the culture of another group, you may attempt to understand the common tendencies of that group's members by **stereotyping**—predicting individuals' behaviour or character on the basis of their membership in a particular group or class. For example, Japanese visitors often stereotype Americans as people who walk fast, are wasteful in using space, speak directly, ask too many questions in the classroom, don't respect professors, are disrespectful of age and status, lack discipline, and are extravagant.[25]

Stereotyping can be useful, but only as a first step in learning about another culture.

Stereotyping may be useful in the beginning, but your next step is to move beyond it to relationships with real people. Unfortunately, when ethnocentric people stereotype, they tend to do so on the basis of limited, general, or inaccurate evidence. They frequently develop biased attitudes toward a group, and they fail to move beyond that initial step.[26] So instead of talking with Abdul Karhum, unique human being, ethnocentric people are talking to "an Arab." They may believe that all Arabs are, say, hagglers, so Abdul Karhum's personal qualities cannot alter such preconceptions. His every action is forced to fit the preconceived image, even if that image is wrong.

To overcome ethnocentrism, follow a few simple suggestions:

- **Acknowledge distinctions.** Don't ignore the differences between another person's culture and your own.

- **Avoid assumptions.** Don't assume that others will act the same way you do, that they will operate from the same assumptions, or that they will use language and symbols the same way you do.
- **Avoid judgments.** When people act differently, don't conclude that they are in error, that their way is invalid, or that their customs are inferior to your own.

Too often, both parties in an intercultural exchange are guilty of ethnocentrism and prejudice. Little wonder, then, that misunderstandings arise when communicating across cultures.

Polishing Your Written Intercultural Skills

To help you prepare effective written communications for multicultural audiences, remember these tips:[27]

Eight tips will help you improve your written intercultural skills.

- **Use plain English.** Use short, precise words that say exactly what you mean.
- **Be clear.** Rely on specific terms and concrete examples to explain your points.
- **Address international correspondence properly.** The order and layout of address information vary from country to country, so follow the conventions that appear in the company's letterhead.
- **Cite numbers carefully.** Use figures (27) instead of spelling them out (twenty-seven).
- **Avoid slang, idioms, jargon, and abbreviations.** Acronyms (such as CAD/CAM) and unfamiliar product names may also lead to confusion.
- **Be brief.** Construct sentences that are short and simple.
- **Use short paragraphs.** Each paragraph should stick to one topic.
- **Use transitional elements.** Help readers follow your train of thought.

Polishing Your Oral Intercultural Skills

When speaking in English to people who speak English as a second language, you may find these tips helpful:

Twelve tips will help you improve your oral intercultural skills.

- **Try to eliminate noise.** Pronounce words clearly, stop at distinct punctuation points, and make one point at a time.
- **Look for feedback.** Be alert to signs of confusion in your listener. Realize that nods and smiles don't necessarily mean understanding. If the other person's body language seems at odds with the message, take time to clarify the meaning.
- **Speak slowly and rephrase your sentence when necessary.** If someone doesn't seem to understand you, choose simpler words; don't just repeat the sentence in a louder voice.
- **Clarify your true intent with repetition and examples.** Try to be aware of unintentional meanings that may be read into your message.
- **Don't talk down to the other person.** Try not to overenunciate, and don't "blame" the listener for not understanding. Say, "Am I going too fast?" rather than "Is this too difficult for you?"
- **Use objective, accurate language.** Avoid throwing around adjectives such as *fantastic* and *fabulous*, which people from other cultures might consider unreal and overly dramatic.
- **Learn foreign phrases.** Learn common greetings and a few simple phrases in the other person's native language. Key phrases are usually listed in travel books and in a separate section of most travel dictionaries.
- **Listen carefully and patiently.** Let other people finish what they have to say. If you interrupt, you may miss something important. You'll also show a lack of respect. When you do not understand a comment, ask the person to repeat it.

- **Adapt your conversation style to the other person's.** For instance, if the other person appears to be direct and straightforward, follow suit.
- **Check frequently for comprehension.** Make one point at a time and pause to check on comprehension before moving on.
- **Clarify what will happen next.** At the end of a conversation, be sure that you and the other person agree on what has been said and decided. If appropriate, follow up by writing a letter or a memo summarizing the conversation and thanking the person for meeting with you.
- **Observe body language.** Be alert to roving eyes, glazed looks, and other facial expressions that signal the listener is lost or confused.

In short, take advantage of the other person's presence to make sure that your message is getting across and that you understand his or her message too.

Improving Your Workplace Sensitivity

Today's culturally diverse workforce is made up of men and women from various nations, ethnic backgrounds, age groups, and races.

The Canadian workforce includes immigrants and people from a variety of ethnic backgrounds (such as Canadians from Chinese, Indian, and Filipino cultures) who often bring their own languages and cultural customs to the workplace. Today's workforce is made up of more and more people who differ in race, gender, age, culture, family structure, religion, and educational background. Nineteen percent of Canadian wage earners in 2001 were born outside the country.[28] Such **cultural diversity** affects how business messages are conceived, planned, sent, received, and interpreted in the workplace. To communicate more effectively with people at work, learn all you can about the cultures of the people around you. Read books and articles about these cultures, and talk to people who have done business with members of these cultures.

The trick is to learn useful general information while remaining aware of and open to variations and individual differences. You can communicate more effectively if you heed the following tips from successful intercultural business people:[29]

Fifteen tips help you communicate effectively in a culturally diverse workforce.

- **Assume differences until similarity is proved.** Don't assume that others are more similar to you than they actually are.
- **Take responsibility for communication.** Don't assume it's the other person's job to communicate with you.
- **Withhold judgment.** Learn to listen to the whole story and accept differences in others without judging them.
- **Show respect.** Learn how respect is communicated in various cultures (through gestures, eye contact, and so on).
- **Empathize.** Before sending a message, put yourself in the receiver's shoes. Imagine the receiver's feelings and point of view.
- **Tolerate ambiguity.** Learn to control your frustration when placed in an unfamiliar or confusing situation.
- **Look beyond the superficial.** Don't be distracted by things such as dress, appearance, or environmental discomforts.
- **Be patient and persistent.** If you want to communicate with someone from another culture, don't give up easily.
- **Recognize your own cultural biases.** Learn to identify when your assumptions are different from the other person's.
- **Be flexible.** Be prepared to change your habits and attitudes when communicating with someone from another culture.
- **Emphasize common ground.** Look for similarities from which to work.
- **Send clear messages.** Make both your verbal and your nonverbal signals clear and consistent.

- **Deal with the individual.** Communicate with each person as an individual, not as a stereotypical representative of another group.
- **Learn when to be direct.** Investigate each culture so that you'll know when to send your message in a straightforward manner and when to be indirect.
- **Treat your interpretation as a working hypothesis.** Once you think you understand a foreign culture, carefully assess the feedback provided by recipients of your communication to see if it confirms your hypothesis.

This advice will help you communicate with anybody, regardless of culture.

Reviewing Key Points

In this chapter you learned that communication is important to the way organizations function. Changes in technology have increased the speed, frequency, and reach of business communication. As a communicator, you must focus messages on action and make them easy to scan to help readers manage information overload. To be a successful communicator, especially in team-based organizations, you need to be aware of audience needs and cultural differences.

You also learned about the six phases of communication—sending, encoding, transmitting, receiving, decoding, and giving feedback—and that effective business communication is ethical, audience centred, and sensitive to cultural differences. High-context cultures such as China and Japan rely on nonverbal actions and environment to convey meaning whereas low-context cultures such as Canada, the United States, and Germany rely more on words and less on circumstances and cues.

You can be sensitive to diversity in the workplace and overcome cultural barriers by

- Withholding judgment and recognizing differences
- Understanding varying social customs regarding gestures, sense of time, and use of space
- Being flexible
- Keeping messages simple and limited in scope
- Using repetition
- Using plain English

Test Your Knowledge

1. What benefits does effective communication give you and your organization?

2. How is technology changing communication in the workplace?

3. How can information overload affect communication?

4. What effects do globalization and workforce diversity have on communication?

5. How are teams changing business communication?

6. In which phases of the communication process are messages encoded and decoded?

7. Define ethics, and explain what ethical communication encompasses.

8. What is an audience-centred approach to communication?

9. In what four general areas can you expect to observe cultural differences?

10. What are tips for communicating effectively in a diverse workplace?

Apply Your Knowledge

1. Why do you think communication is the lifeblood of business organizations? Explain briefly.

2. How does your understanding of the communication process help you conduct business more effectively?

3. Your company has relocated to Vancouver, where a Vietnamese subculture is strongly established. Many employees will be from this subculture. As a member of the human resources department, what suggestions can you make to improve communication between management and the Vietnamese Canadians your company is hiring?

4. Do you think that written or spoken messages would be more susceptible to cultural misunderstanding? Why?

5. **Ethical Choices** Because of your excellent communication skills, your boss always asks you to write his reports for him. But when the CEO compliments him on his logical organization and clear writing style, your boss responds as if he'd written all those reports himself. What kind of ethical choice does this represent? What can you do in this situation? Briefly explain your solution and your reasoning.

Practise Your Knowledge

Activities

For live links to all Web sites discussed in this chapter, visit this text's Web site at www.pearsoned.ca/bovee. Just log on, select Chapter 1, and click on "Student Resources." Locate the page or the URL related to the material in the text. For the "Best of the Web" exercises, you'll also find navigational directions. Click on the live link to the site.

1. **Analyze This Document** Your boss wants to send a brief e-mail message welcoming employees recently transferred to your department from your Hong Kong branch. They all speak English, but your boss asks you to review her message for clarity. What would you suggest your boss change in the following e-mail message—and why? Would you consider this message to be audience centred? Why or why not?

   I wanted to welcome you ASAP to our little family here in B.C. It's high time we shook hands in person and not just across the sea. I'm pleased as punch about getting to know you, and I for one will do my level best to sell you on Canada.

2. **Ethical Choices** In less than a page, explain why you think each of the following is or is not ethical.

   a. De-emphasizing negative test results in a report on your product idea
   b. Taking a computer home to finish a work-related assignment
   c. Telling an associate and close friend that she'd better pay more attention to her work responsibilities or management will fire her
   d. Recommending the purchase of excess equipment to use up your allocated funds before the end of the fiscal year so that your budget won't be cut next year

3. **The Changing Workplace: Always in Touch** Technological devices such as faxes, cellular phones, electronic mail, and voice mail are making business people easily accessible at any time of day or night, at work and at home. What kind of impact might frequent intrusions have on their professional and personal lives? Please explain your answer in less than a page.

4. **Internet** As a manufacturer of aerospace, energy, and environmental equipment, Lockheed Martin has developed a code of ethics that it expects employees to abide by. Visit Lockheed Martin's Web site at www.lockheedmartin.com. Click on "Ethics" (in the pull-down menu under "About Us") then follow the link to "Partners in Setting the Standards" and review the company's code of ethics. In a brief paragraph, describe three specific examples of things you could do that would violate these provisions. Now scroll down and study the list of "Warning Signs" of ethics violations and take the "Quick Quiz." In another brief paragraph, describe how you could use this advice to avoid ethical problems as you write business letters, memos, and reports. Submit both paragraphs to your instructor.

5. **Ethical Choices** Your boss often uses you as a sounding board for her ideas. Now she seems to want you to act as an unofficial messenger. You are to pass her ideas along to the staff, without mentioning her involvement. Then she wants you to inform her of what staff members say, without telling them you're going to repeat their responses. What questions should you ask yourself as you consider the ethical implications of this situation? Write a short paragraph explaining the ethical choice you will make in this situation.[30]

6. **Self-Introduction** Write a paragraph or prepare a two-minute oral presentation introducing yourself to your instructor and your class. Include such things as your background, interests, achievements, and goals.

7. **Teamwork** Your boss has asked your work group to research and report on corporate child-care facilities. Of course, you'll want to know who (besides your boss) will be reading your report. Working with two team members, list four or five other things you'll want to know about the situation and about your audience before starting your research. Briefly explain why each of the items on your list is important.

8. **Communication Process: Analyzing Miscommunication** Use the six phases of the communication process to analyze a miscommunication you've recently had with a co-worker, supervisor, classmate, teacher, friend, or family member. What idea were you trying to share? How did you encode and transmit it? Did the receiver get the message? Did the receiver correctly decode the message? How do you know? Based on your analysis, what do you think prevented your successful communication in this instance?

9. **Ethical Choices** Your team has been given the critical assignment of selecting the site for your company's new plant. After months of negotiations with landowners, numerous cost calculations, and investments in ecological, social, and community impact studies, your team is about to recommend building the new plant on the Georgian Bay site. Now, just 15 minutes before your team's big presentation to top management, you discover a possible mistake in your calculations: Site-purchase costs appear to be $50 000 more than you calculated, nearly 10 percent over budget. You don't have time to recheck all your figures, so you're tempted to just go ahead with your recommendation and ignore any discrepancies. You're worried that management won't approve this purchase if you can't present a clean, unqualified solution. You also know that many projects run over their original estimates, so you can probably work the extra cost into the budget later. On your way to the meeting room, you make your final decision.

   Your task: In a few paragraphs, explain the decision you made.

10. **Intercultural Sensitivity: Recognizing Differences** Your boss represents a Canadian toy company that's negotiating to buy miniature truck wheels from a manufacturer in Osaka, Japan. In the first meeting, your boss explains that your company expects to control the design of the wheels as well as the materials that are used to make them. The manufacturer's representative looks down and says softly, "Perhaps that will be difficult." Your boss presses for agreement, and to emphasize your company's willingness to buy, he shows the prepared contract he's brought with him. However, the manufacturer seems increasingly vague and uninterested.

    Your task: What cultural differences may be interfering with effective communication in this situation? Explain briefly in an e-mail message to your instructor.

11. **Teamwork** Working with two other students, prepare a list of 10 examples of slang (in your own language) that would probably be misinterpreted or misunderstood during a business conversation with someone from another culture. Next to each example, suggest other words you might use to convey the same message. Do the alternatives mean *exactly* the same as the original slang or idiom?

12. **Intercultural Communication: Studying Cultures** Choose a specific country, such as India, China, Korea, Thailand, or Nigeria, with which you are not familiar. Research the culture and write a brief summary of what a Canadian business person would need to know about concepts of personal space and rules of social behaviour in order to conduct business successfully in that country.

13. **Multicultural Workforce: Bridging Differences** Differences in gender, age, and physical abilities contribute to the diversity of today's workforce. Working with a classmate, role-play a conversation in which

    a. A woman is being interviewed for a job by a male personnel manager
    b. An older person is being interviewed for a job by a younger personnel manager
    c. A person using a wheelchair is being interviewed for a job by a person who can walk

    How did differences between the applicant and the interviewer shape the communication? What can you do to improve communication in such situations?

14. **Intercultural Sensitivity: Understanding Attitudes** You are assistant to the director of marketing for a telecommunications firm based in Germany. You're accompanying your boss to negotiate with an official in Guangzhou, China, who's in charge of selecting a new telephone system for the city. Your boss insists that the specifications be spelled out in detail in the contract. However, the Chinese negotiator argues that in developing a long-term business relationship, such minor details are unimportant.

    Your task: What can you suggest that your boss do or say to break this intercultural deadlock and obtain the contract so that both parties are comfortable? Outline your ideas in a brief e-mail message to your instructor.

Expand Your Knowledge

Best of the Web

Check Out These Resources at the Business Writer's Free Library The Business Writer's Free Library is a terrific resource for business communication material. Categories of information include basic composition skills, basic writing skills, correspondence, reference material, and general resources and advice. Log on and read about the common errors in English, become a word detective, ask Miss Grammar, review samples of common forms of correspondence, fine-tune your interpersonal skills, join a newsgroup, and more. Follow the links and improve your effectiveness as a business communicator.

www.mapnp.org/library/commskls/cmm_writ.htm

Exercises

1. How do the objectives of professional writing differ from the objectives of composition and literature?
2. What is the purpose of feedback?
3. What are some basic guidelines for giving feedback?

Exploring the Web on Your Own

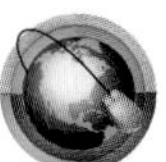

Review these chapter-related Web sites on your own to learn more about achieving communication success in the workplace.

1. Netiquette Home Page, www.albion.com/netiquette. Learn the dos and don'ts of online communication at this site, then take the Netiquette Quiz.
2. You Can Work from Anywhere, www.youcanworkfromanywhere.com. Click on this site's Info and Tech Center and follow the links. Review the tips, tools, articles, ideas, and other helpful resources to improve your productivity as a telecommuter, mobile, or home-based worker.
3. E-Mail Help, www.net-market.com/email.htm. Learn the ins and outs of e-mail at this site so that your e-mail will stand out from the crowd.

Learn Interactively

Interactive Study Guide

Visit the Companion Website at www.pearsoned.ca/bovee. For Chapter 1, take advantage of the interactive "Study Guide" to test your chapter knowledge. Get instant feedback on whether you need additional studying.

This site's "Study Hall" helps you succeed in this course by offering support with writing and study skills, time management, and career skills, as well as numerous other resources.

Peak Performance Grammar and Mechanics

PEAK Use the Peak Performance Grammar and Mechanics CD to test your skill with nouns. In the "Nouns and Pronouns" section, take the Pretest to determine whether you have any weak areas. Then review those areas in the Refresher Course. Take the Follow-Up Test to check your grasp of noun usage. For an extra challenge or advanced practice, take the Advanced Test.

Improve Your Grammar, Mechanics, and Usage

Level 1: Self-Assessment—Nouns

Use the following self-assessment exercises to improve your knowledge of and power over English grammar, mechanics, and usage. Review all of Section 1.1 in the Handbook of Grammar, Mechanics, and Usage that appears at the end of this book. Answers to these exercises appear on page AK-1.

Review all of Section 1.1 in the handbook, and then look at the following 15 items.

In items 1–5, underline the common nouns and circle the proper nouns.

1. Give the balance sheet to Melissa.
2. We'd like to order 50 more satchels for Craigmont Stores, and 3 each for the other stores on our list.
3. Tarnower Corporation donates a portion of its profits to charity every year.
4. Which aluminum bolts are packaged?
5. Please send the Joneses a dozen of the following: stopwatches, canteens, headbands, and wristbands.

In items 6–10, underline the subjects and circle the objects.

6. The technician has already repaired the machine for the client.
7. An attorney will talk to the group about incorporation.
8. After her vacation, the buyer prepared a third-quarter budget.
9. The new flat monitors are serving our department very well.
10. Accuracy overrides speed in importance.

In items 11–15, underline inappropriate noun plurals and possessives, and write the correct form in the space provided:

11. __________ Make sure that all copys include the new addresses.

12. __________ Ask Jennings to collect all employee's donations for the United Way drive.

13. __________ Charlie now has two son-in-laws to help him with his two online business's.

14. __________ Avoid using too many parenthesises when writing your reports.

15. __________ Follow President Nesses rules about what constitutes a weeks work.

Level 2: Workplace Applications

The following items contain numerous errors in grammar, capitalization, punctuation, abbreviation, number style, word division, and vocabulary. Rewrite each sentence in the space provided, correcting all errors. Write *C* in the space after any sentence that is already correct.

1. If a broken down unproductive guy like Carl can get a raise; why can't a take charge guy like me get one?

2. Visit our Web site and sign up for "On Your Toes", our free newsletter that keeps you informed of promotions, discounts and about Internet-only specials.

3. As of March, 2005, the Board of Directors have 9 members including: three women, one First Nations, and one of East Asian descent.

4. As one of the nearly 3,000,000 Maritime Life policyholders eligible to vote, we urge you to approve the new investment advisory agreement.

5. Gerrald Higgins, vice president for marketing, told us reporters that CIBC provides financial services to one-eighth of homes in Canada.

6. Our Customer Relations associates work with people everyday to answer questions, provide assistance, and helping solve problems.

7. If anyone breaches the lease, its likely that the landlord will file legal action against them to collect on the remainder of they're lease.

8. An R.E.S.P. is one of the most common plans for educational savings because of it's ease of setting up and administering.

9. My advise to you is, to put you're mission statement on your web cite.

10. According to Karen Smiths' report small-business owners do'nt recognize the full effect that layoffs and terminations are liable to have on the motivation of surviving employees'.

11. To exacerbate the processing of your Revenue Canada tax return, use the mailing label and bar coded envelope that comes with your tax package.

12. The student association has implemented a exciting array of programs that make it more easy for opinions and concerns to be voiced by you.

13. Keep in mind the old saying "When we laugh the world laugh with us, when you cry you cry alone."

14. Albert Edmunds and me are Owners of the real estate firm of Edmunds & Cale, which have recently opened a new office in Cornerbrook, NL.

15. The memo inferred that the economic downturn will have a greater affect on the company's bottom line then we previously assumed, this was the worse news we could of gotten.

Level 3: Document Critique

The following document contains errors in grammar, capitalization, punctuation, abbreviation, number style, word division, and vocabulary. Correct all errors using standard proofreading marks (see Appendix C).

Memo

TO: All Employees

FROM: R. Smith, Personnel Director

DATE: December 28, 2004

SUBJECT: Time Cards

After reviewing our Current Method of keeping track of employee hours; we have concluded that time cards leave a lot to be desired. So starting Monday, we have a new system, a time clock. You just have to punch in and punch out; whenever you will come and go from your work area's.

The new system may take a little while to get used to, but should be helpful to those of us who are making a new years resolution to be more punctual.

Happy New Year to all!

eg

Test Your Intercultural Knowledge

Never take anything for granted when you're doing business in a foreign country. All sorts of assumptions that are valid in one place can cause you problems elsewhere if you fail to consider that customs may vary. Here are several true stories about business people who blundered by overlooking some simple but important cultural differences. Can you spot the wrong assumptions that led these people astray?

1. You're tired of the discussion and you want to move on to a new topic. You ask your Australian business associate, "Can we table this for a while?" To your dismay, your colleague keeps right on discussing just what you want to put aside. Are Australians that inconsiderate?
2. You finally made the long trip overseas to meet the new German director of your division. Despite slow traffic, you arrive only four minutes late. His door is shut, so you knock on it and walk in. The chair is too far away from the desk, so you pick it up and move it closer. Then you lean over the desk, stick out your hand, and say, "Good morning, Hans, it's nice to meet you." Of course, you're baffled by his chilly reaction. Why?
3. Your meeting went better than you'd ever expected. In fact, you found the Japanese representative for your new advertising agency to be very agreeable; she said yes to just about everything. When you share your enthusiasm with your boss, he doesn't appear very excited. Why?
4. You've finally closed the deal, after exhausting both your patience and your company's travel budget. Now, two weeks later, your Chinese customers are asking for special considerations that change the terms of the agreement. How could they do this? Why are they doing it? And, most important, what should you do?

In each case the problems have resulted from inaccurate assumptions. Here are the explanations of what went wrong:

1. To "table" something in Australia means to bring it forward for discussion. This is the opposite of what North Americans usually mean. The English that's spoken in Australia is closer to British than to North American English. If you are doing business in Australia, become familiar with the local vocabulary. Note the tendency to shorten just about any word whenever possible, and adding "ie" to it is a form of familiar slang: for example, *brolly* (umbrella) and *lollie* (candy). And yes, it's true: "G'day" is the standard greeting. Use it.
2. You've just broken four rules of German polite behaviour: punctuality, privacy, personal space, and proper greetings. In time-conscious Germany, you should never arrive even a few minutes late. Also, Germans like their privacy and space, and they adhere to formal greetings of "Frau" and "Herr," even if the business association has lasted for years.
3. The word *yes* may not always mean "yes" in the Western sense. Japanese people may say *yes* to confirm they have heard or understood something but not necessarily to indicate that they agree with it. You'll seldom get a direct no. Some of the ways that Japanese people say no indirectly include "It will be difficult," "I will ask my supervisor," " I'm not sure," "We will think about it," and "I see."
4. For most North American business people, the contract represents the end of the negotiation. For Chinese business people, however, it's just the beginning. Once a deal is made, Chinese negotiators view their counterparts as trustworthy partners who can be relied on for special favours—such as new terms in the contract.

Applications for Success

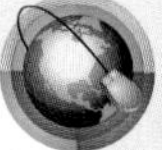

Learn how to improve your cultural savvy and gain an international competitive advantage. Visit Cultural Savvy (www.culturalsavvy.com) by Joyce Millet & Associates and read the country reports and cultural tips. Follow the site's links to interviews, profiles, articles, books, and more.

Answer the following questions:

1. Why should you avoid humour when communicating with people of a different culture?
2. Every culture has its own business protocol. What should you know about a culture's business protocol before you transact business with that culture?
3. What are some examples of cultural gift-giving taboos?

Communicating in Teams: Listening, Nonverbal, and Meeting Skills

2

From the Real World

"Good listeners will achieve more business success in their careers."

–Tony Martino
Vice-President, Human Resources, Communication, & Corporate Affairs
Xerox Canada

After studying this chapter, you will be able to

1 Explain how teams contribute to an organization's decision-making process
2 Outline four elements that are necessary to plan a productive meeting
3 Explain four ways to increase productivity during meetings
4 List and briefly explain the five phases of the listening process
5 Discuss three barriers to effective listening and some strategies for overcoming them
6 List several of the techniques for improving the way you answer phone calls, make phone calls, and use voice mail
7 Identify six categories of nonverbal communication

As vice-president responsible for human resources, communication, and corporate affairs for Xerox Canada, Tony Martino relies on effective communication among team members and between teams and upper management. He uses meetings to bring people together to solve business problems and help ensure that participants will be committed to the implementation. "To succeed," says Martino, "you need to gather as much input as possible to develop a good business solution. Listening, clarifying, testing understanding, and truly hearing what people are saying makes the difference in teamwork and success."

Working in Teams

Team members have a shared mission and are collectively responsible for their work.

A **team** is a unit of two or more people who work together to achieve a goal. Team members share a mission and the responsibility for working to achieve it.[1] Teams are important in today's workplace. At their best, teams offer an extremely useful forum for making key decisions. Teams help organizations succeed by[2]

Teams contribute to an organization's performance.

- **Increasing information and knowledge.** By aggregating the resources of several individuals, teams bring more information and expertise to the decision-making process.
- **Increasing the diversity of views.** Team members bring a variety of perspectives to decision-making tasks.
- **Increasing the acceptance of a solution.** Because team members share in making a decision, they are more likely to support that decision enthusiastically and encourage others to accept it.

- **Increasing performance levels.** Working in teams can unleash vast amounts of creativity and energy in workers who share a sense of purpose and mutual accountability. Teams also contribute to performance levels by filling the individual worker's need to belong to a group, reducing employee boredom, increasing feelings of dignity and self-worth, and reducing tension between workers.

At their worst, teams are unproductive and frustrating, and they waste everyone's time. Team members must be careful to avoid the following:

Teams are unproductive when

- Members feel pressured to conform and agree to unwise decisions
- Group members' personal motives interfere with the group's efforts
- Some team members don't contribute
- The cost of coordinating a team runs high

- **Groupthink.** When belonging to a team is more important to members than making the right decision, that team may develop **groupthink,** the willingness of individuals to set aside their personal opinions and go along with everyone else, even if everyone else is wrong. Groupthink not only leads to poor decisions and ill-advised actions but can even induce people to act unethically.
- **Hidden agendas.** Some team members can have private motives that affect the group's interaction. Sam might want to prove that he's more powerful than Laura, Laura might be trying to share the risks of making a decision, and Don might be looking for a chance to postpone doing "real" work. Each person's hidden agenda can detract from a team's effectiveness.
- **Free riders.** Some team members don't contribute their fair share to the group's activities because they aren't being held individually accountable for their work. The free-ride attitude can cause certain tasks to go unfulfilled.
- **High coordination costs.** Aligning schedules, arranging meetings, and coordinating individual parts of a project can eat up a lot of time and money.

Effective teams

- Understand their purpose
- Communicate openly
- Build consensus
- Think creatively
- Stay focused
- Resolve conflict

Effective teams have a clear sense of purpose, communicate openly and honestly, reach decisions by consensus, think creatively, remain focused, and resolve conflict effectively.[3] The purpose of developing an effective team is to get members to collaborate on necessary tasks, and much of that collaboration takes place in meetings.

Preparing, Conducting, and Attending Meetings

A great deal of the oral communication that takes place in the workplace happens in small-group meetings. Unfortunately, too many meetings are unproductive. Some managers have recently reported that little more than half their meetings were actually productive and that a quarter of them could have been handled by a phone call or a memo.[4] To ensure productivity, take great care when planning, conducting, and attending meetings, and make sure to follow up.

Preparing for Team Meetings

The best preparation for a meeting is having a specific goal that would be best handled in a face-to-face situation.

Before you call a meeting, be sure that one is truly needed. Perhaps you could accomplish your purpose more effectively in a memo or through individual conversations. If you do require the interaction of a group, be sure to bring the right people together in the right place for just enough time to accomplish your goals. The key to productive meetings is careful planning of purpose, participants, location, and agenda:

An effective agenda tells participants

- What must be done
- What issues are important
- What information is necessary for discussion
- Who is attending
- When and where the meeting is being held
- The order in which business will be handled

- **Decide on your purpose.** Most meetings are one of two types: In *informational meetings,* participants share information and sometimes coordinate action. Briefings may come from each participant or from the leader. In *decision-making meetings,* participants persuade, analyze, and solve problems. They are often involved in brainstorming sessions and debates.
- **Select participants.** Try to invite only those people whose presence is essential. If the session is purely informational and one person will be doing most of the talking, you can include a relatively large group. However, if you're trying to solve a prob-

lem, develop a plan, or reach a decision, try to limit participation to between 6 and 12 people.[5]

- **Choose an appropriate location.** Decide where you'll hold the meeting, and reserve the location. For work sessions, morning meetings are usually more productive than afternoon sessions. Also, consider the seating arrangements. Are rows of chairs suitable, or do you need a conference table? Plus, pay attention to room temperature, lighting, ventilation, acoustics, and refreshments.
- **Set and follow an agenda.** Meeting agendas help prepare the participants. Although small, informal meetings may not require a formal agenda, even they benefit if you prepare at least a list of matters to be discussed. Distribute the agenda to participants several days before the meeting so that they know what to expect and can come prepared to respond to the issues at hand.

A typical agenda format (shown in Figure 2.1) may seem stiff and formal, but it helps you start and end your meetings on time and stay on track. Doing so sends a signal of good organization and allows attendees to meet other commitments.

Productive meetings have the right purpose, include the right people, take place at the right location and time, and have a clear agenda.

FIGURE 2.1 Meeting Agenda

schedule (syllabus)

AGENDA

PLANNING COMMITTEE MEETING

Monday, October 21, 2004
10:00 A.M. to 11:00 A.M.

Executive Conference Room

		Person	Proposed Time
1.	Call to Order		
2.	Approval of Agenda		
3.	Approval of Minutes from Previous Meeting		
4.	Chairperson's Report on Site Selection Progress		
5.	Subcommittee Reports		
	a. New Markets	Alan	5 minutes
	b. New Products	Jennifer	5 minutes
	c. Finance	Craig	5 minutes
6.	Old Business—Decide Pricing Policy for New Products	Terry	10 minutes
7.	New Business		
	a. Review Carson and Canfield Data on New Product Sales	Sarah	10 minutes
	b. Decide restructuring of Product Territories due to New Product Introductions	Edith	10 minutes
8.	Announcements		
9.	Adjournment		

An effective agenda focuses on action, answering three key questions: (1) What do we need to do in this meeting to accomplish our goals? (2) What issues are of greatest importance? (3) What information must be available in order to discuss these issues?[6] Agendas also include the names of the participants, the time, the place, and the order of business. Make sure agenda items are specific, in order to help all attendees prepare in advance with facts and figures.

Conducting and Attending Meetings

The success of any meeting depends largely on the effectiveness of its leader. If the leader is prepared and has selected participants carefully, the meeting will generally be productive.

Keep the Meeting on Track

A good meeting is a cross-flow of discussion and debate, not a series of dialogues between individual members and the leader. Good leaders occasionally guide, mediate, probe, stimulate, and summarize, but mostly they let others thrash out their ideas. That's why it's important for leaders to avoid being so domineering that they close off suggestions. Of course, they must also avoid being so passive that they lose control of the group. A meeting leader is responsible for

- **Developing and circulating an agenda in advance so that participants come prepared.**
- **Keeping the meeting moving along.** If the discussion lags, call on those who haven't been heard.
- **Pacing the presentation and discussion.** Limit the time spent on each agenda item so that you'll be able to cover them all.
- **Summarizing meeting achievements.** As time begins to run out, interrupt the discussion and summarize what has been accomplished; however, don't be too rigid. Allow enough time for all the main ideas to be heard, and give people a chance to raise related issues.

Don't be so rigid that you cut off discussion too quickly.

Encourage Participation

Don't let one or two members dominate the meeting.

The best meetings are those in which everyone participates, so don't let one or two people dominate your meeting while others doodle on their notepads.To draw out the shy types, ask for their input on issues that particularly pertain to them. You might say something like, "Roberta, you've done a lot of work in this area. What do you think?" For the overly talkative, simply say that time is limited and others need to be heard from. As you move through your agenda, stop at the end of each item, summarize what you understand to be the feelings of the group, and state the important points made during the discussion.

If you're a meeting participant, try to contribute to both the subject of the meeting and the smooth interaction of the participants. Use your listening skills and powers of observation to size up the interpersonal dynamics of the people; then adapt your behaviour to help the group achieve its goals. Speak up if you have something useful to say, but don't monopolize the discussion.

Close Effectively

Productive meetings end with a review of what's been accomplished and who's responsible for doing what.

At the conclusion of the meeting, tie up the loose ends. Either summarize the general conclusion of the discussion or list the actions to be taken. Wrapping things up ensures that all participants agree on the outcome, and it gives people a chance to clear up any misunderstandings. Before the meeting breaks up, briefly review who has agreed to do what by what date.

Following Up

Minutes of the meeting remind everyone of what happened and who needs to take action.

As soon as possible after the meeting, make sure all participants receive a copy of the minutes or notes, showing recommended actions, schedules, and responsibilities. Generally, the secretary who attends the meeting or a person appointed to record prepares a set of minutes for distribution to all attendees and other interested parties. An informal meeting may not require minutes. Instead, attendees simply make their own notes on their copies of the agenda. Follow-up is then their responsibility, although the meeting leader may need to remind them to do so through an e-mail or a phone call.

Listening to Others

Just as follow-up is the responsibility of team members, so is each person's ability to listen. Without effective listening skills on the part of every team member, meetings could not take place. Your ability to listen effectively is directly related to your success in meetings, conversations, phone calls, and other group relationships. Unfortunately, most of us listen at or below a 25 percent efficiency rate: We remember only about half of what's said in a 10-minute conversation, and we forget half of that within 48 hours.[7] In addition, when questioned about material we've just heard, we are likely to get the facts mixed up. That's because although we listen to words, we don't necessarily hear their meaning.[8]

Most people need to improve their listening skills.

The Listening Process

By understanding the process of listening, you begin to understand why oral messages are so often lost. Listening involves five related activities, which usually occur in sequence:[9]

Listening involves five steps.

1. **Receiving:** Physically hearing the message and taking note of it. Physical reception can be blocked by noise, impaired hearing, or inattention.
2. **Interpreting:** Assigning meaning to sounds according to your own values, beliefs, ideas, expectations, roles, needs, and personal history. The speaker's frame of reference may be quite different from yours, so you may need to determine what the speaker really means.
3. **Remembering:** Storing a message for future reference. As you listen, you retain what you hear by taking notes or by making a mental outline of the speaker's key points.
4. **Evaluating:** Applying critical thinking skills to weigh the speaker's remarks. You separate fact from opinion and evaluate the quality of the evidence.
5. **Responding:** Reacting once you've evaluated the speaker's message. If you're communicating one on one or in a small group, the initial response generally takes the form of verbal feedback. If you're one of many in an audience, your initial response may take the form of applause, laughter, or silence. Later on, you may act on what you have heard.

Obstacles to Effective Listening

A large part of becoming a good listener is the ability to recognize and overcome a variety of physical and mental barriers, including

- **Prejudgment.** To function in life, people must operate on some basic assumptions. However, these assumptions can be incorrect or inappropriate in new situations. Moreover, some people listen defensively, viewing every comment as a personal attack, so they distort messages by tuning out anything that doesn't confirm their assumptions.
- **Self-centredness.** Some people tend to take control of conversations, rather than listen. If a speaker mentions a problem, self-centred listeners eagerly relate their own problems, trivializing the speaker's concerns by pointing out that their own difficulties are much worse. No matter what the subject, these people know more than the speaker does, and they're determined to prove it.

Effective listening is blocked when

- You jump to conclusions and close your mind to additional information
- Self-centred listeners shift their attention from the speaker to themselves
- Selective listeners tune out the speaker

- **Selective listening.** When you listen selectively (also called *out-listening*), you let your mind wander to things such as whether you brought your dry-cleaning ticket to work. You tune out until you hear something that gets your attention. Thus, you don't remember what the speaker *actually* said; you remember what you *think* the speaker *probably* said.[10]

Your mind can process information more than four times faster than the rate of speech.

One reason people's minds tend to wander is that they think faster than they speak. Most people speak at about 120 to 150 words per minute. However, studies indicate that, depending on the subject and the individual, people can process information at 500 to 800 words per minute.[11] This disparity between rate of speech and rate of thought can be used to pull one's thoughts together, but some listeners let their minds wander and just tune out.

Strategies for Effective Listening

Effective listening strengthens organizational relationships, enhances product delivery, alerts the organization to innovation from both internal and external sources, and allows the organization to manage growing diversity both in the workforce and in the customers it serves.[12] Good listening gives you an edge and increases your impact when you speak (see Table 2.1). However, effective listening requires a conscious effort and a willing mind. To improve your listening skills, heed the following tips:

Ten tips will help you improve your listening.

- **Find areas of interest.** Look beyond the speaker's style by asking yourself what the speaker knows that you don't.
- **Judge content, not delivery.** Evaluate and criticize the content, not the speaker. Review the key points. Do they make sense? Are the concepts supported by facts?
- **Keep quiet.** Don't interrupt. Depersonalize your listening so that you decrease the emotional impact of what's being said and are better able to hold your rebuttal until you've heard the total message.
- **Listen for ideas.** Listen for concepts and key ideas as well as for facts, and know the difference between fact and principle, idea and example, and evidence and argument.
- **Take careful notes.** Take meaningful notes that are brief and to the point.
- **Work at listening.** Look for unspoken messages. Often the speaker's tone of voice or expressions will reveal more than the words themselves. Provide feedback. Let the speaker know you're with him or her. Maintain eye contact. Provide appropriate facial expressions.

Table 2.1 Distinguishing Good Listeners from Bad Listeners

The Bad Listener	The Good Listener
Tunes out dry subjects	Opportunizes; asks "What's in it for me?"
Tunes out if delivery is poor	Judges content; skips over delivery errors
Tends to enter into argument	Doesn't judge until comprehension is complete; interrupts only to clarify
Listens for facts	Listens for central themes
Takes extensive notes	Takes fewer notes
Fakes attention	Works hard; exhibits active body state
Is distracted easily	Fights or avoids distractions; knows how to concentrate
Resists difficult expository material	Uses heavier material as exercise for the mind
Reacts to emotional words	Interprets emotional words; does not get hung up on them
Tends to daydream with slow speakers	Listens between the lines; weighs the evidence; mentally summarizes

- **Block out competing thoughts.** Fight distractions by closing doors, turning off radios or televisions, and moving closer to the speaker.
- **Paraphrase the speaker's ideas.** Paraphrase or summarize when the speaker reaches a stopping point.
- **Stay open-minded.** Keep an open mind by asking questions that clarify understanding; reserve judgment until the speaker has finished.
- **Capitalize on the fact that thought is faster than speech.** Stay ahead of the speaker by anticipating what will be said next and by thinking about what's already been said.

Listening to what someone is saying is crucial to business success, whether you're conversing with someone face to face, listening to a speaker during a meeting, or having a conversation over the phone. But telephone conversations and voice mail involve more than simply listening.

Using Telephones and Voice Mail

Just as important as how you plan, conduct, and participate in meetings is how you communicate using the telephone and voice mail. In fact, some experts estimate that 95 percent of most companies' daily contacts come via the telephone.[13]

Telephones and voice mail are essential for organizations to conduct business effectively.

When using the telephone and voice mail, your communication loses a great deal of the nonverbal richness that accompanies face-to-face conversations. Even so, your attitude and tone of voice can convey your confidence and professionalism effectively. Your voice and attitude can impress others with your eagerness to help, your willingness to listen, and your ability to communicate clearly.

Receiving Telephone Calls Effectively

When people call your place of business, they want to know, first, that they will reach someone who can help them and, second, that doing so will be quick and easy. They don't want to be passed from department to department. They don't want to hold while their party finishes up with someone else. And they don't want to get stuck talking with someone who lacks the knowledge or the ability to get them the information or the action they need.

If you answer the phone for someone who is unable to take the call right away, note the caller's name, telephone number, and a brief but accurate message—assuring the caller that the appropriate person will get the message and return the call. Likewise, if you will be away from your telephone for any length of time, forward your calls so that anyone calling you won't have to be transferred again and again.[14]

To be as effective as possible when receiving calls, observe the following helpful tips:[15]

Six tips will help you answer telephone calls effectively.

- **Answer promptly and with a smile.** Answer within two or three rings. Also, answering with a smile makes you sound friendly and positive. Speak clearly, and don't rush your greeting. Speak slowly enough for people to understand what you're saying.
- **Identify yourself.** Announce the company name, the department, and your own name. Keep your manner friendly and professional so that the conversation begins pleasantly and positively, building an instant relationship with your caller.
- **Establish the needs of your caller.** Immediately ask, "How may I help you?" If you know the caller's name, use it to affirm a sense of warmth and personal interest. Also, use continuity expressions to show that you're listening (e.g., "Oh yes," "I see," or "That's right."). Keep focused on the subject at hand, and don't interrupt with pointless questions.
- **Be positive.** If you can, answer callers' questions promptly and efficiently. If you can't help, tell them what you can do for them. Explain that you will find the necessary

Handle calls in a confident, positive, helpful manner.

information. Avoid conveying a lack of confidence; that is, don't use vague phrases, such as "I'm really not sure whether . . . " or "It may be that . . . "

- **Take complete, accurate messages.** Obtain as much information as you can so that you know how to process the call. Repeat names, telephone and fax numbers, e-mail addresses, and dates to make sure you have them right. Always take a return number, even if the caller assures you it is known. And don't forget to write neatly so that whoever gets your message can read it.
- **Give reasons for your actions.** If you absolutely must put a caller on hold briefly or transfer the call, explain to the caller what you are doing and why. Don't leave callers on hold for long periods of time. If it's necessary to hunt for information or to take another call, offer to call back.

Making Effective Telephone Calls

Plan your calls so that you can be efficient.

The key to making effective telephone calls is planning. Know precisely why you're calling and exactly what you need from the person you're calling. Before you make the call, gather all the materials you may need to refer to, and briefly outline or jot down notes about what you're going to say. To be as effective as possible when making phone calls, keep in mind the following tips:[16]

Seven tips will help you make telephone calls more effectively.

- **Be ready before you call.** Anticipate the conversation and plan ahead how you will handle any possible outcomes. Make an outline or notes and have them in front of you, along with a pad for taking notes. Also make sure you have at your fingertips any other necessary materials: account numbers, catalogues, electronic files, cost figures, and so on.
- **Schedule the call.** Decide ahead of time when you will call. Consider your own readiness, the time of day, and whether your contact is located in a different time zone. Don't call people first thing in the morning when they are answering mail and starting their day. Likewise, don't call anyone last thing at night when they're heading out of the office.
- **Eliminate distractions.** Don't call from a noisy pay phone or from an area where background noise will interfere with your concentration and your ability to hear and be heard. Similarly, don't tap a pencil or make other noises that might be picked up and amplified over the phone wires.
- **Make a clear, comprehensive introduction.** Immediately identify the person you're calling, give your own name and organization, briefly describe the reason for your call, and greet the person. This opening starts the call on a positive note. Keep your tone friendly, and always ask, "Is this a good time to talk briefly, or should I call you back?"
- **Don't take up too much time.** Avoid talking too slowly, spending too much time in small talk, or complaining about how difficult it is to get in touch with this person. Speak quickly and clearly, and get right to the point of the call.
- **Maintain audience focus throughout the call.** Ask questions and give clear answers so that both of you understand the call and can decide together what action is needed.
- **Close in a friendly, positive manner.** Double-check all vital information by summarizing what you've discussed. Check to see that you both agree on any action that either party will take. Thank the other person for his or her time, and if you promise to phone back, make sure you do so.

Using Voice Mail Effectively

Voice mail lets you send, store, and retrieve verbal messages. Voice mail is part of what is now called *voice processing,* which can include an automatic attendant, automatic call distribution, e-mail and paging integration, call forwarding, call screening, and many other features.[17]

Voice mail can be used to replace short memos and phone calls that need no response. It is most effective for short, unambiguous messages. Like e-mail, it solves time-zone difficulties and reduces a substantial amount of interoffice paperwork.[18]

Recording a Greeting

Use voice mail for short, straightforward messages.

Before recording your outgoing greeting for your own voice mail system, organize your thoughts.[19] You want your message to be accurate and concise. The following tips may also help you make your voice mail greeting more effective:[20]

Seven tips will help you record a more effective voice mail greeting.

- **Be brief.** Your message should not take longer than 30 seconds.
- **Be accurate.** Specifically state what callers should do.
- **Sound professional.** Make sure your voice is businesslike but cheerful. Never eat, drink, chew gum, or suck candy while recording a message. Speak slowly. Don't say names or phone numbers so fast that they can't be understood.
- **Keep your callers in mind.** Encourage callers to leave detailed messages. Also remind them to leave a phone number (especially frequent callers who may assume you have it handy).
- **Make options logical and helpful.** Limit options to three or four. Make one of the options an easy way to reach a live operator without bouncing from one menu option to another. When describing options, state the action first and then the key to press.
- **Keep your personal greeting current.** Update your greetings to reflect your schedule and leave special announcements. Don't forget to change your message when you go on vacation or plan to be away from your desk for an extended period of time.
- **Respond promptly.** Check your voice mail messages regularly and return all necessary calls within 24 hours.

Leaving a Message

Plan messages in advance to focus on the main ideas and be concise.

When you leave a message on someone else's voice mail system, think about your message in advance, and plan it carefully. Remember the following tips:[21]

Six tips will help you leave more effective voice mail messages.

- **Keep the message simple.** Save the complicated details to give in person. Leave your name, number, and purpose for calling. Designate a specific time when you can be reached (or arrange to call the person back at a specific time). Give just enough detail to get your message across so that the receiver can evaluate whether to call you back. Don't forget to repeat your name and phone number at the end of the message.
- **Sound professional.** Give your message a headline so that the listener can quickly judge its priority. Speak clearly, slowly, and loudly. Remember to smile while recording, so that your tone will be pleasant. Avoid background noise as much as possible, and before using a cellphone, consider the effect of a bad connection or interruption.
- **Avoid personal messages.** Remember, someone else may be in the room when your message is played back.
- **Replay your message before leaving the system.** Use this option whenever it is available, in order to listen to your message objectively and make sure it is clear.
- **Don't leave multiple, repetitious messages.** Rather than a series of messages with the same information, simply leave one detailed message and follow that up with a fax or an e-mail.
- **Never hide behind voice mail.** Don't use it to escape unpleasant encounters, and make sure to give praise in person.[22]

Understanding Nonverbal Communication

When using telephones and voice mail, the way you sound is important—your tone and your attitude shape the way other people perceive you and your message. Tone goes beyond the words you use. Although sound, tone, and attitude are nonverbal, they communicate an important message to your receivers. Your ability to use and interpret nonverbal communication is just as important as all the other skills discussed so far.

The most basic form of communication is **nonverbal communication**: all the cues, gestures, facial expressions, spatial relationships, and attitudes toward time that enable people to communicate without words. Nonverbal communication differs from verbal methods in terms of intent and spontaneity. You generally think about verbal messages, if only for a moment. However, when you communicate nonverbally, you sometimes do so unconsciously—you don't mean to raise an eyebrow or to blush.

The Importance of Nonverbal Communication

Actions do speak louder than words. In fact, most people can deceive others much more easily with words than they can with their bodies. Words are relatively easy to control; body language, facial expressions, and vocal characteristics are not. By paying attention to a person's nonverbal cues, you can detect deception or affirm a speaker's honesty.

Nonverbal communication is more reliable and more efficient than verbal communication.

Also, nonverbal communication is efficient. When you have a conscious purpose, you can often achieve it more economically with a gesture than with words. A wave of the hand, a pat on the back, a wink—all are streamlined expressions of thought. Even so, nonverbal communication usually blends with speech, carrying part of the message to augment, reinforce, and clarify the spoken word.

The Types of Nonverbal Communication

The thousands of forms of nonverbal communication can be grouped into some general categories. Just remember, the interpretation of these nonverbal signals varies from culture to culture (as discussed in Chapter 1).

Facial Expression

The face and eyes command particular attention as sources of nonverbal messages.

Your face is the primary site for expressing your emotions; it reveals both the type and the intensity of your feelings.[23] Your eyes are especially effective for indicating attention and interest, influencing others, regulating interaction, and establishing dominance. In fact, eye contact is so important in North America that even when your words send a positive message, averting your gaze can lead your audience to perceive a negative one.[24] Some people try to manipulate their facial expressions to simulate an emotion they do not feel or to mask their true feelings.

Gesture and Posture

Body language reveals a lot about a person's emotions and attitudes.

By moving your body, you can express both specific and general messages, some voluntary and some involuntary. Many gestures—a wave of the hand, for example—have a specific and intentional meaning, such as "hello" or "goodbye." Other types of body movement are unintentional and express a more general message. Slouching, leaning forward, fidgeting, and walking briskly are all unconscious signals that reveal whether you feel confident or nervous, friendly or hostile, assertive or passive, powerful or powerless.

Vocal Characteristics

Your tone of voice carries meaning, whether intentional or not.

Like body language, your voice carries both intentional and unintentional messages. Consider the sentence "What have you been up to?" If you repeat that question four or five times, changing your tone of voice and stressing various words, you can intentionally convey quite different messages. However, your vocal characteristics also reveal many things you're unaware of. Your tone and volume, your accent and speaking pace, and all the little *um*'s and *ah*'s that creep into your speech say a lot about who you are, your relationship with the audience, and the emotions underlying your words.

Personal Appearance

People respond to others on the basis of their physical appearance. Because you see yourself as others see you, their expectations are often a self-fulfilling prophecy—that is, when people think you're capable and attractive, you feel good about yourself, and that feeling affects your behaviour, which in turn affects other people's perceptions of you. Although body type and facial features impose limitations, most people are able to control their attractiveness to some degree. Grooming, clothing, accessories, "style"—all modify a person's appearance. If your goal is to make a good impression, adopt the style of the people you want to impress.

Physical appearance and personal style contribute to one's identity.

Touching Behaviour

Touch is an important vehicle for conveying warmth, comfort, and reassurance. Perhaps because it implies intimacy, touching behaviour is governed in various circumstances by relatively strict customs that establish who may touch whom and how. The accepted norms vary, depending on the gender, age, relative status, and cultural background of the persons involved. In business situations, touching suggests dominance, so a higher-status person is more likely to touch a lower-status person than the other way around. Touching has become controversial, however, because it can sometimes be interpreted as sexual harassment.

Touching behaviour is governed by customs.

Use of Time and Space

Like touch, time and space can be used to assert authority. Some people demonstrate their importance by making other people wait; others show respect by being on time. People can also assert their status by occupying the best space. In Canadian and U.S. companies, the chief executive often has the corner office and the best view. Apart from serving as a symbol of status, space can determine how comfortable people feel talking with each other. When others stand too close or too far away, we are likely to feel ill at ease. Again, attitudes toward punctuality and comfort zones vary from culture to culture.

Punctuality and comfort zones vary by culture and authority.

Ways to Improve Your Nonverbal Communication

When communicating orally, pay attention to your nonverbal cues, and avoid giving others conflicting signals.[25] You can improve your nonverbal communication by following these tips:

Twelve tips will help you improve your nonverbal skills.

- Avoid giving conflicting signals.
- Be as honest as possible in communicating your emotions.
- Smile genuinely. Faking a smile is obvious to observers.
- Maintain the eye contact your audience expects.
- Be aware of your posture and of the gestures you use.
- Try to use appropriate vocal signals while minimizing unintentional messages.
- Imitate the appearance of the people you want to impress.
- Respect your audience's comfort zone.
- Adopt a handshake that matches your personality and intention.
- Be aware of varying attitudes toward time.
- Use touch only when appropriate.
- Be aware that people may give false nonverbal cues.

Keep in mind that few gestures convey meaning in and of themselves; they must be interpreted in clusters, and they should reinforce your words, not replace them. You'll have plenty of practice with nonverbal communication in meetings, whether you are leading or participating.

Reviewing Key Points

In this chapter you learned how effective teams contribute to an organization's success by involving employees in decision making, by increasing the diversity of perspectives and amount of information brought to tasks, and by increasing a sense of belonging among employees. In meetings, staff members get together to share ideas and solve problems.

When you are the meeting leader, you

- Organize the agenda
- Keep people on track
- Clarify and summarize results

When you are a meeting participant, listen actively, present ideas concisely, and help facilitate the group's work. Good listeners

- Stay focused on the topic being discussed
- Avoid interrupting
- Block out competing thoughts
- Keep open minds

When you work with others, interpret and send nonverbal messages by being aware of what is conveyed in tone of voice, attitude, gestures, facial expressions, and sounds.

The chapter also provides tips on using the telephone, advising you to plan ahead so that calls and voice mail can be focused and concise. Handle calls in an organized and polite manner to create positive impressions with clients and co-workers.

Participating in teams and meetings, listening, and managing nonverbal communication and telephone communication are all important for career success.

Test Your Knowledge

1. In what four ways do organizations benefit from team decision making?

2. What four things must effective teams avoid?

3. How should a meeting leader prepare?

4. What questions should an agenda answer?

5. What activities make up the listening process?

6. Name the three main barriers to effective listening.

7. Of the 10 strategies listed to help you listen effectively, list and explain five.

8. Explain why your attitude and tone of voice are so important when using the telephone and voice mail.

9. In what six ways can an individual communicate nonverbally?

10. Of the dozen tips listed to improve nonverbal communication, list and explain five.

Apply Your Knowledge

1. Whenever your boss asks for feedback, she blasts anyone offering criticism, which causes people to agree with everything she says. You want to talk to her about it, but what should you say? List some of the points you want to make when you discuss this issue with your boss.

2. At your last department meeting, three people monopolized the entire discussion. What might you do at the next meeting to encourage other department members to participate voluntarily?

3. Jason never seems to be paying attention during weekly team meetings. He has never contributed to the discussion, and you've never even seen him take notes. He says he wants to support the team but that he finds it difficult to focus during routine meetings. List some ideas you could give him that might improve his listening skills.

4. How can nonverbal communication help you run a meeting? For example, how can it help you call a meeting to order, emphasize important topics, show approval, express reservations, regulate the flow of conversation, and invite a colleague to continue with a comment?

5. **Ethical Choices** As team leader, you've just received a voice mail message from Tanya Moore, asking to lead next week's meeting. She's been with the company for six weeks and with your team for three. From what you've already observed, she's opinionated (a bit of a know-it-all), and she tends to discourage the more reserved team members from speaking up.

   You can't allow her to run next week's meeting, and without improvement in her attitude toward others, she may never be ready to lead. You consider three options for explaining your view of her position: (1) leaving her a friendly voice mail message, (2) meeting with her, or (3) sending her a friendly e-mail message. What should you do? Explain your choice.

Practise Your Knowledge

Activities

For live links to all Web sites discussed in this chapter, visit this text's Web site at www.pearsoned.ca/bovee. Just log on and select Chapter 2, and click on "Student Resources." Locate the page or the URL related to the material in the text. For the "Best of the Web" exercises, you'll also find navigational directions. Click on the live link to the site.

1. **Analyze This Document** A project leader has made notes about covering the following items at the quarterly budget meeting. Prepare a formal agenda by putting these items into a logical order and rewriting them, where necessary, to phrase items in parallel form and to focus clearly on needed action.

   Budget Committee Meeting to be held on December 12, 2004, at 9:30 a.m.
   - I will call the meeting to order.
   - Site director's report: A closer look at cost overruns on Greentree site.

- The group will review and approve the minutes from last quarter's meeting.
- I will ask the finance director to report on actual vs. projected quarterly revenues and expenses.
- I will distribute copies of the overall divisional budget and announce the date of the next budget meeting.
- Discussion: How can we do a better job of anticipating and preventing cost overruns?
- Meeting will take place in Conference Room 3.
- What additional budget issues must be considered during this quarter?

2. **Teamwork** With a classmate, attend a local community or campus meeting where you can observe group discussion. Take notes individually during the meeting and then work together to answer the following questions:

   a. What is your evaluation of this meeting? In your answer, consider (1) the leader's ability to clearly state the meeting's goals, (2) the leader's ability to engage members in a meaningful discussion, and (3) the group's listening skills.
   b. How well did the individual participants listen? How could you tell?
   c. Compare the notes you took during the meeting with those of your classmate. What differences do you notice? How do you account for these differences?

3. **Team Communication** Every month, each employee in your department is expected to give a brief oral presentation on the status of his or her project. However, your department has recently hired an employee with a severe speech impediment that prevents people from understanding most of what he has to say.

   Your task: As assistant department manager, how will you resolve this dilemma? Please explain.

4. **Meeting Productivity: Analyzing Agendas** Obtain a copy of the agenda from a recent campus or work meeting. Does this agenda show a start time or end time? Is it specific enough that you, as an outsider, would be able to understand what was to be discussed? If not, how would you improve the agenda?

5. **Listening Skills: Overcoming Barriers** Identify some of your bad listening habits and make a list of some ways you could correct them. For the next 30 days, review your list and jot down any improvements you've noticed as a result of your effort.

6. **Listening Skills: Self-Assessment** How good are your listening skills? Rate yourself on each of the following elements of good listening; then examine your ratings to identify where you are strongest and where you can improve, using the tips in this chapter.

Element of Listening	Always	Frequently	Occasionally	Never
1. I look for areas of interest when people speak.	____	____	____	____
2. I focus on content rather than delivery.	____	____	____	____
3. I wait to respond until I understand the content.	____	____	____	____
4. I listen for ideas and themes, not isolated facts.	____	____	____	____
5. I take notes only when needed.	____	____	____	____
6. I really concentrate on what speakers are saying.	____	____	____	____
7. I stay focused even when the ideas are complex.	____	____	____	____
8. I keep an open mind despite emotionally charged language.	____	____	____	____

7. **Telephones and Voice Mail** You are interested in the hiring policies of companies in your area. You want information about how often entry positions need to be filled, what sort of qualifications are required for these positions, and what range of pay is offered. Plan out your phone call. Think about what you will say (1) to reach the person who can help you, (2) to gain the information you need, (3) in a voice mail message. Once you've planned out your approach, call three companies in your area, and briefly summarize the results of these calls.

8. **Nonverbal Communication: Analyzing Written Messages** Select a business letter and envelope that you have received at work or at home. Analyze their appearance. What nonverbal messages do they send? Are these messages consistent with the content of the letter? If not, what could the sender have done to make the nonverbal communication consistent with the verbal communication?

9. **Nonverbal Communication: Analyzing Body Language** Describe what the following body movements suggest when they are exhibited by someone during a conversation. How do such movements influence your interpretation of spoken words?

   a. Shifting one's body continuously while seated
   b. Twirling and playing with one's hair
   c. Sitting in a sprawled position
   d. Rolling one's eyes
   e. Extending a weak handshake

Expand Your Knowledge

Best of the Web

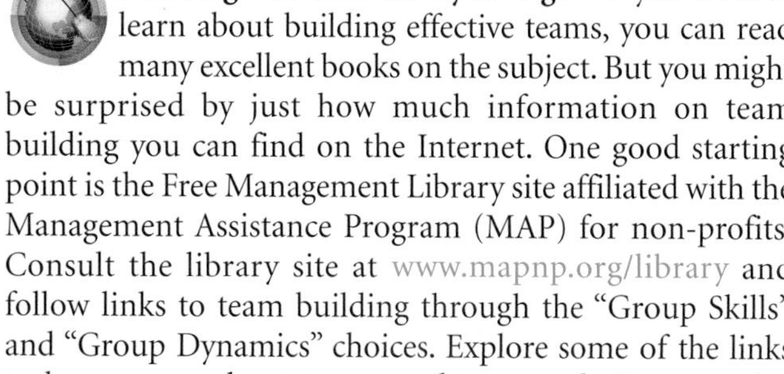

Building Teams in the Cyber Age If you want to learn about building effective teams, you can read many excellent books on the subject. But you might be surprised by just how much information on team building you can find on the Internet. One good starting point is the Free Management Library site affiliated with the Management Assistance Program (MAP) for non-profits. Consult the library site at www.mapnp.org/library and follow links to team building through the "Group Skills" and "Group Dynamics" choices. Explore some of the links to learn more about teams and teamwork. You can also consult the MAP site at www.mapfornonprofits.com.

Exercises

1. Click on "Dialoguing" and choose "Introduction to Dialogue." What is the difference between "dialogue" and "debate?"

2. Under "Related Library Links" select "Team Building." Click on "Being an Effective Team Member" to find "Being a Valuable Team Member." Of the meeting roles discussed here, which roles come naturally to you? Which of the negative roles mentioned affect groups in which you participate?

3. Under "Basics of Team Building" find "Developing Your Skills for Building Your Team" and take the assessment test. What should you concentrate on to improve your teamwork?

Exploring the Web on Your Own

Review these chapter-related Web sites on your own to learn more about achieving communication success in the workplace.

1. Teamworks: The Virtual Team Assistant, www.vta.spcomm.uiuc.edu, is a Web site dedicated to providing support for group communication processes and teams.

2. Center for the Study of Work Teams, www.workteams.unt.edu, has many links, articles, and research reports on the subject matter of teams.

3. 3M Meeting Network, www.mmm.com/meetingnetwork, has dozens of articles and tips on how to run effective meetings—from the basics to advanced facilitation skills.

Learn Interactively

Interactive Study Guide

Visit the Companion Website at www.pearsoned.ca/bovee. For Chapter 2, take advantage of the interactive "Study Guide" to test your chapter knowledge. Get instant feedback on whether you need additional studying. This site's "Study Hall" helps you succeed in this course by offering support with writing and study skills, time management, and career skills, as well as numerous other resources.

Peak Performance Grammar and Mechanics

Use the Peak Performance Grammar and Mechanics CD to test your skill with pronouns. In the "Nouns and Pronouns" section, take the Pretest to determine whether you have any weak areas. Then review those areas in the Refresher Course. Take the Follow-Up Test to check your grasp of noun usage. For an extra challenge or advanced practice, take the Advanced Test.

Improve Your Grammar, Mechanics, and Usage

Level 1: Self-Assessment—Pronouns

Review Section 1.2 in the Handbook of Grammar, Mechanics, and Usage, and then look at the following 15 items.

In items 1–5, replace the underlined nouns with the correct pronouns:

1. __________ To which retailer will you send your merchandise?
2. __________ Have you given John and Nancy a list of parts?
3. __________ The main office sent the invoice to Mr. and Mrs. Litvak on December 5.
4. __________ The company settled the company's accounts before the end of the year.
5. __________ Which person's umbrella is this?

In items 6–15, write the correct pronouns in the spaces provided:

6. The sales staff is preparing guidelines for __________ (*their, its*) clients.
7. Few of the sales representatives turn in __________ (*their, its*) reports on time.
8. The board of directors has chosen __________ (*their, its*) officers.
9. Donna and Eileen have told __________ (*her, their*) clients about the new program.
10. Each manager plans to expand __________ (*her, their, his or her*) sphere of control next year.
11. Has everyone supplied __________ (*his, their, his or her*) social insurance number?
12. After giving every employee __________ (*his, their, a*) raise, George told __________ (*them, they, all*) about the increased workload.
13. Bob and Tim have opposite ideas about how to achieve company goals. __________ (*Who, Whom*) do you think will win the debate?
14. City Securities has just announced __________ (*who, whom*) it will hire as CEO.
15. Either of the new products would readily find __________ (*their, its*) niche in the marketplace.

Level 2: Workplace Applications

The following items contain numerous errors in grammar, capitalization, punctuation, abbreviation, number style, word division, and vocabulary. Rewrite each sentence in the space provided, correcting all errors. Write *C* in the space after any sentence that is already correct.

1. Anita Doig from Data Providers will outline their data interpretations as it relates to industry trends, additionally Miss Doig will be asked to comment on how their data should be ultilized.

2. You're order for 2000 mylar bags has been received by us; please be advised that orders of less than 5000 bags only get a 20 percent discount.

3. Just between you and I, the new 'customer centric' philosophy seems pretty confusing.

4. Whether dealing with a catastrophe, or with the many problems that afflict a great city on a daily basis; Mayor Taylor has relied on a systematic methodical approach that can work for any manager, in any sized business.

5. Among the specialties of Product Marketers International is promotional efforts for clients, including presence on the Internet, radio, and on television.

6. An overview of a typical marketing plan will be covered in the introduction to this report, to give you an idea of what's in it.

7. Franchise sales can be a discreet source of income and compliment your overall sales.

8. Special events ranging from author breakfasts and luncheons to awards programs and reception's offers a great way to make industry contacts.

9. We will show you how not only to meet the challenges of information rich material but also the challenges of electronic distance learning.

10. To site just one problem, the reason that the market is in such a state of confusion is the appalling lack of standards whether for hardware, software or for metadata.

11. Two leading business consultants Doug Smith and Carla McNeil will share their insights on how specialty stores can effectively compete in a world of Corporate Superstores.

12. One of the big questions we need to address are "How does buying effect inventory levels"?

13. The closing of many industry digital entities have greatly affected the perception of e-books as a viable platform.

14. A competent, motivated, and enthusiastic staff can be a managers' most important asset in a competitive marketplace.

15. Come by the Technology Lounge where you can log on to computers and plug into laptops and check out demos of sponsor's Web sites.

Level 3: Document Critique

The following document contains errors in grammar, capitalization, punctuation, abbreviation, number style, and vocabulary. Correct all errors using standard proofreading marks (see Appendix C).

Date: Thurs, 14 November 2005 11:07:33 -0800

From: rick glissmeyer < rickg@aol.com>

To: richard herman < rcherman@ddc.com>

CC:

BCC:

Attached:

Subject: Please supply shipping costs

Dear Richard:

As you requested heres the complete order for seed mixes required by Roberta Mcdonald in Vancouver:

* Thirty two kilograms 80/20 canary seed mix @ $7.99
* 30 kg soak seed @ $9.50
* Total order: $540.68

The seeds are to be shipped to:

Roberta C. McDonald

1725 w. Third Av.

Vancuover, BC, V5M-5R6

We will mail our cheque, as soon as you reply with the amount of shipping costs. Roberta says “her flock’s getting ready for breeding,” and she needs the soak seed by the end of this month.

Thanks for your Quick Srevice

Rick Glissmeyer

What You Should Know About Videoconferencing Versus Face-to-Face Meetings

Ever since AT&T unveiled a videophone at the 1964 World's Fair, two-way TV has been touted as the next revolution in communication. Videoconferencing has always been a good idea, but its high costs and technical complexity had put off widespread acceptance—until now.

Today's videoconferencing equipment is better, faster, and more user friendly. System quality makes participants feel as if they are in the same room. Furthermore, the costs of installing videoconferencing systems have dropped dramatically in the last few years. Installations range in price from $10 000 for a portable TV monitor unit to $250 000 for a fully outfitted conference room with a giant screen and remote-control video camera. In some cases, the time and cost savings from reduced corporate travel could pay for these systems in less than one year.

Spurred by such cost savings and a heightened fear of flying, cancelled flights, and long airport delays following the September 11, 2001, terrorist attacks, sales of videoconferencing equipment are soon expected to top $40 billion. Companies that have considered videoconferencing for years are now being pressured by customers and suppliers to install such services. In fact, the hottest first-class seat is no longer on an airplane—instead, it's in front of a videoconferencing camera.

Will videoconferencing make face-to-face meetings obsolete? Probably not. You still need to seal important deals with personal handshakes—especially when conflicts or emotions are involved or when a relationship requires personal interaction to flourish. But videoconferencing will likely change the way people meet. For instance, lower-priority meetings and even details of merger talks could take place without participants leaving their hometown offices. "There's been far too much travelling around the country for 30-minute meetings," says one corporate executive. "It's foolish to have 15 people from different places fly thousands of miles to sit opposite each other at a conference table . . . It doesn't make any sense. It never made any sense." As one frequent business traveller put it, with videoconferencing, "there is no reason to get on a plane unless you absolutely need to."

Applications for Success

Hone your videoconferencing skills by visiting www.ADCOM.com. ADCOM, headquartered in Toronto, has offices in Calgary, Edmonton, Ottawa, Montreal, and Halifax, and in countries around the world. Choose "Training," then follow links to "Videoconferencing" and "Etiquette and Protocol" for tips on presenting. Assume you are an assistant to the director of communications at Morris & McWhinney, a law firm with branches in Vancouver, Calgary, and Toronto. The partners have asked your boss to investigate whether the firm should purchase all the equipment necessary for videoconferencing. To begin, your boss asks you to examine the general pros and cons.

Do the following:

1. Summarize your own opinion about whether videoconferencing is appropriate for all types of meetings that your firm conducts. Are there any meetings that would not be right for videoconferencing?
2. Make a list of videoconferencing's advantages and disadvantages for Morris & McWhinney.
3. Based on the results of your examination (and assuming that money is no object), make your own recommendation to your boss either to purchase the equipment or not.

3 Planning Business Messages

After studying this chapter, you will be able to

1. Describe the three-step writing process
2. List four questions that can help you test the purpose of your message
3. Discuss six ways to satisfy your audience's information needs
4. Identify six elements to consider when choosing a channel and medium
5. Specify six ways to establish a good relationship with your audience
6. Explain how to use the "you" attitude when writing messages
7. Give examples of bias-free language and explain its importance

From the Real World

"Timely and effective communication with key stakeholders is critical to the success of any business strategy. With more than 12 million clients and 60 000 employees worldwide, staying in touch with them is vitally important to ensure we stay ahead of changes in the markets we serve. We rely on a multi-channel communications approach—from brochures to e-mails, telephones to Internet, advertising to direct mail, newsletters to videoconferencing, as well as emerging technologies such as satellite TV and Internet Protocol Television—to make sure our employees and clients receive the information that they need."

–Anne Sutherland
Senior Vice–President
Client Segment Strategies
RBC Royal Bank

From its beginning as a small regional bank in Halifax in 1875 to its international presence in global financial services, RBC Financial Group has built its success by creating strategies to accommodate changes in markets, customers, and employee needs. Today, RBC has 60 000 employees serving customers in branches, online, and through automated services.[1] Its network has grown to nearly 2000 branches in Canada and the United States, more than 4000 automated banking machines, and more than 2.5 million online clients. Communicating face to face with their various audiences is not always an option for RBC staff. Instead, they must make use of a wide range of available channels and media, as well as new technologies, to make their messages effective.

Creating Audience-Centred Messages

Like RBC Royal Bank's managers, you'll face a variety of communication assignments in your career, both oral and written. Some of your tasks will be routine, needing little more than jotting down a few sentences; others will be more complex, requiring reflection, research, and careful document preparation. Whatever the situation, you can make your messages more effective by making them

- **Purposeful.** Business messages provide information, solve a problem, or request the resources necessary to accomplish a goal. Every message has a specific purpose.
- **Audience-centred.** Business messages help audiences understand issues, collaborate on tasks, or take action. Each message considers the audience's needs, background, and viewpoint.
- **Concise.** Business messages respect everyone's time by presenting information clearly and efficiently. Every message should be as short as it can be without detracting from the subject.

One of the best ways to create effective business messages is to follow a systematic writing process.

What Is the Three-Step Process?

The writing process outlined in Figure 3.1 on page 44 can help you write more effective messages. As the figure shows, this process may be viewed as three simple steps: planning, writing, and completing.

The three-step writing process covers planning, writing, and completing business messages.

Planning

First, think about the fundamentals of your message. Clarify your purpose in communicating and analyze audience members so that you can tailor your message to their needs and expectations. Gather the information that will inform, persuade, or motivate your audience. Then adapt your message by selecting the channel and medium that will suit both your needs and those of your audience. Finally, establish a good relationship with your audience. Planning is the focus of this chapter.

Writing

Once you've planned your message, the next step is to organize your ideas and compose your first draft. In this stage, you commit your thoughts to words, create sentences and paragraphs, and select illustrations and details to support your main idea. Writing business messages is discussed in Chapter 4.

Completing

After writing your first draft, it's time to step back to review the content and organization for overall style, structure, and readability. You'll want to revise and rewrite until your message comes across clearly and effectively; then edit your message for details such as grammar, punctuation, and format. The next task is to produce your message, putting it into the form that your audience will receive. The last step is to proof the final document for typos, spelling errors, and other mechanical problems. Completing business messages is discussed in Chapter 5.

How Does the Three-Step Process Work?

Because so many of today's business messages are composed under pressure, allocating your time among these three steps can be a challenge. But whether you have 30 minutes or two days, try using roughly half of your time for planning—for deciding on your purpose, getting to know your audience, and immersing yourself in your subject matter. Devote less than a quarter of your time to actually writing your document. Then use more than a quarter of your time for completing the project (so that you don't shortchange important final steps such as revising and proofing).[2]

Try to budget your time for each step.

There is no right or best way to write all business messages. As you work through the writing process presented in Chapters 3, 4, and 5, try not to view it as a list of how-to directives but as a way to understand the various tasks involved in effective business writing.[3] Effective communicators complete all three steps, although they may not necessarily complete them in 1-2-3 order. Some jump back and forth from one step to another; some compose quickly and then revise; others revise as they go along. But for the sake of organization, we'll start with planning, the first step of the writing process.

The order of the three steps is flexible.

Analyzing the Situation and Identifying Your Audience

When planning a business message, the first thing you need to think about is your purpose. For a business message to be effective, its purpose and its audience must complement each other.

FIGURE 3.1 The Three-Step Writing Process

Planning	Writing	Completing
Analyze the Situation Identify your purpose and profile your audience. **Investigate the Topic** Gather information through formal or informal research methods. **Adapt to the Audience** Choose the right channel and medium; then establish a good relationship with your audience.	**Organize the Message** Define your main idea, group your points, and choose the direct or indirect approach. **Compose the Message** Control your style through level of formality and conversational tone. Choose your words carefully to create effective sentences and paragraphs.	**Revise the Message** Evaluate content and organization. Edit and rewrite for conciseness and clarity. **Produce the Message** Use effective design elements. Check that emphasis is given to key ideas. **Proofread the Message** Review for errors in layout, spelling, and mechanics.
1	2	3

Define Your Purpose

Business messages have an "action" purpose.

All business messages have a **general purpose:** to inform, to persuade, or to collaborate with your audience. Business messages also have a **specific purpose.** To help you define the specific purpose of your message, ask yourself what you hope to accomplish with your message and what your audience should **DO** or think after receiving your message. Focus on the action you want. Often when people write in business, it is because something needs to happen or has happened. What action do you want? One technique to develop an action-based purpose statement is to complete this sentence: *"I want my reader to...* Use a verb to express your action purpose. Also consider the context or circumstances in which you are communicating when developing your purpose statement. Ask yourself these questions:

- **Is my purpose realistic?** If your purpose involves a radical shift in action or attitude, go slowly. Consider proposing the first step and using your message as the beginning of a learning process.
- **Is this the right time?** If an organization is undergoing changes of some sort, you may want to defer your message until things stabilize and people can concentrate on your ideas.
- **Is the right person delivering this message?** Although you may have done all the work, having your boss deliver your message could get better results because of his or her higher status.
- **Is my purpose acceptable to the organization?** Even though you want to fire off an angry reply to an abusive letter attacking your company, your supervisors might prefer that you regain the customer's goodwill. Your response must reflect the organization's priorities.

Once you have identified a clear purpose in communicating, take a good look at your intended audience.

Develop an Audience Profile

Ask yourself some key questions about your audience.

Who are your audience members? What are their attitudes? What do they need to know? And why should they care about your message? The answers to such questions will indicate which material you'll need to cover and how to cover it (see Figure 3.2).

FIGURE 3.2 Audience Analysis Helps You Plan Your Message

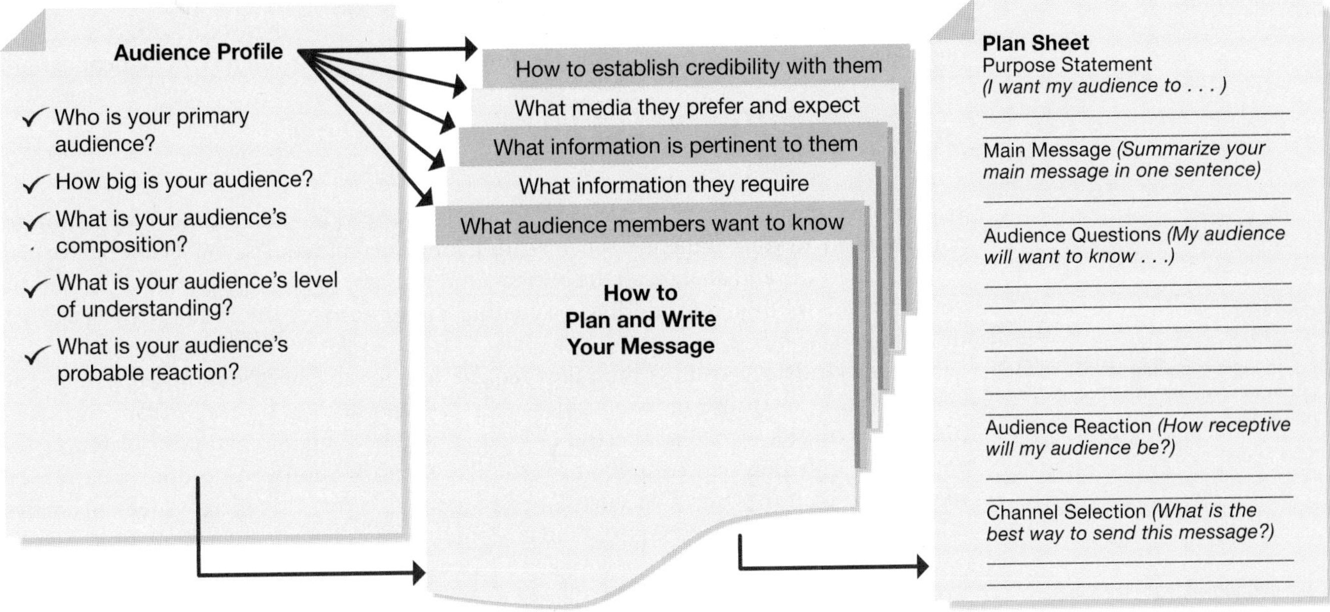

Analyze the Audience

To satisfy your audience's information needs, begin by identifying your primary audience. If you can reach the decision makers or opinion moulders in your audience, other audience members will fall into place.

Profile your audience by

- Identifying key decision makers
- Determining audience size
- Looking for common interests
- Estimating audience understanding
- Predicting audience reactions and questions about your topic.

- **Determine the size of your audience.** A report for a large audience requires a more formal style, organization, and format than one directed to three or four people in your department. Also, respond to the particular concerns of key individuals. The head of marketing would need different facts than the head of production or finance would need.
- **Define your audience's composition.** Look for common interests that tie audience members together across differences in culture, education, status, or attitude. Include evidence that touches on everyone's area of interest. To be understood across cultural barriers, consider how audience members think and learn, as well as what style they expect.[4]
- **Gauge your audience's level of understanding.** If audience members share your general background, they'll understand your material without difficulty. If not, you must educate them. Include only enough information to accomplish your objective, gearing your coverage to your primary audience (the key decision makers).
- **Estimate your audience's probable reaction.** If you expect a favourable response, you can state conclusions and recommendations up front and offer minimal supporting evidence. If you expect scepticism, you can introduce conclusions gradually, with more proof. Chapter 4 discusses how audience reaction affects message organization.

Use a Plan Sheet

To develop ideas for the content of your messages, use the plan sheet in Figure 3.2. Once you focus yourself by stating an action purpose, write your main message in one sentence. This summary statement can be part of the introduction to your communication and it will help focus the receiver.

The plan sheet can also help you generate content to include in your communication. Pretend the audience has read the main message, then predict what questions would follow. List the audience questions on the plan sheet. Later, you can use these questions to select the content, organize it, and create headings—thus creating a reader-oriented document design.

Investigating the Topic

Before you compose your message, you'll most likely need to gather some information to communicate to your audience. When writing long, formal reports, you'll conduct formal research to locate and analyze all the information relevant to your purpose and your audience. Formal techniques for finding, evaluating, and processing information are discussed in Chapter 11.

For many messages, collect information informally through networking.

Other kinds of business messages require less formal information gathering. For example, you may simply try to consider others' viewpoints. Put yourself in someone else's position to consider what that person or group might be thinking, feeling, or planning. Or your company's files may be a good source of the information you need for a particular memo or e-mail message. Consider company annual reports, financial statements, news releases, memos, marketing reports, and customer surveys for helpful information.

Ask the audience for feedback.

Chatting with supervisors, colleagues, or customers can help you gather information. Conducting telephone or personal interviews is a convenient way to investigate. And don't forget to ask your audience for input. If you're unsure of what audience members need from your message, ask them through casual conversation (face to face or over the phone), informal surveys, or unofficial interviews.

Be careful when deciding what information to include in your messages. Make sure your information is

- **Complete.** One good way to test the thoroughness of your message is to use the journalistic approach: Check to see whether your message answers *who, what, when, where, why,* and *how.*

Double-check your information.

- **Accurate.** Your organization is legally bound by any promises you make, so be sure your company can follow through. Check with the appropriate people *before* you make the commitment. Also, review all mathematical or financial calculations, check all dates and schedules, and examine your own assumptions and conclusions.
- **Ethical.** Messages can be unethical simply because information is omitted. You need to include enough detail to avoid misleading your audience. Include as much information as you believe best fits your definition of complete.
- **Pertinent.** Choose and emphasize the points that affect your audience the most. Whereas engineers may be interested in customer reaction to product design, shipping managers might want to know when customers receive the product. For an unknown audience, use your common sense to identify points of particular interest. Factors such as job, location, income, or education can give you a clue.

Adapting Your Message to Your Audience and Purpose

By now you know why you're writing, you know the audience you're writing to, and you have most of the information you need. But before beginning to write your message, think of how to make it serve both your audience and your purpose. To adapt your message, select a channel and a medium that fit your purpose and satisfy your audience's expectations. In addition, you need to establish a good relationship with your audience.

Select the Best Channel and Medium

Different types of messages require different communication channels and media.

Selecting the best channel and medium for your message can make the difference between effective and ineffective communication.[5] You must choose between the oral and written channels, and you must consider all the media within each one.

The *oral channel* includes media such as face-to-face conversation, telephone calls, speeches, presentations, and meetings. The chief advantage of oral communication is the opportunity it provides for immediate feedback. Your choice between a face-to-face conversation and a telephone call would depend on audience location, message importance, and your need for the sort of nonverbal feedback that only body language can reveal.

In general, use an oral channel if your purpose is to collaborate with the audience.

The *written channel* includes media that range from the scribbled notes people use to jog their own memories to formal reports that rival magazines in graphic quality. The most common written media are letters, memos, and reports (see Appendix A for business document formats). Written messages have one big advantage: They let you plan and control the message.

A written channel increases the sender's control but eliminates the possibility of immediate feedback.

In addition to the traditional forms of oral and written media, both channels have electronic forms. Oral media also include voice mail, audiotape and videotape, teleconferencing and videoconferencing, closed-circuit television, and many more. Written media also include e-mail, faxing, computer conferencing (with groupware), Web sites, instant messaging, and more.

The trick to choosing the best channel and medium is to select the tool that does the best overall job in each situation (see Table 3.1). To choose the channel and medium that will best match your purpose and audience, consider the following elements:

- **Message style and tone.** You wouldn't write a report with the same level of informality that you might use in an e-mail message. To emphasize the formality of your message, use a more formal medium, such as a memo or a letter.
- **Possibility for feedback.** Different media offer varying levels of feedback. The more feedback possible, the richer the medium. Face-to-face conversation is richest because

When choosing a channel and medium, consider six elements:

- Message style
- Opportunity for feedback
- Audience perception
- Timing
- Cost
- Audience expectation

Table 3.1 Choosing the Best Channel and Medium

Use Written Channels When

- You need no immediate feedback
- Your message is detailed, complex, or requires careful planning
- You need a permanent, verifiable record
- Your audience is large and geographically dispersed
- You want to minimize the distortion that can occur when messages pass orally from person to person
- Immediate interaction with the audience is either unimportant or undesirable
- Your message has no emotional component

Use Oral Channels When

- You want immediate feedback from the audience
- Your message is relatively simple and easy to accept
- You need no permanent record
- You can assemble your audience conveniently and economically
- You want to encourage interaction to solve a problem or reach a group decision
- You want to read the audience's body language or hear the tone of their response
- Your message has an emotional component

Use Electronic Forms When

- You need speed
- You're physically separated from your audience
- Time zones differ
- You must reach a dispersed audience personally

it provides immediate verbal and nonverbal feedback. On the other hand, unaddressed documents such as fliers are leanest because they offer no feedback at all. Use leaner media (notes, memos, letters) for simple, routine messages; use richer media (meetings, videos) for complex, nonroutine messages; and use phone calls, e-mail, and voice mail for messages in between.

- **Audience perception.** To emphasize the confidentiality of a message, use voice mail rather than a fax, send a letter rather than a memo, or plan on a private conversation rather than a meeting. To instill an emotional commitment, consider videotape or a videoconference. If you can get together, face-to-face conversation, however, can be more complete.[6]
- **Time.** If your message is urgent, you'll probably use the phone, send a fax, or send your message by next-day mail.
- **Cost.** You wouldn't think twice about telephoning an important customer overseas if you just discovered your company had erroneously sent the wrong shipment. But you'd probably choose to fax or e-mail a routine order acknowledgement to your customer in Australia.
- **Audience expectation.** Consider which media your audience expects or prefers.[7] You expect your university or college to deliver your degree/diploma by hand at graduation or in the mail, not by fax. Moreover, culture influences channel preference. People in Canada and Germany prefer written messages, whereas people in Japan prefer oral ones.[8] North American workers prefer e-mail and voice mail because it helps with the continent's multiple time zones; whereas German and French workers prefer traditional paper-based media and find long, detailed voice mails irritating. [9]

Establish a Good Relationship with Your Audience

Once you've chosen an appropriate channel and medium, you're still not ready to start writing. Effective communicators do more than simply convey information. They make sure that they establish a good relationship with their audience.

To give the right impression in your message, think carefully about who you are and who your audience is. Since a good relationship is based on sincerity, respect, and courtesy, show yours by using the "you" attitude, emphasizing the positive, establishing your credibility, being polite, using bias-free language, and projecting the company's image.

Use the "You" Attitude

Express your message in terms of the audience's interests and needs.

To project your audience-centred approach, adopt a **"you" attitude**—that is, speak and write in terms of your audience's wishes, interests, hopes, and preferences. On the simplest level, you replace terms that refer to you and your company with terms that refer to your audience. Use *you* and *yours* instead of *I, me, mine, we, us,* and *ours:*

Instead of	Use
To help us process this order, we must ask for another copy of the requisition.	So that your order can be filled promptly, please send another copy of the requisition.
We are pleased to announce our new flight schedule from Montreal to Toronto, which is any hour on the hour.	Now you can take a plane from Montreal to Toronto any hour on the hour.

Don't overdo the "you" attitude.

However, using *you* and *yours* requires finesse. If you overdo it, you're likely to create some rather awkward sentences, and you run the risk of sounding like a high-pressure carnival barker.[10] The "you" attitude is not intended to be manipulative or insincere. You can use *you* 25 times in a single page and still ignore your audience's true concerns. It's the thought and sincerity that count, not the pronoun. If you're talking to a retailer, try to think like a retailer; if you're writing to a dissatisfied customer, imagine how you would feel at the other end of the transaction. The important thing is your attitude toward audience members and your appreciation of their position.

In fact, on some occasions you'll do better to avoid using *you*. For instance, using *you* in a way that sounds dictatorial is impolite. Or, when someone makes a mistake, you may want to minimize ill will by pointing out the error impersonally. You might say, "We have a problem," instead of "You caused a problem."

Avoid using *you* and *yours* when doing so

- Makes you sound dictatorial
- Makes someone else feel guilty
- Goes against your organization's style

Be sure to consider the attitudes and policies of your organization and those of other cultures. In some cultures, it is improper to single out one person's achievements because the whole team is responsible for the outcome; using the pronoun *we* or *our* is more appropriate. Similarly, some companies have a tradition of avoiding references to *you* and *I* in their memos and formal reports. If you work for a company that expects a formal, impersonal style, confine your use of personal pronouns to informal letters and memos.

Emphasize the Positive

Another way of establishing a good relationship with your audience is to emphasize the positive side of your message.[11] Stress what is or will be instead of what isn't or won't be. Most information, even bad news, has some redeeming feature. If you can make your audience aware of that feature, your message will be more acceptable.

Explain what you have done, what you can do, and what you will do—not what you haven't done, can't do, or won't do.

Avoid Being Negative	Say What You *Can* Do
It is impossible to repair your vacuum cleaner today.	Your vacuum cleaner will be ready by Tuesday.
We apologize for inconveniencing you during our remodelling.	The renovations now underway will help us serve you better.

If you're trying to persuade the audience to buy a product, pay a bill, or perform a service for you, emphasize audience benefits by pointing out what's in it for them. Don't focus on why *you* want them to do something. An individual who sees the possibility for personal benefit is more likely to respond positively to your appeal.

Show audience members how they will benefit from complying with your message.

Avoid Focusing on Your Needs	Focus on Reader Benefits
Please buy this book so that I can make my sales quota.	The plot of this novel will keep you in suspense to the last page.
We need your contribution to the Variety Club.	You can help a child make friends and build self-confidence through your donation to the Variety Club.

In general, try to state your message without using words that might hurt or offend your audience. Substitute mild terms (euphemisms) for those that have unpleasant connotations. You can be honest without being harsh:

Avoid Harsh Language	Use Subtle Language
cheap merchandise	bargain prices
toilet paper	bathroom tissue

On the other hand, don't carry euphemisms to extremes. If you're too subtle, people won't know what you're talking about. You won't be helping your audience by "derecruiting" workers to the "mobility pool" instead of telling them that they have six weeks to find another job.

Establish Your Credibility

If you're unknown to your audience members, you'll have to earn their confidence before you can win them to your point of view. You want people to trust that your word is

People are more likely to react positively to your message when they have confidence in you.

dependable and that you know what you're doing. Your **credibility** (or believability) is based on how reliable you are and how much trust you evoke in others.

If you're communicating with a familiar group, your credibility has probably already been established, so you can get right down to business. But if audience members are complete strangers or, worse, if they start off with doubts about you, you'll need to devote the initial portion of your message to gaining credibility.

To enhance your credibility

- Show that you understand the other person's situation
- Explain your own credentials or ally yourself with a credible source
- Back up your claims with evidence, not exaggerations
- Use words that express confidence
- Believe in yourself and your message

Try to show an understanding of your audience's situation. Sometimes you can call attention to the things you have in common. If your audience shares your professional background, you might say, "As a fellow engineer [or lawyer, doctor, teacher, or whatever], I'm sure you can appreciate this situation." Also, use technical or professional terms that identify you as a peer.

You can explain your credentials. Your title or the name of your organization might be enough to impress your audience with your abilities. You might mention the name of someone who carries some weight with your audience ("Professor Goldberg suggested that I contact you") or quote a recognized authority on your subject. Just be careful not to sound pompous.

Avoid exaggerating your claims. A mail-order catalogue promised: "You'll be absolutely amazed at the incredible blooms on this healthy plant." Terms such as *amazing, incredible, extraordinary, sensational,* and *revolutionary* exceed the limits of believability, unless they're supported with some sort of proof. Similarly, support compliments with specific points. Don't appear to be currying favour with compliments that are overblown and insincere.

Avoid Exaggerating	Be Specific
My deepest heartfelt thanks for the excellent job you did. It's hard these days to find workers like you. You are just fantastic! I can't stress enough how happy you have made us with your outstanding performance.	Thanks for the fantastic job you did filling in for Gladys at the convention with just an hour's notice. Despite the difficult circumstances, you managed to attract several new orders with your demonstration of the new line of coffee makers. Your dedication and sales ability are truly appreciated.

Finally, avoid revealing any lack of confidence. Try not to undermine your credibility with vague sentiments or by using words such as *if, hope,* and *trust.* Avoid communicating an uncertain attitude that undermines your credibility. State your case with authority so that your audience has no doubts.

Avoid Creating Doubt	Be Definite
We hope this recommendation will be helpful.	We're glad to make this recommendation.
If you'd like to order, mail us the reply card.	To order, mail the reply card.

Be Polite

Try to express the facts in a kind and thoughtful manner.

Being polite is another good way to earn your audience's respect. By being courteous to members of your audience, you show consideration for their needs and feelings. Express yourself with kindness and tact. Venting your emotions rarely improves the situation and can jeopardize your audience's goodwill. Instead, be gentle when expressing yourself:

Avoid Accusation	Be Tactful
You really fouled things up with that last computer run.	Let's go over what went wrong with the last computer run so that the next run goes smoothly.
You've been sitting on my order for two weeks, and we need it now!	We are eager to receive our order. When can we expect delivery?

In general, written communication requires more tact than oral communication. When you're speaking, your words are softened by your tone of voice and facial expression. Plus, you can adjust your approach according to the feedback you get. But written communication is stark and self-contained. If you hurt a person's feelings in writing, you can't soothe them right away.

Use Bias-Free Language

Bias-free language avoids unethical, embarrassing blunders in language related to gender, race, ethnicity, age, and disability. Good communicators make every effort to correct biased language (see Table 3.2). To keep your messages bias-free, avoid the following:

Avoid biased language that might offend your audience.

- **Gender bias.** Avoid sexist language by using the same label for everyone (don't use *chairperson* for a woman and then use *chairman* for a man). Reword sentences to use *they* or to use no pronoun at all. Remember, the preferred title for women in business is *Ms.*, unless the individual asks to be addressed as *Miss* or *Mrs.* or has some other title, such as *Dr.*

Table 3.2 Tips for Overcoming Bias in Language

Examples	Unacceptable	Preferable
Gender Bias		
Using words containing "man"	Man-made	Artificial, synthetic, manufactured, constructed
	Businessman	Executive, business manager, business person
	Salesman	Sales representative, salesperson, clerk, sales agent
	Foreman	Supervisor
Using female-gender words	Authoress, actress, stewardess	Author, actor, flight attendant
Using special designations	Woman doctor, male nurse	Doctor, nurse
Using "he" to refer to "everyone"	The average worker . . . he	The average worker . . . he or she
Identifying roles with gender	The typical executive spends four hours of his day in meetings.	Most executives spend four hours a day in meetings.
	the nurse/teacher . . . she	nurses/teachers . . . they
Identifying women by marital status	Ian Hanomansing and Sandi Ian Hanomansing and Ms. Renaldo	Ian Hanomansing and Sandi Renaldo Mr. Hanomansing and Ms. Renaldo
Racial and Ethnic Bias		
Assigning stereotypes	My Indian assistant speaks more articulately than I do.	My assistant speaks more articulately than I do
	Jim Wong is an unusually tall Asian.	Jim Wong is tall.
Identifying people by race or ethnicity	Adrienne Clarkson, Chinese-Canadian journalist and governor general of Canada	Adrienne Clarkson, journalist and governor general of Canada
Age Bias		
Including age when irrelevant	Mary Kirazy, 58, has just joined our trust department.	Mary Kirazy has just joined our trust department.
Disability Bias		
Putting the disability before the person	Crippled workers face many barriers on the job.	Workers with physical disabilities face many barriers on the job.
	An epileptic, Tracy has no trouble doing her job.	Tracy's epilepsy has no effect on her job performance.

- **Racial and ethnic bias.** The central principle is to avoid language suggesting that members of a racial or an ethnic group have stereotypical characteristics. The best solution is to avoid identifying people by race or ethnic origin unless such a label is relevant.
- **Age bias.** As with gender, race, and ethnic background, mention the age of a person only when it is relevant. When referring to older people, avoid such stereotyped adjectives as *spry* and *frail.*
- **Disability bias.** No painless label exists for people with a physical, mental, sensory, or emotional impairment. Avoid mentioning a disability unless it is pertinent. However, if you must refer to someone's disability, avoid terms such as *handicapped, crippled,* or *retarded.* Put the person first and the disability second.[12]

Project the Company's Image

Subordinate your own style to that of the company.

Even though establishing a good relationship with the audience is your main goal, give some thought to projecting the right image for your company. When you communicate with outsiders, on even the most routine matter, you serve as the spokesperson for your organization. The impression you make can enhance or damage the reputation of the entire company. Thus, your own views and personality must be subordinated, at least to some extent, to the interests and style of your company.

Reviewing Key Points

In this chapter you learned about the first stage of the writing process: planning. When planning a message, you should

- Define a specific purpose.
- Analyze audience needs by assessing interests, educational background, and job needs and by predicting audience questions.
- Gather relevant information by asking questions, reviewing company files, and interviewing informally.
- Check information accuracy, completeness, and relevance.
- Select an appropriate channel and medium—choose written (such as letters, memos, reports) when the message is complex and detailed or when you need a record; choose oral (such as face to face, meetings, presentations, telephone) for immediate feedback or collaboration, or when messages are simple or highly emotional. Choose electronic forms (such as e-mail, voice mail, fax) for speed or convenience, or when you have time zone differences.
- Adapt your style to the audience.
- Use "you" attitude, bias-free language, and a positive approach to build a relationship, be credible, and be sincere.

Test Your Knowledge

1. What are the three steps in the writing process?

2. What two types of purposes do all business messages have?

3. What do you need to know in order to develop an audience profile?

4. What are four methods of informal information gathering?

5. When including information in your message, what four conditions must you satisfy?

6. What are the main advantages of oral communication? Of written media?

7. What six elements must you consider when choosing a channel and medium?

8. What is the "you" attitude, and how does it differ from an "I" attitude?

9. Why is it important to establish your credibility when communicating with an audience of strangers?

10. How does using bias-free language help communicators establish a good relationship with their audiences?

Apply Your Knowledge

1. Some writers argue that planning messages wastes time because they inevitably change their plans as they go along. How would you respond to this argument? Briefly explain.

2. As a member of the public relations department, what medium would you recommend using to inform the local community that your toxic-waste cleanup program has been successful? Why?

3. When composing business messages, how can you be yourself and project your company's image at the same time?

4. Considering how fast and easy it is, should e-mail replace meetings and other face-to-face communication in your company? Why or why not?

5. **Ethical Choices** The company president has asked you to draft a memo for her signature to the board of directors, informing them that sales in the new line of gourmet fruit jams have far exceeded anyone's expectations. As a member of the purchasing department, you happen to know that sales of moderately priced jams have declined quite a bit (many customers have switched to the more expensive jams). You were not directed to add that tidbit of information. Should you write the memo and limit your information to the expensive gourmet jams? Or should you include the information about the decline in moderately priced jams? Please explain.

Practise Your Knowledge

Exercises for Perfecting Your Writing

Specific Purpose For each of the following communication tasks, state a specific purpose (if you have trouble, try beginning with "I want to tell you that . . .").

1. A report to your boss, the store manager, about the outdated items in the warehouse

2. A memo to clients about your booth at the upcoming trade show

3. A letter to a customer who hasn't made a payment for three months

4. A memo to employees about the office's expensive water service bills

5. A phone call to a supplier checking on an overdue parts shipment

6. A report to future users of the computer program you have chosen to handle the company's mailing list

Audience Profile For each communication task below, write brief answers to three questions: (1) Who is my audience? (2) What is my audience's general attitude toward my subject? (3) What does my audience need to know? Predict a list of audience questions.

7. A final-notice collection letter from an appliance manufacturer to an appliance dealer, sent 10 days before initiating legal collection procedures

8. An unsolicited sales letter asking readers to purchase computer disks at near-wholesale prices

9. Fliers to be attached to doorknobs in the neighbourhood, announcing reduced rates for chimney lining or repairs

10. A cover letter sent along with your resumé to a potential employer

11. A request (to the seller) for a price adjustment on a piano that incurred $150 in damage during delivery to a banquet room in the hotel you manage

Media and Purpose Describe a message you have received lately (such as direct-mail promotions, letters, e-mail messages, phone solicitations, and lectures). Determine the general and the specific purpose; then answer the questions listed.

12. General purpose:

13. Specific purpose:

14. Was the message well timed?

15. Did the sender choose an appropriate medium for the message?

16. Did the appropriate person deliver the message?

17. Was the sender's purpose realistic?

18. What action did the writer want to happen? Where was the action stated?

Audience and Purpose Read the scenario below. Identify a specific (action) purpose, describe a few characteristics of the audience, sum up your main message, then predict and list audience questions that need to be answered in the communication. Select an appropriate channel for communicating your message.

You work as a supervisor at Sport Right, a sports clothing retailer, in the local mall. It bothers you that the merchandise is frequently lying over racks or on the floor by the end of a shift and that the items are often misplaced around the store. The manager, Sandi Johal, has been out of the store for the last few weeks in training courses. Even when she is around, though, things get pretty messy out on the floor. Each shift has enough people but they don't seem to worry about the appearance of the store. You decide to approach Sandi to solve this problem.

19. Use the plan sheet in Figure 3.2 to develop a plan. Make up the details you need to complete your plan.

The "You" Attitude Rewrite the following sentences to reflect your audience's viewpoint.

20. We request that you use the order form supplied in the back of our catalogue.

21. We insist that you always bring your credit card to the store.

22. We want to get rid of all our 15-inch monitors to make room in our warehouse for the 19-inch screens. Thus we are offering a 25 percent discount on all sales this week.

23. I am applying for the position of bookkeeper in your office. I feel that my grades prove that I am bright and capable, and I think I can do a good job for you.

24. As requested, we are sending the refund for $25.

Emphasizing the Positive Revise these sentences to be positive rather than negative.

25. To avoid the loss of your credit rating, please remit payment within 10 days.

26. We don't make refunds on returned merchandise that is soiled.

27. Because we are temporarily out of Baby Cry dolls, we won't be able to ship your order for 10 days.

28. You failed to specify the colour of the blouse that you ordered.

29. You should have realized that waterbeds will freeze in unheated houses during winter. Therefore, our guarantee does not cover the valve damage and you must pay the $9.50 valve-replacement fee (plus postage).

Emphasizing the Positive Revise the following sentences to replace unflattering terms (in italics):

30. The new boss is __________ (*stubborn*) when it comes to doing things by the book.

31. When you say we've doubled our profit level, you are __________ (*wrong*).

32. Just be careful not to make any __________ (*stupid*) choices this week.

33. Jim Riley is __________ (*incompetent*) for that kind of promotion.

34. Glen monopolizes every meeting by being __________ (*a loudmouth*).

Courteous Communication Revise these sentences to make them more courteous:

35. You claim that you mailed your cheque last Thursday, but we have not received it.

36. It is not our policy to exchange sale items, especially after they have been worn.

37. You neglected to sign the enclosed contract.

38. I received your letter, in which you assert that our shipment was three days late.

39. We are sorry you are dissatisfied.

40. You failed to enclose your instructions for your new will.

41. We request that you send us the bond by registered mail.

Bias-Free Language Rewrite each of the following sentences to eliminate bias:

42. For an Indian, Maggie certainly is outgoing.

43. He needs a wheelchair, but he doesn't let his handicap affect his job performance.

44. A pilot must have the ability to stay calm under pressure, and then he must be trained to cope with any problem that arises.

45. Candidate Renata Parsons, married and the mother of a teenager, will attend the debate.

Activities

For live links to all Web sites discussed in this chapter, visit this text's Web site at www.pearsoned.ca/bovee. Just log on and select Chapter 3, and click on "Student Resources." Locate the page or the URL related to the material in the text. For the "Best of the Web" exercises, you'll also find navigational directions. Click on the live link to the site.

1. **Analyze This Document** Read the following document; then (1) analyze the strengths and weaknesses of each sentence and (2) revise the document so that it follows this chapter's guidelines.

   I am a new publisher with some really great books to sell. I saw your announcement in *Quill & Quire* about the bookseller's show you're having this summer, and I think it's a great idea. Count me in, folks! I would like to get some space to show my books. I thought it would be a neat thing if I could do some airbrushing on T-shirts live to help promote my hot new title, *T-Shirt Art.* Before I got into publishing, I was an airbrush artist, and I could demonstrate my techniques. I've done hundreds of advertising illustrations and have been a sign painter all my life, so I'll also be promoting my other book, hot off the presses, *How to Make Money in the Sign Painting Business.*

   I will be starting my PR campaign about May 2005 with ads in Q & Q and some art trade papers, so my books should be well known by the time the show comes around in August. In case you would like to use my appearance there as part of your publicity, I have enclosed a biography and photo of myself.

   P.S. Please let me know what it costs for booth space as soon as possible so that I can figure out whether I can afford to attend. Being a new publisher is mighty expensive!

2. **Message-Planning Skills: Self-Assessment** How good are you at planning business messages? Use the following chart to rate yourself on each of the following elements of planning an audience-centred business message. Then examine your ratings to identify where you are strongest and where you can improve.

Element of Planning	Always	Frequently	Occasionally	Never
1. I start by defining my purpose.	___	___	___	___
2. I analyze my audience before writing a message.	___	___	___	___
3. I investigate what my audience wants to know.	___	___	___	___
4. I check that my information is accurate, ethical, and pertinent.	___	___	___	___
5. I consider my audience and purpose when selecting media.	___	___	___	___
6. I adopt the "you" attitude in my messages.	___	___	___	___
7. I emphasize the positive aspects of my message.	___	___	___	___
8. I establish my credibility with audiences of strangers.	___	___	___	___
9. I express myself politely and tactfully.	___	___	___	___
10. I use bias-free language.	___	___	___	___
11. I am careful to project my company's image.	___	___	___	___

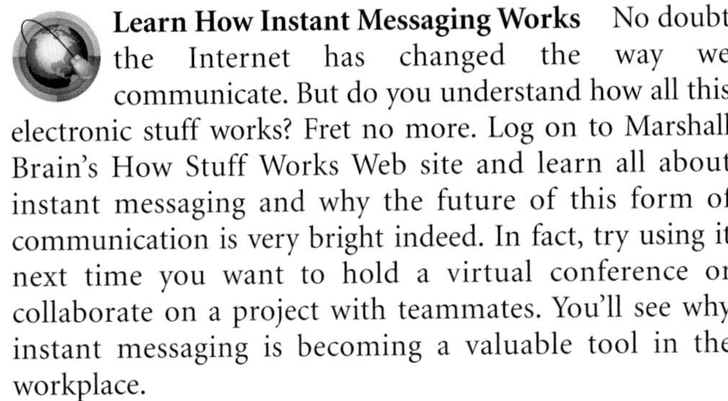

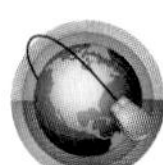

Expand Your Knowledge

Best of the Web

Learn How Instant Messaging Works No doubt the Internet has changed the way we communicate. But do you understand how all this electronic stuff works? Fret no more. Log on to Marshall Brain's How Stuff Works Web site and learn all about instant messaging and why the future of this form of communication is very bright indeed. In fact, try using it next time you want to hold a virtual conference or collaborate on a project with teammates. You'll see why instant messaging is becoming a valuable tool in the workplace.

www.howstuffworks.com/instant-messaging.htm

Exercises

1. What are the key advantages of instant messaging?
2. What is the difference between a chat room and instant messaging?
3. Is instant messaging a secure way to communicate?

Exploring the Web on Your Own

Review these chapter-related Web sites on your own to learn more about achieving communication success in the workplace:

1. Learn more about the writing process, English grammar, style and usage, words, and active writing at Garbl's Writing Resources Online, www.garbl.com.
2. Improve your organization and learn how to write better by paying attention to the sound advice and writing tips at Writing Better, an electronic Handbook for Amherst Students, www.amherst.edu/~writing/writingbetter.
3. Discover how e-mail works and how to improve your e-mail communications by following the steps at About Internet for Beginners—Harness E-Mail, www.learnthenet.com/english/section/email.html.

Learn Interactively

Interactive Study Guide

Visit the Companion Website at www.prenhall.ca/bovee. For Chapter 3, take advantage of the interactive "Study Guide" to test your chapter knowledge. Get instant feedback on whether you need additional studying.

This site offers a variety of additional resources: The "Research Area" helps you locate a wealth of information to use in course assignments. The "Study Hall" helps you succeed in this course by offering support with writing and study skills, time management, and career skills, as well as numerous other resources.

Peak Performance Grammar and Mechanics

PEAK Use the Peak Performance Grammar and Mechanics CD to test your skill with verbs. In the "Verbs" section, take the Pretest to determine whether you have any weak areas. Then review those areas in the Refresher Course. Take the Follow-Up Test to check your grasp of noun usage. For an extra challenge or advanced practice, take the Advanced Test.

Improve Your Grammar, Mechanics, and Usage

Level 1: Self-Assessment—Verbs

Review Section 1.3 in the Handbook of Grammar, Mechanics, and Usage, and then complete the following 15 items.

In items 1–5, provide the verb form called for in the following exercises:

1. I __________ (present perfect, *become*) the resident expert on repairing the copy machine.
2. She __________ (past, *know*) how to conduct an audit when she came to work for us.
3. Since Joan was promoted, she __________ (past perfect, *move*) all the files to her office.
4. Next week, call John to tell him what you __________ (future, *do*) to help him set up the seminar.
5. By the time you finish the analysis, he __________ (future perfect, *return*) from his vacation.

For items 6–10, rewrite the sentences so that they use active voice instead of passive:

6. The report will be written by Leslie Cartwright.

7. The failure to record the transaction was mine.

8. Have you been notified by the claims department of your rights?

9. We are dependent on their services for our operation.

10. The damaged equipment was returned by the customer before we even located a repair facility.

In items 11–15, circle the correct verb form provided in parentheses:

11. Everyone upstairs (*receive/receives*) mail before we do.

12. Neither the main office nor the branches (*is/are*) blameless.

13. C&B sales (*is/are*) listed in the directory.

14. When measuring shelves, 17 cm (*is/are*) significant.

15. About 90 percent of the employees (*plan/plans*) to come to the company picnic.

Level 2: Workplace Applications

The following items contain numerous errors in grammar, capitalization, punctuation, abbreviation, number style, word division, and vocabulary. Rewrite each sentence in the space provided, correcting all errors. Write *C* in the space after any sentence that is already correct.

1. Cut 5 cm off trunk and place in a water stand, and fill with water.

2. The newly-elected officers of the Board are: John Rogers, president, Robin Doig, vice-president, and Mary Sturhann, secretary.

3. Employees were stunned when they are notified that the trainee got promoted to Manager only after her 4th week with the company.

4. Seeking reliable data on market trends, the *Financial Post* is by far the best source.

5. Who did you wish to speak to?

6. The keynote address will be delivered by Jeffrey Simpson, who is an author of popular books, and writes a column for "The Globe and Mail."

7. Often the reputation of an entire company depend on one employee that officially represents that company to the public.

8. The executive director, along with his staff, are working quickly to determine who should receive the Award.

9. Him and his co-workers, the top bowling team in the tournament, will represent our Company in the league finals on saturday.

10. Listening on the extension, details of the embezzlement plot were overheard by the Security Chief.

11. The acceptance of visa cards are in response to our customer's demand for a more efficient and convenient way of paying for parking here at Pearson International airport.

12. The human resources dept. interviewed dozens of people, they are seeking the better candidate for the opening.

13. Libraries' can be a challenging; yet lucrative market if you learn how to work the "system" to gain maximum visibility for you're products and services.

14. Either a supermarket or a discount art gallery are scheduled to open in the Mall.

15. I have told my supervisor that whomever shares my office with me cannot wear perfume, use spray deodorant, or other scented products.

Level 3: Document Critique

The following document may contain errors in grammar, capitalization, punctuation, abbreviation, number style, vocabulary, and spelling. You will also find errors relating to topics in this chapter. Concentrate on using the "you" attitude, emphasizing the positive, being polite, and using bias-free language as you improve this memo. Correct all errors using standard proofreading marks (see Appendix C).

MEMO

To: Blockbuster mngrs.

From: Sid Ryan, deputy chairmen, Viacom, Inc.

in care of Blockbuster Entertainment Canada

1201 Elm street; Toronto, ON M3P 2T6

Date May 8 2005

Sub: Recent Cash Flow and consumer response—Survey

Now that our stores have been re-organized with your hard work and cooperation, we hope revenues will rise to new heights; if we re-emphasize video rentals as Blockbusters core business and reduce the visibility of our sideline retail products. Just in case though, we want to be certain that these changes are having the postive affect on our cash flow that we all except and look forward to.

To help us make that determination, respond to the following survey questions and fax them back. Answer concisely; but use extra paper if necessary—for details and explanations.

When you finish the survey it will help headquarters improve service to you; but also, help us all improve service to our customers. Return your survay before before May 15 to my attention. Then blockbuster hopefully can thrive in a marketplace, that critics say we cannot conquer. Blockbuster must choose wisely and serve it's customers well in a difficult video-rental business environment.

Times are very tough but if we work hard at it its possible we might make Blockbuster 'the man on the streets favorite 'place to go to rent videos!'

Technology

Business Communication Notebook

Caution! E-mail Can Bite

Gone are the days when memos were dictated, typed, revised, retyped, photocopied, and circulated by interoffice "snail" mail. Today, e-mail messages are created, sent, received, and forwarded in the blink of an eye, and at the stroke of a key. But this quick and efficient method of communication can cause a great deal of trouble for companies.

One of the greatest features—and dangers—of e-mail is that people tend to treat it far more informally than other forms of business communication. They think of e-mail as casual conversation and routinely make unguarded comments. Moreover, they are led to believe that "deleting" e-mail destroys it permanently. But that's a dangerous misunderstanding of technology.

Even after you delete an e-mail message, it can still exist on the system's hard drive and backup storage devices at both the sender's and the recipient's location. Deleting files only signals the computer that the space required to store the message is no longer needed. The space is so marked, but the data that occupy that space continue to exist until the computer overwrites it with new data. Thus, deleted messages are recoverable—even though doing so is an involved and expensive process—and they can be used as court evidence against you and your company. Embarrassing e-mail has played a big role in corporate battles. In the high-profile Microsoft court battle, for instance, e-mail emerged as the star witness.

So how can companies guard against potential e-mail embarrassment and resulting litigation? Besides restricting the use of e-mail by employees, monitoring employees' e-mail, developing company e-mail policies, and reprimanding or terminating offenders, companies can train their employees to treat e-mail as any other form of written communication. Perhaps one of the best ways to ensure that employee messages won't come back to haunt the company is to teach employees that e-mail messages are at least as permanent as letters and memos—if not more so.

To make sure that you use e-mail effectively, efficiently, and safely, follow these guidelines:

- Don't send large files (including large attachments) without prior notice.
- Proofread every message.
- Respect other people's electronic space by sending messages only when necessary.
- Respond to messages quickly.
- Avoid overusing the label "urgent."
- Be careful about using the "reply all" button.
- Remember that e-mail isn't always private.

Applications for Success

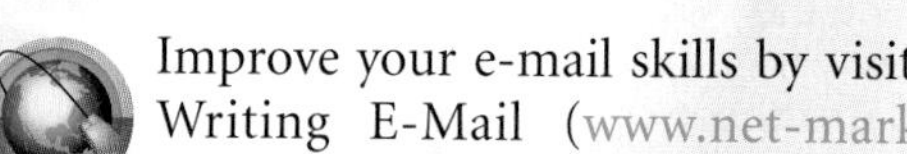

Improve your e-mail skills by visiting The Art of Writing E-Mail (www.net-market.com/email.htm). Whether you're working for a company or for yourself, be sure to give your e-mail messages as much consideration as you give more formal types of communication.

Answer the following questions:

1. Why do you think that most people treat e-mail so casually?
2. What kinds of things do you think a company should address in an e-mail policy?
3. Do you think that companies have the right to monitor employees' e-mail? Please explain.

Writing Business Messages

4

After studying this chapter, you will be able to

1 Explain why good organization is important to both you and your audience
2 List the four activities required to organize business messages effectively
3 Summarize five features of an effective outline
4 Identify three factors you must consider before choosing a direct or an indirect approach
5 Explain four things you should avoid to achieve a conversational tone in business messages
6 Describe five techniques for selecting the best words when writing business messages
7 Discuss three measures you can take to help you create more effective sentences
8 List four methods of establishing transitions to make paragraphs coherent

From the Real World

"My college professor said to take what you know, close your eyes, and pretend you're running home and opening the door and saying, 'Hey, Mom, guess what?' The next words will be your first line."

–Julie Galle
Writer/Producer
weather.com

Julie Galle is writer/producer for the official Web site of The Weather Channel, weather.com. Whether writing a short news item about a snowstorm on the prairies or a lengthy report on the effects of global warming, Galle must organize and compose her messages so that members of her audience can easily understand the information, believe it, and quickly apply it to their own lives. Galle limits the scope of her articles and carefully organizes them. Although short news stories may require only the briefest notes of a few facts, Galle prepares outlines for long pieces. For non-news items and long reports, she usually writes three drafts: for style, for covering meteorological points, and for proofing grammar and punctuation.[1]

Organizing Your Message

Poor organization costs time, efficiency, and relationships.

Misinterpreted messages waste time, lead to poor decision making, and shatter business relationships. So you can see how valuable clear writing and good organization can be.[2] Successful communicators like Julie Galle rely on good organization to make their messages meaningful.[3]

What exactly makes a particular organization "good"? Although the definition of good organization varies from country to country, in Canada and the United States it generally means creating a linear message that proceeds point by point and delivers the main message near the beginning. Consider Figure 4.1. The poorly written draft displays weak organization, but the organization is much improved in the revised version. Before you begin to write, think about what you're going to say and how you're going to say it.

FIGURE 4.1 Letter with Improved Organization

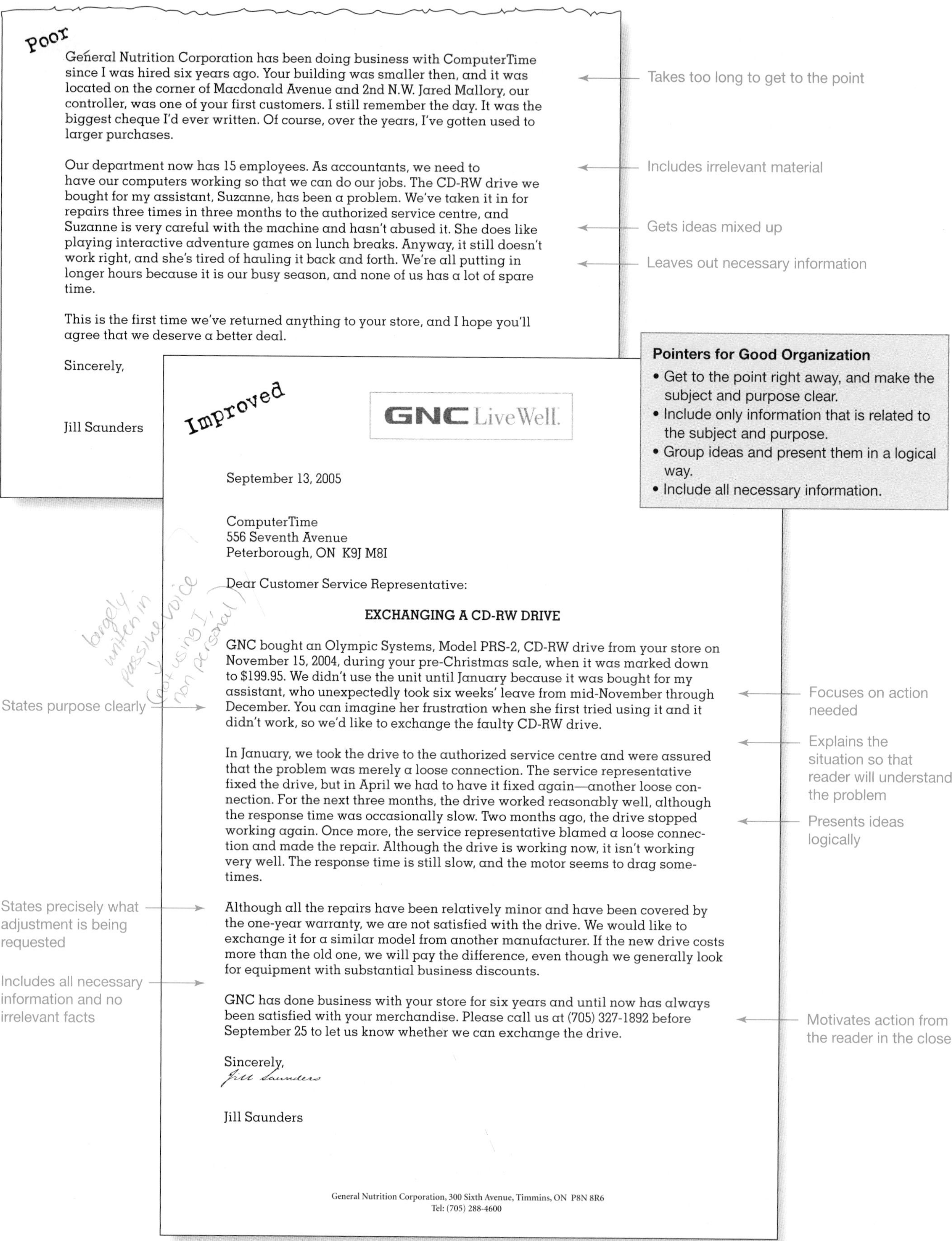

Poor

General Nutrition Corporation has been doing business with ComputerTime since I was hired six years ago. Your building was smaller then, and it was located on the corner of Macdonald Avenue and 2nd N.W. Jared Mallory, our controller, was one of your first customers. I still remember the day. It was the biggest cheque I'd ever written. Of course, over the years, I've gotten used to larger purchases.

Our department now has 15 employees. As accountants, we need to have our computers working so that we can do our jobs. The CD-RW drive we bought for my assistant, Suzanne, has been a problem. We've taken it in for repairs three times in three months to the authorized service centre, and Suzanne is very careful with the machine and hasn't abused it. She does like playing interactive adventure games on lunch breaks. Anyway, it still doesn't work right, and she's tired of hauling it back and forth. We're all putting in longer hours because it is our busy season, and none of us has a lot of spare time.

This is the first time we've returned anything to your store, and I hope you'll agree that we deserve a better deal.

Sincerely,

Jill Saunders

Pointers for Good Organization

- Get to the point right away, and make the subject and purpose clear.
- Include only information that is related to the subject and purpose.
- Group ideas and present them in a logical way.
- Include all necessary information.

Improved

GNC LiveWell.

September 13, 2005

ComputerTime
556 Seventh Avenue
Peterborough, ON K9J M8I

Dear Customer Service Representative:

EXCHANGING A CD-RW DRIVE

GNC bought an Olympic Systems, Model PRS-2, CD-RW drive from your store on November 15, 2004, during your pre-Christmas sale, when it was marked down to $199.95. We didn't use the unit until January because it was bought for my assistant, who unexpectedly took six weeks' leave from mid-November through December. You can imagine her frustration when she first tried using it and it didn't work, so we'd like to exchange the faulty CD-RW drive.

In January, we took the drive to the authorized service centre and were assured that the problem was merely a loose connection. The service representative fixed the drive, but in April we had to have it fixed again—another loose connection. For the next three months, the drive worked reasonably well, although the response time was occasionally slow. Two months ago, the drive stopped working again. Once more, the service representative blamed a loose connection and made the repair. Although the drive is working now, it isn't working very well. The response time is still slow, and the motor seems to drag sometimes.

Although all the repairs have been relatively minor and have been covered by the one-year warranty, we are not satisfied with the drive. We would like to exchange it for a similar model from another manufacturer. If the new drive costs more than the old one, we will pay the difference, even though we generally look for equipment with substantial business discounts.

GNC has done business with your store for six years and until now has always been satisfied with your merchandise. Please call us at (705) 327-1892 before September 25 to let us know whether we can exchange the drive.

Sincerely,
Jill Saunders

Jill Saunders

General Nutrition Corporation, 300 Sixth Avenue, Timmins, ON P8N 8R6
Tel: (705) 288-4600

What does good organization do for you? First and foremost, it saves you time. Your draft goes more quickly because you're not putting ideas in the wrong places or composing material you don't need. In addition, you can use your organizational plan to get some advance input from your audience, making sure you're on the right track before spending hours working on your draft. And, if your project is large and complex, you can even use your organizational plan to divide the writing job among co-workers.

Most disorganized communication suffers from problems with clarity, relevance, grouping, and completeness.

Good organization saves time, strengthens relationships, and improves efficiency.

In addition to helping you, good organization helps your audience:

- **Good organization helps your audience understand your message.** By making your main point clear at the outset, and by focusing on audience interests, your well-organized message will satisfy your audience's need for information.
- **Good organization helps your audience accept your message.** Even when your message is logical, you need to select and organize your points in a diplomatic way. Softening refusals and leaving a good impression enhance credibility and add authority to your messages.
- **Good organization saves your audience time.** Audience members receive only the information they need, and because that information is relevant, brief, and logically placed, your audience can follow your thought pattern without a struggle.

Good organization helps audience members understand your message, accept your message, and save time.

When writing messages at weather.com, Julie Galle achieves good organization by defining the main idea, limiting the scope, grouping supporting points, and establishing their sequence by selecting either a direct or an indirect approach.

To organize a message

- Define your main idea
- Limit the scope
- Group your points
- Choose the direct or indirect approach

Define the Main Idea

In addition to having a general purpose and a specific purpose, all business messages gain focus when they begin with a **main idea** or general interest statement that sums up the message. The rest of your document supports, explains, or demonstrates this point. Your main idea is not the same as your topic. The broad subject of your message is the **topic,** and your main idea makes a statement about that topic. The topic is "*what*" you are writing about. The main idea is the "*so what*" about the topic.

The topic is the broad subject; the main idea makes a statement about the topic.

In longer documents and presentations, you'll need to unify a mass of material, so you'll need to define a main idea that encompasses or summarizes all the individual points you want to make. For tough assignments like these, you may want to take special measures to define your main idea.

Limit the Scope

Determine the scope of your message (its length and detail) by analyzing your audience's needs. Decide how much to write by predicting what questions the audience would have about your main idea.

Regardless of how long the message will be, focus on three or four major points—five at the very most. According to communication researchers, that's all your audience will remember.[4] Instead of introducing additional points, you can more fully develop complex issues by supporting your points with a variety of evidence.

Focus on three or four major points (not more than five), regardless of message length.

Group Your Points in an Outline

Once you have narrowed the scope of your message, you must provide supporting details in the most logical and effective way. Constructing an outline of your message is a great way to visualize how your major points and supporting details will fit together. Whether you use the outlining features provided with word-processing software or simply jot down three or four points on the back of an envelope, your outline will keep you on track and help you cover the important information. You're no doubt familiar with the basic outline format (see Figure 4.2 on page 70).

An outline or a schematic diagram will help you visualize the relationship among parts of a message.

Remember that outlines

- use numbers (or letters and numbers) to identify each point.
- indent points to show which ideas are of equal status.
- divide a topic into at least two parts.
- ensure that each group of ideas is separate and distinct.

FIGURE 4.2 Common Outline Forms

ALPHANUMERIC OUTLINE

I. First Major Part
  A. First subpoint
  B. Second subpoint
    1. Evidence
    2. Evidence
II. Second Major Point
  A. First subpoint
    1. Evidence
    2. Evidence
  B. Second subpoint

DECIMAL OUTLINE

1.0 First Major Part
  1.1 First subpoint
  1.2 Second subpoint
    1.2.1 Evidence
    1.2.2 Evidence
2.0 Second Major Point
  2.1 First subpoint
    2.1.1 Evidence
    2.1.2 Evidence
  2.2 Second subpoint

The main idea states the action you want your audience to take and why.

Figure 12.3 (in Chapter 12) shows you an outline of a 30-minute presentation. When outlining your message, begin with a purpose statement and your main idea. To help you establish the goals and general strategy of your message, the main idea summarizes two things: (1) what you want audience members to do or think and (2) why they should do so. Everything in your message must either support the main idea or explain its implications.

Major supporting points clarify your main idea.

Next, you state the major supporting points. Try to identify between three and five major points that support and clarify your message in more concrete terms. If you come up with more, go back and look for opportunities to combine some of your ideas.

Finally, illustrate your major supporting points with evidence—facts and examples that help your audience understand and remember your message. In a long, complex message, you may need to carry the outline down several levels; in short, informal business documents, numbers are rarely used. Just remember that every level is a step along the chain from the abstract to the concrete, from the general to the specific. The lowest level contains the individual facts and figures that make up your evidence.

Choose Between the Direct and Indirect Approaches

Once you've defined your ideas and outlined your message, you choose the basic approach you'll use to present your points. When addressing a Canadian or U.S. audience with few cultural differences, you have two options:

Use direct order if the audience's reaction is likely to be positive and indirect order if it is likely to be negative.

- **Direct approach (deductive).** The main idea comes first (a recommendation, conclusion, or request), followed by the evidence. Use this approach when your audience will be neutral about your message or pleased to hear from you.
- **Indirect approach (inductive).** The evidence comes first, and the main idea comes later. Use this approach when your audience may be displeased about or may resist what you have to say.

Before you can choose one of these approaches, you must have a good idea of how your audience is likely to react to your purpose and message. Consider whether the culture of the audience has a preference for an indirect approach. The direct approach is generally fine when audience members will be receptive—if they are eager, interested, pleased, or even neutral. But you may have better results with the indirect approach if audience members are likely to resist your message—if they are displeased, uninterested, or unwilling (see Figure 4.3).

Audience reaction can range from eager to unwilling.

FIGURE 4.3 Audience Reaction Affects Organizational Approach

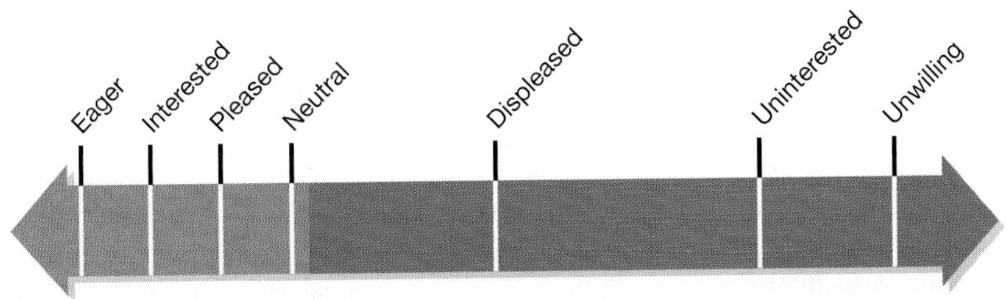

	Direct approach	Indirect approach	
Audience reaction	Eager/interested/ pleased/neutral	Displeased	Uninterested/unwilling
Message type	Routine, good news, goodwill	Bad news	Persuasive
Message opening	Start with the main idea, the request, or the good news.	Start with a neutral statement that acts as a transition to the reasons for the bad news.	Start with a statement or question that captures attention.
Message body	Provide necessary details.	Give reasons to justify a negative answer. State or imply the bad news, and make a positive suggestion.	Arouse the audience's interest in the subject. Build the audience's desire to comply.
Message close	Close with a cordial comment, a reference to the good news, or a statement about the specific action desired.	Close cordially.	Request action.

Bear in mind, however, that each message is unique. No simple formula will solve all your communication problems. Sometimes you'll want to get directly to the point, even if your message is unpleasant. Also, the direct approach may be better for long messages, regardless of your audience's attitude, because delaying the main idea could cause confusion and frustration. So before choosing a direct or an indirect approach, consider all three of the following factors:

Choice of approach depends on audience reaction, message length, and message type.

- **Audience reaction:** Positive, neutral, or negative
- **Message length:** Short memos and letters (discussed in Unit 3) or long reports, proposals, and presentations (discussed in Unit 4)
- **Message type:** (1) routine, good-news, and goodwill messages; (2) bad-news messages; or (3) persuasive messages (all of which are discussed in Unit 3)

Just remember, your first priority is to make your message clear. In the following brief discussions, note how the opening, body, and close all play an important role in getting your message across, regardless of message type.

Composing Your Message

Once you've completed the planning process and organized your message, you're ready to begin composing your first draft. If your schedule permits, put aside your outline for a day or two. Then review it with a fresh eye, looking for opportunities to improve the flow of ideas. Once you begin writing, you may discover as you go along that you can improve on your outline. Feel free to rearrange, delete, and add ideas, as long as you don't lose sight of your purpose.

Composition is the process of drafting your message; polishing it is a later step.

As you compose your first draft, try to let your creativity flow. Don't try to draft and edit at the same time or worry about getting everything perfect. Just put down your ideas as quickly as you can. You'll have time to revise and refine the material later. Once you have all your thoughts and ideas jotted down, begin shaping your message. Start by paying attention to your style and tone. Try to select words that match the tone you want to achieve. Next, create effective sentences and develop coherent paragraphs. The following sections discuss each of these elements.

Control Your Style and Tone

When composing your message, you can vary the style to create a tone that suits the occasion.

Style is the way you use words to achieve a certain **tone,** or overall impression. You can vary your style—your sentence structure and vocabulary—to sound forceful or objective, personal or formal, colourful or dry. The right choice depends on the nature of your message and your relationship with your audience.

Use a Conversational Tone

Most business messages aim for a conversational tone, using plain language that sounds businesslike without being stuffy, stiff, wordy, or full of jargon. To achieve a conversational tone in your messages, try to avoid obsolete and pompous language, intimacy, humour, and preaching or bragging.

To achieve a warm but businesslike tone

- Don't use obsolete language
- Don't be too familiar
- Use humour only with great care
- Don't preach or brag

Avoid Obsolete Language Business language used to be much more formal than it is today, and some out-of-date phrases still remain. You can avoid using such language if you ask yourself, "Would I say this if I were talking with someone face to face?"

Obsolete	Up to Date
In due course	today, tomorrow (or a specific time)
permit me to say that	(omit—permission is not necessary)
we are in receipt of	we have received
pursuant to	(omit)
In closing, I'd like to say	(omit)
we wish to inform you	(omit—just say it)
attached please find	enclosed is
please be advised that	(omit)

Avoid False Familiarity Don't mention anything about anyone's personal life unless you know the individual very well. Avoid phrases such as "just between you and me" and "as you and I are well aware." Be careful about sounding too folksy or chatty; such a familiar tone may be seen as an attempt to seem like an old friend when, in fact, you're not.

Avoid Humour Using humour can backfire, especially if you don't know your audience very well. What seems humorous to you may be deadly serious to others. Plus, what's funny today may not be in a week or a month. Moreover, when you're communicating across cultures, chances are slim that your audience will appreciate your humour or even realize that you're trying to be funny.[5]

Use Plain English

Plain English is close to spoken English and can be easily understood.

Plain English is a way of writing and arranging technical materials so that your audience can understand your meaning. Because it's close to the way people normally speak, plain English is easily understood by people with a grade eight or nine education. If you've ever tried to make sense of an overwritten or murky passage in a legal document or credit agreement, you can understand why governments and corporations endorse the plain-English movement.[6]

Avoid Overwriting	Use Simple, Clear Language
The applicability of the general information and administrative procedures set forth below accordingly will vary depending on the investor and the record-keeping system established for a shareholder's investment in the Fund. Participants in RRSP's and other plans should first consult with the appropriate persons at their employer or refer to the plan materials before following any of the procedures below.	If you are investing through a large retirement plan or other special program, follow the instructions in your program material.

Plain English lacks the precision necessary for scientific research, intense feeling, and personal insight, but it is invaluable in general business messages. Even though it's intended for audiences who speak English as their primary language, plain English can also help you simplify the messages you prepare for audiences who speak English only as a second or even third language. For example, by choosing words that have only one interpretation, you will surely communicate more clearly with your intercultural audience.[7]

Plain English is best for intercultural communication.

Select the Best Words

To compose effective messages, you must choose your words carefully.[8] Good business writing is learned by imitation and practice. As you read business journals, newspapers, and even novels, make a note of the words you think are effective and keep them in a file. Then look through them before you draft your next letter or report. Try using some of these words in your document. You may be surprised at how they can strengthen your writing.

First, pay close attention to correctness. Using words correctly is important. If you make grammatical or usage errors, you lose credibility with your audience, and grammatical errors are distracting. If you have doubts about what is correct, look up the answer. Memorize the words listed in the Handbook of Grammar, Mechanics, and Usage, at the end of this text on pages H-27–H-28. You can also consult any number of special reference books and resources available in libraries, in bookstores, and on the Internet. Most authorities agree on the basic conventions.

Correctness is the first consideration when choosing words.

Just as important as selecting the correct word is selecting the most suitable word for the job at hand. Word effectiveness is generally more difficult to achieve than correctness, particularly in written communication. Good writers work at their craft to produce messages that are clear, concise, and accurate.

Effectiveness is the second consideration when choosing words.

Blend Abstract and Concrete Words

An **abstract word** expresses a concept, quality, or characteristic. Abstractions are usually broad, encompassing a category of ideas. They are often intellectual, academic, or philosophical. *Love, honour, progress, tradition,* and *beauty* are abstractions.

A **concrete word** stands for something you can touch or see. Concrete terms are anchored in the tangible, material world. *Chair, table, horse, rose, kick, kiss, red, green,* and *two* are concrete words; they are direct, clear, and exact.

Abstractions permit us to rise above the common and tangible. They allow us to refer to concepts such as *morale, productivity, profits, quality, motivation,* and *guarantees.* Even though they're indispensable, abstractions can be troublesome. They tend to be fuzzy and subject to many interpretations. They also tend to be boring. It isn't always easy to get excited about ideas, especially if they're unrelated to concrete experience. The best way to minimize such problems is to blend abstract terms with concrete ones, the general with the specific. State the concept, then pin it down with details expressed in more concrete terms. Instead of referring to a *sizable loss,* talk about a *loss of $32 million.* Save the abstractions for ideas that cannot be expressed any other way.

In business communication, use concrete, specific terms whenever possible; use abstractions only when necessary.

Choose Strong Words

Good business communicators choose strong words.

Choose words that express your thoughts most clearly, specifically, and dynamically. Nouns and verbs are the most concrete, so use them as much as you can. Adjectives and adverbs have obvious roles, but use them sparingly—they often evoke subjective judgments. Verbs are especially powerful because they tell what's happening in the sentence, so make them dynamic and specific; for example, replace *rise* or *fall* with *soar* or *plummet.*

Avoid Weak Phrases	Use Strong Terms
wealthy business person	tycoon
business prosperity	boom
hard times	slump

Choose Familiar Words

For effective messages, choose familiar words.

You'll communicate best with words that are familiar to your readers. Avoid using pompous language that contains big words, overly complicated phrases, and trite expressions. However, when trying to choose familiar words, remember that words familiar to one reader might be unfamiliar to another.

Avoid Unfamiliar Words	Use Familiar Words
ascertain	find out, learn
consummate	close, bring about
peruse	read, study
circumvent	avoid
increment	growth, increase
unequivocal	certain

Avoid Clichés

To make a good impression, avoid clichés.

Although familiar words are generally the best choice, beware of terms and phrases so common that they have become virtually meaningless. Because clichés are used so often, readers tend to slide right by them to whatever is coming next. Most people use these phrases not because they think it makes their message more vivid and inviting but because they don't know how to express themselves otherwise.[9]

Avoid Clichés	Use Plain Language
scrape the bottom of the barrel	strain shrinking resources
an uphill battle	a challenge
writing on the wall	prediction
call the shots	be in charge
take by storm	attack
cost an arm and a leg	expensive
a new ball game	a fresh start
worst nightmare	strong competitor, disaster
fall through the cracks	be overlooked

Avoid Jargon

Handle technical or professional terms with care. As Julie Galle puts it, meteorological terminology and jargon can add precision and authority to a weather message, but many people don't understand the jargon. When deciding whether to use technical jargon, let your audience's knowledge guide you. For example, when addressing a group of engineers or scientists, it's probably fine to refer to *meteorological effects on microwave propagation;* otherwise, refer to the *effects of weather on radio waves.*

Use jargon only if your readers know the term.

Create Effective Sentences

In English, words don't make much sense until they're combined in a sentence to express a complete thought. Thus the words *Jill, receptionist, the, smiles,* and *at* can be organized into "Jill smiles at the receptionist." Now that you've constructed the sentence, you can begin exploring the possibilities for improvement, looking at how well each word performs its particular function. Nouns and noun equivalents are the topics (or subjects) that you're communicating about. Verbs and related words (or predicates) make statements about those subjects. In a complicated sentence, adjectives and adverbs modify the nouns and verbs, and various connectors hold the words together. You can make your sentences more effective by using all four types of sentences, emphasizing key thoughts through sentence style, and selecting active or passive voice.

In English, word order is important when constructing sentences.

Use All Four Types of Sentences

Sentences come in four basic varieties: simple, compound, complex, and compound-complex. A **simple sentence** has one main clause (a single subject and a single predicate), although it may be expanded by nouns and pronouns serving as objects of the action and by modifying phrases. Here's a typical example (with the subject underlined once and the predicate verb underlined twice):

You can choose from four types of sentences:

- Simple
- Compound
- Complex
- Compound-complex

> Profits have increased in the past year.

A **compound sentence** has two main clauses that express two or more independent but related thoughts of equal importance, usually joined by *and, but,* or *or.* In effect, a compound sentence is a merger of two or more simple sentences (independent clauses) that are related. For example:

> Wage rates have declined by 5 percent, and employee turnover has been high.

The independent clauses in a compound sentence are always separated by a comma or by a semicolon (in which case the conjunction—*and, but, or*—is dropped).

A **complex sentence** expresses one main thought (the independent clause) and one or more subordinate thoughts (dependent clauses) related to it, often separated by a comma. The subordinate thought, which comes first in the following sentence, could not stand alone:

> Although you may question Gerald's conclusions, you must admit that his research is thorough.

A **compound-complex sentence** has two main clauses, at least one of which contains a subordinate clause:

> Profits have increased in the past year, and although you may question Gerald's conclusions, you must admit that his research is thorough.

To make your writing as effective as possible, balance all four sentence types. If you use too many simple sentences, you won't be able to properly express the relationships among your ideas. If you use too many long, compound sentences, your writing will sound monotonous. On the other hand, an uninterrupted series of complex or compound-complex sentences is hard to follow.

Vary your style by balancing the four types of sentences.

Emphasize Key Thoughts with Sentence Style

Sentence style varies from culture to culture. In English, try to make your sentences grammatically correct, efficient, readable, interesting, and appropriate for your audience. For most business audiences, clarity and efficiency take precedence over literary style, so strive for straightforward simplicity. In every message, some ideas are more important than others. You can emphasize these key ideas through your sentence style.

Emphasize important ideas by

- Using sentence type to reflect the relationship between ideas
- Giving important ideas more space
- Making the important idea the subject of the sentence
- Putting important ideas at the beginning or at the end of the sentence

Reflect Relationships with Sentence Type One obvious technique for emphasizing key ideas is to choose the type of sentence to match the relationship of the ideas you want to express. If you have two ideas of equal importance, express them as two simple sentences or as one compound sentence. However, if one of the ideas is less important than the other, place it in a dependent clause to form a complex sentence. By making the first thought subordinate to the second, you establish a cause-and-effect relationship:

> Because the chemical products division is the strongest in the company, its management techniques should be adopted by the other divisions.

Emphasize key ideas.

Allocate More Space to the Important Ideas Another way to emphasize key ideas is to give important points the most space. When you want to call attention to a thought, use extra words to describe it. Consider this sentence:

> The chairperson of the board called for a vote of the shareholders.

To emphasize the importance of the chairperson, you might describe her more fully:

> Having considerable experience in corporate takeover battles, the chairperson of the board called for a vote of the shareholders.

You can increase the emphasis even more by adding a separate, short sentence to augment the first:

> The chairperson of the board called for a vote of the shareholders. She has considerable experience in corporate takeover battles.

Make Important Ideas the Subject You can also call attention to a thought by making it the subject of the sentence. In the following example, the emphasis is on the person:

> *I* can write letters much more quickly using a computer.

However, by changing the subject, the computer takes centre stage:

> The *computer* enables me to write letters much more quickly.

Place Important Ideas First or Last Another way to emphasize an idea is to place it at either the beginning or the end of a sentence:

> **Less Emphatic:** We are cutting the *price* to stimulate demand.
>
> **More Emphatic:** To stimulate demand, we are cutting the *price.*
>
> **Most Emphatic:** *Price* cuts will stimulate demand.

Beginnings and endings are emphatic positions in sentences.

If you want to emphasize the idea, put it at the beginning or end. If you want to downplay the idea, put it in the middle of the sentence.

> **Less Emphatic:** Mexico, *which has lower wage rates,* was selected as the production point for the electronic parts.

More Emphatic: *Wage rates are lower in Mexico so,* the electronic parts are manufactured there.

Most Emphatic: The electronic parts are manufactured in Mexico, *which has lower wage rates than Canada.*

Techniques like these give you a great deal of control over the way your audience interprets what you have to say.

Choose Active or Passive Voice

Your choice of active or passive voice also affects the tone of your message. You're using **active voice** when the subject (the "actor") comes before the verb and the object (the "acted upon") follows the verb: "John rented the office." You're using **passive voice** when the object comes before the verb and the subject follows the verb: "The office was rented by John." As you can see, the passive voice combines the helping verb *to be* with a form of the verb that is usually similar to the past tense.

Use Active Voice in General

Active sentences generally sound less formal and usually make it easier for the reader to figure out who performed the action. Passive voice de-emphasizes the subject and implies action done by something or someone.

Passive	Active
The new procedure is thought by the president to be superior.	The president thinks the new procedure is superior.
There are problems with this contract.	This contract has problems.
It is necessary that the report be finished by next week.	The report must be finished by next week.

Active sentences are stronger than passive ones.

Using the active voice produces shorter, stronger sentences and makes your writing more vigorous, concise, and generally easier to understand.[10] Using the passive voice, while not wrong grammatically, is cumbersome, wordy, and often unnecessarily vague, and it can make sentences longer.

Use Passive Voice for Diplomacy or Objectivity

Using the passive voice makes sense in some situations because it can help you focus on your audience and demonstrate the "you" attitude. Use the passive when you want to

Use passive sentences to soften bad news, to put yourself in the background, or to create an impersonal tone.

- be diplomatic about pointing out a problem or error of some kind (the passive version seems less like an accusation)
- point out what's being done without taking or attributing either the credit or the blame (the passive version leaves the actor completely out of the sentence)
- avoid personal pronouns in order to create an objective tone (the passive version may be used in a formal report, for example)

Active Voice Focuses on the Actor	Passive Voice Can Leave out the Actor
You lost the shipment.	The shipment was lost.
I am analyzing the production line to determine the problem.	The production line is being analyzed to determine the problem.
We have established criteria to evaluate capital expenditures.	Criteria have been established to evaluate capital expenditures.

Develop Coherent Paragraphs

A paragraph contains sentences that pertain to a single thought.

A *paragraph* is a cluster of sentences all related to the same general topic. It is a unit of thought, separated from other units by skipping a line or indenting the first line. A series of paragraphs makes up an entire composition. Each paragraph is an important part of the whole, a key link in the train of thought. As you compose your message, think about the paragraphs and their relationship to one another.

Adapt Paragraph Length

Paragraphs vary widely in length and form. You can communicate effectively in one short paragraph or in pages of lengthy paragraphs, depending on your purpose, your audience, and your message. The typical paragraph contains three basic elements: a topic sentence, related sentences that develop the topic, and transitional words and phrases.

Use Development Techniques

Six ways to develop paragraphs:

- Illustration
- Comparison or contrast
- Cause and effect
- Classification
- Problem and solution
- Chronology

Paragraphs can be developed in many ways. Six of the most common techniques are illustration, comparison or contrast, cause and effect, classification, problem and solution, and chronology. Your choice of technique depends on your subject, your intended audience, and your purpose:

- **Illustration:** Giving examples that demonstrate the general idea
- **Comparison or contrast:** Using similarities or differences to develop the topic
- **Cause and effect:** Focusing on the reasons for something
- **Classification:** Showing how a general idea is broken into specific categories
- **Problem and solution:** Presenting a problem and then discussing the solution
- **Chronology:** Following the sequence of occurrence.

In practice, you'll often combine two or more methods of development in a single paragraph. To add interest, you might begin by using illustration, shift to comparison or contrast, and then shift to problem and solution. However, before settling for the first approach that comes to mind, consider the alternatives. Think through various methods before committing yourself. If you fall into the easy habit of repeating the same old paragraph pattern time after time, your writing will be boring.

Achieve Unity and Coherence

The topic sentence

- Reveals the subject of the paragraph
- Indicates how the subject will be developed

Every properly constructed paragraph is *unified*—it deals with a single topic. The sentence that introduces this topic is called the **topic sentence.** In business, the topic sentence is generally explicit, rather than implied, and is often the first sentence in the paragraph. The topic sentence gives readers a summary of the general idea that will be covered in the rest of the paragraph.

Paragraphs are developed through a series of related sentences that provide details about the topic sentence.

The sentences that explain the topic sentence round out the paragraph. These related sentences must all have a bearing on the general subject and must provide enough specific details to make the topic clear. These developmental sentences are all more specific than the topic sentence. Each one provides another piece of evidence to demonstrate the general truth of the main thought. Also, each sentence is clearly related to the general idea being developed; the relation between the sentences and the idea is what gives the paragraph its unity. A paragraph is well developed when it contains enough information to make the topic sentence convincing and interesting.

Because each paragraph covers a single idea, use transitional words and phrases to show readers how paragraphs relate to each other.

In addition to being unified and well developed, effective paragraphs are *coherent;* that is, they are arranged in a logical order so that the audience can understand the train of thought. When you complete a paragraph, your readers automatically assume that you've finished with a particular idea. You achieve coherence by using transitions to show the relationship between paragraphs and among sentences within paragraphs. **Transitions** are words or phrases that tie ideas together and show how one thought is related to another. They help readers understand the connections you're trying to make. You can establish transitions in various ways:

- Use connecting words: *and, but, or, nevertheless, however, in addition,* and so on.
- Use key term repeats. Echo a word or phrase from a previous paragraph or sentence: "A system should be established for monitoring inventory levels. *This system* will provide . . ."

- Use a pronoun that refers to a noun used previously: "Ms. Arthur is the leading candidate for the president's position. *She* has excellent qualifications."
- Use words that are frequently paired: "The machine has a *minimum* output of . . . Its *maximum* output is . . ."

Here is a list of transitions frequently used to move readers smoothly between sentences and paragraphs:

Additional detail:	moreover, furthermore, in addition, besides, first, second, third, finally
Causal relationship:	therefore, because, accordingly, thus, consequently, hence, as a result, so
Comparison:	similarly, here again, likewise, in comparison, still
Contrast:	yet, conversely, whereas, nevertheless, on the other hand, however, but, nonetheless
Condition:	although, if
Illustration:	for example, in particular, in this case, for instance
Time sequence:	formerly, after, when, meanwhile, sometimes
Intensification:	indeed, in fact, in any event
Summary:	in brief, in short, to sum up
Repetition:	that is, in other words, as I mentioned earlier

Although transitional words and phrases are useful, they're not sufficient in themselves to overcome poor organization. Your goal is first to put your ideas in a strong framework and then to use transitions to link them even more strongly.

Consider using a transition device whenever it might help the reader understand your ideas and follow you from point to point. You can use transitions inside paragraphs to tie related points together and between paragraphs to ease the shift from one distinct thought to another. In longer reports, transitions that link major sections or chapters are often complete paragraphs that summarize the ideas presented in the section just ending and serve as mini-introductions to the information that will be covered in the next section. Here's an example:

You can use transitions inside paragraphs, between paragraphs, and between major sections.

> Given the nature of this product, the alternatives are limited. As the previous section indicates, we can stop making it altogether, improve it, or continue with the current model. Each of these alternatives has advantages and disadvantages, which are discussed in the following section.

Reviewing Key Points

In this chapter you learned how to

- Organize your message according to your audience's needs.
- Assess whether reaction to your idea will be positive, neutral, or negative so that you could choose an appropriate approach. If reaction is neutral, positive, or only mildly negative, choose a direct approach so that you can put the main idea near the beginning of the document. Use an indirect approach if resistance to your idea is strong.
- Compose by writing down your ideas and then revising to vary sentences and to choose effective words for a concise, clear, and friendly style and tone.
- Use plain English, familiar words, and active voice.
- Think about what ideas need emphasis and make those ideas prominent by leaving space around them or by making them the subjects of sentences.

- Ensure that your paragraphs are developed with a main idea and supporting details and examples.
- Build unity and coherence through use of transitional phrases and connecting words.

Test Your Knowledge

1. How does planning help you organize more effective messages?

2. How does good organization help your audience?

3. What four steps help you organize messages more effectively?

4. What three elements do you consider when choosing between a direct and an indirect approach?

5. How do you achieve a conversational tone?

6. How does an abstract word differ from a concrete word?

7. In what three situations should you use passive voice?

8. How can you use sentence style to emphasize key thoughts?

9. What is the purpose of the topic sentence?

10. What functions do transitions serve?

Apply Your Knowledge

1. Does good organization help you or your audience more? Please explain.

2. Some people feel that preparing an outline for a business message is a waste of time. Do you agree or disagree? Please explain.

3. Would you use a direct or an indirect approach to ask employees to work overtime to meet an important deadline? Please explain.

4. Which approach would you use to let your boss know that you'll be out half a day this week to attend your father's funeral—direct or indirect? Why?

5. **Ethical Choices** Do you think that using an indirect approach to overcome audience resistance is manipulative? Discuss the ethical issues in your answer.

Practise Your Knowledge

Exercises for Perfecting Your Writing

Choosing the Approach Indicate whether the direct or the indirect approach would be best in each of the following situations. Write *direct* or *indirect* in the space provided.

1. ________ A letter asking when next year's automobiles will be put on sale locally
2. ________ A letter from a recent college graduate requesting a letter of recommendation from a former instructor
3. ________ A letter turning down a job applicant
4. ________ An announcement that because of high heating costs, the plant temperature will be held at 18°C during winter.
5. ________ A final request to settle a delinquent debt

Drafting Persuasive Messages If you were trying to persuade people to take the following actions, how would you organize your argument? Write *direct* or *indirect* in the space provided.

6. ________ You want your boss to approve your plan for hiring two new people.
7. ________ You want to be hired for a job.
8. ________ You want to be granted a business loan.
9. ________ You want to collect a small amount from a regular customer whose account is slightly past due.
10. ________ You want to collect a large amount from a customer whose account is seriously past due.

Selecting Specific and Precise Words In the following sentences, replace vague phrases (underlined or in italics) with concrete phrases. Make up any details you might need.

11. We will be opening our new facility <u>sometime this spring</u>.

12. You can now purchase our new Leaf-Away yard and lawn blower <u>at a substantial savings</u>.

13. After the reception, we were surprised that <u>such a large number attended</u>.

14. The new production line has been operating <u>with increased efficiency</u> on every run.

15. Over the holiday, we hired a crew to <u>expand the work area</u>.

16. The two reporters __________ (*ran after*) every lead enthusiastically.

17. Even large fashion houses have to match staff size to the normal __________ (*seasonal ups and downs*).

18. The __________ (*bright*) colours in that ad are keeping customers from seeing what we have to sell.

19. Health costs __________ (*suddenly rise*) when management forgets to emphasize safety issues.

20. Once we solved the zoning issue, new business construction __________ (*moved forward*), and the district has been flourishing ever since.

Avoiding Clichés Rewrite these sentences to replace the clichés with fresh, personal expressions:

21. Being a jack-of-all-trades, Dave worked well in his new selling job.

22. Moving Leslie into the accounting department, where she was literally a fish out of water, was like putting a square peg into a round hole, if you get my drift.

23. I knew she was at death's door, but I thought the doctor would pull her through.

24. Movies aren't really my cup of tea; as far as I am concerned, they can't hold a candle to a good book.

25. It's a dog-eat-dog world out there in the rat race of the asphalt jungle.

Choosing Simple and Familiar Words In the following sentences, replace long words (in italics) with short, simple ones:

26. Management __________ (*inaugurated*) the recycling policy six months ago.
27. I'll miss working with you when my internship __________ (*terminates*).
28. You can convey the same meaning without __________ (*utilizing*) the same words.
29. No one __________ (*anticipated*) that Mr. Hughes would retire so soon.
30. When Julian asked for my __________ (*assistance*), I grabbed the chance to learn more about accounting.
31. You'll never be promoted unless you __________ (*endeavour*) to be more patient.
32. I have to wait until payday to __________ (*ascertain*) whether or not I got the raise.
33. On your way back from lunch, don't forget to __________ (*procure*) more photocopy paper.
34. We'll send you an invoice when we __________ (*consummate*) the job.
35. Please __________ (*advise*) me when you're ready to begin the test.
36. John will send you a copy, once he's inserted all the __________ (*alterations*) you've requested.
37. The contract was __________ (*forwarded*) to you for your signature on July 19.
38. Grand Tree __________ (*fabricates*) office furniture that is both durable and attractive.
39. I understand from your letter that you expect a full refund, __________ (*nevertheless*) your warranty expired more than a year ago.
40. I have received __________ (*substantial*) support on this project from Claire Devon and Randy Smith.

Removing Outdated Words Rewrite the following sentences, replacing obsolete phrases with up-to-date versions. Write *none* if you think there is no appropriate substitute.

41. I have completed the form and returned it to my insurance company, as per your instructions.

42. Attached herewith is a copy of our new contract for your records.

43. Even though it will increase the price of the fence, we have decided to use the cedar in lieu of the chain link.

44. Saunders & Saunders has received your request for the Greenwood file, and in reply I wish to state that we will send you copies of Mr. Greenwood's documents only after Judge Taylor makes her ruling and orders us to do so.

45. Please be advised that your account with Credit Union Atlantic has been compromised, and we advise you to close it as soon as possible.

Using Active Voice Rewrite each sentence in active voice.

46. The raw data are submitted to the data processing division by the sales representative each Friday.

47. High profits are publicized by management.

48. The policies announced in the directive were implemented by the staff.

49. Our computers are serviced by the company.

50. The employees were represented by Janet Hogan.

Using Transitions Add transitional elements to the following sentences to improve the flow of ideas. (Note: You may need to eliminate or add some words to smooth out your sentences.)

51. Tim Hortons first opened in 1964 in Hamilton, Ontario. The first Tim Hortons sold only coffee and doughnuts. The chain has more than 2200 restaurants in Canada and more than 160 in the United States. Tim Hortons is growing. The chain plans to add

170 to 180 restaurants each year for the next few years. Tim Hortons plans to open restaurants in western Canada and Ontario. The chain enjoys wide popularity with Canadians. Canadians eat three times as many doughnuts per capita as Americans. Canadians consume more doughnuts per capita than any other country in the world.[11]

52. Facing some of the toughest competitors in the world, Harley-Davidson had to make some changes. The company introduced new products. Harley's management team set out to rebuild the company's production process. New products were coming to market and the company was turning a profit. Harley's quality standards were not on par with those of its foreign competitors. Harley's costs were still among the highest in the industry. Harley made a U-turn and restructured the company's organizational structure. Harley's efforts have paid off.

53. Whether you're indulging in a doughnut in Mississauga or California, Krispy Kreme wants you to enjoy the same delicious taste with every bite. The company maintains consistent product quality by carefully controlling every step of the production process. Krispy Kreme tests all raw ingredients against established quality standards. Every delivery of wheat flour is sampled and measured for its moisture content and protein levels. Krispy Kreme blends the ingredients. Krispy Kreme tests the doughnut mix for quality. Krispy Kreme delivers the mix to its stores. Krispy Kreme knows that it takes more than a quality mix to produce perfect doughnuts all the time. The company supplies its stores with everything they need to produce premium doughnuts—mix, icings, fillings, equipment—you name it.

Activities

For live links to all Web sites discussed in this chapter, visit this text's Web site at www.pearsoned.ca/bovee. Just log on and select Chapter 4, and click on "Student Resources." Locate the page or the URL related to the material in the text. For the "Best of the Web" exercises, you'll also find navigational directions. Click on the live link to the site.

1. **Analyze This Document** A writer is working on an insurance information brochure and is having trouble grouping the ideas logically into an outline. Prepare the outline, paying attention to appropriate subordination of ideas. If necessary, rewrite phrases to give them a more consistent sound.

   Accident Protection Insurance Plan

   - Coverage is only pennies a day
   - Benefit is $100 000 for accidental death on common carrier
   - Benefit is $100 a day for hospitalization as result of motor vehicle or common carrier accident
   - Benefit is $20 000 for accidental death in motor vehicle accident
   - Individual coverage is only $17.85 per quarter; family coverage is just $26.85 per quarter
   - No physical exam or health questions
   - Convenient payment—billed quarterly
   - Guaranteed acceptance for all applicants
   - No individual rate increases
   - Free, no-obligation examination period

- Cash paid in addition to any other insurance carried
- Covers accidental death when riding as fare-paying passenger on public transportation, including buses, trains, jets, ships, trolleys, subways, or any other common carrier
- Covers accidental death in motor vehicle accidents occurring while driving or riding in or on automobile, truck, camper, motor home, or nonmotorized bicycle

2. **Teamwork** Working with six other students, divide the following six topics and write one paragraph on your selected topic. Be sure one student writes a paragraph using the illustration technique, one using the comparison-or-contrast technique, one using a discussion of cause and effect, one using the classification technique, one using a discussion of problem and solution, and one using the chronology technique. Then exchange paragraphs within the team and pick out the main idea and general purpose of the paragraph one of your teammates wrote. Was everyone able to correctly identify the main idea and purpose? If not, suggest how the paragraph might be rewritten for clarity.

   a. Types of cameras (or dogs or automobiles) available for sale
   b. Advantages and disadvantages of eating at fast-food restaurants
   c. Finding that first full-time job
   d. Good qualities of my car (or house, or apartment, or neighbourhood)
   e. How to make a favourite dessert (or barbecue a steak or make coffee)
   f. How to get a driver's licence

Expand Your Knowledge

Best of the Web

Compose a Better Business Message At Purdue University's Online Writing Lab (OWL), you'll find tools to help you improve your business messages. For advice on composing written messages, for help with grammar, and for referrals to other information sources, you'll be wise to visit this site. Purdue's OWL offers online services and an introduction to Internet search tools. You can also download a variety of handouts on writing skills. Check out the resources at the OWL home page and learn how to write a professional business message.

http://owl.english.purdue.edu

Exercises

1. Explain why positive wording in a message is more effective than negative wording. Why should you be concerned about the position of good news or bad news in your written message?
2. What points should you include in the close of your business message? Why?

Although Purdue University's Online Writing Lab is acknowledged as one of the best online writing sites available on the Internet, many Canadian universities and colleges also have online writing resources. Explore a few of these sites to find help with grammar, writing, documentation, and ESL-related resources, and for links to other online writing centres.

University of New Brunswick at Saint John Writing Centre
http://www.unbsj.ca/stu_serv/write/links.html
Queen's University—The Writing Centre
http://qsilver.queensu.ca/~wcentre/
The University of Ottawa Writing Centre. "Hypergrammar" tutorials at:
http://www.uottawa.ca/academic/arts/writcent/hypergrammar/

Exploring the Web on Your Own

Review these chapter-related Web sites on your own to learn more about writing business messages.

1. Write it right by paying attention to the writing tips at Bull's Eye Business Writing Tips, www.basic-learning.com/wbwt.

Learn Interactively

Interactive Study Guide

Visit the Companion Website at www.pearsoned.ca/bovee. For Chapter 4, take advantage of the interactive "Study Guide" to test your chapter knowledge. Get instant feedback on whether you need additional studying.

This site offers a variety of additional resources: The "Research Area" helps you locate a wealth of information to use in course assignments. You can even send a message to online research experts, who will help you find exactly the information you need. The "Study Hall" helps you succeed in this course by offering support with writing and study skills, time management, and career skills, as well as numerous other resources.

Peak Performance Grammar and Mechanics

Use the Peak Performance Grammar and Mechanics CD to test your skill with adjectives. In the "Adjectives and Adverbs" section, take the Diagnostic Test to determine whether you have any weak areas. Then review those areas in the Refresher Course. Take the Follow-Up Test to check your grasp of adjective usage. For an extra challenge or advanced practice, take the Fine-Points Test.

Improve Your Grammar, Mechanics, and Usage

Level 1: Self-Assessment—Adjectives

Review Section 1.4 in the Handbook of Grammar, Mechanics, and Usage, and then look at the following 15 items.

In items 1–5, fill in the appropriate form of the adjective that appears in parentheses:

1. Of the two products, this one has the __________ (*great*) potential.
2. The __________ (*perfect*) solution is *d*.
3. Here is the __________ (*interesting*) of all the ideas I have heard so far.
4. Our service is __________ (*good*) than theirs.
5. The __________ (*hard*) part of my job is firing people.

In items 6–10, insert hyphens wherever required:

6. A highly placed source revealed Dotson's last ditch efforts to cover up the mistake.
7. Please send an extra large dust cover for my photocopier.
8. A top secret document was taken from the president's office last night.
9. A 30 year old person should know better.
10. If I write a large scale report, I want to know that it will be read by upper level management.

In items 11–15, insert required commas between adjectives:

11. The two companies are engaged in an all-out no-holds-barred struggle for dominance.

12. A tiny metal shaving is responsible for the problem.
13. She came to the office with a bruised swollen knee.
14. A chipped cracked sheet of glass is useless to us.
15. You'll receive our usual cheerful prompt service.

Level 2: Workplace Applications

The following items contain numerous errors in grammar, capitalization, punctuation, abbreviation, number style, word division, and vocabulary. Rewrite each sentence in the space provided, correcting all errors. Write *C* in the space after any sentence that is already correct.

1. Its time that you learned the skills one needs to work with suppliers and vendors to get what you want and need.
2. Easy flexible wireless calling plans start for as little as $19 dollars a month.
3. There's several criteria used to select customer's to receive this offer.
4. PetFood Warehouse officially became PETsMART, Jim left the co. due to health reasons.
5. First quarter sales gains are evident in both the grocery store sector (up 1.03%) and the restaurant sector (up 3.17 per cent) according to Food Institute estimates.
6. Whatever your challenge, learning stronger "negotiating" tactics and strategies will improve the way people work and the results that comes from their efforts.
7. To meet the increasing demand for Penta bottled-drinking-water, production capacity is being expanded by Bio-Hydration Research Lab by 80 percent.

8. Seminars begin at 9 am and wrap up at 4:00 p.m.

9. Burns Foods, a subsidiary of McCains has bought a facility in Scarborough, ON, that it will use to distribute products to customers such as convenience stores, stores that sell items at a discount, and mass merchants.

10. The British Retail Consortium are releasing the 3rd edition of its Technical Standards on Apr. 22, reported the National Post.

11. The reason SkillPath is the fastest growing training company in the world is because of our commitment to providing clients with the highest-quality learning experiences possible.

12. According to professor Charles Noussair of the economics department of McGill University, opinion surveys "Capture the respondent in the role of a voter, not in the role of a consumer".

13. The Study found that people, exposed to Purina banner ads, were almost 50 percent more likely to volunteer Purina as the first Dog Food brand that came to mind.

14. In a consent decree with Health Canada, E'Ola International a dietary supplement maker agreed not to sell any more products containing the drug, ephedrine.

15. Dennis Dickson is looking for a company both to make and distribute plaidberries under an exclusive license, plaidberries is blackberries that are mixed with extracts and they are used as a filling.

Level 3: Document Critique

The following document may contain errors in grammar, capitalization, punctuation, abbreviation, number style, vocabulary, and spelling. You will also find errors relating to topics in this chapter. Concentrate on using the "you" attitude, emphasizing the positive, being polite, and using bias-free language as you improve this letter. Correct all errors using standard proofreading marks (see Appendix C).

Burdette's

• Special Sizes •

For Special Ladies and Gentlemen

820 Yonge Street, Toronto, ON M5T 2T9 • (416) 967-5170 • Fax: (416) 967-1235 • www.burdettes.com

10/19/05

Mrs. Bruce Crandall

1597 Church Street

Brantford, ON P3A 3V8

Dear Mrs. Crandall,

Order no. 89-97526-277

We were so happy to recieve your order—We know you'll be enjoying the dress you've selected from our fall catalogue. We feel its a popular number because its so versitile and flatters our heavier customers. We think you'll get alot of use out of it on your trip to Niagara Falls.

Unfortunately, you forgot to indicate what size you need. We can't ship your dress until you tell us your size. Plus, if you don't mail in the postage paid card that we've enclosed for you to use very soon we can't be guaranteeing that your attractive new dress will arrive in time for your trip!

Sincerely,

Melodie Proteau

Workplace Skills

Business Communication Notebook

Beating Writer's Block: Ten Workable Ideas to Get Words Flowing

Putting words on a page or on a screen can be a real struggle. Some people get stuck so often that they develop a mental block. If you get writer's block, here are some ways to get those words flowing again:

- **Use positive self-talk.** Stop worrying about how well or easily you write, and stop thinking of writing as difficult, time-consuming, or complicated. Tell yourself that you're capable and that you can do the job. Also, recall past examples of your writing that were successful.
- **Know your purpose.** Be specific about what you want to accomplish with this particular piece of writing. Without a clear purpose, writing can indeed be impossible.
- **Visualize your audience.** Picture audience backgrounds, interests, subject knowledge, and vocabulary (including the technical jargon they use). Such visualization can help you choose an appropriate style and tone for your writing.
- **Create a productive environment.** Write in a place that's for writing only, and make that place pleasant. Set up "writing appointments." Scheduling a session from nine-thirty to noon is less intimidating than an indefinite session. Also, keep your mind fresh with scheduled breaks.
- **Make an outline or a list.** Even if you don't create a formal outline, at least jot down a few notes about how your ideas fit together. As you go along, you can revise your notes, as long as you end up with a plan that gives direction and coherence.
- **Just start.** Put aside all worries, fears, distractions—anything that gives you an excuse to postpone writing. Then start putting down any thoughts you have about your topic. Don't worry about whether these ideas can actually be used; just let your mind range freely.
- **Write the middle first.** Start wherever your interest is greatest and your ideas are most developed. You can follow new directions, but note ideas to revisit later. When you finish one section, choose another without worrying about sequence. Just get your thoughts down.
- **Push obstacles aside.** If you get stuck at some point, don't worry. Move past the thought, sentence, or paragraph, and come back to it later. Prime the pump simply by writing or talking about why you're stuck: "I'm stuck because . . ." Also try brainstorming. Before you know it, you'll be writing about your topic.
- **Read a newspaper or magazine.** Try reading an article that uses a style similar to yours. Choose one you'll enjoy so that you'll read it more closely.
- **Work on nontext segments.** Work on a different part of the project, such as formatting or creating graphics or verifying facts and references.

Remember, when deadlines loom, don't freeze in panic. Concentrate on the major ideas first, and save the details for later, after you have something on the page. If you keep things in perspective, you'll succeed.

Applications for Success

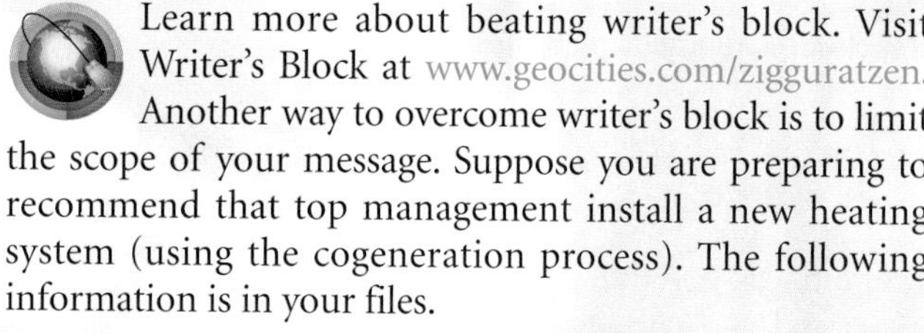

Learn more about beating writer's block. Visit Writer's Block at www.geocities.com/zigguratzen. Another way to overcome writer's block is to limit the scope of your message. Suppose you are preparing to recommend that top management install a new heating system (using the cogeneration process). The following information is in your files.

- History of the development of the cogeneration heating process
- Scientific credentials of the developers of the process
- Risks assumed in using this process
- Your plan for installing the equipment in your building
- Stories about its successful use in comparable facilities
- Specifications of the equipment that would be installed
- Plans for disposing of the old heating equipment
- Costs of installing and running the new equipment
- Advantages and disadvantages of using the new process
- Detailed 10-year cost projections
- Estimates of the time needed to phase in the new system
- Alternative systems that management might wish to consider

Do the following:

1. Limit the scope of this message by eliminating any topics that aren't essential.
2. Arrange the remaining topics so that your report will give top managers a clear understanding of the heating system and a balanced, concise justification for installing it.
3. List the ways you procrastinate, and discuss what you can do to break these habits.
4. Analyze your own writing experiences. What negative self-talk do you use? What might you do to overcome this tendency?

Completing Business Messages

5

After studying this chapter, you will be able to

1. List the main tasks involved in completing a business message
2. Identify nine techniques for improving the clarity of your writing
3. Discuss four methods for making your writing more concise
4. Explain how four design elements affect your document's appearance
5. Clarify the types of errors you look for when proofreading
6. Describe seven ways to improve your proofreading process

From the Real World

"In Government, the constant challenge of communications is to take complex material, prepared by experts, and present it in a format that is visually appealing, easy to understand, and consistent with the overall communications goals of the organization. This requires a rigorous attention to detail, combined with a clear and straightforward style."

–Jamie Baillie, Chief of Staff
Office of the Premier
Province of Nova Scotia

As senior adviser to the premier, Jamie Baillie runs the Office of the Premier, ensuring that the government's agenda is communicated to the public as clearly and concisely as possible. He writes memoranda, strategic plans, and briefing notes for the premier and reviews communication plans, major speeches, and paid media campaigns. "I have been known to revise an important document eight or nine times in order to ensure that the message fits with the overall communications goals of government. The tolerance for error or even mixed messages is low, so it is essential to revise and edit to get details right."[1]

Revising Your Message

Successful business people care about saying precisely the right thing in precisely the right way. Look back at the diagram of the three-step writing process (Figure 3.1 on page 44). You can see that completing your message consists of three tasks: revising, producing, and proofreading your message.

Revision takes place during and after preparing the first draft.

Although the tendency is to separate revision from composition, revision occurs throughout the writing process. You revise as you go along; then you revise again after you've completed the first draft. Ideally, you should let your draft age a day or two before you begin the revision process, so that you can approach the material with a fresh eye. Then read through the document quickly to evaluate its overall effectiveness (its content, organization, style, and tone) before you begin revising for finer points such as clarity and conciseness.

The beginning and end of a message have the greatest impact on readers.

In your first pass, spend a few extra moments on the beginning and ending of the message. These are the sections that have the greatest impact on the audience. Be sure that the opening of a letter or memo has the main message summarized and is geared to the reader's probable reaction. Ask, "What should be emphasized?" Is "reader action" located in an emphatic spot? In longer messages, check to see that the first few paragraphs establish the subject, purpose, and organization of the material. Review the conclusion to be sure that it summarizes the main idea and leaves the audience with a positive impression.

As you revise your messages, you'll find yourself rewriting sentences, passages, and even whole sections to improve their effectiveness. Look closely at the revised message in Figure 5.1. It has been edited using the proofreading marks shown in Appendix C. As you can see, the revisions provide the requested information in a more organized fashion, in a friendlier style, and with clearer mechanics.

Solve some problems by deleting them.

Sometimes you'll find that you can solve the most difficult problem in a sentence simply by removing it. When you come upon a troublesome element, ask yourself, "Do I need it at all?" You may find that the element was causing a problem because it was trying to do an unnecessary job.[2]

FIGURE 5.1 Sample Edited Letter (Excerpt)

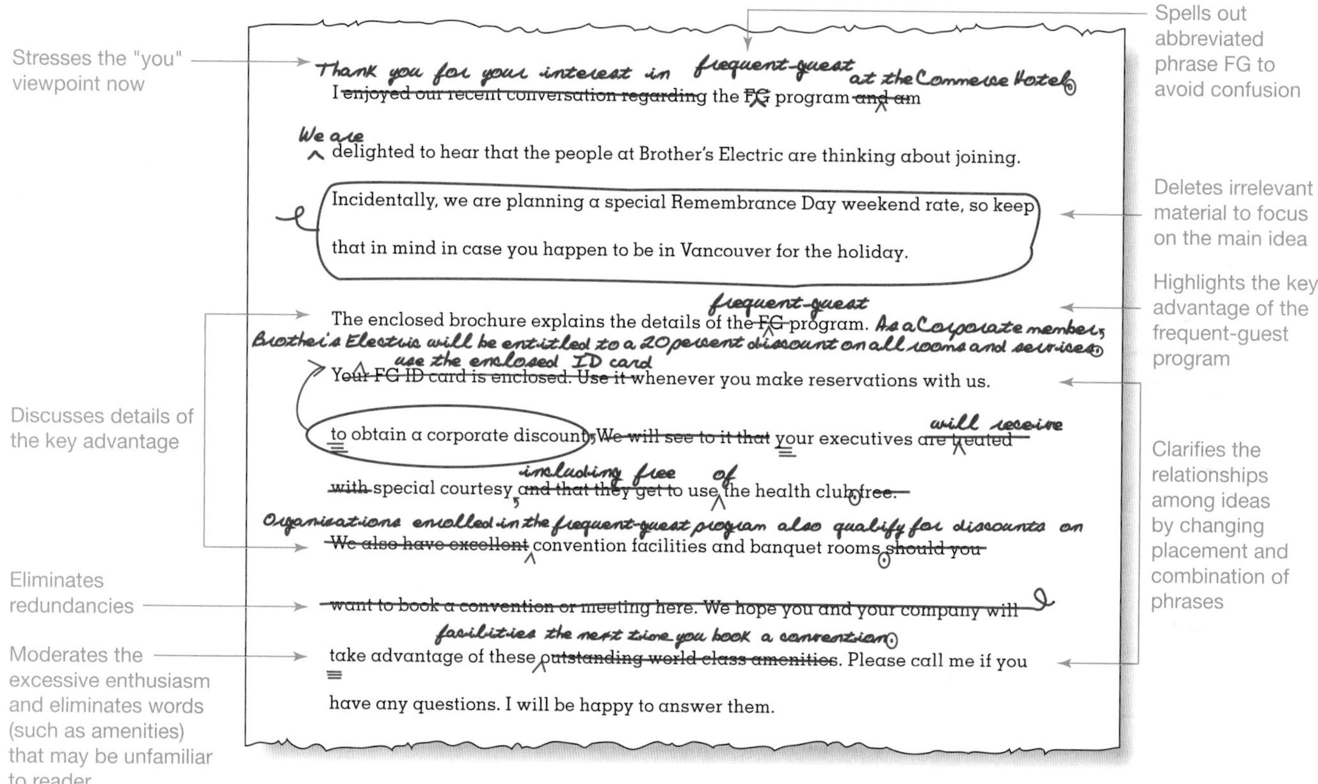

Rewrite and Edit for Clarity

Clarity avoids confusion.

Once you've reviewed your message for overall effectiveness, you'll want to make sure that your message is clear. Perhaps a sentence is so cluttered that the reader can't unravel it, or it's constructed in such a way that the reader can interpret it in several ways.[3] The goal is to enable the audience to read the document once and understand one precise meaning.

Break up Overly Long Sentences

In many cases, the parts of a compound sentence should be separated into two sentences.

Don't connect too many clauses with *and.* If you find yourself stuck in a long sentence, you're probably trying to make the sentence do more than it can reasonably do, such as express two dissimilar thoughts. You can often clarify your writing style by separating a string into individual sentences. Try not to take compound sentences too far, as shown in the following table.

Too Long	Improved
The magazine will be published January 1, and I'd better meet the deadline if I want my article included.	The magazine will be published January 1. I'd better meet the deadline if I want my article included.

Rewrite Hedging Sentences

Sometimes you have to write *may* or *seems* to avoid stating a judgment as a fact. Nevertheless, when you have too many such hedges, you aren't really saying anything. Avoid overqualifying your sentences:

Don't be afraid to present your opinions without qualification.

Hedging	Definite
I believe that Mr. Johnson's employment record seems to show that he may be capable of handling the position.	Mr. Johnson's employment record shows that he is capable of handling the position.

Impose Parallelism

When you have two or more similar (parallel) ideas to express, use the same grammatical pattern for each related idea—parallel construction. Repeating the pattern makes your message more readable: It tells readers that the ideas are comparable, and it adds rhythm. Parallelism can be achieved by repeating the pattern in words, phrases, clauses, or entire sentences.

When you use the same grammatical pattern to express two or more ideas, you show that they are comparable thoughts.

Not Parallel	Parallel
Miss Simms had been drenched with rain, bombarded with telephone calls, and her boss shouted at her.	Miss Simms had been drenched with rain, bombarded with telephone calls, and shouted at by her boss.
Ms. Reynolds dictated the letter, and next she signed it and left the office.	Ms. Reynolds dictated the letter, signed it, and left the office.
To waste time and missing deadlines are bad habits.	Wasting time and missing deadlines are bad habits.
Interviews are a matter of acting confident and to stay relaxed.	Interviews are a matter of acting confident and staying relaxed.

Correct Dangling Modifiers

Sometimes a modifier is not just an adjective or an adverb but an entire phrase modifying a noun or a verb. Be careful not to leave this type of modifier dangling with no connection to the subject of the sentence. The first unacceptable example in the following group implies that the red sports car has both an office and the legs to walk there. The second example shows one frequent cause of dangling modifiers: passive construction. Avoid placing modifiers close to the wrong nouns and verbs:

Make sure that modifier phrases are really related to the subject of the sentence.

Dangling Modifiers	Corrected
Walking to the office, a red sports car passed her.	A red sports car passed her while she was walking to the office.
Working as fast as possible, the budget was soon ready.	Working as fast as possible, the committee soon had the budget ready.
After a three-week slump, we increased sales.	After a three-week slump, sales increased.

Reword Long Noun Sequences

Stringing together a series of nouns may save a little space, but it causes confusion.

Avoid stringing too many nouns together. When nouns are strung together as modifiers, the resulting sentence is hard to read. You can clarify such a sentence by putting some of the nouns in a modifying phrase. Although you add a few more words, your audience won't have to work as hard to understand the sentence.

Too Many Nouns	Clear
The aluminum window sash installation company will give us an estimate on Friday.	The company that installs aluminum window sashes will give us an estimate on Friday.

Replace Camouflaged Verbs

Turning verbs into nouns or adjectives weakens your writing style.

Watch for word endings such as *ion, tion, ing, ment, ant, ent, ence, ance,* and *ency.* Most of them change verbs into nouns and adjectives. Liberate the verbs to create a more powerful style.

Noun Forms	"Liberated" Verbs
The manager undertook implementation of the rules.	The manager implemented the rules.
Verification of the shipments occurs weekly.	Shipments are verified weekly.

Also try not to transform verbs into nouns (writing "we performed an analysis of" rather than "we analyzed"). To prune and enliven your messages, use verbs instead of noun phrases:

Wordy Noun Forms	Concise, Powerful Verbs
reach a conclusion about	conclude
make a discovery of	discover
give consideration to	consider

Clarify Sentence Structure

Subject and predicate should be placed as close together as possible, as should modifiers and the words they modify.

Keep the subject and predicate of a sentence as close together as possible. When subject and predicate are far apart, readers have to read the sentence twice to figure out who did what. Try not to separate subject and predicate:

Scattered	Focused
A 10 percent decline in market share, which resulted from quality problems and an aggressive sales campaign by Armitage, the market leader in the Maritimes, was the major problem in 2004.	The major problem in 2004 was a 10 percent loss of market share, which resulted from both quality problems and an aggressive sales campaign by Armitage, the market leader in the Maritimes.

Similarly, adjectives, adverbs, and prepositional phrases usually make the most sense when they're placed as close as possible to the words they modify:

Misplaced Modifier	Clear
Our antique desk is suitable for busy executives with thick legs and large drawers.	With its thick legs and large drawers, our antique desk is suitable for busy executives.

Clarify Awkward References

To save words, business writers sometimes use expressions such as *the above-mentioned, as mentioned above, the aforementioned, the former, the latter,* and *respectively.* These words cause readers to jump from point to point, which hinders effective communication. Use specific references, even if you must add a few more words:

Be specific in your references.

Awkward	Clear
The Law Office and the Accounting Office distribute computer supplies for legal secretaries and beginning accountants, respectively.	The Law Office distributes computer supplies for legal secretaries; the Accounting Office distributes those for beginning accountants.

Moderate Your Enthusiasm

An occasional adjective or adverb intensifies and emphasizes your meaning, but too many can ruin your writing. Try not to display too much enthusiasm:

Business writing shouldn't be gushy.

Over the Top	Businesslike
We are extremely pleased to offer you a position on our staff of exceptionally skilled and highly educated employees. The work offers extraordinary challenges and a very large salary.	We are pleased to offer you a position on our staff of skilled and well-educated employees. The work offers challenges and an attractive salary.

Rewrite and Edit for Conciseness

Many business documents today are swollen with words and phrases that do no new work. In fact, a majority of executives responding to one survey complained that most written messages are too long.[4] Because executives are more likely to read documents that efficiently say what needs to be said, it's especially important to weed out unnecessary material. As you rewrite and edit your messages, concentrate on how each word contributes to an effective sentence and how that sentence develops a coherent paragraph.

Conciseness means efficiency.

Most first drafts can be cut by 50 percent.[5] Eliminate every word that serves no function, replace every long word that could be a short word, and remove every adverb that adds nothing to the meaning already carried in the verb.

To test whether every word counts, try removing phrases or words that don't appear to be essential. If the meaning is unchanged, leave those elements out. For instance, *very* can be a useful word to achieve emphasis, but more often it's clutter. There's no need to call someone "very methodical." The person is either methodical or not. As you begin your editing task, simplify, prune, and strive for order.

Delete Unnecessary Words and Phrases

Some combinations of words have one-word equivalents that are more efficient. Avoid using wordy phrases:

Be on the lookout for inefficient phrases and excessive or confusing relative pronouns and articles.

Wordy	Concise
for the sum of	for
in the event that	if
on the occasion of	on
prior to the start of	before

in the near future	soon
have the capability of	can
at this point in time	now
due to the fact that	because
in view of the fact that	because
until such time as	when
with reference to	about

In addition, avoid the clutter of too many or poorly placed relative pronouns (*who, that, which*). Even articles can be excessive (mostly too many *the*'s):

Awkward	Clear
Cars that are sold after January will not have a six-month warranty.	Cars sold after January will not have a six-month warranty.
Employees who are driving to work should park in the underground garage.	Employees driving to work should park in the underground garage.

However, well-placed relative pronouns and articles prevent confusion. Make sure to use enough relative pronouns to be clear:

Confusing	Clear
The project manager told the engineers last week the specifications were changed.	The project manager told the engineers last week *that* the specifications were changed.
	The project manager told the engineers *that* last week the specifications were changed.

Shorten Long Words and Phrases

Short words are generally more vivid and easier to read than long ones are. The idea is to use short, simple words, *not* simple concepts.[6] Try to get rid of overly long words:

Inflated	Plain English
During the preceding year, the company accelerated productive operations.	Last year the company sped up operations.
The action was predicated on the assumption that the company was operating at a financial deficit.	The action was based on the belief that the company was losing money.

Short words and infinitives are generally more vivid than long words and phrases, and they improve the readability of a document.

By using infinitives in place of some phrases, you not only shorten your sentences but also make them clearer. Be careful to use infinitives rather than wordy phrases:

Wordy	Concise
He went to the library for the purpose of studying.	He went to the library to study.
The employer increased salaries so that she could improve morale.	The employer increased salaries to improve morale.

Eliminate Redundancies

Remove unneeded repetition.

In some word combinations, the words tend to say the same thing. For instance, "visible to the eye" is redundant because *visible* is enough; nothing can be visible to the ear. Try not to repeat meanings:

Redundant	Concise
absolutely complete	complete
basic fundamentals	fundamentals
follows after	follows
reduce down	reduce
free and clear	free
refer back	refer
repeat again	repeat
collect together	collect
future plans	plans
return back	return
important essentials	essentials
midway between	between
end result	result
actual truth	truth
final outcome	outcome
uniquely unusual	unique
surrounded on all sides	surrounded

In addition, avoid using double modifiers with the same meaning.

Redundant	Concise
modern, up-to-date equipment	modern equipment

Recast "It Is/There Are" Starters

Avoid starting sentences with *it* and *there.*

If you start a sentence with an indefinite pronoun (an expletive) such as *it* or *there,* odds are that the sentence could be shorter. Make sure that your sentences start with a strong subject.

Wordy	Focused
It would be appreciated if you would sign the lease today.	Please sign the lease today.
There are five employees in this division who were late to work today.	Five employees in this division were late to work today.

Producing Your Message

Before you can proofread your final version, you must produce it in some readable form.

Once you have revised and refined your message from start to finish, you are ready to produce it. You want to give your message an attractive, contemporary appearance by designing your document carefully. Also, make sure that your design uses graphics and visual elements to reinforce key ideas.

Select the Right Design Elements

To Reflect a Modern Appearance

Design affects the impression your message makes.

The way you package your ideas has a lot to do with how successful your communication will be. The first thing your readers notice about your message is its appearance. If your document looks tired and out of date, it will give that impression to your readers—even if your ideas are innovative. Good looks can help you get your message across, especially to busy readers.

To Emphasize Main Parts

When designing your message, balancing graphics and text is important. The visual elements should be carefully selected to highlight key points. Consider the memo in Figure 5.2. The bar chart in this memo is centred to give a formal impression, and the colour used in the graphic is balanced by the letterhead logo. The headings emphasize the organizational divisions and important content.

FIGURE 5.2 The Importance of Appearance

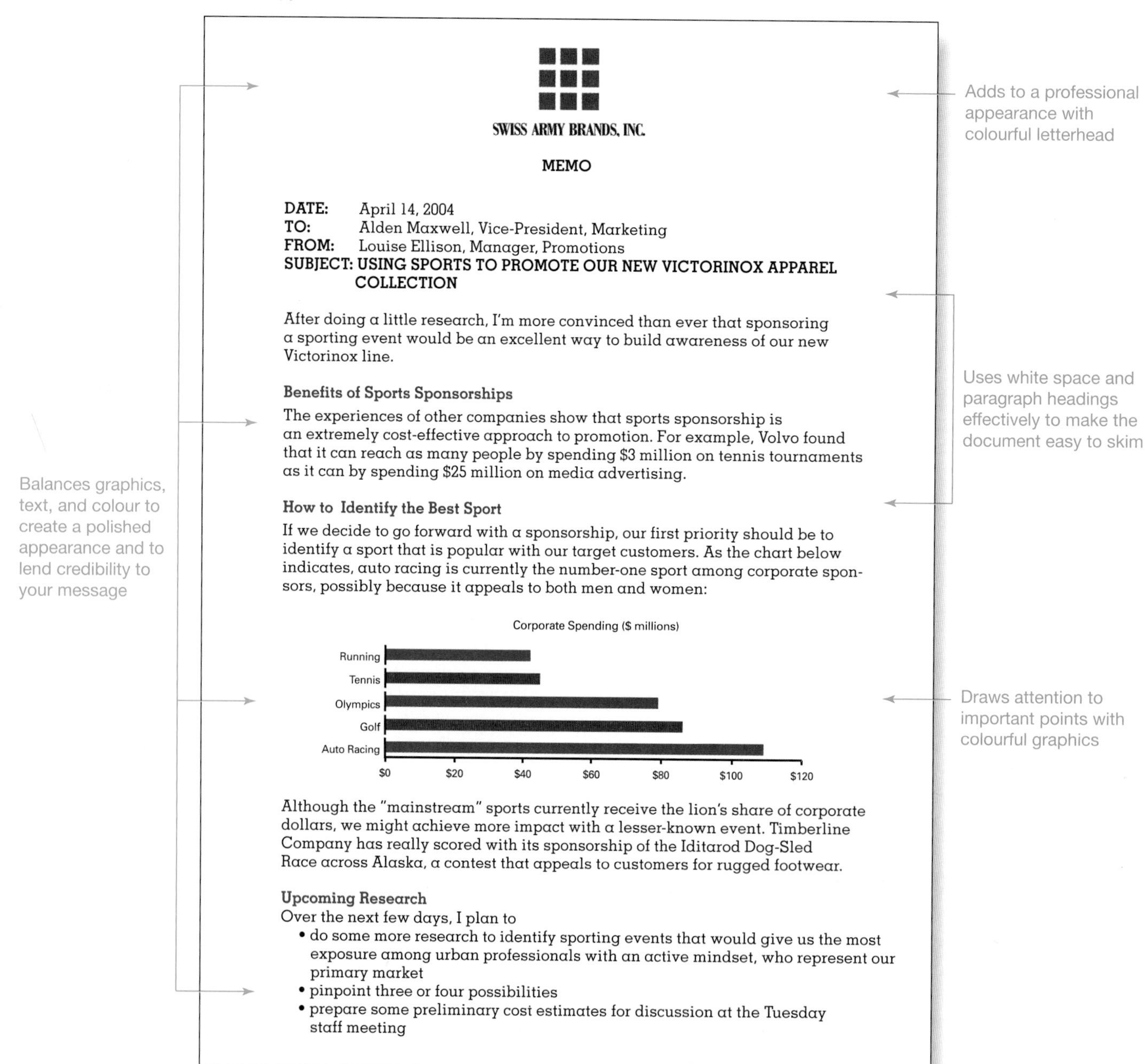

Adds to a professional appearance with colourful letterhead
Uses white space and paragraph headings effectively to make the document easy to skim
Balances graphics, text, and colour to create a polished appearance and to lend credibility to your message
Draws attention to important points with colourful graphics

SWISS ARMY BRANDS, INC.

MEMO

DATE: April 14, 2004
TO: Alden Maxwell, Vice-President, Marketing
FROM: Louise Ellison, Manager, Promotions
SUBJECT: USING SPORTS TO PROMOTE OUR NEW VICTORINOX APPAREL COLLECTION

After doing a little research, I'm more convinced than ever that sponsoring a sporting event would be an excellent way to build awareness of our new Victorinox line.

Benefits of Sports Sponsorships

The experiences of other companies show that sports sponsorship is an extremely cost-effective approach to promotion. For example, Volvo found that it can reach as many people by spending $3 million on tennis tournaments as it can by spending $25 million on media advertising.

How to Identify the Best Sport

If we decide to go forward with a sponsorship, our first priority should be to identify a sport that is popular with our target customers. As the chart below indicates, auto racing is currently the number-one sport among corporate sponsors, possibly because it appeals to both men and women:

Corporate Spending ($ millions)
Running
Tennis
Olympics
Golf
Auto Racing
$0
$20
$40
$60
$80
$100
$120

Although the "mainstream" sports currently receive the lion's share of corporate dollars, we might achieve more impact with a lesser-known event. Timberline Company has really scored with its sponsorship of the Iditarod Dog-Sled Race across Alaska, a contest that appeals to customers for rugged footwear.

Upcoming Research

Over the next few days, I plan to

- do some more research to identify sporting events that would give us the most exposure among urban professionals with an active mindset, who represent our primary market
- pinpoint three or four possibilities
- prepare some preliminary cost estimates for discussion at the Tuesday staff meeting

You can use a variety of design elements, such as white space, margin and line justification, typefaces, and type styles to make your message look professional, interesting, and up to date. You can use text boxes to emphasize important information. But be careful—too many design elements will confuse your audience. If you will be designing a lot of documents that contain a variety of elements, you would be wise to take a course in page layout or at least to read further about effective design techniques.

Use White Space to Show Organization

White space is the part of a document that is free of text or artwork. It provides visual contrast for your readers, and perhaps even more important, it gives their eyes a resting point. White space includes the open area surrounding headings and margin areas, the vertical space between columns, the space created by ragged line endings, the paragraph indents or extra space between unindented paragraphs, and the horizontal space between lines of text. White space is used to show organizational divisions such as with the double spacing between paragraphs. White space opens up the page and prevents crowding. In today's busy workplace, readers want to scan quickly for information. Crowded text cannot be scanned.

White space provides contrast and prevents crowding.

Improve Readability through Margins and Layout

Margins define the space around your text and between text columns. They're influenced by the way you place lines of type, which can be set (1) justified (flush on the left and flush on the right), (2) flush left with a ragged right margin, (3) flush right with a ragged left margin, or (4) centred. Ample margins improve the reader's ability to move through text quickly. The column of space left in the margin of this text allows the summary notes to be highlighted for speed-reading and review.

Margins frame your text.

Justified type "darkens" your message's appearance, because the uniform line lengths lack the white space created by ragged margins. It also tends to make your message look more like a form letter and less like a customized message. Justified type is often considered more difficult to read.

Flush-left, ragged-right type "lightens" your message's appearance. It gives a document an informal, contemporary feeling of openness. Spacing between words is the same, and only long words that fall at the ends of lines are hyphenated.

Flush-left, ragged-right type gives your message an open feeling.

Choose Easy-to-Read Typefaces

Typeface refers to the physical design of letters, numbers, and other text characters. Most computers offer many choices of fonts or typefaces. Each typeface influences the tone of your message, making it look authoritative, friendly, expensive, classy, casual, and so on. Choose fonts that are appropriate for your message.

Serif typefaces have small crosslines (called serifs) at the ends of each letter stroke (see Table 5.1). Serif faces such as Times Roman (packaged with most laser printers) are commonly used for text; they can look busy and cluttered when set in large sizes for headings or other display treatments. Typefaces with rounded serifs can look friendly; those with squared serifs can look official.

Serif typefaces are commonly used for text.

Sans serif typefaces have no serifs. Faces such as Helvetica (packaged with most laser printers) are ideal for display treatments that use larger type. Sans serif faces can be difficult to read in long blocks of text. They look best when surrounded by plenty of white space—as in headings or in widely spaced lines of text.

Sans serif typefaces are commonly used for headings.

Table 5.1 Common Typefaces

Sample Serif Typeface	Sample Sans Serif Typeface
Times Roman is often used for text.	Helvetica is often used for headings.
TIMES ROMAN IS HARDER TO READ IN ALL CAPS.	HELVETICA IS A CLEANER FACE, EVEN IN ALL CAPS.

Limit the number of typefaces in a single document.[7] In general, use no more than two typefaces on a page. Many great-looking documents are based on a single sans serif typeface for heads and subheads, with a second serif typeface for text and captions. Using too many typefaces clutters the document and reduces your audience's comprehension.

Use Type Styles to Dramatize Important Information

Type style refers to any modification that lends contrast or emphasis to type. Most computers offer underlining, boldface, italic, and other highlighting and decorative styles. Using boldface type for subheads breaks up long expanses of text. Too much boldfacing will darken the appearance of your message and make it look heavy. You can set isolated words in boldface type in the middle of a text block to draw more attention to them. However, if you boldface too many words, you might create a "checkerboard" appearance in a paragraph.

Use italic type to set off text but notice that italic is a weak typeface. Boldface will create a more dramatic effect. Italics can also be used to identify a quote or to indicate the title of a publication and are often used in captions. Boldface type and italics are most effective when reserved for key words—those words that help readers understand the main point of the text.

Avoid using type styles that slow your readers down.

As a general rule, don't use any style that slows your audience's progress through your message. For instance, using underlining or all-uppercase letters can interfere with your reader's ability to recognize the shapes of words and thus slow the reader's progress.

Make sure the size of your type is proportionate to the importance of your message and the space allotted. Small type in a sea of white space appears lost. Large type squeezed into a small area is hard to read and visually cramped. For most business messages, use a type size of 10 to 12 points.

Make Design Elements Effective

For effective design, pay attention to

- Consistency
- Balance
- Restraint
- Detail

Make all design elements work together. Effective document design guides your readers through your message, so be sure to focus on being consistent, maintaining balance, showing restraint, being detail-oriented, and using whatever technological tools you can (see Table 5.2).

Avoid last-minute compromises. Don't reduce type size or white space to squeeze in text. If you've planned your message so that your purpose, your audience, and your message are clear, you can design your document to be effective.[8] Start by thinking about your medium (press release, magazine or newsletter article, brochure, direct-mail package, slide presentation, formal report, business letter, or internal memo). Once you've decided on a medium for your message, make it look interesting and easy to read and understand.

Use Computers to Improve Your Documents

The most common means for creating printed documents is word-processing software.

Whether you're composing your message, adding graphics, or revising your first draft, technology helps you do so more efficiently, and it helps you produce more professional-looking results. Word processors give you the ability to delete and move text easily, with features such as automatic list numbering, page numbering, and dating.

Use Software

For Editing When it's time to revise and polish your message, your word processor helps you add, delete, and move text with functions such as *cut and paste* (taking a block of text out of one section of a document and pasting it in somewhere else) and *search and replace* (tracking down words or phrases and changing them if you need to). In addition, the AutoCorrect feature allows you to store words you commonly misspell or mistype, along with their correct spelling. So if you frequently type *teh* instead of *the,* AutoCorrect will automatically correct your typo for you. Finally, software tools such as revision marks

Table 5.2 Five Pointers for Making Design Elements Effective

1. Balance all visual elements
Create a pleasing design by balancing the space devoted to text, artwork, and white space.

2. Strive for simplicity in design
Don't clutter your message with too many design elements, too much highlighting, or too many decorative touches.

3. Be consistent throughout a message
Keep margins, typeface, type size, and spacing consistent from document to document (and sometimes even from message to message). Also be consistent when using recurring design elements, such as vertical lines, columns, and borders.

4. Pay attention to design details
When headings and subheadings appear at the bottom of a column or a page, readers can be offended because the promised information doesn't appear until the next column or page. Plus, narrow columns with too much space between words can be distracting.

5. Use the best technology available
Word-processing and desktop publishing programs help you combine text and graphics for a professional, inviting appearance. They add a first-class finish with attractive typefaces and colour graphics. They also let you manage document style with formatting commands that you can save and apply as needed—to ensure consistency from section to section and from document to document. Technology can turn a plain piece of text into a dazzling, persuasive document.

keep track of proposed editing changes electronically and provide a history of a document's revisions. The revisions appear in a different font colour from the original text, giving you a chance to review changes before accepting or rejecting them.

For Checking Spelling and Grammar Three advanced software functions can help bring out the best in your documents: a *spell checker,* a *thesaurus,* and a *grammar checker.* Just don't rely on grammar or spell checkers to do all your revision work. For example, spell checkers cannot tell the difference between *their* and *there.* Moreover, some of the "errors" they do detect may actually be proper names, technical words, words that you misspelled on purpose, or simply words that weren't included in the spell checker's dictionary. Grammar checkers are even more limited, so it's up to you to decide whether each flagged item should be corrected or left alone, and it's up to you to find the errors that your spell and grammar checkers have overlooked.[9]

Spell checkers, grammar checkers, and computerized thesauruses can all help with the revision process, but they can't take the place of good writing and editing skills.

Spelling and grammar checkers have their limitations.

For Making Graphics *Graphics software* can help you create simple diagrams and flow charts (see Chapter 11) or you can create your pictures from scratch, use *clip art* (collections of uncopyrighted images), or scan in drawings or photographs.

You can use graphics software to add visual elements to your message.

Proofreading Your Message

Most readers view attention to detail as a sign of your professionalism. Whether you're writing a one-paragraph memo or a 500-page report, if you let mechanical errors slip through, your readers wonder whether you're unreliable. For example, a resumé with a typo in it may be rejected.

Your credibility is affected by your attention to the details of mechanics and form.

What to Look for When Proofreading

To ensure that your message is letter perfect, proofread it. Give some attention to your overall format. Have you followed accepted conventions and company guidelines for laying out the document on the page (margin width, number of columns, page numbering)? Have you included all the traditional elements that belong in documents of the type you're creating? Have you been consistent in handling heading styles, exhibit titles, source notes, and other details? (To resolve questions about format and layout, see Appendix A.)

The types of details to look for when proofreading include language errors, missing material, design errors, and typographical errors.

Check your document for correct grammar, usage, and punctuation (for a quick review, see the Handbook of Grammar, Mechanics, and Usage at the end of this textbook). Also look for common spelling errors and typos. Check for missing material: a missing source note, exhibit, or paragraph. Look for design errors; for example, make sure that all headings and text appear in the right typeface and that columns within tables and exhibits are aligned. Graphic characters such as ampersands and percent signs may appear when they should be spelled out, and numerical symbols might be incorrect. Look closely at the type to spot problems such as extra spacing between lines or between words, a short line of type ending a paragraph at the top of a new page, a heading that's been left hanging at the bottom of a page, or incorrect hyphenation.

How to Adapt the Proofreading Process

Allow time for thorough proofreading.

How many and what sorts of errors you catch when proofreading depend on how much time you have and what type of document you are preparing. The more routine your document, the less time you'll need to spend proofreading it. Proofreading may require patience, but it adds credibility to your document. To help make your proofreading more effective and ensure that your document is error free, remember the following pointers:

Look for one thing at a time.

- **Multiple passes.** Go through the document several times, focusing on a different aspect each time. The first pass might be to look for omissions and errors in content. The second pass could be for layout, spacing, and other aesthetic features. A final pass might be to check for typographical, grammatical, and spelling errors.
- **Perceptual tricks.** Your brain has been trained to ignore typos. Try (1) reading each page from the bottom to the top (starting at the last word in each line), (2) placing your finger under each word and reading it silently, (3) making a slit in a sheet of paper that reveals only one line at a time, and (4) reading the document aloud and pronouncing each word carefully.
- **Impartial reviews.** Have a friend or colleague proofread the document for you. Others are likely to catch mistakes that you continually fail to notice. (All of us have blind spots when it comes to reviewing our own work.)
- **Distance.** If you have time, set the document aside and proofread it the next day.
- **Vigilance.** Avoid reading large amounts of material in one sitting, and try not to proofread when you're tired.
- **Focus.** Concentrate on what you're doing. Try to block out distractions, and focus as completely as possible on your proofreading task.
- **Caution.** Take your time. Quick proofreading is not careful proofreading.

Reviewing Key Points

This chapter describes what to do in the third step of the three-step writing process. To complete a business document be sure to

- Allow time for thorough revision.
- Start with checking the content. Pay attention to the opening—does it say what the document is about? Is the body of the document complete? Are all predicted reader

questions answered in the document? Where is the action you want readers to take—is it noticeable and emphasized because it is in the beginning and end, the most emphatic parts of the document?

- Revise sentences to ensure that they are free of redundancies, long strings of nouns, camouflaged verbs, extra words, and ineffective sentence starters. Ensure that sentences and lists are in parallel structure. Check for dangling and misplaced modifiers.
- Check that simplicity, balance, consistency, and emphasis are achieved in the document's overall appearance and form.
- Make the document easy to scan or read at a glance:
  - Use boldface headings to provide accessibility to the content and to give emphasis to important points.
  - Leave ample margin and white space to avoid crowding the information.
  - Choose fonts that match your purpose.
- Use software to edit and to check spelling and grammar.
- Make several passes to find mistakes in spelling, grammar, and punctuation. Pay attention to detail to show professionalism and build credibility.

Test Your Knowledge

1. What are the three main tasks involved in completing a business message?

2. What is a hedging sentence, and how can you correct one?

3. What is parallel construction, and why is it important?

4. Why is it a good idea to use verbs instead of noun phrases?

5. What are some ways you can make your message more concise?

6. What are design elements?

7. How do readers benefit from white space?

8. How can you make design elements more effective?

9. What computer tools can you use when revising messages?

10. Why is proofreading an important part of the writing process?

Apply Your Knowledge

1. Why should you let your draft "age" a day before you begin the revision process?

2. Why is it important that your business messages be clear?

3. Why is it important that your business messages be concise?

4. How does design contribute to a document's overall effectiveness?

5. **Ethical Choices** You have been asked to write a document explaining how your customers can appeal a decision made in the company's favour during a dispute. What are the ethical implications of using hard-to-read type styles such as underlining and all capitals in your message?

Practise Your Knowledge

Exercises for Perfecting Your Writing

Reducing Sentence Length

1. The next time you write something, check your average sentence length in a 100-word passage, and if your sentences average more than 16 to 20 words, see whether you can break up some of the sentences.

2. Unfortunately, no gadget will produce excellent writing, but using a yardstick like the Fog Index gives us some guideposts to follow for making writing easier to read because its two factors remind us to use short sentences and simple words.

3. Know the flexibility of the written word and its power to convey an idea, and know how to make your words behave so that your readers will understand.

Trimming Unnecessary Words Cross out unnecessary words in the following:

4. The board cannot act without a consensus of opinion.
5. To surpass our competitors, we need new innovations both in products and in company operations.
6. George McClannahan has wanted to be head of engineering a long period of time, and now he has finally gotten the promotion.

Using Simple Words

7. The antiquated calculator is ineffectual for solving sophisticated problems.

8. It is imperative that the pay increments be terminated before an inordinate deficit is accumulated.

9. The impending liquidation of the company's assets was cause for jubilation among the company's competitors.

Using Infinitives to Be Concise

10. For living, I require money.

11. They did not find sufficient evidence for believing in the future.

12. Bringing about the destruction of a dream is tragic.

Removing Unnecessary Words Condense these sentences to as few words as possible:

13. We are of the conviction that writing is important.

14. In all probability, we're likely to have a price increase.

15. Our goals include making a determination about that in the near future.

16. When all is said and done at the conclusion of this experiment, I'd like to summarize the final windup.

Removing Unnecessary Modifiers

17. Tremendously high pay increases were given to the extraordinarily skilled and extremely conscientious employees.
18. The union's proposals were highly inflationary, extremely demanding, and exceptionally bold.

Removing Hedging

19. It would appear that someone apparently entered illegally.

20. It may be possible that sometime in the near future the situation is likely to improve.

21. Your report seems to suggest that we might be losing money.

Beginning with the Main Idea Rewrite these sentences to eliminate the indefinite starters:

22. There are several examples here to show that Nadia can't hold a position very long.

23. It would be greatly appreciated if every employee would make a generous contribution to Mildred Cook's retirement party.

24. It has been learned in Ottawa today from generally reliable sources that an important announcement will be made shortly by the prime minister.

25. There is a rule that states that we cannot work overtime without permission.

Improving Parallelism Present the ideas in these sentences in parallel form:

26. Mr. Hill is expected to lecture three days a week, to counsel two days a week, and must write for publication in his spare time.

27. She knows not only accounting, but she also reads Latin.

28. Both applicants had families, university degrees, and were in their thirties, with considerable accounting experience but few social connections.

29. This book was exciting, well written, and held my interest.

Revising Dangling Modifiers Rewrite these sentences to clarify the dangling modifiers:

30. Running down the railroad tracks in a cloud of smoke, we watched the countryside glide by.

31. Lying on the shelf, Madhu saw the seashell.

32. Being cluttered and filthy, Sandy took the whole afternoon to clean up her desk.

Eliminating Noun Sequences Rewrite the following sentences to eliminate the long strings of nouns:

33. The focus of the meeting was a discussion of the bank interest rate deregulation issue.

34. Following the government task force report recommendations, we are revising our job applicant evaluation procedures.

35. The production department quality assurance program components include employee training, supplier cooperation, and computerized detection equipment.

Improving Sentence Structure Rearrange the following sentences to bring the subjects closer to their verbs:

36. Trudy, when she first saw the bull pawing the ground, ran.

37. It was Terri who, according to Ted, who is probably the worst gossip in the office (Tom excepted), mailed the wrong order.

38. Judy Schimmel, after passing up several sensible investment opportunities, despite the warnings of her friends and family, invested her inheritance in a ginseng plantation.

Revising Camouflaged Verbs Rewrite each sentence so that the verbs are no longer camouflaged:

39. Adaptation to the new rules was performed easily by the employees.

40. The assessor will make a determination of the tax due.

41. Verification of the identity of the employees must be made daily.

42. The board of directors made a recommendation that Mr. Ronson be assigned to a new division.

Activities

For live links to all Web sites discussed in this chapter, visit this text's Web site at www.pearsoned.ca/bovee. Just log on and select Chapter 5, and click on "Student Resources." Locate the page or the URL related to the material in the text. For "Best of the Web" exercises, you'll also find navigational directions. Click on the live link to the site.

1. **Analyze This Document** Read the following document; then (1) analyze the strengths and weaknesses of each sentence and (2) revise the document so that it follows the guidelines in Chapters 3 through 5.

   The move to our new offices will take place over this coming weekend. For everything to run smooth, everyone will have to clean out their own desk and pack up the contents in boxes that will be provided. You will need to take everything off the walls too, and please pack it along with the boxes.

   If you have alot of personal belongings, you should bring them home with you. Likewise with anything valuable. I do not mean to infer that items will be stolen, irregardless it is better to be safe than sorry.

   On Monday, we will be unpacking, putting things away, and then get back to work. The least amount of disruption is anticipated by us, if everyone does their part. Hopefully, there will be no negative affects on production schedules, and current deadlines will be met.

2. **Internet** Visit the stock market page of Bloomberg's Web site at www.bloomberg.com and evaluate the use of design in presenting the latest news. What design improvements can you suggest to enhance readability of the information posted on this page?

3. **Proofreading Messages: E-Mail** Proofread the following e-mail message and revise it to correct any problems you find:

   Our final company orrientation of the year will be held on Dec. 20. In preparation for this sesssion, please order 20 copies of the Policy handbook, the confindentiality agreenemt, the employee benefits Manual, please let me know if you anticipate any delays in obtaining these materials.

Expand Your Knowledge

Best of the Web

Write It Right: Rethink and Revise Are you sure that readers perceive your written message as you intended? If you want help revising a message that you're completing, use the Paradigm Online Writing Assistant (POWA). With this interactive writer's guide, you can select topics to get tips on how to edit your work, reshape your thoughts, and rewrite for clarity. Read discussions about perfecting your writing skills, and for practice, complete one of the many online activities provided to reinforce what you've learned. Or select the Forum to "talk" about writing. At POWA's Web site, you'll learn how to improve the final draft of your message.

www.powa.org

Exercises

1. Why is it better to write out ideas in a rough format and later reread your message to revise its content? When revising your message, what questions can you ask about your writing?
2. Name the four elements of the "writing context." Imagine that you're the reader of your message. What questions might you ask?
3. When you revise a written message, what is the purpose of "tightening"? What is one way to tighten your writing as you complete a message?

Exploring the Web on Your Own

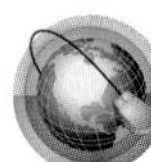

Review these chapter-related Web sites on your own to learn more about writing business messages.

1. Take the fog out of your documents and improve their readability by visiting the Training Post, trainingpost.org/3-2-res.htm, and following the hotlinks to the Gunning Fog Index.
2. Produce flawless messages by reviewing the material at the Guide to Grammar and Writing, http://ccc.commnet.edu/grammar.
3. Need help with grammar? Visit the Grammar Slammer at englishplus.com/grammar and find out why it promotes itself as the complete English grammar resource.

Learn Interactively

Interactive Study Guide

Visit the Companion Website at www.pearsoned.ca/bovee. For Chapter 5, take advantage of the interactive "Study Guide" to test your chapter knowledge. Get instant feedback on whether you need additional studying.

This site offers a variety of additional resources: The "Research Area" helps you locate a wealth of information to use in course assignments. You can even send a message to online research experts, who will help you find exactly the information you need. The "Study Hall" helps you succeed in this course by offering support with writing and study skills, time management, and career skills, as well as numerous other resources.

Peak Performance Grammar and Mechanics

PEAK

Use the Peak Performance Grammar and Mechanics CD to test your skill with adverbs. In the "Adjectives and Adverbs" section, take the Pretest to determine whether you have any weak areas. Then review those areas in the Refresher Course. Take the Follow-Up Test to check your grasp of adverb usage. For an extra challenge or advanced practice, take the Advanced Test.

Improve Your Grammar, Mechanics, and Usage

Level 1: Self-Assessment—Adverbs

Review Section 1.5 in the Handbook of Grammar, Mechanics, and Usage and then look at the following 15 items.

In items 1–5, select the correct word (in italics), and write it in the space provided:

1. Their performance has been ________ (*good/well*).
2. I ________ (*sure/surely*) do not know how to help you.
3. He feels ________ (*sick/sickly*) again today.
4. Customs dogs are chosen because they smell ________ (*good/well*).
5. The redecorated offices look ________ (*good/well*).

In items 6–10, provide the correct form of the adverb in parentheses:

6. Which of the two programs computes (*fast*) ________?
7. Kate has held 5 jobs over 13 years, and she was (*recently*) ________ employed by Graphicon.
8. Could they be (*happily*) ________ employed than they are now?
9. Of the two we have in stock, this model is the (*well*) ________ designed.
10. Of all the arguments I've ever heard, yours is the (*logically*) ________ reasoned.

In items 11–15, rewrite the sentences to correct double negatives.

11. He doesn't seem to have none.

12. That machine is scarcely never used.

13. They can't get no replacement parts until Thursday.

14. It wasn't no different from the first event we promoted.

15. We've looked for it, and it doesn't seem to be nowhere.

Level 2: Workplace Applications

The following items contain numerous errors in grammar, capitalization, punctuation, abbreviation, number style, word division, and vocabulary. Rewrite each sentence in the space provided, correcting all errors. Write *C* in the space after any sentence that is already correct.

1. All too often, whomever leaves the most out of his cost estimate is the one who wins the bid - if you can call it winning.

2. CEO, Dennis Kozlowski, called the plan to break up Safeco a 'mistake', considering the sluggish economy, spending cutbacks, and jitters on bay street over corporate accounting.

3. Shoppers were disinterested in the Web initially because many hyped services, offered no real cost or convenience advantages over offline stores.

4. Different jobs and different customers call for different pricing, estimating, and negotiating strategies.

5. Get to know the customer and their expectations, get the customer to talk about their primary use for you're product.

6. To homeowners, who feel they have found a competent contractor who has they're best interest's at heart, price will not matter nearly as much.

7. If I was you, I would of avoided investing in large conglomerates in light of the collapse of energy trader, Enron Corp., over accounting irregularities.

8. Outdoor goods retailer MEC has had significant, success with in-store kiosks that let customers choose between several types of merchandise.

9. To people in some areas of cyberspace "Advertising" is a four letter word but "Marketing" is perfectly acceptable.

10. In any business effort, making money requires planning. Strategic marketing, a good product, good customer service, considerable shrewdness—and much hard work.

11. Investors must decide weather to put their capitol into bonds or GICs.

12. Running at full capacity, millions of Nike shoes are being produced by manufacturing plants every day.

13. Metropolis' stationary has a picture of the CN tower on it.

14. Starbucks are planning to add fruit drinks to their menu in provinces throughout the west.

15. Credit ratings ain't what they used to be.

Improving Your Writing for the Web

The Web is unlike any other medium you may be required to write for. People visit the Web because they want to get information efficiently. So you need to grab a reader's attention and make your main points immediately. In addition to incorporating the business-writing skills discussed in this textbook, you must modify the structure and style of your writing for this medium.

Before beginning to write for the Web, understand what Web users need and expect. Most are impatient, and because their time is limited, they tend to scan text rather than read it, moving between sites instead of spending a lot of time on a single Web page. This skim-and-scan style demands extreme brevity. Moreover, reading on a computer monitor is more difficult than reading from the printed page, and written information on a Web page can take up multiple screens, forcing readers to scroll through the document. Although most readers move through a printed document in a fairly linear path from beginning to end, Web users move about a document and its related screens in any order they please.

A Web page has no beginning, middle, or end. Readers usually access a Web site from another site's link. Once readers arrive, getting an overview of a Web site could take hours, requiring readers to click on every page of the site. Plus, cyber content is constantly changing, so readers find it nearly impossible to quantify or gauge the depth of a site's material. In addition, links to other Web sites can increase the scope of a document to the entire cyberworld.

Successful Web writers help their readers along by breaking information into smaller screen-sized chunks that may be accessed in any order. *Hyperlinks* are the in-text tags that allow readers to click on a screen element and be instantly transported to information somewhere else. Using hyperlinks, Web writers can create three-dimensional documents that are minutely tailored to the needs of various members of their audience.

The following pointers summarize the ways that you can improve your Web writing:

1. **Develop a well-organized hyperlink structure:**
   - Plan your navigation first.
   - Let readers decide how they will access the information on your site—how much they will read, in what order, and when.
   - Provide a search engine in your document.
   - Make your structure obvious with a hyperlinked site map or a table of contents at the top or bottom of your page.
2. **Modify your message style:**
   - Use a lighter, less-formal writing style.
   - Avoid clever, humorous, or jargon-filled phrases that could be misunderstood by readers from other cultures.
   - Modify your messages for global audiences, perhaps localizing material so that it reflects your customers' native language, norms, weights, measures, time, currency, and so on—making your site and material appear as if they were originally developed in the local region.
3. **Modify your message format:**
   - Break information into independent chunks (self-contained, readable pages of information) and connect the chunks with hyperlinks.
   - Don't repeat information; instead, link your reader to the page where that information already resides.
   - Don't burden others with unwanted detail. Place specific details on subsequent pages.
   - Try to keep longer pieces to a maximum of three scrollable screens, if possible.
   - Avoid randomly breaking a single, linear article (even a lengthy one) into a series of pages once you've determined its concept cannot be further subdivided.
   - Include a downloadable, printable version of longer documents for offline reading.
   - Adopt an inverted pyramid style so that readers can quickly see your topic, main idea, and conclusion.
   - Put your most important concept in the first 50 words, in case search engines pick up those words to describe your site.
4. **Help readers skim text for the information they need:**
   - Write shorter sentences and paragraphs to ease the reading process and to fit in narrow columns.
   - Cut traditional print by about 40 percent and try to keep chunks to 75 words or less.
   - Tighten your writing by avoiding passive voice, needless prepositional phrases, and wordiness.

- Avoid tightening your prose to the point that it's choppy and abrupt.
- Delete superfluous details, and stick to what's relevant.
- Use bulleted and numbered lists.
- Use boldface, colour, and other typographical elements conservatively.
- Write informative headings that stand on their own and are consistent in their wording.
- Write concise summaries and descriptions that are informative and crystal clear.

5. **Write effective links and place them strategically:**
   - Use a combination of textual and graphical hyperlinks, but don't overdo graphics, since they slow down document loading time.
   - Avoid self-referential terms such as "click here" or "follow this link."
   - Use absolute directions.
   - Write informative hyperlinks so that the content of subsequent pages is obvious.
   - Place your links strategically and carefully.
6. **Establish your credibility (important because anyone can post material on a Web site):**
   - Include your name and the name of your sponsor (if applicable) on every Web page.
   - Provide contact information (at least an e-mail address) so that readers can get in touch with you or your sponsor easily.
   - Include posting and revision dates for your information.
   - Make sure your content is error free.

Applications for Success

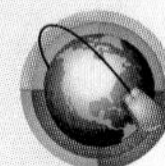

Writing for the Web (www.useit.com/papers/webwriting) offers you a huge amount of information on Web writing. Visit this site and access research on how users read on the Web and the official Sun Microsystems guidelines booklet, and find links to other Web-writing sites.

Do the following:

1. Select any Web page and critique the headings. Do they make sense on their own? Do they include hyperlinks? Does the author use colour or boldface effectively? What changes, if any, would you recommend?
2. Select any Web page and critique the effectiveness of the written hyperlinks. Does the author use self-referential terms or absolute directions? Is the writing concise? Are linked words embedded in a sentence or paragraph to provide the reader with context? Are the hyperlinks placed effectively?
3. Select a short article from any print magazine or newspaper. Now rewrite the article in a format suitable for the Web, using the techniques discussed in this workshop. Focus on writing only one Web page. Include some hyperlinks on that page and in your article (but don't take the time to develop material for the linked page).

Working with Letters, Memos, and E-mail Messages

6

After studying this chapter, you will be able to

1 Explain the difference between internal and external communication
2 Discuss how letters, memos, and e-mail messages differ in format
3 Summarize four techniques you can use to improve message readability
4 Distinguish between descriptive and informative headings
5 Describe four methods you can use to improve the readability of e-mail messages
6 Define e-mail etiquette and give examples

From the Real World

"Considering most people don't read much of what is written, you must be brief and direct."

–Colin Ferguson
Partner
Ferguson Walker Marketing Communications

Based in Winnipeg, Ferguson Walker Marketing Communications has handled communication for many prominent businesses such as Canada Safeway, McDonald's Restaurants of Canada, James Richardson & Sons Limited, GM, and the Pan American Games. "All messages need to be carefully planned. For instance, understanding your audience and subject matter are critical in deciding the tone and formality of the message," says Colin Ferguson. You need to know when to use a casual tone and when to be formal. You also need to know when to send a memo, transmit an e-mail, or send a letter.[1]

Sending Memos, E-mails, and Letters

Understanding the differences among memos, e-mails, and letters is important.

Although a lot of business communication is oral (taking place in face-to-face conversations, in meetings, during phone conversations, and in voice mail), a significant amount of your time will be spent writing e-mails, memos, and letters. Getting written information to the people who need it and receiving written information from the people who have it are easier if you understand the differences among memos, e-mails, and letters.

First, think about whether your message is internal or external and then whether it requires a formal or informal approach.

Internal or External Communication

Internal communication is the way employees exchange information within an organization.

Use memos and e-mail for internal communication.

External communication is the way employees exchange information with the world outside the organization.

Internal communication refers to the exchange of information and ideas within an organization. You use memos and e-mail for the routine, day-to-day communication within the organization. Internal communication helps employees develop a clear sense of the organization's mission, identify potential problems, and react quickly to changes.

Just as internal communication carries information throughout the organization, **external communication** carries it into and out of the organization. Companies constantly exchange messages in e-mails and letters with customers, vendors, distributors, competitors, investors, journalists, and community representatives.

Use letters and e-mail for external communication.

These external messages also perform an important public relations function.

E-mail is often used for external communication (1) in response to e-mail messages that you receive, (2) when the purpose of your message is informal, and (3) when your audience accepts e-mail as appropriate. External communication helps employees create a favourable impression of their company, plan for and respond to crises, and gather useful information.

Format Differences

Different media have varying levels of formality:

- Formal = letters
- Less formal = memos
- Least formal = e-mail messages

Most memos, e-mails, and letters are relatively brief, generally less than two pages long (often less than a page for e-mail). Letters are the most formal of the three. Memos are less formal, and e-mail messages are the least formal of all. For in-depth format information, see Appendix A: Format and Layout of Business Documents. When trying to distinguish among these three types of documents, keep the following format differences in mind.

Memos

Memos have elements such as

- Title
- "To, From, Date, Subject" heading

Being less formal than letters, most memos begin with a title, such as *Memo, Memorandum,* or *Interoffice Correspondence.* They use *To, From, Date,* and *Subject* headings to emphasize the needs of the readers (who usually have time only to skim messages). Figure 6.1 is a typical memo at Carnival Corporation (responding to a request for data on passenger capacity). The comments in the left margin point out typical memo format elements.

The Carnival writer might have chosen to respond using e-mail. However, the data being provided are clearest in table form, and tabular material comes out more reliably in print.

Memos do not have salutations. Good memos discuss only one topic and use a conversational tone. Memos generally have no complimentary close or signature. Because of their open construction and informal method of delivery (either interoffice mail or e-mail), memos are less private than letters.

E-mail Messages

E-mail messages have elements such as

- Heading (often brief, including information about copies and attachments)
- Salutation (optional but highly recommended)
- Complimentary closing (optional but highly recommended)
- Typed name of sender
- Contact information (optional but recommended)

Like memos, e-mail messages begin with *To, From, Date,* and *Subject* information. The heading section also may include information about copies and attachments. The date is automatically inserted into the document by the program. Figure 6.2 on page 124 is a typical e-mail message (a request for capacity data at Carnival Corporation). The comments in the left margin point out typical e-mail format elements.

For e-mail messages a salutation is optional; however, a greeting can add a friendly tone. Because the information in the header is often very brief, you may want to include contact information with your name at the end of the e-mail, especially if the e-mail is going outside the company.

E-mail has a reputation for speed and informality. Nevertheless, you'll want to write your e-mail messages carefully. Appearance, organization, and style are just as important for electronic messages as for any other type of business message.

Letters

Letters have elements such as

- Letterhead
- Date
- Inside address
- Salutation
- Subject line
- Complimentary close
- Signature block

Although the format for a letter depends on the traditions of the organization, it does have some generally accepted characteristics. For example, consider the letter in Figure 6.3 on page 125. Alberta's Save the Wolves Foundation seeks to raise funds for relocating wolves from other Canadian provinces into selected wilderness areas in North America. The foundation tries to educate the public and garner support, so it communicates externally. Figure 6.3 is a letter from the foundation to representatives of the mass media. Comments in the left margin point out format elements.

Most business letters appear on letterhead stationery, which includes the company's name and address and other contact information. The first thing to appear after the letterhead is the date. Next comes the inside address, which identifies the person receiving the letter. And after that comes the salutation, usually in the form of *Dear Mr.* or *Ms. Last*

FIGURE 6.1 A Typical Memo

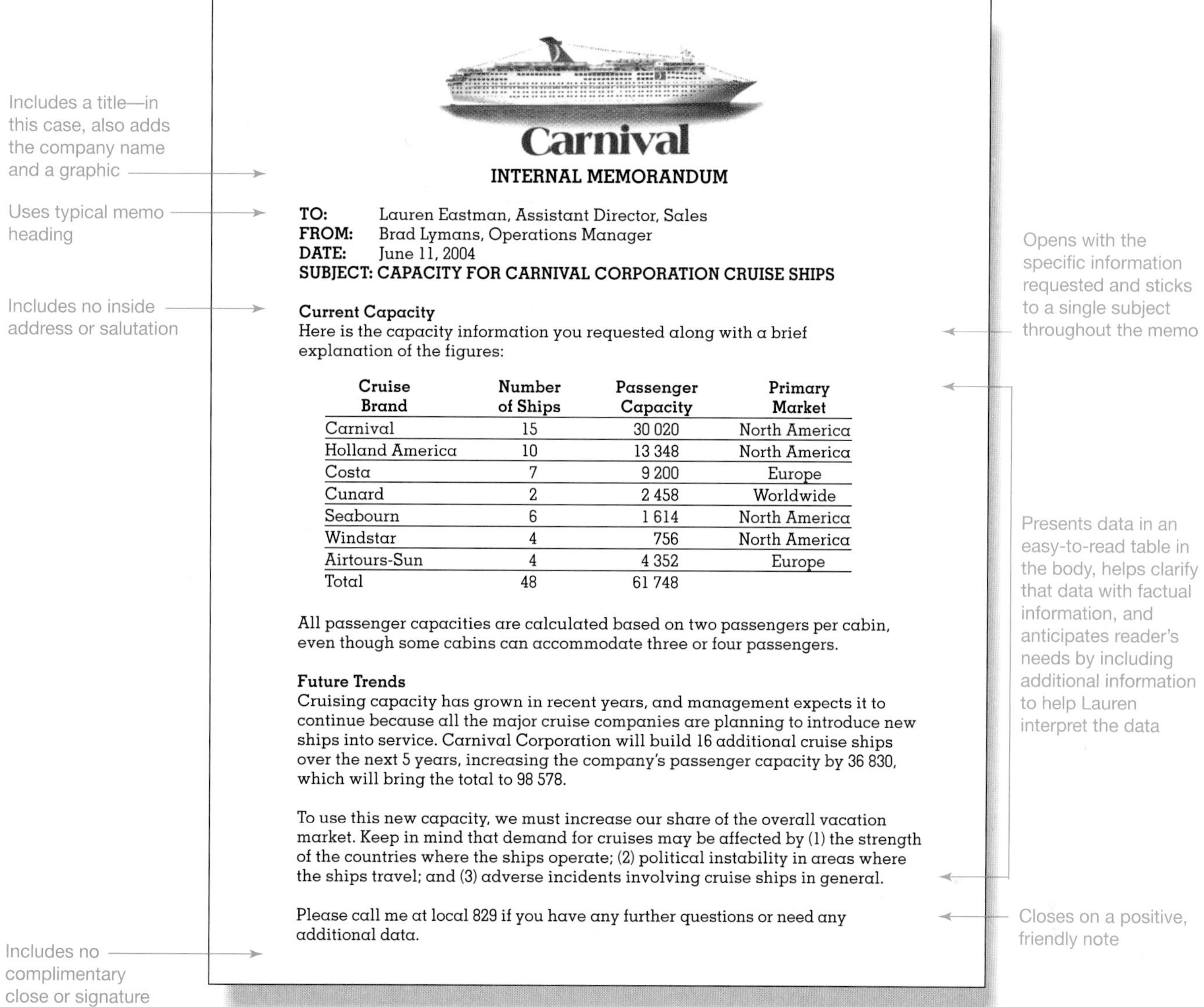
Includes a title—in this case, also adds the company name and a graphic
Uses typical memo heading
Includes no inside address or salutation
Includes no complimentary close or signature
Opens with the specific information requested and sticks to a single subject throughout the memo
Presents data in an easy-to-read table in the body, helps clarify that data with factual information, and anticipates reader's needs by including additional information to help Lauren interpret the data
Closes on a positive, friendly note

Carnival

INTERNAL MEMORANDUM

TO: Lauren Eastman, Assistant Director, Sales
FROM: Brad Lymans, Operations Manager
DATE: June 11, 2004
SUBJECT: CAPACITY FOR CARNIVAL CORPORATION CRUISE SHIPS

Current Capacity
Here is the capacity information you requested along with a brief explanation of the figures:

Cruise Brand	Number of Ships	Passenger Capacity	Primary Market
Carnival	15	30 020	North America
Holland America	10	13 348	North America
Costa	7	9 200	Europe
Cunard	2	2 458	Worldwide
Seabourn	6	1 614	North America
Windstar	4	756	North America
Airtours-Sun	4	4 352	Europe
Total	48	61 748	

All passenger capacities are calculated based on two passengers per cabin, even though some cabins can accommodate three or four passengers.

Future Trends
Cruising capacity has grown in recent years, and management expects it to continue because all the major cruise companies are planning to introduce new ships into service. Carnival Corporation will build 16 additional cruise ships over the next 5 years, increasing the company's passenger capacity by 36 830, which will bring the total to 98 578.

To use this new capacity, we must increase our share of the overall vacation market. Keep in mind that demand for cruises may be affected by (1) the strength of the countries where the ships operate; (2) political instability in areas where the ships travel; and (3) adverse incidents involving cruise ships in general.

Please call me at local 829 if you have any further questions or need any additional data.

Name. A subject line summarizes the topic and acts as a title and filing reference. The message comes next, often running several paragraphs and sometimes running over to a second page. After the message is the complimentary close, usually *Sincerely* or *Yours truly.* And last comes the signature block: space for the signature, followed by the sender's printed name and title.

Improving Readability in Short Business Messages

Most business writers know that busy readers seldom read every word of a message on their first pass. Instead, they typically skim a message, reading only certain sections carefully to assess the value of the document. If they determine that the document contains valuable information or requires a response, they will read it more carefully when time permits. You can adopt a number of techniques to make your message easier to skim: varying sentence length, using shorter paragraphs, using lists and bullets, and adding effective headings and subheadings.

Make your messages easy to skim.

FIGURE 6.2 A Typical E-Mail Message

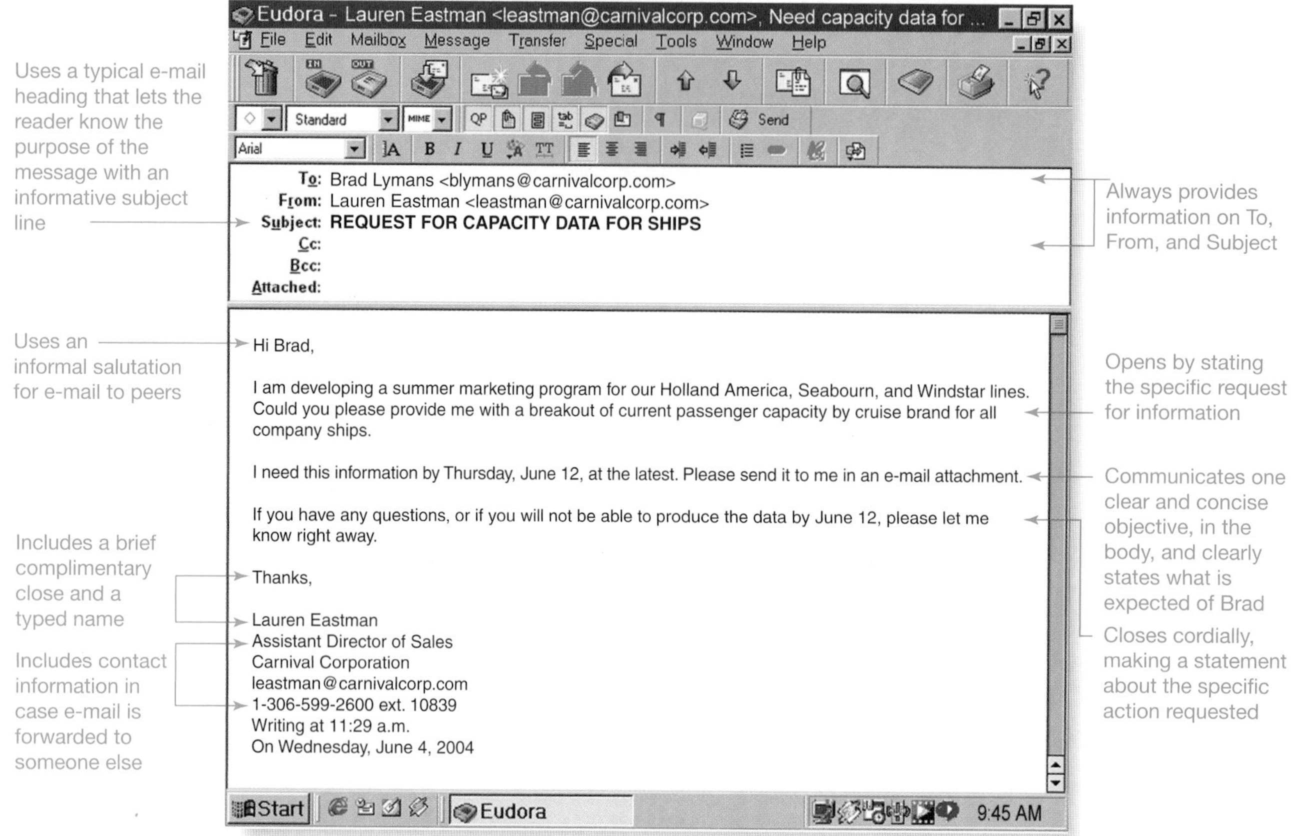

Vary Sentence Length

Using a variety of short, medium, and long sentences makes your message more interesting.

Although good business writers use short sentences most of the time, too many short sentences in a row can make your writing choppy. To increase interest, use a variety of both short and long sentences:

- Long sentences are well suited for grouping or combining ideas, listing points, and summarizing or previewing information.
- Medium-length sentences (those with about 20 words) are useful for showing the relationships among ideas.
- Short sentences emphasize important information.

Most good business writing has an average sentence length of 20 words or fewer. (Varying sentence length can create translation problems for international readers, so stick to short sentences for audiences abroad.)[2]

Keep Paragraphs Short

Short paragraphs are easier to read than long ones.

Most business readers are put off by large blocks of text. Unless you break up your thoughts somehow, you'll end up with a three-page paragraph that's guaranteed to intimidate even the most dedicated reader. Short paragraphs (of seven lines or fewer) are easier to read than long ones, and they make your writing look inviting.

As you write your message, try to use a variety of paragraph lengths. But be careful to use one-sentence paragraphs only occasionally and only for emphasis. When you want to package a big idea in short paragraphs, break the idea into subtopics and treat each subtopic in a separate paragraph—being careful to provide plenty of transitional elements.

FIGURE 6.3 A Typical Letter

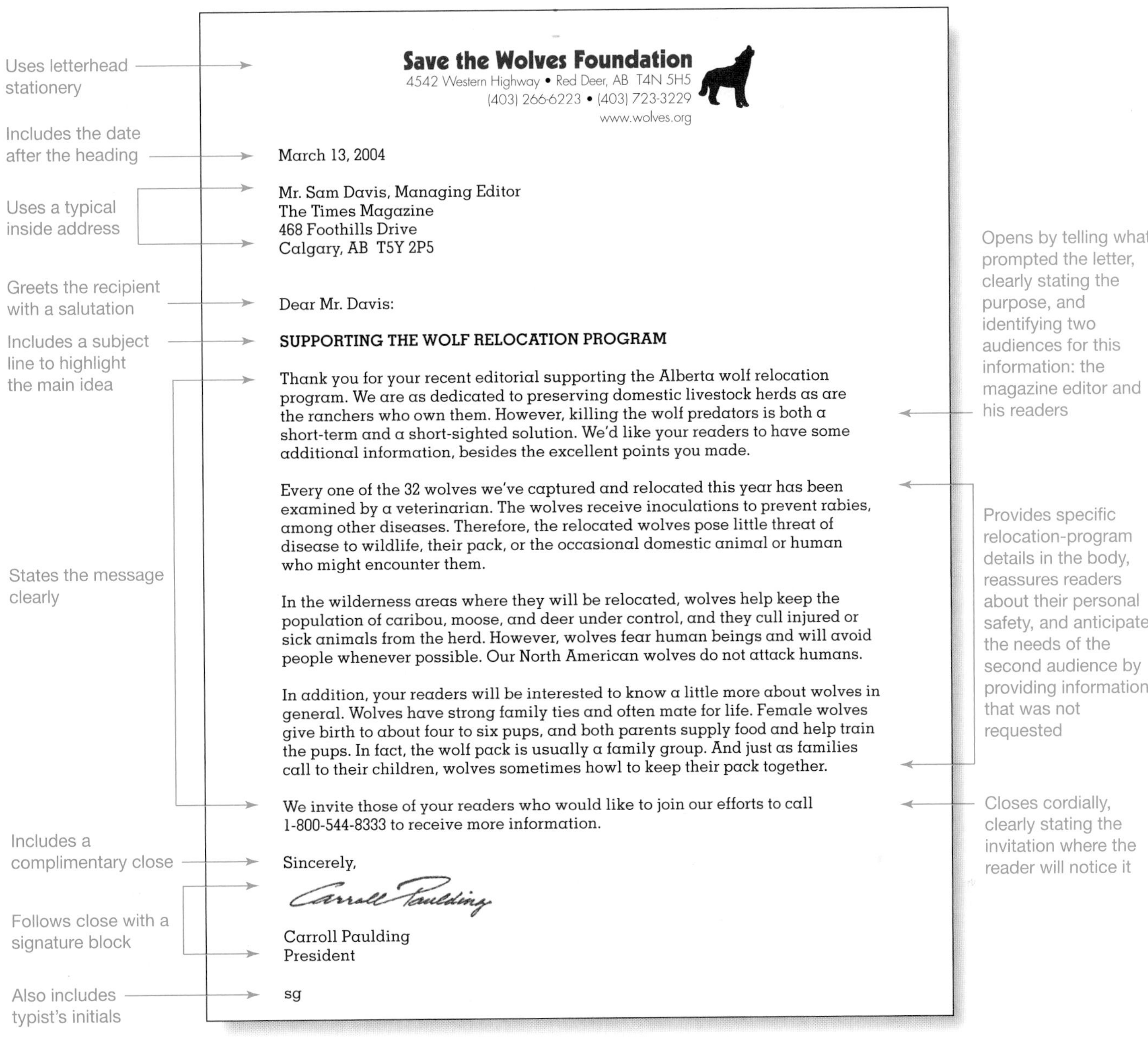
Uses letterhead stationery
Includes the date after the heading
Uses a typical inside address
Greets the recipient with a salutation
Includes a subject line to highlight the main idea
States the message clearly
Includes a complimentary close
Follows close with a signature block
Also includes typist's initials
Opens by telling what prompted the letter, clearly stating the purpose, and identifying two audiences for this information: the magazine editor and his readers
Provides specific relocation-program details in the body, reassures readers about their personal safety, and anticipates the needs of the second audience by providing information that was not requested
Closes cordially, clearly stating the invitation where the reader will notice it

Save the Wolves Foundation
4542 Western Highway • Red Deer, AB T4N 5H5
(403) 266-6223 • (403) 723-3229
www.wolves.org

March 13, 2004

Mr. Sam Davis, Managing Editor
The Times Magazine
468 Foothills Drive
Calgary, AB T5Y 2P5

Dear Mr. Davis:

SUPPORTING THE WOLF RELOCATION PROGRAM

Thank you for your recent editorial supporting the Alberta wolf relocation program. We are as dedicated to preserving domestic livestock herds as are the ranchers who own them. However, killing the wolf predators is both a short-term and a short-sighted solution. We'd like your readers to have some additional information, besides the excellent points you made.

Every one of the 32 wolves we've captured and relocated this year has been examined by a veterinarian. The wolves receive inoculations to prevent rabies, among other diseases. Therefore, the relocated wolves pose little threat of disease to wildlife, their pack, or the occasional domestic animal or human who might encounter them.

In the wilderness areas where they will be relocated, wolves help keep the population of caribou, moose, and deer under control, and they cull injured or sick animals from the herd. However, wolves fear human beings and will avoid people whenever possible. Our North American wolves do not attack humans.

In addition, your readers will be interested to know a little more about wolves in general. Wolves have strong family ties and often mate for life. Female wolves give birth to about four to six pups, and both parents supply food and help train the pups. In fact, the wolf pack is usually a family group. And just as families call to their children, wolves sometimes howl to keep their pack together.

We invite those of your readers who would like to join our efforts to call 1-800-544-8333 to receive more information.

Sincerely,

Carroll Paulding

Carroll Paulding
President

sg

Use Lists and Bullets

Lists help you focus your reader's attention on important points.

Set off important ideas in a **list**—a series of words, names, or items. Lists can show the sequence of your ideas, heighten visual impact, and help readers find your key points. In addition, lists simplify complex subjects, ease the skimming process for busy readers, and give the reader a breather.

You can separate list items with numbers, letters, or bullets (a general term for any kind of graphical element that precedes each item). Bullets are generally preferred over numbers or letters, unless the sequence of events is critical (if the steps in a process must be completed in a specific order, for example).

Introduce lists clearly.

When using lists, introduce them clearly so that people know what they're about to read. One way to introduce a list is to use an introductory or lead-in sentence:

> The board of directors met to discuss the revised annual budget. To keep expenses in line with declining sales, the directors voted to
>
> - Cut everyone's salary by 10 percent
> - Close the employee cafeteria
> - Reduce travel expenses

If necessary, add further discussion after the lists to complete your thought. Another way to introduce a list is to use a complete introductory sentence, followed by a colon:

> To accomplish our mission, our team will follow three steps:
>
> 1. Find out how many employees would use on-site daycare facilities.
> 2. Determine how much space the daycare centre would require.
> 3. Estimate the cost of converting conference rooms for the on-site facility.

Make sure list items are parallel in structure.

The items in a list should be in parallel form. If one list item begins with a verb, all list items should begin with a verb. If one is a noun phrase, all should be noun phrases:

Avoid Nonparallel List Items	Use Parallel List Items
■ Improve our bottom line	■ Improving our bottom line
■ Identification of new foreign markets for our products	■ Identifying new foreign markets for our products
■ Global market strategies	■ Developing our global market strategies
■ Issues regarding pricing and packaging size	■ Resolving pricing and packaging issues

For additional discussion of parallelism, see "Rewrite and Edit for Clarity" in Chapter 5.

Use Headings and Subheadings

Headings and subheadings help readers decipher the content of your message.

A **heading** is a brief title that cues readers to the content of the section that follows. Headings and subheadings serve several important functions:

- **Organization.** Headings show your reader at a glance how the document is organized. They are labels that group related paragraphs together, organizing your material into short sections.
- **Attention.** Informative, inviting, and in some cases intriguing headings grab the reader's attention, make the copy easier to read, and help readers find the parts they need to read—or skip.
- **Connection.** Using headings and subheadings visually indicates shifts from one idea to the next, helping readers see the relationship between subordinate and main ideas.

Informative headings allow readers to skim your subject matter.

Headings fall into two categories. **Descriptive headings** ("Cost Considerations") identify a topic but do little more. **Informative headings** (Reducing Costs by Changing Suppliers) sum up the content of the text below them. A well-written informative heading is self-contained; readers can understand it without reading the rest of the document. Keep your headings brief, and use parallel construction as you would for an outline, a list, or a series of words.

Improving Readability in E-mail Messages

E-mail can be as informal and casual as a conversation between old friends. But it can also emulate "snail mail" by using conventional business language, a respectful style, and a more formal format—by using a traditional greeting, formalized headings, and a formal closing and signature.[3] As with any business communication, how formal you make your message depends on your audience and your purpose.

Be sure to use correct spelling and proper grammar for your electronic messages. Spelling, grammar, capitalization, and punctuation still count in cyberspace.[4] To improve e-mail readability even more, be sure to make your subject lines informative, make your message easy to follow, personalize your messages, and observe basic e-mail etiquette.

You can improve e-mail readability by

- Writing informative subject lines
- Making messages visually easy to follow
- Personalizing your messages
- Observing basic e-mail etiquette

Make Subject Lines Informative

Subject lines in e-mail messages and memos should identify message content and build interest.

Always use subject lines in memos, e-mails, and letters. To capture your audience's attention, make your subject line informative. Do more than just describe or classify message content. Build interest with key words, actions, or benefits. Make subject lines short, specific, and action-oriented. Using verbs, especially participle forms ("ing") will make the style active. Keep subject lines positive or neutral in tone. If the message is negative, use a topic subject line that does not disclose the message. Otherwise, tell the whole story in this one short phrase.[5]

Ineffective Subject Line	Effective Subject Line
July sales figures	Sending figures for July sales
Tomorrow's meeting	Bringing consultant's report to Friday's meeting
Marketing report	Supplying budget for marketing report
Employee parking	Revised resurfacing schedule for parking lot
Status report	Warehouse remodelling is on schedule

Subject lines should be

- a phrase (short)
- specific (informative)
- focused on action

Change Subject Lines When Replying

In e-mails, if you are exchanging multiple e-mails on the same topic, periodically modify the subject line of your message to reflect the revised message content. Most e-mail programs will copy the subject line when you click the Reply button. Multiple messages in your e-mail electronic files with the same subject line can be confusing. Moreover, they may have absolutely nothing to do with the original topic. Modifying the subject line with each new response will prevent reader confusion and can make it easier to locate a message at a later date.

Modify your subject line over multiple messages.

Make Your E-mail Messages Easy to Follow

Avoid lines that run off screen or wrap oddly by using the Enter key to limit lines to 80 characters (60 if e-mail will be forwarded). Avoid styled text (boldface, italics), unless your receiver's system can read it.[6] Write short, focused, logically organized paragraphs. And try to limit e-mail to one screen; otherwise, write like a reporter—starting with the "headline" and adding detail in descending order of importance.[7] That way you'll be sure to get your point across as early as possible, in case your reader doesn't have the time or interest to finish reading your message.

You can make e-mail messages easier to follow by

- Ensuring the subject line is precise
- Using lines of the proper length
- Using unstyled text
- Writing well-organized content
- Limiting message length
- Covering the most important points first

Personalize E-mail Messages

Adding a salutation to your e-mail message makes it more personal. Naturally, whether you use a formal greeting (*Dear Professor Ingersol*) or a more casual one (*Hi Marty*) depends on your audience and your purpose. Your complimentary closing and signature

You can personalize your e-mail messages by adding a salutation, a complimentary closing, and perhaps even a signature file that includes a digital copy of your handwritten signature.

also personalize your e-mail message. In most cases, use simple closings, such as *Thanks* or *Regards,* rather than more traditional business closings such as *Sincerely yours.* However, you may want to use a more formal closing for international e-mail.

For your signature, you can simply type your name on a separate line. Or you may want to use a *signature file,* a short identifier that can include your name, company, postal address, fax number, other e-mail addresses, and so on. You can also use a digital copy of your handwritten signature, which is becoming acceptable as legal proof in business transactions, especially when accompanied by the date stamp that is automatically inserted by your e-mail program.

Observe Basic E-mail Etiquette

The best business communicators know how to communicate quickly and courteously. They know how to refrain from putting into writing anything that could come back to haunt them. And they know how important it is to proofread e-mail messages before sending them. Following basic e-mail etiquette means being courteous, brief, and careful.

Be Courteous

Being courteous pertains to more than just what you write; it also pertains to how you go about writing.

Common courtesy is an important consideration when sending any communication. Since e-mail creates a false sense of intimacy, it is tempting to write less carefully than you would when composing a memo or letter. However, you should always think about how your messages affect your various audiences; that includes thinking about more than just message content.

- **Compose your message offline.** Consider drafting your message in a word processor and then cutting and pasting it into your e-mail. This way, you'll conserve network resources and save significant Internet connect charges.
- **Send only necessary messages.** Do your best not to add to your audience's information overload.
- **Know who your audience is.** Before clicking on the Send button, double-check your addressees to make sure you've included everyone necessary and no one else.
- **Know your audience's culture.** Don't assume that your audience reads and understands your language. Make sure you know the culture and language of your readers before you begin to write.
- **Be clear about time.** In international e-mail, be sure to use a 24-hour military time format (say 18:00 instead of 6:00 P.M.). Also, indicate the appropriate time zone—Eastern Standard Time (EST), Pacific Daylight Time (PDT), and so on.
- **Respect your audience's schedule.** Identify messages that require no response by including words such as "for your information only" in your subject line or opening comments. And don't waste time sending jokes or chain letters.
- **Don't flame.** A negative e-mail message containing insensitive, insulting, or critical comments is called a *flame.* If you're upset about something or angry with someone, compose yourself before composing your e-mail.
- **Use the priority feature with care.** Many e-mail programs allow you to assign a priority to your message, such as *high, normal,* or *low.* Make sure the priority assigned to your message matches its urgency. Do not overuse "urgent."

Be Brief

Avoid wasting readers' time.

Make sure that you craft tight, meaningful messages. Cover only what is necessary. Identify the issue, add the relevant facts, suggest a resolution, offer possible obstacles, present a timetable for response, and ask for agreement.

- **Narrow your scope.** Stick to one purpose. If you find yourself with two or three purposes, write separate e-mails. This narrow scope not only helps your readers focus on your message but also facilitates filing and forwarding.

- **Write short messages.** Short, direct messages have a much better chance of being understood and acted on than long, roundabout ones. However, don't edit your e-mail messages so much that your readers cannot understand them.
- **Rely on short sentences.** Long sentences are particularly hard to read on screen. Whenever possible, break up long sentences into short, concise ones. If you need to write longer sentences now and then, make sure they are logically and clearly written.

Be Careful

E-mail's speed is its greatest benefit and can also be its greatest drawback. When we sit down at the keyboard, our mindset is typically to empty our e-mail box and move on to other business. E-mail prompts such quick responses that we forget to organize our thoughts. Successful e-mail is written carefully.

Write your e-mail carefully, but also be careful about addressing and replying to e-mail messages.

- **Be sure you hit the right reply button.** When you receive an e-mail message, it may be addressed to you alone or to dozens of others. It may be "copied" to others or "blind copied" to recipients you don't know about. Make sure you hit the correct reply button so that only intended recipients receive your message.
- **When you choose to "reply to all," do so wisely.** Even though the original e-mail sender may think it's a good idea to update everyone on the team, not all team members may need to see every recipient's reply.
- **Understand the use of the cc and bcc fields.** When you add addresses to the cc (courtesy copy) field, make sure that you want all recipients to see who is receiving a copy of your message. Otherwise, use the bcc (blind courtesy copy) field.
- **Slow down.** Every word matters. Even though the fast pace of technology encourages us to respond to others instantaneously, take your time and proceed at your own comfortable pace. The other party will wait.
- **Reread your message.** Avoid sending important e-mail messages immediately after you write them. Ideally, reread them the next morning and make changes.
- **Edit e-mail carefully.** Double-check your e-mail message before sending it. Proofread every e-mail message for completeness, content, fluency, punctuation, and grammar. Finally, make sure that promised documents are indeed attached.

Reviewing Key Points

This chapter introduces the forms and uses of memos, e-mails, and letters. The chapter explains how to choose to format, based on whether the message is intended for internal or external communication and whether the message form suits the formality of the situation.

Memos are used inside companies, while letters are used for more formal external communication. E-mails are used in both internal and informal external communication.

You learned how to improve overall readability in short business messages by

- Using short paragraphs of no more than seven lines
- Varying sentence patterns and length but limiting sentence length to no more than 16–20 words
- Using lists and bullets to highlight key information and items in a sequence or process
- Making list items parallel and giving them an introductory or lead-in sentence
- Giving every message a short, specific, informative, and action-oriented subject line
- Using informative headings and subheadings phrased in parallel construction to highlight sections of your documents to allow readers to find information quickly or to speed-read the material
- Following proper protocols for the professional appearance of memos, e-mails, and letters.

You also learned basic e-mail etiquette such as

- Changing the subject line of reply e-mails
- Being brief, courteous, and mindful of the recipient's time
- Keeping messages short and easy to follow
- Avoiding overfamiliarity, chain e-mails, and humour

Test Your Knowledge

1. Which message forms are used for internal communication? Why?

2. Which message forms are used for external communication? Why?

3. What format elements make letters more formal than memos and e-mail?

4. How can you increase the readability of your short business messages?

5. What functions do headings serve?

6. How can you increase the readability of your e-mail messages?

7. What are the characteristics of an effective subject line for a memo, an e-mail, or a letter?

8. In what ways can you be courteous when preparing your e-mail messages?

9. Besides wording the content of your e-mail message, what other steps should you take before sending the message?

10. What are the characteristics of a well-written heading?

Apply Your Knowledge

1. Why do you think good internal communication improves employee attitudes and performance? Explain briefly.

2. What do you think is important about matching the formality of your message to the formality of the situation and audience expectations?

3. Does it matter whether you personalize your e-mail messages? Please explain.

4. Is it ever okay to use an indirect approach when writing e-mail? How can you put off the bad news when you have to state your purpose in the subject line? Explain.

5. **Ethical Choices** Your boss wants you to send a message to the production staff, thanking all six members for their hard work and overtime to get the new manufacturing line set up and running on schedule. Your boss has been working a lot of overtime herself; she's been under a lot of pressure, and it's beginning to show. She wants to send the thank-you message by e-mail and asks you to work on the wording. You think each member of the production staff should receive a formal letter to keep for future promotions or other jobs. You know your boss won't like being interrupted about an issue that she thinks is off her desk, and you know how valuable her time is.

a. Should you draft the letter and produce six copies so that you don't have to bother your boss?
b. Should you simply draft the e-mail message as requested to save everyone time?
c. Should you discuss the issue with your boss, regardless of taking her away from the tasks she so desperately needs to get done?

Practise Your Knowledge

Exercises for Perfecting Your Writing

Form and Audience Barbara Marquardt is in charge of public relations for a cruise line that operates out of Vancouver, B.C. She is shocked to read a letter in a local newspaper from a disgruntled passenger, complaining about the service and entertainment on a recent cruise. Marquardt will have to respond to these publicized criticisms in some way.

1. What audiences will she need to consider in her response?
2. For each of these audiences, should Marquardt send her message via letter, memo, or e-mail?

Teamwork Your team has been studying a new method for testing the durability of your company's electric hand tools. Now your team needs to summarize the findings in three separate reports: (a) one for company administrators who will decide whether to purchase the new testing equipment needed for this new method, (b) one for company engineers who design and develop the hand tools, and (c) one for the trainers from the test equipment company, who will be showing your workers how to use the new testing equipment. Your team leader emphasizes that all three reports need to reach receivers so that your team can receive responses in less than a month. Working with at least two other students, answer the following questions for each of the three reports:

3. Should your team send the report by letter, memo, or e-mail?
   a. Administrators
   b. Engineers
   c. Trainers
4. Should the language be formal or conversational?
   a. Administrators
   b. Engineers
   c. Trainers

Using Bullets Rewrite the following paragraph using a bulleted list:

5. With our alarm system, you'll have a 24-hour security guard who signals the police when there is any indication of an intruder. You'll also appreciate the computerized scanning device that determines exactly where and when the intrusion occurred. No need to worry about electrical failure, either, thanks to our backup response unit.[8]

Keeping Paragraphs Short Using proofreading marks, indicate where to break the following paragraph into shorter paragraphs:

6. Donner Corporation faced a major transformation, growing from a small, single-product company to a large, broadly based corporation in just three years. This changeover involved much more than simply adding on to the plant and hiring more people, because the quality of the existing staff and products was not good enough for a first-rate operation. The task therefore required both physical expansion and quality improvement. The physical expansion alone represented a major undertaking. The investment in facilities required $18 million. Over a three-year period, the organization spent more on the new plant and equipment than it had spent in the past 17 years of its operation. To raise its competitive capability, the company had to develop new programs and organizational units and, at the same time, expand and upgrade its existing operations. It also needed to double the size of its staff by recruiting high-calibre people from many fields. This staffing had to be accomplished in an increasingly competitive labour market and without benefit of an experienced human resources department.

Varying Sentence Length Using proofreading marks, revise the following paragraph to vary the length of the sentences and to shorten the paragraph so that readers find it more readable:

7. Although major league hockey remains popular, more people are attending minor league hockey games because they can spend less on admission, snacks, and parking and still enjoy the excitement of Canada's favourite game. For example, in the 2001–02 season more than seven million fans attended regular games and one million attended the playoffs. Saskatchewan has three teams—the Moose Jaw Warriors, Saskatoon Blades, and the Regina Pats—and Manitoba has the Brandon Wheat Kings. These teams play in relatively small rinks, so fans are close enough to see and hear everything, including the sounds of the players hitting the boards or the goalie catching the puck. Best of all, the cost of a family outing to see rising stars play in a local minor league game is just a fraction of what the family would spend to attend a major league game in a much larger, more crowded arena.

Making Subject Lines Informative Use your imagination to make the following subject lines more informative:

8. New budget figures

9. Your opinion on our current marketing brochure

10. Production schedule

Activities

For live links to all Web sites discussed in this chapter, visit this text's Web site at www.pearsoned.ca/bovee. Just log on and select Chapter 6, and click on "Student Resources." Locate the page or the URL related to the material in the text. For "Exploring the Best of the Web" exercises, you'll also find navigational directions. Click on the live link to the site.

1. **Analyze This Document** Read the following document; then (1) analyze the strengths and weaknesses of each sentence and (2) revise the document so that it follows the guidelines in Chapters 3 through 6.

   Dear Ms. Giraud:

   Enclosed herewith please find the manuscript for your book, *Careers in Woolgathering.* After perusing the first two chapters of your 1500-page manuscript, I was forced to conclude that the subject matter, handicrafts and artwork using wool fibres, is not coincident with the publishing program of Framingham Press, which to this date has issued only works on business endeavours, avoiding all other topics completely.

   Although our firm is unable to consider your impressive work at the present time, I have taken the liberty of recording some comments on some of the pages. I am of the opinion that any feedback that a writer can obtain from those well versed in the publishing realm can only serve to improve the writer's authorial skills.

   In view of the fact that your residence is in the Toronto area, might I suggest that you secure an appointment with someone of high editorial stature at Pearson Press, which I believe might have something of an interest in works of the nature you have produced.

   Wishing you the best of luck in your literary endeavours, I remain

   Arthur J. Cogswell

   Editor

2. **Analyze This Document** Read the following document; then (1) analyze the strengths and weaknesses of each sentence and (2) revise the document so that it follows the guidelines in Chapters 3 through 6.

   For delicious, air-popped popcorn, please read the following instructions: The popper is designed to pop 1/2 cup of popcorn kernels at one time. Never add more than 1/2 cup. A half cup of corn will produce three to four quarts of popcorn. More batches may be made separately after completion of the first batch. Popcorn is popped by hot air. Oil or shortening is not needed for popping corn. Add only popcorn kernels to the popping chamber. Standard grades of popcorn are recommended for use. Premium or gourmet-type popping corns may be used. Ingredients such as oil, shortening, butter, margarine, or salt should never be added to the popping chamber. The popper, with popping chute in position, may be preheated for two minutes before adding the corn. Turn the popper off before adding the corn. Use electricity safely and wisely. Observe safety precautions when using the popper. Do not touch the popper when it is hot. The popper should not be left unattended when it is plugged into an outlet. Do not use the popper if it or its cord has been damaged. Do not use the popper if it is not working properly. Before using the first time, wash the chute and butter/measuring cup in hot soapy water. Use a dishcloth or sponge. Wipe the outside of the popper base. Use a damp cloth. Dry the base. Do not immerse the popper base in water or other liquid. Replace the chute and butter/measuring cup. The popper is ready to use.

3. **Planning a Memo: Learn While You Earn—Memo Announcing Burger King's Educational Benefits**

Herb Lipsey, owner of the Burger King store in Moncton, is worried about employee turnover. He needs to keep 50 people on the payroll to operate the outlet, but recruiting and retaining those people is tough. The average employee leaves after about seven months, so Lipsey has to hire and train 90 people a year just to maintain a 50-person crew. At a cost of $1500 per hire, the price tag for all that turnover is approximately $60 000 a year.

Lipsey knows that a lot of his best employees quit because they think that flipping burgers is a dead-end job. But what if it weren't a dead-end job? What if a person could really get some place flipping burgers? What if Lipsey offered to pay his employees' way through college if they remained with the store? Would that keep them behind the counter?

He's decided to give educational incentives a try. Employees who choose to participate will continue to earn their usual salary, but they will also get free books and college tuition, keyed to the number of hours they work each week. Those who work from 10 to 15 hours a week can take one free course at nearby New Brunswick Community College; those who work 16 to 25 hours can take two courses; and those who work 26 to 40 hours can take three courses. The program is open to all employees, regardless of how long they have worked for Burger King, but no one is obligated to participate.

Your task If you were Herb Lipsey, or if you worked for him, how would you plan and write a memo announcing the new educational incentives? The purpose is clear (to inform employees about the new offer), the audience has already been defined (all Moncton Burger King employees), and the medium has been chosen (a written memo). Now use the following questions to continue your planning, choosing the best answer for each one. Then, creating sentences of your own, draft the memo based on what you've learned from this planning exercise.

1. Which sentence best expresses the memo's main idea?
   - **a.** Turnover at the Moncton Burger King costs approximately $60 000 a year.
   - **b.** Flipping burgers doesn't have to be a dead-end job.
   - **c.** The Moncton Burger King is offering its employees an exciting new educational program.
   - **d.** The new educational incentive program is open to all employees, no matter how long they've worked for Burger King.
2. Which of these sentences will help you establish a good relationship with your audience?
   - **a.** We are hoping that many of you will take advantage of the new program because it will reduce our turnover.
   - **b.** Employees need not attend college to continue working for us.
   - **c.** We hope that you will find the program useful.
   - **d.** Now you can earn free college tuition while you work at Burger King.
3. What must the body of your message accomplish? (Choose all that apply.)
   - **a.** Tell employees how to take advantage of the educational offer.
   - **b.** Explain how working hours relate to tuition payments.
   - **c.** Describe how Mr. Lipsey came up with his idea.
   - **d.** Influence employees to attend college.

4. Which of the following methods will be best for conveying the relationship between hours worked and tuition paid?
   a. A two-column table with the headings: "Those Who Work" (listing hours per week) and "May Take" (listing number of courses paid for).
   b. A paragraph explaining the connection between hours worked and courses paid for.
   c. A bulleted list with parallel entries such as, "If you work 10 to 15 hours, you'll get one free course; If you work 16 to 25 hours, you'll get two free courses;" etc.
   d. A paragraph suggesting that details can be obtained from Mr. Lipsey's office for those interested in taking advantage of the program.

5. To close the memo, which of the following sentences is the best choice?
   a. We hope you'll take advantage of this offer, since doing so will help us reduce our turnover problem.
   b. You don't have to take college courses to continue working for us.
   c. I'll be happy to answer any questions you might have about how working for Burger King can help you earn free college tuition; just ask me.
   d. If you're thinking of quitting, this may give you second thoughts.

Now imagine that you are Herb Lipsey and draft your own memo in your own words.

4. **Revising a Memo: Break-Time Blues—Memo Requesting a New Employee Procedure** The following memo contains numerous errors related to what you've learned about planning and writing business messages. First, list the flaws you find in this version. Then follow the steps below to plan and write a better memo:

Memo

To: Billing Department

From: Felicia August, Sr. Supervisor

Date: December 28, 2004

Subject: Compliance with new break procedure

Some of you may not like the rules about break times; however, we determined that keeping track of employees while they took breaks at times they determined rather than regular breaks at prescribed times was not working as well as we would have liked it to work. The new rules are not going to be an option. If you do not follow the new rules, you could be docked from your pay for hours when you turned up missing, since your direct supervisor will not be able to tell whether you were on a "break" or not and will assume that you have walked away from your job. We cannot be responsible for any errors that result from your inattentiveness to the new rules. I have already heard complaints from some of you and I hope this memo will end this issue once and for all. The decision has already been made.

Starting Monday, January 1, you will all be required to take a regular 15-minute break in the morning and again in the afternoon, and a regular thirty-minute lunch at the times specified by your supervisor, NOT when you think you need a break or when you "get around to it."

There will be no exceptions to this new rule!

---

1. Describe the flaws you discovered in this memorandum:
2. Develop a plan for rewriting the memo. Use the following steps to organize your efforts before you begin writing:
   a. Determine the purpose
   b. Identify and analyze your audience
   c. Define the main idea
   d. Outline the major supporting points
   e. Choose between a direct and an indirect approach
3. Now rewrite the memo. Don't forget to leave ample time for revision of your own work before you turn it in.

5. **Revising a Memo: Moving Day—Memo Informing Employees About an Office Relocation** From what you've learned about planning and writing business messages, you should be able to identify numerous errors made by the writer of the following memo. List them below, then plan and write a better memo, following the guidelines given.

Memorandum

To: All Office Personnel

From: David Burke, Manager

Date: September 27, 2004

Subject: Get Ready

We are hoping to be back at work soon, with everything running smoothly, same production schedule and no late projects or missed deadlines. So you need to clean out your desk, put your stuff in boxes, and clean off the walls. You can put the items you had up on your walls in boxes, also.

We have provided boxes. The move will happen this weekend. We'll be in our new offices when you arrive on Monday.

We will not be responsible for personal belongings during the move.

nd

---

1. Describe the flaws you discovered in this memorandum.
2. Develop a plan for rewriting the memo. Use the following steps to organize your efforts before you begin writing:
   a. Determine the purpose
   b. Analyze and identify your audience
   c. Define the main idea
   d. Outline the major supporting points
   e. Choose between direct and indirect approaches

3. Now rewrite the memo. Don't forget to leave ample time for revision of your own work before you turn it in.

Expand Your Knowledge

Best of the Web

Improve Your Use of E-mail You've probably used e-mail for personal communication, but writing business e-mail can be both risky and daunting. Before you begin, brush up your skills with Mary Houten-Kemp's Everything E-Mail Web site. You'll learn "netiquette" (network etiquette) standards for some of the more advanced applications of e-mail. You'll also find simple technical advice on how to make your messages readable in all types of e-mail programs, how to attach documents, and how to include URLs (Web site addresses) as links that your readers can follow. Also, tips on style and usage help you convey a professional image, free of blunders that might offend business e-mail veterans.

everythingemail.net/email_help_tips.html

Exercises

1. When is it okay to promote your business in an e-mail discussion group? If you break this rule, what do you think might happen?
2. What's wrong with using common e-mail jargon and abbreviations in business e-mail, such as BTW (by the way) or IMHO (in my humble opinion)?
3. What is an *autoresponder?* If you're operating a Web site, how might it improve the effectiveness of your e-mail communication? Can you think of situations in which it might work against your business interests?

Exploring the Web on Your Own

Review these chapter-related Web sites on your own to learn more about writing business messages.

1. Become fluent in your e-mail usage, from basic set-up to advanced techniques, by taking the tutorial at www.webteacher.org/home-windows/index.html. On the home page, click "Communicating," then select "E-mail."
2. Master e-mail's unique challenges by studying suggestions for developing clear content, using special cues, and creating context at A Beginner's Guide to Effective E-Mail, www.webfoot.com/advice/email.top.html.
3. Gain more insight into the parts of a memo and their effective use by reading the handbook notes at www.ecf.toronto.edu/~writing/handbook-memo.html.

Learn Interactively

Interactive Study Guide

Visit the Companion Website at www.pearsoned.ca/bovee. For Chapter 6, take advantage of the interactive "Study Guide" to test your chapter knowledge. Get instant feedback on whether you need additional studying.

This site offers a variety of additional resources: The "Research Area" helps you locate a wealth of information to use in course assignments. You can even send a message to online research experts, who will help you find exactly the information you need. The "Study Hall" helps you succeed in this course by offering support with writing and study skills, time management, and career skills, as well as numerous other resources.

Peak Performance Grammar and Mechanics

PEAK Use the Peak Performance Grammar and Mechanics CD to test your skill with prepositions and conjunctions. In the "Prepositions, Conjunctions, and Articles" section, take the Pretest to determine whether you have any weak areas. Then review those areas in the Refresher Course. Take the Follow-Up Test to check your grasp of preposition and conjunction usage. For an extra challenge or advanced practice, take the Advanced Test.

Cases

Apply each step in Figure 3.1 on page 44 to the following cases, as assigned by your instructor.

E-MAIL SKILLS 1. No exaggeration: Short e-mail describing internship duties

You've been labouring all summer at an internship, learning how business is conducted. You've done work nobody else wanted to do, but that's okay. Even the smallest tasks can make a good impression on your future resumé.

This morning, your supervisor asks you to write a description of the job you've been doing. "Include everything, even the filing," she suggests, "and address it to me in an e-mail message."

She says a future boss might assign such a task prior to a performance review. "You can practise describing your work without exaggeration—or too much modesty," she says, smiling.

Your Task Using good techniques for short messages and relying on your real-life work experience, write an e-mail that will impress your supervisor.

WEB SKILLS 2. Satisfaction guaranteed: Letter from Tilley Endurables granting a claim

One of the nicest things about working in customer service for sporting goods and clothing retailer Tilley Endurables is that company policy guarantees satisfaction, "no questions asked." This means you always get to say yes to angry customers who want a refund.

In your hand is a package from Arvin Bummel (212 Borealis Drive, Iqaluit, Nunavut X0A 0H0). You open it to find (a) one pair of wool covert twill trousers, stiff and shrunken, (b) an outfitter's guide shirt (regular), also two sizes smaller than it should be, and (c) an angry letter from Mr. Bummel saying the clothes were ruined the first time he washed them.

You're not surprised, since they all clearly say, "Dry Clean Only."

Your Task Write a letter to Mr. Bummel granting him a refund, to be credited to his MasterCard. Visit the Tilley Endurables Web site, www.tilley.com, to verify current prices and to find suggestions for washable clothing he might want to try. But remember not to blame him in your letter; a Tilley customer is always right.

TEAM SKILLS 3. Measuring suppliers: Memo requesting reviews at Microsoft

Microsoft evaluates employees regularly to determine their performance—so why not do the same with the independent contractors the company hires to perform key functions? Nearly every department uses outside providers these days—a practice called *outsourcing*. So if there's a gap between what Microsoft expects from contractors and what the contractors actually deliver, shouldn't Microsoft tell them how they can improve their performance?

You've been discussing these questions all morning in a meeting with other members of the Employee Services Group. Your boss is convinced that regular reviews of independent contractors are essential.

"It's all about improving clarity in terms of goals and expectations," he says, adding that if contractors receive constructive feedback, Microsoft can develop good relationships with them instead of having to look for new service suppliers all the time.

Your boss assigns your team the task of informing all Microsoft departments that they'll be required to evaluate subcontractors every six months, beginning immediately. The goal of the review is to determine the performance of independent contractors so that Microsoft can (1) give them constructive feedback and continue a strong relationship or (2) end the relationship if service is substandard. Departments will need to rate each contractor on a scale of 1 (poor) to 5 (excellent) for each of several factors that your group is going to determine. Departments will be sending their reports to Roxanna Frost, group program manager for Microsoft's Executive Management and Development Group.

Your Task Working as a team with your classmates, develop a list of factors that will help you rate the overall service of independent contractors. You'll need to consider "cost," "quality of work," "innovation," "delivery," and other factors similar to those you'd encounter in a job performance review. Then compose a memo to all Microsoft department managers: Explain the new review requirements and include your list of factors to be rated on the 1-to-5 scale.[9]

E-MAIL SKILLS 4. Pizza promises: Message from an unknown parent, VF Corporation

The human relations director at VF Corporation is grinning at you. "We can't let them go on in ignorance, and I know just what will get their attention."

As his assistant, you're listening to your boss defeat a problem. A spot survey taken yesterday showed that none of the 40 000 line workers at VF's subsidiaries recognized the corporate parent's name. They didn't even know they had a parent company. They're working in factories that make Lee, Wrangler, and other clothing brands, and those are the only names they know.

Your Task You're to write an e-mail message to be sent to all 40 000 employees, explaining that tomorrow 15 000 pizzas will be delivered to their factories at lunchtime, compliments of their corporate parent, VF Corporation.[10]

5. Wakeboard mania: Letter from Performance Ski & Surf inquiring about availability

Your boss, Bill Porter, owner of Performance Ski & Surf in Peterborough, Ontario, hasn't seen a sport this popular since in-line skating took off.

"I hope these kids don't get hurt trying to imitate the pros," Porter says. You're both admiring a picture of a professional wakeboarder catching air as he trails behind a boat on nearby Rice Lake. He's five metres in the air, with the short, stubby fibreglass board strapped to his feet—only he's upside down. His grimace shows the flip isn't as easy as it looks.

"Don't worry," you say. "Extreme sports are hot. Think of snowboarding. I guarantee, you'll see wakeboarding at the Olympics soon."

"Well, meanwhile, we've got to get these Wake Techs, Neptunes, and Full Tilts in stock," Porter replies. "They're outselling traditional water skis 20 to 1."

Your Task Draft a letter Porter can send to manufacturers to inquire about availability throughout Ontario's busy summer season. It's winter now and you're well stocked, but when summer returns, your sales will rocket.

6. Nap time: Memo announcing new sleeping room at Phidias & Associates

"We're going to do what?" you ask in astonishment. But your boss is standing over your desk and he isn't smiling. Jonas T. Phidias is senior partner of Phidias & Associates, a Vancouver architectural firm, and he's completely serious.

"A nap room," he says somewhat impatiently. "We've hired a subcontractor to convert those two back offices that we haven't been using. You know what pressures our people are under to handle the stress of long hours and still be creative. Well, we'll soon be offering them the opportunity to rejuvenate with a quick, creative nap."

From his snappish tone, you realize that your response wasn't what he had expected. Quickly you compose yourself. As you think about it, his idea makes a lot of sense. You've felt the need yourself—after working late on a rush job, you've wondered how you're supposed to be creatively inspired when you can barely get your eyes to focus. "Why, naps could be great!" you finally manage.

"Yes," he interrupts before you can go on. "Thomas Edison knew the creative value of a quick nap. I've just read *The Art of Napping* by William A. Anthony, and the benefits of a nap room are too great to ignore.

"Other companies are proving that naps can improve employees' mental function sufficiently to affect the bottom line. I've decided that no matter what they think of it, Phidias & Associates employees are going to take naps during working hours. Draft a memo to tell them of my decision, and I want no arguments from them!" he instructs as he strides away.

Your Task As Phidias's assistant, write a straightforward memo informing employees that the new "nap room" will be ready for their convenience in approximately three weeks, and that they will be expected to make good use of it. Try to keep humour out of your memo, since it will be sent from Jonas T. Phidias.

E-MAIL SKILLS 7. Environmental planning: E-mail announcing a committee meeting

You've probably worked as a volunteer on a committee or with team members for class assignments. You know how hard it is to get a diverse group of individuals together for a productive meeting. Maybe you've tried different locations—one member's home, or a table at the library. This time you're going to suggest a local restaurant.

The committee you're leading is a volunteer group planning a trash-clearing project at an area park. Your meeting goal is to brainstorm ways to encourage public participation in this environmental event, to be held next Earth Day.

Your Task Develop a short e-mail message telling committee members about the meeting. Include time, date, duration, and location (choose a place you know). Mention the meeting goal to encourage attendance.

WEB SKILLS 8. Mercedes merchandise: Letter announcing exclusive online gift shop

Mercedes-Benz owners take their accessories seriously, which is why you get angry letters when they buy fake Mercedes merchandise produced by "sweatshop entrepreneurs," as your boss calls them. Too often, these unauthorized imitations fall apart, and it's Mercedes' high-class image that suffers.

That's why Mercedes started producing and promoting its own high-quality accessories, from T-shirts and toddler's jumpers to travel alarm clocks. First the company hired top-of-the-line manufacturers and designers to produce a glossy, full-colour catalogue of "Mercedes-Benz Personal and Automotive Accessories." Now the catalogue has moved online.

At www.mercedes-benz.ca, home page for Mercedes, shoppers can follow links to the online gift shop. But first they need to know it exists.

Your Task As assistant for Steve Beaty, vice-president of accessories marketing, you're to draft an informative letter to Mercedes owners telling them about the online gift shop. Visit the Web site to learn more about it, then write the letter using a style you think suits the car manufacturer's image.

E-MAIL SKILLS 9. Bolga boo-boo: E-mail to Getrade (Ghana) Ltd. from Pier 1 Imports

When you were hired as an assistant buyer for Pier 1 Imports, you thought it would be an exciting introduction to the import-export business—the job you've always dreamed about. What a romantic way to earn a living—travelling overseas, buying products, and then shipping them back to Canada for sale. But now you've learned some of the realities of the job, and your romantic ideas are fading.

For example, Pier 1 sent a buyer to Accra, Ghana, to find local handicrafts to satisfy your customers' unquenchable thirst for African art. So far the local entrepreneurs are having trouble meeting the demand from large-quantity buyers like Pier 1 (and your rival, Cost Plus). A good example of what's been going wrong is the shipment that just arrived from Getrade (Ghana) Ltd., one of your best Ghanaian suppliers. You sympathize with Ladi Nylander, chairman and managing director of Getrade, who is trying hard to adapt to the specific tastes of Canadian buyers. He's hiring local artisans to carve, shape, and weave all sorts of artifacts—often from designs provided by Pier 1.

Your Pier 1 customers love bowl-shaped Bolga baskets, traditionally woven by the Fra-fra people of northern Ghana. You can't keep the baskets in stock, so this was to be a huge shipment—3000 Bolga baskets. Your order requested 1000 green, 1000 yellow, and 1000 magenta baskets in the traditional shape.

However, when the order came in, you found 3000 mixed-colour, flat Bolga baskets. Your overseas buyer reported that the Body Shop had ordered baskets similar to yours but with mixed-colour patterns and a flatter shape. Pier 1 may have received the Body Shop's order by mistake.

Your Task As assistant buyer, you need to send an e-mail message to Nylander at Nylander@Getrade.co.za, informing him of the error in your order. You can mention that your order and the Body Shop's may have been mixed up, a mistake that should be relatively easy to fix.

Improve Your Grammar, Mechanics, and Usage

Level 1: Self-Assessment—Prepositions and Conjunctions

Review Sections 1.6.1 and 1.6.2 in the Handbook of Grammar, Mechanics, and Usage, and then look at the following items.

Rewrite items 1–5, deleting unnecessary words and prepositions, and adding required prepositions:

1. Where was your argument leading to?

2. I wish he would get off of the phone.

3. This is a project into which you can sink your teeth.

4. BMO Mercantile must become aware and sensitive to its customers' concerns.

5. We are responsible for aircraft safety in the air, the hangars, and the runways.

In items 6–10, write the correct preposition in the blank:

6. Dr. Namaguchi will be talking __________ the marketing class, but she has no time for questions.

7. Matters like this are decided after thorough discussion __________ all seven department managers.

8. We can't wait __________ their decision much longer.

9. Their computer is similar __________ ours.

10. This model is different __________ the one we ordered.

In items 11–15, rewrite the sentences in the space provided to make phrases parallel:

11. She is active in not only a civic group but also in an athletic organization.

12. That is either a mistake or was an intentional omission.

13. The question is whether to set up a booth at the convention or be hosting a hospitality suite.

14. We are doing better in both overall sales and in profits.

15. She had neither the preferred educational background, nor did she have suitable experience.

Level 2: Workplace Applications

The following items contain numerous errors in grammar, capitalization, punctuation, abbreviation, number style, word division, and vocabulary. Rewrite each sentence in the space provided, correcting all errors. Write *C* in the space after any sentence that is already correct.

1. Peabody Energys commitment to environmental excellence is driven by the companies' mission statement which states that when mining is complete, the company will leave the land in a condition equal or better than it was before mining.

2. In 1998, Interco opened a state of the art distribution center in St. Thomas, Ontario, just South of the company's London, Ontario, Headquarters.

3. Miss Tucci was responsible for developing Terraspring's business plan, establishing the brand, and for launching the company.

4. The principle goals of the new venture will be to offer tailored financial products and meeting the needs of the community.

5. Nestle Waters North America are the number one bottled water company in Canada and the US.

6. The reason egg prices dropped sharply is because of a Post Easter reduction in demand.

7. Joining bank officials during the announcement of the program were Canadian member of parliament Svend Robinson, Carlos Remirez, Mexican Ambassador to Canada, and "Don Francisco", the leading hispanic entertainment figure on the North American Continent.

8. The summer advertising campaign is the most unique in 7-Eleven's history.

9. Upon introducing it's new Quadruple Fudge flavor, consumers are expected to flock to Baskin-Robbins ice cream parlors.

10. The signing of a Trade Pact between the european union and Chile, is being delayed by european negotiators who insist the deal includes an agreement requiring Chile to stop using the names Cognac, Champagne, and Burgundy.

11. Canadian health advocate, Mrs. Sheila F. Anthony called on the dietary supplement industry to institute better self regulation, and called on the media to refuse ads containing claims that are obviously false.

12. Founded in 1971, GSD&M has grown to become a nationally-acclaimed advertising agency with more than 500 employees and having billings of over $1 billion dollars.

13. Although marketing may seem to be the easier place to cut costs during a downturn its actually the last place you should look to make strategic cuts.

14. After closing their plant in Kelowna, Western Star Truck will have less than 200 employees.

15. The purchasing needs of professional's differ from blue collar workers.

Level 3: Document Critique

The following document may contain errors in grammar, capitalization, punctuation, abbreviation, number style, vocabulary, and spelling. You will also find errors relating to topics in this chapter. For example, consider the format, organization, paragraph length, and subject line as you improve this memo. Correct all errors using standard proofreading marks (see Appendix C).

Memo

To: George Kimball

From: John Mason

Subject: My trip back East

May 31, 2004

Dear George:

I went back to Montreal for apresentation the 15th of this month and I found it very informative. The sponsor of my visat was Vern Grouper. Vern is the Manager of the data processing-operation at headquarters; that is, their centralized data procesing operation. They've got quite a bit of power out there. And they do encourage us to utilize their capibilities, there services, and experiences to whatever extent will be beneficial to us. However, you could say it would be my observation that although they have a tremendous amount of computing capability that capability is directed toward a business dimension very different than ours and unlike anything we have. However, their are certain services that might be performed in our behalf by headquarters. For example, we could utilize people such as Vern to come and address our data-processing advisory group since I am planning on convening that group on a monthly basis.

By the way, I need to talk to you about the data-processing advicory group when you get a chance. I have 1 or 2 thoughts about some new approaches we can take with it I'd like to run by you if you don't mind. Its not too complicated just some simple ideas.

Let me know what you think of this idea about Vern coming here. If you like it than I will go ahead and set things in motion with Vern.

Sincerely,

John Mason

Supervisor

Spin Cycle: Deciphering Corporate Doublespeak

If there's one product North American businesses can manufacture in large amounts, it's doublespeak. Doublespeak is language that only pretends to say something but that in reality hides, evades, or misleads. Like most products, doublespeak comes in many forms, from the popular buzzwords that everyone uses but no one really understands—such as *competitive dynamics* and *empowerment*—to words that try to hide meaning, such as *re-engineering, synergy,* and *restructuring.*

With doublespeak, bribes and kickbacks are called *rebates* or *fees for product testing,* used-car-parts dealers have become *auto dismantlers and recyclers,* and travel agents are called *vacation specialists, destination counsellors,* or *reservation specialists.* Plus, just about everyone's job title has the word *chief* in it: chief nuclear officer, chief learning officer, chief cultural officer, chief ethics officer, chief turnaround officer, and chief creative officer. After all the "operations improvement" that corporations have undergone, you have to wonder who all those "chiefs" are leading. Never before have so many led so few.

With doublespeak, banks don't have *bad loans* or *bad debts;* they have *nonperforming credits* that are *rolled over* or *rescheduled.* And corporations never lose money; they just experience *negative cash flow, deficit enhancement,* or *negative contributions to profits.*

Of course, no one gets fired these days. People high enough in the corporate pecking order *resign for personal reasons.* Those below the lofty heights of corporate power are *involuntarily terminated* as the result of *downsizing, workforce adjustments,* and *headcount reductions.* Some companies even *implement a skills mix adjustment* or *eliminate redundancies in the human resources area.* One automobile company (that closed an entire assembly plant and eliminated more than 8000 jobs) called the action *a volume-related production schedule adjustment.*

But don't worry, if you're *dehired, deselected, surplused,* or *uninstalled,* corporations will offer you a *career change opportunity* or *vocational relocation.* In fact, hardly anyone is laid off these days. "We don't characterize it as a layoff," said one corporate doublespeaker (sometimes called a spin doctor). "We're managing our staff resources. Sometimes you manage them up, and sometimes you manage them down."

The goal of good writing is to communicate, not to confuse; to be understood, not to hide behind words. Look at this confusing excerpt from an investment document:

> The applicability of the general information and administrative procedures set forth below accordingly will vary depending on the investor and the record-keeping system established for a shareholder's investment in the Fund. Participants in RRSPs and other plans should first consult with the appropriate persons at their employer or refer to the plan materials before following any of the procedures below.

As discussed in Chapter 4, *plain English* is a way of writing and arranging technical materials so that your audience can understand your meaning. Restating our excerpt in plain English reveals one simple thought: "If you are investing through a large retirement plan or other special program, follow the instructions in your program material."

Some companies are concerned that writing documents in plain English will increase their liability, but many companies are finding just the opposite. "In many ways," notes one Bell Atlantic employee, "we reduced our liability because we have created a document that is much clearer and less ambiguous." Similarly, when Citibank introduced promissory notes written in plain English, the number of collection lawsuits fell dramatically. The clearer writing simply made it easier for borrowers to understand their obligations.

Some lawyers may purposely choose obscure language to control vital information, to take advantage of those who don't know what they're signing, or profit from people who hire them to interpret the difficult language. But many legal professionals strongly endorse the plain-English movement. The plain-English movement has generated great momentum; perhaps confusing language will become obsolete.

Applications for Success

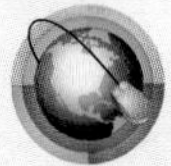

For more on the subject of doublespeak, read the article "Life Under the Chief Doublespeak Officer" at www.dt.org/html/Doublespeak.html. Answer the following questions:

1. What do you think? Isn't corporate doublespeak just another way to emphasize the positive in business situations? Or is it unethical to use business buzzwords and corporate doublespeak to ease negative impressions? Explain your position in a one-page memo or an e-mail message to your instructor.
2. If it's unethical to use doublespeak, would you classify it as an ethical dilemma or an ethical lapse? Explain your position in a one-page memo or e-mail message to your instructor.
3. Do the people in your field appear to value the jargon and buzzwords of their industry? If you use plain English, do you risk your reputation as a professional in your field? Please explain in a one-page memo or e-mail message to your instructor.
4. The president of one company just learned that some of his employees have been playing a popular game called "buzzword bingo," in which participants ridicule doublespeak by tracking the jargon their bosses use during staff meetings on bingo-like cards. Some managers are complaining that it's getting out of control. In fact, as one meeting dragged on, employees tried to steer the conversation to use all the buzzwords on their cards. What can managers do to avoid these silly games?
5. Visit one of the following buzzword bingo Web sites and print out a card or two:

   www.executivespeak.com/buzzword_bingo.html
   isd.usc.edu/~karl/Bingo
   www.esc3.net/wm/bbbingo

Read the current business section of your favourite newspaper. How many buzzwords did you find?

Unit 3

BRIEF BUSINESS CORRESPONDENCE

7

Writing Routine, Good-News, and Goodwill Messages

From the Real World

"When we write at work, it is often about action—asking people for action that needs to happen, telling about things that have happened. When we ask for action, most people appreciate it when you tell them directly what you want, how it affects them, and why it is important to do it. At the same time we are making these requests, we also have to build or maintain a positive relationship with the reader. A positive impression will help you get the action you want."

–Fred G. Withers
Managing Partner
Ernst & Young
Vancouver

After studying this chapter, you will be able to

1 Apply the three-step writing process to routine positive messages
2 Illustrate the strategy for writing routine requests
3 Discuss the differences among three types of routine requests
4 Illustrate the strategy for writing routine replies and positive messages
5 Explain the main differences among messages granting a claim when the company, the customer, or a third party is at fault
6 Clarify the importance of goodwill messages, and describe how to make them effective

Ernst & Young is one of the world's largest providers of professional services, with offices in 670 locations in 140 countries. Ernst & Young Canada operates in 14 Canadian cities, offering accounting, business, and financial consulting services to a variety of industries. The company also has a strong sense of corporate responsibility and has a reputation of creating goodwill through actively supporting the arts. As a managing partner, Fred Withers communicates widely with professional staff and clients. "Some people think that accountants only work with numbers," says Withers, "but the key is being able to explain them to people in a clear, professional manner." Whether requesting information from clients, or responding to routine inquires, Withers believes concise, accurate, open communication can create a positive impression for the business.[1]

Using the Three-Step Writing Process for Routine Messages

Even for routine situations, you need to plan, write, and complete your messages.

Like Fred Withers, you'll probably compose a lot of routine, good-news, and goodwill messages: orders, company policies, claims, credit, information about employees, products, operations, and so on. To produce the best messages possible, apply the three-step writing process (see Figure 7.1 on page 150):

- **Step 1: Planning routine messages.** For routine messages, you may need only a few moments to analyze your purpose and audience, investigate audience needs, and adapt your message to your readers.
- **Step 2: Writing routine messages.** Organizing and composing routine messages can be direct and quick; however, be sure to verify the customs of your intercultural audiences before deciding to use the direct approach.

- **Step 3: Completing routine messages.** No matter how short or straightforward your message, make it professional by allowing plenty of time to revise, produce, and proofread it.

Making Routine Requests

Whenever you ask for something—information, action, products, adjustments, references—you are making a request. A request is routine if it's part of the normal course of business and you anticipate that your audience will want to comply. Don't make unnecessary requests. If you can find information yourself, don't risk your credibility and burden others by asking them to find it for you.

Strategy for Routine Requests

Use the direct approach. Open with your main idea (a clear statement of your request). In the body give details and justify your request. Then close by requesting specific action and concluding cordially.

Organize your routine messages according to the direct approach.

Begin with the Request

To begin, ask yourself what you want readers to **do** or to understand as a result of reading your message. Place your request first; however, be careful not to be abrupt or tactless. Follow these guidelines:

Keep your direct approach from being harsh or discourteous.

- **Pay attention to tone.** Even though you expect a favourable response, instead of demanding action ("Send me your catalogue no. 33A"), soften your request with words such as *please.*
- **Assume your audience will comply.** Assume that once the reason is clearly understood, your audience will comply with your request. An impatient demand is unnecessary.
- **Avoid beginning with personal introductions.** Don't start with, "I am the senior corporate writer at UnumProvident, and I'm looking for information on . . . " Such a beginning buries the main idea so that the actual request may be lost.
- **Punctuate questions and polite requests differently.** A polite request in question form requires no question mark ("Would you please help us determine whether Kate Kingsley is a suitable applicant for this position"). A direct question does require a question mark ("Did Kate Kingsley demonstrate an ability to work smoothly with clients?").
- **Be specific.** State precisely what you want. For example, if you request the latest census figures from a government agency, be sure to say whether you want a page or two of summary figures or a detailed report running several thousand pages.

Explain and Justify Your Request

Use the body of your message to explain your request. Try to make the explanation grow smoothly and logically from your opening remarks. When you request information, tell readers why you need the information and explain how they might benefit from granting the request.

You can use the body of your routine request to list a series of questions. You might ask about the technical specifications, exact dimensions, and precise use of a complex piece of machinery. When listing a series of questions, just keep a few basics in mind:

Numbered lists help readers sort through multiple related items or multiple requests.

- **Ask the most important questions first.** Number your questions, and list them logically in descending order of importance. If cost is your main concern, begin by asking, "What does the C-704 cost?" Then you can ask related but more specific questions, perhaps about the availability of a product ("How many C-704s do you usually have in stock?") or its warranty ("What warranty do you provide with the C-704?").

FIGURE 7.1 **Applying the Three-Step Writing Process to Routine Messages**

Planning	Writing	Completing
Analyze the Situation • Make your purpose specific. • Know whether readers will react positively. • Learn more about them if necessary. **Investigate the Topic** • Find out what readers need to know. • Have all the relevant information. • Gather more information if needed. **Adapt to the Audience** • Verify the effectiveness of the written channel. • If written, choose the best medium. • Use the "you" attitude. • Keep your language positive and polite.	**Organize the Message** • Define the main idea before beginning. • Group relevant points logically. • Adopt the direct approach. ∘ Open by clearly stating the main idea. ∘ Put all necessary details in the body. ∘ Close cordially. **Compose the Message** • Adapt the style and tone. • Use a conversational tone. • Use plain English.	**Revise the Message** • Evaluate the overall effect of the message. • Be sure you've said what you want to. • Put content in the order you want. • Make the message easy to read, concise, and clear. **Produce the Message** • Design the document to suit your readers. • Use effective design elements. • Use appropriate delivery methods. **Proofread the Message** • Check for typos. • Check for spelling and mechanical errors. • Look for alignment problems. • Make sure print quality is acceptable.
1	2	3

- **Ask only relevant questions.** Don't waste your reader's time; ask only those questions central to your request. If your questions need simple yes-or-no answers, provide boxes to check; otherwise, use open-ended questions to elicit the information you want: Ask "How fast can you ship the unit?" or "When will you ship the unit?" rather than "Can you ship the unit?"
- **Deal with only one topic per question.** Break down multiple requests. If you have an unusual or complex request, list the request and then provide supporting details in a separate, short paragraph. Use paragraph headings to make your reader's job easier.

Request Specific Action in a Courteous Close

Even routine messages require special attention to the close.

Close your message with three important elements:

- **A specific request for action.** Restate your request and ask that readers respond by a specific time ("Please send the figures by April 5 so that I can return first-quarter results to you before the May 20 conference").
- **Contact information.** Help your reader respond easily by including your phone number, office hours, and other contact information.
- **An expression of appreciation or goodwill.** Sincerely express your goodwill and appreciation; however, don't thank readers "in advance" for cooperating. If a reader's response warrants a thank you, send it after you've received the reply.

Types of Routine Requests

The types of routine requests are numerous, from asking favours to requesting credit. Many of the routine messages that you'll be writing will likely fall into major categories.

The following sections discuss three of these categories: placing orders, requesting information and action, and making claims and requesting adjustments.

Placing Orders

Today, many companies make paperless orders by using computer-generated order forms. These forms provide a list of products with a description of each item and information such as the catalogue number, name or trade name, colour, size, and unit price. Your job is to fill in the quantity, compute the total amount due, and provide the shipping address.

If you do need to draft an order letter, follow the same format as you would on an order blank.

When placing orders, be thorough and clear.

- **Opening.** Start with the general request.
- **Body.** Include specific information about the items you want. Put this information in columns, double-space between the items, and total the price at the end.
- **Close.** Specify the delivery address, which may differ from the billing address. Also indicate how the merchandise is to be shipped. Finally, in any letter including a payment, mention the amount enclosed and explain how the amount was calculated.

Here's an example of an effective order:

Please send the following items to the above address. I am ordering from your current spring–summer catalogue: ← States general request first

COUNT	STOCK I.D.	DESCRIPTION	ITEM PRICE	TOTAL PRICE
3	139-24	Daily appointment books (black)	$ 8.95	$ 26.85
50	289-90	Mechanical pencils (0.5 mm/black)	1.69	84.50
5	905-18	Wrist pads (grey)	6.99	34.95
10	472-67	CD-R disks (50/box)	17.99	179.90
			TOTAL SALES	$326.20
			SHIPPING	FREE
			AMOUNT DUE	$326.20

← Provides all necessary details in a format similar to an order form

← Calculates the total amount due (from information on tax and shipping that was provided in the catalogue)

My cheque #1738 for $326.20 is enclosed. Please ship these supplies via Purolator to the address in the letterhead. ← Includes additional important information in the close

Requesting Information and Action

Basically, a simple request says, "This is what I want to know or what I want you to do, why I'm making the request, and why it may be in your interest to help me." In more complex situations, readers might be unwilling to respond unless they understand how the request benefits them, so be sure to include this information in your explanation. Follow the direct approach:

When requesting information or action, as with any business message, keep your purpose clearly in mind.

- **Opening.** Start with a clear statement of your reason for writing.
- **Body.** Provide whatever explanation is needed to justify your request.
- **Close.** Provide a specific account of what you expect, and include a deadline if appropriate.

Internal requests to fellow employees are often oral and rather casual, but sending a clear, thoughtfully written memo or e-mail message can save time and questions by helping readers understand precisely what you want (see Figure 7.2 on page 152). Requests to outsiders are often made by letter, although some are sent via e-mail. These messages are usually short and simple (see Figure 7.3 on page 153).

Follow the same strategy for both internal and external requests.

Planning	Writing	Completing
Analyze the Situation Purpose is to request feedback from fellow employees. **Investigate the Topic** Gather accurate, complete information on program benefits and local gym. **Adapt to the Audience** Office memo or e-mail is appropriate medium. Use "you" attitude, and make responding easy.	**Organize the Message** Main idea is saving money while staying healthy. Save time and meet audience expectations using the direct approach. **Compose the Message** Keep style informal but business-like. Using a "we" attitude includes readers in the decision-making process.	**Revise the Message** Keep it brief. Weed out overly long words and phrases. Avoid unnecessary details. **Produce the Message** No need for fancy design elements in this memo. Include a response form. **Proofread the Message** Review carefully for both content and typographical errors.
1	2	3

FIGURE 7.2 Memo Requesting Action from Company Insiders

ACE Ace Hardware Corporation

INTERNAL MEMORANDUM

Routes message efficiently, with all needed information

TO: All Employees
FROM: Tony Ramirez, Human Resources
DATE: October 15, 2004
SUBJ: **NEW WELLNESS PROGRAM OPPORTUNITY**

The benefits package committee has asked me to contact everyone about an opportunity to save money and stay healthier in the bargain. As you know, we've been meeting to decide on changes in our benefits package. Last week, we sent you a memo detailing the Synergy Wellness Program. Now we would like to know whether you are interested in participating in the program.

States purpose and request in opening to avoid wasting busy readers' time

Presents the situation that makes the inquiry necessary

In addition to the package as described in the memo (life, major medical, dental, hospitalization), Synergy has sweetened the pot by offering ACE Hardware a 10 percent discount. To meet the requirements for the discount, we have to show proof that at least 25 percent of our employees participate in aerobic exercise at least 3 times a week for at least 20 minutes. (Their actuarial tables show a resulting 10 percent reduction in claims.)

After looking around, we discovered a gymnasium just a few blocks south on Haley Boulevard. Sports Action will give our employees unlimited daytime access to their indoor track, gym, and pool for a group fee that comes to approximately $4.50 per month per employee if at least half of us sign up.

In addition to using the track and pool, we can play volleyball, jazzercise, form our own intramural basketball teams, and much more. Our spouses and children can also participate at a deeply discounted monthly fee. If you have questions, please e-mail or call me (or any member of the committee). Let us know your wishes on the following form.

Lists reader benefits and requests action

Sign and return the following no later than Friday, October 29.

= =

Provides an easy-to-use response form

_____ Yes, I will participate in the Synergy Wellness program and pay $4.50 a month.
_____ Yes, I am interested in a discounted family membership.
_____ No, I prefer not to participate.

Signature ______________________________

Employee ID Number ______________________________

FIGURE 7.3 Letter Requesting Information from a Company Outsider

Pralle Realty

823 Viewpoint Avenue
Kingston, ON N5Y 5R6
(519) 633-3018 fax: (519) 663-3020

September 24, 2004

Mr. Harold Westerman
Agri-Lawn Services
1796 West Commercial Ave.
Kingston, ON N6T 8V2

Dear Mr. Westerman:

INFORMATION ON LAWN SERVICES

Would you please send us information about the lawn services you provide. Pralle Realty owns approximately 27 pieces of rental property in Kingston and we're looking for a lawn service to handle all of them. We are making a commitment to provide quality housing in this universtiy town, and we are looking for an outstanding firm to work with us.

In addition to brochures or other literature, please respond to the following:

1. **Lawn care.** What is your annual charge for each location for lawn maintenance, including mowing, fertilizing, and weed control?
2. **Shrubbery.** What is your annual charge for each location for the care of deciduous and evergreen bushes, including pruning, fertilizing, and replacing as necessary?
3. **Contract.** How does Agri-Lawn Services structure such large contracts? What additional information do you need from us?

Please let us hear from you by February 15. We must have a lawn-care firm in place by March 15.

Sincerely,

Kathleen Moriarity

Kathleen Moriarity
Senior Partner

al

Makes overall request in polite question form (no question mark)

Avoids making an overly broad request by using a series of specific questions

Avoids useless yes-or-no answers by including open-ended questions

Keeps reader's interest by hinting at possibility of future business

Itemizes questions in a logical sequence

Specifies a time limit in the courteous close

Pointers for Making a Routine Request

Direct Statement of the Request

- Be direct since your readers will respond favourably.
- Open by stating the main idea clearly and simply.
- Write in a polite, undemanding, personal tone.
- Before complex requests, include a brief explanation.

Justification, Explanation, and Details

- Justify the request, or explain its importance.
- Explain the benefit of responding.
- State desired actions in a positive, supportive manner.
- Itemize a complex request in a logical, numbered list.
- Limit any question to one topic.

Courteous Close with Request for Specific Action

- Courteously request a specific action.
- Make it easy to comply by including contact information.
- Indicate your gratitude.
- Clearly state any important deadline or time frame.

Making Claims and Requesting Adjustments

Putting your claim in writing

- Documents your dissatisfaction
- Requires courtesy, clarity, and conciseness

When you're dissatisfied with a company's product or service, you make a **claim** (a formal complaint) or request an **adjustment** (a claim settlement). Although a phone call or visit may solve the problem, a written claim letter documents your dissatisfaction. Moreover, if you're angry or frustrated, writing the letter will help you cool off and adopt a more objective tone. After all, a courteous, clear, concise explanation will make a far more favourable impression than an abusive, angry letter.

In most cases, and especially in your first letter, assume that a fair adjustment will be made, and follow the plan for direct requests:

- **Opening.** Begin with a straightforward statement of the problem.
- **Body.** Give a complete, specific explanation of the details, providing any information an adjuster would need to verify your claim.
- **Close.** Politely request specific action or convey a sincere desire to find a solution. And don't forget to suggest that the business relationship will continue if the problem is solved satisfactorily.

Be prepared to document your claim. Send copies and keep the original documents.

Companies usually accept the customer's explanation of what's wrong, so ethically it's important to be entirely honest when filing claims. Also, be prepared to back up your claim with invoices, sales receipts, cancelled cheques, dated correspondence, catalogue descriptions, and any other relevant documents. Send copies and keep the originals for your files. Be sure to supply your contact information and the best time to call so that the company can discuss the situation with you if necessary. For more insights into writing these kinds of messages, compare the poor and improved versions of the claim letter in Figure 7.4.

Sending Routine Replies and Positive Messages

Your routine replies and positive messages have four specific goals.

When responding positively to a request, giving good news, or sending a goodwill message, you have several goals: (1) to communicate the information or good news, (2) to answer all questions, (3) to provide all required details, and (4) to leave your reader with a good impression of you and your firm. Routine positive messages can be quite brief and to the point, but remember to be courteous, stay upbeat, and maintain a you-oriented tone.

Strategy for Routine Replies and Positive Messages

Like requests, routine replies and positive messages will generally be of interest to your readers, so you'll usually use the direct approach. Open with your main idea (the positive reply or the good news). Use the body to explain all the relevant details. Then close cordially, perhaps highlighting a benefit to your reader.

Start with the Main Idea

Before you begin, have a clear idea of what you want to say.

Begin your positive message with the main idea or good news and prepare your audience for the detail that follows. Try to make your opening clear and concise. Look at the following introductory statements. They make the same point, but one is so cluttered with unnecessary information that it buries the purpose; the other is brief, to the point, and clear:

Instead of	Write
I am pleased to inform you that after deliberating the matter carefully, our human resources committee has recommended you for appointment as a staff accountant.	Congratulations. You've been selected to join our firm as a staff accountant, beginning March 20.

FIGURE 7.4 Letter Making a Claim

Poor

We have been at our present location only three months, and we don't understand why our December utility bill is $815.00 and our January bill is $817.50. Businesses on both sides of us, in offices just like ours, are paying only $543.50 and $545.67 for the same months. We all have similar computer and office equipment, so something must be wrong.

Opens with emotion and details

Small businesses are helpless against big utility companies. How can we prove that you read the meter wrong or that the November bill from before we even moved in here got added to our December bill? We want someone to check this meter right away. We can't afford to pay these big bills.

Uses a defensive tone and blames the meter reader

This is the first time we've complained to you about anything, and I hope you'll agree that we deserve a better deal.

Closes with irrelevant information and a weak defence

Sincerely,

Laura Covington

Laura Covington
Proprietor

Improved

The European Connection
Specialist Purveyors of European Antiques
for over 30 years
P.O. Box 804 • Saint John, NB E2L 3V1
Telephone: (506) 979-7727 Fax: (506) 979-2828
EuroConnect@bellca.net

February 23, 2004

Customer Service Representative
City of Saint John Utilities
955 Cabot Street
Saint John, NB E4Y 1Z1

Dear Customer Service Representative:

REQUEST FOR METER CHECK

The utility meter in our store may not be accurate. Please send someone to check it.

Opens by clearly and calmly stating the problem

Explains details in the body so that reader can understand why Covington thinks a problem exists

We have been at our current location since December 1, almost three months. Our monthly bill is nearly triple those of neighbouring businesses in this building, yet we all have similar storefronts and equipment. In December we paid $815.00, and our January bill was $817.50—the highest bills that neighbouring businesses have paid were $543.50 and $545.67.

Presents details clearly, concisely, and completely

Requests specific action in the closing and provides contact information to make responding easy

If your representative could visit our store, he or she could do an analysis of how much energy we are using. We understand that you regularly provide this helpful service to customers.

We would appreciate hearing from you this week. You can reach me by calling 979-7727 during business hours.

Sincerely,

Laura Covington

Laura Covington
Proprietor

Pointers for Making a Claim

- Gain reader understanding by praising some aspect of the product—at least explain why the product was purchased.
- Maintain a confident, factual, fair, unemotional tone.
- Present facts clearly, politely, and honestly.
- Show confidence in the reader's fairness—eliminate threats, sarcasm, hostility, and exaggeration, and use a nonargumentative tone.
- Make no accusation against any person or company—unless you can back it up with facts.

Provide Necessary Detail and Explanation

In the body, explain your point completely so that the audience will experience no confusion or lingering doubt. In addition to providing details in the body, maintain the supportive tone you already established in the opening. This tone is easy to continue when your message is purely good news, as in this example:

> Your educational background and internship have impressed us, and we believe you would be a valuable addition to Green Valley Properties. As discussed during your interview, your salary will be $3300 per month, plus benefits. In that regard, you will meet with our benefits manager, Paula Vellani, on Monday, March 20, at 8:00 a.m. She will assist you with all the paperwork necessary to tailor our benefit package to your family situation. She will also arrange various orientation activities to help you adapt to our company.

Embed any slightly negative information in a positive context.

However, if your routine message is mixed and must convey mildly disappointing information, put the negative portion of your message into as favourable a context as possible:

Instead of	Write
No, we no longer carry the Sportsgirl line of sweaters.	The new Olympic line has replaced the Sportsgirl sweaters that you asked about. Olympic features a wider range of colours and sizes and more contemporary styling.

The more complete description is less negative and emphasizes how the audience can benefit from the change. However, be careful using even only slightly negative information in this type of message: Use it *only* if you're reasonably sure the audience will respond positively. Otherwise, use the indirect approach (discussed in Chapter 8).

End with a Courteous Close

Make sure the audience understands what to do next and how that action will benefit them.

Your message is most likely to succeed if your readers are left feeling that you have their personal welfare in mind. Accomplish this task either by highlighting a benefit to the audience or by expressing appreciation or goodwill. If follow-up action is required, clearly state who will do what next.

Types of Routine Replies and Positive Messages

Innumerable types of routine replies and positive messages are used in business every day. Many of these messages fall into three main categories: granting requests for information and action, granting claims and requests for adjustments, and sending goodwill messages.

Granting Requests for Information and Action

If your answer to a request is yes or is straightforward information, use the direct plan: Open with the main idea (or good news), use the body for explanation and detail, and close courteously. Your prompt, gracious, and thorough response will positively influence how people think about your company, its products, your department, and you. For a good example of this type of message, see Herman Miller Inc.'s response to Julian Zamakis's request for information about employment opportunities (see Figure 7.5).

Many companies use form responses to reply to similar requests.

Many of the requests you receive will be routine and can get a standardized response. For example, a human resources department gets numerous routine inquiries about job openings. To handle repetitive queries like these, companies usually develop form responses. Although such messages are often criticized as being cold and impersonal, you can put a great deal of thought into wording them, and you can use computers to personalize and mix paragraphs. Thus, a computerized form letter prepared with care may be personal and sincere.

Granting Claims and Requests for Adjustment

Satisfied customers bring additional business to a firm; angry, dissatisfied customers do not. Plus, they complain to anyone who'll listen, creating poor public relations. So even though claims and adjustments may seem unpleasant, progressive business people treat them as golden opportunities for building customer loyalty.[2]

The claims you receive are your chance to build strong relationships with customers and clients.

Few people go to the trouble of requesting an adjustment unless they actually have a problem. So the most sensible reaction to a routine claim is to assume that the claimant's account of the transaction is an honest statement of what happened—unless the same customer repeatedly submits dubious claims or the dollar amount is very large. When you receive a complaint, investigate the problem first to determine what went wrong and why. In addition, determine whether your company, your customer, or a third party is at fault.

Finding out who is at fault helps you know how to respond to a claim.

When Your Company Is at Fault Refer to company errors carefully. Explain your company's efforts to do a good job, and imply that the error was an unusual incident. Here are some tips on what *not* to do:

When a complaint is the result of company error, word your response carefully.

- Don't blame an individual or a specific department.
- Don't use lame excuses such as "Nobody's perfect" or "Mistakes will happen."
- Don't promise that problems will never happen again (such guarantees are unrealistic and often beyond your control).

Many response letters are written as a personal answer to a unique claim. Such letters start with a clear statement of the good news: the settling of the claim according to the customer's request. For example, when a customer complained about a defective product, Klondike Gear (a large mail-order company) responded with the personal answer in Figure 7.6.

Companies also receive many claims that are quite similar. Klondike Gear has numerous customers who claim they haven't received exactly what was ordered. So the company created a form letter (see Figure 7.6), which can be customized through word processing and then individually signed.

When the Customer Is at Fault When your customer is at fault (perhaps washing a dry-clean-only sweater in hot water), either you refuse the claim and attempt to justify your refusal or you simply do what the customer asks. Remember, if you refuse the claim, you may lose your customer—as well as many of the customer's friends, who will hear only one side of the dispute. You must weigh the cost of making the adjustment against the cost of losing future business from one or more customers.

If you choose to grant the claim, open with the good news: You're replacing the merchandise or refunding the purchase price. However, the message body needs special attention. After all, if the customer fails to realize what went wrong, you'll be committing your firm to an endless procession of returned merchandise. Your job is to help the customer understand that the merchandise was mistreated, but you must do so without being condescending ("Perhaps you failed to read the instructions carefully") or preachy ("You should know that wool shrinks in hot water"). If you insult the customer, your cash refund will be wasted because you'll lose that customer anyway. Without being offensive, the letter in Figure 7.7 on page 161 educates a customer about how to treat his in-line skates.

When complying with an unjustified claim, let the customer know that the merchandise was mistreated, but maintain a respectful and positive tone.

When a Third Party Is at Fault Sometimes neither you nor the claimant is at fault. Perhaps the carrier damaged merchandise in transit. Or perhaps the original manufacturer is responsible for some product defect. When a third party is at fault, you have three options:

You have three options when a third party is at fault.

- **Simply honour the claim.** This option is the most attractive. You satisfy your customer with a standard good-news letter and no extra explanation. You maintain your reputation for fair dealing but bear no cost (since the carrier, manufacturer, or other third party reimburses you).

FIGURE 7.5 E-Mail Replying to a Request for Information

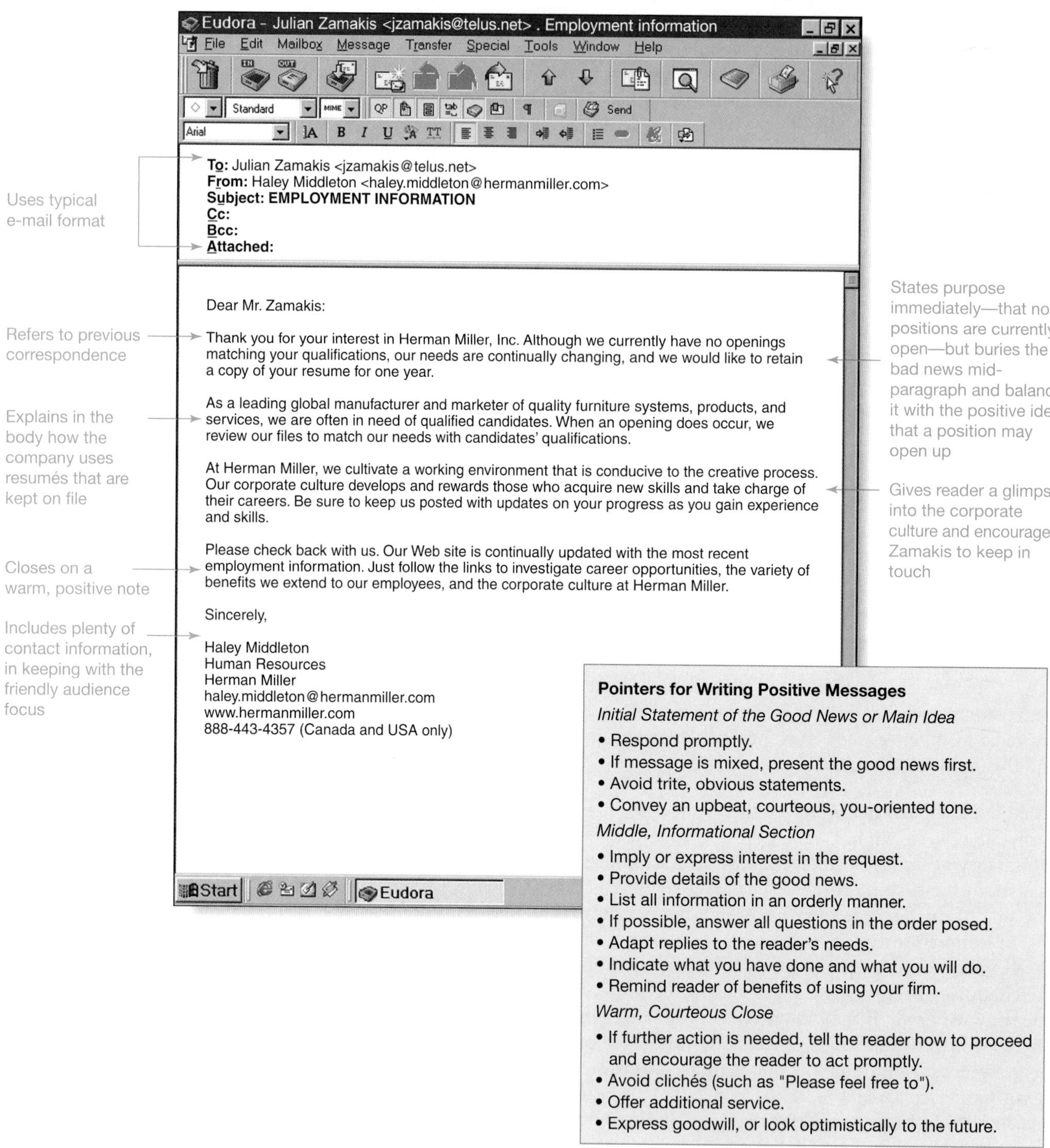

Pointers for Writing Positive Messages

Initial Statement of the Good News or Main Idea

- Respond promptly.
- If message is mixed, present the good news first.
- Avoid trite, obvious statements.
- Convey an upbeat, courteous, you-oriented tone.

Middle, Informational Section

- Imply or express interest in the request.
- Provide details of the good news.
- List all information in an orderly manner.
- If possible, answer all questions in the order posed.
- Adapt replies to the reader's needs.
- Indicate what you have done and what you will do.
- Remind reader of benefits of using your firm.

Warm, Courteous Close

- If further action is needed, tell the reader how to proceed and encourage the reader to act promptly.
- Avoid clichés (such as "Please feel free to").
- Offer additional service.
- Express goodwill, or look optimistically to the future.

- **Honour the claim but explain you're not at fault.** This option corrects any impression that the damage was caused by your negligence. You can still write the standard good-news letter, but stress the explanation.
- **Refer the reader to the third party.** This option is usually a bad choice because you fail to satisfy the reader's needs. However, use this option when you're trying to dissociate yourself from any legal responsibility for the damaged merchandise, especially if it has caused a personal injury, in which case you would send a bad-news message (see Chapter 8).

FIGURE 7.6 Personalized and Form Letters Responding to Complaints

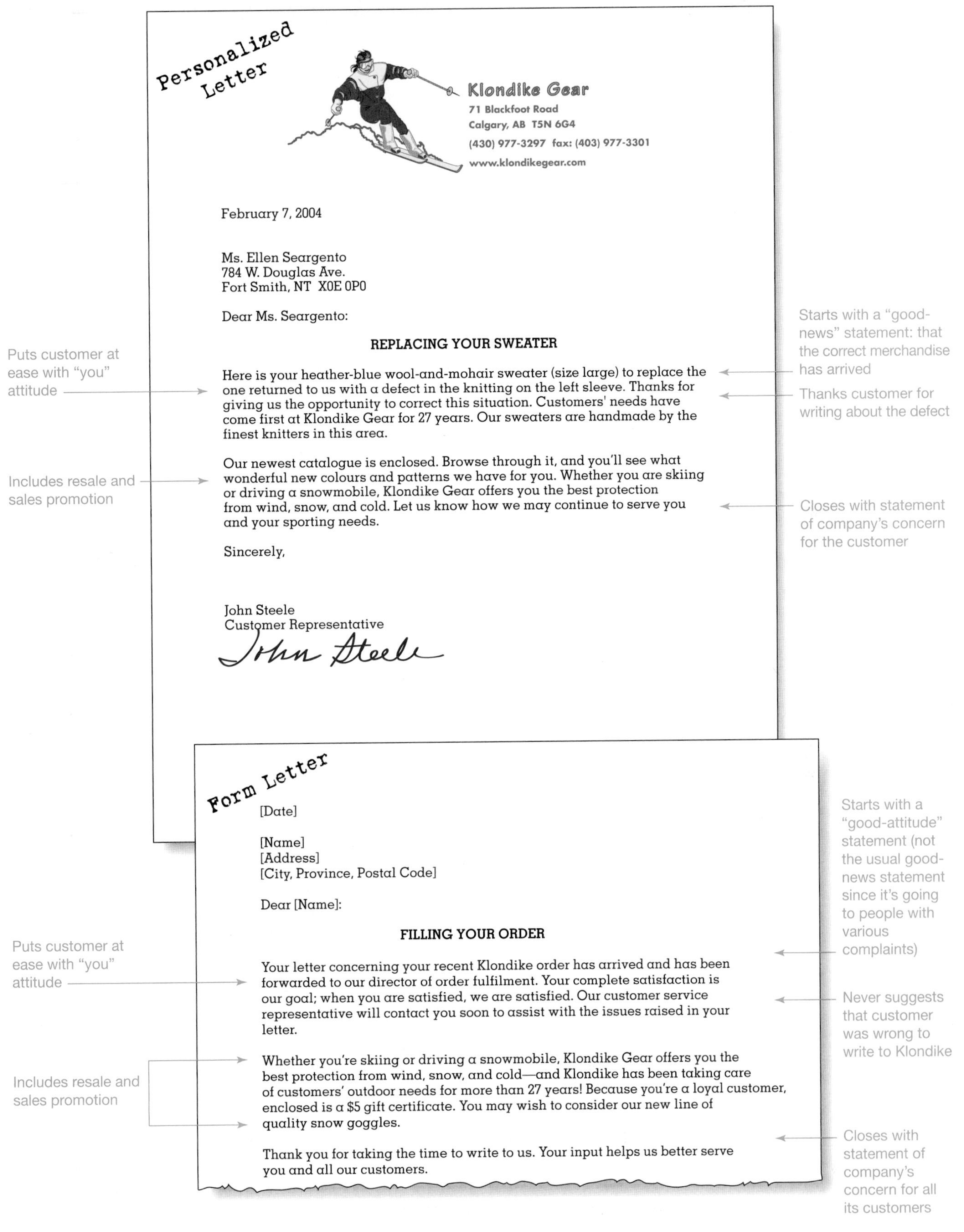

Personalized Letter

Klondike Gear
71 Blackfoot Road
Calgary, AB T5N 6G4
(430) 977-3297 fax: (403) 977-3301
www.klondikegear.com

February 7, 2004

Ms. Ellen Seargento
784 W. Douglas Ave.
Fort Smith, NT X0E 0P0

Dear Ms. Seargento:

REPLACING YOUR SWEATER

Here is your heather-blue wool-and-mohair sweater (size large) to replace the one returned to us with a defect in the knitting on the left sleeve. Thanks for giving us the opportunity to correct this situation. Customers' needs have come first at Klondike Gear for 27 years. Our sweaters are handmade by the finest knitters in this area.

Our newest catalogue is enclosed. Browse through it, and you'll see what wonderful new colours and patterns we have for you. Whether you are skiing or driving a snowmobile, Klondike Gear offers you the best protection from wind, snow, and cold. Let us know how we may continue to serve you and your sporting needs.

Sincerely,

John Steele
Customer Representative

Puts customer at ease with "you" attitude
Includes resale and sales promotion
Starts with a "good-news" statement: that the correct merchandise has arrived
Thanks customer for writing about the defect
Closes with statement of company's concern for the customer

Form Letter

[Date]

[Name]
[Address]
[City, Province, Postal Code]

Dear [Name]:

FILLING YOUR ORDER

Your letter concerning your recent Klondike order has arrived and has been forwarded to our director of order fulfilment. Your complete satisfaction is our goal; when you are satisfied, we are satisfied. Our customer service representative will contact you soon to assist with the issues raised in your letter.

Whether you're skiing or driving a snowmobile, Klondike Gear offers you the best protection from wind, snow, and cold—and Klondike has been taking care of customers' outdoor needs for more than 27 years! Because you're a loyal customer, enclosed is a $5 gift certificate. You may wish to consider our new line of quality snow goggles.

Thank you for taking the time to write to us. Your input helps us better serve you and all our customers.

Puts customer at ease with "you" attitude
Includes resale and sales promotion
Starts with a "good-attitude" statement (not the usual good-news statement since it's going to people with various complaints)
Never suggests that customer was wrong to write to Klondike
Closes with statement of company's concern for all its customers

Planning	Writing	Completing
Analyze the Situation Purpose is to grant a customer's claim, gently educate him, and encourage further business. **Investigate the Topic** Gather information on product care, warranties, and resale information. **Adapt to the Audience** Use letter format to reinforce businesslike tone. Give customer relationship utmost attention.	**Organize the Message** Main idea is that you're replacing the wheel assembly—even though you are not required to do so. **Compose the Message** Use an upbeat, conversational style, but remain businesslike. Choose words carefully, especially when educating the customer. Include resale information to reinforce future business.	**Revise the Message** Revise for tone, focusing on conciseness, clarity, and the "you" attitude. **Produce the Message** Avoid confusing your positive message with fussy design elements. Keep it simple. **Proofread the Message** Review for the usual errors, and include all promised enclosures.
1	2	3

Sending Goodwill Messages

You can enhance your relationships with customers, colleagues, and other business people by sending friendly, unexpected notes for special occasions. Effective goodwill messages must be sincere, honest and avoid exaggeration. Back up any compliments with specific points. Remember, readers often regard restrained praise as being more sincere:

Instead of	Write
Words cannot express my appreciation for the great job you did. Thanks. No one could have done it better. You're terrific! You've made the whole firm sit up and take notice, and we are ecstatic to have you working here.	Thanks again for taking charge of the meeting in my absence. You did an excellent job. With just an hour's notice, you managed to pull the legal and public relations departments together so that we could present a united front in the negotiations. Your dedication and communication abilities have been noted and are truly appreciated.

Taking note of significant events in someone's personal life helps cement the business relationship.

Congratulations Reasons for sending congratulations include the highlights in people's personal lives—weddings, births, graduations, and successes. A prime opportunity for sending goodwill messages is to congratulate someone for a significant business achievement—perhaps for being promoted or for attaining an important civic position. The improved congratulatory note in Figure 7.8 on page 162 moves swiftly to the good news.

You may congratulate business acquaintances on their own achievements or on the accomplishments of a spouse or child. You may also take note of personal events, even if you don't know the reader well. Of course, if you're already friendly with the reader, you can get away with a more personal tone.

A message of appreciation documents a person's contributions.

Appreciation An important business quality is the ability to recognize the contributions of employees, colleagues, suppliers, and other associates. Your praise does more than just make the person feel good; it encourages further excellence. Moreover, a message that expresses appreciation may become an important part of someone's personnel file. So when you write, specifically mention the person or people you want to praise. The brief e-mail message that follows expresses gratitude and reveals the happy result:

> Thank you for sending the air-conditioning components via overnight delivery. You allowed us to satisfy the needs of two customers who were getting very impatient with the heat.

FIGURE 7.7 Letter Responding to a Claim When the Buyer Is at Fault

Skates Alive!

209 Fraser Way
London, ON N5Y 3R6
(519) 332-7474 • Fax: (519) 336-5297
skates@rogers.net

August 7, 2005

Mr. Steven Cox
1172 Amber Court
Summerside, PE C1A 4Z1

Dear Mr. Cox:

REPLACING YOUR SKATE WHEELS

Thank you for contacting us about your in-line skates. Even though your six-month warranty has expired, Skates Alive! is mailing you a complete wheel assembly replacement free of charge. The enclosed instructions make removing the damaged wheel line and installing the new one relatively easy.

Acknowledges reader communication, keeps opening positive by avoiding words such as "problem," and conveys the good news right away

The "Fastrax" (model NL 562) you purchased is our best-selling and most reliable skate. However, wheel jams may occur when fine particles of sand block the smooth rotating action of the wheels. These skates perform best when used on roadways and tracks that are relatively free of sand. We suggest that you remove and clean the wheel assemblies (see enclosed directions) once a month and have them checked by your dealer about every six months.

Explains the problem without blaming the customer by avoiding the pronoun "you" and by suggesting ways to avoid future problems

Includes sales promotion in the body, encouraging the customer to "trade up"

Because of your location, you may want to consider our more advanced "Glisto" (model NL 988) when you decide to purchase new skates. Although more expensive than the Fastrax, the Glisto design helps shed sand and dirt quite efficiently and should provide years of carefree skating.

Adds value by enclosing a newsletter that invites future response from customer

Enjoy the enclosed copy of "Rock & Roll," with our compliments. Inside, you'll read about new products, hear from other skaters, and have an opportunity to respond to our customer questionnaire.

Closes positively, ending on a "feel good" note that conveys an attitude of excellent customer service

We love hearing from our skaters, so keep in touch. All of us at Skates Alive! wish you good times and months of healthy skating.

Sincerely,

Candace Parker

Candace Parker
Customer Service Representative

Enclosure

Pointers for Granting a Claim

- In the opening, state the good news: you're honouring the claim.
- Thank the reader for writing.
- In the body, explain how you'll grant the claim.
- Don't argue with reader's version of events.
- Keep your explanation objective, nonvindictive, and impersonal.
- Apologize only when appropriate; then do so crisply, with no overly dramatic tone.
- Keep your tone supportive.
- In the closing, remind the reader how you are honouring the claim.
- Encourage the reader to look favourably on your company or product.
- Clarify any actions the reader must take.

Special thanks to Susan Brown, who took our initial call and never said, "It can't be done." Her initiative on our behalf is greatly appreciated.

Condolences In times of serious trouble and deep sadness, written expressions of sympathy leave their mark. Granted, this type of message is difficult to write, but don't let such difficulty keep you from responding promptly. Those who have experienced a health problem, the death of a loved one, or a business misfortune appreciate knowing that they're not alone.

In condolence messages, try to find a middle path between being superficial and causing additional distress.

Condolences are seldom written on letterhead. Use a plain note card with matching envelope. Open with a brief statement of sympathy, such as "I was deeply sorry to hear of your loss." In the body, mention the good qualities or the positive contributions made by

Planning	Writing	Completing
Analyze the Situation Purpose is to create goodwill with industry business associates. **Investigate the Topic** Gather information on specific accomplishments of the reader's firm. **Adapt to the Audience** Letter format lets reader use your message (perhaps even reproduce it) as an industry testimonial. 1	**Organize the Message** Main idea is to congratulate the reader. The direct approach is perfect for this welcome news. **Compose the Message** A conversational tone complements the slightly formal style, since this is your first contact with the reader. Avoid generalized praise by mentioning specific, concrete accomplishments. 2	**Revise the Message** Review for consistency in tone, word choice, and sentence structure. **Produce the Message** A simple design avoids distracting your reader from the message. **Proofread the Message** Create a positive first impression by being especially careful to send an error-free message. 3

FIGURE 7.8 Letter Congratulating a Business Acquaintance

Poor

We are so pleased when companies that we admire do well. When we attended our convention in Halifax last month, we heard about your firm's recent selection to design and print media advertisements for the National Association of Business Suppliers (NABS). ← Sounds condescending and self-centred—expressing the reason but failing to actually congratulate the reader

We have long believed that the success of individual franchises is directly linked to the healthy growth of the industry at large. Lambert, Cutchen & Browt is the only firm for the job. ← Seems insincere because of the lack of supporting reasons and the exaggeration ("only you can do the job")

We wish you the best of luck with your new ad campaign. Congratulations on a job well done! ← Congratulating the reader in the close seems like an afterthought

Sincerely,

Janice McCarthy

Janice McCarthy
Director, Media Relations

Improved

Office DEPOT, Canada
200 Fort Garry Road, Winnipeg, MB R3K 6J5 (204) 278-4800

March 3, 2003

Mr. Ralph Lambert, President
Lambert, Cutchen & Browt, Inc.
1435 Leeds Avenue
Hamilton, ON L8N 3T2

Dear Mr. Lambert:

CONGRATULATIONS ON YOUR SUCCESS

Immediately expresses the reason for congratulating the reader →

Congratulations on your firm's recent selection to design print media advertisements for the National Association of Business Suppliers (NABS). We learned of your success at our convention in Halifax last month.

We believe that the success of individual franchises is directly linked to the healthy growth of the industry at large. We can think of no better firm to help our industry achieve wide recognition than Lambert, Cutchen & Browt.

Uses body to make compliment more effective by showing knowledge of the reader's work, while avoiding exaggeration →

We have admired your success in promoting associations of other industries such as soft drinks, snack foods, and recycling. Your "Dream Vision 2003" ads for the bottling industry were both inspirational and effective in raising consumer awareness, and we look for similar positive responses to your ABS campaign.

Closes by expressing interest in following the future success of the firm →

We look forward to seeing the results of the survey you conducted during our convention. We will follow your media campaign with great interest.

Sincerely,

Janice McCarthy

Janice McCarthy
Director, Media Relations

tw

FIGURE 7.9 Note of Condolence

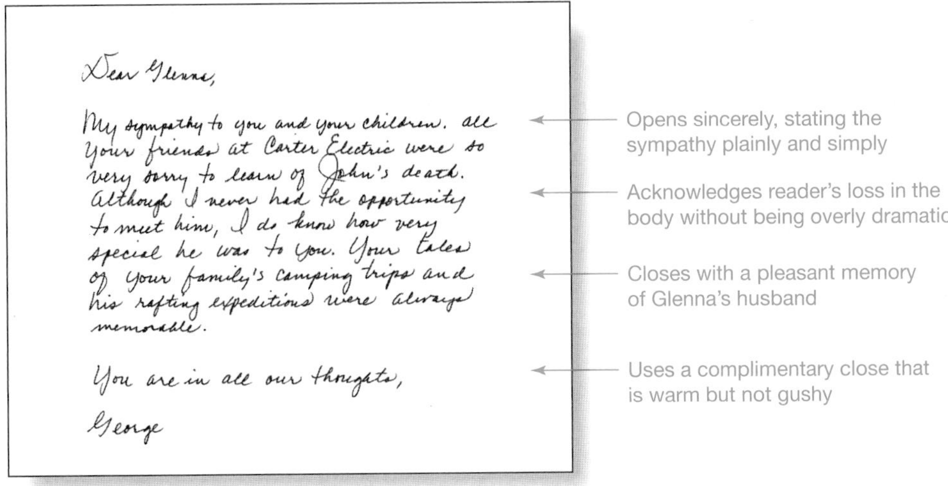

Dear Glenna,

My sympathy to you and your children. All your friends at Carter Electric were so very sorry to learn of John's death. Although I never had the opportunity to meet him, I do know how very special he was to you. Your tales of your family's camping trips and his rafting expeditions were always memorable.

You are in all our thoughts,

George

Opens sincerely, stating the sympathy plainly and simply
Acknowledges reader's loss in the body without being overly dramatic
Closes with a pleasant memory of Glenna's husband
Uses a complimentary close that is warm but not gushy

the deceased. State what the person or business meant to you. In the close, you can offer your condolences and your best wishes. One considerate way to end this type of message is to say something that will give the reader a little lift, such as a reference to a brighter future. Here are a few general suggestions for writing condolence messages:

- **Keep reminiscences brief.** Recount a memory or an anecdote (even a humorous one), but don't dwell on the details of the loss, lest you add to the reader's anguish.
- **Write in your own words.** Write as if you were speaking privately to the person. Don't quote "poetic" passages or use stilted or formal phrases. If the loss is a death, refer to it as such rather than as "passing away" or "departing."
- **Be tactful.** Mention your shock and dismay, but remember that bereaved and distressed loved ones take little comfort in lines such as "Richard was too young to die" or "Starting all over again will be so difficult." Try to strike a balance between superficial expressions of sympathy and heartrending references to a happier past or the likelihood of a bleak future.
- **Take special care.** Be sure to spell names correctly and to be accurate in your review of facts. Try to be prompt.
- **Write about special qualities of the deceased.** You may have to rely on reputation to do this, but let the grieving person know you valued his or her loved one.
- **Write about special qualities of the bereaved person.** A pat on the back helps a bereaved family member feel more confident about handling things during such a traumatic time.[3]

For an example of an effective condolence note, see Figure 7.9 above. George Bigalow sent the message to his administrative assistant, Glenna Case, after learning of the death of Glenna's husband.

Reviewing Key Points

This chapter introduced you to strategies for routine, good-news, and goodwill messages. When you write messages such as routine requests, "yes" replies, claims, and adjustments, follow the direct pattern by

- Stating the request or response at the beginning
- Explaining the details
- Closing politely, facilitating the specific action

When you respond to claim letters, you aim to restore and maintain customer relations, so try to accommodate the claim where possible. In order letters, precise specification is important, and in goodwill messages, sincere, specific examples are most effective.

In routine correspondence, remember to

- Begin by stating the main action
- Explain "why," "what," or "how" in a clear, concise, courteous style and tone
- End by pointing the way to the next step—*who* will do *what*, by *when*

Test Your Knowledge

1. When is a request routine?

2. What are three guidelines for asking a series of questions in a routine request?

3. What information should be included in an order request?

4. Should you use the direct or indirect approach for most routine messages? Why?

5. Where in a routine message should you state your actual request?

6. How does a claim differ from an adjustment?

7. How does the question of fault affect what you say in a message granting a claim?

8. Why do firms sometimes grant claims even when they know the customer was at fault?

9. How can you avoid sounding insincere when writing a goodwill message?

10. What are six guidelines for writing condolence messages?

Apply Your Knowledge

1. When organizing request messages, why is it important to know whether any cultural differences exist between you and your audience? Explain.

2. Your company's error cost an important business customer a new client; you know it and your customer knows it. Do you apologize, or do you refer to the incident in a positive light without admitting any responsibility? Briefly explain.

3. You've been asked to write a letter of recommendation for an employee who has a disability and uses a wheelchair. The disability has no effect on the employee's ability to do the job, and you feel confident about writing the best recommendation possible. Nevertheless, you know the prospective company and its facilities aren't well suited to wheelchair access. Do you mention the employee's disability in your letter? Explain.

4. Every time you send a direct-request memo to Ted Jackson, he delays or refuses to comply. You're beginning to get impatient. Should you send Jackson a memo to ask what's wrong? Complain to your supervisor about Jackson's uncooperative attitude? Arrange a face-to-face meeting with Jackson? Bring up the problem at the next staff meeting? Explain.

5. **Ethical Choices** You have a complaint against one of your suppliers, but you have no documentation to back it up. Should you request an adjustment anyway? Why or why not?

Practise Your Knowledge

Exercises for Perfecting Your Writing

Revising Messages: Direct Approach Revise the following short e-mail messages so that they are more direct and concise; develop a subject line for each revised message.

1. I'm contacting you about your recent order for a High Country backpack. You didn't tell us which backpack you wanted, and you know we make a lot of different ones. We have the canvas models with the plastic frames and vinyl trim and we have the canvas models with leather trim, and we have the ones that have more pockets than the other ones. Plus they come in lots of different colours. Also they make the ones that are large for a big-boned person and the smaller versions for little women or kids.

   Subject line: ____________________

2. Thank you for contacting us about the difficulty you had collecting your luggage at the Toronto airport. We are very sorry for the inconvenience this has caused you. As you know, travelling can create problems of this sort regardless of how careful the airline personnel might be. To receive compensation, please send us a detailed list of the items that you lost and complete the following questionnaire. You can e-mail it back to us.

   Subject line: ____________________

Revising Messages: Direct Approach Rewrite the following sentences so that they are direct and concise.

3. We wanted to invite you to our special 40 percent off by-invitation-only sale. The sale is taking place on November 9.

4. We wanted to let you know that we are giving a tote bag and a free Phish CD with every $50 donation you make to our radio station.

5. The director planned to go to the meeting that will be held on Monday at a little before 11:00 A.M.

6. In today's meeting, we were happy to have the opportunity to welcome Paul Eccelson. He reviewed some of the newest types of order forms. If you have any questions about these new forms, feel free to call him at his office.

Audience Analysis (Teamwork) With another student, conduct an audience analysis of the following message topic: A notice to all employees about the placement of recycling bins by the elevator doors

7. What is the purpose of this message?

8. What is the most appropriate format for communicating this written message?

9. How is the audience likely to respond to this message?

10. Based on this audience analysis, would you use the direct or the indirect approach for this message? Explain your reasoning.

Revising Messages: Closing Paragraphs How would you rewrite each of the following closing paragraphs to be concise, courteous, and specific?

11. I need your response sometime soon so I can order the parts in time for your service appointment. Otherwise your air-conditioning system may not be in tip-top condition for the start of the summer season.

12. Thank you in advance for sending me as much information as you can about your products. I look forward to receiving your package in the very near future.

13. To schedule an appointment with one of our knowledgeable mortgage specialists in your area, you can always call our hotline at 1-800-555-8765. This is also the number to call if you have more questions about mortgage rates, closing procedures, or any other aspect of the mortgage process. Remember, we're here to make the home-buying experience as painless as possible.

Activities

For live links to all Web sites discussed in this chapter, visit this text's Web site at www.pearsoned.ca/bovee. Just log on and select Chapter 7, and click on "Student Resources." Locate the page or the URL related to the material in the text. For "Exploring the Best of the Web" exercises, you'll also find navigational directions. Click on the live link to the site.

1. **Analyze This Document** Read the following document, then (1) analyze the strengths and weaknesses of each sentence and (2) revise the document so that it follows this chapter's guidelines.

   Our university is closing its dining hall for financial reasons, so we want to do something to help the students prepare their own food in residence rooms if they so choose. Your colourful ad in *Campus Magazine* caught our eye. We need the following information before we make our decision.

   1. Would you be able to ship the microwaves by August 15th? I realize this is short notice, but our board of trustees just made the decision to close the dining hall last week and we're scrambling around trying to figure out what to do.
   2. Do they have any kind of a warranty? University students can be pretty hard on things, as you know, so we will need a good warranty.
   3. How much does it cost? Do you give a discount for a big order?
   4. Do we have to provide a special outlet?
   5. Will students know how to use them, or will we need to provide instructions?

   As I said before, we're on a tight time frame and need good information from you as soon as possible to help us make our decision about ordering. You never know what the board might come up with next. I'm looking at several other companies, also, so please let us know ASAP.

2. **Analyze This Document** Read the following document, then (1) analyze the strengths and weaknesses of each sentence and (2) revise the document so that it follows this chapter's guidelines.

   At a local business-supply store, I recently purchased your "Negotiator Pro" for my computer. I bought the CD because I saw your ad for it in *MacWorld* magazine, and it looked as if it might be an effective tool for use in my corporate seminar on negotiation.

   Unfortunately, when I inserted it in my office computer, it wouldn't work. I returned it to the store, but since I had already opened it, they refused to exchange it for a CD that would work or give me a refund. They told me to contact you and that you might be able to send me a version that would work with my computer.

   You can send the information to me at the letterhead address. If you cannot send me the correct disk, please refund my $79.95. Thanks in advance for any help you can give me in this matter.

3. **Analyze This Document** Read the following document, then (1) analyze the strengths and weaknesses of each sentence and (2) revise the document so that it follows this chapter's guidelines.

   We read your letter requesting your deposit refund. We couldn't figure out why you hadn't received it, so we talked to our maintenance engineer as you suggested. He said you had left one of the doors off the hinges in your apartment in order to get a large sofa through the door. He also confirmed that you had paid him $5.00 to replace the door since you had to turn in the U-Haul trailer and were in a big hurry.

This entire situation really was caused by a lack of communication between our housekeeping inspector and the maintenance engineer. All we knew was that the door was off the hinges when it was inspected by Sally Tarnley. You know that our policy states that if anything is wrong with the apartment, we keep the deposit. We had no way of knowing that George just hadn't gotten around to replacing the door.

But we have good news. We approved the deposit refund, which will be mailed to you from our home office in Red Deer, Alberta. I'm not sure how long that will take, however. If you don't receive the cheque by the end of next month, give me a call.

Next time, it's really a good idea to stay with your apartment until it's inspected as stipulated in your lease agreement. That way, you'll be sure to receive your refund when you expect it. Hope you have a good summer.

4. **Internet** Visit the business section of the Blue Mountain site at www.bluemountain.com/index.pd then follow the link to "Career," under "Featured eCards." Analyze one of the electronic greeting cards bearing a goodwill message of appreciation for good performance. Under what circumstances would you send this electronic message? How could you personalize it for the recipient and the occasion? What would be an appropriate close for this message?

5. **Ethical Choices** Your small supermarket chain has received dozens of complaints about the watery consistency of the ketchup sold under the chain's brand name. You don't want your customers to stop buying other store-brand foods, which are made and packaged for your chain by various suppliers, but you do want to address their concerns about the ketchup. In responding to these complaints, should you explain that the ketchup is actually manufactured by a local supplier and then name the supplier, who has already started bottling a thicker ketchup?

6. **Planning a Letter: Air Rage Fiasco** Letter requesting refund from British Airways.

You've been administrative assistant to Samantha Alberts, vice-president of sales for Richter Office Solutions, for two years. You handle all her travel arrangements and you've never seen her so upset. The "air rage" incident happened on Friday and now it's Monday, but she's still pale and shaky.

"There we were, cruising over the Atlantic, and the guy just erupted! I couldn't believe it!" she says for the third time.

She was flying back from a conference in London to make a presentation at your Montreal branch. Then she was to catch a plane home to Edmonton on Saturday. With airline security so tight these days, she expected a calm flight and lots of time to prepare her presentation notes as she crossed the ocean. As it turned out, she spent most of that time fearing for her life.

"What made the guy angry?" you ask.

"Apparently some passengers complained about 'offensive images' he was viewing on his laptop. When the steward politely asked him to stop, the guy went nuts and started hitting people, swearing all the while. At first I thought he was a hijacker and I was going to die on that plane! Thank goodness several crew members and passengers were able to subdue him and handcuff him into a back-row seat. But we still had hours over the Atlantic before the pilot could land, so we had to listen to him screaming profanity. Finally, a passenger who was a pediatrician injected him with a sedative."

"Did they arrest him?" you want to know.

"As soon as we got on the ground. Police cars were everywhere. He just kept muttering, 'I thought they were going to kill me.'" She shudders. "But the flight attendants and airline officials were wonderful. They told us to write to the airline, explain the details, and ask for a refund.

"Of course, I was late and unprepared for my presentation. When they heard what happened, the folks in our Montreal office just handed me a cup of herbal tea, sat me on a couch with a blanket, and told me to forget about making any presentations that day."

Your task: Samantha leaves you her ticket stubs and other documents. She's expecting you to write the refund request to British Airways Ticket Refunds Canada, 1217 Sinclair Avenue, Toronto, ON M3T 5V2. Before you begin, consider these questions.[4]

1. For the purpose of this exercise, what details will you need to make up to write the request?
2. Will you use a direct or indirect approach? Why?
3. What tone should you adopt? What should you avoid?
4. How will you support the claim?
5. What would be an effective closing for this request?

7. Planning a Letter: Intercultural Condolences Letter conveying sympathy at Xerox.

You've been working two years as administrative assistant to Kathleen Wilson, director of global workforce diversity at Xerox Canada's Learning Centre in Toronto, Ontario. After listening to so many of her speeches on maintaining multicultural sensitivity in the workplace, you know you're facing a sensitive situation right now. You need to stop and think before you act.

Your co-worker Chana Panichpapiboon's husband was killed in a bus accident yesterday, along with 19 others. The bus skidded on icy pavement into a deep ravine, tipping over and crushing the occupants before rescue workers could get to them.

You met Chana's husband, Surin, last year at a company banquet. You can still picture his warm smile and the easy way he joked with you and others over chicken Florentine, even though you were complete strangers to him. He was only 32 years old, and he left Chana with two children, a 12-year-old boy, Arsa, and a 10-year-old girl, Veera. His death is a terrible tragedy.

Normally, you'd write a condolence letter immediately. But Chana Panichpapiboon is a native of Thailand, and so was Surin. You know you'd better do a little research first. Is Chana Buddhist or Catholic? Is there anything about the typical Western practice of expressing sympathy that might be inappropriate or offensive?

After making some discreet inquiries among Chana's closest friends at work, you learn that she is Theravada Buddhist, as are most people in Thailand. In a reference book your boss lends you about doing business around the world, you read that in Thailand, "the person takes precedence over rule or law" and "people gain their social position as a result of karma, not personal achievement," which means Chana may believe in reincarnation. However, the book also says that Theravada Buddhists are free to choose which precepts of their religion, if any, they will follow. So Chana's beliefs are still a mystery.

You do know that her husband was very important to her and much loved by all their family. That, at least, is universal. And you're considering using a poetic line you remember, "The hand of time lightly lays, softly soothing sorrow's wound." Is it appropriate?

You've decided to handwrite the condolence note on a blank greeting card you've found that bears a peaceful, "Eastern-flavour" image. You know you're risking a cultural gaffe, but you don't want to commit the offence of not writing at all. Use the following questions to help you think through your choices before you begin writing:[5]

1. If you had to choose among these sentences, which one would make the best opening?
   a. I was so sorry to hear the news about your husband.
   b. What a terrible tragedy you have suffered.
   c. If there's anything I can do for you, Chana, please let me know.
   d. You and your children must be so upset, and who could blame you?
2. In the body of the letter, you want to express something meaningful, but you're concerned about Chana's beliefs and you're not sure what's safe. Choose the best idea from the following:
   a. You could quote the poem about "the hand of time" mentioned in the case.
   b. You might say something about the bus driver's terrible carelessness on slippery pavement.
   c. You could express your sorrow for Chana's children.
   d. You could mention something nice about Surin you learned during your brief meeting.

3. For your closing paragraph, which of these ideas is best?
   a. Take a moment to express your thoughts about death and the hereafter.
   b. Say something positive and encouraging about Chana.
   c. Explain that you don't understand her religious beliefs and aren't sure what's appropriate to say at this time.
   d. All of the above.
4. In the following list, circle all of the words you should avoid as you write:
   a. Death
   b. Departure
   c. Karma
   d. Unbearable

Now write the condolence letter in your own words. Remember that sincerity is the most important tool in overcoming differences of custom or tradition.

8. **Revising a Letter: Betting the Company** A team-written letter from Bombardier replying to questions about new aircraft plans.

You're part of a team in the communication department at Bombardier and you've been handed the following form letter, which was written by a temporary worker assisting the corporate chairman. Clearly the letter needs improvement. Your group has been asked to undertake the project, since this letter replying to routine requests for information will be going out to customers, suppliers, the media, and anyone else who inquires about Bombardier's plans for developing the new Sonic Swift aircraft.

Your task: Working with your classmates as a team, read and discuss the problems you find in the letter, based on what you've learned in this chapter. Then outline a new plan for the letter and choose one person to put your team's ideas in letter form, which you'll all review and discuss before turning in your new, improved version.

Name
Address
City, Province Postal Code
Country

Dear [name]:

We have been inundated with requests for information about Bombardier's plans to produce the new Sonic Swift high-speed jet since our announcement of this revolutionary design, which resulted from hundreds of hours of research into the future of commercial air travel. So please forgive us for responding to you with a form letter, as we cannot respond effectively to each and every individual who has written to us with an inquiry.

The new jets will take off and land safely on shorter runways, fit comfortably with smaller terminals and taxiways, fly longer ranges. For every 4825 km flown, they will shave one hour of traditional flying time because they travel at Mach .95 (20 percent faster than a 747). The new jets will cost airlines less to operate because of reduced flying time, and the new jets will offer consumers faster transport to their destination, featuring a sleek, delta-wing style, and they will be available in 2008.

For the first time, Bombardier's manufacturing division will use outside suppliers for basic parts, so that our engineers can focus their expertise on the sophisticated systems required by the Sonic Swift. We're excited about this new efficiency. We expect to reap many benefits from it as Bombardier continues to meet the future needs of air travellers, carriers, and the communities we serve.

Bombardier envisions that municipalities will be building many more smaller, suburban airports to overcome the traffic congestion now clogging major airport hubs, both in the air and on the ground. To aid in this positive development, we have designed our new Sonic Swift.

Sincerely,

Expand Your Knowledge

Best of the Web

The Medium and the Message Explore About.com's numerous links to sources of information on a variety of subjects. Use the search function to find "Public Relations and Marketing Communications" and follow links to tips on business writing with examples of letters, memos, and press releases. You'll find help from numerous guides on many business-related topics and a link to the Internet Public Library, where you can research your interests. You can even get online help with setting standards for a company's online communication.

www.about.com

Exercises

1. Both the chapter and this site offer guidelines for writing effective messages. List the "Seven C's" that characterize good letters and memos. If you use clear language in a routine message, is it still important to restrict yourself to one topic? Why or why not?
2. Even the best-run businesses sometimes disappoint their customers. Imagine that you have been asked to write a response to an angrily worded e-mail message that charges your company with fraud because a product ordered through the Web has not arrived. Which of the 10 "secrets" of writing business letters do you think would be most useful in shaping your reply?
3. Describe some similarities and differences between a memo and a letter.

Exploring the Web on Your Own

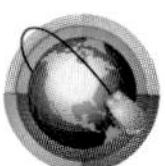

Review these chapter-related Web sites on your own to learn more about writing business messages.

1. Learn how to write effective thank-you notes by reviewing the steps at www.lepapier.invitations.com/content/brightideas/intro.mhtml.
2. Turn praise into prose when writing letters of recommendation by following the steps at resume.monster.ca/coverletter/recommendation.

Learn Interactively

Interactive Study Guide

Visit the Companion Website at www.pearsoned.ca/bovee. For Chapter 7, take advantage of the interactive "Study Guide" to test your chapter knowledge. Get instant feedback on whether you need additional studying.

This site offers a variety of additional resources: The "Research Area" helps you locate a wealth of information to use in course assignments. The "Study Hall" helps you succeed in this course by offering support with writing and study skills, time management and career skills, as well as numerous other resources.

Peak Performance Grammar and Mechanics

Use the Peak Performance Grammar and Mechanics CD to test your skill with punctuation. In the "Punctuation I" section, take the Pretest to determine whether you have any weak areas. Then review those areas in the Refresher Course. Take the Follow-Up Test to check your grasp of punctuation. For an extra challenge or advanced practice, take the Advanced Test.

Cases

Apply each step in Figure 7.1 on page 150 to the following cases, as assigned by your instructor:

1. Unhappy customer: Claim letter from you requesting an adjustment

As a consumer, you've probably bought something that didn't work right, or paid for a service that did not turn out the way you expected. Maybe it was a pair of jeans with a rip in a seam that you didn't find until you got home, or a watch that broke a week after you bought it. Or maybe your family hired a lawn service to do some yard work—and no one from the company showed up on the day promised. When a man finally appeared, he did not do what he'd been hired for, but did other things that wound up damaging valuable plants.

In either case, you'd be wise to write a claim letter asking for a refund, repair, replacement, or other adjustment. You'll need to include all the details of the transaction, plus your contact address and phone number.

Your Task To practise writing claim letters, choose an experience like this from your own background or make up details for these imaginary situations. If your experience is real, you might want to mail the letter. The reply you receive will provide a good test of your claim-writing skills!

2. Step on it: Letter to Floorgraphics requesting information about underfoot advertising

You work for Mary Utanpitak, owner of Better Bike and Ski Shop. You're always unpacking promotional displays and posters from manufacturers, and Mary has you store the extras in the back room or even take some home, since you love ski posters. But now a manufacturer wants to lease a piece of the store's floor!

The Raliegh sales representative, Ruth Beeker, met with Mary yesterday, urging her to sign a contract with Floorgraphics. That company leases floor space from retail stores, and then creates and sells floor ads to manufacturers like Raliegh. Floorgraphics will pay Mary a fee for leasing the floor space, as well as a percentage for every ad it sells. Mary was definitely interested, and turned to you after Beeker left.

"Ruth says that advertising decals on the floor in front of the product reach consumers right where they're standing when making a decision," explained Mary. "She says the ads increase sales from 25 percent to 75 percent."

You both look down at the dusty floor, and Mary laughs. "It seems funny that manufacturers will pay hard cash to put their names where customers are going to track dirt all over them! But if Ruth's telling the truth, we could profit three ways: from the leasing fee, the increased sales, and the share in ad revenues. That's not so funny."

Your Task Mary Utanpitak wants you to write to CEO Richard Rebh at Floorgraphics, Inc. (5 Vaughn Drive., Timmons, ON P8N 8R6) asking for financial details and practical information about the ads. For example, how will you clean your floors? Who installs and removes the ads? Can you terminate the lease if you don't like them? She'll sign the letter, but since you've been studying business communication, she thinks you'll do a better job writing the request.[6]

E-MAIL SKILLS WEB SKILLS 3. A juicy position: E-mail requesting information about careers at Jamba Juice

You did not expect to find a job while working out at 24-Hour Fitness, but you're willing to explore an opportunity when it appears. As you were buying a smoothie at the Jamba Juice bar inside the gym, you overheard the manager there talking about the company's incentives for employees, especially those interested in becoming managers. You ask her about it and she suggests you log on to the company's Web site (www.jambajuice.com) for more information.

You're still in business school, and you need a part-time job. Finding one at a company that offers a good future after graduation would be even better than simply earning some money to keep you going now. You check the Jamba Juice Web site.

You discover that the juice-bar chain has created a good reputation in the health, fitness, and nutrition industry. Also, you can submit your resumé for an entry-level job online. That sounds promising. If you could start now while finishing your degree, you'd be in a prime spot for promotion once you graduate.

But when you look at the jobs section, you find the information a little confusing. The "General Manager J.U.I.C.E. Plan" seems to be about profit-sharing, but the details are not fully explained. You'd like to know more.

Your Task You're going to write an e-mail message requesting additional information about careers and advancement at Jamba Juice. First, visit www.jambajuice.com and the link to "jobs" to learn all that you can. Then compose your message. Ask for clarification on any points you don't understand, or ask for further instructions on submitting your application. You might want to mention that you're still in school, studying business.[7]

4. Lighten up: E-mail reply to a Web site designer at Organizers Unlimited

When Kendra Williams, owner of Organizers Unlimited, wanted to create a Web site to sell her Superclean Organizer, she asked you, her assistant, to find a designer. You researched it and found three promising individuals. Williams chose Pete Womack, whose resumé impressed both of you. Now he's e-mailed his first design proposal and Williams is not happy.

"I detest cluttered Web sites!" she explodes. "This home page has too many graphics and animations, too much 'dancing baloney.' He must have included at least 500 kilobytes of bouncing cotton balls and jogging soap bars! Clever, maybe, but we don't want it! If the home page takes too long to load, our customers won't wait for it and we'll lose sales."

Williams' dislike of clutter is what inspired her to invent the Superclean Organizer in the first place, a neat device for organizing bathroom items.

Your Task "You found him," says Williams, "now you can answer and tell him what's wrong with this design." Before you write the reply to Womack explaining the need for a simpler home page, read some of the articles offering tips at www.sitepoint.com. Use these ideas to support your message.[8]

5. Satellite farming: Letter granting credit from Deere & Company

Your favourite task as a credit assistant at Deere & Company in Saskatoon, Saskatchewan, is writing to farmers like Arlen Ruestman and telling them that yes, the company will grant them credit to purchase new equipment.

Ruestman's farm is in Moose Jaw, Saskatchewan, and he wants to buy your company's new GreenStar satellite system for farmers. This technology, the Global Positioning System (GPS), uses a series of satellites orbiting Earth to pinpoint (to the metre) exactly where a farmer is positioned at any given moment as he drives his GreenStar-equipped combine over a field. For farmers like Ruestman, GPS means that even 4000 hectares of corn or soybeans can be managed down to the last square metre.

For example, using the GreenStar system, farmers can map and analyze characteristics such as acidity, soil type, or crop yields from a given area. Using this information, they know exactly how much herbicide or fertilizer to spread over precisely which spot, thereby eliminating waste and achieving better results. Farmers can analyze why crops are performing well in some areas and not so well in others. They can even program farm equipment to treat only problem areas. For instance, Ruestman might discover and spray an insect infestation only two metres wide, without having to spray the entire field if it's not infested.

Some farms have already saved as much as $25 a hectare on fertilizers alone. For 4000 hectares, that's $10 000 a year. Once Ruestman installs your GreenStar precision package on his old combine, he should have no problem saving enough to pay off the $7350 credit account you're about to grant him.

Your Task Write a letter to Mr. Ruestman (P.O. Box 4067, Moose Jaw, Saskatchewan S7K 3X2), informing him of the good news.[9]

6. Midnight mission: Thank-you letter at the Blue Marble bookstore

Tina Moore, owner of the Blue Marble bookstore in Fredericton, New Brunswick, likes to please her customers. You are her lead salesperson and, with your co-workers, you've been working hard to prepare for the biggest book sales party your store has ever hosted. Tonight's the night.

No one can argue with the popularity of author J. K. Rowling's *Harry Potter* books (and the movies) about a boy who discovers he's a wizard-in-training and attends a special school for wizards only. Rowling's Canadian publisher, Raincoast, calls the book a "phenomenon" in publishing history, "beyond anything we imagined." It's become a bookstore tradition to host a release party when the newest edition in the series becomes available.

By agreement with the publishers, stores in Canada are not allowed to sell the new Harry Potter books they receive until a specific, "strict on-sale" date. Many stores open with a big party at midnight on that day. Parents and their children flock to the stores in pyjamas, and often buy all the copies on hand before morning.

Like other adults, you've enjoyed the clever stories of Harry and his friends at Hogwarts school of wizardry. When Moore brought up the subject of a Harry Potter party, you quickly volunteered to coordinate the preparations.

Tonight, when the clock chimes midnight, customers will be ushered in by you and your co-workers in costume. An animal trainer with an owl that looks like Harry's "Hedwig" will be there. You'll serve oatmeal and Harry's favourite "butter beer" (apple juice and ginger ale over dry ice) from big black cauldrons the staff's been building all week. The kids will get free lightning-bolt stickers (to create forehead scars like Harry's), and black, round-rimmed imitation "Harry Potter spectacles." It's going to be great fun.

Your Task You've all been donating your free time sewing costumes, making hats, and inventing butter-beer recipes. Moore has asked you, as coordinator, to write a thank-you letter to the entire staff, and she wants you to co-sign it with her. She's going to include a $25 gift certificate in each envelope and give them out tonight before the party begins.[10]

7. Come back to us: Letter from EDS to dot-com deserters

"Now's our chance to get them back," announces director Tom Templeton at a human resources staff meeting. You're his assistant, and for a moment you're confused.

"Get who back?"

"Everyone who left to join dot-com start-ups. You know how many people we lost when the Internet's promise of overnight fortunes lured away some of our best employees. But now it's our turn."

"You mean invite back the 550 employees we lost to dot-coms in recent years?" you ask.

"Exactly. I read that 12 000 dot-com jobs were cut in a nine-month period last year. That number is probably higher now."

You see his point and smile. He'll save EDS considerable money and trouble if some of these individuals return. Finding and keeping good employees is one of the greatest costs of operating any business.

"As dot-coms fail, some of our best people may be out there looking for jobs," Templeton adds. "Are we going to let our competitors have them?"

Your Task After the meeting, Templeton asks you to create a form letter he can send to ex-employees, telling them that EDS will welcome them back if their dot-com jobs haven't worked out as expected.[11]

8. Ranch country: Letter offering a regional sales position with Lumenlight

Alberta rancher Jerry Lumen hired you when his invention, the Lumenlight, first started to sell. Now Lumenlight, Inc. earns more than $2 million annually, but you're still Jerry's right-hand assistant.

Lumen invented the portable light to fit on his truck so he wouldn't have to get out in the freezing winters to check on his livestock. Then fishing enthusiasts, hunters, and boaters around the world discovered Lumenlight, and sales representatives were soon working in every province and overseas—all except Alberta. Lumen refused to give up his personal territory until he found the right person.

He's finally decided on Robert Victor, who also grew up on an Alberta ranch. Victor knows the territory, and best of all, he's been doing well selling agricultural equipment in Manitoba for two years. Lumen liked him the moment they shook hands.

"He's got the job if he wants it," Lumen says. "Better send him an offer before someone else grabs him. He can start as soon as he's settled."

Your Task Compose the letter offering Victor salary plus commission "as discussed," with full benefits (paid vacation and health and dental insurance) after six months of employment. Victor's address is P.O. Box 437, Portage La Prairie, MB R3H 0J9.[12]

Improve Your Grammar, Mechanics, and Usage

Level 1: Self-Assessment—Periods, Question Marks, and Exclamation Points

Review Sections 2.1, 2.2, and 2.3 in the Handbook of Grammar, Mechanics, and Usage, and then look at the following 15 items.

In items 1–15, add periods, question marks, and exclamation points wherever they are appropriate.

1. Dr Eleanor H Hutton has requested information on TaskMasters, Inc
2. That qualifies us as a rapidly growing new company, don't you think
3. Our president, Daniel Gruber, is a CGA On your behalf, I asked him why he started the company
4. In the past three years, we have experienced phenomenal growth of 800 percent
5. Contact me at 1358 N Bluff Avenue, Lethbridge, AB T1K 1L6
6. Jack asked, "Why does he want to know Maybe he plans to become a competitor"
7. The debt load fluctuates with the movement of the Bank of Canada prime rate
8. I can't believe we could have missed such a promising opportunity

9. Is consumer loyalty extinct Yes and no.
10. Johnson and Kane, Inc has gone out of business What a surprise
11. Will you please send us a cheque today so that we can settle your account
12. Mr James R Capp will be our new CEO, beginning January 20, 2005
13. The rag doll originally sold for $1098, but we have lowered the price to a mere $599
14. Will you be able to make the presentation at the conference, or should we find someone else
15. So I ask you, "When will we admit defeat" Never

Level 2: Workplace Applications

The following items contain numerous errors in grammar, capitalization, punctuation, abbreviation, number style, word division, and vocabulary. Rewrite each sentence in the space provided, correcting all errors. Write *C* in the space after any sentence that is already correct.

1. Attached to both the transit station and the Fairmont hotel, one doesn't even need to step outside the convention centre to go from train to meeting room.

2. According to national statistics, 61 percent of the countries employers have less than 5 workers.

3. "The problem", said Business Owner Mike Millorn, "Was getting vendor's of raw materials to take my endeavour serious."

4. After pouring over trade journals, quizzing industry experts, and talks with other snack makers, the Harpers' decided to go in the pita chip business.

5. A Mac with half as much RAM and a slower processor is as fast or faster than a PC.

6. The couple has done relatively little advertising, instead they give away samples in person at trade shows, cooking demonstrations, and in grocery stores.

7. CME Information Services started by videotaping doctor's conventions, and selling the recorded presentations to nonattending physicians that wanted to keep track of the latest developments.

8. For many companies, the two biggest challenges to using intranets are: getting people to use it and content freshness.

9. Company meetings including 'lunch and learn' sessions are held online often.

10. Most Children's Orchard franchisees, are women between the ages of 30-50; first time business owners lacking even basic computer skills.

11. Joining the company in 1993, she had watched it expand and grow from a single small office to a entire floor of a skyscraper.

12. One issue that effected practically everyone was that they needed to train interns.

13. The Web site includes information on subjects as mundane as the filling out of a federal express form, and as complex as researching a policy issue.

14. "Some management theories are good, but how many people actually implement them the right way?", says Jack Hartnett President of D. L. Rogers Corp.

15. Taking orders through car windows, customers are served by roller-skating carhops at Sonic restaurants.

Level 3: Document Critique

The following document may contain errors in grammar, capitalization, punctuation, abbreviation, number style, vocabulary, and spelling. You will also find errors relating to topics in this chapter. For example, consider the organization and relevance of material as you improve this routine request for information. Correct all errors using standard proof-reading marks (see Appendix C).

Risa Zenaili

883 Rue St. Hubert Aven.

Chicoutimi, PC G7H 1Z6

418-555-9983

rzenaili@bellca.net

March 13 2004

Tharita Jones Owner

Subway Restaurant

120 Boulevard Cité des Jeunes

Chicoutimi, QC G8P 2A4

Dear Ms. Jones,

I am investigatting careers in vareous fast-food enviroments, since I expect to complete my degree in business administration within the next 3 years and that should leave me enough time to grow into a management position. Subway gave me your name when I asked for a franchise owner who might be willing to answer some questions about managment careers with the company. You may be able to provide the kind of informaton I'll never get from coporate brochures.

For example I'd like to know how long I can expect to work at an entry level before promotions are considered. How many levels must I rise before reaching assistant manager. And how many before I would be considered as manager, assuming I've performed well. Sometimes a person is promoted because they are qualified and sometimes it just because they willing to work long hours, so I want to know this before I commit myself!

I'm looking for a company that will offer me the best future in the most promising environment and since there are so many to choose from I am trying to be very careful in making this choice. I'd be really gratefull if you could take a moment to share any advice or encouragment you might have for me because as you know this kind of decision is one we all must make one day and it will effect us for a long, long time to come

I also like to know: How many hour a week can I expect to work to be on management career track? Once I reach management level: will those hours increase?

What qualifications do you look for in your managers and assitant managers? Plus: Benefits the company offers, special training—availibility and qualifications; how to improve my chances for promation if I choose Subway?

Please let me hear from you before the end of the month.

If you prefer to call than write; you reach me at 418 555-9983 day or evening. My cellphone number is (418) 555-8838. Or you can send a reply to me at the address above or to my e-mail address rzeinali@bellca.net

Sincerely:

Risa Zeinali

How Direct Is Too Direct?

Is it possible to be too direct, even if you're simply requesting information? At an event in Mexico, the president of the United States spoke bluntly of political realities, but the president of France spoke more abstractly—his style more grand, his words more beautiful. One man addressed the issues directly; the other was less direct. Which one had greater impact?

Neither speech changed global relationships, but the U.S. president was seen as a product of his outspoken culture, whereas the French president was seen as at least making his listeners feel better for a while. Countries such as France, Mexico, Japan, Saudi Arabia, Italy, and the Philippines all tend toward high-context cultures (see discussion in Chapter 1). That is, people in those countries depend on shared knowledge and inferred messages to communicate; they gather meaning more from context and less from direct statement. On a continuum of high-to-low context cultures, Canada falls between France, Britain, and the United States, having been influenced by our English and French heritage and by our proximity to the United States. So, although people in the United States believe that being direct is civil, considerate, and honest, people in high-context cultures and mid-context cultures, such as Canada, sometimes view that same directness as abrupt, rude, and intrusive—even dishonest and offensive. You might think you're doing a good thing by offering a little honest and constructive criticism to your Italian assistant, but doing so may actually hurt your assistant's dignity and could even be devastating. In fact, in high-context cultures, don't say outright, "You are wrong." People know when they've made a mistake, but if you put it into words in high-context cultures, you cause them to lose face.

To determine whether your international audience will appreciate a direct or an implied message, consider your audience's attitudes toward four factors: destiny, time, authority, and logic.

- **Destiny.** Do people in this culture believe they can control events themselves? Or are events seen as predetermined and uncontrollable? If you're supervising employees who believe that a construction deadline is controlled by fate, they may not understand your crisp e-mail message requesting them to stay on schedule; they may even find it insulting.
- **Time.** Do people in this culture believe that time is exact, precise, and not to be wasted? Or do they view time as relative, relaxed, and necessary for developing interpersonal relationships? If you believe that time is money and you try to get straight to business in your memo to your Japanese manager, your message may be overlooked in the confusion over your lack of relationship skills and your disregard for social propriety.
- **Authority.** Do the people in this culture conduct business more autocratically or more democratically? In Mexico, rank and status are highly valued, so when communicating with people who have less authority than you do, you may need to be even more direct than you're used to being in Canada. And when communicating with people who have more authority than you do, you may need to be much less direct in Mexico than you're used to being in Canada.
- **Logic.** Do the people in this culture pursue logic in a straight line from point A to point B? Or do they communicate in circular or spiral patterns of logic? If you organize a message in a straightforward and direct manner, your message may be considered illogical, unclear, and disorganized.

You may need to ask not only how direct to be in written messages but also whether to write at all; perhaps a phone call or a visit would be more appropriate. By finding out how much or how little a culture tends toward high-context communication, you can decide whether to be direct or to rely on nuance when communicating with people in that culture.

Applications for Success

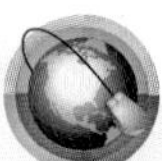

For more information on the subject of intercultural communication, go to www.executiveplanet.com.

Answer the following questions:

1. Research a high-context culture such as Japan, Korea, or China, and write a one- or two-paragraph summary of how someone in that culture would go about requesting information.
2. When you are writing to someone in a high-context culture, would it be better to (a) make the request directly in the interest of clarity or (b) try to match your audience's unfamiliar logic and make your request indirectly? Explain your answer.
3. Germany is a low-context culture; by comparison, France and England are more high-context. These three translations of the same message were posted on a lawn in Switzerland:
   - **a.** German: "Walking on the grass is forbidden."
   - **b.** English: "Please do not walk on the grass."
   - **c.** French: "Those who respect their environment will avoid walking on the grass."

How does the language of each sign reflect the way information is conveyed in the cultural context of each nation? Write a brief (two- to three-paragraph) explanation.

Writing Bad-News Messages

8

After studying this chapter, you will be able to

1 Apply the three-step writing process to bad-news messages
2 Show how to achieve an audience-centred tone and explain why it helps readers
3 Describe the differences between the direct and indirect approaches to bad-news messages, and indicate when it's appropriate to use each one
4 Discuss the three techniques for saying no as clearly and kindly as possible

From the Real World

"Often audiences seem to have a premonition that bad news is coming and just as often move to a worst-case scenario. Similarly, bad news is difficult to contain; rumour often precedes fact. Credibility, for you and your organization, can hinge on the speed with which you get the difficult information out to communities, audiences, or individuals."

–Kevin Gass
Vice-President, Marketing and Communication
B.C. Lotteries Corporation

Bad news in the business world comes in all shapes and sizes. But even though bad news may be commonplace, most business people don't know how to communicate this type of news effectively. Working in public relations for more than 20 years, Kevin Gass has helped dozens of companies communicate bad news on such topics as health-care service cuts, Vancouver's loss of an NBA team, plant closings, and other unfavourable situations. Many companies make the mistake of pulling back from communicating, but as Gass explains, "the key is to deal effectively, fully, and quickly with the bad news. Ideally companies should turn the situation into an opportunity or, at the very least, get back to business as quickly as possible." Of course, communicating bad news isn't always easy, but the proper tone and approach can help people accept and understand your message. Public relations experts tell us that "most people will forgive just about anything if you admit to it, take responsibility for it, explain how it happened, and tell what you are doing to ensure it won't occur again."[1]

Using the Three-Step Writing Process for Bad-News Messages

Saying no is difficult.

Nobody likes bad news—as Kevin Gass can attest. People don't like to get it, and they don't like to give it. Saying no can put knots in your stomach and cost you hours of sleep. The word *no* is terse and abrupt, so negative that a lot of people have trouble saying it. And for most, it's the toughest word to hear or understand. But the most damaging "no" is usually the one you don't explain.[2] The three-step writing process can help you write bad-news messages that are more effective and less damaging (see Figure 8.1 on page 183).

Step 1: Planning Your Bad-News Messages

Analysis, investigation, and adaptation help you avoid alienating your readers.

To be effective, bad-news messages require extremely careful analysis. Analysis helps you know how your readers will receive your message and whether they prefer receiving it directly or indirectly, in person or in writing. Investigation provides you with all the facts your audience will need to accept the negative message. Finally, maintaining a good relationship with your audience is particularly important, in order to avoid alienating readers, so be sure to adapt your medium and tone to your audience.

Step 2: Writing Your Bad-News Messages

Appropriate organization helps readers accept your negative news.

Because your main idea is negative, be careful to define it and cover relevant points thoroughly and logically. Choosing between the direct and indirect approaches takes on added importance in bad-news messages. You need to decide whether to open with the bad news or to prepare your readers with a cogent explanation before giving them the negative bits. Also, pay special attention to word choice so that you can create sentences and paragraphs that are tactful and diplomatic.

Step 3: Completing Your Bad-News Messages

Careful revision ensures that your bad-news message is organized properly, says what you want it to say, and does so concisely and clearly. It gives you a chance to make sure that your design is appropriate for the bad news and contributes to your efforts to be sensitive. As always, proofreading your message helps ensure that misunderstandings won't arise from typos, errors in spelling, or problems with mechanics.

Strategies for Bad-News Messages

Five goals of bad-news messages

- Give the bad news
- Ensure its acceptance
- Maintain the reader's goodwill
- Maintain the organization's good image
- Reduce future correspondence on the matter

Whatever the details of your particular message, when you have bad news, you want your readers to feel that they have been taken seriously, and you want them to agree that your news is fair and reasonable. When delivering bad news, you have five main goals:

- To convey the bad news
- To gain acceptance for it
- To maintain as much goodwill as possible with your audience
- To maintain a good image for your organization
- To reduce or eliminate the need for future correspondence on the matter

Accomplishing so many goals in a single message is not easy. But you can convey negative news more effectively by following these guidelines: First, adopt an audience-centred tone. Second, organize your message to meet your audience's needs and expectations by using either the direct approach, which presents the main idea before the supporting data (fully described in Chapter 7), or the indirect approach, which presents the supporting data before the main idea.

Creating an Audience-Centred Tone

When establishing tone, strive for

- Firmness
- Fairness
- Goodwill
- Respect

Your tone helps your readers accept that your bad news represents a firm decision. Your audience-centred focus helps readers understand that, under the circumstances, your decision was fair and reasonable. Your tone helps your audience remain well disposed toward your business. And not least, your audience-centred tone helps readers preserve their pride.

Experts suggest that conveying bad news in person requires listening to your audience before talking—building trust by letting people say what they feel. Bad news involves emotions, and you must acknowledge these emotions in your communication.[3] However, if you're delivering bad news in writing, you're unable to "listen" to your audience first. Nevertheless, you can certainly do your research up front and learn as much as you can about your audience. Only then are you able to demonstrate in writing that you're aware of your reader's needs, concerns, and feelings.

FIGURE 8.1 Applying the Three-Step Writing Process to Bad-News Messages

Planning	Writing	Completing
Analyze the Situation • Verify specific purpose is worth pursuing. • Know how readers react to bad news. • Know what readers want: bad news or reasons first. **Investigate the Topic** • Ensure information is reliable and accurate. • Ensure facts support negative news. • Gather all relevant facts readers need. **Adapt to the Audience** • Verify effectiveness of written channel. • Adapt medium and tone to audience. • Pay particular attention to readers' feelings. 1	**Organize the Message** • Carefully define negative main idea. • Cover relevant points thoroughly. • Group relevant points logically. • Choose the direct or indirect approach with special care. **Compose the Message** • Adapt style and tone to readers' culture. • Pay special attention to word choice. • Create sentences and paragraphs carefully. 2	**Revise the Message** • Verify message is organized properly. • Be sure it says what you want it to. • Ensure message gives bad news concisely and clearly. **Produce the Message** • Ensure design doesn't detract from bad news. • Ensure design doesn't detract from your efforts to be sensitive. **Proofread the Message** • Correct spelling and mechanical errors. • Correct any alignment problems. • Ensure that the print quality is acceptable. 3

To adopt an audience-centred tone, pay close attention to several techniques:

Several techniques will help you establish an audience-centred tone.

- **Use the "you" attitude.** The "you" attitude is crucial to every message you write, but it's especially important in bad-news messages. Point out how your decision might actually further your audience's goals. Convey concern by looking for the best in your audience. And assume that your audience is interested in being fair, even when they are at fault.
- **Choose positive words.** The words you choose can make a letter either offensive or acceptable. You can ease disappointment by using positive words rather than negative, counterproductive ones (see Table 8.1 on page 184). Just be sure not to hide the bad news.[4] Remember, you want to convey the bad news, not cover it up, even when you use the indirect approach.
- **Use respectful language.** Protect your audience's pride by using language that conveys respect and avoids an accusing tone. For instance, when your audience is at fault, observe the "you" attitude by avoiding the word *you*. Use impersonal language to explain audience mistakes in an inoffensive way. Say, "The appliance won't work after being immersed in water" instead of "The appliance doesn't work because you immersed it in water."

Using the Direct Approach

If you know that your audience prefers the bad news first, or if the situation is minor and the news will cause your audience little disappointment, use the direct approach:

Use the direct approach when your negative answer or information will have little personal impact.

- **Opening.** Start with a clear statement of the bad news.
- **Body.** Proceed to the reasons for the decision (perhaps offering alternatives).
- **Close.** End with a positive statement aimed at maintaining a good relationship with the audience.

Stating the bad news first has two advantages: (1) It makes a shorter message possible, and (2) the audience needs less time to reach the main idea of the message, the bad news itself.

Table 8.1 Choosing Positive Words

Avoid a Negative Tone	Use a Positive Tone
I *cannot understand* what you mean.	Please clarify your request.
There will be a *delay* in your order.	We will ship your order as soon as possible.
Your account is in *error.*	Corrections have been made to your account.
The breakage was not our *fault.*	The merchandise was broken during shipping.
Sorry for your inconvenience.	The enclosed coupon will save you $5 next time.
I was *shocked* to learn that you're unhappy.	Your letter reached me yesterday.
The enclosed statement is *wrong.*	Please recheck the enclosed statement.

Some bad-news situations are more appropriate for directness than others. Use a direct approach when

- You know from experience that your audience prefers reading bad news first in any message.
- Your company prefers internal correspondence to be brief and direct regardless of whether the message is negative.
- The message, although negative, is routine and likely to have little impact.
- The intended readers see bad news frequently and expect it (such as job seekers).[5]
- You want to present an image of firmness.

Using the Indirect Approach

Use the indirect approach when some preparation will help your audience accept your bad news.

Beginning a bad news message with a blunt "no" could prevent some people from reading or listening to your reasons. Some people prefer an explanation first, and for them you would use the indirect approach, easing them into your message by explaining your reasons before delivering the bad news:

- **Opening.** Start with a buffer.
- **Body.** Continue with a logical, neutral explanation of the reasons for the bad news; then follow with a diplomatic statement of the bad news (emphasizing any good news and de-emphasizing the bad).
- **Close.** End with a positive, forward-looking statement that is helpful and friendly.

Presenting your reasons first increases your chances of gaining audience acceptance by gradually preparing readers for the negative news to come. The indirect approach follows a four-part sequence: buffer, reasons, bad news, positive close.

Begin with a Buffer

A buffer is a neutral lead-in to bad news.

A **buffer** is a neutral, noncontroversial statement that is closely related to the point of the message. Some critics believe that using a buffer is manipulative and dishonest, and thus unethical. But buffers are unethical only if they're insincere. Breaking bad news with kindness and courtesy is the humane way. Considering the feelings of others is never dishonest, and that consideration helps your audience accept your message. An effective buffer is tricky to write. A good buffer expresses your appreciation for being thought of, assures the reader of your attention to the request, compliments the reader, or indicates your understanding of the reader's needs. To write effective buffers, try to make them

- **Sincere.** Never insult your audience with insincere flattery or self-promoting blather. An effective buffer never makes readers feel they are being set up or "snowed."
- **Relevant.** Don't use an unrelated buffer. You will seem to be avoiding the issue. You'll appear manipulative and unethical, and you'll lose your audience's respect. In fact, try to base your buffer on statements made by the reader. Doing so shows that you have listened well.
- **Not misleading.** Avoid implying that good news will follow. Building up your audience's expectations at the beginning only makes the actual bad news even more surprising. Imagine your reaction to the following openings:

  Your resumé indicates that you would be well suited for a management trainee position with our company.

  Your resumé shows very clearly why you are interested in becoming a management trainee with our company.

  The second opening emphasizes the applicant's interpretation of her qualifications rather than the company's evaluation, so it's less misleading but still positive.
- **Neutral.** Avoid saying "no." An audience encountering the blunt refusal right at the beginning usually reacts negatively to the rest of the message, no matter how reasonable and well phrased it is.
- **Respectful.** Avoid using a know-it-all tone. When you use phrases such as "you should be aware that," readers expect your lecture to lead to a negative response, so they resist the rest of your message.
- **Succinct.** Avoid wordy and irrelevant phrases and sentences. Sentences such as "We have received your letter," "This letter is in reply to your request," and "We are writing in response to your request" are irrelevant. Make better use of the space by referring directly to the subject of the letter.
- **Assertive.** Avoid apologizing. Unless warranted by extreme circumstances, an apology only weakens the following explanation of your unfavourable news.
- **Brief.** Avoid writing a buffer that is too long. Identify something that both you and your audience are interested in and agree on before proceeding in a businesslike way.

To write an effective buffer, make it sincere, relevant, not misleading, neutral, respectful, succinct, assertive, and brief.

Table 8.2 on page 186 shows several types of buffers you could use to open a bad-news message tactfully. After you've composed a buffer, evaluate it by asking yourself four questions: Is it pleasant? Is it relevant? Is it neutral, saying neither yes nor no? Does it provide for a smooth transition to the reasons that follow? If you can answer yes to every question, you can proceed confidently to the next section of your message.

Follow with Reasons

Cover the more positive points first; then move to the less positive ones. Provide enough detail for the audience to understand your reasons, but be concise; a long, roundabout explanation may make your audience impatient. Your goal is to explain *why* you have reached your decision before you explain *what* that decision is. If you present your reasons effectively, they should convince your audience that your decision is justified, fair, and logical.

Giving reasons shows that your decision is reasonable and fair.

Highlight readers' benefits rather than focusing on why the decision is good for you or your company. For example, when denying a request for credit, you can show how your decision will keep the person from becoming overextended financially. Facts and figures are often helpful when convincing readers that you're acting in their best interests.

Be tactful by focusing on reader benefits, not hiding company policy, and not apologizing.

Avoid hiding behind company policy to cushion the bad news. If you say, "Company policy forbids our hiring anyone who does not have two years' management experience," you seem to imply that you haven't considered the person on her or his own merits. Skilled and sympathetic communicators explain company policy (without referring to it as "policy") so that the audience can try to meet the requirements at a later time.

Table 8.2 Types of Buffers

Buffer	Strategy	Example
Agreement	Find a point on which you and the reader share similar views.	We both know how hard it is to make a profit in this industry.
Appreciation	Express sincere thanks for receiving something.	Your cheque for $127.17 arrived yesterday. Thank you.
Cooperation	Convey your willingness to help in any way you realistically can.	At Employee Services our job is to assist you.
Fairness	Assure the reader that you've closely examined and carefully considered the problem, or mention an appropriate action that has already been taken.	For the past week, we have carefully monitored those using the photocopying machine to see whether we can detect any pattern of use that might explain its frequent breakdowns.
Good news	Start with the part of your message that is favourable.	A replacement knob for your range is on its way, shipped February 10 via UPS.
Praise	Find an attribute or an achievement to compliment.	Your resumé shows an admirable breadth of experience, which should serve you well as you progress in your career.
Resale	Favourably discuss the product or company related to the subject of the letter.	With their heavy-duty, full-suspension hardware and fine veneers, the desks and file cabinets in our Montclair line have become a hit with value-conscious professionals.
Understanding	Demonstrate that you understand the reader's goals and needs.	So that you can more easily find the printer with the features you need, we are enclosing a brochure that describes all the Panasonic printers currently available.

Similarly, avoid apologizing when giving your reasons. Apologies are appropriate only when someone in your company has made a severe mistake or has done something terribly wrong. If no one in the company is at fault, an apology gives the wrong impression. For example, suppose that you're refusing the application of a management trainee. A tactfully worded letter might give these reasons for the decision not to hire:

> Because these management trainee positions are quite challenging, our human relations department has researched the qualifications needed to succeed in them. The findings show that the two most important qualifications are a bachelor's degree in business administration and two years' supervisory experience.

Well-written reasons are

- Detailed
- Tactful
- Individualized
- Unapologetic
- Positive

The paragraph does a good job of stating the reasons for the refusal because it

- Provides enough detail to make the reason for the refusal logically acceptable.
- Implies that the applicant is better off avoiding a program in which he or she would probably fail, given the background of potential co-workers.
- Explains the company's policy as logical rather than rigid.
- Offers no apology for the decision.
- Avoids negative personal expressions ("You do not meet our requirements").

Sometimes detailed reasons should not be provided.

Even though specific reasons help audiences accept bad news, reasons cannot always be given. Don't include reasons when they involve confidential, excessively complicated, or purely negative information or when they benefit only you or your firm (by enhancing the company's profits, for example). Instead, move directly to the next section.

State the Bad News

When the bad news is a logical outcome of the reasons that come before it, the audience is psychologically prepared to receive it. However, the audience may still reject your message if the bad news is handled carelessly. Four techniques are useful for saying no clearly and kindly.

To handle bad news carefully, use four techniques:

- De-emphasize the bad news visually and grammatically.
- Use a conditional statement.
- Tell what you did do, not what you didn't do.
- Be clear.

De-emphasize Bad News

- Minimize the space or time devoted to the bad news.
- Subordinate bad news in a complex or compound sentence ("My department is already shorthanded, so I'll need all my staff for at least the next two months"). This construction pushes the bad news into the middle of the sentence, the point of least emphasis.
- Embed bad news in the middle of a paragraph or use parenthetical expressions ("Our profits, which are down, are only part of the picture").

Use a Conditional Statement Use a conditional (*if* or *when*) statement to imply that the audience could have received, or might someday receive, a favourable answer ("When you have more managerial experience, you are welcome to reapply"). Such a statement could motivate applicants to improve their qualifications.

Say What You *Can* Do Tell the audience what you did do, can do, or will do rather than what you did not do, cannot do, or will not do. Say "We sell exclusively through retailers, and the one nearest you that carries our merchandise is . . ." rather than "We are unable to serve you, so please call your nearest dealer." By implying the bad news, you may not need to actually state it ("The five positions currently open have been staffed with people whose qualifications match our needs"). By focusing on the positive and implying the bad news, you soften the blow.

Don't let the bad news get lost by overemphasizing the positive.

Be Clear When implying bad news, be sure your audience understands the entire message—including the bad news. It would be unethical to overemphasize the positive. So if an implied message might leave doubt, state your decision in direct terms. Avoid overly blunt statements that are likely to cause pain and anger:

Instead of	Use
I *must refuse* your request.	I will be out of town on the day you need me.
We *must deny* your application.	The position has been filled.
I *am unable* to grant your request.	Contact us again when you have established . . .
We *cannot afford* to continue the program.	The program will conclude on May 1.
Much as I would like to attend . . .	Our budget meeting ends too late for me to attend.
We *must reject* your proposal.	We've accepted the proposal from AAA Builders.
We *must turn down* your extension request.	Please send in your payment by June 14.

End with a Positive Close

After giving your audience the bad news, end your message on an upbeat note. You might propose an attainable solution to the audience's problem ("The human resources department has offered to bring in temporary workers when I need them, and they would probably consider doing the same for you"). In a message to a customer or potential customer, an ending can include **resale information** (favourable comments about a product or service that the customer has already purchased) or **sales promotion** (favourable comments that encourage interest in goods or services the reader has not yet committed to purchase). If you've asked readers to decide between alternatives or to take some action, make sure that they know what to do, when to do it, and how to do it with ease. Whatever type of close you choose, follow these guidelines:

Make your close positive, final, optimistic, sincere, and confident.

- **Keep it positive.** Don't refer to, repeat, or apologize for the bad news, and refrain from expressing any doubt that your reasons will be accepted (avoid statements such as "I trust our decision is satisfactory").
- **Limit future correspondence.** Encourage additional communication *only* if you're willing to discuss your decision further (avoid wording such as "If you have further questions, please write").
- **Be optimistic about the future.** Don't anticipate problems (avoid statements such as "Should you have further problems, please let us know").
- **Be sincere.** Steer clear of clichés that are insincere in view of the bad news (avoid saying, "If we can be of any help, please contact us").
- **Be confident.** Don't show any doubt about keeping the person as a customer (avoid phrases such as "We hope you will continue to do business with us").

Types of Bad-News Messages

In the course of your business career, you will write various types of bad-news messages, from refusing credit to refusing requests and giving bad news about orders. Many of the messages that you'll be writing will fall into two major categories: negative answers to routine requests and negative organizational news.

Sending Negative Answers to Routine Requests

As a business person, you can't say yes to everyone. Occasionally, your response to routine requests must simply be "no." It's a mark of your skill as a communicator to be able to say no clearly and yet not cut yourself off from future dealings with the people you refuse.

Refusing Requests for Information

Use either the direct or the indirect approach to tell someone you cannot provide what has been requested.

When people ask you for information and you can't honour the request, you may answer with either the direct approach or the indirect approach. However, using the direct approach may offend readers who are outside the company and may be emotionally involved in the response. Compare the poorly written draft with the improved, revised letter in Figure 8.2 on page 190. The improved letter conveys the same negative message but without sounding offensive. As you think about the different effects of these two letters, you can see why good business writers take the time and the trouble to give negative messages the attention they deserve, even when they are only requesting information.

Refusing Invitations and Requests for Favours

When turning down an invitation or a request for a favour, base your choice of approach on your relationship with the reader.

When you must say no to an invitation or a requested favour, your use of the direct or the indirect approach depends on your relationship with the reader. For example, suppose the president of the local community college asks your company to host graduation on your corporate grounds, but your sales meetings will be taking place at the same time. If you don't know the president well, you'll probably use the indirect approach. See Figure 8.3 on page 191, in which May Yee Kwan delivers this bad news in a helpful and supportive way. If you are friends with the president and work frequently on projects for the college, you might use the direct approach.

> Sandra, thanks for asking us to host your graduation. You know we've always supported the college and would love to do this for you. However, our company sales meetings will be going on during the same time. We'll have so many folks tied up with logistics, we won't have the personnel to adequately take care of the graduation.

> Have you called Jerry Kane over at the Botanical Gardens? I can't think of a prettier site for graduation. Roberta in my office volunteers over there and knows Jerry. She can fill you in on the details, if you'd like to talk to her first.
>
> Thanks again for considering us. Let's have lunch in mid-June to plan our involvement with the college for the next school year. You can think of all kinds of ways to make me sorry I had to say no! I'll look forward to seeing you and catching up on family news.

This letter gets right to the point but still uses some blow-softening techniques: It compliments the person and organization making the request, suggests an alternative, and looks toward future opportunities for cooperation.

Handling Bad News About Orders

For several reasons, businesses must sometimes convey bad news concerning orders. Also, when delivering bad news to existing or would-be customers, you have an additional challenge—resale. To make readers feel good about continuing to do business with your firm, you want to reinforce the customer's confidence in your service or product.

The basic goal of a bad-news letter about orders is to protect or make a sale.

When you must back-order for a customer, you have one of two types of bad news to convey: (1) You're able to send only part of the order, or (2) you're able to send none of the order. When sending only part of the order, you actually have both good news and bad news, so use the indirect approach. The buffer contains the good news (that part of the order is en route) along with a resale reminder of the product's attractiveness. After the buffer come the reasons for the delay of the remainder of the shipment. A strong close encourages a favourable attitude toward the entire transaction. For a customer whose order for a recliner and ottoman will be only partially filled, your e-mail message might read like the one in Figure 8.4 on page 192.

Use the indirect approach for both types of bad news about orders.

Refusing Claims and Requests for Adjustment

Almost every customer who makes a claim is emotionally involved; therefore, the indirect approach is usually the best approach for a refusal. Your job as a writer is to avoid accepting responsibility for the unfortunate situation and yet avoid blaming or accusing the customer. To steer clear of these pitfalls, pay special attention to the tone of your letter. Keep in mind that a tactful and courteous letter can build goodwill even while denying the claim. For example, Village Electronics recently received a letter from Daniel Lindmeier, who believes that his warranty covers one year, when it actually covers only three months. For the reply to his letter, see Figure 8.5 on page 193.

Use the indirect approach in most cases of refusing a claim.

When refusing a claim, avoid language that might have a negative effect on the reader. Instead, demonstrate that you understand and have considered the complaint. Then, even if the claim is unreasonable, rationally explain why you are refusing the request. Remember, don't apologize and don't rely on company policy. End the letter on a respectful note, and try to suggest some alternative action.

When refusing a claim

- Demonstrate your understanding of the complaint
- Explain your refusal
- Suggest alternative action

Sending Negative Organizational News

Refusing a request isn't the only type of bad news. At times, you may have bad news about your company's products or about its operations. Whether you're reporting to a supervisor or announcing your news to the media, the particular situation dictates whether you will use the direct or the indirect approach.

Bad News About Products

Say that you must provide bad news about a product. If you were writing to tell your company's bookkeeping department about increasing product prices, you'd use the direct approach. Although your audience would have to make some arithmetical adjustments,

FIGURE 8.2 Letter Refusing a Request for Information

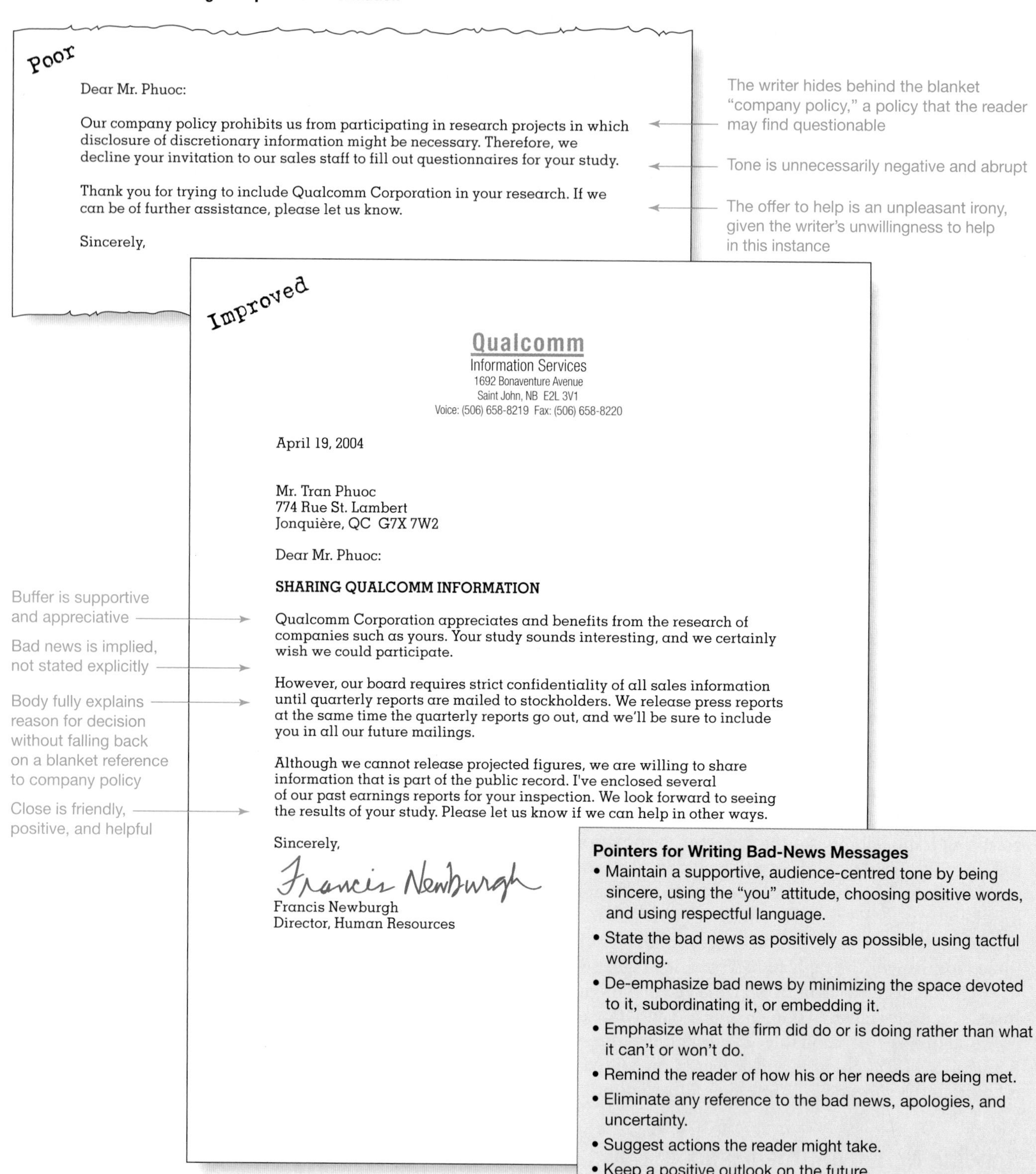

Poor

Dear Mr. Phuoc:

Our company policy prohibits us from participating in research projects in which disclosure of discretionary information might be necessary. Therefore, we decline your invitation to our sales staff to fill out questionnaires for your study.

Thank you for trying to include Qualcomm Corporation in your research. If we can be of further assistance, please let us know.

Sincerely,

The writer hides behind the blanket "company policy," a policy that the reader may find questionable
Tone is unnecessarily negative and abrupt
The offer to help is an unpleasant irony, given the writer's unwillingness to help in this instance

Improved

Qualcomm
Information Services
1692 Bonaventure Avenue
Saint John, NB E2L 3V1
Voice: (506) 658-8219 Fax: (506) 658-8220

April 19, 2004

Mr. Tran Phuoc
774 Rue St. Lambert
Jonquière, QC G7X 7W2

Dear Mr. Phuoc:

SHARING QUALCOMM INFORMATION

Qualcomm Corporation appreciates and benefits from the research of companies such as yours. Your study sounds interesting, and we certainly wish we could participate.

However, our board requires strict confidentiality of all sales information until quarterly reports are mailed to stockholders. We release press reports at the same time the quarterly reports go out, and we'll be sure to include you in all our future mailings.

Although we cannot release projected figures, we are willing to share information that is part of the public record. I've enclosed several of our past earnings reports for your inspection. We look forward to seeing the results of your study. Please let us know if we can help in other ways.

Sincerely,

Francis Newburgh
Director, Human Resources

Bad news is implied, not stated explicitly
Body fully explains reason for decision without falling back on a blanket reference to company policy
Close is friendly, positive, and helpful

Pointers for Writing Bad-News Messages

- Maintain a supportive, audience-centred tone by being sincere, using the "you" attitude, choosing positive words, and using respectful language.
- State the bad news as positively as possible, using tactful wording.
- De-emphasize bad news by minimizing the space devoted to it, subordinating it, or embedding it.
- Emphasize what the firm did do or is doing rather than what it can't or won't do.
- Remind the reader of how his or her needs are being met.
- Eliminate any reference to the bad news, apologies, and uncertainty.
- Suggest actions the reader might take.
- Keep a positive outlook on the future.
- Be confident about keeping the person as a customer.

readers would probably be unemotional about the matter. On the other hand, if you were writing to convey the same information to customers or even to your own sales department, you would probably use the indirect approach. Customers never like to pay more, and your sales reps would see the change as weakening your product's competitive edge, threatening their incomes, and possibly threatening their jobs.

Planning	Writing	Completing
Analyze the Situation Gauge audience's reaction to refusal; gear level of formality to reader familiarity. **Investigate the Topic** Collect information on possible alternatives. **Adapt to the Audience** For a more formal response, letterhead is best. Maintain the relationship with the "you" attitude, and focus on the reader's problem.	**Organize the Message** Main idea is to refuse a request. Respect your reader by showing that the request received serious consideration. Use an indirect approach. **Compose the Message** Make your style conversational but keep it businesslike. Keep the letter brief, clear, and helpful.	**Revise the Message** Maintain a friendly tone by eliminating overly formal words and phrases. Ensure your tone is positive. **Produce the Message** Use letterhead with a straight-forward format. **Proofread the Message** Be careful to review for accuracy, spelling, and mechanics.
1	2	3

FIGURE 8.3 Letter Declining a Favour

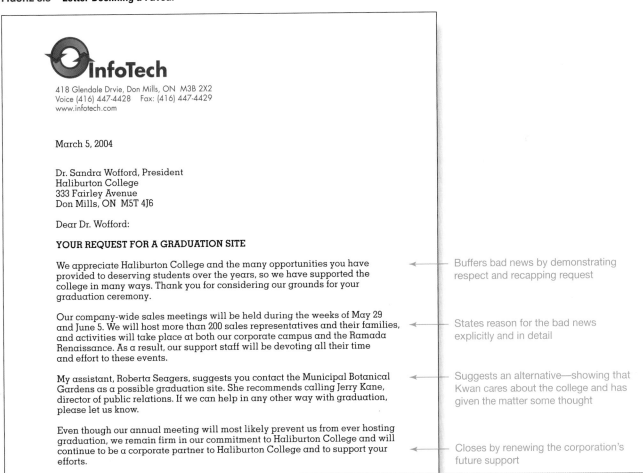

418 Glendale Drvie, Don Mills, ON M3B 2X2
Voice (416) 447-4428 Fax: (416) 447-4429
www.infotech.com

March 5, 2004

Dr. Sandra Wofford, President
Haliburton College
333 Fairley Avenue
Don Mills, ON M5T 4J6

Dear Dr. Wofford:

YOUR REQUEST FOR A GRADUATION SITE

We appreciate Haliburton College and the many opportunities you have provided to deserving students over the years, so we have supported the college in many ways. Thank you for considering our grounds for your graduation ceremony.

← Buffers bad news by demonstrating respect and recapping request

Our company-wide sales meetings will be held during the weeks of May 29 and June 5. We will host more than 200 sales representatives and their families, and activities will take place at both our corporate campus and the Ramada Renaissance. As a result, our support staff will be devoting all their time and effort to these events.

← States reason for the bad news explicitly and in detail

My assistant, Roberta Seagers, suggests you contact the Municipal Botanical Gardens as a possible graduation site. She recommends calling Jerry Kane, director of public relations. If we can help in any other way with graduation, please let us know.

← Suggests an alternative—showing that Kwan cares about the college and has given the matter some thought

Even though our annual meeting will most likely prevent us from ever hosting graduation, we remain firm in our commitment to Haliburton College and will continue to be a corporate partner to Haliburton College and to support your efforts.

← Closes by renewing the corporation's future support

Sincerely,

May Yee Kwan

May Yee Kwan
Public Relations Director

Pointers for Writing Buffers and Giving Reasons

Buffer

- Express appreciation, cooperation, fairness, good news, praise, resale, or understanding.
- Introduce a relevant topic.
- Avoid apologies and negative-sounding words *(won't, can't, unable to)*.
- Be brief and to the point.

Reasons

- Smooth the transition from the favourable buffer to the reasons.
- Show how the decision benefits your audience.
- Avoid apologies and expressions of sorrow or regret.
- Offer enough detail to show the logic of your position.
- Include only factual information and only business reasons, not personal ones.
- Carefully word the reasons so that readers can anticipate the bad news.

FIGURE 8.4 E-mail Message Advising of a Back Order

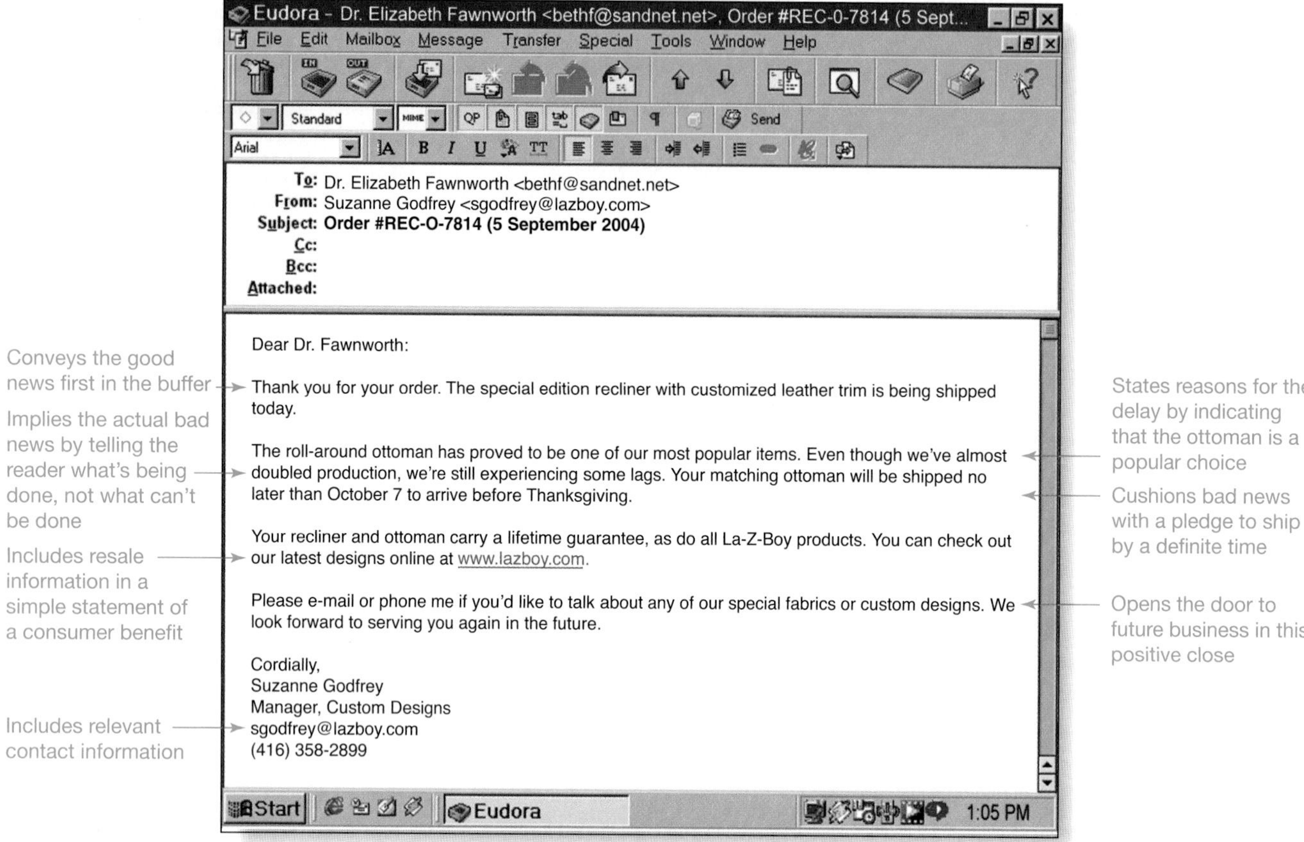

Eudora - Dr. Elizabeth Fawnworth <bethf@sandnet.net>, Order #REC-0-7814 (5 Sept...

To: Dr. Elizabeth Fawnworth <bethf@sandnet.net>
From: Suzanne Godfrey <sgodfrey@lazboy.com>
Subject: **Order #REC-O-7814 (5 September 2004)**
Cc:
Bcc:
Attached:

Dear Dr. Fawnworth:

Thank you for your order. The special edition recliner with customized leather trim is being shipped today.

The roll-around ottoman has proved to be one of our most popular items. Even though we've almost doubled production, we're still experiencing some lags. Your matching ottoman will be shipped no later than October 7 to arrive before Thanksgiving.

Your recliner and ottoman carry a lifetime guarantee, as do all La-Z-Boy products. You can check out our latest designs online at www.lazboy.com.

Please e-mail or phone me if you'd like to talk about any of our special fabrics or custom designs. We look forward to serving you again in the future.

Cordially,
Suzanne Godfrey
Manager, Custom Designs
sgodfrey@lazboy.com
(416) 358-2899

Conveys the good news first in the buffer
Implies the actual bad news by telling the reader what's being done, not what can't be done
Includes resale information in a simple statement of a consumer benefit
Includes relevant contact information
States reasons for the delay by indicating that the ottoman is a popular choice
Cushions bad news with a pledge to ship by a definite time
Opens the door to future business in this positive close

Pointers for Informing Customers About Back Orders

Buffer

- Include all details to identify the order.
- Extend a welcome to a new customer.
- Use resale information to build the customer's confidence in the original choice.
- For partial shipments, include the good news about the fulfilled part.

Reasons

- State the facts without laying blame.
- Specify shipping dates.
- Explain why the item is out of stock (such as exceptional demand, which may stimulate the customer's desire for the item).
- Reinforce the customer's confidence (for consumers, emphasize personal attention, credit, repair services, free delivery, special discounts, telephone shopping, and other services; for dealers, emphasize free counter and window displays, advertising materials, sales manuals, factory guarantees, and nearby warehousing).

The Bad News

- Stress how the reader benefits from the decision to buy.
- Offer a substitute product, if available.

Positive, Friendly, Helpful Close

- Adopt a tone that shows you remain in control of the situation and will continue to give customers' orders personal attention.
- Use resale information to clinch the sale.

Planning	Writing	Completing
Analyze the Situation Purpose is to explain that the warranty has expired and to offer repairs that the reader can pay for. **Investigate the Topic** Briefly gather information on product warranties, terms for repair, and resale information. **Adapt to the Audience** Use letter format and focus on customer relationship. 1	**Organize the Message** Main idea is that you're offering repairs, even though the warranty has expired. Use the indirect approach to help reader accept your message. **Compose the Message** Make the style conversational. Choose your words carefully, and enclose a catalogue to encourage future business. 2	**Revise the Message** Review for logical order and tone. Be clear but friendly. **Produce the Message** Use a clean letter format on letterhead. **Proofread the Message** Review for accuracy and correctness. Be sure to include promised enclosures. 3

FIGURE 8.5 Letter Refusing a Claim

48 College Street, Toronto, ON M5B 1H8
Voice: (416) 591-1312 • (416) 591-1316

May 3, 2004

Mr. Daniel Lindmeier
12 Wellington Square
Brantford, ON N3T 4H7

Dear Mr. Lindmeier:

REPAIRING YOUR CAMERA

Thank you for your letter about the battery release switch on your JVC digital camera. We believe, as you do, that electronic equipment should be built to last. That's why we stand behind our products with a 90-day warranty.

Even though your JVC camera is a year old and therefore out of warranty, we can still help. Please package your camera carefully and ship it to our store in St. Catharine's. Include your complete name, address, phone number, and a brief description of the malfunction, along with a cheque for $35. After examining the unit, we will give you a written estimate of the needed parts and labour. Then just let us know whether you want us to make the repairs—either by phone or by filling out the prepaid card we'll send you with the estimate.

If you choose to repair the unit, the $35 will be applied toward your bill, the balance of which is payable by cheque or credit card. If you decide not to repair the unit, the $35 will pay for the technician's time examining the unit. JVC also has service centres available in your area. If you would prefer to take the unit to one of them, please see the enclosed list.

Thanks again for inquiring about our service. I've enclosed a catalogue of our latest cameras and accessories. In June JVC is offering a "Trade-Up Special," at which time you can receive trade-in credit for your digital camera when you purchase a newer model. Come to visit Village Electronics soon.

Sincerely,

Walter Brodie

Walter Brodie
President

mk

Enclosures: List of service centres
Catalogue

Margin notes:

- Buffers the bad news by emphasizing a point that reader and writer both agree on
- States bad news indirectly, tactfully leaving the repair decision to the customer
- Puts company's policy in a favourable light
- Helps soothe the reader with a positive alternative action
- Closes by blending sales promotion with an acknowledgement of customer's interests

Pointers for Refusing Claims

- In the buffer, indicate your full understanding of the complaint.
- Avoid all areas of disagreement and any hint of your final decision.
- In the body, provide an accurate, factual account of the transaction.
- Avoid using a know-it-all tone, and use impersonal, passive language.
- Make the refusal clear, using tactful language (avoid words such as reject and claim).
- Avoid any hint that your decision is less than final.
- Offer a counterproposal, a compromise, or a partial adjustment.
- Include resale information for the company or product.
- Emphasize your desire for a good relationship in the future.
- Offer to replace the product or to provide a replacement part at the regular price.
- In the close, make no reference to your refusal.
- Refer to enclosed sales material.
- Make any suggested action easy for readers to comply with.

Company Decisions Affecting Customers

When conveying bad news about your company, focus on the reasons and on possible benefits.

At least three situations require bad-news letters about company operations or performance: (1) a change in company policy or future plans that will have a negative effect on the reader, (2) problems with company performance, and (3) controversial or unpopular company operations. In trying situations, apologies may be in order. If an apology is appropriate, good writers usually make it brief and bury it somewhere in the middle of the letter. Moreover, they try to leave readers with a favourable impression by closing on a positive note.

When a change in company policy will have a negative effect on your audience, state the reasons for the change clearly and carefully. The explanation section of the message convinces readers that the change was necessary and, if possible, explains how the change will benefit them. For example, if your company decided to drop orthodontic coverage from its employee dental plan, you could explain the decision this way:

> By eliminating this infrequently used benefit, we will not have to increase the monthly amount withheld from your paycheque for insurance coverage.

If your company is having serious performance problems, your customers and shareholders want to learn of the difficulty from you, not from newspaper accounts or from rumours. Even if the news leaks out before you announce it, counter with your own explanation as soon as possible. Business is based on mutual trust; if your customers and shareholders can't trust you to inform them of your problems, they may choose to work with someone they can trust. When you do inform stakeholders, use your common sense and present the bad news in as favourable a light as possible.

If your company loses a major business customer or if an important deal falls through, you could present the bad news as an opportunity to focus on smaller, growing businesses or on new products, as the e-mail in Figure 8.6 does. In this example, rather than dwell on the bad news, the company focuses on possible options for the future. The upbeat close and focus on action diminish the effect of the bad news.

FIGURE 8.6 E-mail Message Providing Bad News About Company Operations

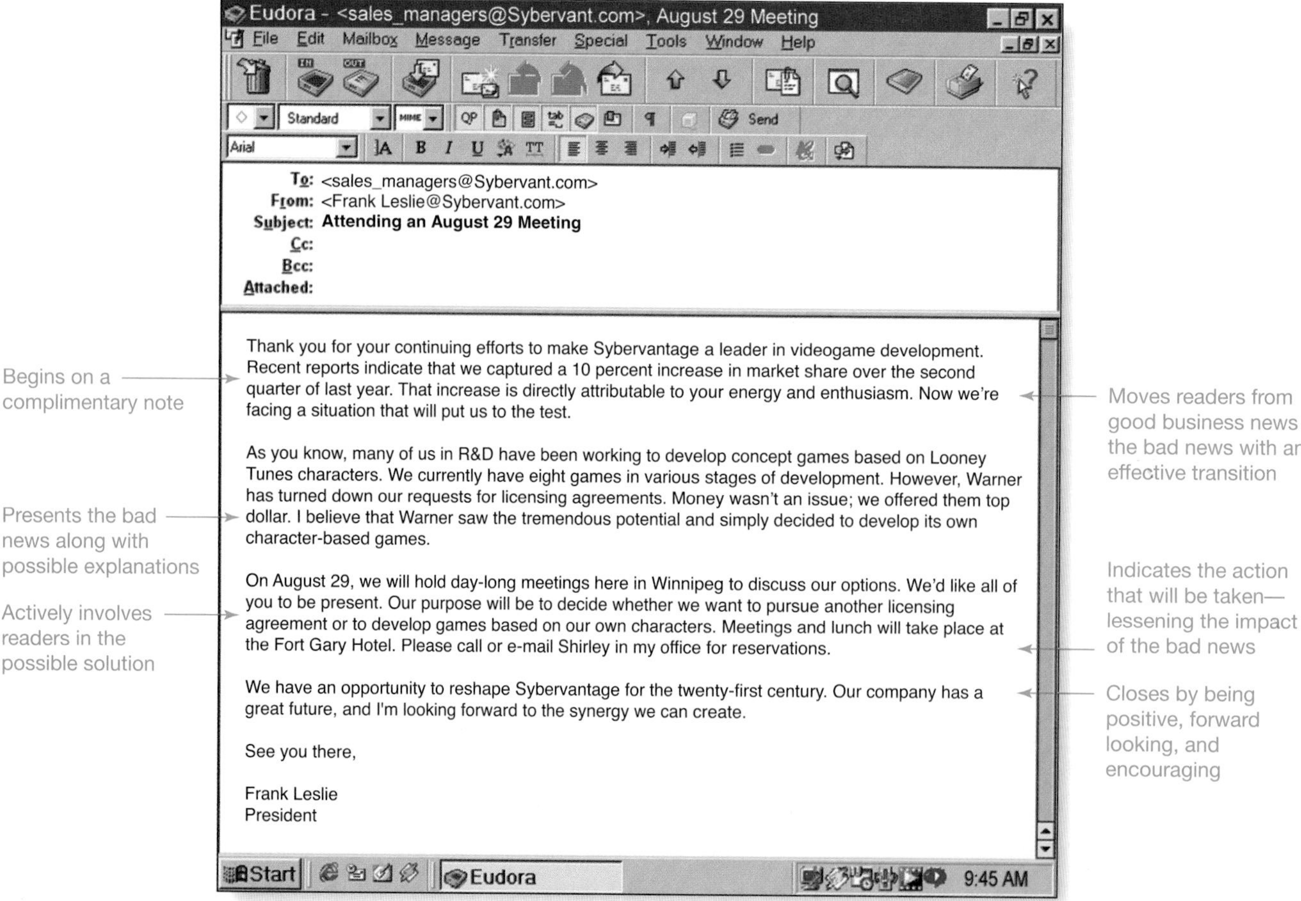

Reviewing Key Points

This chapter shares strategies for bad-news messages. Since no one likes to receive bad news, you'll want to pay attention to readers' feelings when you have to convey negative messages. In this chapter, you learned how to

- Send effective bad-news messages by creating an audience-centred tone.
- Choose the direct approach when you know the reader prefers bad news first, when the situation is minor, or when writing inside your organization and the company practice is to be very direct.
- Choose the indirect approach when you expect the news to be hard to accept, and to avoid having the reader reject your message before getting to the reasons. The indirect pattern for bad news includes
  - A buffer (a point of agreement, appreciation, good news, or fairness)
  - Reasons for the refusal (carefully and objectively explained with relevant facts)
  - The refusal (to de-emphasize the negativity, the refusal could be placed at the bottom of the reasons paragraph, subordinated, or implied)
  - A positive close (in which you may offer alternatives or resale information)
- Handle negative responses to requests, orders, and claims without laying blame and by restoring a goodwill relationship.
- Advise people inside and outside the company about problems with products or company operations by being straightforward, telling what you can do, and being optimistic about the future.

Test Your Knowledge

1. What are the five main goals in delivering bad news?

2. Why is it particularly important to adapt your medium and tone to your audience's needs and preferences when writing a bad-news message?

3. What are the advantages of using the direct approach to deliver the bad news at the beginning of a message?

4. What is the sequence of elements in a bad-news message that is organized using the indirect approach?

5. What is a buffer, and why do some critics consider it unethical?

6. When using an indirect approach to announce a negative decision, what is the purpose of presenting your reasons before explaining the decision itself?

7. What are four techniques for de-emphasizing bad news?

Apply Your Knowledge

1. Why is it important to end your bad-news message on a positive note? Explain.

2. If company policy changes, should you explain those changes to employees and customers at about the same time, or should you explain them to employees first? Why?

3. If the purpose of your letter is to convey bad news, should you take the time to suggest alternatives to your reader? Why or why not?

4. When a company suffers a setback, should you soften the impact by letting out the bad news a little at a time? Why or why not?

5. **Ethical Choices** Is intentionally de-emphasizing bad news the same as distorting graphs and charts to de-emphasize unfavourable data? Why or why not?

Practise Your Knowledge

Exercises for Perfecting Your Writing

Teamwork Working alone, revise the following statements to de-emphasize the bad news. (*Hint:* Minimize the space devoted to the bad news, subordinate it, embed it, or use the passive voice.) Then team up with a classmate and read each other's revisions. Did you both use the same approach in every case? Which approach seems to be most effective for each of the revised statements?

1. The airline can't refund your money. The "Conditions" segment on the back of your ticket states that there are no refunds for missed flights. Sometimes the airline makes exceptions, but only when life and death are involved. Of course, your ticket is still valid and can be used on a flight to the same destination.
2. I'm sorry to tell you, we can't supply the custom decorations you requested. We called every supplier and none of them can do what you want on such short notice. You can, however, get a standard decorative package on the same theme in time. I found a supplier that stocks these. Of course, it won't have quite the flair you originally requested.
3. We can't refund your money for the malfunctioning lamp. You shouldn't have placed a 250-watt bulb in the fixture socket; it's guaranteed for a maximum of 75 watts.

Using Buffers Answer the following questions pertaining to buffers:

4. You have to tell a local restaurant owner that your plans have changed and you have to cancel the 90-person banquet scheduled for next month. Do you need to use a buffer? Why or why not?
5. Write a buffer for a letter declining an invitation to speak at an association's annual fundraising event. Show your appreciation for being asked.
6. Write a buffer for a letter rejecting a job applicant who speaks three foreign languages fluently. Include praise for the applicant's accomplishments.

Selecting Indirect or Direct Approach Select which approach you would use (direct or indirect) for the following bad-news messages:

7. A memo to your boss informing her that one of your key clients is taking its business to a different accounting firm

8. An e-mail message to a customer informing her that one of the books she ordered over the Internet is temporarily out of stock

9. A letter to a customer explaining that the tape backup unit he ordered for his new custom computer is on back order and that, as a consequence, the shipping of the entire order will be delayed

Activities

For live links to all Web sites discussed in this chapter, visit this text's Web site at www.pearsoned.ca/bovee. Just log on and select Chapter 8, and click on "Student Resources." Locate the page or the URL related to the material in the text. For the "Exploring the Best of the Web" exercises, you'll also find navigational directions. Click on the live link to the site.

1. **Analyze This Document** Read the following document; then (1) analyze the strengths and weaknesses of each sentence and (2) revise the document so that it follows this chapter's guidelines.

   Your spring party sounds like fun. We're glad you've again chosen us as your caterer. Unfortunately, we have changed a few of our policies, and I wanted you to know about these changes in advance so that we won't have any misunderstandings on the day of the party.

   We will arrange the delivery of tables and chairs as usual the evening before the party. However, if you want us to set up, there is now a $100 charge for that service. Of course, you might want to get some friends to do it, which would save you money. We've also added a small charge for cleanup. This is only $3 per person (you can estimate because I know a lot of people come and go later in the evening).

   Other than that, all the arrangements will be the same. We'll provide the skirt for the band stage, tablecloths, bar setup, and of course, the barbecue. Will you have the tubs of ice with soft drinks again? We can do that for you as well, but there will be a fee.

   Please let me know if you have any problems with these changes and we'll try to work them out. I know it's going to be a great party.

2. **Analyze This Document** Read the following document; then (1) analyze the strengths and weaknesses of each sentence and (2) revise the document so that it follows this chapter's guidelines.

   I am responding to your letter of about six weeks ago asking for an adjustment on your fax/modem, model FM39Z. We test all our products before they leave the factory; therefore, it could not have been our fault that your fax/modem didn't work.

   If you or someone in your office dropped the unit, it might have caused the damage. Or the damage could have been caused by the shipper if he dropped it. If so, you should file a claim with the shipper. At any rate, it wasn't our fault. The parts are already covered by warranty. However, we will provide labour for the repairs for $50, which is less than our cost, since you are a valued customer.

   We will have a booth at the upcoming trade fair there and hope to see you or someone from your office. We have many new models of office machines that we're sure you'll want to see. I've enclosed our latest catalogue. Hope to see you there.

3. **Ethical Choices** The insurance company where you work is planning to raise all premiums for health-care coverage. Your boss has asked you to read a draft of her letter to customers announcing the new, higher rates. The first two paragraphs discuss some exciting medical advances and the expanded coverage offered by your company.

Only in the final paragraph do customers learn that they will have to pay more for coverage starting next year. What are the ethical implications of this draft? What changes would you suggest?

4. **Planning a Memo: Bad News About Polyester at Coca-Cola** Polyester went out of style in the 1980s, when no fashionable person would consider the synthetic material. Now polyester is making a comeback in both fashion and food, and the product development department at Coca-Cola wants to use it in the company's plastic drink containers.

To support this proposal, they've presented stacks of material from the chemical companies that produce polyester, such as Amoco, Dow, and Shell. These experts insist that mixing some of their new-generation polyester (polyethylene naphthalate or PEN) into the current plastic used for drink containers (polyethylene terephthalate or PET) will create a harder plastic that will eliminate carbonation loss and solve heat-sensitivity problems. They also say that the resulting material will appeal to consumers because it's clear, lightweight, resealable, and recyclable.

As a marketing assistant, you've now helped conduct research among a major market segment for soft drinks: young adults. Of all the container materials proposed in the market survey of 1000 young adults, aluminum ranked highest, with 84 percent of them preferring it. They said they like the feel of the aluminum cans (plastic feels slippery and is harder to hold) and believe that aluminum keeps drinks colder. They also believe that aluminum keeps the carbonation longer, creating a "mouth buzz," whereas plastic lets the fizz out. And finally, they think that aluminum cans look "cool" and that plastic containers look "dorky." They're not likely to buy your drinks in the proposed new containers.

Your research team came up with some suggestions for improving plastic's image among young adults. One approach would be an ad campaign showing "cool young people" drinking from plastic bottles. Another would be ads showing that new technology is helping the plastic containers to hold in the "fizz."

Meanwhile, Shell Chemical's director of polyester research and development, David Richardson, is pushing your company to use the new polyester. "In a few years," he says, "I'll be able to fix you a nice meal, and everything in it will come out of a polyester container." Richard Marion, an executive at Canco Corporation's Canco Chemical Company, suggests that "plastic is less deadly than glass when you throw it at a soccer match," so Coca-Cola would be doing the world a good turn, as well.

Your task: You need to report the market research findings to your boss, Tom Ruffenbach, director of marketing at Coca-Cola, in a form he can pass along to other departments during meetings on the proposed conversion to polyester containers. Before you start writing, answer the following questions to help you organize your thinking.

1. The best format for conveying the information will be
   - **a.** Notes you've made from the study results, organized in neat outline form
   - **b.** An informal e-mail that alerts your boss to the problem uncovered by the study
   - **c.** A formal letter using subheadings to detail the bad news, point by point
   - **d.** A memo that summarizes the bad news from the market study and includes suggestions for overcoming this consumer resistance
2. Using the direct approach, a good opening sentence for your message would be
   - **a.** "Tom, we've got a problem."
   - **b.** "We can't use plastic containers for our soft drinks."
   - **c.** "Although the proposals for the new polyester are convincing and based on scientific data, our market research has uncovered a potential problem with youthful consumers."
   - **d.** "I think you should consider the results of our market study before you proceed."
3. Explain why you chose your answer for question 2. Then explain why you did not choose each of the other selections.

4. In the body of your message, you'll want to
   a. Explain the scope of the market study
   b. Summarize the study results, possibly using lists
   c. Suggest positive steps to counteract the bad news
   d. All of the above

5. What's a good way to close this memo to your boss?
   a. With a restatement of the problem/bad news
   b. On a positive note
   c. With your recommendation for action
   d. With your contact information for further communication

Now that you've thought through these elements, write the bad-news memo in your own words.[6]

5. **Revising an E-mail Message: Budgetary Cutbacks at Black & Decker** The following bad-news e-mail about travel budget cutbacks contains numerous blunders. Using what you've learned in the chapter, read the message carefully and analyze its faults. Then use the questions below to outline and write an improved message.

Date: Fri, 28 May 2004 4:20:15 -0800
From: M. Juhasz, Travel & Meeting Services <mjuhasz@blackanddecker.com>
To: [mailing list]
CC:
BCC:
Attached:
Subject: Travel Budget Cuts Effective Immediately

Dear Travelling Executives:

We need you to start using some of the budget suggestions we are going to issue as a separate memorandum. These include using videoconference equipment instead of travelling to meetings, staying in cheaper hotels, arranging flights for cheaper times, and flying from less-convenient but also less-expensive suburban airports.

The company needs to cut travel expenses by 50 percent, just as we've cut costs in all departments of Black & Decker. This means you'll no longer be able to stay in fancy hotels and make last-minute, costly changes to your travel plans.

You'll also be expected to avoid hotel phone surcharges. Compose your e-mail offline when you're in the hotel. And never return a rental car with an empty tank! That causes the rental agency to charge us a premium price for the gas they sell when they fill it up upon your return.

You'll be expected to make these changes in your travel habits immediately.

Sincerely,

M. Juhasz

Travel & Meeting Services

1. Describe the flaws you discovered in this bad-news e-mail about company operations.
2. Develop a plan for rewriting the e-mail, using the direct approach for company insiders. The following steps will help you organize your efforts before you begin writing:
   a. Create an opening statement of the bad news, using the "you" attitude.
   b. Decide what explanation is needed to justify the news.
   c. Determine whether you can use lists effectively.
   d. Choose some positive suggestions you can include to soften the news.
   e. Develop an upbeat closing.
3. Now rewrite the e-mail. Don't forget to leave ample time for revision of your own work before you turn it in.

6. **Teamwork: Revising a Letter—Refusal from Home Depot to New Faucet Manufacturer** The following letter rejecting a faucet manufacturer's product presentation contains many errors in judgment. Working with your classmates in a team effort, you should be able to improve its effectiveness as a bad-news message. First, analyze and discuss the letter's flaws. How can it be improved? Use the questions below to help guide your discussion and development of an improved version.

July 15, 2004

Pamela Wilson, Operations Manager
Sterling Manufacturing
133 Industrial Avenue
Red Deer, AB T5D 2D6

Dear Ms. Wilson:

We regret to inform you that your presentation at Home Depot's recent product review sessions in Edmonton did not meet our expert panellists' expectations. We require new products that will satisfy our customers' high standards. Yours did not match this goal.

Our primary concern is to continue our commitment to product excellence, customer knowledge, and price competitiveness, which has helped make Home Depot a top-performing company with more than a thousand stores Canada-wide. The panel found flaws in your design and materials. Also, your cost per unit was too high.

The product review sessions occur annually. You are allowed to try again; just apply as you did this year. Again, I'm sorry things didn't work out for you this time.

Sincerely,

1. Describe the problems you found with this letter rejecting a product presentation.
2. Develop a plan for rewriting the letter, using the indirect approach. First, organize your thinking before you begin writing:
   a. Select a buffer for the opening, using the "you" attitude.
   b. Choose the reasons you'll use to explain the rejection.
   c. Develop a way to soften or embed the bad news.
   d. Create a conditional (if/then) statement to encourage the recipient to try again.
   e. Find a way to close on a positive, encouraging note.
3. Now rewrite the letter. Don't forget to leave ample time for revision of your own work before you turn it in.

Expand Your Knowledge

Best of the Web

Learn from Professionals. Find out more about ethical considerations of delivering bad news by visiting the Canadian Public Relations Society Web site and clicking on "Code of Professional Standards." Learn how important truthful communication is to a practising professional in this field.

www.cprs.ca

Visit the Public Relations Consultants Association Web site to read Mandanmohan Rao's review of a book by Don Middleberg titled *Winning PR in the Wired World: Powerful Communication Strategies for the Noisy Digital Space* (New York: McGraw-Hill, 2001). By reading the review, you can learn how the Internet has changed the public's expectation of information sharing during times of crisis.

www.prcai.org/resources/articles_6.htm

Excercises

1. How has the Internet influenced the practice of public relations?
2. What difference do these changes in society make to companies who have bad news to deliver?
3. How has the Internet changed the way companies should communicate in a crisis?

Exploring the Web on Your Own

Review these chapter-related Web sites on your own to learn more about the bad-news issues human resources departments are facing today.

1. Don Rosner's "Working Wounded" column on the Workopolis Web site, www.globeandmail.workopolis.com, offers some advice for delivering bad news to your boss. Read some of the other articles to find out what kinds of issues managers have to resolve in the workplace. What are the top "headaches" reported by employees?
2. Human Resources Development Canada offers extensive human resources management advice and information on its Web site. Visit www.hrmanagement.ca to read about workplace trends, labour law affecting employers, recruiting, benefits, staffing, and more.

Learn Interactively

Interactive Study Guide

Visit the Companion Website at www.pearsoned.ca/bovee. For Chapter 8, take advantage of the interactive "Study Guide" to test your chapter knowledge. Get instant feedback on whether you need additional studying.

This site offers a variety of additional resources: The "Research Area" helps you locate a wealth of information to use in course assignments. The "Study Hall" helps you succeed in this course by offering support with writing and study skills, time management, and career skills, as well as numerous other resources.

Peak Performance Grammar and Mechanics

PEAK

Use the Peak Performance Grammar and Mechanics CD to test your skill with punctuation. In the "Punctuation II" section, take the Pretest to determine whether you have any weak areas. Then review those areas in the Refresher Course. Take the Follow-Up Test to check your grasp of punctuation. For an extra challenge or advanced practice, take the Advanced Test.

Apply each step in Figure 8.1 on page 183 to the following cases, as assigned by your instructor.

WEB SKILLS 1. Too anomalous: Letter declining an invitation from the Disclosure Project

You work part-time for the president of the Alberta Flying Club, an organization that offers discounts on flying lessons and small plane rentals. In exchange, you get free flying lessons from the president, John Zuniga.

Like most pilots-to-be, you're interested in anomalous aerial phenomena (UFOs), so you paid close attention when Zuniga was asked if the club would sponsor a free public event in Calgary, a "Campaign for Disclosure." The request came from two club members, both retired airforce pilots who are well respected around the airport, Bill West and Chuck Macdonald. You've overheard some of their stories about their UFO encounters during airborne military manoeuvres. You also heard them say that they were threatened by superiors to "forget what they'd seen."

These two members met with Zuniga in his office, presenting him with a book and videotape from a non-profit research organization in the United States called the Disclosure Project. It was founded by Dr. Steven Greer, an emergency-room physician who gave up his doctor's salary to document the testimony of more than 400 witnesses to UFO and extraterrestrial events. These witnesses are from the United States, Canada, Britain, Russia, Australia, and other countries, and from the armed services, the CIA, NASA, CSIS, and other agencies.

When Zuniga emerges from the meeting, his face is grim, determined. "These fellas are really into it, but we can't do it," he tells you when you ask about the sponsorship.

"It's my job to encourage pilots to join this flying club, " he explains. "No matter what I believe personally, this isn't an event we should sponsor. I can't have folks referring to us as 'those kooks over in Hangar 5,' much as I'd love to hear Dr. Greer speak. He's got a powerful agenda and I'd love to support him—but officially, I just can't do it."

Your Task Zuniga wants you to write a letter to Bill West (12468 16 St NW, Calgary, AB T1V 4Y2), declining the sponsorship invitation. "First take a look at the Disclosure Web site, www.disclosureproject.org, and you'll know why we can't sponsor this. Then write a polite refusal. Use what you've learned to let the doctor know we've given this event our serious consideration. Be encouraging, if you can, and let me sign the letter."[7]

WEB SKILLS E-MAIL SKILLS 2. Disappearing baby bibs: E-mail from Home Shopping Network's Craftopia

At Craftopia online, part of the Home Shopping Network (HSN) Web site, the $12.99 Stamped Cross-Stitch Baby-Bib sewing kit is always popular. Now an on-air TV promotion has totally depleted your stock of the do-it-yourself kits. New kits won't be ready to ship for six weeks.

Your Task As customer service supervisor, write a form message to be sent by e-mail to notify customers of the delay in receiving their stitchery kits. Soften this news with some resale. First, go online to find resale information you can include in the message. Log on to the HSN home page at www.HSN.com/cs, then follow the link to Craftopia. Customers who don't want to wait six weeks can call 1-800-373-0343 to request a refund.[8]

3. Cyber-surveillance: Letter refusing claim from Silent Watch victim

You work in human resources for a company called Advertising Inflatables, which designs and builds the huge balloon replicas used for advertising atop retail stores, tire outlets, used-car lots, fast-food outlets, fitness clubs, and so on. Since you started, you've seen balloon re-creations of everything from a 17-m King Kong to a "small" 3-m pizza.

Not long ago, company management installed the "cyber-surveillance" software, Silent Watch, to track and record employees' computer usage. At the time, you sent out a memo informing all employees that they should limit their computer use and e-mail to work projects only. You also informed them that their work would be monitored. At your boss's request, you did not mention that Silent Watch would record every keystroke of their work or that they could be monitored from a screen in their manager's office.

As it turned out, Silent Watch caught two of the sales staff spending between 50 percent and 70 percent of their time surfing Internet sites unrelated to their jobs. The company docked (withheld) their pay accordingly, without warning. Management sent them a memo notifying them that they were not fired but were on probation. You considered this wise, because when they work, both employees are very good at what they do, and talent is hard to find.

But now salesman Jarod Harkington has sent you a letter demanding reinstatement of his pay and claiming he was "spied on illegally." On the contrary, company lawyers have assured management that the courts almost always side with employers on this issue, particularly after employees receive a warning such as the one you wrote. The computer equipment belongs to Advertising Inflatables, and employees are paid a fair price for their time.

Your Task Write a letter refusing Mr. Harkington's claim.[9] His address is 267 Hale Avenue, Peterborough, ON K9J 7B1.

4. Not this time: Letter to VanCity customer denying ATM debit adjustments

You work in operations in the ATM Error Resolution Department at VanCity Credit Union. Your department often adjusts customer accounts for multiple ATM debit errors. Mistakes are usually honest ones—such as a merchant swiping a customer's debit card two or three times, thinking the first few times didn't "take" when they actually did.

Whenever customers call the bank about problems on their statements, they're instructed to write a claim letter to your department describing the situation and to enclose copies of receipts. Customers are notified of the outcome within 10 to 20 business days.

You usually credit their account. But this time, your supervisor is suspicious about a letter you've received from Margaret Caldwell, who maintains several hefty joint accounts with her husband at VanCity.

Three debits to her chequing account were processed on the same day, credited to the same market, Wilson's Gourmet. The debits carry the same transaction reference number, 1440022-22839837109, which is what caught Mrs. Caldwell's attention. But you know that number changes daily, not hourly, so multiple purchases made on the same day often carry the same number. Also, the debits are for different amounts ($23.02, $110.95, and $47.50), so these transactions weren't a result of repeated card swipes. No receipts are enclosed.

Mrs. Caldwell writes that the store was trying to steal from her, but your supervisor doubts that and asks you to contact Wilson's Gourmet. Manager Simon Lau tells you that he's had no problems with his equipment and mentions that food shoppers commonly return at different times during the day to make additional purchases, particularly for beverages or to pick up merchandise they forgot the first time.

Your supervisor decides this was neither a bank error nor an error on the part of Wilson's Gourmet. It doesn't matter whether Mrs. Caldwell is merely confused or trying to commit an intentional fraud. Bank rules are clear for this situation: You must politely deny her request.

Your Task Write to Margaret Caldwell, 2789 Cedar Parkway, Richmond, BC VYR 2E5, explaining your refusal of her claim number 7899. Remember, you don't want to lose this wealthy customer's business.[10]

5. Product recall: Letter from Perrigo Company to retailers about children's painkiller

You work at Perrigo Company in customer service, where the atmosphere has been tense lately. Your company discovered that one batch of its cherry-flavoured children's painkiller contains too much acetaminophen, and it must immediately inform retailers and the public of this dangerous error. Full and prompt disclosure is especially crucial when consumer health is involved.

Perrigo manufactures more than 900 store-brand, over-the-counter (OTC) pharmaceuticals and nutritional products. Store brands are packaged under store names, such as Save-On or London Drugs. They're priced lower than brand-name products such as Tylenol, Motrin, and NyQuil, but they offer "comparable quality and effectiveness."

Your marketing department calculates that 6500 118-mL bottles of the "children's nonaspirin elixir" (a Tylenol look-alike) are already in the hands of consumers. That leaves 1288 bottles on store shelves. The lab says the acetaminophen contained in the painkilling liquid is up to 29 percent more than labels state, enough to cause an overdose in young children, which can cause liver failure. Fortunately, only lot number 1AD0228 is affected.

The painkiller is sold under the Save-On, London Drugs, and Good Sense labels at stores throughout Canada. Consumers must be told not to give the product to children. They must check the lot number, and if the bottle is from the affected batch, they must return it to the store they bought it from for a refund.

Your Task Company news releases have already notified the media about the product recall, but for legal purposes, you've been asked to write a formal letter to retailers. Explain the recall, and instruct stores to remove the product from their shelves for return to your company. Perrigo will reimburse them for refunds to customers. Include a phone number they can call with questions and pass on to customers: 1-800-321-0105.[11]

TEAM SKILLS 6. Safe selling: Memo from the Sports Authority headquarters about dangerous scooters

You are a merchandising assistant at the Pacific regional office of The Sports Authority and you recently noted that the Consumer Product Safety Commission (CPSC) in the United States has issued a consumer advisory on the dangers of motorized scooters. You're not surprised—these trends are common in Canada, too. You have even tried the scooters yourself and lived to regret forgetting to wear elbow pads.

The popular electric or gas-powered scooters, which feature two wheels similar to in-line skates, travel 14 km to 23 km per hour. As sales have grown, so have the reports of broken arms and legs, scraped faces, and bumped heads. The problem is that, unlike a motorcycle or bicycle, a scooter can be mastered by first-timers almost immediately. Both children and adults are hopping on and riding off—without helmets or other safety gear.

Over a six-month period, the CPSC says 2250 motorized scooter injuries and 3 deaths were reported by emergency rooms around the United States. The riders who were killed, ages 6, 11, and 46, might all have lived if they'd been wearing helmets. Some provinces and states have already enacted laws restricting scooter operations.

Your stores sell a wide selection of both the foot-powered ($25 to $150) and motorized scooters ($350 to $1000). The merchandising experts you work for are as concerned about the rise in injuries as they are about the CPSC advisory's potential negative effect on sales and liability. Many consumers in Canada pay attention to these advisories. You've been assigned to a team that will brainstorm ideas for improving the situation.

For example, one team member has suggested developing a safety brochure to give to customers; another wants to train salespeople to discuss safety issues with customers before they buy. "We'd like to see increased sales of reflective gear ($6 to $15), helmets ($24), and elbow and knee pads ($19)," a store executive tells your team, "not to improve on The Sports Authority's annual revenue, but to save lives."

Your Task Working as a team with classmates, discuss how the Sports Authority can use positive actions, including those mentioned in the case, to soften the effect of the CPSC advisory. Choose the best ideas and decide how to use them in a bad-news memo notifying the chain's 15 store managers in the Pacific region about the consumer advisory. Then write the memo your team has outlined.[12]

7. The cheque's in the mail—almost: Letter from Sun Microsystems explaining late payments

Like everyone else working for Sun Microsystems, you were amazed that the installation of the computer company's new management information system did not go smoothly. When the new computer program was installed, errors were made that caused information to be lost. This embarrassment wasn't discovered until Sun's suppliers started clamouring for payments they never received.

Terence Lenaghan (the corporate controller and your boss) has to tell 6000 vendors why Sun Microsystems has failed to pay its bills on time—and why it might be late with payments again.

"Until we get these errors corrected," Lenaghan confesses to you, "we're going to have to finish some of the accounting work by hand. That means that some of our payments to vendors will probably be late next month too. I need you to write to our suppliers and let them know that there's nothing wrong with the company's financial status. The last thing we want is for our vendors to think our business is going under."

Your Task Write a form letter for your boss to send to Sun Microsystem's vendors explaining that problems with your new management information system are responsible for the delays in payment.[13]

E-MAIL SKILLS 8. Cellphone violations: E-mail message to associates at Wilkes Artis law firm

"Company policy states that personnel are not to conduct business using cellphones while driving," David Finch reminds you. He's a partner at the law firm of Wilkes Artis in Toronto, where you work as his administrative assistant.

You nod, waiting for him to explain. He already issued a memo about this rule last year, after that 15-year-old girl was hit and killed by a lawyer from another firm. Driving back from a client meeting, the lawyer was distracted while talking on her cellphone. The girl's family sued the firm and won $30 million, but that's not the point. The point is that cellphones can cause people to be hurt, even killed.

Finch explains, "Yesterday one of our associates called his secretary while driving his car. We can't allow this. Heck, one province, some of the states, and a few countries have banned the use of hand-held cellphones while driving. From now on, any violation of our cellphone policy will result in suspension without pay, unless the call is a genuine health or traffic emergency."

Your Task Finch asks you to write an e-mail message to all employees, announcing the new penalty for violating company policy.[14]

Improve Your Grammar, Mechanics, and Usage

Level 1: Self-Assessment—Semicolons and Colons

Review Sections 2.4, 2.5 and 2.6 in the Handbook of Grammar, Mechanics, and Usage, and then look at the following 15 items.

In items 1–15, insert all required semicolons, colons, and commas:

1. This letter looks good that one doesn't.
2. I want to make one thing perfectly clear neither of you will be promoted if sales figures don't improve.
3. The Zurich airport has been snowed in therefore I won't be able to meet with you before January 4.
4. His motivation was obvious to get Meg fired.
5. Only two firms have responded to our survey J. J. Perkins and Tucker & Tucker.
6. Send a copy to Mary Kwan Marketing Director Robert Bache Comptroller and Dennis Mann Sales Director.
7. Please be sure to interview these employees next week Henry Gold Doris Hatch and George Iosupovich.
8. We have observed your hard work because of it we are promoting you to manager of your department.
9. You shipped three items on June 7 however we received only one of them.
10. The convention kit includes the following response cards, giveaways, brochures, and a display rack.
11. The workers wanted an immediate wage increase they had not had a raise in nearly two years.
12. This, then, is our goal for 2005 to increase sales 35 percent.
13. His writing skills are excellent however he still needs to polish his management style.
14. We would like to address three issues efficiency profitability and market penetration.
15. Remember this rule When in doubt, leave it out.

Level 2: Workplace Applications

The following items contain numerous errors in grammar, capitalization, punctuation, abbreviation, number style, word division, and vocabulary. Rewrite each sentence in the space provided, correcting all errors. Write *C* in the space after any sentence that is already correct.

1. Hector's, Julie's, and Tim's report was well-received by the Committee.

2. Everyone who are interested in signing up for the training seminar must do so by 3:00 o'clock PM on friday.

3. David Stern is a management and training expert that has spent a major part of his career coaching, counselling, and giving advise both to managers and workers.

4. Be aware and comply with local "zoning ordnances" and building codes.

5. Garrett didn't seem phased when her supervisor didn't except her excuse for being late, she forgot to set her alarm.

6. Copyright laws on the Internet is not always clearly defined, be sure your research doesn't extend to "borrowing" a competitors' keywords or copy.

7. Sauder Woodworking, in Sydney, NS, sell a line of ready to assemble computer carts, desks, file cabinets, and furniture that is modular that can be mixed and matched to meet each business owners' personal taste.

8. Spamming is the most certain way to loose you're e-mail account, Web site, and you're reputation.

9. Us programmers have always tried to help others learn the tricks of the trade, especially Roger and myself.

10. The person whom was handling Miss Gill's account told her that an error had been made by the bank in her favour.

11. "The trouble with focus groups" says Marketing Expert Frances Knight, "Is that consumers rarely act in real life they way they do in a "laboratory" setting."

12. In a industry in which design firms tend to come and go Skyline has licensed seventy products and grown to 8 employees.

13. If youv'e ever wondered why fast food restaurants are on the left and gift shops are on the right as you walk toward the gate into a newly-constructed airport you should read Malcolm Gladwells article, 'The Science of Shopping,' in the *Maclean's*.

14. Anyone whose starting a business should consider using their life story, as a way to generate customer's interest.

15. Having been in business since 1993, over 1000s of sales calls has been made by Mr. Jurzang, on prospects for his minority owned company.

Level 3: Document Critique

The following document may contain errors in grammar, capitalization, punctuation, abbreviation, number style, vocabulary, and spelling. You may also discover problems with wordiness, usage, and appropriateness of tone for bad-news messages. Correct all errors using standard proofreading marks (see Appendix C).

MEMORANDUM

To: all employees

Subject: Health insurance—Changes

Date: Octbr. 22, 2004

From: Lucinda Goodman, Benefits Mangr., Human resources

Unlike many companies, Bright Manufacturing has always paid a hundred % of medical insurance for it's employees, absorbing the recent 10-20 percent annual cost increases in order to provide this important benefit. This year; Maritime Life gave us some terrible news: the cost increase for our employee's medical coverage would be a staggering fourty percent per month next year

To mange the increase and continue to offer you and your family highquality medical coverage we have negotiated several changes with Maritime Life; a new cost saving alternative is also being offered by us:

1. Under the Maritime Life Plus plan, copay amounts for office visits will be ten dollars next year/ $50 for emergency room visits.
2. 80% of employees' insurance coverage (including 10 percent of the cost increase) will be paid by Bright next year and 100 % of the prescription drug costs (including a 23 percent cost increase). The remaining twenty percent of medical coverage will be deducted by us monthly from your salary, if you choose to remain on a Maritime Life Plus plan. We realize this is alot, but its still less than many companies charge their employees.
3. A fully paid alternative health plan, Maritime Life, will now be provided by Bright at no cost to employees. But be warned that there is a deadline. If you want to switch to this new plan you must do so during our open enrollment period, Nov. 20 to December 1 2004, and we will not consder applications for the change after that time so don't get your forms in late.

There are forms available in the Human Resources office for changing your coverage. They must be returned between November 20 and December 1, 2004. If you wish to remain on a Maritime Life Plus policy, you do not need to notify us; payroll deductions for company employees on the plan will occur automatic beginning January first, 2005.

If you have questions, please call our new Medical Benefits Information line at ext. 3392. Our Intranet sight will also provide you easy with information about health care coverage online if you click the "Medical Benefits" icon. Since our founding in 1946, we have provided our company employees with the best medical coverage available. We all hate rising costs and although things are looking bleak for the future but we're doing all we can do to hold on to this helpful benefit for you.

Ethics

Business Communication Notebook

Should Employers Use E-mail to Deliver Negative Messages?

Most people are more comfortable delivering bad news via e-mail than in person or on the phone. But is it appropriate to avoid the dreaded task of explaining layoffs and spending cuts in person by using e-mail to break such bad news? Some think it is.

Few executives advise using e-mail in extremely personal situations such as firing an employee, but some think it's perfectly fine to use e-mail for other uncomfortable scenarios such as job cuts, travel restrictions, hiring freezes, and other significant spending changes. Consider these examples:

- Amazon.com called an in-person meeting to announce job cuts, but telecommuters who couldn't attend the meeting were informed via e-mail. "I want you to know that this was a very difficult decision for the company to make . . . we know this must be very painful to hear," the e-mail read.
- Discovery Communications used e-mail to alert Discover.com workers that staffing changes would take place before announcing layoffs of some of its dot-com full-time employees.
- Motorola sent e-mail to employees in its semiconductor sector explaining layoffs and other cost-cutting steps. Workers being let go were told in person, but word of what was happening went out electronically.
- Ameritrade online brokerage notified more than 2000 call-centre workers of layoffs via e-mail.

Employers who use e-mail to deliver bad news claim that it's a quick and effective way to get information to all employees—especially those in remote locations or home offices. With face-to-face or even voice-to-voice communication, people have a tendency to tune out the worst and sugarcoat the bad news. But delivering bad news via e-mail lets people be more honest. E-mail facilitates straight talk because senders don't see the discomfort of their recipients.

However, critics cry foul when companies break job-related bad news via e-mail. As they see it, e-mail is too impersonal. "The only advantage is that it gives management an opportunity to duck and dodge angry employees," says one communication expert. If you want to maintain good relationships with your employees, "these kinds of things should be done in person."

Applications for Success

For more information about e-mail and employer/employee communication, go to www.atkinson.yorku.ca/~hrresall/dbn.PDF.

1. Do you think employers should deliver negative messages via e-mail? Explain your answer.
2. Why does e-mail facilitate straight talk?
3. If you are sending bad news in an e-mail message, how can you use an indirect approach and still include an informative subject line? Won't the subject line give away your message before you have the chance to explain your reasons? Briefly explain in a one- to two-paragraph memo or e-mail to your instructor.

Writing Persuasive Messages

9

After studying this chapter, you will be able to

1 Discuss the planning tasks that need extra attention when preparing persuasive messages
2 Distinguish between emotional and logical appeals, and discuss how to balance them
3 Describe the AIDA plan for persuasive messages
4 List six strategies for sending sales messages
5 Explain how to adapt the AIDA plan to sales messages
6 Compare sales messages with fundraising messages

From the Real World

"Winning someone over generally has a lot to do with past proven performance, as well as your ongoing relationship with that individual. If you said you were going to do something, then you had better deliver on it."

–Mary Kreuk
Vice-President, Marketing
CTV

As vice-president, marketing at CTV, Mary Kreuk persuades advertisers and agencies across the country. Mary sums up her department's approach as "meeting an advertiser's need and eliminating any potential roadblock—before it is raised. Relationship building is the key." In addition to persuading external clients, CTV's marketing group also persuades internal audiences, working with programming, sales, communications, promotions, research, and television producers. In internal communication, the marketing group provides the "reason why" and always relates that reason to a particular audience's interests. For instance, when selling an idea to a producer, the "reason why" may be potential revenue, but that persuasive message by itself might fail if the proposal does not also accommodate the producer's need to maintain editorial control. Kreuk knows that recognizing the interests of the audience is an essential part of persuasive communication.

In persuasive messages, Kreuk targets the needs of audience members—not to manipulate them but to use information, logic, and reason to help them make intelligent, informed decisions[1]. She also augments these individual messages with ongoing relationship building to better work with clients on a long-term basis and to develop a level of trust that helps smooth out the rough spots. Either way, success depends on being able to identify client needs and develop strategies to meet those needs.

Using the Three-Step Writing Process for Persuasive Messages

Savvy business people often accomplish communication goals by using techniques of **persuasion**—the attempt to change an audience's attitudes, beliefs, or actions.[2] Effective persuasion is "the ability to present a message in a way that will lead others to

Persuasion is the attempt to change someone's attitudes, beliefs, or actions.

support it," says Jay Conger, author of *Winning 'Em Over.* "It makes audiences feel they have a choice, and they choose to agree."[3] In today's competitive marketplace, successful business people must be able to put together a persuasive argument. Applying the three-step writing process to your persuasive messages will help you make them as effective as possible (see Figure 9.1).

Step 1: Planning Persuasive Messages

For a persuasive message, some planning tasks require more effort.

Unlike routine positive messages (discussed in Chapter 7), persuasive messages aim to influence audiences who are inclined to resist. Therefore, persuasive messages are generally longer, are usually more detailed, and often depend heavily on careful planning. Persuasive messages require that you pay particular attention to analyzing your purpose, analyzing your audience, establishing your credibility, and striving for high ethical standards.

Analyze Your Purpose

Persuasive requests encounter two problems:

- Audiences are busy.
- Audiences receive many competing requests.

When writing a persuasive message, your purpose is to persuade people to do something different or to try something new. But people are busy, so they're reluctant to act, especially if the action takes time and offers no guarantee of any reward in return. Moreover, people receive competing requests from everywhere. When writing persuasive requests, you must be absolutely sure that your purpose is clear, necessary, and appropriate for written media. Focus on the action you want from the reader.

Analyze Your Audience

Chapter 3 discusses the basics of audience analysis, but the process can become much more involved for persuasive messages. Learning about your audience's needs or concerns can take weeks—even months. Everyone's needs differ, so everyone responds differently to any given message.

The questions you ask before writing a persuasive message go beyond those you would ask for other types of messages.

Using Questions to Gauge Audience Needs The best persuasive messages are closely connected to your audience's existing desires and interests.[4] Ask yourself these important questions:

- Who is my audience?
- What are their needs?
- What do I want them to do?
- How might they resist?
- Are there alternative positions I need to examine?
- What does the decision maker consider the most important issue?
- How might the organization's culture influence my strategy?

To assess various individual needs, you can refer to specific information. **Demographics** is information about the age, gender, occupation, income, education, and other quantifiable characteristics of your audience. **Psychographics** is information about the personality, attitudes, lifestyle, and other psychological characteristics of an individual. Both types of information are strongly influenced by culture.

Cultural differences influence your persuasion attempts.

Considering Cultural Differences Persuasion is different in different cultures. To satisfy the needs of audience members and gain their respect, you must understand and respect their cultural differences. For example, in France, using an aggressive, hard-sell technique would probably antagonize your audience. In Germany, where people tend to focus on technical matters, plan on verifying any figures you use for support, and make sure they are exact. In North America, audiences are usually concerned with more practical matters.[5] By taking into account the cultural expectations and practices of the people in your audience, you will be able to use the appropriate appeal and organize your message in a way that seems familiar and comfortable to them.

FIGURE 9.1 Applying the Three-Step Writing Process to Persuasive Messages

Planning	Writing	Completing
Analyze the Situation • Identify an "action" purpose. • Gauge audience needs. • Adapt the persuasive argument to cultural differences. **Investigate the Topic** • Ensure information is reliable and accurate. • Ensure facts support your argument. • Gather all relevant facts readers need. • Identify reader benefits. **Adapt to the Audience** • Verify effectiveness of written channel. • Establish your credibility. 1	**Organize the Message** • Define your main idea, limit the scope, and group related points. • Use the direct approach when: ∘ Readers prefer the "bottom line" first. ∘ Your firm encourages directness. ∘ Your message is long or complex. ∘ Your authority warrants doing so. • Choose the indirect approach when emotions are high. **Compose the Message** • Adapt the style and tone to readers. • Choose positive words. 2	**Revise the Message** • Judge your argument objectively. • Carefully match the purpose and organization to audience needs. **Produce the Message** • Ensure design emphasizes benefits. • Ensure the delivery method fits your purpose and audience expectations. **Proofread the Message** • Strengthen your persuasive message by correcting spelling and mechanical errors. • Correct any alignment problems. • Make sure the print quality is acceptable. 3

Establish Your Credibility

To persuade a sceptical or hostile audience, you must convince people that you know what you're talking about and that you're not trying to mislead them. Your *credibility* is your capability of being believed because you're reliable and worthy of confidence. Without such credibility, your efforts to persuade will seem manipulative. Some of the best ways to gain credibility are to

Your credibility is defined by how reliable, believable, and trustworthy you are.

You can do a lot to establish your credibility.

- **Support your message with facts.** Testimonials, documents, guarantees, statistics, and research results all provide seemingly objective evidence for what you have to say, which adds to your credibility. The more specific and relevant your proof, the better.
- **Name your sources.** Telling your audience where your information comes from and who agrees with you always improves your credibility, especially if your sources are already respected by your audience.
- **Establish your expertise.** Your knowledge of the subject area builds credibility.
- **Establish common ground.** Those beliefs, attitudes, and background experiences that you have in common with members of your audience will help them identify with you.
- **Be enthusiastic and positive.** Your excitement about your subject can infect your audience.
- **Be objective.** Your ability to understand and acknowledge all sides of an issue helps you present fair and logical arguments in your persuasive message.
- **Be sincere.** Your concern, genuineness, good faith, and truthfulness help you focus on your audience's needs.

Strive for High Ethical Standards

Some people view the word *persuasion* as negative. They associate persuasion with dishonest and unethical practices, such as coaxing, urging, and even tricking people into accepting an idea, buying a product, or taking an unwanted or unneeded action. However,

Positive persuasion leaves your audience free to choose.

successful business people make persuasion positive. They influence audience members by providing information and aiding understanding, which allows audiences the freedom to choose.[6]

To maintain the highest ethics, try to persuade without manipulating.

To maintain the highest standards of business ethics, make every attempt to persuade without manipulating. Choose words that won't be misinterpreted, and be sure you don't distort the truth. Focus on the members of your audience by showing honest concern for their needs and interests. Ethical business people show audiences that the benefits of an idea, a group, a product, or an action will satisfy a need they truly have.

Step 2: Writing Persuasive Messages

When writing persuasive messages, you will define your main idea, limit the scope of your message, and group your points in a meaningful way. But you must focus even more effort on choosing the direct or indirect approach. Some persuasive messages use the indirect approach, explaining reasons and building interest before revealing their purpose. However, many situations call for the direct approach.

Use the indirect approach when your audience will react unfavourably to your message. Use the direct approach when your message is long or complex, or when your reader prefers directness.

If audience members are objective, or if you know they prefer the "bottom line" first (perhaps because it saves them time), the direct approach might be the better choice. You'll also want to use the direct approach when your corporate culture encourages directness. In addition, when a message is long or complex, your readers may become impatient if the main idea is buried seven pages in, so you may want to choose the direct approach for these messages as well.

Sandi Sidhu is administrative assistant to the athletic director at UBC University. Each year, after hockey season tickets have been mailed, the cost of the athletic department's toll-free phone number skyrockets as fans call with questions about their seats, complaints about receiving the wrong number of tickets, or orders for last-minute tickets. Sidhu came up with an idea that could solve the problem, so she composed an e-mail message that uses the direct approach (see Figure 9.2). Sidhu supports her idea with benefits, not only for the athletic department but also for the fans who buy season tickets. Plus, her reasons are so logical that the message sounds both confident and convincing.

If you use the direct approach, keep in mind that even though your audience prefers the main point up front, you'll still want to include a justification or explanation, just as Sandi Sidhu did. Don't expect your reader to accept your idea on blind faith. For example, consider the following two openers:

Poor	Improved
I recommend building our new retail outlet on the West Main Street site.	After comparing the four possible sites for our new retail outlet, I recommend West Main Street as the only site that fulfils our criteria for visibility, proximity to mass transportation, and square footage.

Choice of approach is also influenced by your position (or authority within the organization) relative to your audience's.

Your choice between a direct and an indirect approach is also influenced by the extent of your authority, expertise, or power in an organization. As a first-line manager writing a persuasive message to top management, you may try to be diplomatic and use an indirect approach. However, your choice could backfire if some managers perceive your indirectness as manipulative and time wasting. On the other hand, you may try to save your supervisors time by using a direct approach, which might be perceived as brash and presumptuous. Similarly, when writing a persuasive message to employees, you may use the indirect approach to ease into a major change, but your audience might see your message as weak, even wishy-washy. You need to think carefully about your corporate culture and what your audience expects before selecting your approach.

FIGURE 9.2 E-mail Message Selling an Idea to a Boss

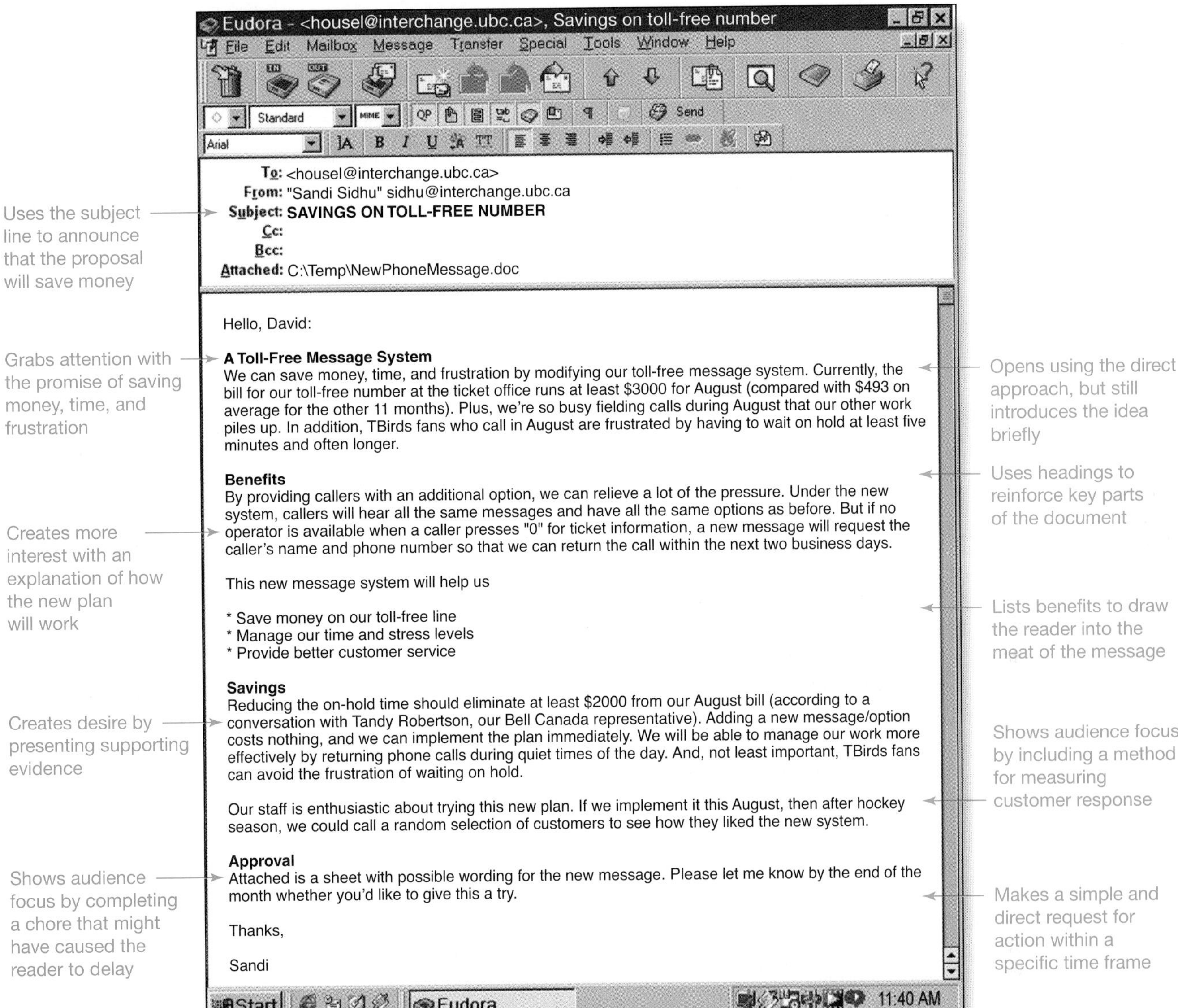

Step 3: Completing Persuasive Messages

The length and complexity of persuasive messages make applying Step 3 even more crucial to your success. When you evaluate your content, try to judge your argument objectively and appraise your credibility. When revising for clarity and conciseness, carefully match the purpose and organization to audience needs.

As with other business messages, Step 3 of the writing process helps guarantee the success of your persuasive messages.

Use design elements to complement (not detract from) your argument. For example, use headings and lists to highlight benefits as Sandi does in Figure 9.2. Finally, meticulous proofreading will identify any mechanical or spelling errors that would detract from the credibility of your persuasive message.

Strategies for Persuasive Messages

Whether you use a direct or an indirect approach, you must convince your reader that your request or idea is reasonable by identifying benefits that appeal to reader needs. Strike a balance between emotional and logical appeals, and master the AIDA (Attention, Interest, Desire, Action) organizational approach.

Balancing Emotional and Logical Appeals

Both emotional and logical appeals are needed to write successful persuasive messages.

One way to persuade people is to appeal to their hearts and minds. Most persuasive messages include both emotional and logical appeals. However, finding the right balance between these two types of appeals depends on four factors: (1) the actions you wish to motivate, (2) your reader's expectations, (3) the degree of resistance you must overcome, and (4) how far you feel empowered to go in selling your point of view.[7]

When you're persuading someone to accept a complex idea, take a serious step, or make a large and important decision, lean toward logic and make your emotional appeal subtle. However, when you're persuading someone to purchase a product, join a cause, or make a donation, rely a bit more on emotion.

Emotional Appeals

Emotional appeals are best if subtle.

An **emotional appeal** is based on audience feelings or sympathies; however, such an appeal must be subtle.[8] For instance, you can make use of the emotion surrounding certain words. The word *freedom* evokes strong feelings, as do words such as *success, prestige, credit record, savings, free, value,* and *comfort.* Such words put your audience in a certain frame of mind and help them accept your message. However, emotional appeals aren't necessarily effective by themselves. Emotion works with logic in a unique way: People need to find rational support for an attitude they've already embraced emotionally.

Logical Appeals

Logical appeals can use

- Analogy
- Induction
- Deduction

A **logical appeal** calls on human reason. In any argument you might use to persuade an audience, you make a claim and then support your claim with reasons or evidence. When appealing to your audience's logic, you might use three types of reasoning:

- **Analogy.** With analogy, you compare your idea to something familiar to your audience. For instance, to persuade employees to attend a planning session, you might use a town meeting analogy, comparing your company to a small community and your employees to valued members of that community.
- **Induction.** With induction, you reason from specific evidence to a general conclusion. To convince potential customers that your product is best, you might report the results of test marketing in which individuals preferred your product over others. After all, if some individuals prefer it, so will others.
- **Deduction.** With deduction, you might reason from a generalization to a specific conclusion. To persuade your boss to hire additional employees, you might point to industrywide projections and explain that industry activity (and thus your company's business) will be increasing rapidly over the next three months, so you'll need more employees to handle increased business.

Using AIDA for Indirect Plans

Most persuasive messages follow an organizational plan that goes beyond the indirect approach used for negative messages. The opening does more than serve as a buffer; it grabs your audience's attention. The explanation section is expanded to two sections. The first incites your audience's interest, and the second changes your audience's attitude. Finally, your close ends on a positive note with a statement of what action is needed and emphasizes reader benefits, motivating readers to take specific action. More intense than the indirect approach of bad-news messages, this persuasive approach is called the **AIDA plan.** In his letter in Figure 9.3, Randy Thumwolt uses the AIDA plan in a persuasive memo about his program to reduce Fairmont West's annual plastics costs while curtailing consumer complaints about the company's recycling record. In persuasive messages, use the AIDA plan to intensify audience reactions in each of four phases:

Organize persuasive messages using the AIDA plan:

- Attention
- Interest
- Desire
- Action

- **Attention.** Make your audience want to hear about your problem or idea. Write a brief and engaging opening sentence, with no extravagant claims or irrelevant points. And

FIGURE 9.3 Persuasive Memo Using the AIDA Plan

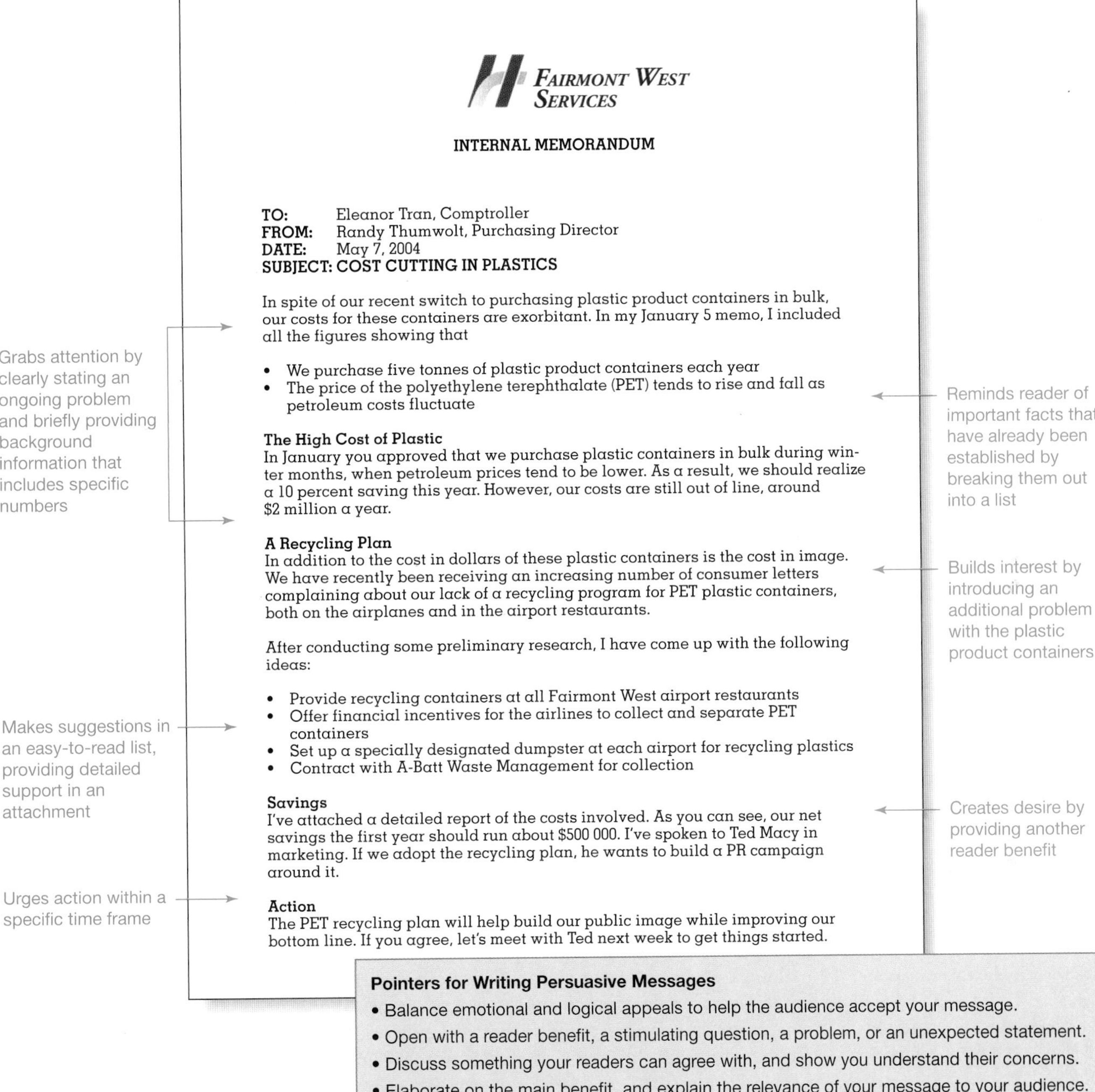

FAIRMONT WEST SERVICES

INTERNAL MEMORANDUM

TO: Eleanor Tran, Comptroller
FROM: Randy Thumwolt, Purchasing Director
DATE: May 7, 2004
SUBJECT: COST CUTTING IN PLASTICS

In spite of our recent switch to purchasing plastic product containers in bulk, our costs for these containers are exorbitant. In my January 5 memo, I included all the figures showing that

- We purchase five tonnes of plastic product containers each year
- The price of the polyethylene terephthalate (PET) tends to rise and fall as petroleum costs fluctuate

The High Cost of Plastic
In January you approved that we purchase plastic containers in bulk during winter months, when petroleum prices tend to be lower. As a result, we should realize a 10 percent saving this year. However, our costs are still out of line, around $2 million a year.

A Recycling Plan
In addition to the cost in dollars of these plastic containers is the cost in image. We have recently been receiving an increasing number of consumer letters complaining about our lack of a recycling program for PET plastic containers, both on the airplanes and in the airport restaurants.

After conducting some preliminary research, I have come up with the following ideas:

- Provide recycling containers at all Fairmont West airport restaurants
- Offer financial incentives for the airlines to collect and separate PET containers
- Set up a specially designated dumpster at each airport for recycling plastics
- Contract with A-Batt Waste Management for collection

Savings
I've attached a detailed report of the costs involved. As you can see, our net savings the first year should run about $500 000. I've spoken to Ted Macy in marketing. If we adopt the recycling plan, he wants to build a PR campaign around it.

Action
The PET recycling plan will help build our public image while improving our bottom line. If you agree, let's meet with Ted next week to get things started.

Grabs attention by clearly stating an ongoing problem and briefly providing background information that includes specific numbers
Reminds reader of important facts that have already been established by breaking them out into a list
Builds interest by introducing an additional problem with the plastic product containers
Makes suggestions in an easy-to-read list, providing detailed support in an attachment
Creates desire by providing another reader benefit
Urges action within a specific time frame

Pointers for Writing Persuasive Messages

- Balance emotional and logical appeals to help the audience accept your message.
- Open with a reader benefit, a stimulating question, a problem, or an unexpected statement.
- Discuss something your readers can agree with, and show you understand their concerns.
- Elaborate on the main benefit, and explain the relevance of your message to your audience.
- Make audience members want to act by explaining how the action will benefit them.
- Back up your claims with relevant evidence.
- Confidently ask for the audience's cooperation, and stress the positive results of the action.
- Include the due date (if any) for a response, and tie it in with audience benefits.
- Include one last reminder of the audience benefit, and make the desired action easy.

find some common ground on which to build your case. Thumwolt's letter gains attention by explaining the specifics of the problem he's trying to solve (see Figure 9.3).

- **Interest.** Explain the relevance of your message to your audience. Continuing the theme you started with, paint a more detailed picture with words. Get your audience thinking. Thumwolt's interest section introduces an additional, unforeseen problem with plastic product containers (see Figure 9.3). Moreover, Thumwolt emphasizes his suggestions with an easy-to-read list.

- **Desire.** Make readers want to change by explaining how the change will benefit them. Reduce resistance by thinking up and answering in advance any questions readers might have. Explain how you would implement complex ideas. Back up your claims to increase reader willingness to take the suggested action. Ensure that all evidence is relevant to your audience. Thumwolt emphasizes a monetary benefit and a possible public relations benefit. Most managers want to save time and money.
- **Action.** Urge readers to take the action you suggest. Make it more than a statement such as "Please institute this program soon" or "Send me a refund." Remind readers of the benefits of taking action, and make the action easy. You might ask your audience to use an enclosed order form or call a toll-free number. Thumwolt's letter suggests a meeting for further discussion. Include a deadline when applicable.

Using AIDA with the indirect approach allows you to save your idea for the action phase; using it with the direct approach allows you to use your main idea as your attention-getter.

The AIDA plan is tailor-made for using the indirect approach, allowing you to save your main idea for the action phase. However, it can also be used for the direct approach, in which case you use your main idea as an attention-getter, build interest with your argument, create desire with your evidence, and emphasize your main idea in the action phase with the specific action you want your audience to take.

When your AIDA message uses an indirect approach and is delivered by memo or e-mail, keep in mind that your subject line usually catches your readers' eye first. Your challenge is to make it interesting and relevant enough to capture reader attention without revealing your main idea. If you put your request in the subject line, you're likely to get a quick "no" before you've had a chance to present your arguments.

Direct	Indirect
Proposal to Install New Phone Message System	Savings on Toll-Free Number

When using the AIDA plan, narrow your objectives. Focus on your primary goal when presenting your case. For example, if your main idea is to convince your company to install a new phone-messaging system, leave discussions about switching long-distance carriers until another day—unless it's relevant to your argument.

Types of Persuasive Requests

Make only reasonable requests.

Highlight the direct and indirect benefits of complying with your request.

People write innumerable persuasive requests inside and outside an organization. When making a persuasive request, highlight both the direct and the indirect benefits of fulfilling it. For example, if you want to persuade your supervisor to institute flextime, a direct benefit for that person might be the reduced workload or the enhanced prestige. An indirect benefit might be better employee morale once flextime is instituted. As examples of persuasive requests, let's look at requests for action, claims, and adjustments.

Persuasive Requests for Action

When making a persuasive request for action, be sure to use the AIDA plan to frame your argument.

Whether you're requesting a favour or a budget increase, plan your message by asking yourself what questions the reader will have about your request. Typically, when readers are asked to do something they may be unwilling to do, they will want to know

- What exactly are you asking me to do?
- Why should I do it?
- What will I get from doing it? What will we gain?
- What will it cost?
- How will it work?

Use these questions to plan the content of your message and use AIDA to organize it:

- **Attention.** Begin with an attention-getting device. Show readers that you know something about their concerns before giving the main reason for making the request.
- **Interest and desire.** Answer the predicted reader questions; provide facts and figures, the benefits of helping, and any history or experience that will enhance your appeal.
- **Action.** Close with a request for some specific action. Make the action easy to do.

Leslie Jorgensen wrote the memo in Figure 9.4 on page 220. She's excited about the new Airbus A380 and believes that purchasing this plane for appropriate markets could help Qantas Airlines meet its growth needs while lowering its operating costs. She needs her boss's approval for a study of the plane's market potential.

Use the direct approach whenever you can.

When requesting a favour that is routine (such as asking someone to attend a meeting in your absence), use the direct approach and the format for routine messages (see Chapter 7). However, when asking for a special favour (such as asking someone to chair an event or to serve as the team leader because you can no longer fill that role), use persuasive techniques to convince your reader of the value of the project. Include all necessary information about the project and any facts and figures that will convince your reader that his or her contribution will be enjoyable, easy, important, and of personal benefit. If a request is sent first in writing, Mary Kreuk of CTV advises that business writers must "follow up with a call. You'd be surprised how many requests I get in a day, and no one follows up," says Kreuk.

Persuasive Claims and Requests for Adjustments

Although persuasive claims and adjustment requests are sometimes referred to as complaint letters, your goal is to persuade someone to make an adjustment in your favour, not merely to complain. You accomplish your goal by demonstrating the difference between what you expected and what you actually got.

The goal of a persuasive claim or request for adjustment is to convince someone to make an adjustment in your favour.

Most claim letters are routine messages and use the direct approach discussed in Chapter 7. However, suppose you purchase something and, after the warranty expires, you discover that the item was defective. You write the company a routine request asking for a replacement, but your request is denied. You're not satisfied, and you still believe you have a strong case. Perhaps you just didn't communicate it well enough the first time. Persuasion is necessary in such cases.

You can't threaten to withhold payment (the item has already been paid for), so try to convey the essentially negative information in a way that will get positive results. Fortunately, most people in business are open to settling your claim fairly. It's to their advantage to maintain your goodwill and to resolve your problem quickly.

Make your persuasive claims

- Complete and specific when reviewing the facts
- Confident and positive in tone

Two key ingredients of a good persuasive claim are (1) a complete and specific review of the facts and (2) a confident and positive tone. Assume that the reader is not trying to cheat you but that you have the right to be satisfied with the transaction. Talk only about the complaint at hand, not about other issues involving similar products or other complaints about the company. Your goal is to solve a particular problem, and your audience is most likely to help if you focus on the audience benefits of doing so (rather than focusing on the disadvantages of neglecting your complaint).

- **Attention.** Begin by stating the basic problem (or with a sincere compliment, rhetorical question, agreeable assertion, or brief review of what's been done about the problem). Include a statement that both you and your audience can agree with or that clarifies what you wish to convince your audience about. Be as specific as possible about what you want to happen.
- **Interest and desire.** Give your reader a good reason for granting your claim. Show how your audience is responsible for the problem, and appeal to your reader's sense of fair play, goodwill, or moral responsibility. Explain the problem without complaining too much, and don't make threats. Make sure your request is calm and reasonable.

FIGURE 9.4 Persuasive Memo Requesting Action—Direct Approach

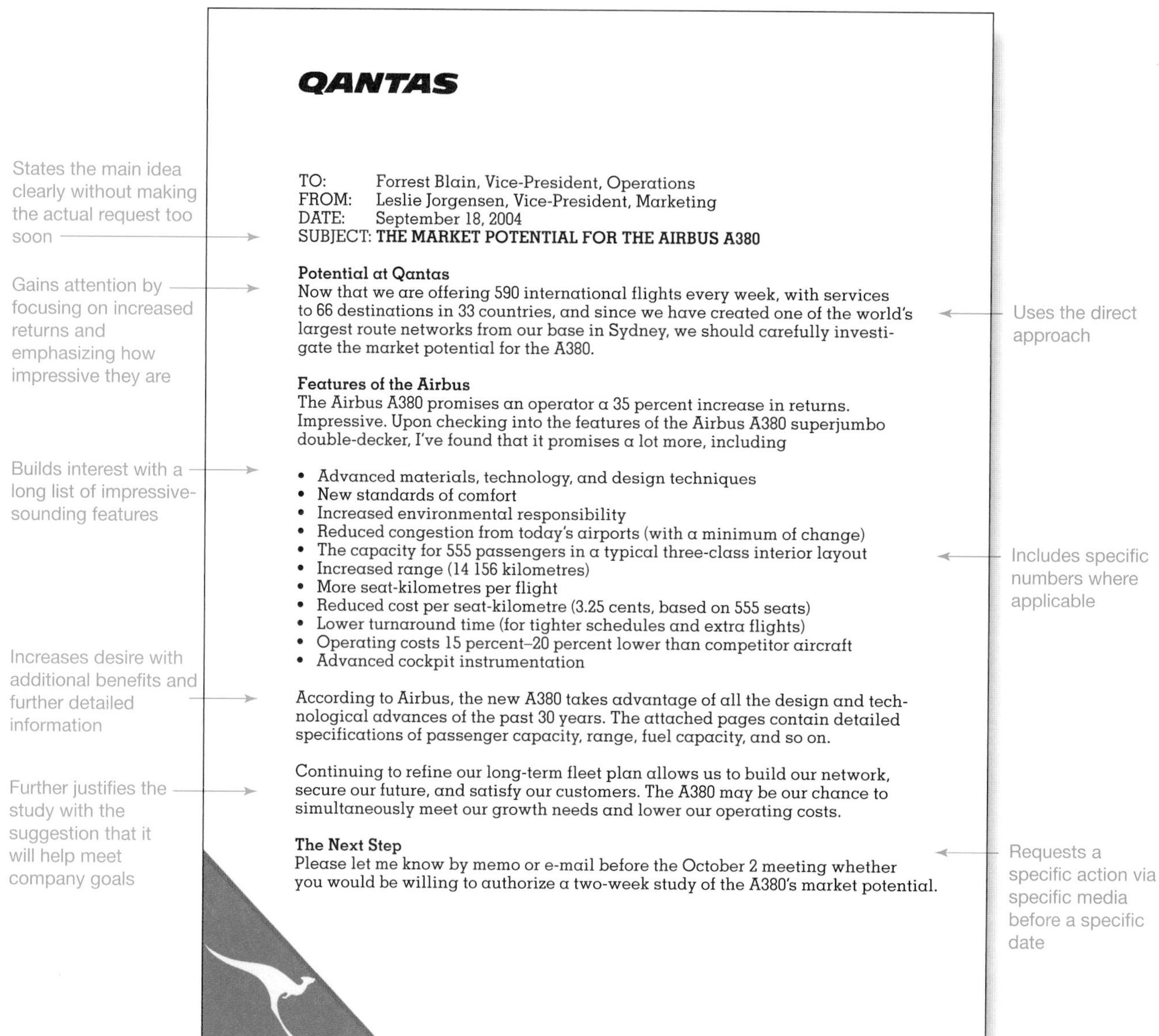

QANTAS

TO: Forrest Blain, Vice-President, Operations
FROM: Leslie Jorgensen, Vice-President, Marketing
DATE: September 18, 2004
SUBJECT: **THE MARKET POTENTIAL FOR THE AIRBUS A380**

Potential at Qantas
Now that we are offering 590 international flights every week, with services to 66 destinations in 33 countries, and since we have created one of the world's largest route networks from our base in Sydney, we should carefully investigate the market potential for the A380.

Features of the Airbus
The Airbus A380 promises an operator a 35 percent increase in returns. Impressive. Upon checking into the features of the Airbus A380 superjumbo double-decker, I've found that it promises a lot more, including

- Advanced materials, technology, and design techniques
- New standards of comfort
- Increased environmental responsibility
- Reduced congestion from today's airports (with a minimum of change)
- The capacity for 555 passengers in a typical three-class interior layout
- Increased range (14 156 kilometres)
- More seat-kilometres per flight
- Reduced cost per seat-kilometre (3.25 cents, based on 555 seats)
- Lower turnaround time (for tighter schedules and extra flights)
- Operating costs 15 percent–20 percent lower than competitor aircraft
- Advanced cockpit instrumentation

According to Airbus, the new A380 takes advantage of all the design and technological advances of the past 30 years. The attached pages contain detailed specifications of passenger capacity, range, fuel capacity, and so on.

Continuing to refine our long-term fleet plan allows us to build our network, secure our future, and satisfy our customers. The A380 may be our chance to simultaneously meet our growth needs and lower our operating costs.

The Next Step
Please let me know by memo or e-mail before the October 2 meeting whether you would be willing to authorize a two-week study of the A380's market potential.

States the main idea clearly without making the actual request too soon
Gains attention by focusing on increased returns and emphasizing how impressive they are
Builds interest with a long list of impressive-sounding features
Increases desire with additional benefits and further detailed information
Further justifies the study with the suggestion that it will help meet company goals
Uses the direct approach
Includes specific numbers where applicable
Requests a specific action via specific media before a specific date

- **Action.** State your request specifically and confidently. Make sure your request proceeds logically from the problem and the facts you've explained. Specify a deadline for action (when necessary or desirable) and remind your audience of the main benefit of granting your claim.

As Figure 9.5 illustrates, the best approach to resolving problems is to engage in a reasonable exchange rather than an adversarial struggle.

Sending Sales and Fundraising Messages

Sales and fundraising letters are distinctive types of persuasive messages that often come in special direct-mail packages.

Two distinctive types of persuasive messages are sales and fundraising messages. These messages are often sent in special direct-mail packages that can include brochures, reply forms, or other special inserts. Both types of messages are often written by specialized and highly skilled professionals.

FIGURE 9.5 Letter Making a Persuasive Claim

WORKING WORDS
EDITORIAL AND WRITING SERVICES
761 Rideau Drive, Ottawa, ON K1K 4R3 (613) 225-9231 Fax: (613) 225-9241

June 15, 2003

Ms. Ella Carver, Customer Service Representative
Del Mar Home Fashions
834 Boulevard Cité des Jeunes
Hull, QC J8Y 6T3

Dear Ms. Carver:

REPLACING A SHADE

Our office purchased five Del Mar cellular window shades through Cellini's Paint and Wall Covering. We bought four shades in June 2001, which were installed in four west-facing double-hung windows. Then in August 2002, we bought an additional shade, which was installed in a much larger north-facing garden window.

A couple of months ago, the individual cells in three of the west-facing shades began coming unglued. Cellini's helped us replace all three shades, in accordance with your company's lifetime guarantee for original owners who have kept the shades in their original windows and who have the original receipts.

Now another of our Del Mar shades has come unglued, and we would like you to replace it. This shade was purchased in August 2002, and the sticker under the endcap carries the following information:

No.	Product	Colour	Width	Height
C1116	Enchante (7/16) Petite cellular shade	Indigo Seas	42 1/4"	69"

Cellini's has informed us that it no longer sells Del Mar products. Although we have the receipts for the four shades purchased in June (see enclosed photocopies), we simply cannot locate the receipt for the single shade purchased in August.

Please help us replace this shade. Knowing your exceptional reputation for quality, fairness, and service, we would be happy to work with you directly or to visit a retailer in our area who handles your products. It's crucial to replace this shade as soon as possible, since July and August are our warmest and brightest months.

Sincerely,

Katherine Graham

Katherine Graham
President

Gains attention with the fact that a number of products have already been purchased from Del Mar

Creates desire to grant the coming request by relating the ease of past replacements and citing Del Mar's guarantee

Refers to attached receipts in the hope they will prove original ownership of the fifth shade

Closes by restating the adjustment requested, by exhibiting a cooperative attitude, and by quietly assuming that the claim will be granted

Implies a deadline

Increases interest by demonstrating full understanding of product guarantee provisions

Makes the request in positive language that follows logically from the problem and the facts described, including all necessary information

Explains extenuating circumstances after the request

Provides reader with a reason to grant the adjustment (Del Mar's reputation)

Pointers for Persuasive Claims and Adjustment Requests

- Begin by stating something you and your audience can agree on.
- Provide a description that shows readers that their firm is responsible for the problem.
- Make your request factual, logical, and reasonable.
- Appeal to the reader's sense of fair play, desire for customer goodwill, need for a good reputation, or sense of legal or moral responsibility.
- Tell the audience how you feel, without being overly emotional.
- Make the action request a logical conclusion based on the problem and the stated facts.
- Specify a due date for action (when desirable).
- State the main audience benefit as a reminder of benefits in earlier statements.

How do sales messages differ from fundraising messages? Sales messages are usually sent by for-profit organizations persuading readers to spend money on products for themselves. However, fundraising messages are usually sent by non-profit organizations persuading readers to donate money or time to help others. Aside from these differences, sales and fundraising messages are quite similar. Both require a few more steps than other types of persuasive messages, and both generally use the AIDA sequence.

Strategies for Sales Messages

When planning a sales message

- Know your product
- Know your audience

Since your purpose in writing a sales message is to sell a product, one of the first things to do is gain a thorough understanding of that product. What does it look like? How does it work? How is it priced? Are there any discounts? How is it packaged? How is it delivered?

At the same time, you'll need to carefully analyze your audience and focus on their needs, interests, and emotional concerns—just as you would for any persuasive message. But in addition to the usual questions, also ask yourself: What might audience members want to know about this product? How can this product help them? Are they driven by bottom-line pricing, or is quality more important to them?

Determining Selling Points and Benefits

Sales letters require you to know your product's selling points and how each point benefits your particular audience.

Selling points focus on the product; benefits focus on the user.

As Table 9.1 shows, **selling points** are the most attractive features of an idea or product; **benefits** are the particular advantages that readers will realize from those features. Selling points focus on the product. Benefits focus on the user. For example, if you say that your shovel has "an ergonomically designed handle," you've described a good feature. But to persuade someone to buy that shovel, say "the ergonomically designed handle will reduce your risk of back injury." That's a benefit. For your letter and your overall sales efforts to be successful, your product's distinguishing benefit must correspond to your readers' primary needs or emotional concerns.

Table 9.1 Features Versus Benefits

Product Feature (Selling Point)	Consumer Benefit
No money down, no interest payments for 24 months.	You can buy what you want right now at no additional costs.
This printer prints 17 pages a minute.	This printer can turn out one of your 100-page proposals in 6 minutes.
Our shelter provides 100 adult beds and 50 children's beds for the needy.	Your donation will provide temporary housing for 100 women who don't want to return to abusive husband or partners.
Your corporate sponsorship of the seminar will pay for the keynote speaker's travel and lodging.	Your corporate sponsorship of the seminar will allow your site manager a five-minute introduction at the beginning of the program to summarize your services.

For example, the sales letter in Figure 9.6 persuades students to buy a SecureAbel dorm-room alarm system. The features of the system are that it can be installed with a screwdriver, it has an activator that hooks to your key chain or belt loop, and it has a blinking red light to warn intruders to stay away. The benefits are ease of installation, ease of activation, and a feeling of safety and security—all obtainable without investing in a full-blown permanently installed alarm system.

When composing sales messages, be sure to focus on relatively few product benefits. Ultimately, you'll single out one key benefit. Safety is the key benefit emphasized by SecureAbel Alarms.

Using Action Terms

Action words give strength to any business message, but they are especially important in sales letters. Compare the following:

Instead of	Write
The NuForm desk chair is designed to support your lower back and relieve pressure on your legs.	The NuForm desk chair supports your lower back and relieves pressure on your legs.

FIGURE 9.6 Letter Selling a Product

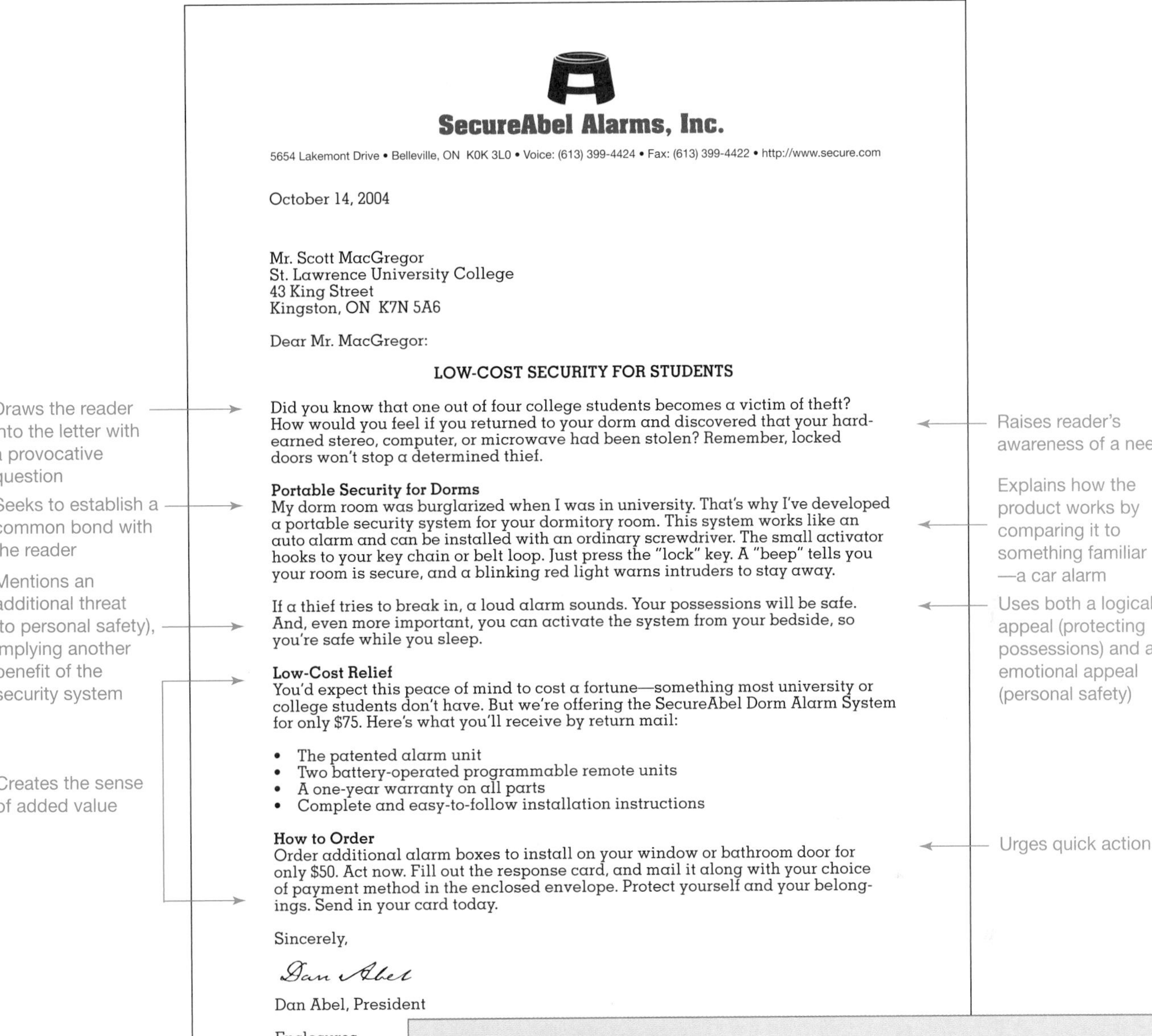

SecureAbel Alarms, Inc.

5654 Lakemont Drive • Belleville, ON K0K 3L0 • Voice: (613) 399-4424 • Fax: (613) 399-4422 • http://www.secure.com

October 14, 2004

Mr. Scott MacGregor
St. Lawrence University College
43 King Street
Kingston, ON K7N 5A6

Dear Mr. MacGregor:

LOW-COST SECURITY FOR STUDENTS

Did you know that one out of four college students becomes a victim of theft? How would you feel if you returned to your dorm and discovered that your hard-earned stereo, computer, or microwave had been stolen? Remember, locked doors won't stop a determined thief.

Portable Security for Dorms
My dorm room was burglarized when I was in university. That's why I've developed a portable security system for your dormitory room. This system works like an auto alarm and can be installed with an ordinary screwdriver. The small activator hooks to your key chain or belt loop. Just press the "lock" key. A "beep" tells you your room is secure, and a blinking red light warns intruders to stay away.

If a thief tries to break in, a loud alarm sounds. Your possessions will be safe. And, even more important, you can activate the system from your bedside, so you're safe while you sleep.

Low-Cost Relief
You'd expect this peace of mind to cost a fortune—something most university or college students don't have. But we're offering the SecureAbel Dorm Alarm System for only $75. Here's what you'll receive by return mail:

- The patented alarm unit
- Two battery-operated programmable remote units
- A one-year warranty on all parts
- Complete and easy-to-follow installation instructions

How to Order
Order additional alarm boxes to install on your window or bathroom door for only $50. Act now. Fill out the response card, and mail it along with your choice of payment method in the enclosed envelope. Protect yourself and your belongings. Send in your card today.

Sincerely,

Dan Abel

Dan Abel, President

Enclosures

Draws the reader into the letter with a provocative question
Seeks to establish a common bond with the reader
Mentions an additional threat (to personal safety), implying another benefit of the security system
Creates the sense of added value
Raises reader's awareness of a need
Explains how the product works by comparing it to something familiar —a car alarm
Uses both a logical appeal (protecting possessions) and an emotional appeal (personal safety)
Urges quick action

Pointers for Writing Sales Letters

- Get attention with a question, a fact, a solution, an offer/gift, a testimonial, and so on.
- Promise a benefit to the reader.
- Develop the central selling point, vividly relating details to the reader's concerns.
- Describe objective details of the product (size, shape, colour, scent, sound, texture, etc.).
- Anticipate and answer reader questions, and use an appropriate form of evidence.
- Offer a free trial or a guarantee, and refer to samples if they are included.
- Note any enclosures in conjunction with a selling point or a reader benefit.
- Clearly state the action you desire, along with specifics on how to order the product.
- Ease action with reply cards, pre-addressed envelopes, phone numbers, and so on.
- Supply a final reader benefit and offer a special inducement to act now.
- In a postscript, convey important donation information or an important sales point.

To give force to a message

- Use action terms
- Use colourful verbs and adjectives

The second version says the same thing in fewer words and emphasizes the chair's benefit to the user ("supports") rather than the design team's intentions ("is designed to support"). Use colourful verbs and adjectives that convey a dynamic image. Be careful, however, not to overdo it: "Your factory floors will sparkle like diamonds" is hard to believe and may prevent your audience from believing the rest of your message.

Talking About Price

You can prepare readers for your product's price by subtle choice and arrangement of words.

Decide whether to highlight or downplay the price of your product. Here's an example from a sales letter offering a product at a bargain price:

> **All the Features of Name-Brand Pantyhose at Half the Price!**
>
> Why pay for fancy packaging or for that little tag with a famous name on it when you can enjoy cotton lining, reinforced toes, and matchless durability for only $1.99?

To de-emphasize price

- Bury actual figures in the middle of a paragraph near the end
- Mention benefits and favourable money matters before the actual price
- Break a quantity price into units
- Compare the price with the cost of some other product or activity

In this excerpt the price falls right at the end of the paragraph, where it stands out. In addition, the price is featured in a bold headline. This technique may even be used as the opening of a letter, if (1) the price is the most important feature and (2) the audience for the letter is value conscious.

If price is not a major selling point, you can handle it in several ways. You could leave the price out altogether or mention it only in an accompanying brochure. Or de-emphasize the price by burying it in the middle of a paragraph close to the end of your sales letter, well after you've presented the benefits and selling points.

Emphasizes the rarity of the edition to signal value and thus prepare the reader for the big-ticket price that follows →

> Only 100 prints of this exclusive, limited-edition lithograph will be created. On July 15, they will be made available to the general public, but you can reserve one now for only $350, the special advance reservation price. Simply send the enclosed reservation card back today so that your order is in before the June 15 publication date.

← Buries the actual price in the middle of a sentence and ties it in with another reminder of the exclusivity of the offer

Another technique is to break a quantity price into units. Instead of saying that a case of wine costs $144, say that each bottle costs $12. One more technique is to compare your product's price with the cost of some other product or activity: "The cost of owning your own exercise equipment is less than you'd pay for a health-club membership." Your aim is to make the cost seem as small and affordable as possible, thereby eliminating price as a possible objection.

Supporting Your Claims

You can't assume that people will believe what you say about your product. You'll have to prove your claims. Support is especially important if your product is complicated, costs a lot, or represents some unusual approach.

Types of support for product claims:

- Samples
- Brochures
- Examples
- Testimonials
- Statistics
- Guarantees

Support for your claims may take several forms. Samples and brochures, often with photographs, can be enclosed in a sales package and referred to in the letter. The letter can also describe or typographically highlight examples of how the product has benefited others. It could include testimonials (quotations from satisfied customers), cite statistics from scientific studies of the product's performance, or offer a guarantee. Try to anticipate every question your audience may want to ask. Put yourself in your audience's place so that you can discover, and solve, all the "what if" scenarios.[9]

Strategies for Fundraising Messages

Fundraising letters focus on the benefits of donating.

Most of the techniques used to write sales letters can also be used to write fundraising letters, as long as your techniques match your audience, your goals, and the cause or organization you're representing. Motivating action is a challenge when you're trying to raise funds. Establish value in the minds of your donors and include the "what's in it for me?" information—for example, telling your readers how good they'll feel by making a donation.[10]

FIGURE 9.7 Letter to Raise Funds

Pointers for Writing Fundraising Letters

- Begin by reading donor letters to learn as much as you can about your audience.
- Research competitor fundraising letters to see what works.
- Emphasize donor benefits.
- Design an attention-getter that uses a human-interest story.
- Don't let your letter sound like a business communication of any kind.
- Don't assume that your organization's goals are more important than readers' concerns.
- Show how important it is for readers to help.
- Spell out exactly what amount of help is being requested.
- Blend cold facts with warm feelings.
- Include detail about how donations are spent, using recognized accounting/auditing firms.

1960 Bloor Street • Toronto, ON M5T 2T9 • (416) 489-6100

June 17, 2004

Mr. William Hanover, President
Hanover, Jude, and Larson
12785 Crestview Dr.
Toronto, ON M9W 5L7

Ernie needs your help!

Includes a photo to further personalize the message and strengthen the emotional appeal

Dear Mr. Hanover:

Gains attention by personalizing the message with a real-life story

Avoids sounding like a business communication while getting right to the point

Ernie deserves a loving home. When Sheila Jenkins found him in the alley behind her apartment, the poor little guy was weak from hunger, infested with fleas, and dragging a broken leg. Under skilful care at the local animal shelter, Ernie recovered fully and won the hearts of all with his indomitable spirit, his quick intelligence, and his perky devotion.

Increases interest by providing hard (even painful) numbers and details of just what PETsMART Charities does

Ernie has been waiting patiently for a family to love, but sometimes homes are hard to find. More than five million pets are euthanized every year in North America simply because they have no family or home to call their own. So in 1992 PETsMART decided not to sell cats and dogs. Instead, the company created PETsMART Charities' Adoption Centres—in-store space that is donated to help local animal welfare organizations make homeless pets available for adoption.

Creates a desire to be involved by sharing specific successes of the program

Uses a carefully constructed transition to move reader from what PETsMART has done to what the reader can do

Over the past decade, PETsMART Charities has donated $24 million to animal welfare programs, and through our in-store adoption programs, in North America we've helped save the lives of more than 1 million pets, one by one. These accomplishments are the result of devotion, hard work, and contributions from our own associates and from companies like yours. Money we raise in your province stays in your province to help local animals. And to continue saving lives, we need your help more than ever.

Makes the request by stating the benefits of the reader's donation to others as well as to the reader

Takes special pains to focus on the reader and his company

Mr. Hanover, you and your associates have proved that you care about your community. You know business is about more than merely selling a product or service. Now, with a one-time donation of $100, your company can save the lives of many faithful pet companions. With a yearly or a scheduled monthly donation, you can do even more to rescue these loving family members. Your gift saves lives, makes you feel great, and strengthens your firm's reputation as a caring and responsible company.

Closes by echoing the real-life story that opened the message and repeating the request for specific action

Please help Ernie find a good home. Just fill out the enclosed reply form and send it along with your donation in the envelope provided. Ernie can't make it without you, and neither can we.

Sincerely,

Rita E. Gomez

Rita E. Gomez
Director

Enclosure

Reply form is complete and thorough

TO HELP PETsMART CHARITIES SAVE LIVES

________________________________ **(company)**

________________________________ **(address)**

WISHES TO DONATE

❑ **$100**	❑ **By cheque (enclosed)**
❑ **$____ each year**	❑ **By credit card:**
❑ **$____ a month (for 12 mos.)**	**____Visa ____MasterCard**
	Card no.: ____________
	Signature: ____________
	Position: ____________

Human interest stories interest readers.

Strong fundraising letters

- Explain a specific need thoroughly
- Show how important it is for readers to help
- Spell out exactly what amount of help is being requested
- Describe in detail the benefits of helping

Because fundraising letters depend so heavily on emotional appeals, keep your message personal. A natural, real-life lead-in is usually the best. People seem to respond best to slice-of-life stories. Storytelling is perfect when your narrative is unforced and goes straight to the heart of the matter.[11] As director of PETsMART Charities, Rita Gomez has the task of raising millions of dollars to help save the lives of and find families for thousands of homeless pets. Her letter in Figure 9.7 makes a compelling case for donations.

Reviewing Key Points

This chapter discussed strategies for persuasive messages, including persuasive requests, claims, and sales and fundraising letters.
In the planning stage

- Analyze the audience to identify needs, values, and interests and to build relationships
- Consider cultural and corporate values in assessing strategies and appeals
- Establish credibility by following through with clients, by supporting points with facts and logical reasons, and by using credible sources
- Have ethical standards and be sincere

In the writing stage

- Use a direct pattern when you anticipate low resistance and for internal communication when the company expects directness
- Use an indirect pattern when resistance is high and the receiver is likely to be unreceptive
- Balance logical and emotional appeals (depending on your topic and audience)
- Use the AIDA pattern for claims and sales messages: get attention, build interest and desire, and motivate readers to act
- Choose positive, definite words

By using these techniques, you can create messages that come across to readers as sincere, sensible, and appealing.

Test Your Knowledge

1. What are some questions to ask when gauging the audience's needs during the planning of a persuasive message?

2. What role do demographics and psychographics play in audience analysis during the planning of a persuasive message?

3. What are four of the ways you can build credibility with an audience when planning a persuasive message?

4. How do emotional appeals differ from logical appeals?

5. What three types of reasoning can you use in logical appeals?

6. What is the AIDA plan, and how does it apply to persuasive messages?

7. What are the similarities and differences between sales messages and fundraising messages?

8. What are six strategies to use when preparing sales messages?

9. How do benefits differ from features?

10. What four strategies will help your fundraising letters succeed?

Apply Your Knowledge

1. When writing persuasive messages, why is it so important to give special attention to the analysis of your purpose and audience?

2. How are persuasive messages different from routine messages?

3. When is it appropriate to use the direct organizational approach in persuasive messages?

4. As an employee, count how many of your daily tasks require persuasion. List as many as you can think of. Who are your audiences, and how do their needs and characteristics affect the way you develop your persuasive messages at work?

5. **Ethical Choices** Are emotional appeals ethical? Why or why not?

Practise Your Knowledge

Analyzing Persuasive Messages: Teamwork With another student, analyze the persuasive memo at Fairmont West (Figure 9.3 on page 217) by answering the following questions:

1. What techniques are used to capture the reader's attention?

2. Does the writer use the direct or the indirect organizational approach? Why?

3. Is the subject line effective? Why or why not?

4. Does the writer use an emotional or a logical appeal? Why?

5. What reader benefits are included?

6. How does the writer establish credibility?

7. What tools does the writer use to reinforce his position?

Composing: Subject Lines Compose effective subject lines for the following persuasive memos:

8. A request to your supervisor to purchase a new high-speed laser printer for your office. You've been outsourcing quite a bit of your printing to AlphaGraphics, and you're certain this printer will pay for itself in six months.

9. A direct mailing to area residents soliciting customers for your new business, "Meals à la Car," a carryout dining service that delivers from most local-area restaurants. All local restaurant menus are on the Internet. Mom and Dad can dine on egg rolls and chow mein while the kids munch on pepperoni pizza.

10. A special request to the company president to allow managers to carry over their unused vacation days to the following year. Apparently, many managers cancelled their fourth-quarter vacation plans to work on the installation of a new company computer system. Under their current contract, vacation days not used by December 31 aren't accruable.

Focusing on Benefits Determine whether the following sentences focus on features or benefits; rewrite as necessary to focus all the sentences on benefits.

11. All-Cook skillets are coated with a durable, patented nonstick surface.

12. You can call anyone and talk as long you like on Saturdays and Sundays with this new wireless telephone service.

13. We need to raise $25 to provide each needy child with a backpack filled with school supplies.

Activities

For live links to all Web sites discussed in this chapter, visit this text's Web site at www.prenhall.ca/bovee. Just log on, select Chapter 9, and click on "Student Resources." Locate the page or the URL related to the material in the text. For the "Exploring the Best of the Web" exercises, you'll also find navigational directions. Click on the live link to the site.

1. **Analyze This Document** Read the following document, then (1) analyze the strengths and weaknesses of each sentence and (2) revise the document so that it follows this chapter's guidelines:

   At Tolson Auto Repair, we have been in business for more than 25 years. We stay in business by always taking into account what the customer wants. That's why we are writing. We want to know your opinions to be able to better conduct our business.

   Take a moment right now and fill out the enclosed questionnaire. We know everyone is busy, but this is just one way we have of making sure our people do their job correctly. Use the enclosed envelope to return the questionnaire.

   And again, we're happy you chose Tolson Auto Repair. We want to take care of all your auto needs.

2. **Analyze This Document** Read the following document, then (1) analyze the strengths and weaknesses of each sentence and (2) revise the document so that it follows this chapter's guidelines:

   Dear Gateway:

   I'm writing to you because of my disappointment with my new TelePath x2 Faxmodem. The modem works all right, but the volume is set wide open and the volume knob doesn't turn it down. It's driving us crazy. The volume knob doesn't seem to be connected to anything but simply spins around. I can't believe you would put out a product like this without testing it first.

   I depend on the modem to run my small business and want to know what you are going to do about it. This reminds me of every time I buy electronic equipment from what seems like any company. Something is always wrong. I thought quality was supposed to be important, but I guess not.

   Anyway, I need this fixed right away. Please tell me what you want me to do.

3. **Analyze This Document** Read the following document, then (1) analyze the strengths and weaknesses of each sentence and (2) revise the document so that it follows this chapter's guidelines:

   We know how awful dining hall food can be, and that's why we've developed the "Mealaweek Club." Once a week, we'll deliver food to your dormitory or apartment. Our meals taste great. We have pizza, buffalo wings, hamburgers and curly fries, veggie roll-ups, and more!

   When you sign up for just six months, we will ask what day you want your delivery. We'll ask you to fill out your selection of meals. And the rest is up to us. At "Mealaweek," we deliver! And payment is easy. We accept MasterCard and Visa or a personal cheque. It will save money, especially when compared with eating out.

Just fill out the enclosed card and indicate your method of payment. As soon as we approve your credit or cheque, we'll begin delivery. Tell all your friends about Mealaweek. We're the best idea since sliced bread!

4. **Ethical Choices** Your boss has asked you to draft a memo requesting that everyone in your department donate money to the company's favourite charity, an organization that operates a special summer camp for children with physical disabilities. You wind up writing a three-page memo packed with facts and heartwarming anecdotes about the camp and the children's experiences. When you must work that hard to persuade your audience to take an action such as donating money to a charity, aren't you being manipulative and unethical? Explain.

5. **Revising a Letter: Request for a Rent Refund from Kuykendahl Joint, Inc.** The following persuasive request for adjustment contains many flaws. Using what you've learned in the chapter, read the message carefully and analyze its faults. Then use the questions below to outline and write an improved message.

CONTRACT
MANAGEMENT
SERVICES
INCORPORATED

3638 University Boulevard, Suite 302, Edmonton, AB T8N 4S2
(403) 458-3899 fax: (403) 458-3803 www.cmsi.com

March 22, 2005

Mr. Robert Bechtold, Manager

Kuykendahl Joint, Inc.
88 North Park Road
Edmonton, AB T8N 3H5
Re: Last Warning
Dear Mr. Bechtold:

Enclosed is a summary of recent ETS-related court cases in which landlords and owners were held responsible for providing toxin-free air for their tenants. In most of these cases, owners were also required to reimburse rents and pay damages for the harm done before the environmental tobacco smoke problem was remedied.

We've been plagued with this since we moved in on January 2, 2004. You haven't acted on our complaints, or responded to our explanations that secondhand smoke is making us sick, filtering in from nearby offices. You must act now or you will be hearing from our lawyers. We've told you that we were forced to hire contractors to apply weather stripping and seal openings. This cost us $3000 (bills attached) and we expect reimbursement. But the smoke is still coming in. We also want a refund for the $9000 we've paid you in rent since January. Call us immediately at (403) 458-3899, or our lawyers will be calling you.

Cigarette smoke from tenants on either side of us, and perhaps above and below as well, has been infiltrating our space, and you have done nothing, despite our pleas, to stop it. This is unacceptable. This is a known human carcinogen. Ask the Environmental Protection Agency, which classified it as Group A toxin. It causes lung, breast, cervical, and endocrine cancer in nonsmokers. You wouldn't want to breathe it, either.

One employee already quit who suffered from asthma. Another is threatening because he's a high risk for heart attack. Migraines, bronchitis, respiratory infections—all caused by the 4600 chemicals in ETS, including poisons such as cyanide, arsenic, formaldehyde, carbon monoxide, and ammonia. We've had them all—the illnesses, that is.

Secondhand smoke is even more dangerous than what smokers inhale, since the inhalation process burns off some of the toxins. Sick time has already cost CMSI valuable business and lowered productivity. Plus many of us are considering finding other jobs unless our office air becomes safe to breathe again. But as the court cases prove, the responsibility for fixing this problem is yours. We expect you to live up to that responsibility immediately. Frankly, we're fed up with your lack of response.

Kathleen Thomas

Manager

1. Describe the flaws you discovered in this persuasive request for adjustment.
2. Develop a plan for rewriting the letter. The following steps will help you organize your thoughts before you begin writing:
   a. Should you use a direct or an indirect approach?
   b. How can you use the "you" attitude to gain attention in the opening?
   c. What can you do to establish your credibility?
   d. How can you improve the order of material presented in the body of the letter?
   e. Create an appropriate closing.
3. Now rewrite the letter. Don't forget to leave ample time for revision of your own work before you turn it in.

6. **Revising a Sales Letter: From ScrubaDub About Its Car Care Club** The following sales letter falls short of its objectives. Use what you know about sales letters to analyze its flaws. Then follow the steps below to produce a better version.

11 locations in Ontario and Quebec
Bob and Dan Paisner, Owners

Dear Customers:

We are pleased to announce that ScrubaDub has added a new service, the Car Care Club.

It costs $5.95 for a lifetime membership (your car's lifetime) and features our computer automation. You'll be given a bar-coded sticker for your windshield so our computers can identify you as a club member when you pull in. If you sign up within the next 30 days, we will grant you a SuperWash for free.

The new club offers the standard ScrubaDub Touch-less systems to protect your finishes, our private formula Superglo detergent to clean your car safely and thoroughly, wheel sensors to prescribe the right treatment for whitewalls, wire, or chrome, soft, heated well water to eliminate spots, soft-cloth drying for final gloss. We also recycle our water and grant you a free wash on your birthday.

In addition, club members only will have access to a 48-hour guarantee (free rewashes) or 4 days if you purchased the premium Super Wash, Luxury Wash, Special or Works Wash. After 10 washes, our computer will award you a free wash. Also available only to club members are $5 rebates for foam waxes (Turtle Wax, Simonize, or Blue Coral). Some additional specials will be granted by us to car club members, on an unplanned basis.

We can handle special requests if you inquire of our Satisfaction Supervisors. We honour our customers with refunds if they remain unsatisfied after a rewash. This is our Bumper-to-Bumper Guarantee.

Sincerely,

Bob and Dan Paisner

1. Describe the mistakes made by the writers of this sales letter.
2. Develop a plan for improving the letter. The following questions will help you organize your thinking:
   a. How can you improve the letterhead, salutation, or subject line (missing here)?
   b. What can you assume about the audience, which is made up of regular customers?
   c. How can you use this information to develop a better opening?
   d. Since customers already know ScrubaDub, what can you do to improve the body of the letter? Can you identify selling points versus benefits? What about the use of language and/or tone of the letter? Formatting?

   e. What can you use as a P.S. to boost sales potential? Could you also make up a special offer to include?

3. Now rewrite the sales letter. Don't forget to leave ample time for revision of your work before you turn it in.

7. Revising a Persuasive Memo: E-cruiting at Boulder Construction This "persuasive" memo probably won't work effectively. Can you identify the mistakes the writer has made? Follow the steps below to analyze and improve on this persuasive request for action.

To: Sheila Young, Human Resources Director
From: Shelby Howard, Vice-President
Subject: Recruiting tactics
Date: February 15, 2004

Dear Sheila: I think we should try e-cruiting. I want you to use the huge data banks of resumés now listed on the Internet. They provide the software for your searches through these thousands of resumés they receive, so it shouldn't be too difficult. But you will have to define the qualifications you want first. Then they'll supply the resumés that fit.

Eventually, you can develop a Web site for our company that will post job listings. Then you'll get replies from the kinds of people who might not otherwise post their resumés online. Some of them may be good employees we've been looking for.

Costs breakdowns are: About $1300 apiece per candidate for traditional (newspaper ad) hiring. Plus your time for pre-screening. For e-cruiting, approximately $183 per candidate, with prescreening supplied by jobsearch databases such as monster.ca, hotjobs.com, or careermosaic.com. They will, however, charge us about $100–300 per month to list our jobs, rather than the $1000 the local paper charges us for a Sunday ad. Online job posting word length: unlimited.

You might have to wade through the 30 000 to 100 000 Internet sites now devoted to recruiting. Better stick with the names I've already mentioned. You'll be accessing about 150 million Internet users in North America, 74 percent of them over the age of 18 looking for jobs.

Right now, our competitors aren't using this method and I can't figure out why. I'm thinking it could be a way to reach talent we might otherwise miss. Maybe they just haven't figured this out yet. You know the ones I mean—the talented individuals we compete for with other construction companies, even though we offer good jobs and benefits.

I read that Bank of Montreal relied on e-cruiting this year. They say they saved $1 million, but we'll have to see how accurate that is with our own trial. Only 2 percent of building industry employers use e-cruiting. Sixty percent of computer companies use it, probably because surfing the Internet is no hassle for them. They insist hiring time per candidate is reduced from six weeks to one hour, but I'll have to see that to believe it! Something about not having to wait for snail mail resumés. But then they also don't get to screen candidates by sight first, so maybe it's a toss-up. On the other hand, they can e-mail questions back and forth.

Well, why don't we give it a go anyway?

1. Describe the flaws in approach and execution of this persuasive request for action.
2. Develop a plan for improving the memo. The following questions should help to stimulate your ideas:
   a. Starting with the subject line, how can you focus on your audience's needs?
   b. What would be a better opening? Why?
   c. How can you reorganize the body of the memo to improve the reader's interest and receptivity to the new idea?
   d. How can you handle facts, statistics, benefits, and appeals more skilfully?
   e. What should be included in the conclusion to the memo?
3. Now rewrite this persuasive request for action. Don't forget to leave ample time for checking your work.

8. **Analyzing a Sales Package: Learning from the Direct-Mail Pros** The daily mail often brings a selection of sales messages to your front door. Find a direct-mail package from your mailbox that includes a sales letter. Then answer the following questions to help you analyze and learn from the approach used by the communication professionals who prepare these glossy sales messages. Your instructor might also ask you to share the package and your observations in a class discussion.

   1. Who is the intended audience?
   2. What are the demographic and psychographic characteristics of the intended audience?
   3. What is the purpose of the direct-mail package? Has it been designed to solicit a phone-call response, make a mail-order sale, obtain a charitable contribution, or do something else?
   4. What, if any, technique was used to encourage you to open the envelope?
   5. What kind of letter is included? Is it fully printed, printed with a computer fill-in of certain specific information, or fully computer-typed? Is the letter personalized with your name or your family's name? If so, how many times?
   6. Did the letter writer follow the AIDA plan? If not, explain the letter's organization.
   7. What needs does it appeal to?
   8. What emotional appeals and logical arguments does the letter use?
   9. What selling points and consumer benefits does the letter offer?
   10. How many and what kinds of enclosures (such as brochures and order cards) were included for support?
   11. Does the letter or package have an unusual format? Does it use eye-catching graphics?
   12. Is the message in the letter and on the supporting pieces believable? Would the package sell the product or service to you? Why or why not?

Expand Your Knowledge

Best of the Web

Influence an Official and Promote Your Cause
At the Welcome to Canada's Parliament site, created jointly by the Senate, House of Commons, and the Library of Parliament, you'll discover voluminous information about federal legislation, members of Parliament, and committee lists. You can also access committee home pages and numerous links to government agencies, current issues, and historical documents. You can review all kinds of regulatory information, including laws and relevant issues that might affect you in the business world. Visit the site and stay informed. Maybe you'll want to convince a government official to support a business-related issue that affects you.

www.parl.gc.ca

Exercises

1. What key ideas would you include in an e-mail message to persuade your Member of the Legislative Assembly (MLA) or MP to support an issue important to you?
2. In a letter to an MLA or MP, what information would you include to convince the reader to vote for an issue supporting small business?
3. When sending a message to someone who daily receives hundreds of written appeals, what attention-getting techniques can you use? How can you get support for a cause that concerns you as a business person?

Exploring the Web on Your Own

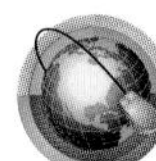

Review these chapter-related Web sites on your own to learn more about writing persuasive messages.

1. Visit Industry Canada's Office of Consumer Affairs Web site, strategis.gc.ca. Click on "Consumer Information" to gather tips and examples of how to resolve problems effectively and find warnings about products.

   Choose "Company Directions" for information on Canadian companies or click on the Strategies guide "Researching Markets" for information on doing business abroad. Take a look at statistics on e-commerce or review databases of importers. At the top of the strategis.gc.ca site, click on "Canada Site" to find lists of government contacts with e-mail, telephone, and street addresses.
2. Learn some aggressive sales strategies without going overboard from Guerrilla Marketing at www.gmarketing.com.

Learn Interactively

Interactive Study Guide

Visit the Companion Website at www.pearsoned.com/bovee. For Chapter 9, take advantage of the interactive "Study Guide" to test your chapter knowledge. Get instant feedback on whether you need additional studying.

This site offers a variety of additional resources: The "Research Area" helps you locate a wealth of information to use in course assignments. The "Study Hall" helps you succeed in this course by offering support with writing and study skills, time management, and career skills, as well as numerous other resources.

Peak Performance Grammar and Mechanics

Use the Peak Performance Grammar and Mechanics CD to test your skill with punctuation. In the "Punctuation II" section, take the Pretest to determine whether you have any weak areas. Then review those areas in the Refresher Course. Take the Follow-Up Test to check your grasp of punctuation. For an extra challenge or advanced practice, take the Advanced Test.

Cases

Apply each step in Figure 9.1 on page 213 to the following cases, as assigned by your instructor.

WEB SKILLS

1. No more driving: Persuasive memo about telecommuting to Bachman, Trinity, and Smith

Sitting in your Montreal office at the accounting firm of Bachman, Trinity, and Smith, clacking away on your calculator, you wonder whether you could be doing this work from your home. You haven't spoken to any co-workers in more than two hours. If you completed your work on time, would your location matter?

As an entry-level accountant, you've participated in location audits at major companies for nearly a year now. If your bosses trust you to work while staying at a hotel, why not let you work from home, where you already have an office with computer, phone, and fax machine? You'd love to regain those two hours you lose commuting to and from work every day.

Your Task To support this idea, visit the Web site of InnoVisions Canada at www.ivc.ca. You'll find statistics and other support for a memo persuading your boss, senior partner Marjorie Bachman, to grant you a six-month trial as a telecommuter.[12]

E-MAIL SKILLS

2. A laughing matter: Persuasive e-mail to Kinko's manager about making work more fun

You've found that working at Kinko's can be tense. By design, the round-the-clock copy and business service centre attracts people who are facing deadlines. They bring a lot of stress in the door with their urgent projects. You and your co-workers pick up their tension, and by the end of the day, your shoulders are aching and your head hurts.

When the economy slows, it's worse. Customers pour in with their resumés and everyone is under pressure. Your co-workers call in sick, your manager gets frustrated, mistakes increase, and morale sinks.

You've read that laughter in the workplace can improve morale and productivity by reducing tension. With a little research, you find support for this idea:

- Dr. Tracy Gaudet, a women's physician and consultant to Oprah Winfrey, says that laughter helps the immune system, lowers blood pressure, decreases heart strain, and lowers blood levels of the stress hormone cortisol. It also releases endorphins, which are the body's pain relievers. A good belly laugh gives the lungs and heart an aerobic workout, she says, and reduces stress by relaxing muscles.
- Other companies have introduced "fun" activities in the workplace (ice cream socials, pet-matching contests) and found they increased enthusiasm, released creativity, and reduced absenteeism.

Having fun on the job doesn't mean workers are lazy. But it may save them from stress-related illnesses or injuries. At Kinko's, it might also improve customer relations!

Your Task Send a persuasive e-mail to your manager, Brad Attlebury, convincing him to try "laugh therapy" at Kinko's.[13]

3. Ouch, that hurts! Persuasive letter at Technology One requesting equipment upgrade

Working in human resources at Technology One, you've seen three complaints about repetitive stress injuries (RSIs) already this month. With 50 computer programmers on the payroll, this could develop into a serious problem for the software development company.

The three programmers, along with four from last month, are planning to file worker's compensation claims. They're suffering sharp wrist pains, numbness, and decreased range of motion. Company medical consultants have suggested exercises and wrist splints, but if these don't work, your technical experts could be facing surgery or even permanent disability.

Your boss is Philippe Bonsall, director of human resources. He noticed that these complaints began shortly after the company bought a truckload of new computer equipment at a local merchant's going-out-of-business sale, and he has hired an outside consultant to check the used equipment. Mary Li, owner of Li and Associates Ergonomic Consulting, reports back that desk and chair heights are fine, but the old-style keyboards and mousing devices are causing the problem. She suggests replacing the keyboards with divided "ergonomic" keyboards, which allow the wrists to stay straight and relieve pressure on the forearm. She also recommends supplying trackballs, an advanced form of computer mouse that also reduces hand movement by eliminating the need to pick up and roll the pointing device.

Replacing equipment will be expensive, but not nearly as expensive as costs that will arise if more technical workers come in with RSI complaints.

Your Task Bonsall asks you to draft a letter he can use to persuade company controller Katherine Wilson to replace the equipment. You must convince her of the urgent need to make the upgrades recommended by Li and Associates Ergonomic Consulting.[14]

TEAM SKILLS

4. Always urgent: Letter pleading case for hosting a Canadian Blood Services blood drive

This morning before heading off to your job in the food services department at the Sundown Casino Entertainment Centre in Richmond, B.C., you heard on the news that Canadian Blood Services (CBS) has put out a call for blood. National supplies have fallen dangerously low. Donated blood lasts only 72 hours, and CBS is responsible for more than half the nation's supply of emergency and routine blood and blood products for victims of accidents and diseases. Thousands depend on the CBS for daily transfusions.

You're one of only 5 percent of eligible donors who think of giving blood. However, today, you're going to do more than just roll up your own sleeve. You want Sundown Casino to host the local CBS chapter's bloodmobile for a community blood drive. As soon as you get to work, you quickly convince other members of the food services staff to help you out. Working together, you'll have all the skills necessary to organize the event.

Not only is it the right thing to do, but the event will improve

- The casino's community image by demonstrating its interest in the public's welfare
- Sundown employees' sense of self-esteem, by helping others
- Sundown customers' personal satisfaction, by having a convenient way to do a good deed
- The CBS's blood supply, since Sundown's hundreds of employees and customers are all potential donors

You also remind your co-workers that the local CBS chapter is part of an international humanitarian organization. As part of its mission to "prevent and alleviate human suffering wherever it may be found," all assistance is given free of charge, made possible by people who donate their time, money, and skills.

Your Task With your team of co-workers (classmates), brainstorm additional support for the event. Then work together to write a persuasive letter to the Sundown board of directors, 145 Ocean View Way, Richmond, BC V5Y 29S, convincing readers to host the bloodmobile. Research (or make up) details, such as your team's qualifications to organize the event, anecdotes to add emotional appeal, and so on. To donate blood, call 1-800-GIVE-LIFE.[15]

5. Identity theft: Persuasive request to eliminate social insurance numbers from Crossland Data ID cards

As your employer insists, you've always carried your Crossland Data ID card in your wallet. You need the card to get into security doors at work and for other identification purposes outside the office. The problem is that the card prominently features your social insurance number. So when your wallet was stolen recently, you feared that your identity might also be stolen.

According to RCMP Inspector John Sliter of the Economic Crimes Branch, "There's been an explosion of identify theft in the past few years." According to Sliter, 20 000 new cases occurred in 2002. This new type of crime involves using a person's unique, identifying information to tap into bank and credit accounts to steal money. With a few key pieces of information, thieves can set up new accounts, apply for credit, make large purchases, even apply for a new driver's licence in your name.

Meanwhile, you might not discover the theft until a suspicious merchant calls your home. Or you might find huge debts on your credit record. Even after the crooks are arrested, some victims have spent hundreds of dollars and hours of phone calls trying to clean up their credit records. To avoid this financial nightmare, law enforcement experts now warn against carrying social insurance numbers in your wallet.

Your Task Write a persuasive letter to Crossland Data's human resources department, requesting that they eliminate social insurance numbers from employee ID cards.[16]

6. No choking matter: Persuasive letter from the Healthy Environment and Consumer Safety Department about fast-food giveaways

You work in the Product Safety Program in the Healthy Environments and Consumer Safety Department. Your manager, Ann Brown, is concerned about some U.S.-based research she read that discussed increasing incidents involving young children and fast-food giveaway toys.

In 1999 two babies died after suffocating on plastic Pokémon balls that their parents got from Burger King. Then three children choked on "Scooter Bugs" that they were given at McDonald's. They weren't seriously injured, but McDonald's undertook a costly recall of 234 000 giveaway toys.

Burger King gives away nearly 100 million toys annually; McDonald's distributes 1.5 billion worldwide. The entire industry accounts for one-third of all toys distributed in North America, and millions of them have been recalled after children were hurt.

Brown worries that toddlers are being given toys meant for older children. Manufacturing defects also pose a problem. The toys are produced cheaply overseas, and often small parts break off to become serious choking hazards.

Burger King now uses safety tests before, during, and after manufacture to catch hazards in advance. McDonald's developed a testing doll with artificial lungs to check suffocation risks. They've loaned "McBaby" to your department so that other restaurants can copy the design. These industry leaders recognize that protecting child safety is to their advantage. Brown wants other fast-food companies to follow their lead and start checking toys before distribution.

Your Task You decide to approach fast-food vendors province by province. Develop a letter to fast-food vendors in Ontario, urging them to pretest giveaway toys. Use facts, anecdotes, and benefits to support your position.[17]

WEB SKILLS 7. Let's not swim with the sharks: Memo persuading IBM to relocate its annual sales event

As assistant to Anna Wilson, director of meeting planning at IBM, you help make travel plans for the annual sales-incentive weekend. That's when the company sends its top salespeople for a warm-weather holiday in the United States as a reward for work well done. This year, the "Weekend Adventure in Paradise" is scheduled for West Palm Beach, Florida, always popular with snow birds. But Wilson is concerned about shark attacks and hurricanes.

Florida leads the world in shark attacks, which usually aren't fatal but which grew more vicious last month as sharks were spotted prowling shallow beach waters. A young boy lost an arm, a woman lost her foot and her companion was killed, and another young boy died from massive blood loss after attacks in shallow water. Relatively minor "bites" were recorded up and down Florida's east coast, and many beaches were closed.

Meanwhile, recent climate changes are making hurricanes appear out of season. High winds, heavy rains, and flooding have sent vacationers scurrying for cover.

Wilson thinks management should move the weekend to California, where shark attacks are rare and hurricanes don't exist. "I've heard that the Hotel Del Coronado in San Diego has a classy reputation. Check it out for me," she instructs you, "and then you can help me convince them."

Your Task Explore the Web sites of San Diego's Hotel Del Coronado at www.hoteldel.com and the Shark Attack files at www.flmnh.ufl.edu/fish/Sharks/Statistics/statsus.htm. Then use facts, statistics, and anecdotes to write a memo to IBM management, persuading them to relocate the incentive weekend.[18]

8. Not too late for others: Letter to the Canadian Food Inspection Agency requesting recall of Westshire Farms meat products

As administrative assistant to Veronica Chang, marketing manager at TriTech, Inc., you often purchase food for her lunch meetings. You've never had a problem before.

On the afternoon of January 22, you bought lunch meats from Bob and Jill's Market in Halifax and refrigerated them. Yesterday, January 23, eight people attended Chang's lunch meeting, ate the cold cuts you bought, and by 8 P.M., were all at Halifax City Hospital's emergency room, undergoing treatment for food poisoning.

According to Dr. Samuel Jenkins, the culprit was salmonellosis, which can be fatal. He suggested that the Westshire Farms cooked, sliced beef or ham might have been contaminated at the factory and should be investigated and recalled to protect others. He gave Chang the address of the agency to contact.

Your Task Chang asks you to write the letter urging a recall of these lunch meats. Address the letter to Elijah Walker, Deputy Minister, Health Canada, Food Inspection Agency, 220 Government Street, Ottawa, ON K1K 2P8. Send a copy to Westshire Farms.[19]

E-MAIL SKILLS 9. Tangled web: Persuasive e-mail to PurelySoftware regarding an online order duplication

Last week you ordered new design software for your boss, Martin Soderburgh, at ArtAlive, the small art-consulting business where you work. As he requested, you used his Visa card to order Adobe InDesign, Version 1.5, and Adobe Photoshop, Version 6.0, from an Internet vendor, Purely Software.com.

When you didn't receive the usual e-mail order confirmation, you called the company's toll-free number. The operator said the company's Web site was having problems, and he took a second order over the phone: $649 for Adobe InDesign, $564 for Adobe Photoshop, including tax and shipping. Four days later, ArtAlive received two shipments of the software, and your boss's credit card was debited twice for a total of $2426.

Your Task Technically, you authorized both orders. But you understood during the phone call that the first order was cancelled, although you have no written proof. Send a persuasive e-mail to customerservice@purelysoftware.com, requesting (1) an immediate credit to your boss's Visa account and (2) a postage-paid return label for the duplicate order.[20]

10. Cow-spotty text: Letter to Gateway requesting warranty extension

Words Unlimited is a "microbusiness"—just two owners and you, the all-round office assistant. From a small office with two computers, you three provide editorial services to businesses.

When your employers, Tom and Miranda Goodman, decided to add a third computer, they ordered a Professional S1300 business system from Gateway, with a "flat screen" monitor that was supposed to offer superior visual display. They didn't realize that the monitor, recommended by salesman Chris Swanson, uses liquid crystal display (LCD) technology. That's great for graphics, but text is produced as disconnnected dots that are hard on the eyes. What they really need is an old-fashioned CRT monitor that displays text as a solid line.

They returned to the store and found one with a fast refresh rate, costing only $20 more, under Gateway's 30-day exchange program. But when they got to the register, they discovered that their 30-day exchange period had run out 5 days ago. Gateway wouldn't take back the LCD monitor, and the Goodmans would have to pay full price for the CRT.

"How did the time run out?" you ask when they return.

"Remember how Swanson forgot to include a modem in our original order, and we had to wait for it to be delivered from the factory?" Tom says. "Then UPS delivered the package to the wrong address. When we finally retrieved it, the installation technician was out sick and we had to wait for his return."

Miranda adds, "And then it took Tom forever to set up the new system, between phone calls and other jobs. By the time we saw the flat screen in action, our 30 days had already elapsed."

"At least Swanson apologized," Tom adds. "He thinks his manager will extend our 30-day exchange period if we write her a letter."

Your Task Since your bosses are busy, they've asked you to draft the persuasive letter to Casey Wilson, Manager, Gateway Country Store, 2900 Pine Lake Road, Timmins, ON P8N 8R6. So far Gateway employees have been courteous, quick, and eager to help, despite the mix-ups. You all have high hopes.[21]

11. Broadband blues: Persuasive claim letter to ZippieNet about cable modem failures

When your cable company offered ZippieNet—high speed, cable modem Internet access—you signed up. You figured $49.95 a month was a bargain for Internet speed.

Your career as a freelance journalist requires you to compete with staff writers at the various publications that buy your work. You need to deliver stories fast to meet short deadlines. Having access to Internet sources "five times faster" than your old dial-up modem should have made your work easier.

At first you were pleased. When the system worked, it worked beautifully. Then the problems began. Three days a week for four weeks, the system failed and you were stuck offline. When you called ZippieNet's support lines, you were put on hold for 30 minutes, and when someone finally answered, they seemed poorly trained and overworked. All you got were vague promises that the system was being repaired.

That was three months ago. Since then, you've experienced total shutdowns at least twice a month. During periods of high usage, the "zippy" speeds that ZippieNet promised slow down to a trickle—not much better than your old dial-up connection.

And now the unthinkable has happened. Last week you were working on an article that you had contracted to sell to *Arete* magazine for $1000, and the system went down for more than 24 hours. You couldn't access critical information, your story was late, and you lost the sale. Moreover, the editor who'd hired you was so angry, he said he'll never work with you again.

Your Task Write a letter to ZippieNet, 1203 rue Belle Fois, Chicoutimi, QC 6H7 1Z6, demanding a refund for your four months of service, plus $1000 for lost income on the lost article sale (include a copy of your contract), and $3000 toward the loss of future sales to the same publication. If ZippieNet pays the $1000, you'll be satisfied, but don't tell them that. Instead, suggest that you will remain a customer if they can deliver improved service within three weeks. When it works, you love broadband.[22]

12. Selling your goods: Sales letter promoting a product of your own invention

You never intended to become an inventor, but you saw a way to make something work more easily, so you set to work. You developed a model, found a way to mass-produce it, and set up a small manufacturing studio in your home. You know that other people are going to benefit from your invention. Now all you need is to reach that market.

Your Task Imagine a useful product that you have invented—perhaps something related to a hobby. For example, one musician wanted to add bass accompaniment to his guitar strumming, so he invented the "Porchboard (Floor) Bass"—a wooden panel you tap with your foot to produce an electronic bass sound. A woman wanted a way to exercise in her short pool, and she invented stretchable "tethers" so that she could keep swimming without hitting the pool's edge.

Now list the benefits and features of your imaginary product (or use one of the examples above). Then write a sales letter for it, using what you've learned in this chapter and making up details as you need them.

Improve Your Grammar, Mechanics, and Usage

Level 1: Self-Assessment—Commas

Review Section 2.6 in the Handbook of Grammar, Mechanics, and Usage, and then look at the following 15 items.

In items 1–15, insert required commas:

1. Please send us four cases of filters two cases of wing nuts and a bale of rags.
2. Your analysis however does not account for returns.
3. As a matter of fact she has seen the figures.
4. Before May 7 1999 they wouldn't have minded either.
5. After Martha has gone talk to me about promoting her.
6. Stoneridge Inc. will go public on September 9 2005.
7. We want the new copier not the old model.
8. "Talk to me" Sandra said "before you change a thing."
9. Because of a previous engagement Dr. Stoeve will not be able to attend.
10. The company started attracting attention during the long hard recession of the mid-1970s.
11. You can reach me at this address: 717 Darby Place Summerside PE C1N 3T4.
12. Transfer the documents from Sherbrooke Quebec to Don Mills Ontario.
13. Sam O'Neill the designated representative is gone today.
14. With your help we will soon begin.
15. She may hire two new representatives or she may postpone filling those territories until spring.

Level 2: Workplace Applications

The following items contain numerous errors in grammar, capitalization, punctuation, abbreviation, number style, word division, and vocabulary. Rewrite each sentence in the space provided, correcting all errors. Write *C* in the space after any sentence that is already correct.

1. A pitfall of internal promotions is, that a person may be given a job beyond their competence.

2. What makes this development possible is the technological advances in todays workplace.

3. We have up to date physical safeguards, such as secure areas in buildings, electronic safeguards, such as passwords and encryption, and we have procedural safeguards, such as customer authentication procedures.

4. When asked why BASF need to bring in a consultant after so many years, process development quality assurance manager Merritt Sink says that experience is extremely important on these type of projects.

5. Looking at just one growth indicator imports to the United States from China "ballooned" to $102 billion in 2001; compared with 15 billion in 1990.

6. Levi Strauss was the first major manufacturer to develop and do publicity about a formal Code of Conduct for it's contract manufacturers.

7. In foreign countries, while the local labour laws may be comparable or even more stringent than in Canada, law enforcement mechanisms are weak or nonexistent often.

8. Hyundai Motor Co., South Koreas' largest-automotive producer are building a $1 billion assembly and manufacturing plant in Windsor, Ontario.

9. The long term success of some Internet products rest heavily on broadbands wide acceptance.

10. Being creative, flexibility, and dynamic planning are the critical elements of any successful, manufacturing process.

11. "Starbucks expanded the Frappucciono family to satisfy customers by offering a broader array of blended beverages," said Howard Behar, Starbucks president, North American Operations.

12. Internationally-renowned interior designer, Jacques Garcia will be designing the hotel's interiors; the gardens will also be designed by him.

13. Anyone who thinks they know what a CEO does is probably wrong, according to Eric Kriss; a professional Chief Executive.

14. Michael Walker, who founded the Fraser institute, headquartered in Vancouver, Brit Col has spent decade's studying economics.

15. The best job-description in the world wont provide you with a trusted executive, finely-honed interviewing skills only will help one do that.

Level 3: Document Critique

The following document may contain errors in grammar, capitalization, punctuation, abbreviation, number style, vocabulary, and spelling. You may also discover problems with wordiness, usage, organization, and tone for a sales message. Correct all errors using standard proofreading marks (see Appendix C).

Date: Monday, 23 June 2004

From: Sasha Morgenstern < smorgenstern@quotesmith.com>

To: < Promotional Customer List2>

Subject: Insurence Service

Dear potential buyers:

You will be able to compare prices from more than three hundredinsurance companies'. Or find the lower rates for any insurance, such as Term life Automobile; Medical. dental. "No-exam" whole life, workers' compensation, Medicare supplements; Fixed annuities

$500 Dollar Guaranttes

We'll find you the lowest rates for term life insurance, or we'll deliver $500 to you overnight. Plus, every quote will carry a $five hundred dollar guarrantee of uptotheday accurracy.

"Quotesmith.com provides rock-bottom quotes."—The Globe & Mail

All quotes are free and accurrate;

We offer Lightning-Fast ServicE

What their saying about us can be found at www.quotesmith.com. Our speedy service is being talked about by everyone, which has received high ratings and postive reviews from "Report on Business" "BC Business" "Toronto Star"

EXPERT ADVISE WILL BE PROVIDED WITH NO SALES PITCH:

You will not be dealing with insurance agents to save you time and money. But if you want advise our saleried insurance experts are available at our toll-free customer service number. We hope you will take a moment to peruse our webstie, www.quotesmith.com today if possible.

Very truly yours,

Sasha Morgenstern

Ethics

Business Communication Notebook

What You May Legally Say in a Sales Letter

As you prepare to write your sales letter, think carefully about your choice of words. False or misleading statements could land you in court, so make sure your language complies with legal and ethical standards. To keep your sales letters within the limits of the law, review the legal considerations of these typical sales phrases:

- **"Our product is the best on the market."** This statement is acceptable for a sales letter because the law permits you to express an opinion about your product. In the process of merchandising a product, statements of opinion are known as "puffery," which is perfectly legal as long as you make no deceptive or fraudulent claims.
- **"Our product will serve you well for many years to come."** This statement from a sales brochure triggered a lawsuit by a disgruntled customer who claimed the manufacturer's product lasted only a few years. The courts ruled that the statement was an acceptable form of puffery because the manufacturer did not promise that the product would last for a specific number of years.
- **"We're so confident you'll enjoy our products that we've enclosed a sample of our most popular line. This sample can be yours for only $5.00! Please send your payment in the enclosed, prepaid envelope."** If you include a product sample with your sales letter, your readers may keep the merchandise without paying for it. Under the law, consumers may consider unordered goods as gifts. They are not obligated to return the items to you or submit payments for unsolicited merchandise.
- **"Thousands of high school students—just like you—are already enjoying this fantastic CD collection! Order before March 1 and save!"** If your sales letter appeals to minors, you are legally obligated to honour their contracts. At the same time, however, the law permits minors to cancel their contracts and return the merchandise to you. Sellers are legally obligated to accept contracts voided by minors and any goods returned by them. Legal adult status is defined differently from province to province, ranging from age 18 to age 21.
- **"You'll find hundreds of bargains at our annual 'scratch and dent' sale! All sales are final on merchandise marked 'as is.' "** When you use the term *as is* in your sales letter, you are not misleading customers about the quality of your products. By warning consumers that the condition of sale items is less than perfect, you are not legally obligated to issue refunds to customers who complain about defects later on.

Applications for Success

1. You probably receive sales letters through the mail all the time. Review two of these sales letters for content. List the "puffery" statements in each letter.
2. Note any statements in these sales letters that appear questionable to you. Rewrite one of the statements, carefully choosing words that won't be misleading to consumers.
3. What do you think? Are these sales letters convincing? How have they persuaded you? If you don't believe they are convincing, explain how they have failed to persuade you.

10 Understanding and Planning Business Reports and Proposals

After studying this chapter, you will be able to

1 Describe four types of informational reports and two types of analytical reports
2 Specify the function of a request for proposal (RFP)
3 Identify seven elements often included in a formal work plan
4 Distinguish between primary and secondary information
5 List the resources you might consult when looking for information in a library
6 Explain how to avoid plagiarism when using research in reports
7 Define what a conclusion is, and list four things that make a conclusion sound
8 Relate how recommendations differ from conclusions

From the Real World

"Written reports are essential for evaluating business opportunities. Without the facts, boards can't act."
–Gerry Roy
Chief Corporate Officer and Legal Counsel
Inualiut Regional Corporation

The Inualiut Regional Corporation (IRC) was established in 1984 to manage the affairs of the first aboriginal Canadians from the Northwest Territories to negotiate a comprehensive land claim settlement with the Government of Canada. Today, IRC's principal business subsidiaries and interests include the land, the investment or "heritage fund," and diverse industries such as environmental services, property management, hospitality, construction, transportation, manufacturing, and oil and gas. Reports are designed to speak to many audiences; Gerry Roy writes reports that facilitate decision making among the boards of directors in this unique business setting. "Conveying an understanding of what we do and where we do it with such a diverse audience," says Roy, "requires careful message planning." Decision makers depend on well-planned reports to summarize carefully researched data, define problems, discuss pertinent issues, and analyze information.

Working with Business Reports and Proposals

Like Gerry Roy, most managers make decisions and solve problems based on the information and analyses they receive in **reports,** written factual accounts that objectively communicate information about some aspect of business. Reports come in all shapes and sizes, from fleeting images on a computer screen and preprinted forms to memos, letters, and formal three-volume bound manuscripts. Regardless of length or formality, most reports are used for one of six general purposes:

Business reports help companies make decisions and solve business problems.

1. To oversee and manage company operations
2. To carry out company rules and ways of doing things
3. To obey government and legal requirements

Reports may be classified in several ways:

- Voluntary or authorized
- Routine or special
- Internal or external
- Short or long
- Informational or analytical

4. To inform others of what's been done on a project
5. To guide decisions on particular issues
6. To get products, plans, or projects accepted by others

Informational Reports

The purpose of informational reports is to explain.

Informational reports present data and facts without analyses or recommendations. Common types of informational reports include monitor/control reports, policy/procedure reports, compliance reports, and progress reports.

Reports for Monitoring and Controlling Operations

Monitor/control reports expose any problems that exist.

Managers rely on reports to learn what's happening to the operations under their control. Monitor/control reports focus on data, so they require special attention to accuracy, thoroughness, and honesty. These reports uncover problems to get them out in the open before it is too late, so they avoid covering up bad news and emphasizing only accomplishments.

Some monitor/control reports, such as strategic plans and annual budgets, establish guidelines for future action. Others, such as monthly sales reports, corporate annual reports, and scouting reports, provide detailed information about operations (see Figure 10.1). Finally, some monitor/control reports describe what occurred during some personal activity, such as a conference, convention, or trip.

Reports for Implementing Policies and Procedures

Policy/procedure reports help managers communicate the company's standards.

Managers provide policy and procedure reports to be read by anyone who wants a question answered. These reports present information in a straightforward manner. The rules of an organization make up lasting guidelines (such as the process for standardizing quality-control procedures or directions for how to reserve the conference room for special meetings). Less permanent issues are treated as they arise in nonrecurring reports (such as a position paper on the need for extra security precautions after a rash of burglaries in the area).

Reports for Complying with Government Regulations

Compliance reports document and explain what a company is doing to conform to government regulations.

All compliance reports are written in response to regulations of one sort or another, most of them imposed by government agencies. The regulatory agency issues instructions on how to write the necessary reports. The important thing in such reports is to be honest, thorough, and accurate. Annual compliance reports include income tax returns and annual shareholder reports. Interim compliance reports include reports from licensed institutions such as nursing homes and child-care facilities.

Reports for Documenting Progress

Reports documenting progress on a client's contract or an internal project provide all the information readers need.

Whether you're writing a progress report for a client or for your boss, you need to anticipate your reader's needs and provide the required information clearly and tactfully. Interim progress reports give an idea of the work that has been accomplished to date (see Figure 10.2 on page 248). In many cases these interim reports are followed by a final report at the conclusion of the contract or project. Final reports are generally more elaborate than interim reports and serve as a permanent record of what was accomplished. They focus on final results rather than on progress along the way.

Analytical Reports

To make informed decisions, managers rely on the supporting information, analyses, and recommendations presented in analytical reports. Typically, an analytical report presents a decision (or solution to a problem), often with recommendations for a number of actions. The body of the report presents all the facts (both good and bad) and persuades

FIGURE 10.1 Monitor/Control Report—Informational

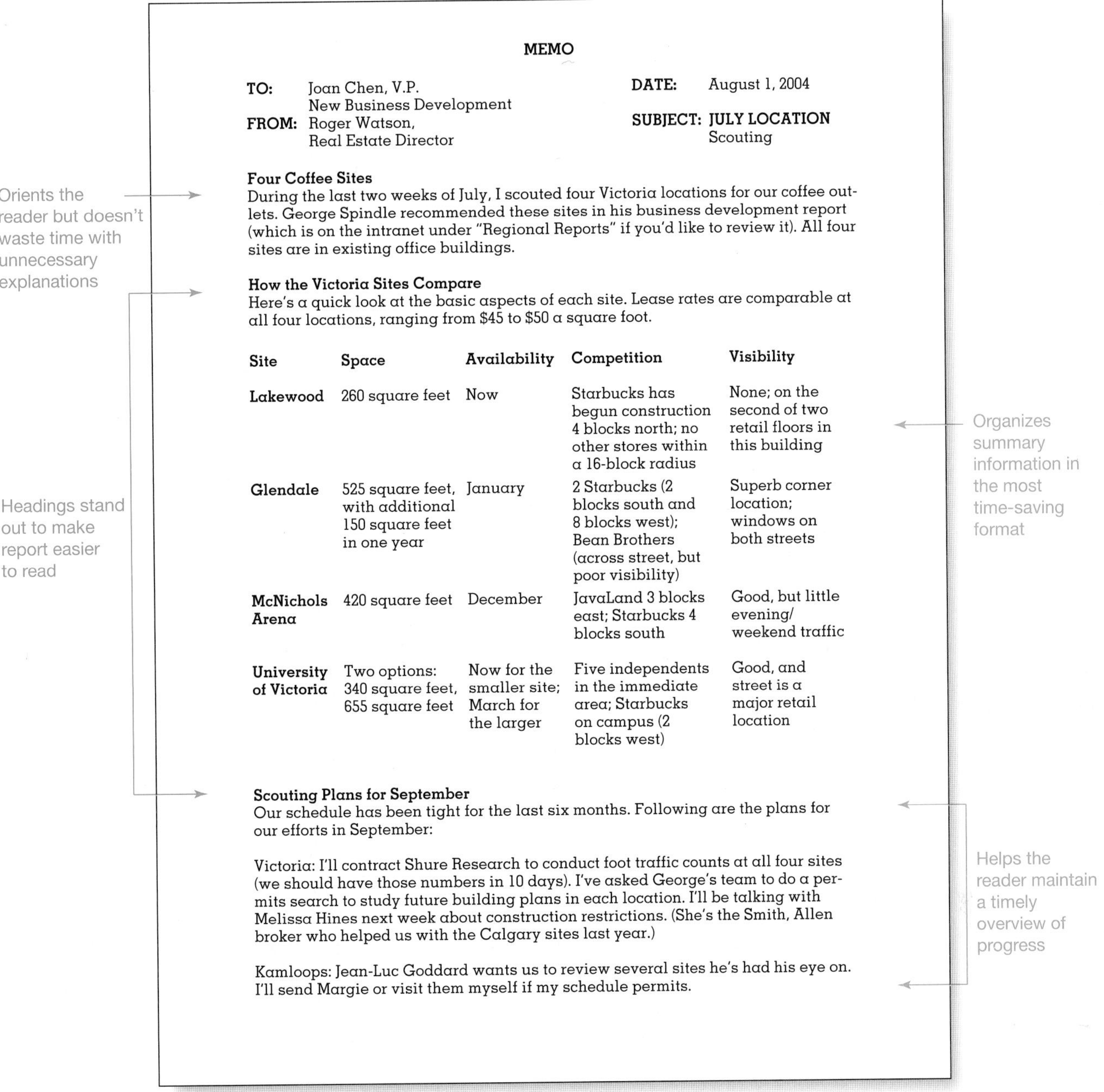

MEMO

TO: Joan Chen, V.P.
New Business Development
FROM: Roger Watson,
Real Estate Director

DATE: August 1, 2004

SUBJECT: JULY LOCATION Scouting

Four Coffee Sites
During the last two weeks of July, I scouted four Victoria locations for our coffee outlets. George Spindle recommended these sites in his business development report (which is on the intranet under "Regional Reports" if you'd like to review it). All four sites are in existing office buildings.

How the Victoria Sites Compare
Here's a quick look at the basic aspects of each site. Lease rates are comparable at all four locations, ranging from $45 to $50 a square foot.

Site	Space	Availability	Competition	Visibility
Lakewood	260 square feet	Now	Starbucks has begun construction 4 blocks north; no other stores within a 16-block radius	None; on the second of two retail floors in this building
Glendale	525 square feet, with additional 150 square feet in one year	January	2 Starbucks (2 blocks south and 8 blocks west); Bean Brothers (across street, but poor visibility)	Superb corner location; windows on both streets
McNichols Arena	420 square feet	December	JavaLand 3 blocks east; Starbucks 4 blocks south	Good, but little evening/ weekend traffic
University of Victoria	Two options: 340 square feet, 655 square feet	Now for the smaller site; March for the larger	Five independents in the immediate area; Starbucks on campus (2 blocks west)	Good, and street is a major retail location

Scouting Plans for September
Our schedule has been tight for the last six months. Following are the plans for our efforts in September:

Victoria: I'll contract Shure Research to conduct foot traffic counts at all four sites (we should have those numbers in 10 days). I've asked George's team to do a permits search to study future building plans in each location. I'll be talking with Melissa Hines next week about construction restrictions. (She's the Smith, Allen broker who helped us with the Calgary sites last year.)

Kamloops: Jean-Luc Goddard wants us to review several sites he's had his eye on. I'll send Margie or visit them myself if my schedule permits.

Orients the reader but doesn't waste time with unnecessary explanations
Headings stand out to make report easier to read
Organizes summary information in the most time-saving format
Helps the reader maintain a timely overview of progress

readers to accept the decision, solution, or recommendations that are detailed throughout the report. To persuade the reader, the writer carefully analyzes the facts and presents a compelling argument. Two of the more common examples of analytical reports are problem-solving reports and proposals.

The purpose of analytical reports is to convince the audience that the conclusions and recommendations developed in the text are valid.

Reports for Solving Problems

When solving problems, managers need both basic information and detailed analysis. Problem-solving reports typically require secondary or primary research. They are used when a problem exists and someone must investigate and propose a solution. These troubleshooting reports usually start with some background information on the problem, then analyze alternative solutions, and finally recommend the best approach.

Feasibility and justification reports study and qualify courses of action—feasibility reports are prepared before the action is taken, and justification reports are prepared after.

From time to time, employees and managers write problem-solving reports to evaluate the practicality and advisability of pursuing a course of action (such as buying equipment,

FIGURE 10.2 Progress Report—Informational (Excerpt)

Uses letter format, common for many external interim progress reports (final reports would usually be longer and would often be in manuscript form)

Johnson Landscaping

820 Grandview Avenue, Saint John, NB E2L 3V9 · (506) 658-8636 / Fax: 658-6361

May 31, 2004

Mr. Steve Gamvrellis, Facilities Manager
The Fairwinds Hotel
240 Kings Street
Saint John, NB E4P 2Y1

Dear Mr. Gamvrellis:

Emphasizes what has been accomplished during the reporting period (if it were a final report, it would focus on results rather than on progress)

PROGRESS ON MAY LANDSCAPING

This report will bring you up to date on the landscaping done for your company by Johnson Landscaping during the month of May 2004.

Initial ground preparation and sprinkler system installation is complete. A total of 25 000 square feet of lawn and flower beds were tilled, raked and leveled. Installation of the sprinkler system for 15 000 square feet of lawn and beds was completed on May 20.

Eases reader's understanding by making headings correspond to the tasks performed

BED PLANTING

From May 21 to May 30, shrubs and ornamental perennials were planted in 7000 square feet of beds. Beds were prepared for 3000 square feet of annuals.

PROBLEM AREAS

Doesn't hesitate to bring up problems that need to be solved, but offers a possible solution for further investigation

We've resolved the flooding problem discovered last month near the south end of the shipping and receiving dock. It appears that an old plumbing repair had begun to come apart under the employee cafeteria, causing water to flow under the building and occasionally flood a small portion of the new lawn area.

Unfortunately, we have uncovered a potential problem in several of the perennial borders we've created along the east side of the main building. A series of soil samples indicates an extremely high level of acidity, much higher than would occur under natural conditions. We suspect that the problem may have been caused by a small chemical spill at some point in the past. We'll try to resolve the problem next month, and I'll contact you if the solution to this problem is likely to affect your budget planning.

PLANS FOR JUNE

Outlines plans for the coming period

1. Distribute bark mulch and plant remaining annuals.
2. Resolve the soil quality issue in the perennial bed and make soil amendments as needed.
3. Monitor and adjust the automated sprinkling system to ensure adequate watering.

changing a procedure, or hiring a consultant). These feasibility reports study proposed options to assess whether any or all of them are sound (see Figure 10.3). Justification reports are written after a course of action has been taken to justify what was done. Audits are written to assess company compliance with regulatory requirements.

Proposals

Proposals present ideas and persuade audiences to accept them.

A **proposal** is a special type of analytical report designed to get products, plans, or projects accepted by others. Proposals can be one or two pages, or they can be hundreds of pages if they involve large, complex jobs. Regardless of the size and scope, these special types of reports analyze an audience's problem, present a solution, and persuade the audience that the solution presented is the best approach. Proposals are usually read by people in positions of authority.

Solicited proposals are generally prepared at the request of external parties who need something done; however, they may also be requested by such internal sources as management or the board of directors. Some external parties prepare an invitation to bid on their contract. Called a **request for proposal (RFP),** such an invitation includes instructions that specify the exact type of work to be performed, along with guidelines on how and when the company wants the work completed.

Effective solicited proposals address each item listed in the RFP.

FIGURE 10.3 Problem-Solving Report—Analytical

MEMO

TO: Board of Directors, Executive Committee members
FROM: Alycia Jenn, Business Development Manager
DATE: July 6, 2004
SUBJECT: ESTABLISHING AN INTERNET RETAILING SITE

Clarifies the purpose and origin of the report in the introduction

In response to your request, my staff and I investigated the potential for establishing a retailing site on the Internet. After analyzing the behaviour of our customers and major competitors and studying the overall development of electronic retailing, we recommend

1. Establishing an online presence within the next six months.
2. Hiring a firm that specializes in online retailing to design and develop the Web site.
3. Integrating online retailing with our store-based and mail-order operations.

Clarifies what's needed by wording recommendations simply and to the point

SETTING UP A WEB SITE

Presents logical and clear reasons for recommending that the firm establish a Web site

First, does a Web site make financial sense? Studies suggest that our competitors are not currently generating significant revenue from their Web sites. Stallini's is the leader so far, but its sales haven't broken the $1 million mark. Moreover, at least half of our competitors' online sales are from current customers who would have purchased the same items in-store or by mail order. The cost of setting up a retailing site is around $120 000, so it isn't possible to justify a site solely on the basis of current financial return.

Second, do we need to establish a presence now in order to remain competitive in the future? The online situation is too fluid and unpredictable to answer this question in a quantitative profit-and-loss way, but a qualitative view of strategy indicates that we should set up a site:

- As younger consumers (more comfortable with online shopping) reach their peak earning years (ages 35–54), they'll be more likely to buy online than today's peak spenders.
- The Web is erasing geographical shopping limits, presenting both a threat and an opportunity. Even though our customers can now shop Web sites anywhere in the world (so that we have thousands of competitors instead of a dozen), we can now attract customers from anywhere in the world.
- If the growth in online retailing continues, the e-market will eventually be viable. Establishing a site now and working out any problems will prepare us for high-volume online business in the years ahead.

ENGAGING A CONSULTANT TO IMPLEMENT THE SITE

Includes not only the recommendation to establish a Web site but also one to hire a consultant to implement the Web site and integrate it with existing systems

Implementing a competitive retailing site can take anywhere from 1000 to 1500 hours of design and programming time. We have some of the expertise needed in-house, but the marketing and information systems departments have only 300 person-hours in the next six months. I recommend that we engage a Web design consultant to help us with the design and to do all the programming.

INTEGRATING THE WEB INTO EXISTING OPERATIONS

Emphasizes the need for integration

The studies we reviewed showed that the most successful Web retailers are careful to integrate their online retailing with their store- and mail-based retailing. Companies that don't integrate carefully find themselves with higher costs, confused customers, and Web sites that don't generate much business. Before we begin designing our Web site, we should develop a plan for integrating the Web into our existing marketing, accounting, and production systems. The online site could affect every department in the company, so it's vital that everyone has a chance to review the plans before we proceed.

SUMMARY

Closes by briefly summarizing the recommendations and the reasons behind them

1. Establish a Web site now to avoid losing future business.
2. Use the services of a Web designer to ensure we have enough person hours to complete the project.
3. Integrate the Web site with existing operations, particularly in marketing, accounting, and production.

Unsolicited proposals are usually written to obtain business or funding without a specific invitation from management or a potential client. In other words, with an unsolicited proposal, the writer makes the first move. Since readers may not know about the problem, the writer must convince them that a problem exists and that he or she can solve it. Thus, unsolicited proposals generally spend considerable time explaining why readers should take action and convincing them of the benefits of buying (or funding) something.

An unsolicited proposal must first establish that a problem exists.

Internal Proposals **Internal proposals** are submitted to decision makers in one's own organization. They have two primary purposes: (1) to seek approval for a course of action (such as changing recruiting procedures, revising the company's training programs, or reorganizing a department) or (2) to request additional resources (such as new equipment, more employees, or extra operating funds).

Because most internal proposals advocate change, you must take extra care to understand whether your audience will feel threatened by your plan. A good internal proposal is completely unbiased and explains why a project or course of action is needed, what it will involve, how much it will cost, and how the company will benefit (see Figure 10.4 on pages 251–252).

Effective internal proposals are unbiased and thoroughly explain the need, application, cost, and benefits of the proposed action.

External Proposals **External proposals** are submitted outside an organization to current or potential clients and government agencies. Like internal proposals, they solicit approval for projects or funds, but they differ in several ways. First, because they're directed to outsiders, external proposals are more formal. Second, external proposals are legally binding. Once approved, they form the basis of a contract, so they are prepared with extreme care, spelling out precisely what your company will provide under specific terms and conditions.

Third, audience members may not know your company, so your proposal must convince them that your organization is the best source of a product or service. You can do so by explaining your experience, qualifications, facilities, and equipment. Also, show that you clearly understand your audience's problem or need (see Figure 10.5 on pages 253–254).[1]

If accepted, external proposals become legally binding documents.

Applying the Three-Step Writing Process to Business Reports and Proposals

The three-step writing process applies to reports as well as to other business messages.

As with other business messages, your reports and proposals benefit when you follow the three-step writing process: (1) planning, (2) writing, and (3) completing business messages. Since much of the three-step process is covered in Chapters 3, 4, and 5, the following sections discuss only those tasks that differ for reports and proposals. The rest of this chapter focuses on Step 1, planning business reports and proposals. Chapter 11 focuses on Steps 2 and 3, writing and completing formal business reports and proposals.

Step 1: Planning Business Reports and Proposals

When planning reports and proposals, you focus on the same three tasks as for other business documents: analysis, investigation, and adaptation. Adapting your report to your audience and purpose is no different from adapting other business documents. You choose the best channel and medium, and you establish a good relationship with your audience. However, you have a few special considerations when analyzing and investigating business reports and proposals.

Analysis for Reports and Proposals

When writing reports, pay special attention to analysis tasks such as defining the problem, writing the statement of purpose, developing a preliminary outline, and preparing the work plan.

When planning reports and proposals, you will of course need to analyze your audience and purpose. Define the problem, define your specific purpose, compose a preliminary outline, and develop a work plan.

FIGURE 10.4 Internal Proposal—Analytical (Unsolicited)

MEMO

TO: Jamie Engle
FROM: Shandel Cohen
DATE: July 8, 2004
SUBJECT: PROPOSED AUTOMATIC MAIL-RESPONSE SYSTEM

Slow Response to Customer Requests for Information

Describes the problem carefully in a positive light (in terms of the company's success) and shows why a new system is needed

Our new produce line has been very well received, and orders have surpassed our projections. This very success, however, has created a shortage of printed catalogues and data sheets, as well as considerable overtime for people in the customer response centre. As we introduce upgrades and new options, our printed materials quickly become outdated. If we continue to rely on printed materials for customer information, we have two choices: distribute existing materials (even though they are incomplete or inaccurate) or discard existing materials and print new ones.

An Automated Mail-Response System

With minor modifications to our current computer system and very little additional software, we can set up an automated system to respond to customer requests for information. This system can save us time and money and can keep our distributed information current.

Hooks reader on solution by highlighting such economic and operational benefits as ease of implementation, affordability, cost and time savings, currency, and proven results

Benefits

Automated mail-response systems have been tested and proven effective. Companies such as Sunco Systems and Freshpac already use this method to respond to customer information requests, so we won't have to worry about relying on untested technology. Both customer and company responses have been positive.

Uses headings to highlight the benefits of the solution

Ever-Current Information
Rather than discard and print new materials, we would need to update only the electronic files. We would be able to provide customers and our field sales organization with up-to-date, correct information as soon as the upgrades or options are available.

Instantaneous Delivery
Within a very short time of requesting information, customers would have that information in hand. Electronic delivery would be especially advantageous for our northern and international customers. Regular mail to remote locations sometimes takes a week to arrive, by which time the information may already be out of date. Both customers and field salespeople will appreciate the automatic mail-response system.

Minimized Waste
With our current method of sending printed information, we discard tonnes of obsolete catalogues, data sheets, and other materials.

(Continued)

Define the Problem

Sometimes the person authorizing your report will define the problem you address. Other times, you will have to define the problem to be resolved. Be careful not to confuse a topic (campus parking) with a problem (the lack of enough campus parking). To help define the problem that your analytical report will address, ask yourself

The problem you need to resolve may be defined by your superior.

- What needs to be determined?
- Why is this issue important?
- Who is involved or affected?
- Where is the trouble located?
- How did the problem originate?
- When did it start?

FIGURE 10.4 (Continued)

2

Benefits (cont'd)

By maintaining and distributing the information electronically, we would eliminate this waste. We would also free up 30 square metres of floor space and shelving that is required for storing printed materials.

Of course, some of our customers may still prefer to receive printed materials, or they may not have access to electronic mail. For these customers, we could simply print copies of the files when we receive requests.

Lower Overtime Costs
Besides savings in paper and space, we would also realize $20 000 savings in wages. Because of the increased interest in our new products, we have been working overtime or hiring new people to meet the demand. An automatic mail-response system would eliminate this need, allowing us to deal with fluctuating interest without a fluctuating work-force.

Setup and Operating Costs

Carefully explains the costs of the proposal

The necessary equipment and software costs approximately $15 000. System maintenance and upgrades are estimated at $5000 per year.

Annual Savings

We expect the following annual savings from eliminating printed information:

Justifies the cost by detailing projected annual savings

$100 000	Printing costs
25 000	Storage costs
5 000	Postage
20 000	Wages
$150 000	**Total savings**

Closes by offering to answer any questions management may have—rather than trying to anticipate management's questions and including unnecessary detail

The Next Step

I will be happy to answer any questions you have about this system. An automated mail-response system would greatly benefit our company, in savings and customer satisfaction. If you approve, we can have it installed and running in six weeks.

Not all these questions apply in every situation, but asking them helps you define the problem and limit the scope of your discussion.

Write the Purpose Statement

The purpose statement defines the objective of your report.

Writing a purpose statement will help you keep your report writing on task. Whereas defining the problem helps you know *what* you are going to investigate, the **purpose statement** clarifies *why* you are preparing the report. The most useful way to word your purpose statement is to begin with an infinitive phrase (*to* plus a verb). Doing so encourages you to take control and decide where you're going before you begin. For instance, in an informational report, your purpose statement can be as simple as these:

> To update clients on the progress of the research project (progress report)
>
> To develop goals and objectives for the coming year (monitor/control report)
>
> To explain the building access procedures (policy/procedure report)
>
> To submit required information to the Department of Transport (compliance report)

Statements of purpose for analytical reports are often more complex than are those for informational reports.

For analytical reports, the statement of purpose is often more comprehensive. Linda Moreno is the cost accounting manager for Electrovision, a high-tech company based in Montreal, Quebec. She was recently asked to find ways of reducing employee travel-and-entertainment costs (her complete report appears in Chapter 11). Because Moreno was supposed to suggest specific ways of reducing travel and entertainment costs, she phrased her statement of purpose accordingly:

FIGURE 10.5 External Proposal—Analytical (Solicited)

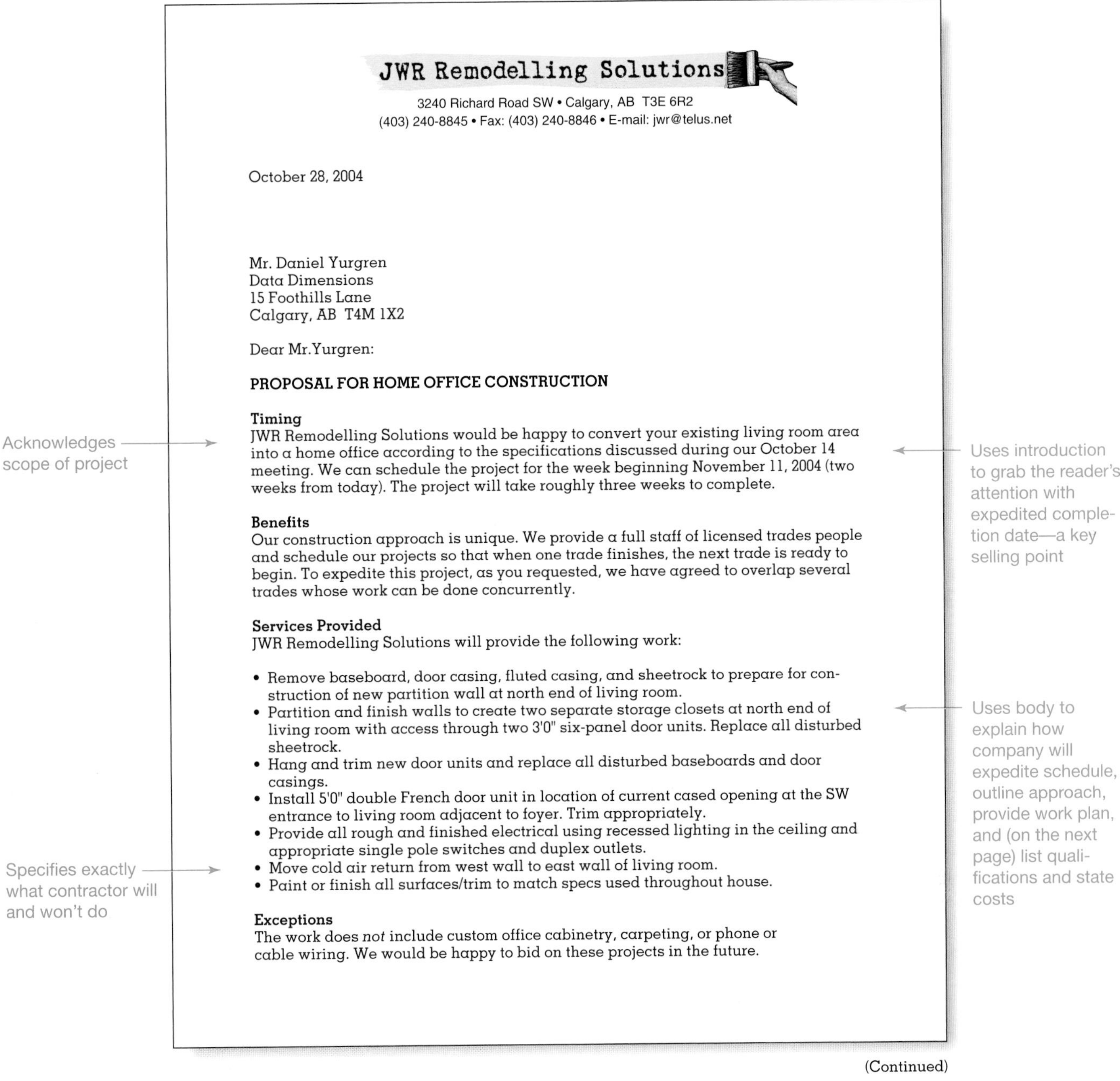

JWR Remodelling Solutions
3240 Richard Road SW • Calgary, AB T3E 6R2
(403) 240-8845 • Fax: (403) 240-8846 • E-mail: jwr@telus.net

October 28, 2004

Mr. Daniel Yurgren
Data Dimensions
15 Foothills Lane
Calgary, AB T4M 1X2

Dear Mr.Yurgren:

PROPOSAL FOR HOME OFFICE CONSTRUCTION

Timing
JWR Remodelling Solutions would be happy to convert your existing living room area into a home office according to the specifications discussed during our October 14 meeting. We can schedule the project for the week beginning November 11, 2004 (two weeks from today). The project will take roughly three weeks to complete.

Benefits
Our construction approach is unique. We provide a full staff of licensed trades people and schedule our projects so that when one trade finishes, the next trade is ready to begin. To expedite this project, as you requested, we have agreed to overlap several trades whose work can be done concurrently.

Services Provided
JWR Remodelling Solutions will provide the following work:

- Remove baseboard, door casing, fluted casing, and sheetrock to prepare for construction of new partition wall at north end of living room.
- Partition and finish walls to create two separate storage closets at north end of living room with access through two 3'0" six-panel door units. Replace all disturbed sheetrock.
- Hang and trim new door units and replace all disturbed baseboards and door casings.
- Install 5'0" double French door unit in location of current cased opening at the SW entrance to living room adjacent to foyer. Trim appropriately.
- Provide all rough and finished electrical using recessed lighting in the ceiling and appropriate single pole switches and duplex outlets.
- Move cold air return from west wall to east wall of living room.
- Paint or finish all surfaces/trim to match specs used throughout house.

Exceptions
The work does *not* include custom office cabinetry, carpeting, or phone or cable wiring. We would be happy to bid on these projects in the future.

Acknowledges scope of project
Specifies exactly what contractor will and won't do
Uses introduction to grab the reader's attention with expedited completion date—a key selling point
Uses body to explain how company will expedite schedule, outline approach, provide work plan, and (on the next page) list qualifications and state costs

(Continued)

. . . to analyze the T&E [travel and entertainment] budget, evaluate the impact of recent changes in airfares and hotel costs, and suggest ways to tighten management's control over T&E expenses.

If Moreno had been assigned an informational report instead, she might have stated her purpose differently:

To summarize Electrovision's spending on travel and entertainment.

You can see from these two examples how much influence the purpose statement has on the scope of your report. Remember, the more specific your purpose statement, the more useful it will be as a guide to planning your report. Also, remember to double-check your purpose statement with the person who authorized the report. The authorizer may decide that the report needs to go in a different direction. Once your statement is confirmed, you can use it as the basis for your preliminary outline.

Once you prepare a written statement of your purpose, review it with the person who authorized the study.

FIGURE 10.5 Continued

Mr. Daniel Yurgren October 28, 2004 Page 2

Qualifications
JWR Remodelling Solutions has been in business in the Calgary area for more than17 years. We have a strong reputation for being a quality builder. We take great pride in our work and we treat all projects with the same high-level attention, regardless of their size or scope. Our trades people are all licensed, insured professionals with years of experience in their respective crafts. Enclosed is a copy of our company brochure discussing our qualifications in greater detail, along with a current client list. Please contact any of the names on this list for references.

Increases desire by highlighting qualifications

Justifies cost by providing detail

Costs
The total cost for this project is $6800, broken down as follows:

Materials and supplies	$3300
Labour	2700
Overhead	800
Total	$6800

An initial payment of $3800 is due upon acceptance of this proposal. The remaining $3000 is due upon completion of the work.

Uses brief closing to emphasize fast turnaround and immediate call for action

Hiring JWR
If you would like to have JWR Remodelling Solutions complete this work, please sign this letter and return it to us with your deposit in the enclosed envelope. We currently anticipate no construction delays, since the materials needed for your job are in stock and our staff of qualified workers is available during the period mentioned. If you have any questions regarding the terms of this proposal, please call me at (403) 946-8845.

Sincerely,

Jordan W. Spurrier
President

Enclosures

Makes letter a binding contract, if signed

Accepted by:

Daniel Yurgren Date

Pointers for Preparing External Proposals

- Review the requirements stated in RFP.
- Define the scope of work.
- Determine the methods and procedures to be used.
- Estimate the requirements for time, personnel, and costs.
- Write the proposal exactly as RFP specifies—following the exact format required and responding meticulously to every point raised.
- Begin by stating the purpose of the proposal, defining the scope of work, presenting background information, and explaining any restrictions that might apply to the contract.
- In the body, give details and specify anticipated results—including methods, schedule, facilities, equipment, personnel, and costs.
- Close by summarizing key points and asking for audience decision.

Develop a Preliminary Outline

A preliminary outline gives you a visual diagram of your report—its important points, the order in which they will be discussed, and the detail to be included (see Figure 10.6). Your preliminary outline will guide your research efforts and help you organize and compose your report. Think of your preliminary outline as a working draft that you'll revise and modify as you go along. It will look quite different from the final outline you develop to write your report. Write informative (talking) headings. Although outlines with informative headings take a little longer to write, they're generally more useful in guiding your work and easier for others to review.

Your preliminary outline establishes the framework for your report and differs from the final outline.

Prepare the Work Plan

Writing a report can be a lengthy task with several phases. In addition to organizing and writing, you'll often need to conduct primary and secondary research and prepare visuals. Developing a work plan is one way to coordinate and monitor your efforts so that you will produce quality reports quickly and efficiently.

If you are preparing the work plan for yourself, it can be relatively informal: a simple list of the steps you plan to take and an estimate of their sequence and timing. If you're conducting a lengthy, formal study, however, you'll want to develop a detailed work plan that can guide the performance of many tasks over a span of time. A formal plan might include the following elements (especially the first two):

Whether you prepare an informal work plan for yourself or a detailed work plan for your team, be sure it identifies all the tasks that must be performed.

- **Problem statement.** The problem statement clearly describes the issue and helps you stay focused.
- **Statement of the purpose and scope of your investigation.** The purpose statement describes what you plan to accomplish and the boundaries of your work. Stating which issues you will and will not cover is especially important with complex, lengthy investigations.

FIGURE 10.6 Preliminary Outline of a Research Report Focusing on Conclusions

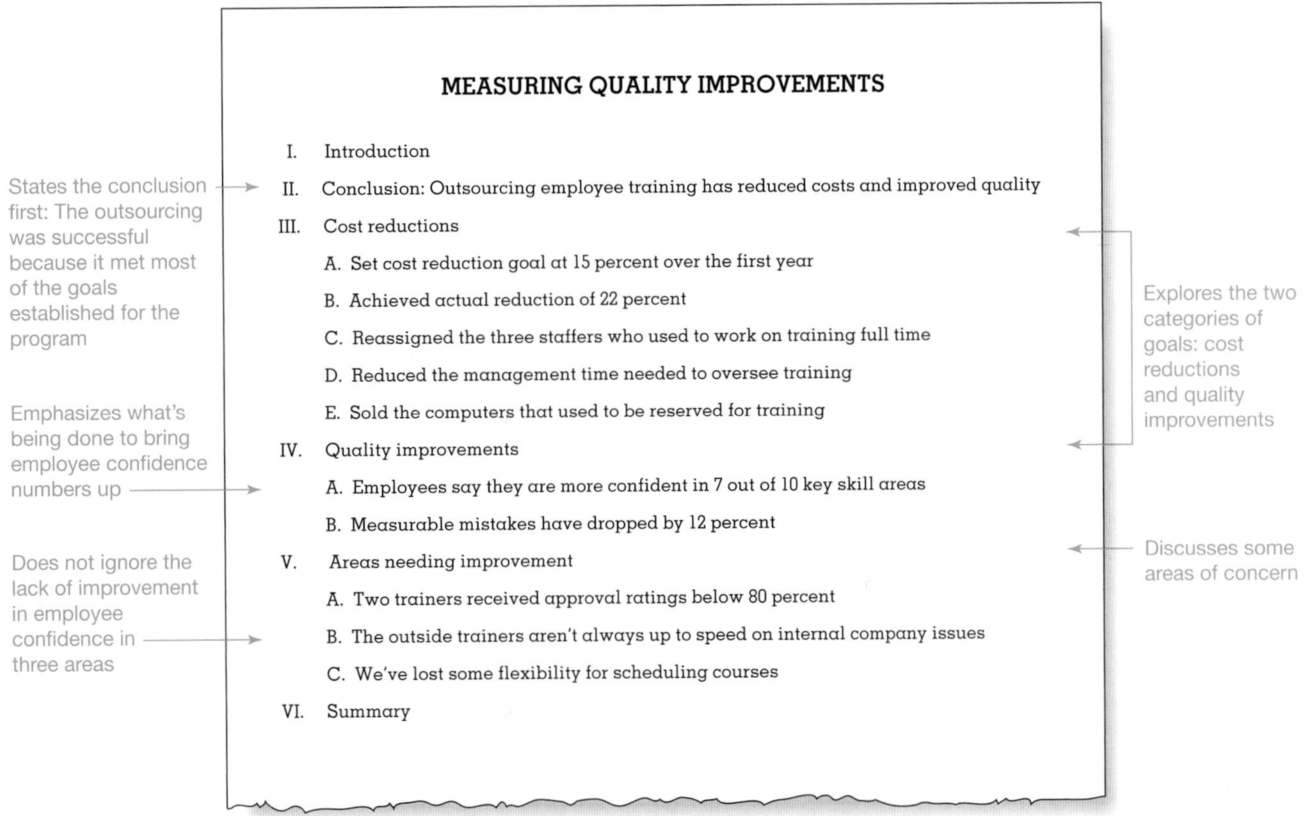
MEASURING QUALITY IMPROVEMENTS

I. Introduction

II. Conclusion: Outsourcing employee training has reduced costs and improved quality

III. Cost reductions

A. Set cost reduction goal at 15 percent over the first year

B. Achieved actual reduction of 22 percent

C. Reassigned the three staffers who used to work on training full time

D. Reduced the management time needed to oversee training

E. Sold the computers that used to be reserved for training

IV. Quality improvements

A. Employees say they are more confident in 7 out of 10 key skill areas

B. Measurable mistakes have dropped by 12 percent

V. Areas needing improvement

A. Two trainers received approval ratings below 80 percent

B. The outside trainers aren't always up to speed on internal company issues

C. We've lost some flexibility for scheduling courses

VI. Summary

- **List of tasks to be accomplished.** For simple reports, the list of things to do will be short and probably obvious. However, longer, complex investigations require an exhaustive list so that you can plan the time needed for each task. Be sure to indicate your sources of information, the research necessary, and any constraints (on time, money, personnel, or data).
- **Description of any products that will result from your investigation.** Often, the only product of your efforts will be the report itself. In other cases, you'll need to produce something beyond a report, perhaps a new marketing plan or even a new product to sell. Make these expectations clear at the outset, and be sure to schedule enough time and resources to get the job done.
- **Review of project assignments, schedules, and resource requirements.** Indicate who will be responsible for what, when tasks will be completed, and how much the investigation will cost. If more than one person will be involved, include a brief section on coordinating report writing and production.
- **Plans for following up after delivering the report.** Follow-up can be as simple as making sure people received the information they need or as complex as conducting additional research to evaluate the results of report recommendations. Even informal follow-up can help you improve future reports and show that you care about your work's effectiveness and its impact on the organization.
- **Working outline.** Some work plans, such as the plan in Figure 10.7, include a tentative outline of the report. This plan was developed for a report on whether to launch a company newsletter.

Investigation for Reports and Proposals

Begin your research by gathering secondary information.

In most cases you'll begin your research by looking for sources of secondary information—information on your subject that already exists and has already been collected, usually in the form of books, periodicals, newspapers, and Web sites. If secondary information doesn't exist or isn't helpful, then you'll need to collect firsthand, primary information for your specific needs.

Gather Secondary Information

Many sources of secondary information are easily accessible in print and online.[2]

Reference librarians are there to assist you with your research efforts.

Finding Information in the Library Libraries are where you'll find business books, electronic databases, newspapers, periodicals, directories, almanacs, and government publications. In additon, you'll find your most important resource: librarians. Reference librarians are trained in research techniques and can show you how to use the library's many resources:

- **Business books.** Although less timely than journal articles, business books provide in-depth coverage of a variety of business topics. You may have better luck finding specialized information at company libraries or at a college or university library.
- **Electronic databases.** These computer-searchable collections of information are often categorized by subject areas (business, law, science, technology, and education). When using an electronic database, try to get a list of the periodicals or publications it includes, as well as the time period it covers so that you can plan to fill in any gaps for items not in the database.
- **Newspapers.** Libraries subscribe to only a select number of newspapers and store a limited number of back issues in print. However, they frequently subscribe to databases containing newspaper articles in full text (available online, on CD-ROM, or on microfilm). Also, most newspapers today offer full-text or limited editions of their papers on the Internet.

FIGURE 10.7 Work Plan for a Formal Study

Clear enough for anyone to understand without background research

STATEMENT OF THE PROBLEM
The rapid growth of our company over the past five years has reduced the sense of community among our staff. People no longer feel like part of an intimate organization where they matter as individuals.

Lays out the tasks to be accomplished and does so in clear, simple terms

Delineates exactly what will be covered in the report

PURPOSE AND SCOPE OF WORK
The purpose of this study is to determine whether a company newsletter would help rebuild employee identification with the organization. The study will evaluate the impact of newsletters in other companies and will attempt to identify features that might be desirable in our own newsletter. Such variables as length, frequency of distribution, types of articles, and graphic design will be considered. Costs will be estimated for several approaches. In addition, the study will analyze the personnel and the procedures required to produce a newsletter.

SOURCES AND METHODS OF DATA COLLECTION
Survey literature in Human Resources Journals about the impact of corporate newsletters on employee morale. Sample newsletters will be collected from 50 companies similar to ours in size, growth rate, and types of employees. The editors will be asked to comment on the impact of their publications on employee morale. Our own employees will be surveyed to determine their interest in a newsletter and their preferences for specific features. Production procedures and costs will be analyzed through conversations with newsletter editors and printers.

A preliminary outline is presented for guidance, even though no description of the end product is included

Includes no plans for following up

PRELIMINARY OUTLINE
The preliminary outline for this study is as follows:

I. Do newsletters affect morale?
   A. Do people read them?
   B. How do employees benefit?
   C. How does the company benefit?
II. What are the features of good newsletters?
   A. How long are they?
   B. What do they contain?
   C. How often are they published?
   D. How are they designed?
III. How should a newsletter be produced?
   A. Should it be written, edited, and printed internally?
   B. Should it be written internally and printed outside?
   C. Should it be totally produced outside?
IV. What would a newsletter cost?
   A. What would the personnel cost be?
   B. What would the materials cost be?
   C. What would outside services costs?
V. Should we publish a company newsletter?
VI. If so, what approach should we take?

States the assignments and the schedules for completing them

WORK PLAN
Each phase of this study will be completed by the following dates:

Survey literature	September 3–14, 2003
Collect/analyze newsletters	September 3–14, 2003
Interview editors by phone	September 16–20, 2003
Survey employees	September 23–27, 2003
Develop sample	September 30–October 11, 2003
Develop cost estimates	October 8–11, 2003
Prepare report	October 14–25, 2003
Submit final report	October 28, 2003

- **Periodicals.** Most periodicals fall into four categories: (1) popular magazines (not intended for business, professional, or academic use), (2) trade journals (providing news and other facts about particular professions, industries, and occupations), (3) business magazines (covering all major industries and professions), and (4) academic journals (publishing data from professional researchers and educators).
- **Directories.** Covering everything from accountants to zoos, business directories provide entries for companies, products, and individuals, and they include the names of key contacts.
- **Almanacs.** Almanacs are handy guides to factual and statistical information about countries, politics, the labour force, and so on.
- **Government publications.** For information on a law, a court decision, or current population patterns and business trends, consult government documents. A librarian can direct you to the information you want.

Finding Business Information on the Internet Today's most popular source of company and industry information is the Internet, offering current news, industry trends, and company-related data on financial performance, products, goals, and employment. Remember that anyone (including you) can post anything on a Web site. Thus, information on the Web may be biased, inaccurate, or exaggerated. Before searching the Web for business information, wait until you've had a chance to learn a bit about your topic from journals, books, and commercial databases. Then you'll be able to detect unreliable information and be more selective about which Web sites and documents you use.

When doing research on the Internet, you need to be selective because anyone can publish anything.

A good place to start on the Web is the Internet Public Library at www.ipl.org. Modelled after a real library, this site will provide you with carefully selected links to high-quality business resources. You can find company profiles, trade data, business news, small-business information, prepared forms and documents, biographies of executives, financial reports, job postings, online publications, and so on. Canadians frequently consult U.S.-based Internet sites for business information, but be aware that U.S. political, legal, and corporate tax information will differ from what is valid in English and French Canada.

To find specific company information, consult The Globe and Mail's Annual Report Service. Go to www.wilink.com to order free copies of annual reports of Canadian companies. Information about Canadian companies, markets, and economic trends can be found on the federal government's Site-By-Site! The International Investment Portal & Research Centre www.site-by-site.com/canada/astock.htm. Also, check the company's Web site (if it maintains one). Company sites generally include detailed information about the firm's products, services, history, mission, strategy, financial performance, and employment needs. Many sites provide links to related company information, such as news releases, and more.

You can find all kinds of information about a company on its Web site.

You can obtain news releases and general company news from news release sites such as PRNewswire (www.prnewswire.com). Select Canada from the country list to find Canada NewsWire. These sites offer free databases of news releases from companies subscribing to their services. News release sites are also good places to look for announcements of new products, management changes, earnings, dividends, mergers, acquisitions, and other company information.

The Web doesn't have everything. You may find nothing about small organizations, or perhaps just their address and phone number. And even if the information exists on the Web, you may not be able to find it. The Internet holds hundreds of millions of Web pages, with hundreds of pages being added every day, and even the best Internet search engines manage to index only about one-third of the pages on the Web.[3]

Understanding Search Engines Search engines identify and screen Web resources. They will often turn up what you're looking for, most likely along with a mountain of stuff you don't need. Not all search engines operate the same way. For instance, some engines index all the pages they find; others index only the most popular pages. Sites such as Yahoo!, Lycos, and Google offer well-known, commercially backed search engines. Google offers the option of searching for "Canada only" sites.

Using Business Databases Many college and university libraries subscribe to important business databases. Check to see whether your library has

- *Canadian Business & Current Affairs*—indexes more than 600 Canadian periodicals and newspapers, making 150 of these available to subscribers in full-text form. The most comprehensive source of business current events information available in Canada.
- *SEDAR*—lists all companies on stock exchanges in Canada.
- *Cancorp Financials*—financial and management information from 13 000 Canadian companies

- *EBSCOhost Web*—includes a number of databases and full-text products including Business Source Premier and Business Wire News
- *Mergent Online*—general and financial information, annual reports, and links to newswire articles, with data on more than 10 000 public U.S. and 17 000 non-public U.S. companies
- *Statistics Canada*—huge repository of accurate data about Canada[4]

Conducting Effective Database Searches Whether you are using a library database or an Internet search engine, follow these tips to improve your search results:[5]

By following a few guidelines, you can improve your database search results.

- **Use multiple search engines.** Don't limit yourself to a single search engine, especially if you are looking for less popular topics. Try your search on several engines by using **metacrawlers,** special engines that search several search engines at once.
- **Translate concepts into key words and phrases.** If you're researching the "effect of TQM on company profits," select the keywords *TQM, total quality management, profits, sales, companies,* and *corporations.* Use synonyms or word equivalents whenever possible.
- **Use capitals and lower case characters correctly.** When a search engine is case sensitive, it will return different documents for the keywords *Chair* and *chair.* If the search engine is not case sensitive, then it will return all documents containing the word *chair,* whether capitalized or not.
- **Use variations of your terms.** Use abbreviations (*CEO, CPA*), synonyms (*man, male*), related terms (*child, adolescent, youth*), different spellings (*dialog, dialogue*), singular and plural forms (*woman, women*), nouns and adjectives (*manager, management, managerial*), and open and compound forms (*online, on line, on-line*).
- **Specify phrases or individual keywords with quotation marks.** To look for an entire phrase ("*total quality management*"), most search engines allow you to use quotation marks around the phrase. Otherwise, the search engine will look for instances where the separate words (*total, quality,* and *management*) appear somewhere on the Web page.
- **Evaluate the precision and quality of your results to refine your search if necessary.** You'll need to refine your search if you end up with more than 60 to 100 links to sort through or if your first page of results doesn't offer something of interest. Also pay attention to whether you are searching in the title, subject, or document field of the database. Each will return different results.

Collect Primary Information

Sometimes what you need is not available from sources of secondary information, or you need something beyond what is covered in secondary information. In that case, you go out into the real world to gather data yourself. The main methods of collecting primary information are examining documents, making observations, conducting experiments, surveying people, and conducting interviews.

Conduct primary research by collecting basic information yourself.

Documents, Observation, and Experiments Often the most useful method of collecting primary information is examining internal documents, such as company sales reports, memos, balance sheets, and income statements. You can find a great deal of information in company databases and files. A single document may be a source of both secondary and primary information. For example, when citing summaries of financial and operations data from an annual report, you're using the report as secondary information. However, the same annual report would be considered a primary source if you were analyzing its design features, comparing it with annual reports from other years, or comparing it with reports from other companies.

Documentary evidence and historical records are sources of primary data.

Another common method of collecting primary business information is making formal observations. For instance, you can observe people performing their jobs or customers interacting with a product. Conducting experiments is another method of collecting primary information, but this method is far more common in technical fields than in general business.

Observation applies your five senses and your judgment to the investigation.

Developing an effective survey questionnaire requires care and skill.

Surveys One of the best methods of collecting primary information is to ask people with relevant experience and opinions. Surveys include everything from a one-time, one-on-one interview to the distribution of thousands of questionnaires. When prepared and conducted properly, surveys can tell you what a cross-section of people think about a given topic. Surveys are useful only when they're reliable and valid. A survey is *reliable* if it produces identical results when repeated. A survey is *valid* if it measures what it's intended to measure. For effective surveys, follow these tips:

- **Provide clear instructions.** Respondents need to know exactly how to fill out your questionnaire.
- **Keep the questionnaire short and easy to answer.** Ask only questions that are relevant to your research. Remember that people are most likely to respond if they can complete your questionnaire within 10 to 15 minutes.
- **Develop questions that provide easy-to-analyze answers.** Numbers and facts are easier to summarize than opinions.
- **Avoid leading questions.** Questions that lead to a particular answer bias your survey. If you ask, "Do you prefer that we stay open in the evenings for customer convenience?" you'll get a yes answer. Instead, ask, "What time of day do you normally do your shopping?"
- **Ask only one thing at a time.** A compound question such as "Do you read books and magazines regularly?" doesn't allow for the respondent who reads one but not the other.
- **Pretest the questionnaire.** Have a sample group identify questions that are subject to misinterpretation.

If you're mailing your questionnaire rather than administering it in person, include a return postage-paid envelope along with a persuasive cover letter that explains why you're conducting the research. Your letter must convince your readers that responding is important. Remember that even under the best of circumstances, you may get no more than a 10 percent to 20 percent response.

Effective interviewers develop a communication plan.

Interviews Getting information straight from an expert can be another effective method for collecting primary information. **Interviews** are planned conversations with a predetermined purpose that involve asking and answering questions. Before you decide to do one, ask yourself whether an interview is really the best way to get the information you need. Although they are relatively easy to conduct, interviews require careful planning and a lot of time.

- **Plan the interview.** Decide in advance what kind of information you want and how you will use it. Analyze your purpose, learn about the other person, and formulate your main idea. Then decide on the length, style, and organization of the interview.
- **Prepare interview questions.** The answers you receive are influenced by the types of questions you ask, the way you ask them, and your subject's cultural and language background.
- **Assign priorities to interview questions.** Rate your questions and highlight the most important ones. If you start to run out of time during the interview, you may have to be selective.
- **Limit the number of questions.** Don't try to cover more questions than you have time for. You can probably handle about 20 questions in a half-hour.
- **Edit your questions.** Try to make your questions as neutral and as easy to understand as possible. Then practise them several times to make sure you're ready for the interview.
- **Process interview information.** After the interview, take a few moments to write down your thoughts, go over your notes, and organize your material. Fill in any blanks while the interview is fresh in your mind.

Document Sources and Give Credit

Whenever you quote or paraphrase, you are using someone else's words or ideas. Doing so without proper credit is **plagiarism.** You can avoid plagiarism by documenting the original source (using one of the systems explained in Appendix B, "Documentation of Report Sources"). Documenting your sources is necessary for books, articles, tables, charts, diagrams, song lyrics, scripted dialogue, letters, speeches—anything that you take from someone else. Even if you paraphrase the material, it's best to give credit to the person you obtained the original information from.

Always give proper credit when you use someone else's material or ideas.

However, you do not have to cite a source for general knowledge or for specialized knowledge that's generally known among your readers. For example, everyone knows that Pierre Trudeau was elected prime minister. You can say so on your own authority, even if you've read an article in which the author says the same thing.

Interpret Your Findings

By themselves, the data you collect won't offer much meaning or insight. You'll need to search for relationships among the facts and the bits of evidence you've compiled. This analysis allows you to interpret your findings and thus answer the questions or solve the problem that required the report in the first place. Once you have thoroughly analyzed your information, your next step is to draw conclusions and, if requested, develop recommendations.

Analyze your results by drawing reasonable and logical conclusions and, if appropriate, developing a set of recommendations.

Drawing Conclusions A **conclusion** is a logical interpretation of the facts in your report. Reaching good conclusions based on the evidence at hand is one of the most important skills you can develop in your business career. Make sure your conclusions are sound: First, your conclusion should fulfil the original statement of purpose. After all, drawing a conclusion is why you took on the project in the first place. Second, base your conclusion strictly on the information included in the rest of the report—all the information. Don't ignore anything, even if it doesn't support your conclusion. Third, don't introduce any new information in your conclusion. And, fourth, make sure your conclusion is logical. A logical conclusion is one that follows accepted patterns of reasoning. Your conclusions are influenced by your personal values and your organization's values; so be aware of how these biases affect your judgment.

Conclusions are interpretations of the facts.

Check the logic that underlies your conclusions.

Developing Recommendations Whereas a conclusion interprets the facts, a **recommendation** suggests what to do about the conclusion. The difference between a conclusion and a recommendation can be seen in the following example:

Recommendations are suggestions for action.

Conclusion	Recommendation
On the basis of its track record and current price, I conclude that this company is an attractive buy.	I recommend that we offer to buy the company at a 10 percent premium over the market value of its stock.

Clarify the relationship between your conclusions and your recommendations. Remember, recommendations are inappropriate in a report when you're not expected to supply them. But when you do provide recommendations in a report, try to develop them without bias. Don't let your assumptions and personal values influence them. To be credible, recommendations must be based on logical analysis and sound conclusions. They must also be practical and acceptable to your readers, the people who have to make the recommendations work. Finally, when making a recommendation, adequately describe the steps that come next. Don't leave your readers scratching their heads and saying, "This all sounds good, but what do I do on Monday morning?" Since recommendations are often the most important information in a report, decide how you can design the document to make the recommendations easily accessible to the reader. Consider using a heading and putting recommendations in a list to emphasize them.

Good recommendations are

- Practical
- Acceptable to readers
- Explained in enough detail for readers to take action

Reviewing Key Points

In this chapter you looked at informational reports for monitoring operations, implementing policies, complying with regulation, and documenting progress on projects. You also learned about analytical reports for solving problems and proposing changes. You viewed internal and external proposals to get products, plans, or projects accepted by authorities. Companies may solicit or invite you to write a proposal that describes how to solve a known problem. Or, you may initiate a proposal and send it unsolicited. When you submit unsolicited proposals, you have to convince the receiver about the problem as well as the solution.

This chapter concentrates on the planning stage of the proposal writing process. In the planning stage of the writing process, you should

- Analyze the audience and write a clear purpose statement
- Define the problem and scope of the document
- Prepare a preliminary outline and a work plan for longer projects
- Research using primary and/or secondary sources to investigate the topic
- Design efficient surveys and interviews with focused, unbiased questions
- Consult important business directories, databases, and indexes such as Canadian Business and Current Affairs, SEDAR, and Strategis to gather facts
- Interpret evidence to identify benefits and develop conclusions

In Chapter 11 you will study the next stages: writing and producing the report or proposal.

Test Your Knowledge

1. How are reports for monitoring and controlling operations used?

2. What functions do progress reports serve?

3. What are the two primary purposes of internal proposals?

4. How do proposal writers use an RFP?

5. How does primary information differ from secondary information?

6. How can you improve your search when using a search engine or a library database?

7. What makes a survey reliable and valid?

8. Why is it important to assign priority to your interview questions?

9. What are the characteristics of a sound conclusion?

10. How does a conclusion differ from a recommendation?

Apply Your Knowledge

1. Why are unsolicited proposals more challenging to write than solicited proposals?

2. If you want to make a specific recommendation in your report, should you include information that might support a different action? Explain your answer.

3. If your report includes only factual information, is it objective? Please explain.

4. After an exhaustive study of an important problem, you have reached a conclusion that you believe your company's management will reject. What will you do? Explain your answer.

5. **Ethical Choices** If you want to make a specific recommendation following your research, should you include information that might support a different recommendation? Explain your answer.

Practise Your Knowledge

Activities

For live links to all Web sites discussed in this chapter, visit this text's Web site at www.prenhall.ca/bovee. Just log on and select Chapter 10, and click on "Student Resources." Locate the page or the URL related to the material in the text. For the "Exploring the Best of the Web" exercises, you'll also find navigational directions. Click on the live link to the site.

1. **Analyze This Document** All public companies file comprehensive annual reports. Many companies post links to these reports on their Web sites along with links to other company reports. Use www.sedar.com to find a company of your choice. View the company's most recent annual report and financial report. Compare the style and format of the two reports. For which audience(s) is the annual report targeted? Who is interested in the financial report? Which report do you find easier to read? More interesting? More detailed?

2. **Understanding Business Reports and Proposals: How Companies Use Reports** Interview several people working in a career you might like to enter, and ask them about the types of written reports they receive and prepare. How do these reports tie in to the decision-making process? Who reads the reports they prepare? Summarize your findings in writing, give them to your instructor, and be prepared to discuss them with the class.

3. **Internet** Read the step-by-step hints and examples for writing a funding proposal at www.learnerassociates.net. Review the entire sample proposal online. What details did the author decide to include in the appendices? Why was this material placed in the appendices and not the main body of the report? According to the author's tips, when is the best time to prepare a Project Overview?

4. **Analyzing the Situation: Statement of Purpose** Sales at the Style Shop, a clothing store for men, have declined for the third month in a row. Your boss is not sure whether this decline is due to a weak economy or if it's due to another, unknown reason. She has asked you to investigate the situation and to submit a report to her highlighting some possible reasons for the decline. Develop a statement of purpose for your report.

5. **Teamwork: Planning an Unsolicited Proposal** Break into small groups and identify an operational problem occurring at your campus—perhaps involving registration, university housing, food services, parking, or library services. Then develop a workable solution to that problem. Finally, develop a list of pertinent facts that your team will need to gather to convince the reader that the problem exists and that your solution will work.

6. **Preparing the Work Plan** The lawn surrounding the Town Centre shopping centre looks as if it could use better care. You're the assistant to the centre's general manager, who must approve any new contracts for lawn service. You want to prepare a formal study of the current state of your lawn's health. Your report will include conclusions and recommendations for your boss's consideration. Draft a work plan, including the problem statement, the statement of purpose and scope, a description of what will result from your investigation, the sources and methods of data collection, and a preliminary outline.

7. **Finding Secondary Information** Business people have to know where to look for secondary information when they conduct research. Prepare a list of the most important magazines and professional journals in the following fields of study:

   a. Marketing/advertising
   b. Insurance
   c. Communications
   d. Accounting

8. **Finding Information: Primary Information** Deciding how to collect primary data is an important part of the research process. Which one or more of the five methods of data collection (examining documents, making observations, surveying people, performing experiments, or conducting interviews) would you use if you were researching these questions?

   a. Has the litter problem on campus been reduced since the cafeteria began offering fewer takeout choices this year?
   b. Has the school attracted more transfer students since it waived the formal application process and allowed students at other colleges simply to send their transcripts and a one-page letter of application?
   c. Have the number of traffic accidents at the school's main entrance been reduced since a traffic light was installed?
   d. Has student satisfaction with the campus bookstore improved now that students can order their books over the Internet and pick them up at several campus locations?

9. **Finding Information: Interviews** You're conducting an information interview with a manager in another division of your company. Partway through the interview, the manager shows clear signs of impatience. How should you respond? What might you do differently to prevent this from happening in the future? Explain your answers.

10. **Processing Information: Documenting Sources** Select five business articles from sources such as journals, books, newspapers, or Web sites. Develop a resource list using Appendix B as a guideline. Practise forming references in APA format by using an interactive Web site developed by Kevin Schoepp at the University of Calgary, www.ucalgary.ca/~dmjacobs/prosem/citing_resources.html.

Expand Your Knowledge

Best of the Web

Pointers for Business Plans What's involved in a business plan? BizPlanIt.com offers tips and advice, consulting services, a free e-mail newsletter, and a sample virtual business plan. You'll find suggestions on what details and how much information to include in each section of a business plan. You can explore the site's numerous links to business plan books and software, online magazines, educational programs, government resources, women and minority resources, and even answers to your business plan questions.

www.bizplanit.com

Exercises

1. Why is the executive summary such an important section of a business plan? What kind of information is contained in the executive summary?
2. What is the product/services section? What information should it contain? List some of the common errors to avoid when planning this part.
3. What type of business planning should you describe in the exit strategy section? Why?

Exploring the Web on Your Own

Review these chapter-related Web sites on your own to learn more about planning and using reports in the workplace.

1. If your report writing involves researching other companies, Wall Street Research Network, www.wsrn.com, is one of the most comprehensive company information sites on the Internet.
2. Looking for a specific company? Try SuperPages at www.bigbook.com where you'll find more than 16 million listings. Select "Canada" to locate Canadian companies.
3. Searching for information on a company or industry? Corporate Information, www.corporateinformation.com, is a good place to begin your online research. It has a link to Wright Investors Source for Canadian profiles.

Learning Interactively

Interactive Study Guide

Visit the Companion Website at www.pearsoned.ca/bovee. For Chapter 10, take advantage of the interactive "Study Guide" to test your chapter knowledge. Get instant feedback on whether you need additional studying.

This site offers a variety of additional resources: The "Research Area" helps you locate a wealth of information to use in course assignments. The "Study Hall" helps you succeed in this course by offering support with writing and study skills, time management, and career skills, as well as numerous other resources.

Peak Performance Grammar and Mechanics

Use the Peak Performance Grammar and Mechanics CD to test your skill with punctuation. In the "Punctuation II" section, take the Pretest to determine whether you have any weak areas. Then review those areas in the Refresher Course. Take the Follow-Up Test to check your grasp of punctuation. For an extra challenge or advanced practice, take the Advanced Test.

Cases

Informal Informational Reports

1. My progress to date: Interim progress report on your academic career

As you know, meeting the requirements involved in getting a degree or certificate can be nearly as challenging as any course you could take.

Your Task Plan an interim progress report detailing the steps you've taken toward completing your graduation or certification requirements. After examining the requirements listed in your catalogue, indicate a realistic schedule for completing those requirements you have yet to complete. In addition to course requirements, include steps such as completing the residency requirement, filing necessary papers, and paying necessary fees. Plan on using a memo format for your report, and address it to anyone who is helping or encouraging you through school.

2. Gavel to gavel: Personal activity report of a meeting

Meetings and conferences can be one-on-one or large gatherings, and you have probably attended your share.

Your Task Plan a personal activity report on a meeting or conference that you recently attended. Plan to use memo format, and direct the report to other students in your class who did not attend.

3. Check that price tag: Informational report on trends in tuition costs

Are tuition costs going up, going down, or remaining the same? Your school's administration has asked you to compare your tuition costs with those of a nearby school and determine which has risen more quickly. Check your school's annual tuition costs for the last four years. Then check the four-year tuition trends for a neighbouring school. For both schools, calculate the percentage change in tuition costs from year to year and between the first and fourth year.

Your Task Plan an informal report (using the letter format) presenting your findings and conclusions to the president of your school. Plan to include graphics that explain and support your conclusions.

4. Get a move on it: Lasting guidelines for moving in with a roommate

Moving in with a roommate is one experience you weren't quite prepared for—lugging your earthly belongings up four flights of stairs in 30-degree heat, channelling electrical cords to the one outlet in the corner of the room, and negotiating with your roommate over who gets the bigger closet. It would have been good to know what is expected of a new roommate on moving day. You feel like an old pro now that you have survived the experience.

Your Task Your part-time job is in the Student Services Office of your college. Your boss heard you talking in the coffee room about your experiences and thought of asking you to help with the Student Handbook. She wants to add a section entitled "Moving in with a Roommate" in next year's edition. She asked if you would prepare a report for anyone moving in with a roommate, outlining the rules and procedures to follow. Lay out the rules, such as establishing a starting time, handling garbage and empty boxes, sorting items permitted and not permitted in apartments or residence rooms, remembering common courtesies, and so on. Be sure to mention any policies for pets, cooking, and overloading electrical circuits. Of course, any recommendations on how to handle disputes with roommates would be helpful. Direct your memo report to fellow students. It will be published in the Student Handbook.

Informal Analytical Reports

5. Career moves: Assessing employment prospects

Your Task Assess the job prospects in your desired occupation and research a company that employs people in this field. Look up the trends and predictions about the occupational category and find out the hiring qualifications. To find information on occupational categories such as accountants, human resource managers, and others, consult the Canadian National Occupational Classification site at www23.hrdc-drhc.gc.ca/2001/e/generic/welcome.shtml. Look on Work Futures sites by province such as www.workfutures.bc.ca. Provincial Work Futures sites contain links to the other provinces and territories.

Use www.sedar.com or www.strategis.ca to locate a company that employs people in the occupational group you have researched. Visit the company's Web site. Find out whether this company would be a good hiring prospect for fellow classmates in your field. If time permits, interview a manager in the company to gather specific information for your report. Write a report that provides information on the company and assesses its employment and future prospects. Develop a conclusion based on the facts you collect and include at least one recommendation.

6. Staying the course: Unsolicited proposal

Think of a course you would love to see added to the core curriculum at your school. Or, if you would like to see a course offered as an elective rather than being required, write your e-mail report accordingly.

Your Task Plan a short e-mail proposal. Plan on submitting it to the academic dean. Be sure to include all the reasons supporting your idea.

7. Planning my program: Problem-solving report

Assume that you will have time for only one course next term.

Your Task Plan a report that lists the pros and cons of four or five courses that interest you, and settle on the course that is best for you to take at this time. Plan to make your report a memo addressed to your counsellor or academic adviser.

8. "Would you carry it?" Unsolicited proposal recommending a product to a retail outlet

Select a product you are familiar with, and imagine that you work for the manufacturer and that you're trying to get a local retail outlet to carry it. Use the Internet and other resources to gather any information you need about the product.

Your Task Plan an unsolicited proposal to be sent in letter format to the owner (or manager) of the store. You want to propose that the store stock your product. Use the information you gathered to describe some of the product's features and benefits to the store. Then make up some reasonable figures, highlighting what the item costs, what it can be sold for, and what services your company provides (return of unsold items, free replacement of unsatisfactory items, necessary repairs, and so on).

9. Restaurant review: Troubleshooting report on a restaurant's food and operations

Visit any restaurant, possibly your school cafeteria. The workers and fellow customers will assume that you are an ordinary customer, but you are really a spy for the owner.

Your Task After your visit, plan a short memo to the owner, explaining (a) what you did and what you observed, (b) any violations of policy that you observed, and (c) your recommendations for improvement. The first part of your report (what you did and what you observed) will be the longest. Plan to include a description of the premises, inside and out. You'll want to tell how long it took for each step of ordering and receiving your meal. Figure out how you'll describe the service and food thoroughly. You are interested in both the good and the bad aspects of the establishment's decor, service, and food. For the second section (violations of policy), use some common sense. If all the servers but one have their hair covered, you may assume that policy requires hair to be covered; a dirty window or restroom obviously violates policy. The last section (recommendations for improvement) involves professional judgment. What management actions will improve the restaurant?

10. On the books: Troubleshooting report on improving the campus bookstore

Imagine that you are a consultant hired to improve the profits of your campus bookstore.

Your Task Visit the bookstore and look critically at its operations. Then plan a memo offering recommendations to the bookstore manager that would make the store more profitable, perhaps suggesting products it should carry, hours it should remain open, or added services it should make available to students. Be sure that you plan how to support your recommendations.

11. Press one for efficiency: Unsolicited proposal on a telephone interviewing system

How can a firm be thorough yet efficient when considering dozens of applicants for each position? One tool that may help is IntelliView, a 10-minute question-and-answer session conducted by Touch-Tone telephone. The company recruiter dials up the IntelliView computer and then leaves the room. The candidate punches in answers to roughly 100 questions about work attitudes and other issues. In a few minutes, the recruiter can call Pinkerton (the company offering the service) and find out the results. On the basis of what the IntelliView interview reveals, the recruiter can delve more deeply into certain areas and, ultimately, have more information on which to base the hiring decision.

Your Task As assistant recruiter for Canadian Tire, you think that IntelliView might help your firm. Plan a brief memo to Paula Wolski, director of human resources, in which you will suggest a test of the IntelliView system. Your memo should tell your boss why you believe your firm should test the system before making a long-term commitment.[6]

12. Day and night: Problem-solving report on stocking a 24-hour convenience store

When a store is open all day, every day, when's the best time to restock the shelves? That's the challenge at Store 24, a retail chain that never closes. As the assistant manager of a Store 24 branch that just opened near your campus, you want to set up a restocking schedule that won't conflict with prime shopping hours. Think about the number of customers you're likely to serve in the morning, afternoon, evening, and overnight hours. Consider, too, how many employees you might have during these four periods.

Your Task Plan a problem-solving report to be in letter form. You'll be sending your report to the store manager (Isabel Chu) and the regional manager (Eric Angstrom), who must agree on a solution to this problem. Plan on discussing the pros and cons of each of the four periods, and include your recommendations for restocking the shelves.

Improve Your Grammar, Mechanics, and Usage

Level 1: Self-Assessment—Dashes and Hyphens

Review Sections 2.7 and 2.8 in the Handbook of Grammar, Mechanics, and Usage, and then look at the following 15 items.

In items 1–15, insert the required dashes (—) and hyphens (-):

1. Three qualities speed, accuracy, and reliability are desirable in any applicant to the data entry department.
2. A highly placed source explained the top secret negotiations.
3. The file on Maria Wilson yes, we finally found it reveals a history of late payments.
4. They're selling a well designed machine.
5. A bottle green sports jacket is hard to find.
6. Argentina, Brazil, Mexico these are the countries we hope to concentrate on.
7. Only two sites maybe three offer the things we need.
8. How many owner operators are in the industry?
9. Your ever faithful assistant deserves without a doubt a substantial raise.
10. Myrna Talefiero is this organization's president elect.
11. Stealth, secrecy, and surprise those are the elements that will give us a competitive edge.
12. The charts are well placed on each page unlike the running heads and footers.
13. We got our small business loan an enormous advantage.
14. Ron Franklin do you remember him? will be in town Monday.
15. Your devil may care attitude affects everyone involved in the decision making process.

Level 2: Workplace Applications

The following items contain numerous errors in grammar, capitalization, punctuation, abbreviation, number style, word division, and vocabulary. Rewrite each sentence in the space provided, correcting all errors. Write *C* in the space after any sentence that is already correct.

1. Commerce One helps its customer's to more efficiently lower administrative costs, improve order times, and to manage contract negotiations.

2. The intermodal bus vehicle seats up to 35 passengers, but is equipped with a 7 metre standardized container in the rear. The same container one sees on ships, trains and on planes.

3. A refusal to except the status quo has just created, in our opinion, Canada's newest and most exciting company to watch," said Gordon Exel, Vice-President Marketing of Westport Innovations.

4. This new, transportation paradigm may have a global affect and the barriers to entry will be extremely costly too overcome.

5. Autobytel also owns and operates Carsmart.com and Autosite.com as well as AIC [Automotive Information Center] a provider of automotive marketing data and technology.

6. Mymarket.com offers a low cost high reward, entry into e-commerce not only for buyers but also suppliers.

7. Bombardier's main competitor are another start-up Skye Air of Hamilton, ON.

8. After identifying the factors that improve a industrial process, additional refining experiments must be conducted to confirm the results.

9. The employment standards Act regulates minimum wages, establishes overtime compensation, and it outlaws labour for children.

10. The Chinese government are supporting use of the Internet as a business tool because it is seen by it as necessary to enhance competitiveness.

11. At a certain point in a company's growth, the entrepreneur, who wants to control everything, can no longer keep up so they look mistakenly for a better manager and call that person a CEO.

12. City Fresh foods is paid by City health agencies to provide Ethnic food to the homebound "elderly" in the Sherbrooke Area.

13. Being in business since 1993, Miss Rosen has boiled down her life story into a 2-minute sound bight for sales prospects.

14. Anyone that wants to gain a new perspective on their product or service must cast aside one's own biases.

15. If I was Bill Gates, I'd handle the U.S. government's antitrust lawsuit much different.

Level 3: Document Critique

The following document may contain errors in grammar, capitalization, punctuation, abbreviation, number style, vocabulary, and spelling. You may also find problems with organization, format, and word use. Correct all errors using standard proofreading marks (see Appendix C).

Memo

SUBJECT: Recruiting and hiring Seminar

To Jeff Black and HR staff

DATE March 14 2004

FROM: Carrie andrews

As you all know the process of recruiting screening and hiring new employees might be a legal minefield. Because we don't have an inhouse lawyer to help us make every decision, its important for all of us to be aware of what actions are legally acceptible and what isn't. Last week I attended a Canadian Federation of Independent Business workshop on this subject. I given enough useful information to warrant updating our online personnel handbook and perhaps developing a quick training session for all interviewing teams. First, heres a quick look at the things I learned.

Avoiding Legal Mistakes

- How to write recruiting ads that accurately portray job openings and not discriminate.
- Complying with the Canadian Human Rights Act
- How to use an employment agency effectively and safe (without risk of legal entanglements)

How to Screen and Interview More Effectively

- How to sort through resumés more efficient (including looking for telltale signs of false information)
- We can avoid interview questions that could get us into legal trouble
- When and how to check criminal records

Measuring Applicants

- Which type of preemployment tests have been proven most effective?
- Which drug-testing issues and recommendations effect us

as you can see the seminar addresed alot of important information. We covering the basic guidelines for much of this already; but a number of specific recommendations and legal concepts should be emphisized and underline.

It will take me a couple of weeks to get the personel handbook updated: but we don't have any immediate hiring plans anyway so that shouldn't be too much of a problem unless you think I should complete it sooner and then we can talk about that.

I'll keep the seminar handouts and my notes on my desk in case you want to peruse them.

After the handbook is updated by me, we can get together and decide whether we need to train the interviewing team members.

Although we have a lot of new information, what people need to be aware of can be highlighted and the new sections can be read as schedules allow, although they might be reluctant to do this and we can also talk about that later, at a time of your conveinence that you can select later.

If you have any questions in the mean-time; don't hesitate to e-mail me or drop by for a chat.

Technology

Business Communication Notebook

Communicating Through the Internet

Understanding the Internet

The *Internet* is the world's largest computer network. Started in 1969 by the U.S. Department of Defense, it is a voluntary, cooperative undertaking; no one individual, organization, or government owns it. The Internet is accessible to individuals, companies, colleges and universities, government agencies, and other institutions all over the world.

Accessing the Net
To use the Internet, you need a computer (with a modem) and an *Internet service provider (ISP)*—a company that connects you to the Internet. For a fee, you can dial into one of the ISP's host computers, which will link you to one of the Internet's networked computers. Although many people use a standard phone line, others pay a bit more for the speed and convenience of a cable connection or a *digital subscriber line (DSL)*, a high-speed phone line that carries both voice and data. You can also connect "on the go," using either a handheld computer or a cellphone that is set up for wireless access.

The most widely used part of the Internet is the World Wide Web. Developed in 1990, the Web enables users to search for, display, and save multimedia resources such as graphics, text, audio, and video files. This information is stored on a *Web site*—a series of *Web pages* that contain related files of multimedia data. To read Web pages, you need a Web *browser*—software such as Netscape Navigator or Microsoft's Internet Explorer.

Navigating the Net
The *home page* of a Web site is the primary screen that users first access when visiting a site. Each page in a Web site is identified by a unique address known as a *uniform resource locator (URL)*. An example is http://www.yahoo.ca. The address begins with *http* (the abbreviation for *hypertext transfer protocol*, the protocol that allows you to navigate the Web). The address continues with *www*, indicating that the site is located on the World Wide Web. The next part of the address is the registered *domain name* (in this case yahoo), a name unique to that site. The abbreviation following the period is the *top-level domain (TLD)*. The TLDs now available include com (company), biz (business), info (general information), pro (professional), museum (museum), aero (aviation), name (individual), coop (cooperative), edu (educational), gov (government), int (international), mil (military), net (network resources), org (nonprofit organizations), and numerous country codes such as fr (France), ca (Canada), or jp (Japan).

A convenient way to navigate the Web is through hyperlinks or *hotlinks*. To automatically jump to another Web page or Web site, just use your mouse to click on words in *hypertext markup language (HTML)*—coloured, underlined, or highlighted words. Once you get to your new destination, you can *bookmark* the site by using a browser feature that places the site's URL in a file on your computer for future use. You can also navigate your trail backward or forward at any time by using the Back and Forward buttons or menus on your browser.

How Businesses Are Using the Internet

The Internet helps businesses make closer connections with other organizations and customers all over the planet. They use the Internet to

- Share text, photos, slides, videos, and other data within the organization
- Permit employees to *telecommute*, or work away from a conventional office, whether at home, on the road, or across the country
- Recruit employees cost-effectively
- Locate information from external sources
- Find new business partners and attract new customers
- Locate and buy parts and materials from domestic and international suppliers
- Promote and sell goods and services to customers in any location
- Provide customers with service, technical support, and product information
- Collaborate with local, national, and international business partners
- Inform investors, industry analysts, and government regulators about business developments

In addition, companies can set up special employee-only Web sites using an *intranet*, a private internal corporate network. Intranets use the same technology as the Internet but restrict the information and access to members of the organization (regardless of a member's actual location). Once a company has an intranet, it can add an *extranet* that allows people to communicate and exchange data within a secure network of qualified people outside the organization—such as suppliers, contractors, and customers who use a password to access the system.

Online Reporting

Thanks to the Internet, more and more companies are using online reports to keep employees, managers, investors, and other stakeholders informed. For example, companies with many branches and operations can have staff enter data into the computer system by following report formats on the screen. These reports are sent electronically to headquarters where corporate managers can track sales, adjust resources, and resolve potential problems much more quickly than if they had to wait for printed reports.

Well-known package-shipper FedEx lets customers access electronic reports to monitor the status of their shipments at any time. This reporting system not only helps FedEx serve its customers better but also puts valuable information in the hands of customers. And like many companies, FedEx posts its annual report and other corporate informational reports on its Web site for interested customers and investors.

Applications for Success

You can learn more about the Internet by taking the tour at www.learnthenet.com or www.netforbeginners.about.com.

Answer the following questions:

1. **Ethical choice:** Do you think companies should monitor their employees' use of the Internet and e-mail? Explain your answer.
2. What kinds of electronic reports might a company want to post on its Web site?
3. What advantages and disadvantages do you see in asking managers to go beyond their informational operations reports and start filing electronic problem-solving reports on the company's intranet?

Unit 4

COMPOSING BUSINESS REPORTS, PROPOSALS, AND PRESENTATIONS

11

Writing and Completing Business Reports and Proposals

From the Real World

"A good proposal reflects whether the writer has a clear idea of the project being proposed: why it is needed, why it is important, and how it will benefit the community."

–Sidney Sawyer
Manager, Community Programs
VanCity Community Foundation

After studying this chapter, you will be able to

1. Discuss what decisions you must make when organizing a business report or proposal
2. Describe the structure of informational reports
3. Describe the structure of analytical reports and proposals
4. List several popular types of graphics and discuss when to use them
5. Name five characteristics of effective report content
6. Explain three tools that writers can use in long reports to help readers stay on track
7. Identify the prefatory parts of a formal report
8. Explain the purpose of an executive summary
9. Name the three supplemental parts of a formal report

The VanCity Community Foundation in Vancouver provides grants and lending advice to non-profit organizations proposing initiatives to improve communities through community economic development. Sidney Sawyer is part of a team that assesses these proposals, evaluating many of them each year. "Proposal writers," says Sawyer, "create positive impressions by providing clear answers, using plain language, and providing facts to support the proposal." Proposals should be concise but contain enough detail to convince the audience that the idea is valuable, practical, and desirable. Proposals must contain a compelling argument—the key to a successful report. [1]

Step 2: Writing Business Reports and Proposals

Once you've planned out your document (see Chapters 3 and 10), you're ready to begin Step 2, writing business reports and proposals. Since so much of Step 2 is discussed in Chapter 4, the following sections cover only those aspects of writing that differ for reports and proposals. Think carefully about all the relevant tasks as you organize and compose your reports and proposals.

Organizing Reports and Proposals

Before you can compose a business report or proposal, you must organize the material you've collected, arranging it in a logical order that meets your audience's needs. You must carefully choose the format, length, order, and structure for your document.

Deciding on Format and Length

When you select the format for your report, you have four options:

You may present a report in one of four formats: preprinted form, letter, memo, or manuscript.

- **Preprinted form.** Used for fill-in-the-blank reports. Most are relatively short (five or fewer pages) and deal with routine information, often mainly numerical.
- **Letter.** Commonly used for reports of five or fewer pages that are directed to outsiders. These reports include all the normal parts of a letter, and they may also have headings, footnotes, tables, and figures.
- **Memo.** Commonly used for short (fewer than 10 pages), informal reports distributed within an organization. Like longer reports, they often have internal headings and sometimes include visual aids.
- **Manuscript.** Commonly used for reports that require a formal approach, whether a few pages or several hundred. As length increases, formal reports require more elements before the text (prefatory parts) and after (supplementary parts). The second half of this chapter explains these elements in more detail.

The length of your report often depends on your subject, your purpose, and your relationship with your audience. When your readers are relative strangers, sceptical, or hostile, or if your material is nonroutine or controversial, you usually have to explain your points in greater detail, which results in a longer document. However, you can afford to be brief if you're on familiar terms with your readers, if they are likely to agree with you, and if the information is routine or uncomplicated.

Length depends on

- Your subject
- Your purpose
- Your relationship with your audience

Choosing the Direct or Indirect Approach

The direct approach is by far the most popular and convenient order for business reports, saving time and making the report easier to follow. It also produces a more forceful report, because stating your conclusions confidently in the beginning makes you sound sure of yourself. However, if your readers have reservations about either you or your material, making strong statements at the beginning may intensify reader resistance. Also, confidence may sometimes be misconstrued as arrogance. So choose the direct approach for reports only when your credibility is high, when your readers trust you, and are willing to accept your conclusions.

The direct approach saves time and makes the report easier to understand by giving readers the main idea first.

If your audience is sceptical or hostile, you may want to use the indirect approach, introducing your complete findings and discussing all supporting details before presenting your conclusions and recommendations. The indirect approach gives you a chance to prove your points and gradually overcome your audience's reservations. Even so, some readers will immediately flip back to the recommendations, thus defeating your purpose. The longer the message, the less effective an indirect approach is likely to be. Also, an indirect argument is harder to follow than a direct one.

The indirect approach helps overcome resistance by withholding the main idea until later in the report.

The indirect approach is not effective for long reports.

Both direct and indirect approaches have merit, so business people often combine them, revealing their conclusions and recommendations as they go along, rather than treating them first or last. Figure 11.1 on page 278 presents the introductions from two reports with the same general outline. In the direct version, a series of statements summarize the conclusion reached about each main topic on the outline. In the indirect version, the same topics are introduced in the same order but without any conclusions about them. Instead, the conclusions appear after evidence given in the report body.

Business people often combine the direct and indirect approaches.

Regardless of the format, length, or order you use, you must still decide how your ideas will be developed. Choose a logical structure that suits your topic and goals and makes the most sense to your audience.

FIGURE 11.1 Direct Approach Versus Indirect Approach in an Introduction

THE DIRECT APPROACH

Since the company's founding 25 years ago, we have provided regular repair service for all our electric appliances. This service has been an important selling point as well as a source of pride for our employees. However, we are paying a high price for our image. Last year, we lost $500 000 on our repair business.

Because of your concern over these losses, you have asked me to study the pros and cons of discontinuing our repair service. With the help of John Hudson and Susan Lefkowitz, I have studied the issue for the past two weeks and have come to the conclusion that we have been embracing an expensive, impractical tradition.

By withdrawing from the electric appliance repair business, we can substantially improve our financial performance without damaging our reputation with customers. This conclusion is based on three basic points that are covered in the following pages:

- It is highly unlikely that we will ever be able to make a profit in the repair business.
- Sevice is no longer an important selling point with customers.
- Closing down the service operation will create few internal problems.

THE INDIRECT APPROACH

Since the company's founding 25 years ago, we have provided repair service for all our electric appliances. This service has been an important selling point as well as a source of pride for our employees. However, the repair business itself has consistently lost money.

Because of your concern over these losses, you have asked me to study the pros and cons of discontinuing our repair service. With the help of John Hudson and Susan Lefkowitz, I have studied the issue for the past two weeks. The following pages present my findings for your review. Three basic questions are addressed:

- What is the extent of our losses, and what can we do to turn the business around?
- Would withdrawal hurt our sales of electric appliances?
- What would be the internal repercussions of closing down the repair business?

Structuring Informational Reports

The nature of the subject dictates the best way to structure the report.

Informational reports provide nothing more than facts. Most readers will respond unemotionally, so you can use the direct approach. However, you need to present the facts logically and accurately so that readers will understand exactly what you mean and be able to use your information easily. For example, when describing a machine, make report headings correspond to each component. Or when describing an event, discuss it chronologically. Let the nature of your subject dictate the structure of your informational reports. Use a **topical organization,** arranging material according to one of the following:

Topical organization is arranging material in order of importance, sequence, chronology, spatial relationships, location, or categories.

- **Importance.** If you're reviewing five product lines, you might organize your report according to product sales, from highest to lowest.
- **Sequence.** If you're studying a process, discuss it step by step—1, 2, 3, and so on.
- **Chronology.** When investigating a chain of events, organize the study according to what happened in January, what happened in February, and so on.
- **Spatial orientation.** If you're explaining how a physical object works, describe it left to right (or right to left in some cultures), top to bottom, outside to inside.
- **Geography.** If location is important, organize your study according to geography, perhaps by region of Canada or by area of a city.
- **Category.** If you're asked to review several distinct aspects of a subject, discuss one category at a time, such as cost, profit, sales, or investment.

Some informational reports (especially compliance reports and internal reports) are prepared on preprinted forms, so they are organized according to the instructions supplied by the person requesting the information.

Structuring Analytical Reports

For analytical reports, your choice of structure depends on the reaction you anticipate. When you expect your audience to agree with you, choose a structure that focuses attention on conclusions and recommendations. When you expect your audience to disagree with you or to be hostile, choose a structure that focuses attention on the reasons behind your conclusions and recommendations. Thus, the two most common approaches to structuring analytical reports are as follows:

The structure of analytical reports depends on audience reaction and whether you focus on

- Conclusions and recommendations
- Logical arguments

- **Direct: Focusing on conclusions and recommendations.** When people are likely to accept your findings, structure your report around conclusions, using a direct approach. Readers interested mainly in your conclusions can grasp them quickly, and those wanting more detail can examine your analysis and data. When asked to solve a problem, structure your report around recommendations, using a direct approach: (1) establish a need for action in the introduction (briefly describing the problem or opportunity), (2) describe your solution to the problem (your conclusion) in general terms, then list the actions required using action verbs for emphasis (your recommendations), (3) introduce the benefits that can result (using action verbs for emphasis), (4) explain each step more fully (giving details of procedures, costs, and benefits), and (5) summarize your recommendations.
- **Indirect: Focusing on logical arguments.** When encouraging readers to weigh all the facts before presenting your conclusions or recommendations, use the indirect approach and arrange your ideas around the reasoning behind your report's conclusions and recommendations. Organize your material to reflect the thinking process that will lead readers to your conclusions.

Structuring Business Proposals

Just as with reports, choosing a structural approach for proposals depends on whether you expect your audience to be receptive. In general, your audience may be more receptive to solicited proposals, since the problem and the solution have already been identified. The writer structures the proposal as specified in the RFP (request for proposal), using a direct approach and focusing on recommendations.

Solicited proposals are best organized by using the client's criteria as the main points.

The indirect approach may be a better choice for unsolicited proposals depending on how much you must convince your audience that a problem exists, and how much you must establish your credibility if you are unknown to the reader. Unfold your solution to the problem by focusing on logical argument, trying to persuade readers to accept your idea and award you a contract, and spelling out the terms of your proposal.

Organizing Graphics

When preparing reports, you'll often include graphics, or visual aids, to convey and emphasize important points. Carefully prepared visuals can help your audience understand your message and make your report more interesting. Even so, don't overdo the number of graphics. Use visuals selectively to support your primary message—to supplement your words, not to replace them.

Use visual aids to simplify, clarify, and emphasize important information.

Some information is clearest in words; other information is clearest as a graphic. For instance, detailed facts and figures may be confusing and tedious in paragraph form, but tables and charts organize and display such detail concisely and conveniently. Information that requires detailed description of physical relationships or procedures is clearest in a flow chart. Or you can simply draw attention to or emphasize a particular fact or detail by reinforcing that information visually.

Be sure to maintain a balance between your visuals and your words. The ideal blend depends on the nature of your subject. But illustrating every point dilutes the effectiveness of visuals. Plus, readers usually assume that the amount of space allocated to a topic indicates its relative importance. So by using visuals to illustrate a minor point, you may be sending a misleading message about its significance.

Choosing the Right Graphic for the Job

Once you decide which points to illustrate visually, select the type of graphic that will present your data most clearly and effectively to your audience. Some types of visuals depict certain kinds of data better than others. Your choice depends on the nature of the message and on the type of data you are presenting. Use Table 11.1 to select the right illustration.

Table 11.1 Choosing the Right Illustration for the Job

When your purpose is to	Choose a
Present a large amount of data so that the reader can analyze the data in detail	Table
Compare up to five variables	Bar graph
Show trends/changes over time	Line graph
Show percentages of a whole	Pie chart
Show relationships	Organization charts or flow charts
Show parts, interrelationships, and features	Illustrations and diagrams

Use tables to help your audience understand detailed information.

Tables To present detailed, specific information, choose a **table,** a systematic arrangement of data in columns and rows, with useful headings along the top and side. When preparing tables, be sure to

- Use common, understandable units, and clearly identify them: dollars, percentages, price per tonne, and so on
- Express all items in a column in the same unit, and round off for simplicity
- Label column headings clearly, and use a subhead if necessary
- Separate columns or rows with lines or extra space to make the table easy to follow
- Document the source of data using the same format as an endnote (see Appendix B)

Bar charts, in which numbers are visually portrayed by rectangular bars, can take a variety of forms.

Bar Charts A **bar chart** portrays numbers by the height or length of its rectangular bars, making a series of numbers easy to read or understand. Bar charts are particularly valuable when you want to

- Compare the size of several items at one time
- Show changes in one item over time
- Indicate the composition of several items over time
- Show the relative size of components of a whole

As Figure 11.2 shows, bar charts allow readers to compare data. Bar charts work best when you want to dramatize a major point with only a few variables. For example, Figure 11.2 shows the change in Canadian immigration patterns.

You can be creative with bar charts in many ways. For instance, you can align the bars either vertically or horizontally (see Figures 11.2 and 11.3).

Use line charts

- To indicate changes over time
- To plot the relationship of two variables

Line Graphs Line graphs can show more complex relationships than bar graphs. A **line graph** illustrates trends over time or plots the relationship of two variables. In line graphs showing trends, the vertical, or *y*, axis shows the amount, and the horizontal, or *x*, axis shows the time or the quantity being measured. Plot lines on the same graph for comparative purposes, as shown in Figure 11.4 on page 282. Try to use no more than three lines on any given graph, particularly if the lines cross. Ordinarily, both scales begin at zero and proceed in equal increments; however, the vertical axis can be broken to show that some of the increments have been left out. A broken axis is appropriate when the data are plotted far above zero, but be sure to clearly indicate the omission of data points.

FIGURE 11.2 Growth of Visible Minorities in Major Canadian Cities, 1981–2001

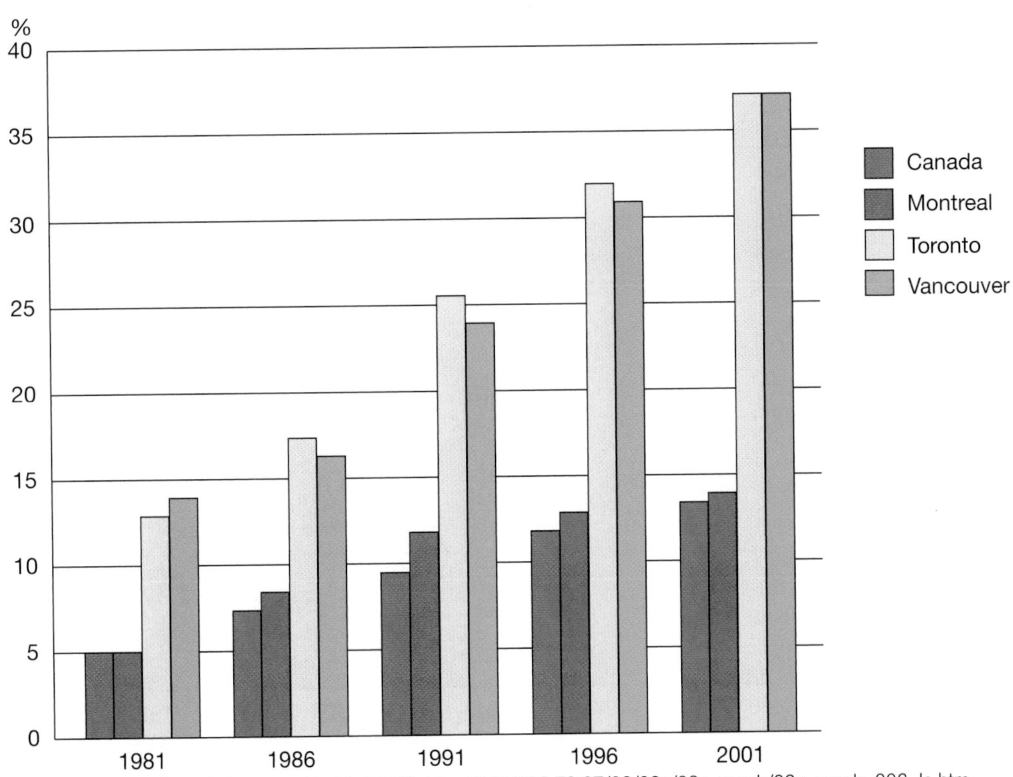

Source: Statistics Canada [accessed 2 July 2003], http://142.206.72.67/02/02a/02a_graph/02a_graph_006_le.htm.

FIGURE 11.3 Household Internet Use, 2001

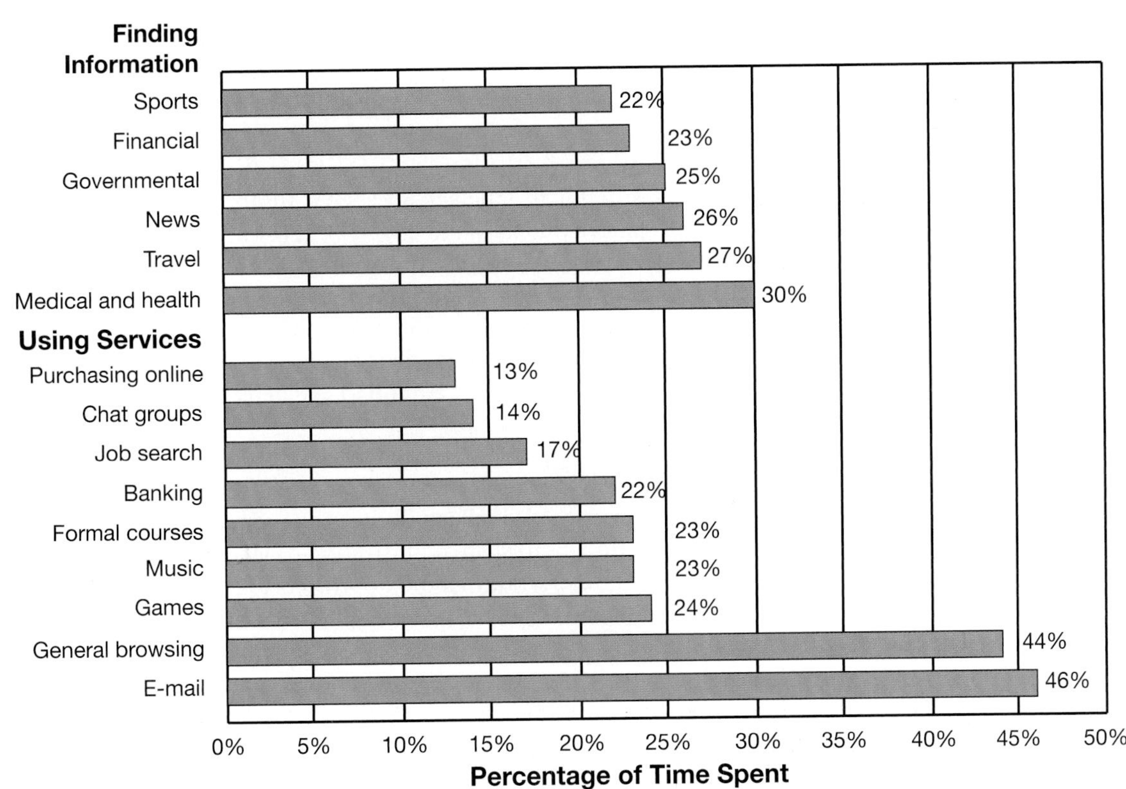

Source: Statistics Canada [accessed 2 July 2003], http://142.206.72.67/03/03d/03dgraph/03dgraph/03d_grouph_001e.htm.

FIGURE 11.4 Trends in Canadian Immigration from Europe and Asia

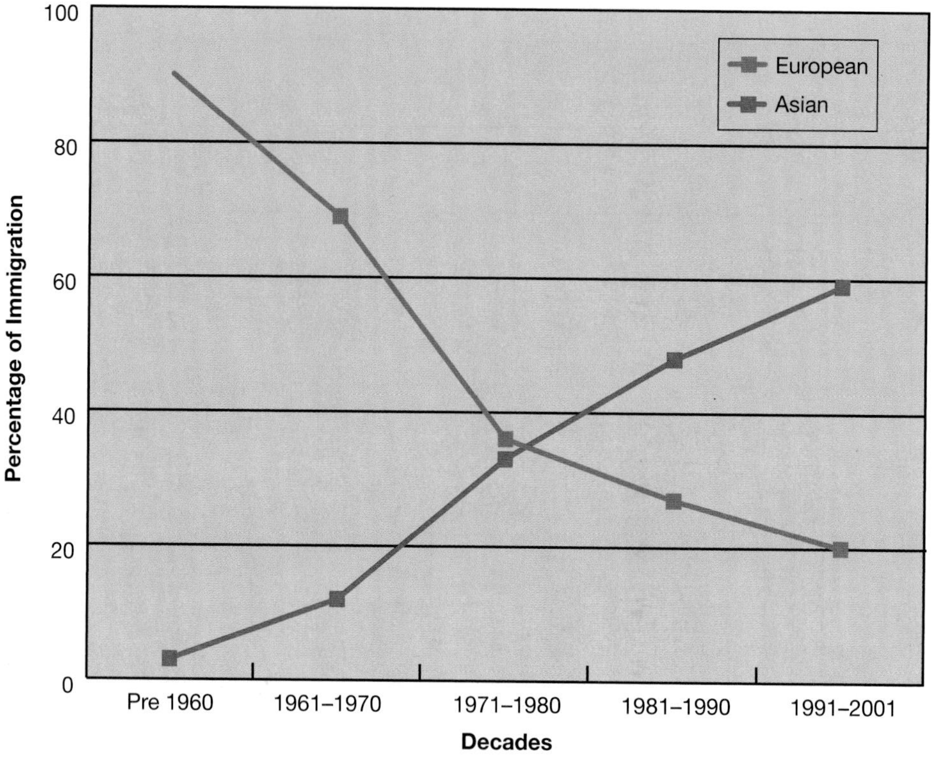

Source: Statistics Canada [accessed 2 July 2003], http://142.206.72.67/02/02a/02a_graph/02a_005_le.htm.

Use pie charts to show the relative sizes of the parts of a whole.

Pie Charts **Pie charts** show how parts of a whole are distributed and are restricted to showing relationships at one point in time. Each segment represents a slice of a complete circle, or *pie.* As you can see in Figure 11.5, pie charts are an effective way to show percentages or to compare one segment with another. You can combine pie charts with tables to expand the usefulness of such visuals.

When composing pie charts, restrict the number of slices in the pie. Otherwise, the chart looks cluttered and is difficult to label. If necessary, lump the smallest pieces together in a "miscellaneous" category. Ideally, the largest or most important slice of the pie is placed at the twelve o'clock position; the rest are arranged clockwise either in order of size or in some other logical progression. Use different colours or patterns to distinguish the various pieces. To emphasize one piece, you can explode it or pull it away from the rest of the pie. Label all segments, and indicate their value either in percentages or in units of measure. Remember, the segments must add up to 100 percent if percentages are used or to the total number if numbers are used.

Use flow charts

- To show a series of steps from beginning to end
- To show sequential relationships

Flow Charts If you need to show physical or conceptual relationships rather than numerical ones, you might want to use a **flow chart,** illustrating a sequence of events from start to finish. Flow charts are indispensable when illustrating processes, procedures, and sequential relationships such as the workflow in a major project. The various elements in the process you want to portray may be represented by pictorial symbols or geometric shapes, as shown in Figure 11.6.

Use organization charts to depict the interrelationships among the parts of an organization.

Organization Charts As the name implies, an **organization chart** illustrates the positions, units, or functions of an organization and the way they interrelate. An organization's normal communication channels are almost impossible to describe without the benefit of a chart like the one in Figure 11.7 on page 284.

FIGURE 11.5 Pie Chart Combined with a Table

Percentage of Time Spent Online by Age Group

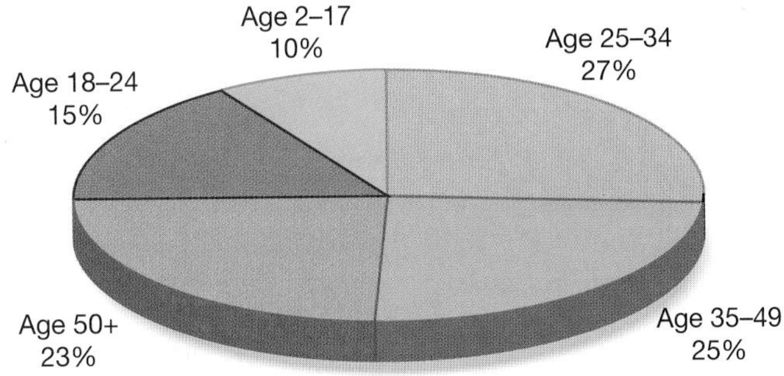

Age Group	Average Minutes per Month	Percent of Time by Age Group
Age 25–34	1642.4	27%
Age 35–49	1496.2	25%
Age 50+	1398.8	23%
Age 18–24	925.9	15%
Age 2–17	605.7	10%

FIGURE 11.6 Flow Chart

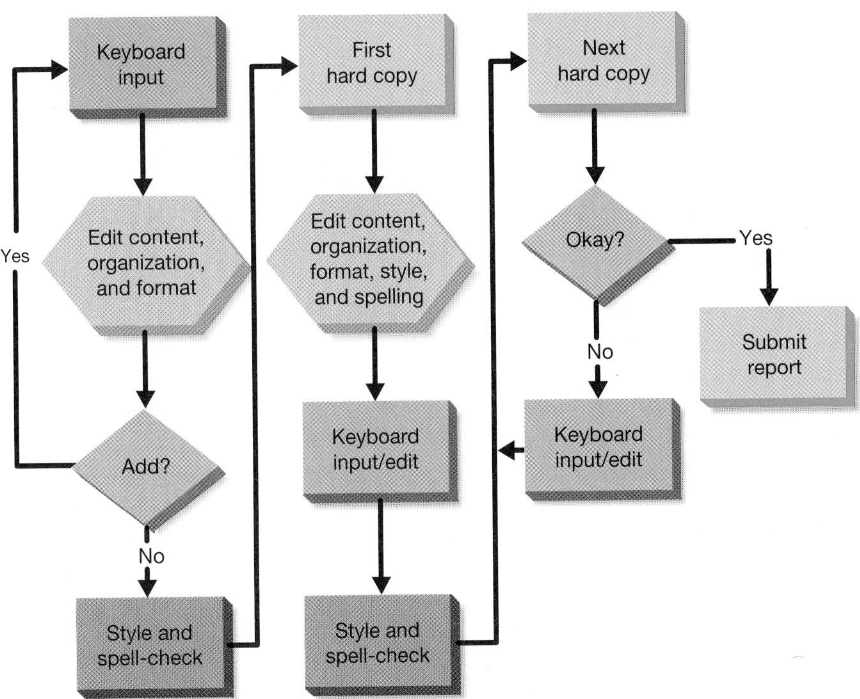

FIGURE 11.7 Organization Chart

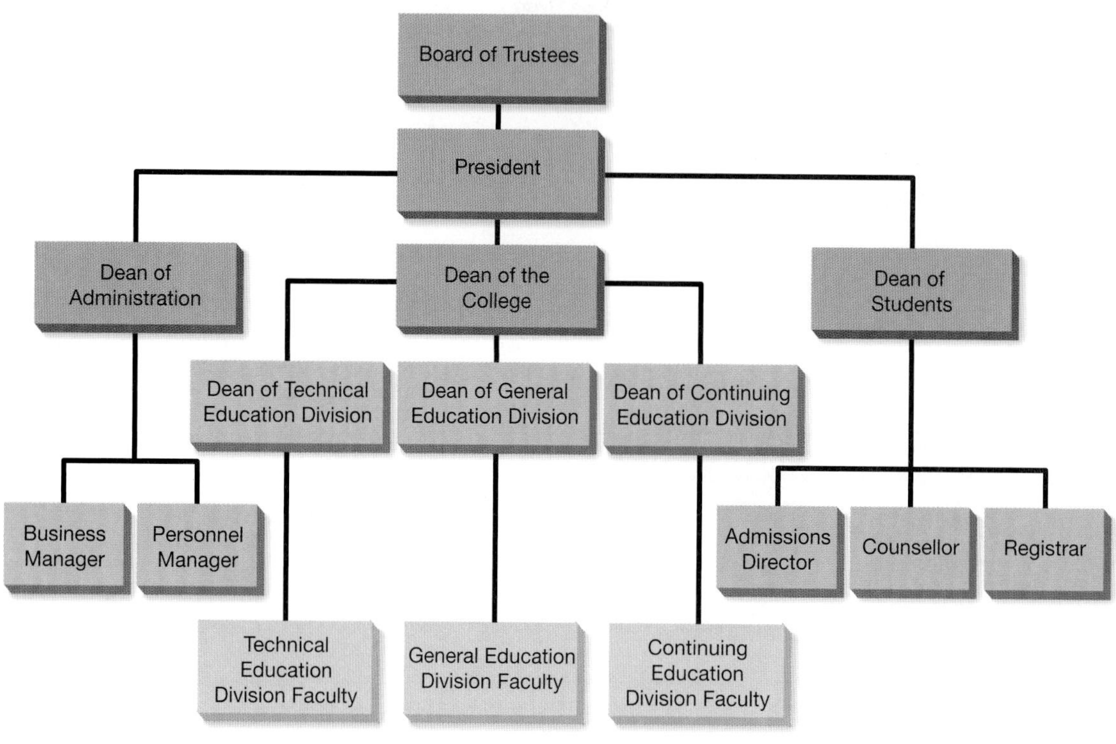

Creating Graphics with Computers

Computer-graphics systems cut the time and cost involved in producing visuals.

Professional-looking graphics used to be extremely expensive and time-consuming to produce, but computer technology now allows business people to turn out professional-looking visuals. Using computer graphics gives you several advantages, including speed, accuracy, and ease of use. You can create freehand drawings, manipulate existing images, and display numbers in graphic form using software programs such as CorelDraw!, PowerPoint, Photoshop, Painter, Excel, and Visio—to name just a few.

The style of your visuals communicates a subtle message about your relationship with your audience. The image you want to project should determine the visual you use.

Composing Reports and Proposals

A final outline is a work in progress.

Effective writers begin composing their first draft by preparing a final outline. In addition to guiding your writing effort, a final outline forces you to re-evaluate the information and visuals you've selected and the order in which you present them. Preparing a final outline also gives you a chance to rephrase your outline points to set the tone of your report.

Once you have a final outline, you are ready to write the report. Additional tasks include drafting the content, using a proper degree of formality, maintaining a consistent time perspective, and providing clues to help readers navigate your document.

Drafting the Content

As with other written business communications, the text of a report or proposal has three major sections: an introduction, a body, and a close. The content and length of each section varies with the type and purpose of the document, the document's organizational structure, the length and depth of the material, the degree of document formality, and the writer's relationship with the audience.

Successful report content is

- **Accurate.** In addition to checking for typos, double-check your facts and references.
- **Complete.** Include all the necessary information—no more, no less.
- **Balanced.** Present all sides of the issue fairly and equitably.
- **Structured clearly and logically.** Write uncluttered sentences and paragraphs that organize your ideas and proceed logically with clear, helpful transitions.[2]
- **Documented properly.** Properly give credit to your sources, as explained in Appendix B.

The most successful reports have certain characteristics.

Guidelines for Proposals Proposals persuade readers to do something (purchase goods or services, fund a project, implement a program). Thus, writing a proposal is similar to writing persuasive sales messages (see Chapter 9). Use the AIDA plan to gain attention, build interest, create desire, and motivate action. In your proposal[3]

For the most successful proposals, use the AIDA plan and follow some important guidelines.

- **Demonstrate your knowledge.** Show readers that you have the knowledge and experience to solve the problem. Provide enough information to win the job without giving away all your ideas so that your services aren't needed.
- **Provide concrete examples.** Avoid vague, unsupported generalizations such as "we are losing money on this program." Instead, include the math. Provide quantifiable details such as the amount of money being lost, how, why, and so on. Explain *how much* money your proposed solution will save. Spell out your plan, and give details on how the job will be done.
- **Research the competition.** Use trade publications and the Internet to become familiar with your competitors' product lines, services, and prices. This strategy is especially important if you are competing against others for a job.
- **Prove that your proposal is workable.** Your proposal must be feasible for the audience. For instance, it would be foolish to recommend a solution that doubles the budget or requires three times the number of current employees.
- **Adopt a "you" attitude.** Relate your product, service, or personnel to the reader's exact needs, either as stated in the RFP for a solicited proposal or as discovered through your own investigation for an unsolicited proposal.
- **Package your proposal attractively.** Make sure your proposal is letter-perfect, inviting, and readable. Readers will judge the type of work you perform by your submitted proposal. If it contains errors, omissions, or inconsistencies, they will likely withhold approval.

Drafting the Introduction In the *introduction,* prepare your readers for the information that follows. Invite them to continue reading by telling them what the report is about, why the audience should be concerned, and how the report is organized. Your introduction should accomplish four tasks:

Your introduction must prepare your audience for information that follows.

- Say why the report or proposal was written and what it proposes to solve.
- Introduce the report's subject (purpose) and indicate why that subject is important.
- Preview the main ideas and the order in which they'll be covered.
- Establish the tone of the document and your relationship with the audience.

In proposals, use the introduction to present the problem you want to solve and to summarize your solution. Orient readers to the remainder of the text. In a solicited proposal, refer to the RFP in your introduction; in an unsolicited one, use the introduction to mention any factors that led you to submit your proposal.

Drafting the Body In the *body* of your reports and proposals, include the major divisions or chapters that present, analyze, and interpret the information you gathered during your investigation. Give complete details of your proposed solution and specify what results you anticipate. The body contains the "proof," the detailed information necessary to support your conclusions and recommendations.

The body contains the substance of your report or proposal.

The close re-emphasizes your main ideas.

Drafting the Close The *close* is the final section of the text in your report or proposal. Leave a strong and lasting impression. This is your last chance to make sure that your report says what you intended.[4] In proposals, the close is your last opportunity to persuade readers to accept your suggestions. In both formal and informal proposals, be brief, assertive, and confident. Your close should accomplish three goals:

- Emphasize the main points of the message.
- Summarize reader benefits (if some change or other course of action is suggested).
- Bring all the action items together in one place and give details about who should do what, when, where, and how.

For examples of some of the topics you might include in the introduction, body, and close of reports and proposals, see Table 11.2.

Choosing the Proper Degree of Formality

For informal reports, adopt a personal style, using the pronouns *I* and *you*.

If you know your readers reasonably well and if your report is likely to meet with their approval, you can generally adopt a fairly informal tone. You can speak to readers in the first person, referring to yourself as *I* and to your readers as *you.* This personal approach is often used in brief memo or letter reports, although there are many exceptions.

Being formal means putting your readers at a distance and establishing an objective, businesslike relationship.

Use a more formal tone for longer reports, especially those dealing with controversial or complex information, and for reports that will be sent to other parts of the organization or to customers or suppliers. Also, communicating with people in other cultures often calls for more formality. Use an impersonal style, and avoid references to *you* and *I* (including *we, us,* and *our*). However, make sure that avoiding personal pronouns doesn't lead to overuse of phrases such as *there is* and *it is,* which are both dull and wordy. Also, be careful not to slip into passive voice more than necessary.

Establishing a Consistent Time Perspective

Be consistent in the verb tense you use, and follow a chronological sequence.

By switching from tense to tense throughout your report, you confuse readers. Use tense consistently.

Also be careful to observe the chronological sequence of events in your report. If you're describing the history or development of something, start at the beginning and cover each event in the order of its occurrence. If you're explaining the steps in a process, take each step in proper sequence.

Helping Readers Find Their Way

Readers can lose their way unless you give them signposts telling them where they are and where they're going.

Readers have no concept of how the various pieces of your report relate to one another. Although you can see how each page fits into the overall structure, readers see your report one page at a time. So give them a preview or road map of your report's structure, and clarify how the various parts are related. Give them a sense of the overall structure of your document by using three tools:

- **Headings.** These brief titles cue readers about the content of a section. They improve readability (see Chapter 6) and clarify a report's framework. *Subheadings* (lower-level headings) help show which ideas are more important. Many companies specify a format for headings; if yours does, use it. Otherwise, use the scheme shown in Figure 11.8 on page 288 or any other scheme that clearly shows the hierarchy.
- **Transitions.** These words or phrases tie ideas together and show how one thought is related to another. Whether words, sentences, or complete paragraphs, use transitions to help readers move from one section of a report to the next. When writing transitions, be sure to list coming topics in the order they are discussed.
- **Previews and reviews.** *Preview sections* introduce an important topic, helping readers get ready for new information. *Review sections* come after a body of material and summarize the information for readers, helping them absorb details while keeping track of the big picture.

Table 11.2 Report and Proposal Contents

Report Contents	Proposal Contents
Introduction	***Introduction***
• **Authorization.** Review who authorized the report (when, how), who wrote it, and when it was submitted. • **Problem/purpose.** Explain the reason for the report's existence and what the report will achieve. • **Scope.** Describe what will and won't be covered in the report—indicating size and complexity. • **Background.** Review historical conditions or factors that led up to the report. • **Sources and methods.** Discuss the primary and secondary sources consulted and methods used. • **Definitions.** List terms and their definitions—including any terms that might be misinterpreted. Terms may also be defined in the body, explanatory notes, or glossary. • **Limitations.** Discuss factors beyond your control that affect report quality—not an excuse for a poor study or bad report. • **Report organization.** Tell what topics are covered in what order.	• **Background or statement of the problem.** Briefly review the reader's situation, establish a need for action, and explain how things could be better. In unsolicited proposals, convince readers that a problem or opportunity exists. • **Solution.** Briefly describe the change you propose, highlighting your key selling points and their benefits to show how your proposal will solve the reader's problem. • **Scope.** State the boundaries of the proposal—what you will and will not do. • **Report organization.** Orient the reader to the remainder of the proposal and call attention to the major divisions of thought.
Body—Main Sections	***Body—Main Sections***
• **Explanations**. Give complete details of the problem, project, or idea. • **Facts, statistical evidence, and trends.** Lay out the results of studies or investigations. • **Analysis of action.** Discuss potential courses of action. • **Pros and cons.** Explain advantages, disadvantages, costs, and benefits of a particular course of action. • **Procedures.** Outline steps for a process. • **Methods and approaches.** Discuss how you've studied a problem (or gathered evidence) and arrived at your solution (or collected your data). • **Criteria.** Describe the benchmarks for evaluating options and alternatives. • **Conclusions and recommendations.** Discuss what you believe the evidence reveals and what you propose should be done about it. • **Support**. Give the reasons behind your conclusions or recommendations.	• **Proposed approach.** Describe your concept, product, or service. • **Facts and evidence to support your conclusions.** Give complete details of the proposed solution and the anticipated results. • **Benefits.** Stress reader benefits and emphasize any advantages you have over your competitors. • **Work plan.** Describe how you'll accomplish what must be done (unless you're providing a standard, off-the-shelf item). Explain the steps you'll take, their timing, the methods or resources you'll use, and the person(s) responsible. State when work will begin, how it will be divided into stages, when you'll finish, and whether follow-up will be needed. • **Statement of qualifications.** Describe your organization's experience, personnel, and facilities—relating it all to readers' needs. Include a list of client references. • **Costs.** Prove that your costs are realistic—break them down so that readers can see the cost of labour, materials, transportation, travel, training, and other categories.
Close	***Close***
• **For direct order.** Summarize key points (except in short memos), listing them in the order they appear in the body. Briefly restate your conclusions or recommendations, if appropriate. • **For indirect order.** You may use the close to present your conclusions or recommendations for the first time—just be sure not to present any new facts. • **For motivating action.** Spell out exactly what should happen next and provide a schedule with specific task assignments.	• **Review of argument.** Briefly summarize the key points. • **Review of reader benefits.** Briefly summarize how your proposal will help the reader. • **Review of the merits of your approach.** Briefly summarize why your approach will be more effective than that of competitors. • **Restatement of qualifications.** Briefly re-emphasize why you and your firm should do the work • **Request.** Ask for a decision from the reader.

FIGURE 11.8 Heading Format for Reports

TITLE

The title is centred at the top of the page in all-capital letters, usually boldfaced, often in a large font (for example, 14 point), and often using a sans serif typeface. When the title runs to more than one line, the lines are usually arranged as an inverted pyramid (longer line on the top).

FIRST-LEVEL HEADING

A first-level heading indicates what the following section is about, perhaps by describing the subdivisions. All first-level headings are grammatically parallel, with the possible exception of such headings as "Introduction," "Conclusions," and "Recommendations." Some text appears between every two headings, regardless of their levels. Still boldfaced and sans serif, the font may be smaller than that used in the title but larger than the typeface used in the text (for example, 12 point) and still in all-capital letters.

Second-Level Heading

Like first-level headings, second-level headings indicate what the following material is about. All second-level headings within a section are grammatically parallel. Still boldfaced and sans serif, the font may either remain the same or shrink to the size used in the text, and the style is now initial capitals with lower case. Never use only one second-level heading under a first-level heading. (The same is true for every other level of heading.)

Headings and subheadings show the content at a glance.

Third-Level Heading

A third-level heading is worded to reflect the content of the material that follows. All third-level headings beneath a second-level heading should be grammatically parallel.

Fourth-Level Heading. Like all the other levels of headings, fourth-level headings reflect the subject that will be developed. All fourth-level headings within a subsection are parallel.

Fifth-level headings are generally the lowest level of heading used. However, you can indicate further breakdowns in your ideas by using a list:

1. *The first item in a list.* You may indent the entire item in block format to set it off visually. Numbers are optional.
2. *The second item in a list.* All lists have at least two items. An introductory phrase or sentence may be italicized for emphasis, as shown here.

Headings allow readers to scan a report and choose which sections to read.

Step 3: Completing Business Reports and Proposals

Producing documents requires some special considerations when working with reports.

The process of writing a report or proposal doesn't end with a first draft. As Chapter 5 points out, once you have finished your first draft, you perform three tasks to complete your document: revise, produce, and proofread. Make sure you've scheduled enough time for production. Corrupted disk files, printing problems, and other glitches can consume hours. If you're preparing a long, formal report, you'll need extra time to prepare and assemble all the various components.

Components of a Formal Report

The three basic divisions of a formal report:

- Prefatory parts
- Text
- Supplementary parts

The parts included in a report depend on the type of report you are writing, the requirements of your audience, the organization you're working for, and the length of your report. The components listed in Figure 11.9 fall into three categories, according to their location in a report: prefatory parts, text, and supplementary parts.

FIGURE 11.9 Parts of a Formal Report

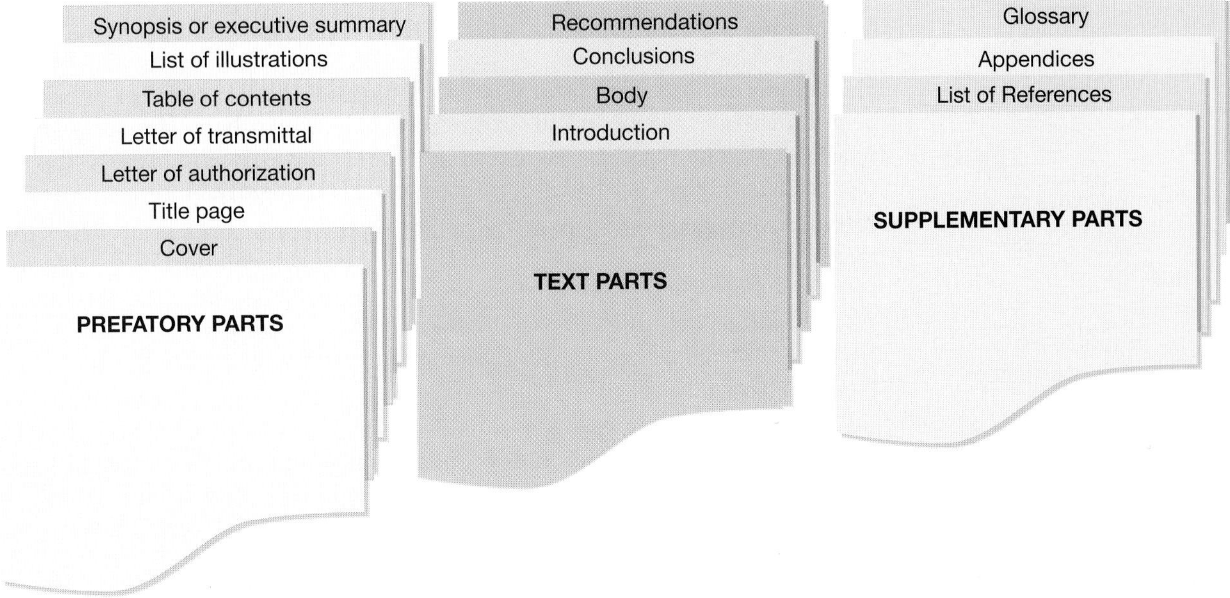

Most prefatory parts (such as the table of contents) should be placed on their own pages. However, the various parts in the report text are often run together and seldom stand alone. If your introduction is only a paragraph long, don't bother with a page break before moving into the body of your report. If the introduction runs longer than a page, however, a page break can signal the reader that a major shift is about to occur in the flow of the report.

For an illustration of how the various parts fit together in an actual report, see Figure 11.10, starting on page 291. This 14-page report was prepared by Linda Moreno, manager of the cost accounting department at Electrovision, a high-tech company. Electrovision's main product is optical character recognition equipment, which is used for sorting mail. Moreno's job is to help analyze the company's travel and entertainment costs. Moreno used direct order and organized her report based on conclusions and recommendations.

Prefatory Parts

Prefatory parts are front-end materials that provide preliminary information so that readers can decide whether to and how to read the report.[5] Many of these parts—such as the table of contents, list of illustrations, and executive summary—are easier to prepare after the text has been completed, because they directly reflect the contents. Other parts can be prepared at almost any time.

Prefatory parts come before the text but may be written after the text has been completed.

- **Cover.** Many companies have standard covers for reports. If your company doesn't provide them, you can find something suitable in a good stationery store. Report titles are often printed on these covers. Think carefully about the title you put on the cover. Give readers all the specific information they need (the who, what, when, where, why, and how of the subject), but be concise.
- **Title page.** The title page includes four blocks of information (see Moreno's Electrovision report): (1) the title of the report; (2) the name, title, and address of the person, group, or organization that authorized the report (usually the intended audience); (3) the name, title, and address of the person, group, or organization that prepared the report; and (4) the date on which the report was submitted.
- **Letter of authorization.** If you received written authorization to prepare the report, you may want to include that letter or memo in your report.

- **Letter of transmittal.** The letter of transmittal is often paper-clipped to the cover of the report or appears just after the title page. This routine document (which can also be a memo) begins with the main idea ("Here is the report you asked me to prepare on . . . "). The opening discusses scope, methods, and limitations. The middle can highlight important sections of the report, suggest follow-up studies, offer details to help readers use the report, and acknowledge help from others. The close can include a note of thanks for the assignment, an expression of willingness to discuss the report, and an offer to assist with future projects (see Figure 11.10).
- **Table of contents.** The contents page lists report parts and text headings to indicate the location and relative importance of the information in the report. You may show only the top two or three levels of headings or only first-level headings. Word headings exactly as they are in the report text. List prefatory parts that come after the contents page and all supplementary parts (see Figure 11.10).
- **List of illustrations.** The list of illustrations gives the titles and page numbers of visual aids. If you have enough space on a single page, include the list of illustrations under its heading directly beneath the table of contents. Otherwise, put the list on the page after the contents page. Tables and figures are numbered separately, so they should also be listed separately. The two lists can appear on the same page if they fit; otherwise, start each list on a separate page.
- **List of appendices.** Supplementary material or oversized documents may be appended to the main report. The list of appendices tells the contents of each appendix you have attached to the report. These items need a title and must be actually mentioned in the text of the report to appear in the appendices. At the back of the report, the appendices are put in the order of mention. For example, if you based your report on surveys or interviews, you might append the list of questions you used to show the scope of your inquiry. Appendices are usually given a letter (A, B, C) and the list would show the title of each and the page number where the items can be found. In very long reports with many appendices, each appendix may have separate page numbering.
- **Executive summary.** An **executive summary** is a fully developed "mini" version of the report itself, which may contain headings, transitions, and even visual aids. Executive summaries are for readers who lack the time or motivation to study the complete text. Keep the length of an executive summary to approximately 10 percent of the length of the report. Linda Moreno's Electrovision report provides one example of an executive summary.

Include a brief summary of any report you write to satisfy readers who may not have time to read the whole report.

Text of the Report

Three main text parts of a report are

- Introduction
- Body
- Close

Although reports may contain a variety of components, the heart of a report is always the text, with its introduction, body, and conclusion. Moreno's executive summary contains key points from each section of the main report.

Linda Moreno's Electrovision report gives you a good idea of the types of supporting detail commonly included in the text body. Pay close attention to her effective use of visuals. Most inexperienced writers have a tendency to include too many data in their reports or to place too many data in paragraph format instead of using tables and charts. Include only the essential supporting data in the body, use relevant graphics and visuals, and place any additional information in an appendix.

In a long report, the closing section may be labelled "Conclusions and Recommendations." Since Moreno organized her report in a direct pattern, her closing is relatively brief. When using the indirect approach, you may use the close to present your conclusions and recommendations, which could make this section relatively extensive.

FIGURE 11.10 Linda Moreno's Formal Report

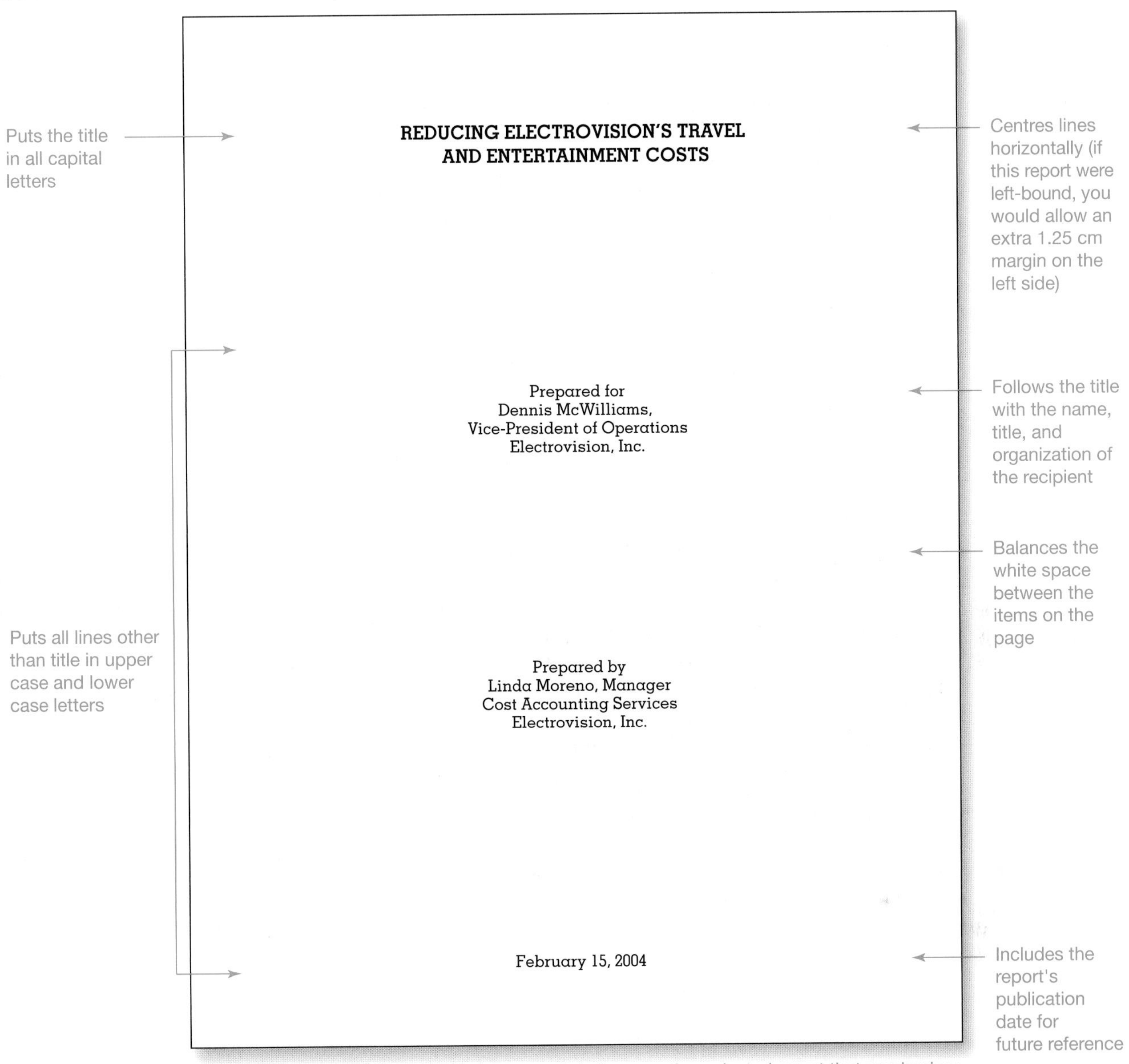

Puts the title in all capital letters
REDUCING ELECTROVISION'S TRAVEL AND ENTERTAINMENT COSTS
Centres lines horizontally (if this report were left-bound, you would allow an extra 1.25 cm margin on the left side)
Prepared for
Dennis McWilliams,
Vice-President of Operations
Electrovision, Inc.
Follows the title with the name, title, and organization of the recipient
Balances the white space between the items on the page
Puts all lines other than title in upper case and lower case letters
Prepared by
Linda Moreno, Manager
Cost Accounting Services
Electrovision, Inc.
February 15, 2004
Includes the report's publication date for future reference

The "how to" tone of Moreno's title is appropriate for an action-oriented report that emphasizes recommendations. A more neutral title, such as "An Analysis of Electrovision's Travel and Entertainment Costs," would be more suitable for an informational report.

Title Page

FIGURE 11.10 Continued

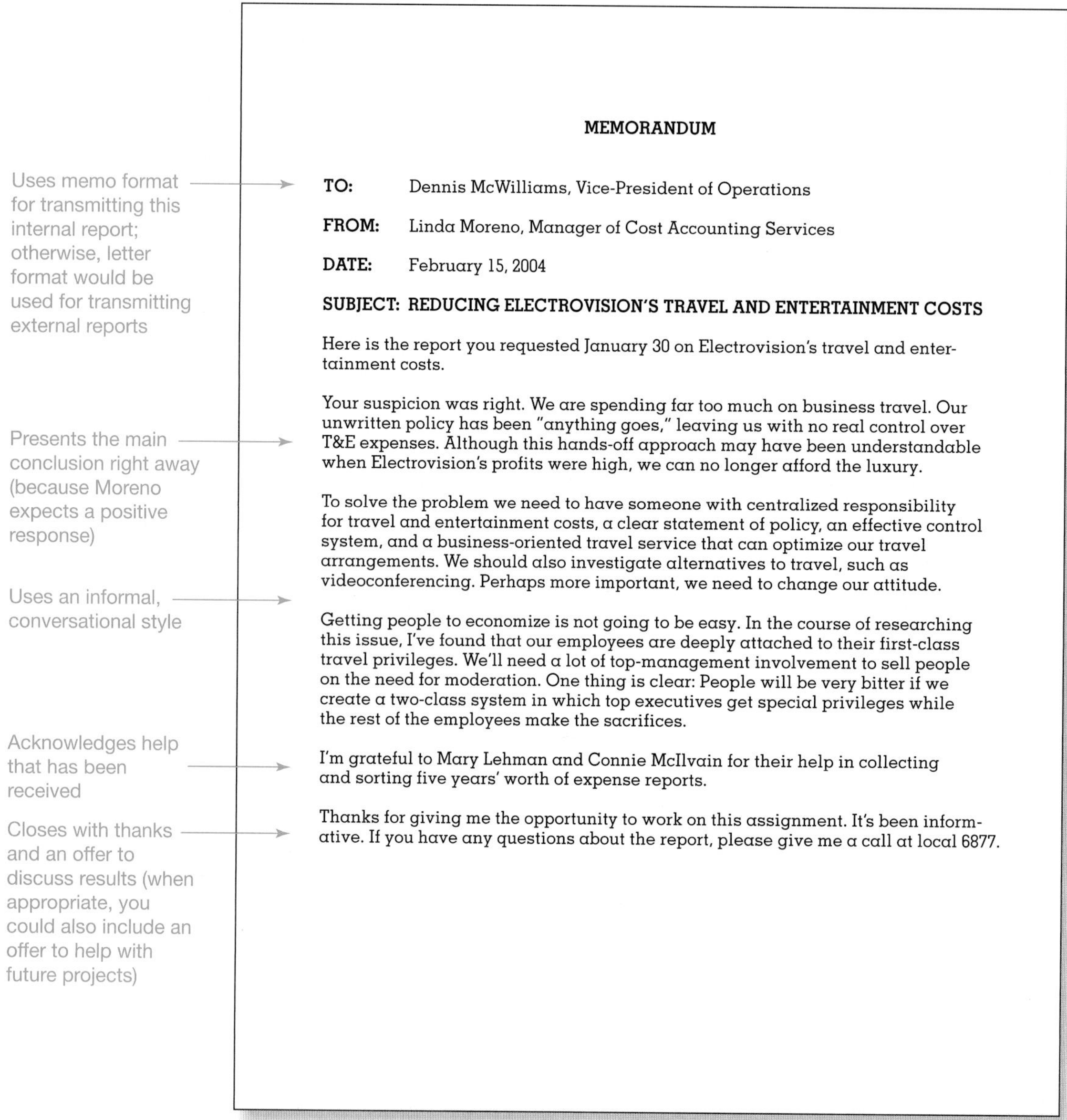

MEMORANDUM

TO: Dennis McWilliams, Vice-President of Operations

FROM: Linda Moreno, Manager of Cost Accounting Services

DATE: February 15, 2004

SUBJECT: REDUCING ELECTROVISION'S TRAVEL AND ENTERTAINMENT COSTS

Here is the report you requested January 30 on Electrovision's travel and entertainment costs.

Your suspicion was right. We are spending far too much on business travel. Our unwritten policy has been "anything goes," leaving us with no real control over T&E expenses. Although this hands-off approach may have been understandable when Electrovision's profits were high, we can no longer afford the luxury.

To solve the problem we need to have someone with centralized responsibility for travel and entertainment costs, a clear statement of policy, an effective control system, and a business-oriented travel service that can optimize our travel arrangements. We should also investigate alternatives to travel, such as videoconferencing. Perhaps more important, we need to change our attitude.

Getting people to economize is not going to be easy. In the course of researching this issue, I've found that our employees are deeply attached to their first-class travel privileges. We'll need a lot of top-management involvement to sell people on the need for moderation. One thing is clear: People will be very bitter if we create a two-class system in which top executives get special privileges while the rest of the employees make the sacrifices.

I'm grateful to Mary Lehman and Connie McIlvain for their help in collecting and sorting five years' worth of expense reports.

Thanks for giving me the opportunity to work on this assignment. It's been informative. If you have any questions about the report, please give me a call at local 6877.

Uses memo format for transmitting this internal report; otherwise, letter format would be used for transmitting external reports
Presents the main conclusion right away (because Moreno expects a positive response)
Uses an informal, conversational style
Acknowledges help that has been received
Closes with thanks and an offer to discuss results (when appropriate, you could also include an offer to help with future projects)

In this report, Moreno decided to write a brief memo of transmittal and include a separate executive summary. Short reports (fewer than 10 pages) often combine the synopsis or executive summary with the memo or letter of transmittal.

Memo of Transmittal

FIGURE 11.10 Continued

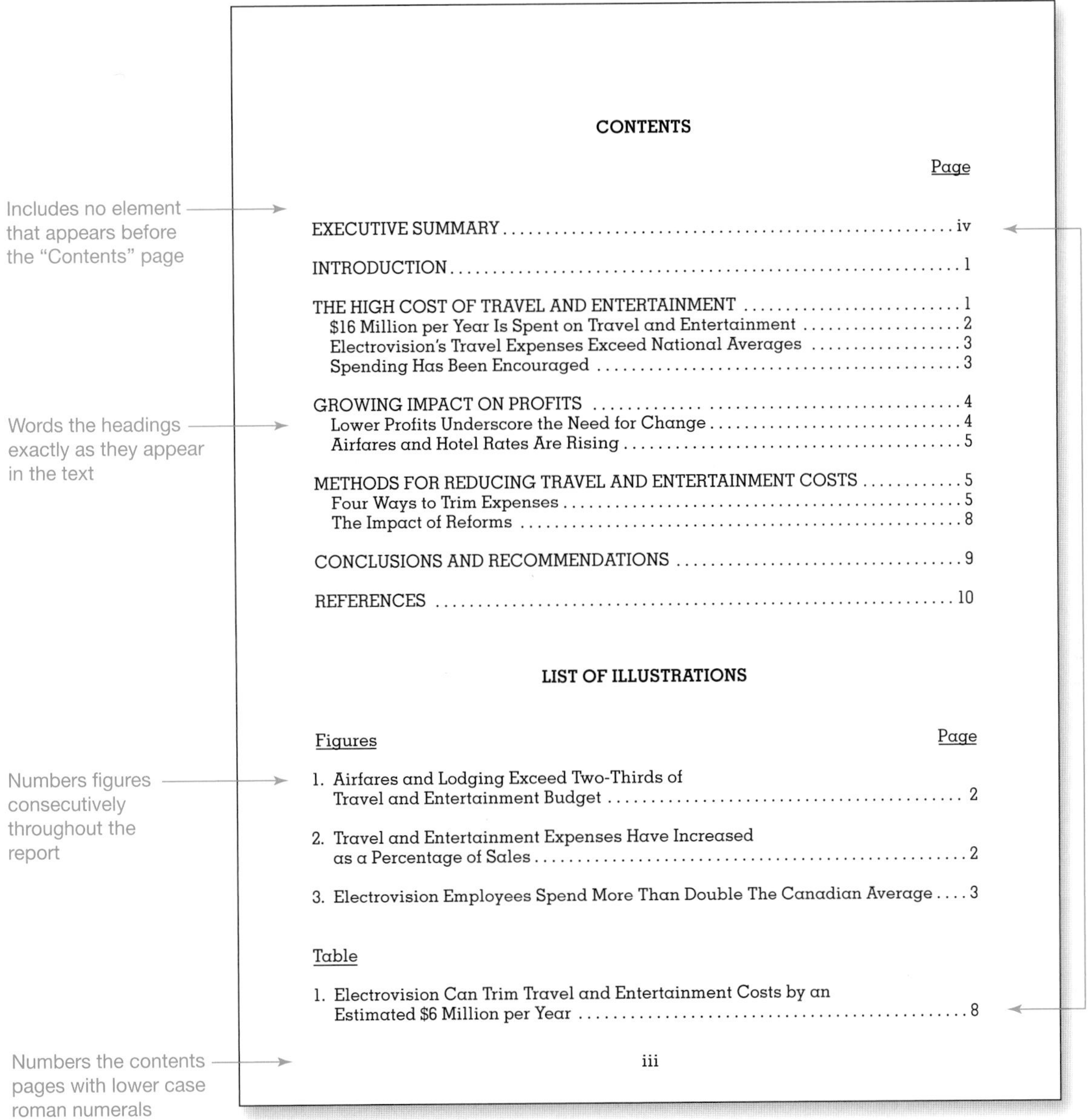

CONTENTS

Page

EXECUTIVE SUMMARY iv

INTRODUCTION 1

THE HIGH COST OF TRAVEL AND ENTERTAINMENT 1
$16 Million per Year Is Spent on Travel and Entertainment 2
Electrovision's Travel Expenses Exceed National Averages 3
Spending Has Been Encouraged 3

GROWING IMPACT ON PROFITS 4
Lower Profits Underscore the Need for Change 4
Airfares and Hotel Rates Are Rising 5

METHODS FOR REDUCING TRAVEL AND ENTERTAINMENT COSTS 5
Four Ways to Trim Expenses 5
The Impact of Reforms 8

CONCLUSIONS AND RECOMMENDATIONS 9

REFERENCES 10

LIST OF ILLUSTRATIONS

Figures Page

1. Airfares and Lodging Exceed Two-Thirds of Travel and Entertainment Budget 2

2. Travel and Entertainment Expenses Have Increased as a Percentage of Sales 2

3. Electrovision Employees Spend More Than Double The Canadian Average 3

Table

1. Electrovision Can Trim Travel and Entertainment Costs by an Estimated $6 Million per Year 8

iii

Includes no element that appears before the "Contents" page

Words the headings exactly as they appear in the text

Numbers figures consecutively throughout the report

Numbers the contents pages with lower case roman numerals centred at the bottom margin

Includes only the page numbers where sections begin

Moreno included only first- and second-level headings in her table of contents, even though the report contains third-level headings. She prefers a shorter table of contents that focuses attention on the main divisions of thought. She used informative titles, which are appropriate for a report to a receptive audience.

Table of Contents and List of Illustrations

FIGURE 11.10 Continued

Begins by stating the purpose of the report

Presents the points in the executive summary in the same order as they appear in the report

Continues numbering the executive summary pages with lower case roman numerals centred about 2.5 cm from the bottom of the page

EXECUTIVE SUMMARY

This report analyzes Electrovision's travel and entertainment (T&E) costs and presents recommendations for reducing those costs.

Travel and Entertainment Costs Are Too High

T&E is a large and growing expense category for Electrovision. The company spends more than $16 million per year on business travel, a cost that is increasing by 12 percent annually. Employees make some 3500 trips a year, each trip averaging $4720. Airfares are the largest expense, followed by hotels and meals.

The nature of Electrovision's business requires extensive travel, but the company's costs seem excessive. Electrovision employees spend more than double what the average business traveller spends. Although the location of company facilities may partly explain this discrepancy, the firm's philosophy and managerial style invite employees to go first class and pay relatively little attention to travel costs.

Cuts Are Essential

Electrovision management now recognizes the need to gain more control over this element of costs. The company is entering a period of declining profits, prompting management to look for every opportunity to reduce spending. Also, rising airfares and hotel rates are making T&E expenses more important to the bottom line.

Electrovision Can Save $6 Million per Year

Electrovision should be able to save up to $6 million per year, based on the experience of other companies. A sensible travel-management program can save firms up to 35 percent a year (Gilligan 2002). Since we purchase more first-class tickets than the average, we should be able to achieve even greater savings.

The first priority should be hiring a director for T&E spending. This director should develop a written T&E policy, establish a cost-control system, retain a national travel agency, and investigate electronic alternatives to travel. Electrovision should make employees aware of the need to reduce T&E spending by forgoing unnecessary travel and by economizing on tickets, hotels, meals, and rental cars.

We should also negotiate preferential rates with travel providers. These changes are likely to hurt short-term morale. Management will need to explain the rationale for reduced spending and set an example by economizing on their own travel arrangements. On the plus side, cutting travel will reduce the burden on employees and help them balance their business and personal lives.

iv

Uses subheadings that summarize the content of the main sections of the report without repeating what appears in the text

Targets a receptive audience with a hard-hitting tone in the executive summary (a more neutral approach would be better for hostile or sceptical readers)

Appears in the same typeface and type style as the text of the report. Uses single spacing because the report is single spaced, and follows the text's format for margins, paragraph indentions, and headings.

Moreno included an executive summary, which provides a short form of the whole report, because her audience was mixed—some readers would be interested in the details of her report and some would prefer to focus on the big picture.

Moreno's impersonal style adds to the formality of her report. She chose an impersonal style for several reasons: (1) several members of her audience were considerably higher up in the organization and she did not want to sound too familiar, (2) she wanted the executive summary to be compatible with the text, and (3) her company prefers the impersonal style for formal reports.

Some writers prefer a more personal approach. Generally, you should gear your choice of style to your relationship with the readers.

Executive Summary

FIGURE 11.10 Continued

Centres the title of the report on the first page of the text, 5 cm from the top of the page (6.25 cm if top-bound)

REDUCING ELECTROVISION'S
TRAVEL AND ENTERTAINMENT COSTS

INTRODUCTION

Begins the introduction by establishing the need for action

Electrovision has always encouraged a significant amount of business travel. To compensate employees for the inconvenience and stress of frequent trips, management has authorized generous travel and entertainment (T&E) allowances. This philosophy has been good for morale, but last year Electrovision spent $16 million on T&E—$7 million more than it spent on research and development.

This year's T&E costs will affect profits even more, due to changes in airfares and hotel rates. Also, the company anticipates that profits will be relatively weak for a variety of other reasons. Therefore, Dennis McWilliams, Vice-President of Operations, asked the accounting department to look into the T&E budget.

The purpose of this report is to analyze the T&E budget, evaluate the effect of changes in airfares and hotel costs, and suggest ways to tighten management's control over T&E expenses. The report outlines several steps to reduce our expenses, but the precise financial impact of these measures is difficult to project. Estimates are a "best guess" view of what Electrovision can expect to save.

For this report, the accounting department analyzed internal expense reports for the past five years to determine how much Electrovision spends on T&E. These figures were compared with average statistics compiled by RBC Dominion Securities as reported in the *Report on Business*'s Travel Index. We also analyzed trends and suggestions published in a variety of business journal articles to see how other companies are coping with the high cost of business travel.

This report reviews the size and composition of Electrovision's T&E expenses, analyzes trends in travel costs, and recommends ways to reduce the T&E budget.

THE HIGH COST OF TRAVEL AND ENTERTAINMENT

Mentions sources and methods to increase credibility and to give readers a complete picture of the study's background

Many companies view T&E as an "incidental" cost of business, but the dollars add up. Electrovision's bill for airfares, hotels, rental cars, meals, and entertainment totalled $16 million last year and has increased by 12 percent per year for the past five years. Compared to the average Canadian business, Electrovision's expenditures are high, largely because of management's generous policy on travel benefits.

Uses the arabic numeral 1 for the first page, centring the number about 2.5 cm from the bottom of the page

1

In her brief introduction, Moreno omitted the subheadings within the introduction and relied on topic sentences and on transitional words and phrases to indicate that she is discussing the purpose, scope, and limitations of the study. Moreno used single spacing and 2.5 cm side margins, common in business reports.

Introduction and Body

FIGURE 11.10 Continued

2

Uses arabic numerals to number the second and succeeding pages of the text in the upper right-hand corner where the top and right-hand margins meet

THE HIGH COST OF TRAVEL AND ENTERTAINMENT

$16 Million per Year Is Spent on Travel and Entertainment

Electrovision's annual T&E budget is 8 percent of sales. Because this is a relatively small expense category, compared with salaries and commissions, it is tempting to dismiss T&E costs as insignificant. But T&E is Electrovision's third-largest controllable expense, directly behind salaries and information systems.

Last year Electrovision personnel made 3390 trips. The average trip cost $4720 and involved a round-trip flight of 4800 km, meals, two to three days of hotel accommodations, and a rental car. About 80 percent of trips were made by 20 percent of the staff—top managers and sales personnel averaged 18 trips per year.

Figure 1 shows how the T&E budget is spent. Airfares and lodging account for $7 out of every $10 employees spend on T&E. This breakdown has been steady for the past five years and is consistent with other companies' distribution.

Introduces visual aids before they appear and indicates what readers should notice about the data

Places the visual aid as close as possible to the point it illustrates

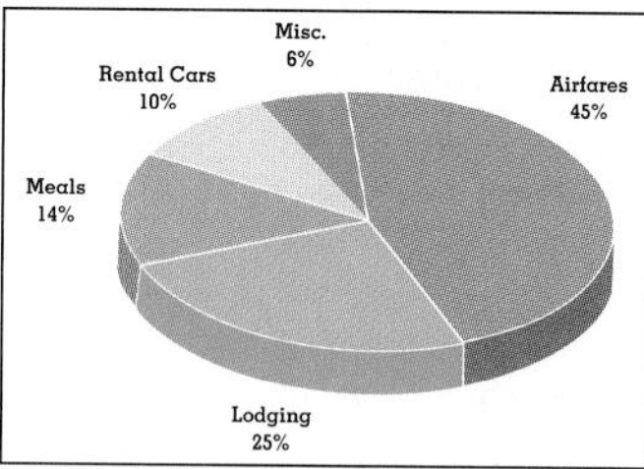

Figure 1
Airfares and Lodging Exceed Two-Thirds of Travel and Entertainment Budget

Makes placement of visual aid titles consistent throughout a report (options for placement include above, below, or beside the visual)

Although the composition of the T&E budget has been consistent, its size has not. With T&E costs increasing 12 percent per year for five years, roughly twice the rate of the company's sales growth (see Figure 2), T&E is Electrovision's fastest-growing expense item.

Numbers the visual aids consecutively and refers to them in the text by their numbers (if your report is a book-length document, you may number the visual aids by chapter; for example, Figure 4.2 would be the second figure in the fourth chapter)

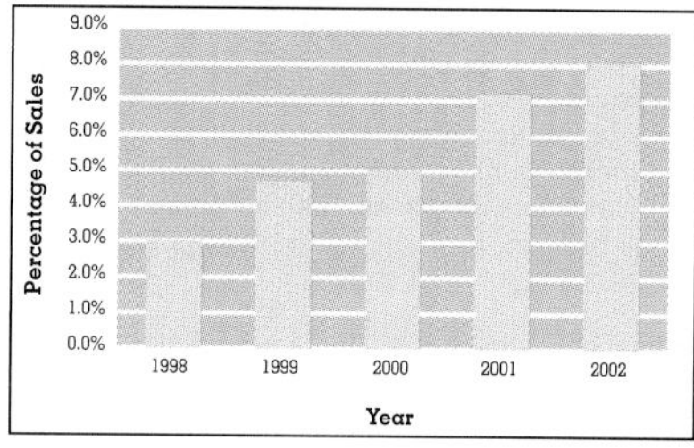

Figure 2
Travel and Entertainment Expenses Have Increased as a Percentage of Sales

Gives each visual aid a title that clearly indicates what it's about

Moreno opened the first main section of the body with a topic sentence that introduces an important fact about the subject of the section. Then she oriented the reader to the three major points developed in the section.

Moreno decided to use a bar chart in Figure 2 to express the main idea in terms of percentage and make the main idea easy to grasp.

FIGURE 11.10 Continued

3

THE HIGH COST OF TRAVEL AND ENTERTAINMENT
Electrovision's Travel Expenses Exceed National Averages

Much of our travel budget is justified. Two major contributing factors are

- Our headquarters are on the west coast and our major customer is on the east coast, so we naturally spend a lot on cross-country flights.
- Corporate managers and division personnel make frequent trips between our headquarters on the west coast and the manufacturing operations in Windsor, Montreal, and Don Mills to coordinate these disparate operations.

However, even with such justifiable expenses, Electrovision spends considerably more on T&E than the average business traveller spends (see Figure 3).

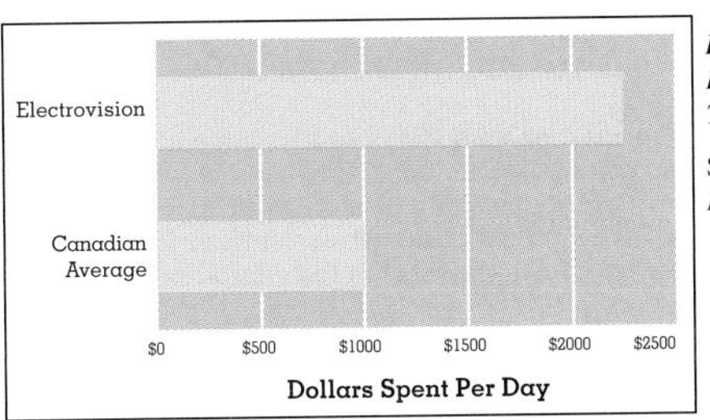

Figure 3
Electrovision Employees Spend More Than Double the Canadian Average

Source: *The Globe and Mail Report on Business and company records*

RBC Dominion's Travel Index calculates the average cost per day of business travel in Canada, based on average rates for airfare, hotel, and rental car. This average fluctuates weekly as travel companies change their rates, but it has been running about $1000 per day for the last year or so. In contrast, Electrovision's average daily expense over the past year has been $2250—125 percent higher than average. This figure is based on the average trip cost of $4720 and an average trip length of 2.1 days.

Leaves a bit more white space above a heading than below to help readers associate that heading with the text it describes

Spending Has Been Encouraged

Although a variety of factors may contribute to this differential, Electrovision's relatively high T&E costs are at least partially due to the company's philosophy and management style. Since many employees do not enjoy business travel, management has tried to make the trips more pleasant by authorizing first-class airfare, luxury hotel accommodations, and full-size rental cars. The sales staff is encouraged to entertain clients at top restaurants and to invite them to cultural and sporting events.

The chart in Figure 3 is very simple, but it creates an effective visual comparison. Moreno included just enough data to make her point. She was as careful about the appearance of her report as she was about its content.

FIGURE 11.10 Continued

Uses bulleted list to make it easy for readers to identify and distinguish related points

Uses informative headings to focus reader attention on the main points (such headings are appropriate when a report is in direct order and intended for a receptive audience; however, descriptive headings are more effective when a report is in indirect order and readers are less receptive)

4

THE HIGH COST OF TRAVEL AND ENTERTAINMENT

The cost of these privileges is easy to overlook, given the weakness of Electrovision's system for keeping track of T&E expenses:

- Monthly financial reports have no separate T&E category; this information is buried in Cost of Goods Sold and in Selling and General Expenses.
- Department heads can approve expense reports, no matter how large.
- Receipts are not required for expenditures of less than $100.
- Individuals are allowed to make their own travel arrangements.
- No one has responsibility for controlling the company's total T&E spending.

GROWING IMPACT ON PROFITS

During the past three years, the company's healthy profits have disguised the need for tighter controls over all aspects of the business. However, as we all know, the projection is for flat to declining profits over the next two years, which has prompted all of us to search for ways to cut costs. Also, rising airfares and hotel rates have increased the impact of T&E expenses on the company's finances.

Lower Profits Underscore the Need for Change

The next two years promise to be difficult for Electrovision. After several years of steady spending increases, Canada Post is tightening procurement policies for automated mail-handling equipment. Funding for our A-12 optical character reader has been cancelled. As a result, our marketing people expect sales to drop 15 percent. Even though Electrovision is negotiating several R&D contracts with nongovernment clients, the marketing department foresees no major procurements for two to three years.

At the same time, Electrovision is facing cost increases on several fronts. As we have known for several months, the new production facility now under construction in Montreal, is behind schedule and over budget. Labour contracts in Windsor and Don Mills will expire within the next six months, and plant managers there anticipate that significant salary and benefits concessions may be necessary to avoid strikes.

Moreover, marketing and advertising costs are expected to increase as we attempt to strengthen these activities to better cope with competitive pressures. Given the expected decline in revenues and increase in costs, the executive committee's prediction that profits will fall by 12 percent in the coming fiscal year does not seem overly pessimistic.

Moreno designed her report to include plenty of white space so that pages having no graphics would appear inviting and easy to read.

FIGURE 11.10 Continued

5

GROWING IMPACT ON PROFITS

Airfares and Hotel Rates Are Rising

Business travellers got used to frequent fare wars and discounting in the travel industry. Excess capacity and aggressive price competition made travel a relative bargain. However, that situation has changed as many competitors have been forced out and the remaining players are keeping rates high. Last year we saw some of the steepest rate hikes in years. Business airfares jumped 40 percent in many markets. The trend is expected to continue, with rates increasing another 5 percent to 10 percent overall (Phillips 2005; Dahl 2003).

Documents the facts to add weight to Moreno's argument →

Since air and hotel costs account for 70 percent of Electrovision's T&E budget, the trend toward higher prices in these two categories will have serious effects on the company's expenses, unless management takes action to control these costs.

METHODS FOR REDUCING TRAVEL AND ENTERTAINMENT COSTS

By implementing a number of reforms, management can expect to reduce Electrovision's T&E budget by as much as 40 percent. This estimate is based on the general assessment made by Global Travel Inc. (Gilligan 2002) and our chance to reduce or eliminate first-class travel. However, these measures are likely to be unpopular with employees. To gain acceptance for such changes, management will need to sell employees on the need for moderation in T&E allowances.

Gives recommendations an objective flavour by pointing out both the benefits and the risks of taking action →

Four Ways to Trim Expenses

By researching what other companies are doing to curb T&E expenses, the accounting department has identified four prominent opportunities that should enable Electrovision to save about $6 million annually in travel-related costs.

1. Institute Tighter Spending Controls

One person should be appointed director of travel and entertainment to lead the T&E budget-control effort. More than a third of all large companies now employ travel managers to keep costs in line ("Businesses Use Savvy Managers" 2004). Reporting to the vice-president of operations, the director should be familiar with the travel industry and well versed in both accounting and information technology. The director should establish a written T&E policy and implement a system for controlling T&E costs. Electrovision currently has no written policy on travel and entertainment, a step widely recommended by air travel experts (Smith 2004). Creating a policy would clarify management's position and serve as a vehicle for

Because airfares represent Electrovision's biggest T&E expense, Moreno included a subsection that deals with the possible impact of trends in the airline industry. Airfares are rising, so it is especially important to gain more control over employees' air travel arrangements.

Moreno created a forceful tone by using action verbs in the third-level subheadings of this section. This approach is appropriate to the nature of the study and the attitude of the audience. However, in a status-conscious organization, the imperative verbs might sound a bit too presumptuous coming from a junior member of the staff.

Moreno carries over major headings to the next page so that readers can orient themselves to the report's organizational structure.

FIGURE 11.10 Continued

Breaks up text with bulleted lists, which not only call attention to important points but also add visual interest (you can also use visual aids, headings, and direct quotations to break up large, solid blocks of print)

6

METHODS FOR REDUCING TRAVEL AND ENTERTAINMENT COSTS

communicating the need for moderation. At a minimum, the policy should include provisions such as the following:

- Limiting all T&E to business purposes and getting approval in advance
- Ensuring that all employees travel by coach and stay in mid-range business hotels (with rare exceptions to be approved on a case-by-case basis)
- Applying policy equally to employees at all levels

To implement the new policy, Electrovision must create a system for controlling T&E expenses. Each department should prepare an annual T&E budget. These budgets should be presented in detail so that management can evaluate how T&E dollars will be spent and can recommend appropriate cuts. To help management monitor performance relative to these budgets, the T&E director should prepare monthly financial statements showing actual T&E expenditures by department.

The director of travel should also be responsible for retaining a business-oriented travel service that will schedule all employee business trips and look for the best travel deals, especially in airfares. In addition to centralizing Electrovision's reservation and ticketing activities, the agency will negotiate reduced group rates with hotels and rental car agencies. The agency should have offices nationwide so that all Electrovision facilities can channel their reservations through the same company. This step is particularly important in light of the differing airfares available from city to city. It's common to find dozens of fares along commonly travelled routes (Rowe 2003). Plus, the director can help coordinate travel across the company to secure group discounts when possible (Barker 2004; Miller 2001).

Specifies the steps required to implement recommendations

2. Reduce Unnecessary Travel and Entertainment

One of the easiest ways to reduce expenses is to reduce the amount of travelling and entertaining that occurs. An analysis of last year's expenditures suggests that as much as 30 percent of Electrovision's T&E is discretionary. The professional staff spent $2.8 million attending seminars and conferences last year. Some of these gatherings are undoubtedly beneficial, but the company could save money by sending fewer people and eliminating the less valuable functions.

Electrovision could also economize on trips between headquarters and divisions by reducing these visits and sending fewer people each time. Although face-to-face meetings are often necessary, management could try to resolve more internal issues through telephone, electronic, and written communication.

Electrovision can urge employees to economize by flying tourist instead of first class or by taking advantage of discount fares. Instead of taking clients to dinner, Electrovision personnel can hold breakfast meetings, which tend to be less costly.

Moreno uses references to research to support her claims.

FIGURE 11.10 Continued

7

METHODS FOR REDUCING TRAVEL AND ENTERTAINMENT COSTS

Rather than ordering a $50 bottle of wine, employees can select a less expensive bottle or dispense with alcohol entirely. People can book rooms at moderately priced hotels and drive smaller rental cars.

3. Obtain Lowest Rates from Travel Providers

Apart from urging individual employees to economize, Electrovision can also save money by searching for the lowest available rates for airfares, hotels, and rental cars. Few Electrovision employees have the time or specialized knowledge to seek out travel bargains, making the most convenient and comfortable arrangements. However, by contracting with a professional travel service, the company will have access to professionals who can more efficiently obtain lower rates.

Judging by the experience of other companies, Electrovision may be able to trim 30 percent to 40 percent from the travel budget by looking for bargains in airfares and negotiating group rates with hotels and rental car companies. The company should be able to achieve these economies by analyzing travel patterns, identifying frequently visited locations, and selecting a few hotels that are willing to reduce rates in exchange for guaranteed business. Also, the company should be able to save up to 40 percent on rental car charges by negotiating a corporate rate.

The possibilities for economizing are promising; however, making the best arrangements is a complicated undertaking, requiring trade-offs such as the following:

- The best fares may not always be the lowest (e.g., indirect flights often cost less than direct ones, but they take longer, costing more in lost work time).
- The cheapest tickets may need to be booked far in advance, often impossible.
- Nonrefundable discount tickets are a drawback if the trip must be cancelled.

Points out possible difficulties to show that all angles have been considered and to build reader confidence in the writer's judgment

4. Replace Travel with Technological Alternatives

We might be able to replace a major portion of our interdivisional travel with electronic meetings, such as videoconferencing or real-time on-screen document sharing. Many companies use these tools to cut costs and reduce employee stress.

Rather than make specific recommendations in this report, I suggest that the new T&E director conduct an in-depth study of the company's travel patterns. An analysis of why employees travel and what they accomplish will highlight any opportunities for replacing face-to-face meetings. Part of this study should include limited testing of various electronic systems as a way of measuring their effect on both workplace effectiveness and overall costs.

Note how Moreno makes the transition from section to section. The first sentence under the first heading on this page refers to the subject of the previous paragraph and signals a shift in thought.

FIGURE 11.10 Continued

8

METHODS FOR REDUCING TRAVEL AND ENTERTAINMENT COSTS

The Impact of Reforms

By implementing tighter controls, reducing unnecessary expenses, negotiating more favourable rates, and exploring "electronic travel," Electrovision should be able to reduce its travel and entertainment budget significantly. As Table 1 illustrates, the combined savings should be in the neighbourhood of $6 million, although precise figures are somewhat difficult to project.

Uses informative title in the table, which is consistent with the way headings are handled and is appropriate for a report to a receptive audience

Table 1

Electrovision Can Trim Travel and Entertainment Costs by an Estimated $6 Million per Year

Table title is worded to help readers focus immediately on the point of the table

Source of Savings	Amount Saved
Switching from first-class to coach airfare	$2 300 000
Negotiating preferred hotel rates	940 000
Negotiating preferred rental car rates	460 000
Systematically searching for lower airfares	375 000
Reducing interdivisional travel	675 000
Reducing seminar and conference attendance	1 250 000
TOTAL POTENTIAL SAVINGS	**$6 000 000**

Includes dollar figures to help management envision the impact of the suggestions, even though estimated savings are difficult to project

To achieve the economies outlined in the table, Electrovision will incur expenses for hiring a director of travel and for implementing a T&E cost-control system. These costs are projected at $95 000: $85 000 per year in salary and benefits for the new employee and a one-time expense of $10 000 for the cost-control system. The cost of retaining a full-service travel agency is negligible because agencies receive a commission from travel providers rather than a fee from clients.

The measures required to achieve these savings are likely to be unpopular with employees. Electrovision personnel are accustomed to generous travel and entertainment allowances, and they are likely to resent having these privileges curtailed. To alleviate their disappointment

- Management should make a determined effort to explain why the changes are necessary.
- The director of corporate communication should develop a multi-faceted campaign to communicate the importance of curtailing T&E costs.
- Management should set an example by adhering strictly to the new policies.
- The limitations should apply equally to employees at all levels in the organization.

Note how Moreno calls attention in the first paragraph to items in the following table, without repeating the information in the table.

The table puts Moreno's recommendations in perspective. She calls attention to the most important sources of savings and also spells out the costs required to achieve those results.

FIGURE 11.10 Continued

Uses a descriptive heading for the last section of the text (in informational reports, this section is often called "Summary"; in analytical reports, it is called "Conclusions" or "Conclusions and Recommendations")

9

CONCLUSIONS

Electrovision is currently spending $16 million per year on travel and entertainment. Although much of this spending is justified, the company's costs are high relative to competitors', mainly because Electrovision has been generous with its travel benefits.

Electrovision's liberal approach to T&E expenses made sense during years of high profitability; however, the company is facing the prospect of declining profits for the next several years. Thus, management is motivated to cut costs in all areas of the business. Reducing T&E spending is particularly important because the impact of these costs will increase as airfares and hotel accommodations increase.

Electrovision should be able to reduce T&E costs by as much as 40 percent by taking four important steps:

Summarizes conclusions in the first two paragraphs—a good approach because Moreno organized her report around conclusions and recommendations, so readers have already been introduced to them

RECOMMENDATIONS

Emphasizes the recommendations by presenting them in list format

1. *Institute tighter spending controls.* Management should hire a T&E director to assume overall responsibility for relevant activities. Within the next six months, this director should develop a written travel policy, institute a T&E budget and a cost-control system, and retain a professional, business-oriented travel agency.

2. *Reduce unnecessary travel and entertainment.* Electrovision should encourage employees to economize on T&E spending. Management can authorize fewer trips and urge employees to be more conservative in their spending.

3. *Obtain lowest rates from travel providers.* Electrovision should focus on obtaining the best rates on airline tickets, hotel rooms, and rental cars. By channelling all arrangements through a professional travel agency, the company can optimize its choices and gain clout in negotiating preferred rates.

4. *Replace travel with technological alternatives.* With the number of computers already installed in our facilities, it seems likely that we could take advantage of desktop videoconferencing and other distance-meeting tools. This won't be quite as feasible with customer sites, since these systems require compatible equipment at both ends of a connection, but it is certainly a possibility for communication with Electrovision's own sites.

Uses a verb-first structure to emphasize actions.

Because these measures may be unpopular with employees, management should make a concerted effort to explain the importance of reducing travel costs. The director of corporate communication should be given responsibility for developing a plan to communicate the need for employee cooperation.

Moreno introduces no new facts in this entire section.

FIGURE 11.10 Continued

Lists references alphabetically by the author's last name, and when the author is unknown, by the title of the reference (see Appendix B for additional details on preparing reference lists)

10

REFERENCES

Barker, Julie. (2004, February). How to Rein in Group Travel Costs. *Successful Meetings*, p. 31.

Businesses Use Savvy Managers to Keep Travel Costs Down. (2004, July 17). *Christian Science Monitor*, p. 4.

Dahl, Jonathan. (2003, December 29). 2003: The Year Travel Costs Took Off. *The Globe and Mail*, section B6, p. 10.

Gilligan, Edward P. (2002, November). Trimming Your T&E Is Easier Than You Think. *Managing Office Technology*, pp. 39–41.

Miller, Lisa. (2005, July 7). Attention, Airline Ticket Shoppers. *National Post*, section B, p. 12.

Phillips, Edward H. (2005, January 8). Airlines Post Record Traffic. *Aviation Week & Space Technology*, p. 331.

Rowe, Irene Vilitos. (2003, October 12). Global Solution for Cutting Travel Costs. *European*, p. 30.

Smith, Carol. (2004, November 2). Rising Erratic Airfares Make Company Policy Vital. *Los Angeles Times*, section D4, p. 9.

Travel Costs Under Pressure. (2004, Februrary 15). *Purchasing*, p. 30.

Moreno's list of references follows APA style.

References

Supplementary Parts

Supplementary parts present additional details and come after the text.

Supplementary parts follow the text of the report and provide information for readers who seek more detailed discussion. Supplements are more common in long reports than in short ones. They typically include appendices, a bibliography, and an index.

- **Appendices.** An appendix contains additional information for those readers who want it—information related to the report but not included in the text because it is too lengthy, is too bulky, or lacks direct relevance. Appendices contain sample questionnaires and cover letters, sample forms, computer printouts, spreadsheets, and so on. Include each type of material in a separate appendix, mention all appendices in the text, and list them in the table of contents. Arrange them in the order of mention.
- **List of References or Bibliography.** The bibliography lists the secondary sources you consulted. In Moreno's report, she labelled her bibliography "References" because she listed only the works that were mentioned in the report, according to APA format. Moreno's Electrovision report uses the author-date system. An alternative is to use numbered endnotes (put at the end of the report). For more on citing sources, see Appendix B, "Documentation of Report Sources."
- **Glossary.** A glossary is a list of definitions of terms used in the report. It is useful when some readers need definitions and some do not. Putting the definitions in a glossary at the back of the report gives readers a choice about reading them.

Components of a Formal Proposal

Formal proposals contain many of the same components as other formal reports (see Figure 11.11). The difference lies mostly in the text, although a few of the prefatory parts are also different. With the exception of an occasional appendix, most proposals have few supplementary parts.

FIGURE 11.11 Parts of a Formal Proposal

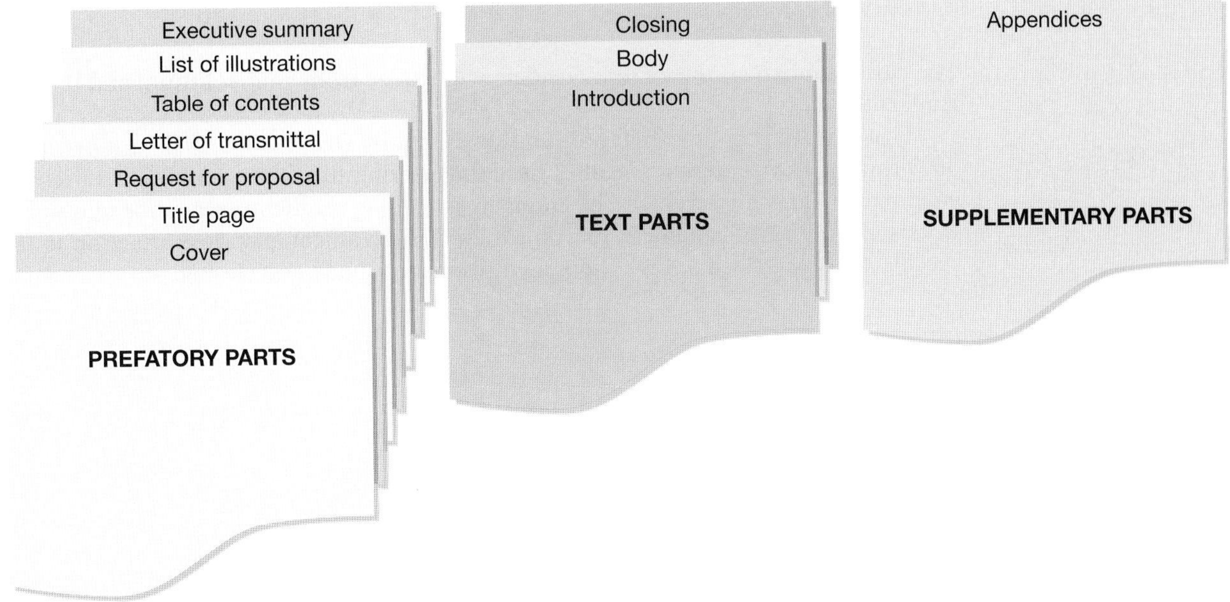

Prefatory Parts

The cover, title page, table of contents, and list of illustrations, and executive summary are handled the same as in other formal reports. However, other prefatory parts are handled quite differently, such as the copy of the RFP and the letter of transmittal:

Formal proposals contain most of the same prefatory parts as other formal reports.

- **Copy of the RFP.** Instead of having a letter of authorization, a formal proposal may have a copy of the request for proposal (RFP), which is a letter or memo soliciting a proposal or a bid for a particular project. If the RFP includes detailed specifications, it may be too long to bind into the proposal; in that case, you may want to include only the introductory portion of the RFP. Another option is to omit the RFP or append it and simply refer to it in your letter of transmittal.
- **Letter of transmittal.** If the proposal is solicited, the transmittal letter follows the pattern for good-news messages, highlighting those aspects of your proposal that may give you a competitive advantage. If the proposal is unsolicited, the transmittal letter follows the pattern for persuasive messages (see Chapter 9). The letter must persuade the reader that you have something worthwhile to offer that justifies reading the entire proposal. Because the transmittal letter may be all that the client reads, it must be especially convincing.

Contents of the Proposal

Just as with reports, the text of a proposal comprises an introduction, body, and a closing section. The introduction presents and summarizes the problem you intend to solve and your solution. The body includes any benefits the reader will receive from the solution and explains the complete details of the solution:

Just like other business reports, proposals have three divisions of text: introduction, body, and close.

- How the job will be done
- How it will be broken into tasks
- What method will be used to do it (including the required equipment, material, and personnel)
- When the work will begin and end

- How much the entire job will cost (including a detailed breakdown)
- Why your company is qualified

The close emphasizes the benefits readers will realize from your solution, and it urges readers to act.

Figure 11.12 is an informal proposal submitted by Dixon O'Donnell, vice-president of O'Donnell & Associates, a geotechnical engineering firm that conducts a variety of environmental testing services. The company is bidding on the mass grading and utility work specified by AGI Builders. As you review this document, pay close attention to the specific items addressed in the proposal's introduction, body, and closing.

FIGURE 11.12 Dixon O'Donnell's Informal Solicited Proposal

1793 East Westerfield Road, Montreal, QC J4P 2X1
(819) 441-1148 Fax: (819) 441-1149 E-mail: dod@inter.net

July 28, 2004

Ms. Joyce Colton, P.E.
AGI Builders, Inc.
1280 Spring Lake Drive
Montreal, QC J7R 8T2

Dear Ms. Colton:

PROPOSAL NO. F-0087 FOR AGI BUILDERS, SAINT-BRUNO MANUFACTURING PLANT

O'Donnell & Associates is pleased to submit the following proposal to provide construction testing services for the mass grading operations and utility work at the Saint-Bruno Manufacturing Plant, 1230 Parent Street, Saint-Bruno, Quebec. Our company has been providing construction-testing services in the Montreal area since 1972 and has performed more than 100 geotechnical investigations at airports within Ontario and Quebec—including Pearson International Airport, Dorval and Mirabel.

Uses opening paragraph in place of an introduction

Grabs reader's attention by highlighting company qualifications

Background

It is our understanding that the work consists of two projects: (1) the mass grading operations will require approximately six months, and (2) the utility work will require approximately three months. The two operations are scheduled as follows:

Mass Grading Operation	May 2005–October 2005
Utility Work	November 2005–January 2006

Acknowledges the two projects and their required time lines

Proposed Approach and Work Plan

Uses headings to divide proposal into logical segments for easy reading

O'Donnell & Associates will perform observation and testing services during both the mass grading operations and the excavation and backfilling of the underground utilities. Specifically, we will

- perform field density tests on the compacted material as required by the job specifications using a nuclear moisture/density gauge
- conduct appropriate laboratory tests such as ASTM D-1557 Modified Proctors
- prepare detailed reports summarizing the results of our field and laboratory testing

Fill materials to be placed at the site may consist of natural granular materials (sand), processed materials (crushed stone, crushed concrete, slag), or clay soils.

Describes scope of project and outlines specific tests the company will perform

(continued)

FIGURE 11.12 Continued

O'Donnell & Associates, Inc. July 28, 2004 Page 2

Staffing

Explains who will be responsible for the various tasks

Encloses resumé rather than listing qualifications in the document

O'Donnell & Associates will provide qualified personnel to perform the necessary testing. Mr. Kevin Patel will be the lead field technician responsible for the project. A copy of Mr. Patel's resumé is included with this proposal for your review. Kevin will coordinate field activities with your job site superintendent and make sure that appropriate personnel are assigned to the job site. Overall project management will be the responsibility of Mr. Joseph Proesel. Project engineering services will be performed under the direction of Mr. Dixon O'Donnell, P.E. All field personnel assigned to the site will be familiar with and abide by the Project Site Health and Safety Plan prepared by Carlson Environmental, Inc., dated April 2004.

Qualifications

O'Donnell & Associates has been providing quality professional services since 1972 in

- Geotechnical engineering
- Materials testing and inspection
- Pavement evaluation
- Environmental services
- Engineering and technical support (CADD) services

Grabs attention by mentioning distinguishing qualifications

The company provides Phase I and Phase II environmental site assessments, preparation of LUST site closure reports, installation of groundwater monitoring wells, and testing of soil/groundwater samples for environmental contaminants. Geotechnical services include all phases of soil mechanics and foundation engineering, including foundation and lateral load analysis, slope stability analysis, site preparation recommendations, seepage analysis, pavement design, and settlement analysis.

O'Donnell & Associates' materials testing laboratory is certified by AASHTO Accreditation Program for the testing of Soils, Aggregate, Hot Mix Asphalt, and Portland Cement Concrete. A copy of our laboratory certification is included with this proposal. In addition to in-house training, field and laboratory technicians participate in a variety of certification programs, including those sponsored by American Concrete Institute (ACI), Quebec Chapter.

Gains credibility by describing certifications

Costs

On the basis of our understanding of the scope of the work, we estimate the total cost of the two projects to be $100 260.00, as shown in the table.

(continued)

FIGURE 11.12 Continued

O'Donnell & Associates, Inc. July 28, 2004 Page 3

Table of Cost Estimates

Cost Estimate: Mass Grading	**Units**	**Rate ($)**	**Total Cost ($)**
Field Inspection			
Labour	1320 hours	$38.50	$ 50 820.00
Nuclear Moisture Density Meter	132 days	35.00	4 620.00
Vehicle Expense	132 days	45.00	5 940.00
Laboratory Testing			
Proctor Density Tests (ASTM D-1557)	4 tests	130.00	520.00
Engineering/Project Management			
Principal Engineer	16 hours	110.00	1 760.00
Project Manager	20 hours	80.00	1 600.00
Administrative Assistant	12 hours	50.00	600.00
Subtotal			***$ 65 860.00***
Cost Estimate: Utility Work	**Units**	**Rate ($)**	**Total Cost ($)**
Field Inspection			
Labour	660 hours	$ 38.50	$ 25 410.00
Nuclear Moisture Density Meter	66 days	35.00	2 310.00
Vehicle Expense	66 days	45.00	2 970.00
Laboratory Testing			
Proctor Density Tests (ASTM D-1557)	2 tests	130.00	260.00
Engineering/Project Management			
Principal Engineer	10 hours	110.00	1 100.00
Project Manager	20 hours	80.00	1 600.00
Administrative Assistant	15 hours	50.00	750.00
Subtotal			***$ 34 400.00***
Total Project Costs			**$100 260.00**

This estimate assumes full-time inspection services. However, our services may also be performed on an as-requested basis, and actual charges will reflect time associated with the project. We have attached our standard fee schedule for your review. Overtime rates are for hours in excess of 8.0 hours per day, before 7:00 a.m., after 5:00 p.m., and on holidays and weekends.

Builds interest by describing all services provided by the company

Itemizes costs by project and gives supporting detail

Provides alternative option in case full-time service costs exceed client's budget

(continued)

FIGURE 11.12 Continued

Uses brief closing to emphasize qualifications and ask for client decision

O'Donnell & Associates, Inc. July 28, 2004 Page 4

Authorization

With a staff of more than 30 personnel, including registered professional engineers, resident engineers, geologists, construction inspectors, laboratory technicians, and drillers, we are convinced that O'Donnell & Associates is capable of providing the services required for a project of this magnitude.

If you would like our firm to provide the services as outlined in this proposal, please sign this letter and return it to us along with a certified cheque for $10 000 (our retainer) by August 15, 2004. Please call me if you have any questions regarding the terms of this proposal or our approach.

Provides deadline and makes response easy

Sincerely,

Dixon O'Donnell

Dixon O'Donnell
Vice-President

Enclosures

Accepted for AGI BUILDERS, INC.

By________________________ Date ________________________

Makes letter a binding contract, if signed

Reviewing Key Points

In this chapter you learned about writing business reports and proposals. When writing a report

- Use a direct pattern when resistance is low. Place conclusions and recommendations near the beginning for reader convenience.
- Use an indirect pattern when resistance is high. Place arguments and evidence before the conclusion and recommendations to help gain reader acceptance of the rationale behind the ideas.
- Include special format requirements when writing long, formal reports, such as
  - An executive summary
  - A table of contents
  - A list of illustrations
  - A list of appendices
  - A title page
- Use an executive summary to provide a condensed version of the whole report to allow the busy reader access to key points and to grasp your conclusions quickly.
- Choose the right graphics according to your purpose; use
  - Tables to summarize numerical data
  - Bar charts for comparisons
  - Line graphs to show trends
  - Charts to show relationships
- Control the style and tone by using the appropriate voice, personal pronouns, and consistent verb tenses. Use active voice when possible. Strive for a style that reflects the image of your organization.

Test Your Knowledge

1. Name four options for report format.

2. What are some ways of organizing informational reports?

3. How would you determine whether to use a direct or indirect approach for structuring an analytical report?

4. What tools can you use to help readers follow the structure and flow of information in a long report?

5. What graphic would you use to compare one part with a whole?

6. What graphic type would you use to show trends?

7. What is an executive summary, and how does it differ from an introduction?

8. What information is included on the title page of a report?

9. What is a letter of transmittal, and where is it included in a formal report submission?

10. How are appendices ordered?

Apply Your Knowledge

1. Should a report always explain the writer's method of gathering evidence or solving a problem? Why or why not?

2. Would you use the direct or indirect approach to document inventory shortages at your manufacturing plant? To propose an employee stock-option plan? Why?

3. What similarities do you see between visuals and nonverbal communication? Explain your answer.

4. You're writing a report to the director of human resources on implementing teams throughout your company. You want to emphasize that since the new approach was implemented six months ago, absenteeism and turnovers have been sharply reduced in all but two departments. How do you visually present your data in the most favourable light? Explain.

5. **Ethical Choices** How would you report on a confidential survey in which employees rated their managers' capabilities? Both employees and managers expect to see the results. Would you give the same report to employees and managers? What components would you include or exclude for each audience? Explain your choices.

Practise Your Knowledge

Activities

For live links to all Web sites discussed in this chapter, visit this text's Web site at www.pearsoned.ca/bovee. Just log on and select Chapter 11, and click on "Student Resources." Locate the page or the URL related to the material in the text. For the "Exploring the Best of the Web" exercises, you'll also find navigational directions. Click on the live link to the site.

1. **Organizing Reports: Deciding on Format** Go to the library or visit the Internet site www.wisi.com. Click on "Wright Research Centre," then select "Company Analyses." select Canada from the Country Profiles list. Select "SEDAR," then "Company Profiles," to find annual reports from hundreds of Canadian companies. Review the annual report recently released by Creo. Be prepared to discuss the following questions in class:
   - **a.** How does Creo discuss its annual performance? Are the data presented clearly so that shareholders can draw conclusions about how well the company performed?
   - **b.** What goals, challenges, and plans does the CEO emphasize in his discussion of results?
   - **c.** How do the format and organization of the report enhance or detract from the information being presented?

2. **Organizing Reports: Choosing the Direct or Indirect Approach** Of the organizational approaches introduced in the chapter, which is best suited for writing a report

that answers the following questions? Briefly explain why. (Note, you will write one report for each question item.)

a. In which market segment—root beer, cola, or lemon-lime—should Fizz Drinks, Inc., introduce a new soft drink to take advantage of its enlarged research and development budget?
b. Should Major Manufacturing, Inc. close down operations of its antiquated Bathurst, Nova Scotia plant despite the adverse economic impact on the town that has grown up around the plant?
c. Should you and your partner adopt a new accounting method to make your financial statements look better to potential investors?
d. Should North Battleford Chemicals buy disposable test tubes to reduce labour costs associated with cleaning and sterilizing reusable test tubes?
e. What are some reasons for the recent data loss at your school's computer centre, and how can we avoid similar problems in the future?

3. **Teamwork: Report Structure** You and a classmate are helping Linda Moreno prepare her report on Electrovision's travel and entertainment costs (see Figure 11.10). This time, however, the report is to be informational rather than analytical, so it will not include recommendations. Review the existing report and determine what changes would be needed to make it an informational report. Be as specific as possible. For example, if your team decides the report needs a new title, what title would you use? Now draft a transmittal memo for Moreno to use in conveying this informational report to Dennis McWilliams, Electrovision's vice-president of operations.

4. **Organizing Reports: Structuring Informational Reports** Assume that your school's president has received many student complaints about campus parking problems. You are appointed to chair a student committee organized to investigate the problems and recommend solutions. The president gives you the file labelled "Parking: Complaints from Students," and you jot down the essence of the complaints as you inspect the contents. Your notes look like this:

- Inadequate student spaces at critical hours
- Poor night lighting near the computer centre
- Inadequate attempts to keep resident neighbours from occupying spaces
- Dim marking lines
- Motorcycles taking up full spaces
- Discourteous security officers
- Spaces (usually empty) reserved for school officials
- Relatively high parking fees
- Full fees charged to night students even though they use the lots only during low-demand periods
- Vandalism to cars and a sense of personal danger
- Inadequate total space
- Resident harassment of students parking on the street in front of neighbouring houses

Now prepare an outline for an informational report to be submitted to committee members. Use a topical organization for your report that categorizes this information.

5. **Choosing the Right Visual** You're preparing the annual report for FretCo Guitar Corporation. For each of the following types of information, select the right chart or visual to illustrate the text. Explain your choices.

a. Data on annual sales for the past 20 years
b. Comparison of FretCo sales, product by product (electric guitars, bass guitars, amplifiers, acoustic guitars), for this year and last year
c. Explanation of how a FretCo acoustic guitar is manufactured
d. Explanation of how the FretCo Guitar Corporation markets its guitars
e. Data on sales of FretCo products in each of 12 countries
f. Comparison of FretCo sales figures with sales figures for three competing guitar makers over the past 10 years

6. **Internet** One of the best places to see how data can be presented visually is in government statistical publications, which are often available on the Internet. For example, Industry Canada's Strategis publishes updates on Canadian trade with other countries. Visit the Strategis Web site at www.strategis.ic.gc.ca and follow the links to "Trade and Investment" and "What's New" to find a recent report. Using what you learned in this chapter, evaluate the charts in the report. Do they present the data clearly? Are they missing any elements? What would you do to improve the charts? Print out a copy of the report to turn in with your answers, and indicate which charts you are evaluating.

7. **Composing Reports: Navigational Clues** Review a long business article in a journal or newspaper. Highlight examples of how the article uses heading, transitions, and previews and reviews to help the readers find their way.

8. **Ethical Choices** Your boss has asked you to prepare a feasibility report to determine whether the company should advertise its custom-crafted cabinetry in the weekly neighbourhood newspaper. Based on your primary research, you think they should. As you draft the introduction to your report, however, you discover that the survey administered to the neighbourhood newspaper subscribers was flawed. Several of the questions were poorly written and misleading. You used the survey results, among other findings, to justify your recommendation. The report is due in three days. What actions might you want to take, if any, before you complete your report?

9. **Producing Reports: Letter of Transmittal** You are president of the Friends of the Library, a non-profit group that raises funds and provides volunteers to support your local library. Every February, you send a report of the previous year's activities and accomplishments to the Municipal Arts Council, which provides an annual grant of $1000 toward your group's summer reading festival. Now it's February 6, and you've completed your formal report. Here are the highlights:

   - The back-to-school book sale raised $2000.
   - The holiday craft fair raised $1100.
   - Promotion and prizes for the summer reading festival cost $1450.
   - Materials for the children's program featuring a local author cost $125.
   - New reference databases for the library's career centre cost $850.
   - Bookmarks promoting the library's Web site cost $200.

   Write a letter of transmittal to Erica Maki, the council's director. Because she is expecting this report, you can use the direct approach. Be sure to express gratitude for the council's ongoing financial support.

10. **Internet** Government reports vary in purpose and structure. Read through Industry Canada's *Monthly Trade Bulletin* report on trade patterns, posted online at www.strategis.gc.ca/sc_ecnmy/mera/engdoc/06.html. What is the purpose of this document? Does the title communicate this purpose? What type of report is this, and what is the report's structure? Which prefatory and supplementary parts are included? Now analyze the visuals. What types are included in this report? Are they all necessary? Are the titles and legends sufficiently informative?

Expand Your Knowledge

Best of the Web

Preview Before You Produce A good way to get ideas for the best style, organization, and format of a report is by looking at copies of professional business reports. To find samples of different types of reports, you can use a metasearch engine, such as Ixquick Metasearch. Ixquick searches many engines simultaneously; in addition to searching in English, you can conduct your search in five other languages. See what Ixquick produces when you enter the phrase "business reports." Choose from various titles or descriptions to compare different kinds of reports. This research could result in your preparing better reports and proposals.

www.ixquick.com

Exercises

1. What is the purpose of the report you read? Who is its target audience? Explain why the structure and style of the report make it easy or difficult to follow the main idea.
2. What type of report did you read? Briefly describe the main message. Is the information well organized? If you answer "yes," explain how you can use the report as a guide for a report you might write. If you answer "no," explain why the report is not helpful.
3. Drawing on what you know about the qualities of a good business report, review a report and describe what features contribute to its readability.

Exploring the Web on Your Own

Review these chapter-related Web sites to learn more about writing reports and proposals.

1. Need some help using graphics software? Get started at the About.com graphics software Web site. Take the tutorials, view the illustrated demonstrations, and read the instructional articles at www.graphicssoft.about.com/cs/howtos/index.htm.
2. Looking for the perfect transitional word? Cues and Transitions for the Reader, at www.managementhelp.org/writing/cuestran.htm, has some recommendations to help you.
3. Develop a better business plan by following the advice at Canadian Business Service Centres at www.cbsc.org, or at Services for Canadian Business at www.businessgateway.ca, or at the Small Business Association Web site, www.sba.gov/starting/indexbusplans.html.

Learn Interactively

Interactive Study Guide

Visit the Companian Website at www.pearsoned.ca/bovee. For Chapter 11, take advantage of the interactive "Study Guide" to test your chapter knowledge. Get instant feedback on whether you need additional studying.

This site offers a variety of additional resources: The "Research Area" helps you locate a wealth of information to use in course assignments. The "Study Hall" helps you succeed in this course by offering support with writing and study skills, time management, and career skills, as well as numerous other resources.

Peak Performance Grammar and Mechanics

Use the Peak Performance Grammar and Mechanics CD to test your skill with punctuation. In the "Punctuation II" section, take the Pretest to determine whether you have any weak areas. Then review those areas in the Refresher Course. Take the Follow-Up Test to check your grasp of punctuation. For an extra challenge or advanced practice, take the Advanced Test.

Cases

The "Cases" section of Chapter 10 asked you to complete planning tasks for 12 informal cases (both informational and analytical). Your instructor may ask you to go back and choose some of those cases to prepare and write as fully developed reports. Following are some formal reports your instructor may assign.

Short Formal Reports

1. Climbing the ladder: Short report summarizing data about corporate opportunities for women (no additional research required)

As assistant to the director of human resources for a large advertising firm, you hear the concerns of many employees. Lately, increasing numbers of women have been complaining about being passed up for promotions and management positions. They feel that men receive preferential treatment, even though many women are more highly qualified.

Your team has already conducted some research into the problem. Table 11.3 shows several key statistics about the men and women working for your company. Table 11.4 depicts how executives in Fortune 1000 companies see the barriers to the advancement of women, and Table 11.5 shows why female executives believe that women should have more opportunities in the corporate world. These data may help shed light on the possibility of sex discrimination at your company. Because your

Table 11.3 Statistics for Male and Female Managers

Employee Statistics	Female Managers	Male Managers
Average number of years with the company	12.3	9.5
Average number of years of management experience	7.2	6.9
Percentage who have an MBA or other advanced degree	74%	63%
Average annual salary	$76 000	$84 000
Average number of times promoted	4.2	4.4

Table 11.4 Why Female Executives Don't Advance into Corporate Leadership Positions

Reason Cited	According to Female Executives	According to Male CEOs
Male stereotyping preconceptions	52%	25%
Exclusion from informal networks	49	15
Lack of general management/line experience	47	82
Inhospitable corporate culture	35	18
Women not in pipeline long enough	29	64

Table 11.5 Why Female Executives Think Companies Should Increase the Number of Female Senior Managers

Reason	Agree	Strongly Agree
Women are large part of management talent pool	29%	69%
Women contribute unique perspective	32	61
Women are large part of consumer base	45	36
Companies have social responsibility	41	10
Shareholders want more executive women	41	7
Customers want more executive women	34	7
Lawsuits are increasing	40	5

company believes in fair and equal treatment for all employees, regardless of gender, you know your boss will be interested in this information.[6] Although the source of the information is from the United States, you know it has relevance for your company.

Your Task Write a short report to the director of human resources, interpreting and summarizing the information in these tables. Suggest a possible course of action to remedy the situation at your company.

WEB SKILLS 2. Picking the better path: Short research report assisting a client in a career choice (additional research required)

You are employed by Open Options, a career-counselling firm, where your main function is to help clients make career choices. Today a client with the same name as yours (what a coincidence!) came to your office and asked for help deciding between two careers—careers that you yourself had been interested in (an even greater coincidence!).

Your Task Research the two careers, and prepare a short report that your client can study. Your report should compare at least five major areas, such as salary, working conditions, and educational requirements. Interview the client to understand her or his personal preferences regarding each of the five areas. For example, what is the minimum salary the client will accept? By comparing the client's preferences with the research material you collect, you will have a basis for concluding which of the two careers is best. The report should end with a career recommendation. Note: Two good places for career-related information are two publications of Human Resources Development Canada, both available in print (in libraries) and online at the sites noted:

- *National Occupational Classification 2001*, online at www23.hrdc-drhc.gc.ca
- Job Futures, online at http://jobfutures.ca

Another good source for detailed information about career opportunities, trends, and qualifications is the *Occupational Outlook Handbook*, published by the U.S. Bureau of Labor Statistics, available in print at the library and online at http://stats.bls.gov/oco/ocoiab.htm.

Long Formal Reports Requiring Additional Research

3. Is there any justice? Report critiquing legislation

Plenty of people complain about their MPs and MLAs, but few are specific about their complaints. Here's your chance.

Your Task Write a formal report about a law that you believe should have been, or should not have been, enacted. Be objective. Write the report using specific facts to support your beliefs. Reach conclusions and offer your recommendation at the end of the report. As a final step, you might send a copy of your report to an appropriate provincial or federal official or member of the legislative assembly in your province or to your member of Parliament.

4. Travel opportunities: Report comparing two destinations for an employee incentive program

You work for a subsidiary of the world's largest publishing company in Toronto as a human resources manager. Your company sends the top Canadian sales representative and his or her family on an all-expenses paid trip to a luxury resort to join top sellers from throughout the company. You have been working with the New York office that has arranged past trips and have been given the responsibility for recommending this year's resort. You have three in mind that you need to research: the Grand Wailea in Maui, Hawaii; the Phoenician in Phoenix, Arizona; and the Chateau Whistler in Whistler, B.C.

Your Task Prepare a report comparing the three resorts. Establish some criteria that you can use to decide which resort to recommend, such as that the price for each attendee's trip (including meals, airfare, car rental, and accommodation) has to be within a budget of CAN $25 000. The trip takes place each February. What other criteria would be useful in assessing these resorts for your purpose? Using resources in your library, on the Internet, and perhaps from travel agencies, analyze the destinations to see which one meets your criteria. At the end of the report, recommend the resort for this year's travel incentive.

5. Secondary sources: Report based on library research

Perhaps one of the following questions has been on your mind:

a. Which is the best university or college at which to pursue an undergraduate degree in business?
b. How can you organize a student group to make your campus safer at night?
c. Which of three companies that you would like to work for has the most responsible environmental policies?
d. What market factors led to the development of a product that you use frequently, and how are those factors different today?
e. Which three Canadian companies have had the best stock price performance over the past 30 years and why?
f. What are the best small-business opportunities available today?

Your Task Answer one of those questions, using secondary sources for information. Be sure to document your sources in the correct form (see Appendix B). Give conclusions and recommendations in your report.

6. Doing business abroad: Report summarizing the social and business customs of a foreign country

Your company would like to sell its products overseas. But first, management must have a clear understanding of the social and business customs of the foreign countries where they intend to do business.

Your Task Choose a non-English-speaking country, and write a long formal report summarizing the country's social and business customs. Review appropriate sections of Chapter 1 as a guide for the types of information you could include in your report.

7. Brewing up sales: Formal proposal to supply coffee to Peter's Doughnuts

You are assistant to the president of Lighthouse Roasters, a small but growing coffee-roasting company. Lighthouse has made a name for itself by offering fresh, dark-roasted gourmet coffees; however, Lighthouse Roasters does not operate its own stores (unlike Starbucks and other competitors). Instead, Lighthouse sells roasted gourmet coffee beans to retailers such as restaurants, bakeries, and latte carts. These retailers use the Lighthouse beans to make the coffee beverages they sell.

Lighthouse's total cost to produce a kilogram of roasted gourmet beans is $2.75. The company wholesales a kilogram of roasted gourmet beans for an average price of $4.50. Competitors who sell regular coffee beans typically charge about $3.00 per kilogram. However, the average price of a gourmet coffee beverage is $1.50, about $0.50 more than beverages made with regular coffee (including both brewed coffee and espresso drinks). Each kilogram of coffee yields about 40 beverages.

With 76 doughnut shops across five provinces, Peter's Doughnuts has seen its sales decline in recent months, after Starbucks began opening stores close by Peter's shops. Starbucks not only sells gourmet coffee but also carries a selection of pastries that compete with doughnuts. Peter's management figures that by offering gourmet coffee, it will win back customers who like doughnuts but who also want darker-roasted gourmet coffees. Therefore, Peter's has invited you to submit a proposal to be its exclusive supplier of coffee. Peter's anticipates that it will need 400 kg of coffee a month during the colder months (October–March) and 300 kg during the warmer months (April–September). The company has said it wants to pay no more than $6.95 per kilogram for Lighthouse coffee.

Your Task Using your imagination to supply the details, write a proposal describing your plan to supply coffee to Peter's Doughnuts. Considering your costs, will you meet Peter's pricing demands, or will you attempt to gain a higher price?

Improve Your Grammar, Mechanics, and Usage

Level 1: Self-Assessment—Quotation Marks, Parentheses, Ellipses, Underscores, and Italics

Review Sections 2.10, 2.11, 2.12, and 2.13 in the Handbook of Grammar, Mechanics, and Usage, and then look at the following 15 items.

In items 1–15, insert quotation marks, parentheses, ellipses, and underscores (for italics) wherever necessary:

1. Be sure to read How to Sell by Listening in this month's issue of B.C. Business.
2. Her response see the attached memo is disturbing.
3. Contact is an overused word.
4. We will operate with a skeleton staff during the holiday break December 21 through January.
5. The SBP's next conference, the bulletin noted, will be held in Winnipeg.

6. Sara O'Rourke a reporter from the Edmonton Star will be here on Thursday.
7. I don't care why you didn't fill my order; I want to know when you'll fill it.
8. The term up in the air means undecided.
9. Her assistant the one who just had the baby won't be back for four weeks.
10. The state has no business in the bedrooms of the nation is the beginning of a famous quotation from Pierre Elliot Trudeau.
11. Whom do you think Time magazine will select as its Person of the Year?
12. Do you remember who sang Snowbird?
13. Refinements in robotics may prove profitable. More detail about this technology appears in Appendix A.
14. The resignation letter begins Since I'll never regain your respect and goes on to explain why that's true.
15. You must help her distinguish between i.e. which means that is and e.g. which means for example.

Level 2: Workplace Applications

The following items contain numerous errors in grammar, capitalization, punctuation, abbreviation, number style, word division, and vocabulary. Rewrite each sentence in the space provided, correcting all errors. Write *C* in the space after any sentence that is already correct.

1. For the 1st time, thank's to largely deals with the big chains like Stop & Shop, Sheila's Snak Treetz are showing a profit.
2. The premise for broadband, sometimes called the 'next generation of Internet', is that consumers need a more fast pipeline for getting digital information in our homes.
3. After moving into they're own factory, the Anderson's found theirselves in the market for an oven with airflow controls.
4. Cash-strapped entrepreneurs have learned penny-pinching, cost-cutting, credit-stretching techniques.

5. Designs in the Rough send out some 7 million catalogues a year yet until recently the company did'nt need a warehouse and they hadn't hardly any carrying costs.

6. Blockbuster estimates that 70 percent of the US population live within a 10 minute drive of a Blockbuster store.

7. Nestle Waters North America are the exclusive importer of globally-recognized brands such as: Perrier and Vittel from France and, S. Pelligrino from Italy,

8. The B.C. East Asian community; the second largest Minority Group in the province; commands impressive political power.

9. We conducted a six-month pilot in Halifax, to insure the affectiveness of the program.

10. A series of 7-Eleven television spots help make the term brain freeze part of every day North American language.

11. The ad agencies accounts include the following consumer-brands; Wal-Mart, Westjet airlines, Kinko's, Rocky Mountain Bicycles, and Krispy Kreme.

12. PETsMART allows pets and their humans to together stroll the aisles of its stores; the number one Specialty Retailer of pet supplies.

13. Signature Fruit Co. is expanding it's Ontario warehouses this Fall.

14. To unite the company's 91 franchisees around a common corporate identity WingsToGo have setup a corporate intranet.

15. It would be well for you to contract with an Internet service provider—a ISP - to both run and to maintain your Web site.

Level 3: Document Critique

The following document may contain errors in grammar, capitalization, punctuation, abbreviation, number style, vocabulary, and spelling. You may also find problems with organization, format, and word use. Correct all errors using standard proofreading marks (see Appendix C).

Memorandum

From: Kris Beiersdorf

Date: 18 April 2005

RE PROJECT: Contract no. 05371 St. Cyril

To: Ken Estes, Drummondville concrete

Memco Construction is pleased to submit a road construction proposal for the above project. Our company has been providing quality materials and subcontracting services for highway reconstruction projects for over twenty-three years. Our most recent jobs in Quebec have included Highway Cap-de-là Madeleine resurfacing, and reconstructing Highway 1, St. Hyacinthe Bypass.

Should you have any questions about this proposal please contact me at the company 819-672-0344, direct extension #30) or by e-mail at kbeirsdorf@memcocon.com.

Based on the scope of the work outlined: the total cost of this job is projected by us to run ninety-nine thousand, two hundred eighty-three dollars. Because material quantities can vary once a project gets underway a separate page will be attached by us to this memorandum detailing our per-unit fees. Final charges will be based on the exact quantity of materials used for the job, and anything that accedes this estimate will be added of course.

Our proposal assumes that the following items will be furnished by other contractors (at no cost to Memco). All forms, earthwork and clearing; All prep work; Water at project site; Traffic control setup, devices, and maintenance—Location for staging, stockpiling, and storing material and equipment at job sight.

If we win this bid, we are already to begin when the apropriate contracts have been signed by us and by you.

Business Communication Notebook

Ethics

Top Tips for Writing Reports That Tell the Truth

Put nothing in writing that you're unwilling to say in public, and write nothing that may embarrass or jeopardize your employer. Does this mean you should cover up problems? Of course not. However, when you're dealing with sensitive information, be discreet. Present the information in such a way that it will help readers solve a problem. Avoid personal gripes, criticisms, alibis, attempts to blame other people, sugarcoated data, and unsolicited opinions.

To be useful, the information must be accurate, complete, and honest. But remember, being honest is not always a simple matter. Everyone sees reality a little differently, and individuals describe what they see in their own way. To restrict the distortions introduced by differences in perception, follow these guidelines:

- **Describe facts or events in concrete terms.** Indicate quantities whenever you can. Say that "Sales have increased 17 percent," or that "Sales have increased from $40 000 to $43 000 in the past two months." Don't say, "Sales have skyrocketed."
- **Report all relevant facts.** Regardless of whether these facts support your theories or please your readers, they must be included. Omitting the details that undermine your position may be convenient, but it is misleading and inaccurate.
- **Put the facts in perspective.** Taken out of context, the most concrete facts are misleading. If you say "Stock values have doubled in three weeks," you offer an incomplete picture. Instead, say "Stock values have doubled in three weeks, rising from $2 to $4 per share."
- **Give plenty of evidence for your conclusions.** Statements such as "We have to reorganize the sales force or we'll lose market share" may or may not be true. Readers have no way of knowing unless you provide enough data to support your claim.
- **Present only verifiable conclusions.** Check facts, and use reliable sources. Don't draw conclusions too quickly (one rep may say that customers are unhappy, but that doesn't mean they all are). And don't assume that one event caused another (sales may have dipped right after you switched ad agencies, but that doesn't mean the new agency is at fault—the general state of the economy may be responsible).
- **Keep your personal biases in check.** Even if you feel strongly about your topic, keep those feelings from influencing your choice of words. Don't say, "Locating a plant in Kingston is a terrible idea because the people there are mostly students who would rather play than work and who don't have the ability to operate our machines." Such language not only offends but also obscures the facts and provokes emotional responses.

Applications for Success

1. When would you use vague language instead of concrete detail? Would this action be unethical or merely one form of emphasizing the positive?
2. Recent budget cuts have endangered the daycare program at your local branch of a national company. You're writing a report for headquarters about the grave impact on employees. Describe the situation in a single sentence that reveals nothing about your personal feelings but that clearly shows your position.
3. When writing an unsolicited proposal to a potential client, you need to persuade your audience to consider hiring your firm or purchasing your product. How can you be persuasive and completely truthful at the same time?

Unit 4

COMPOSING BUSINESS REPORTS, PROPOSALS, AND PRESENTATIONS

12

Planning, Writing, and Delivering Oral Presentations

From the Real World

"When you speak before an audience, have some fun with it. Stop concentrating on 'Will they like me?' and instead focus on 'What will they gain from hearing me?' "
–Leanne Anderson
Owner, Anderson Business Resources

After studying this chapter, you will be able to

1. Explain how planning an oral presentation differs from planning a written document
2. Describe the five tasks that go into organizing oral presentations
3. List three challenges you must keep in mind while composing your presentation
4. Discuss four elements involved in creating effective slides
5. List 10 ways to overcome your anxiety and feel more confident
6. Discuss two factors in presenting visuals effectively
7. Discuss six guidelines for handling questions effectively

Leanne Anderson helps businesspeople become better public speakers by training them to focus on their audience's needs. She believes that knowing your audience is the most important element of a successful speech. She also advocates being a ruthless editor, because a good way to make your presentation stand out from others is to write a well-organized speech that is clear, concise, and focused. "Economy of language is the real key to good communication," she says. "That means choosing the best way of saying something to get the desired result."[1]

The Three-Step Oral Presentation Process

Like Leanne Anderson, chances are you'll have an opportunity to deliver a number of oral presentations throughout your career. You may not speak before large audiences of employees or the media, but you'll certainly be expected to present ideas to your colleagues, make sales presentations to potential customers, or engage in other kinds of spoken communication. For instance, if you're in the human resources department, you may give orientation briefings to new employees or explain company policies, procedures, and benefits at assemblies. If you're familiar with your department's procedures, you may conduct training programs. Regardless of your job or the purpose of your presentation, you will be more effective if you adopt an oral presentation process that follows three familiar steps (see Figure 12.1):

The process for preparing oral presentations has three familiar steps.

1. Plan your presentation.
2. Write your presentation.
3. Revise and rehearse your presentation.

FIGURE 12.1 The Three-Step Oral Presentation Process

Planning	Writing	Revising and Rehearsing
Analyze the Situation Study your purpose, lay out your schedule, and profile your audience.	**Organize the Message** Define your main idea, limit the scope, choose your approach, prepare your outline, and decide on a style.	**Revise the Message** Edit the presentation for content, conciseness, and clarity.
Investigate the Topic Gather needed information through formal or informal research methods.	**Compose the Message** Compose your presentation, ensuring that the introduction, body, close, and question-and-answer period all accomplish the necessary tasks for an oral medium.	**Edit the Message** Review visuals for typos; review speech for improper grammar.
Adapt to the Audience Adapt your presentation to the occasion and audience; then establish a good relationship with your audience.		**Prepare for Delivery** Practise your presentation, check the location, and overcome your anxiety.
1	2	3

Step 1: Planning Speeches and Presentations

Planning oral presentations is similar to planning any other business message: It requires analyzing your purpose and your audience, investigating and researching necessary information, and adapting your message to the occasion and your audience so that you can establish a good relationship. However, because presentations are delivered orally under relatively public circumstances, they require a few special communication techniques. For one thing, a presentation is a one-time event; your audience cannot leaf back through printed pages to review something you said earlier. So you must make sure that audience members will hear what you say and remember it. You must capture their attention immediately and keep them interested. Therefore, begin by defining your purpose clearly while thinking of ways to engage your audience.

Preparing oral presentations requires some special communication techniques to ensure your audience hears what you say.

Clarify Your Purpose

The four basic reasons for giving a presentation are to inform, to persuade, to motivate, and to entertain. The purpose of your oral presentation will govern the content you include and the style in which you present the content. Most of your presentations or speeches will be informative, requiring a straightforward statement of the facts. If you're involved in marketing or sales, however, you'll probably be writing and delivering persuasive presentations and speeches using the organizational and writing techniques discussed in Chapter 9. Motivational speeches tend to be more specialized, so many companies bring in outside professional speakers to handle this type of presentation. Entertainment speeches are perhaps the rarest in the business world; they are usually limited to after-dinner speeches and to speeches at conventions or retreats.

The content and style of speeches and presentations vary, depending on your purpose.

Analyze Your Audience

Whatever your purpose, your speech will be more effective if you keep your audience interested in your message. To do so, you must understand who your audience members are and what they need. If you're involved in selecting the audience or if you're speaking to a group of peers at work, you'll certainly have information about listener characteristics. But in many cases, you'll be speaking to a group of people you know very little about. You'll want to investigate their needs and characteristics before showing up to speak. Identify audience interests related to your topic. Research to find relevant facts and examples. You can also ask your host or some other contact person for

What you know about your audience affects your main idea, scope, approach, outline, and style.

help with audience analysis, and you can supplement that information with some educated estimates of your own. For a reminder of how to analyze an audience, review Chapter 3's "Develop an Audience Profile" and see Figure 12.2. For even more insight into audience evaluation (including emotional and cultural issues), consult a good public-speaking textbook.

Step 2: Writing Speeches and Presentations

You may never actually write out a presentation word for word. But that doesn't mean that developing its content will be any easier or quicker than preparing a written document. Speaking intelligently about a topic may actually involve more work and more time than preparing a written document about the same topic.

Organize Your Speech or Presentation

Organize an oral message just as you would organize a written message, by focusing on your audience as you define your main idea, limit your scope, choose your approach, prepare your outline, and decide on the most effective style for your presentation.

The tasks you perform when organizing oral messages are similar to those you perform for written messages.

- **Define the main idea.** What is the one message you want audience members to walk away with? The "you" attitude helps keep your audience's attention and convinces people that your points are relevant.
- **Limit your scope.** Tailor the material to the time allowed, which is often strictly regulated. Speakers can deliver about one paragraph (125 to 150 words) a minute (or between 20 and 25 double-spaced, typed pages per hour). To make three basic points in a 10-minute presentation, allow about 2 minutes (about two paragraphs) to explain each point, devote a minute each to the introduction and the conclusion, and leave 2 minutes for questions.
- **Choose your approach.** If you have 10 minutes or less to deliver your message, organize your presentation like a letter or a brief memo. Organize longer presentations like reports.

FIGURE 12.2 Audience Analysis Checklist

AUDIENCE ANALYSIS CHECKLIST

Determine Audience Size and Composition
- ✓ Estimate how many people will attend.
- ✓ Consider whether they have some political, religious, professional, or other affiliation in common.
- ✓ Analyze the mix of men and women, ages, socio-economic and ethnic groups, occupations, and geographic regions represented.

Predict the Audience's Probable Reaction
- ✓ Analyze why audience members are attending the presentation.
- ✓ Determine the audience's general attitude toward the topic: interested, moderately interested, open-minded, unconcerned, or hostile.
- ✓ Analyze the mood that people will be in when you speak to them.
- ✓ Find out what kind of backup information will most impress the audience: technical data, historical information, financial data, demonstrations, samples, and so on.
- ✓ Consider whether the audience has any biases that might work against you.
- ✓ Anticipate possible objections or questions.

Gauge the Audience's Level of Understanding
- ✓ Analyze whether everybody has the same background and experience.
- ✓ Determine what the audience already knows about the subject.
- ✓ Decide what background information the audience will need to better understand the subject.
- ✓ Consider whether the audience is familiar with your vocabulary.
- ✓ Analyze what the audience expects from you.
- ✓ Think about the mix of general concepts and specific details you will need to present.

FIGURE 12.3 Sample Outline for a 30-Minute Presentation

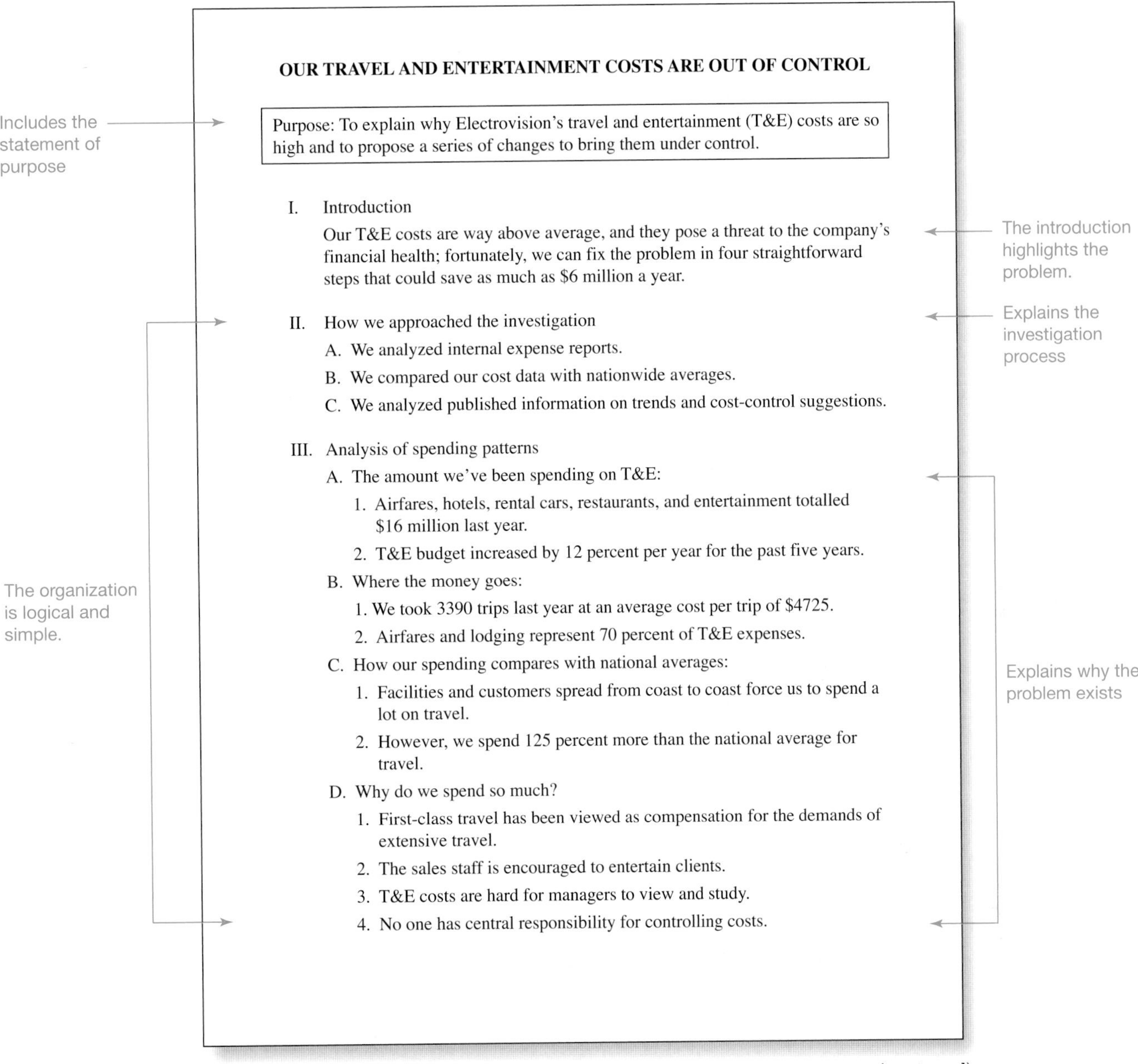

OUR TRAVEL AND ENTERTAINMENT COSTS ARE OUT OF CONTROL

Purpose: To explain why Electrovision's travel and entertainment (T&E) costs are so high and to propose a series of changes to bring them under control.

I. Introduction

Our T&E costs are way above average, and they pose a threat to the company's financial health; fortunately, we can fix the problem in four straightforward steps that could save as much as $6 million a year.

II. How we approached the investigation

A. We analyzed internal expense reports.

B. We compared our cost data with nationwide averages.

C. We analyzed published information on trends and cost-control suggestions.

III. Analysis of spending patterns

A. The amount we've been spending on T&E:

1. Airfares, hotels, rental cars, restaurants, and entertainment totalled $16 million last year.

2. T&E budget increased by 12 percent per year for the past five years.

B. Where the money goes:

1. We took 3390 trips last year at an average cost per trip of $4725.

2. Airfares and lodging represent 70 percent of T&E expenses.

C. How our spending compares with national averages:

1. Facilities and customers spread from coast to coast force us to spend a lot on travel.

2. However, we spend 125 percent more than the national average for travel.

D. Why do we spend so much?

1. First-class travel has been viewed as compensation for the demands of extensive travel.

2. The sales staff is encouraged to entertain clients.

3. T&E costs are hard for managers to view and study.

4. No one has central responsibility for controlling costs.

Includes the statement of purpose
The introduction highlights the problem.
Explains the investigation process
The organization is logical and simple.
Explains why the problem exists

(continued)

Regardless of length, use direct order if the audience is receptive and indirect if you expect resistance. Simplicity of organization is especially valuable in oral presentations, since listeners can't review a paragraph or flip pages back and forth, as they can when reading.

- **Prepare your outline.** Your outline helps you keep your presentation both audience centred and within the allotted time. Figure 12.3 is the outline for a 30-minute analytical presentation based on Linda Moreno's Electrovision report (see Chapter 11). It is organized around conclusions and presented in direct order. If you plan to give your presentation from notes rather than from written text, your outline can also become your final "script."
- **Decide on an appropriate style.** Choose your style to fit the occasion, audience size, subject, purpose, budget, location, and preparation time. When speaking to a small group in a conference room, encourage participation with a casual style. For a large audience at an important event, establish a more formal atmosphere: perhaps speaking from a stage or platform, standing behind a lectern, and using a microphone.

FIGURE 12.3 (Continued)

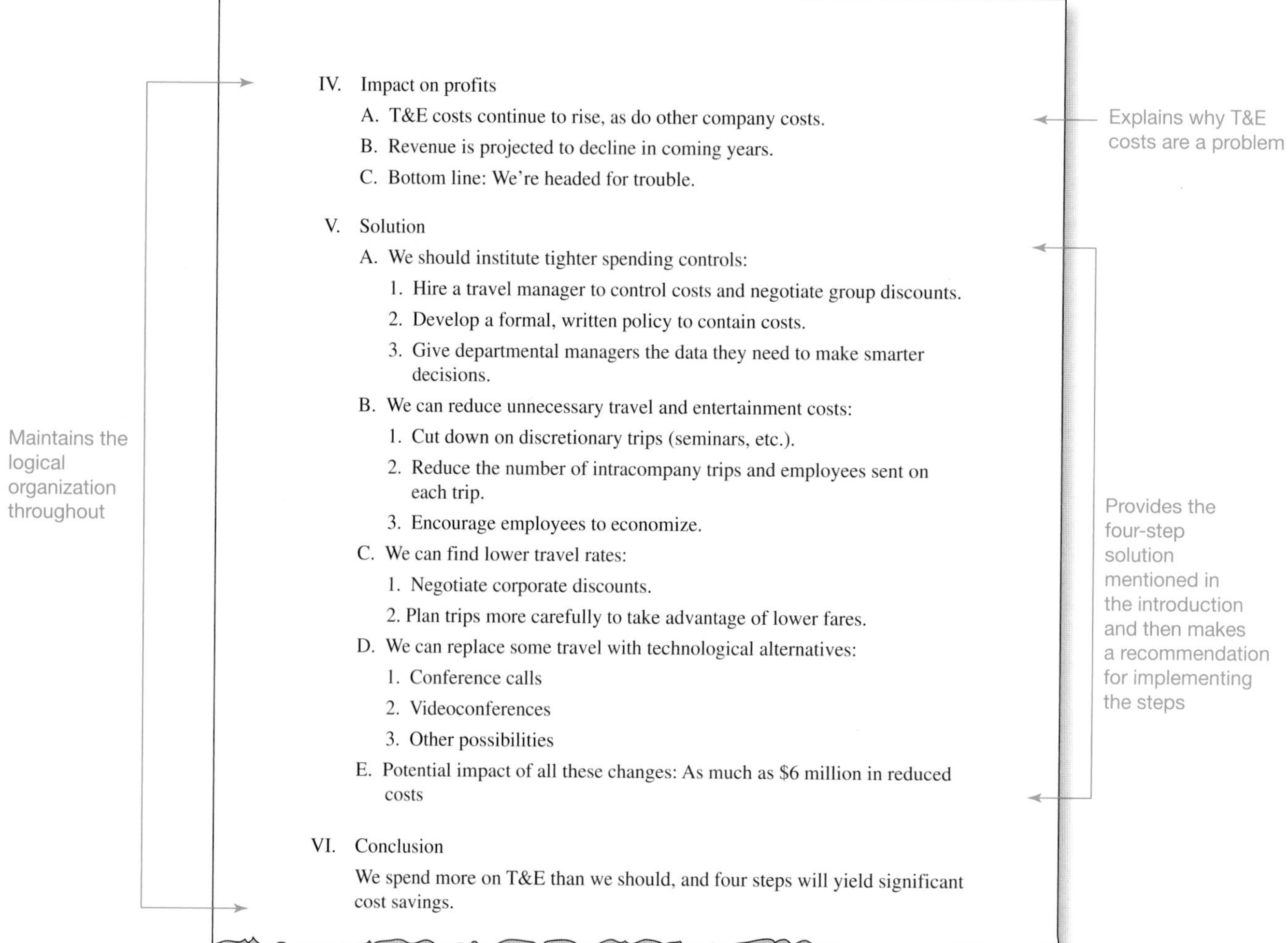
IV. Impact on profits
A. T&E costs continue to rise, as do other company costs.
B. Revenue is projected to decline in coming years.
C. Bottom line: We're headed for trouble.
V. Solution
A. We should institute tighter spending controls:
1. Hire a travel manager to control costs and negotiate group discounts.
2. Develop a formal, written policy to contain costs.
3. Give departmental managers the data they need to make smarter decisions.
B. We can reduce unnecessary travel and entertainment costs:
1. Cut down on discretionary trips (seminars, etc.).
2. Reduce the number of intracompany trips and employees sent on each trip.
3. Encourage employees to economize.
C. We can find lower travel rates:
1. Negotiate corporate discounts.
2. Plan trips more carefully to take advantage of lower fares.
D. We can replace some travel with technological alternatives:
1. Conference calls
2. Videoconferences
3. Other possibilities
E. Potential impact of all these changes: As much as $6 million in reduced costs
VI. Conclusion
We spend more on T&E than we should, and four steps will yield significant cost savings.
Explains why T&E costs are a problem
Maintains the logical organization throughout
Provides the four-step solution mentioned in the introduction and then makes a recommendation for implementing the steps

Compose Your Speech or Presentation

Formal presentations offer opportunities that written reports do not.

Developing a major presentation is much like writing a formal report, except that you need to adjust your technique to an oral channel. Speaking before a group offers certain opportunities:

- **Immediate audience feedback.** You can transmit information, but you can also receive audience feedback without delay.
- **Immediate modification to suit audience needs.** You can adjust both the content and the delivery of your message as you go along, in order to clarify or to be more compelling. Instead of simply expressing your ideas, you can draw ideas from your audience and then reach a mutually acceptable conclusion.
- **Nonverbal reinforcement.** You also have the opportunity to use nonverbal cues to express your meaning and emphasize what's important.

Oral presentations offer challenges that written reports do not.

Using an oral communication channel presents you with challenges you need not face in written reports. As you compose each part of your presentation, think about how you will face each challenge:

- **Maintaining control.** The more you expect to interact with your audience, the less control you'll have of the situation.

- **Helping your audience follow what you're saying.** Since listeners cannot refer back and forth to what has been or will be said, you must work harder to clarify where you're going and help them stay on track.
- **Shifting topics smoothly.** Halfway through your presentation, a comment from someone in the audience might force you to shift topics. If you anticipate such shifts, you can prepare for them as you compose your presentation.

As you develop your speech, think carefully about how to handle each part: introduction, body, and close.

Introduction

A good introduction arouses the audience's interest in your topic, establishes your credibility, and prepares the audience for what will follow. That's a lot to pack into the first few minutes of your presentation. So, of the total time you allocate to writing your oral presentation, plan on spending a disproportionate amount on developing your introduction. In the introduction, you want to

The introduction must capture attention, inspire confidence, and preview the contents.

- **Arouse audience interest.** Get a good start by capturing the audience's attention (several methods are listed in Table 12.1). If you are presenting to a small group, you can involve the audience by encouraging comments from listeners. However, when speaking to a large group, responding to comments can interrupt the flow of information, weaken your argument, and reduce your control of the situation. In that case, it's often best to ask people to hold questions until you're finished—be sure to allow ample time after your remarks.
- **Build your credibility.** Establish your credentials quickly—people will decide about you within a few minutes.[2] Building credibility is easy for a familiar, open-minded audience. For strangers (especially sceptical ones), try letting someone else introduce you. If introducing yourself, keep your comments simple, and don't be afraid to mention your accomplishments:

Mention your credentials to establish credibility.

> I'm Karen Whitney. I've worked in the telemarketing department for the past five years, specializing in small-business markets. Vice-President John Barre asked me to talk to you about our telemarketing methods so that you'll have a better idea of how to get started.

Table 12.1 Five Ways to Get Attention and Keep It

Use humour	Even though the subject of most business presentations is serious, including a light comment now and then can perk up the audience. Just be sure the humour is relevant to the presentation and not offensive to the audience.
Tell a story	Slice-of-life stories are naturally interesting and can be compelling. Be sure your story illustrates an important point.
Pass around a sample	Psychologists say that you can get people to remember your points by appealing to their senses. The best way to do so is to pass around a sample. If your company is in the textile business, let the audience handle some of your fabrics. If you sell chocolates, give everybody a taste.
Ask a question	Asking questions will get the audience actively involved in your presentation and, at the same time, will give you information about them and their needs.
State a startling statistic	People love details. If you can interject an interesting statistic, you can often wake up your audience.

Get attention with specific examples, anecdotes, and audience involvement.

- **Preview your presentation.** Help your audience understand the structure and contents of your message. Give them cues to figure out how the main points of the message fit together. Summarize the main idea, identify the supporting points, and indicate the order in which you'll develop them. Establish the framework so that your audience will understand how the facts and figures are related to your main idea as you move into the body of your presentation.

Body

Simplify the body by covering no more than three or four main points.

The bulk of your speech or presentation is devoted to a discussion of the three or four main points in your outline. Use the same organizational patterns you would use in a letter, memo, or report, but keep things simple—limit the body to three or four main points. Make sure that your organization is clear and that your presentation holds the audience's attention.

Connecting Your Ideas To show how ideas are related, a written report uses typographical and formatting clues: headings, paragraph indentions, white space, and lists. However, an oral presentation must rely on words to link various parts and ideas.

Help your audience follow your presentation by using clear transitions between sentences and paragraphs, as well as between major sections.

For the small links between sentences and paragraphs, use one or two transitional words: *therefore, because, in addition, in contrast, moreover, for example, consequently, nevertheless,* or *finally.* To link major sections of a presentation, use complete sentences or paragraphs, such as "Now that we've reviewed the problem, let's take a look at some solutions." Every time you shift topics, be sure to stress the connection between ideas. Summarize what's been said, then preview what's to come.

Emphasize your transitions by repeating key ideas, using gestures, changing your tone of voice, or introducing a visual aid.

The longer your presentation, the more important your transitions become. If you will be presenting many ideas, audience members may have trouble absorbing them and seeing the relationships among them. Your listeners need clear transitions to guide them to the most important points. Furthermore, they need transitions to pick up any ideas they may have missed. So by repeating key ideas in your transitions, you can compensate for lapses in your audience's attention. When you actually give your presentation, you might also want to call attention to the transitions by using gestures, moving to a new position, changing your tone of voice, or introducing a visual aid (discussed later in this chapter).

Make a special effort to capture wandering attention.

Holding Your Audience's Attention To communicate your points effectively, you must do more than connect your ideas with clear transitions. You also have to hold your audience's attention. Here are a few helpful tips for engaging an audience:

- **Relate your subject to your audience's needs.** People are interested in things that affect them personally. Present every point in light of your audience's needs and values.
- **Anticipate your audience's questions.** Try to anticipate as many questions as you can, and address these questions in the body of your presentation. You'll also want to prepare and reserve additional material to use during the question-and-answer period should the audience ask for greater detail.
- **Use clear, vivid language.** People become bored when they don't understand the speaker. If your presentation will involve abstract ideas, plan to show how those abstractions connect with everyday life. Use familiar words, short sentences, and concrete examples.
- **Explain the relationship between your subject and familiar ideas.** Show how your subject is related to ideas that audience members already understand, so that you give people a way to categorize and remember your points.[3]
- **Ask opinions or pause occasionally for questions or comments.** Getting audience feedback helps you determine whether your listeners have understood a key point. Feedback also gives your audience a change from listening to participating. Plan your pauses, even noting them in your outline so that you won't forget to pause once you're on stage.

Close

The close of a speech or presentation is almost as important as the beginning because audience attention peaks at this point. Plan to devote writing time to the ending. When developing your conclusion, begin by telling listeners that you're about to finish, so that they'll make one final effort to listen intently. Don't be afraid to sound obvious. Consider saying something such as "in conclusion" or "to sum it all up." You want people to know that this is the home stretch.

The close should leave a strong and lasting impression.

- **Restating your main points.** Repeat your main idea in the close. Emphasize what you want your audience to do or think, state the key motivating factor, and restate the three or four main supporting points. A few sentences are enough to refresh people's memories. One speaker ended a presentation by repeating his four specific recommendations and concluding with a memorable statement to motivate his audience:

  We can all be proud of the way our company has grown. If we want to continue that growth, however, we will have to adjust our managers' compensation program to reflect competitive practices. If we don't, our best people will look for opportunities elsewhere.

  In summary, our survey has shown that we need to do four things to improve executive compensation:

  - Increase the overall level of compensation
  - Install a cash bonus program
  - Offer a variety of stock-based incentives
  - Improve our health insurance and pension benefits

  By making these improvements, we can help our company grow to compete on a global scale.

- **Describing the next steps.** If you expect listeners to take action, explain who is responsible for doing what. (You might present a slide listing each item with a completion date and the name of persons responsible.) Alert people to potential difficulties or pitfalls.
- **Ending on a strong note.** Make your final remarks encouraging and memorable. Conclude with a quote, a call to action, or some encouraging words. You might stress the benefits of action, express confidence in the listeners' ability to accomplish the work ahead, or end with a question or statement that leaves people thinking. Your final words give the audience a satisfied feeling of completeness. Don't introduce new ideas or alter the mood of the speech.

Step 3: Revising and Rehearsing Speeches and Presentations

To complete your oral presentation, evaluate the content of your message and edit your remarks for clarity and conciseness—as you would for any business message. Develop any visual aids for your presentation, and coordinate them with your delivery. Finally, master the art of delivery through practice and preparation, by building your confidence, and by polishing the way you present visuals and handle questions.

Using Visual Aids in Your Speech or Presentation

Visual aids can improve the quality and impact of your oral presentation by creating interest, illustrating points that are difficult to explain in words alone, adding variety, and increasing the audience's ability to absorb and remember information. Visual aids help

Visual aids help the audience remember important points.

your audience; they are estimated to improve learning by 400 percent, because humans can process visuals 60 000 times faster than text.[4] Visual aids also help you as speaker; they help you remember the details of your message (no small feat in a lengthy presentation), and they improve your professional image (speakers who use visuals generally appear better prepared and more knowledgeable than other speakers).

Selecting the Right Type of Visual

To enhance oral presentations, you can choose from a variety of visual aids. Among the most popular types are:

When preparing visual aids for oral presentations, you have a variety of media to choose from.

- **Overhead transparency.** This piece of clear plastic contains text or a graphic. You show a transparency by placing it on the lit window of an overhead projector, which casts the image onto a large screen. You can create transparencies by hand, but you're more likely to use word-processing, page-layout, or presentation software. We sometimes refer to transparencies as slides because their content and design elements are so similar to electronic slides.
- **Electronic presentation.** This slide show is a series of electronic slides created and stored on computer. Using software such as Microsoft PowerPoint, Lotus Freelance Graphics, or Corel Draw!, you can incorporate text, photos, sound, video, graphics, and animation into your slides. You show these slides on a personal computer monitor, a special projector that puts the image of a computer monitor onto a large screen, or a liquid crystal display (LCD) projector.[5]
- **Chalkboard or whiteboard.** These writing surfaces are effective tools for recording points made during small-group brainstorming sessions. Because these visual aids are produced on the spot, they offer flexibility; however, they're too informal for some situations.
- **Flip chart.** These large sheets of paper are attached at the top like a tablet and can be propped on an easel so that you can flip the pages as you speak. With felt-tip markers, you can also record ideas generated during a discussion.
- **Other visual aids.** Product or material samples help your audience experience your subject directly. Scale models represent objects conveniently. Slide presentations, television, and videotapes show demonstrations, interviews, and other events. Also, slides, movies, TV, and videos can stand alone (without a speaker) to communicate with dispersed audiences at various times.

Overhead transparencies and electronic presentations both consist of a series of slides.

The two most popular visual aids are overhead transparencies and electronic presentations. Even though these two visual aids differ in some features and delivery, both are a collection of slides that must be well written and well designed to be effective. Once the slides are created, they are either printed on clear plastic sheets (for overhead transparencies) or stored electronically and further embellished with multimedia effects (for electronic presentations). Both overhead transparencies and electronic slides have advantages and disadvantages, as Table 12.2 points out.

Limiting the Number of Visuals

Even if you produce an outstanding set of slides, they'll do you no good if you can't complete your presentation in the allotted time. Having too many visuals can detract from your message. It forces you either to rush through a presentation or to skip visuals—some of which may be critical to your message.

Covering less information in a relaxed style is much better than covering too much information in a hurried and disorganized manner. Build enough time into your presentation for a smile, an anecdote, or further illustration of a point. Remember that audiences won't be angry if you let them out early, but they might be upset if you keep them late.

Limit the number of slides to a few good ones.

Gauging the correct number of visuals depends on the length of your presentation and the complexity of the subject matter. If you are using electronic slides, try to average one slide for every 90 seconds you speak. For a 30-minute presentation, you would create

Table 12.2 Advantages and Disadvantages of Overhead and Electronic Slides

Advantages of Overhead Transparencies	*Advantages of Electronic Slides*
• Inexpensive and easy to create. You can prepare high-quality overheads using a computer and a high-resolution colour inkjet or laser printer. • Simple to use. They require little extra equipment to show: Most conference rooms or classrooms have overhead projectors. • Can be projected in full daylight. Speakers can maintain eye contact with their listeners. • Can be altered during presentation. Speakers can use special markers to write on transparencies as they present information.	• Easy to change in real time. You can change a graphic, add a bulleted phrase, even alter slide sequence with a simple click of the mouse. • Make dazzling professional presentations. You can add animation, video clips, sound, hypertext, and other multimedia effects, as well as preprogram and automate the release of text and graphic elements. • Easy to store, transport, and customize for different audiences. • Allow you to feature one text point at a time.
Disadvantages	***Disadvantages***
• Must be replaced if content changes. • Must be manually renumbered to add or remove a slide from the sequence. • Fragile. They easily chip, flake, scratch, and tear. Protective frames of cardboard or plastic and transparent sleeves are costly and bulky to store and transport. • Must be aligned carefully (one at a time) on the overhead projector, limiting the speaker's ability to move freely about the room.	• Display equipment is expensive, can be complicated to use, and may not be available in all situations. • Most people spend too much time focusing on the technical components of a presentation, paying more attention to the animation and special effects than to the audience. • Inexperienced presenters tend to use too many special effects, creating a visual overload of pictures and graphics that dazzle or hypnotize the audience but blur the key message.

about 20 slides.[6] Of course, you may spend more time discussing some slides than others, so the best way to find the "right" number is to time your presentation as you practise.

Creating Effective Slides

Once you've planned out what a slide is going to say, organize the content as you would for any written message. Then compose and polish the written content before focusing on the slide's design elements.

Slides are most effective when they are simple and are used sparingly.

Simplicity is the key to effective design. Since people cannot read and listen effectively at the same time, your slides must be simple enough for the audience to understand in a moment or two. Use phrases only. Sentences and paragraphs require prolonged reading. Keep content and graphics simple and readable, select design elements that enhance your message without overshadowing it, be consistent in your design selections, and use special effects selectively.

Colour can increase the appeal and impact of your slides.

Choosing Colour Colour is a critical design element. It grabs the viewer's attention, emphasizes important ideas, creates contrast, and isolates slide elements. Colour can make your slides more attractive, lively, and professional (see Table 12.3 on page 334). Indeed, colour visuals can account for 60 percent of an audience's acceptance or rejection of an idea.[7] When choosing colour, remember these important guidelines:

- **Use colour to stimulate the right emotions.** If you wish to excite your audience, add some warm colours such as red and orange to your slides. If you wish to achieve a more relaxed and receptive environment, stick to blue.[8]

Table 12.3 Colour and Emotion

Colour	Emotional Associations	Best Use
	Peaceful, soothing, tranquil, cool, trusting	Background for electronic business presentations (usually dark blue); safe and conservative
	Neutral, innocent, pure, wise	Font colour of choice for most electronic business presentations with a dark background
	Warm, bright, cheerful, enthusiastic	Text bullets and subheadings with a dark background
	Losses in business, passion, danger, action, pain	Promote action or stimulate audience; seldom used as a background
	Money, growth, assertiveness, prosperity, envy, relaxation	Highlight and accent colour

- **Be sensitive to cultural differences.** When creating slides for international audiences, remember that colour may have a different meaning from culture to culture.
- **Limit colour selections to a few complementary ones.** Avoid using too many colours in your slides. Also, remember that some colours work together better than others.
- **Use contrasting colours to increase readability.** For backgrounds, titles, and text, avoid choosing colours that are close in hue: yellow text on a white background, brown on green, blue on black, blue on purple, and so on.[9]
- **Adjust colour choices to room light.** Since most electronic presentations are shown in a dark room, use dark colours such as blue for the background, a midrange of brightness for illustrations, and light colours for text. If you are showing overhead transparencies in well-lit rooms, reverse the colours: Use light colours for the background and dark colours for text.[10]

Choosing Background Designs A slide's background can silently persuade viewers to pay attention or encourage them to look the other way. Many companies hire professional graphic artists to develop a custom background design to be used in all company slides. These custom designs generally include a company logo and company colours.

If you're not using a company design, you have several options. Popular software programs such as Microsoft's PowerPoint come with a collection of professionally developed background designs. Some designs are effective for business presentations; others are too busy or too colourful to be used in business settings. You can also purchase collections of slide backgrounds over the Internet, obtain them from other software packages, or create your own.

Select a background design that fits with your message and your audience.

Regardless of your source, be careful when choosing slide backgrounds. Avoid backgrounds whose heavy colour, busy patterns, or strong graphics compete with your text. Choose a design that is simple, is appropriate for the presentation subject, and will appeal to the audience. Make sure that graphic elements such as borders and company logos repeat on every visual. Such consistency not only makes your slides easier to read but also gives your presentation a clean, professional look. Another way to achieve design consistency is to use the layout templates that are included with most presentation software packages. As Figure 12.4 shows, each layout contains placeholders for specific slide elements such as a title, graphic art, or bulleted text.

Layout templates are easy to use.

Use a strong, simple font.

Choosing Fonts and Type Styles Most software programs offer an immense selection of fonts. However, even though decorative fonts appear attractive, few of them project well on screen.

FIGURE 12.4 PowerPoint's Predefined Layouts

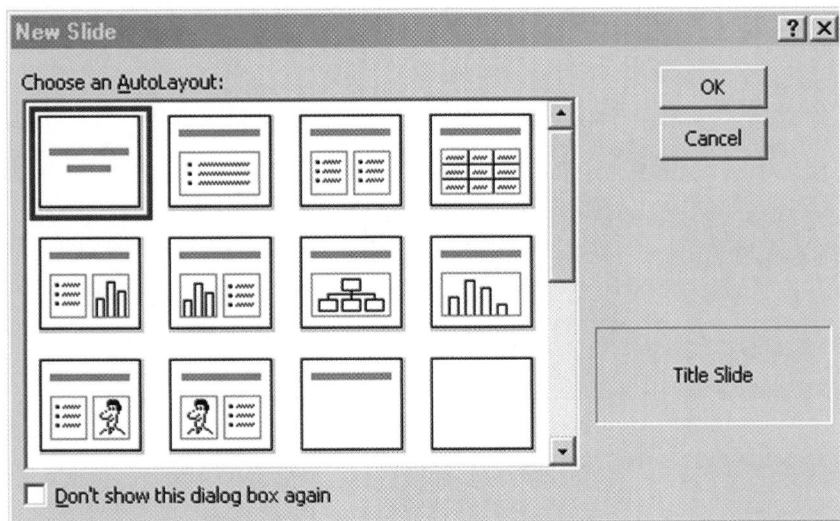

When designing a new slide for a presentation, beginning with one of PowerPoint's preformatted layouts can save you time and improve the consistency of your presentation.

When selecting fonts and type styles for slides, follow these guidelines:

- Avoid script or decorative fonts.
- Limit your fonts to one or two per slide (if two fonts are used, reserve one for headings and the other for bulleted items).
- Use boldface type for electronic slides so that letters won't look washed out.
- Avoid italicized type because it is difficult to read when projected.
- Use both upper case and lower case letters, with extra white space between lines of text.

Bigger is not always better when it comes to type size. Large type can force text from one line to two and diminish the slide's white space. Use between 24- and 36-point type for electronic presentations, reserving the larger size for titles and the smaller size for bullet items. Headings of the same level of importance should use the same font, type size, and colour. Once you've selected your fonts and type styles, test them for readability by viewing sample slides from a distance.

Test your font and typeface selections by viewing slides from the back of a room.

Adding Animation and Special Effects Unlike transparencies, electronic slide shows can include a number of special effects, such as sound, animation, and video. You can even automate your program to move from one slide to the next without the speaker's intervention. The biggest challenge to overcome is the tendency to use too many of these features, which can include

Don't overdo special effects.

- **Transitions.** The way that one electronic slide replaces another on screen is called a *transition.* Effective transitions can make your presentation flow smoothly from slide to slide so that you keep your audience's attention. Most electronic software packages include a number of effective transition effects, such as blind, box, checkerboard, dissolve, wipe, fade, paintbrush, and split. Use the same transitions throughout your presentation.
- **Builds.** The way that text and graphics are released for viewing is called a *build.* You can make your bullet points appear one at a time, line by line, to draw audience attention to the point being discussed. The most basic build effects are flys (making an element appear to fly in) and dissolves (altering the intensity of an element's colour as you discuss it while fading the other colours into the background). Use the same builds throughout your presentation.

FIGURE 12.5 Slide Sorter View

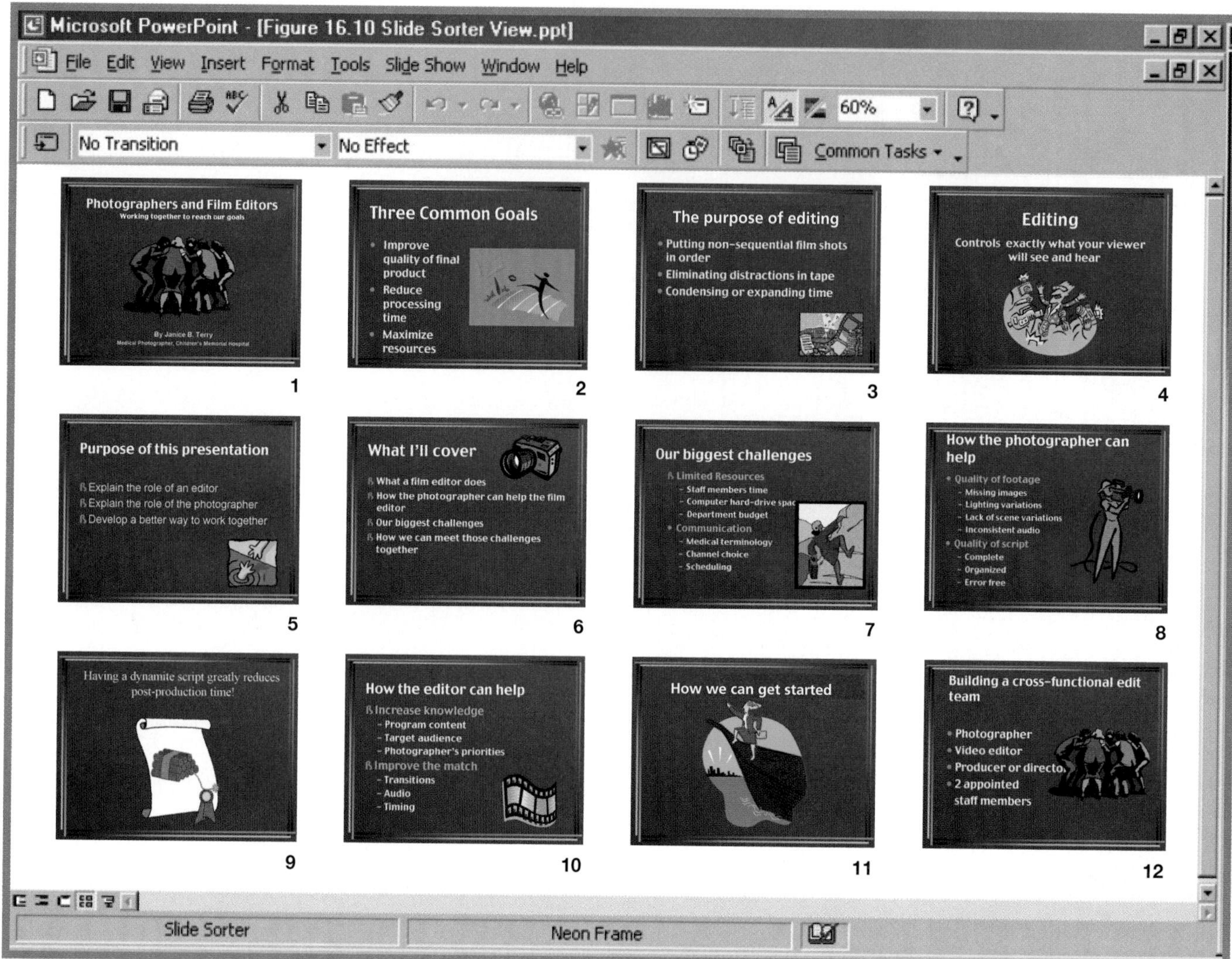

Examining thumbnails of slides on one screen is the best way to check the overall design of your final product. Note how each slide in this group looks uncluttered (not overburdened with text) and uses consistent colours and design elements.

- **Hyperlinks.** By coding text, graphics, or pictures with hypertext markup language, you can build interactivity into electronic slides. When you click on a slide's hyperlink with a mouse, you are taken to a different slide in your presentation, to other files on your computer, or even to a Web page on the Internet. Hyperlinks are a great tool for illustrating fine details without having to incorporate each detail into a slide.

Slide sorter view makes it easier to check your slides for consistency and logical organization.

Electronic presentation software can help you plan, write, and revise your slides. As Figure 12.5 shows, the *slide sorter view* lets you see a file's entire batch of slides at once, making it relatively easy to add and delete slides, reposition slides, and check slides for design consistency. You can also use this view to preview animation and transition effects and experiment with design elements.

Creating Effective Handouts

Good handouts keep the audience informed without overwhelming them with information.

Handouts are a terrific way to offer your audience additional material without overloading your slides with information. Candidates for good handout material include the following.[11]

- **Complex charts and diagrams.** Charts and tables that are too unwieldy for the screen or that demand thorough analysis make good handouts. One common approach is to create a stripped-down version of a chart or graphic for the presentation slide and include a more detailed version in your handout.
- **Report parts.** In most cases lengthy research reports promise information overload and are inappropriate for handouts. But photocopies of specific pages that highlight or underline relevant text are welcome material.

Use handouts to provide detail. If you use magazine articles, seek permission to avoid copyright infractions.

- **Web sites.** Lists of Web sites related to your topic are useful. In addition to providing the URL address, annotate each item with a one- or two-sentence summary of each site's content.
- **Copies of presentation slides.** In many cases, audiences like to have small print versions of the slides used by the speaker (about three to a page) along with accompanying comments and blank lines for note-taking.

Other good handout materials include brochures, pictures, outlines, and a copy of the presentation agenda.

Timing the distribution of handouts is a difficult decision. You must base that decision on the content of your handouts, the nature of your presentation, and whether you plan to use the material during the talk. Some speakers distribute handout materials before the presentation; other speakers advise the audience of the types of handouts but delay distributing anything until they have finished speaking.

Manage handouts carefully to avoid distractions.

To help you decide when to distribute handouts, how many visuals to include, or how to coordinate your slides with what you have to say, you'll need to practise delivering your speech.

Mastering the Art of Delivery

Giving a speech is quite different from preparing one. Once you've planned and written your presentation and developed your visuals, you're ready to begin practising your delivery. You have a variety of delivery methods to choose from, some of which are easier to handle than others:

- **Speaking from notes.** Making a presentation with the help of an outline, note cards, or visual aids is probably the most effective and easiest delivery mode. This approach gives you something to refer to and still allows for eye contact and interaction with the audience. If your listeners look puzzled, you can expand on a point or rephrase it. (Generally, note cards are preferable to sheets of paper, because nervousness is easier to see in shaking sheets of paper.)

Speaking from notes is generally the best way to handle delivery.

- **Memorizing.** Unless you're a trained actor, avoid memorizing your speech, especially a long one. You're likely to forget your lines, and your speech will sound stilted. Besides, you'll often need to address audience questions during your speech, so you must be flexible enough to adjust your speech as you go. However, memorizing a quotation, an opening paragraph, or a few concluding remarks can bolster your confidence and strengthen your delivery.

Avoid both memorized and recited delivery and avoid reading.

- **Reading.** If you're delivering a technical or complex presentation, you may need to read parts of it. Policy statements by government officials are sometimes read because the wording may be critical. If you choose to read your speech, practise enough so that you can still maintain eye contact with your audience. Triple-spaced copy, wide margins, and large type will help. You might even want to include stage cues, such as *pause, raise hands, lower voice.* However, in most business presentations you will be more effective if you do not read. You'll want to connect with the audience.
- **Impromptu speaking.** You might have to give an impromptu, or unrehearsed, speech if you're called on to speak unexpectedly or if you've agreed to speak but neglected to prepare your remarks. Avoid speaking unprepared unless you've spoken countless times on the same topic or are an extremely good public speaker. When you're asked to speak "off the cuff," take a moment to think through what you'll say. Then avoid the temptation to ramble.

Prepare to Speak

Before you speak
- Practise
- Prepare the location
- Consider cultural differences

Regardless of which delivery mode you use, be sure that you're thoroughly familiar with your subject. Knowing what you're talking about is the best way to build your self-confidence. Also, practising helps keep you on track, helps you maintain a conversational tone with your audience, and boosts your confidence and composure. Practise in front of a mirror. If possible, rehearse on videotape to see yourself as your audience will. Practise in front of people.

In addition to knowing your material and practising your delivery, check the room and seating arrangements to ensure that they're appropriate for your needs. Check the outlets, projection equipment, pointer, extension cords, and any other small but crucial items you might need.

Also, make sure you're prepared to address audiences from other cultures. You may need to adapt the content of your presentation or the way you deliver it.

Overcome Anxiety and Stage Fright

If you're nervous about facing an audience and experience stage fright, you're not alone. Even speakers with years of experience feel some anxiety about getting up in front of an audience. Although you might not be able to make your nervous feelings disappear, you can learn to cope with your anxiety.

Feeling More Confident Nervousness shows that you care about your audience, your topic, and the occasion. If your palms get wet or your mouth goes dry, don't think of nerves, think of excitement. Such stimulation can give you the extra energy you need to make your presentation sparkle. Here are some ways to become a more confident speaker:[12]

Several techniques can help you become a more confident speaker.

- **Prepare more material than necessary.** Combined with a genuine interest in your topic, extra knowledge will reduce your anxiety.
- **Rehearse.** The more familiar you are with your material, the less panic you'll feel.
- **Think positively.** See yourself as polished and professional, and your audience will too.
- **Visualize your success.** Use the few minutes before you actually begin speaking to tell yourself you're on and you're ready.
- **Take a few deep breaths.** Before you begin to speak, remember that your audience is silently wishing you success.
- **Be ready.** Have your first sentence memorized and on the tip of your tongue.
- **Be comfortable.** If your throat is dry, drink some water.
- **Don't panic.** If you feel that you're losing your audience during your speech, try to pull them back by involving them in the action; ask for their opinions or pause for questions.
- **Keep going.** Things usually get better as you go.
- **Focus on your message and audience.** Perhaps the best way to feel more confident is to focus outside yourself. If you're busy thinking about your subject and observing your audience's response, you'll tend to forget your fears.

Appearing More Confident As you practise delivering your presentation, try to be aware of the nonverbal signals you're transmitting. Regardless of how you feel inside, your effectiveness greatly depends on how you look and sound.

Don't rush the opening.

Well-delivered presentations start with your first minute at the podium, so don't rush. As you approach the speaker's lectern, walk slowly, breathe deeply, and stand up straight. Face your audience, adjust the microphone, count to three slowly, and then survey the room. When you find a friendly face, make eye contact and smile. Count to three again and begin your presentation.[13] If you are nervous, this slow, controlled beginning will help you establish rapport and appear more confident.

Use eye contact, posture, gestures, and voice to convey an aura of mastery and to keep your audience's attention.

Be particularly careful to practise maintaining eye contact with your audience. Pick out several people positioned around the room, and shift your gaze from one to another. Looking directly at your listeners will make you appear sincere, confident, and trustworthy. It also helps you get an idea of the impression you're creating.

Your posture is also important in projecting more confidence. Stand tall, with your weight on both feet and your shoulders back. Avoid gripping the lectern. In fact, practise stepping out from behind the lectern to help your audience feel more comfortable with you and to express your own comfort and confidence in what you're saying. Use your hands to emphasize your remarks with appropriate gestures. Meanwhile, vary your facial expressions to make the message more dynamic.

Finally, think about the sound of your voice. Studies indicate that people who speak with lower vocal tones at a slightly faster than average rate are perceived as being more credible.[14] Practise speaking in a normal, conversational tone but with enough volume for everyone to hear you. Try to sound poised and confident, varying your pitch and speaking rate to add emphasis. Don't ramble. Use silence instead of meaningless filler words such as *um, you know, okay,* and *like.* Silence adds dramatic punch and gives the audience time to think about the message. Remember, speak clearly and crisply, articulating all the syllables, and sound enthusiastic about what you're saying.

Present Visuals Effectively

When practising your presentation, run through it about five times using your visuals. Your credibility is dramatically enhanced when you move seamlessly through your presentation.

Speaking Without Reading The most common mistake people make when delivering a presentation is reading their slides. When using PowerPoint, touch the "B" key to black out the screen so you can connect directly with your listeners. When you read to audience members, you lose contact with them. As your voice loses its inflection, listeners lose interest and eventually stop paying attention. Plus, listeners expect you to add valuable information not included on the slides. You must know enough about the subject of your presentation to elaborate on your visuals, so do your research.

Don't read your slides to the audience.

As you practise, try not to be dependent on your slides. Some people can deliver a perfect presentation without notes. But for those who require notes, electronic software gives you an added advantage. Speaker's notes (as shown in Figure 12.6) are a helpful tool included with most popular electronic presentation software packages. You can display these notes along with a scaled-down version of your slide on a computer screen so that only you can see the notes. As with visuals, don't read your speaker's notes aloud word for word. Instead, use them to list important facts or to remind yourself of comments you should make as you present the slide. For instance, you might include a note such as "Explain the impact of last year's bad weather on sales."

Use speaker's notes to jog your memory.

Introducing Visuals All visual aids must be properly introduced. Too many speakers show a visual first and then introduce it. Introduce the next visual aid *before* you show it. State your transition out loud:

Introduce your slides before you show them.

"We can get started with this new program by introducing these policies . . . "

"The next segment of my presentation discusses . . . "

"The three most significant issues facing our company are . . . "

Also avoid referring to a slide in your transitional comments. For instance, don't say "The next slide illustrates . . . " Instead, match your words to the slide and let the audience make the proper connection.

If you're using overhead transparencies, introduce the next overhead as you remove the old one and position the new one on the projector. Immediately cover all but the first bulleted phrase with a sheet of paper to prevent the audience from reading ahead. Then step aside to give the audience about five seconds to look it over before you start discussing it. As you advance through your discussion, you can move the paper down the transparency to uncover the next bullet, or use a pointer. When you are finished using the transparency, cover it until you're ready to introduce a new slide. Keep in mind that placing overhead transparencies on a projector takes a bit more time than clicking a mouse. The audience will probably have little interest in reading the old transparency once your comments move forward.[15]

Practise placing overhead transparencies on a projector so it becomes second nature.

FIGURE 12.6 Speaker's Notes

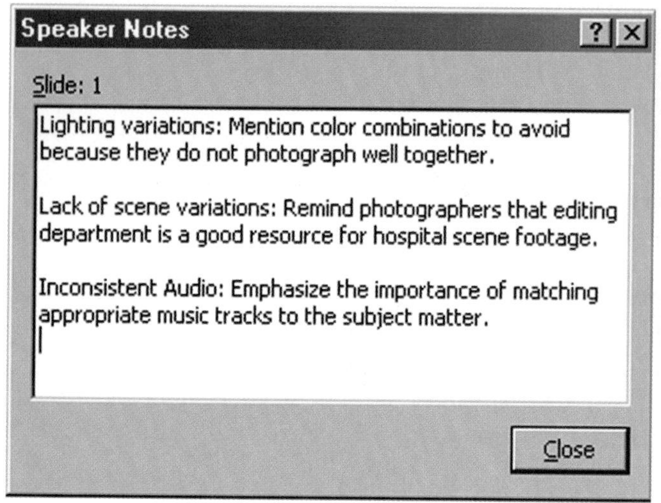

Figure 12.6a Speaker's notes

How the photographer can help

- Quality of footage
  - Missing images
  - Lighting variations
  - Lack of scene variations
  - Inconsistent audio
- Quality of script
  - Complete
  - Organized
  - Error-free

Figure 12.6b Corresponding slide

Speaker's notes, such as the ones displayed in Figure 12.6a, are an added benefit of using electronic presentations. The notes are displayed only on the presenter's screen while the corresponding slide, Figure 12.6b, is presented to the audience.

With electronic slides, you are not tied to the projector or front of the room.

If you are using electronic slides, introduce the slide before you show it and then give the audience a few seconds to view the title and design elements. With electronic slides, you have more control over the release of information. For instance, you can release bulleted points or sections of a graph as you discuss them. This control gives you more flexibility to move about the room. Take advantage of this benefit. Moving around can increase audience involvement and enhance your impact. You may even want to invest in a mouse with an extended cord or a battery-operated remote mouse to maximize your freedom to walk around.

Use a pointer to guide the audience to a specific part of a visual. It is not a riding crop, conductor's baton, leg scratcher, or walking stick. Use the pointer only at the time you need it, then fold it and remove it from sight. If you are using a laser pointer that puts a focused dot of light on the desired part of your visual, don't overdo it. A laser pointer is an excellent tool if used judiciously, but in the hands of the overzealous presenter, it can become a distraction.[16]

Handle Questions Responsively

Anticipate questions and be ready with answers so that you can

- Emphasize your most important points
- Refer to material that didn't fit in the formal presentation
- Overcome audience resistance

The question-and-answer period is one of the most important parts of an oral presentation. At the beginning of your presentation explain when the audience can ask questions and be sure to leave time for them. Questions give you a chance to obtain important information and feedback, to emphasize points you made earlier, to work in material that didn't fit into the formal presentation, and to overcome audience resistance by building enthusiasm for your point of view. Without questions, you might just as well write a report.

Many speakers do well delivering their oral presentation, only to falter during the question-and-answer period. But if you spend time anticipating these questions, you'll be ready with answers. Some experts recommend that you hold back some dramatic statistics as ammunition for the question-and-answer session.[17] If your message is unpopular, you should also be prepared for hostile questions. Treat them as legitimate requests for information. Maintaining your professionalism will improve your credibility. Follow these guidelines to ensure an effective question-and-answer period:

- **Respond appropriately.** Answer the question you're asked. Don't sidestep it, ignore it, or laugh it off. If an adequate answer would take too long, say, "I'm sorry, we don't have time to explore that issue right now, but if you'll see me after the presentation, I'll be happy to discuss it with you." If you don't know the answer, don't pretend to. Say, "I don't have those figures. I'll get them for you as quickly as possible." At the end of your presentation invite the audience to ask questions.

- **Focus on the questioner.** Pay attention to body language and facial expression to determine what the question really means. Nod your head in acknowledgement, and repeat the question aloud to confirm your understanding and ensure that everyone has heard it. If a question is vague, ask for clarification before giving a simple, direct answer. If asked to choose between two alternatives, don't feel you must. Offer your own choice if it makes more sense.[18]
- **Maintain control of the situation.** Prevent anyone from monopolizing this period. State a time or question limit per person. Asking people to identify themselves before they speak helps them behave themselves.[19] Avoid lengthy debate. You might respond with a brief answer before moving on to the next questioner. Or you might admit that you and the questioner have different opinions and offer to get back to the questioner once you've done more research.[20]
- **Maintain self-control.** If a question flusters or angers you, answer honestly but stay cool. Maintain eye contact, answer the question as well as you can, and try not to show your feelings. Don't get into an argument. Defuse hostility by paraphrasing the question and asking the questioner to confirm that you've understood it correctly. Break long, complicated questions into parts. Respond accurately and unemotionally; then move on.
- **Motivate questions.** If listeners are too timid or hostile to ask questions, consider planting your own. If a friend or the event organizer starts off, others will join in. When all else fails, say something like "I know from experience that most questions are asked after the question period. So I'll be around afterwards to talk."[21]
- **Signal the end of your speech.** When your allotted time is up, halt the question-and-answer session, even if people still want to talk. Say, "Our time is almost up. Let's have one last question." After you reply, summarize the main idea of the presentation and thank people for their attention. Conclude the way you began, by looking around the room and making eye contact. Then gather your notes and leave the podium, shoulders straight, head up.

Answer questions effectively by

- Using body language to show you're listening
- Keeping answers short and to the point
- Stating some ground rules to maintain control
- Responding unemotionally
- Helping listeners ask you questions

Reviewing Key Points

In this chapter, you learned to plan your speeches and presentations by studying your purpose and profiling your audience. You learned how to organize and compose your presentation, and how to develop the introduction, body, and close. To make your introduction effective, capture attention, establish credibility, and preview the content. Develop the body by anticipating audience interests, providing specific examples and anecdotes relevant to the audience, and emphasizing the most important points with visual aids. Use analogies, audience-oriented examples, and vivid language to keep the audience's attention. Add transitional phrases, gestures, and visuals to ensure that the audience follows as you move between sections in your talk. In the closing, restate key points, tell what's next, and end with a quote, a provocative question, or a memorable remark.

The chapter suggested following these guidelines for preparing visuals:

- Select the appropriate type of visual (electronic slides, transparencies, flip charts, white boards, or handouts) depending on the formality, size of the venue, and subject matter
- Limit the number of visuals so that they will have maximum effect.
- Make slides easy to scan by keeping them simple, limiting points to phrases only, ensuring a minimum amount of information is on each one, and choosing a simple, boldface font and using upper and lower case letters.

To build confidence and create effective delivery, you should

- Rehearse to practise timing and word choice
- Avoid memorizing, reciting, and reading
- Maintain eye contact with the audience
- Use posture and eye contact to convey a nonverbal message of confidence
- Use movement and gestures to provide emphasis and variety
- Vary your voice in volume, rhythm, and pace
- Avoid reading visuals from the screen
- Invite questions and exercise self-control when answering them

Test Your Knowledge

1. How does the purpose for giving an oral presentation influence how the speaker delivers it?

2. Why is simplicity of organization important in oral communication?

3. What three goals should you accomplish during the introduction of an oral presentation?

4. How can a speaker get and keep the audience's attention?

5. What three tasks should you accomplish in the close of your presentation?

6. When creating slides for oral presentations, which should you do first: select the background design for your slides or write your bulleted phrases? Explain your answer.

7. What is the advantage of practising an oral presentation with visual aids before a live audience?

8. As a speaker, what nonverbal signals can you send to appear more confident?

9. When should you avoid reading from your notes and slides as much as possible?

10. What can speakers do to maintain control during the question-and-answer period of a presentation?

Apply Your Knowledge

1. Why is it important to limit the scope of oral presentations?

2. How might the audience's attitude affect the amount of audience interaction during or after a presentation? Explain your answer.

3. If you were giving an oral presentation on the performance of a company product, what three attention-getters might you use to enliven your talk?

4. From the speaker's perspective, what are the advantages and disadvantages of responding to questions from the audience throughout an oral presentation, rather than just afterwards? From the listener's perspective, which approach would you prefer? Why?

5. **Ethical Choices** How can you use design elements and special effects to persuade an audience? Is it ethical to do so?

Practise Your Knowledge

Activities

For live links to all Web sites discussed in this chapter, visit this text's Web site at www.pearsoned.ca/bovee. Just log on and select Chapter 12, and click on "Student Resources." Locate the page or the URL related to the material in the text. For the "Exploring the Best of the Web" exercises, you'll also find navigational directions. Click on the live link to the site.

1. **Analyze This Document** Pick a speech from *Vital Speeches of the Day,* a publication containing recent speeches on timely and topical subjects. As an alternative, select a speech from an online source such as the speech archives of a large company's Web site. For example, go to www.bombardier.com and follow the links from "What's New" to the "Media Centre" and then click on "Speeches." Select a speech that interests you. Examine both the introduction and the close; then analyze how these two sections work together to emphasize the main idea. What action does the speaker want the audience to take? Next, identify the transitional sentences or phrases that clarify the speech's structure for the listener, especially those that help the speaker shift between supporting points. Using these transitions as clues, list the main message and supporting points; then indicate how each transitional phrase links the current supporting point to the succeeding one. Now, prepare a brief (two- to three-minute) oral presentation summarizing your analysis for your class.
2. **Internet** For many years, Toastmasters has been dedicated to helping its members give speeches. Instruction, good speakers as models, and practice sessions aim to teach members to convey information in lively and informative ways. Visit the Toastmasters Web site at www.toastmasters.org and carefully review the linked pages about listening, speaking, voice, and body. Evaluate the information and outline a three-minute presentation to your class telling why Toastmasters and its Web site would or would not help you and your classmates write and deliver an effective speech.
3. **Mastering Delivery: Analysis** Attend a presentation at your school or in your town, or watch a speech on television. Categorize the speech as one that motivates or entertains, one that informs or analyzes, or one that persuades or urges collaboration. Then compare the speaker's delivery with the concepts presented in this chapter. Write a two-page report analyzing the speaker's performance and suggesting improvements.
4. **Mastering Delivery: Nonverbal Signals** Observe and analyze the delivery of a speaker in a school, work, or other setting. What type of delivery did the speaker use? Was this delivery appropriate for the occasion? What nonverbal signals did the speaker use to

emphasize key points? Were these signals effective? Which nonverbal signals would you suggest to further enhance the delivery of this oral presentation—and why?

5. **Ethical Choices** Think again about the oral presentation you observed and analyzed in Activity 4. How could the speaker have used nonverbal signals to unethically manipulate the audience's attitudes or actions?

6. **Teamwork** You've been asked to give an informative 10-minute talk on vacation opportunities in your home province. Draft your introduction, which should last no more than two minutes. Then pair off with a classmate and analyze each other's introductions. How well do these two introductions arouse the audience's interest, build credibility, and preview the presentation? Suggest how these introductions might be improved.

7. **Completing Oral Presentations: Self-Assessment** How good are you at planning, writing, and delivering oral presentations? Rate yourself on each of the following elements of the oral presentation process. Then examine your ratings to identify where you are strongest and where you can improve, using the tips in this chapter.

Element of Presentation Process	Always	Frequently	Occasionally	Never
1. I start by defining my purpose.	____	____	____	____
2. I analyze my audience before writing an oral presentation.	____	____	____	____
3. I match my presentation length to the allotted time.	____	____	____	____
4. I begin my oral presentations with an attention-getting introduction.	____	____	____	____
5. I look for ways to build credibility as a speaker.	____	____	____	____
6. I cover only a few main points in the body of my presentation.	____	____	____	____
7. I use transitions to help listeners follow my ideas.	____	____	____	____
8. I review main points and describe next steps in the close.	____	____	____	____
9. I practise my presentation beforehand.	____	____	____	____
10. I prepare in advance for questions and objections.	____	____	____	____
11. I conclude oral presentations by summarizing my main idea.	____	____	____	____

8. **Delivering Oral Presentations: Possible Topics** Perhaps one of the following topics interests you:

   a. What I expect to learn in this course
   b. Past public speaking experiences: the good, the bad, and the ugly
   c. I would be good at teaching ________________________.
   d. I am afraid of ________________________.
   e. It's easy for me to ________________________.
   f. I get angry when ________________________.
   g. I am happiest when I ________________________.
   h. People would be surprised if they knew that I ________________________.
   i. My favourite older person
   j. My favourite charity
   k. My favourite place
   l. My favourite sport
   m. My favourite store
   n. My favourite television show
   o. The town you live in suffers from a great deal of juvenile vandalism. Explain to a group of community members why juvenile recreational facilities should be built instead of a juvenile detention complex.

p. You are speaking to the Humane Society. Support or oppose the use of animals for medical research purposes.
q. You are talking to civic leaders of your community. Try to convince them to build an art gallery.
r. You are talking to your community's local soccer club. Tell them why the club should raise funds to light a practice field nearby.
s. You are speaking to a group of travelling salespeople. Convince them that they should wear their seatbelts while driving.
t. You are speaking to a group of elderly people. Convince them to adopt an exercise program.
u. Environmental concerns (energy conservation, global warming, pollution, population control, rare species and wildlife extinction, world hunger, etc.)
v. Financial issues (banking, investing, financial issues in the last decade, the challenges faced by two-income families, single-parent families, etc.)
w. Government (domestic policy, foreign policy, medicare, income taxes, welfare, etc.)
x. Information age and computers (electronic mail, Internet, technophobes, voice mail, etc.)
y. Politics (political parties and elections, campaign fundraising, legislation, etc.)
z. Sports (amateur and professional hockey, football, golf, hang gliding, basketball, skiing, rock climbing, tennis, etc.)

Your task: Choose a topic and prepare a brief presentation (5–10 minutes) to be given before your class.

Expand Your Knowledge

Best of the Web

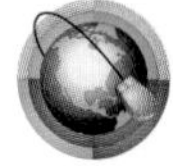

Speak with Flair The Virtual Presentation Assistant offers abundant resources with related links to other Web sites that contain useful articles, reviews, or supplemental materials for planning presentations. You can also connect to popular media and library pages with worldwide research information. You'll find examples of presentation types, suggestions for selecting and focusing your topic, tips on audience analysis, delivery, using visual aids, and various other guidelines to help you prepare and deliver an effective oral presentation. If you need inspiration, check out this site.

www.ukans.edu/cwis/units/coms2/vpa/vpa.htm

Exercises

1. Suppose you have been asked to prepare an oral presentation on a business issue currently in the news. How could you use what you've discovered at the VPA site to help you select a topic? How could you use this site to find additional information or supplementary materials related to your topic?
2. According to this Web site, what factors should you consider when analyzing your audience?
3. What topics or information will entice you to return to this site or its links? (If you don't find the Virtual Presentation Assistant useful, explain why.)

Exploring the Web on Your Own

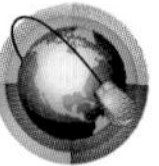

Review these chapter-related Web sites on your own to enhance your oral presentation skills and knowledge.

1. Visit the Advanced Public Speaking Institute, at www.public-speaking.org, and learn how to be the best public speaker you can be.
2. Learn to prepare, write, and polish your oral presentations at SpeechSuccess.com, www.successtips.com.

Learn Interactively

Interactive Study Guide

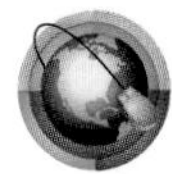

Visit the Companion Website at www.pearsoned.ca/bovee. For Chapter 12, take advantage of the interactive "Study Guide" to test your chapter knowledge. Get instant feedback on whether you need additional studying.

This site offers a variety of additional resources: The "Research Area" helps you locate a wealth of information to use in course assignments. The "Study Hall" helps you succeed in this course by offering support with writing and study skills, time management, and career skills, as well as numerous other resources.

Peak Performance Grammar and Mechanics

PEAK Use the Peak Performance Grammar and Mechanics CD to test your skill with capitalization, numbers, and other mechanics of writing. In the "Mechanics" section, take the Pretest to determine whether you have any weak areas. Then review those areas in the Refresher Course. Take the Follow-Up Test to check your grasp of punctuation. For an extra challenge or advanced practice, take the Advanced Test.

Improve Your Grammar, Mechanics, and Usage

Level 1: Self-Assessment—Capitals and Abbreviations

Review Sections 3.1 and 3.2 in the Handbook of Grammar, Mechanics, and Usage, and then look at the following 15 items.

In items 1–15, indicate proper capitalization by underlining appropriate letters with three underscores. Circle abbreviations that should be spelled out, and insert abbreviations where appropriate.

1. Dr. paul hansen is joining our staff.
2. New caressa skin cream should be in a position to dominate that market.
3. Send this report to mister h. k. danforth, rural route 1, p.o. box 2243, riley, alberta T5S 4S2.
4. You are responsible for training my new assistant to operate the xerox machine.
5. She received her master of business administration degree from the university of new brunswick.
6. The building is located on the corner of champlain and cartier streets.
7. Call me at 8 tomorrow morning, pacific standard time, and I'll have the information you need.
8. When jones becomes ceo next month, we'll need your input asap.
9. Address it to art bowers, chief of production.
10. Please rsvp to sony corp. just as soon as you know your schedule.
11. The data-processing department will begin work on feb. 2, just one wk. from today.
12. You are to meet him on friday at the parliament buildings in ottawa.
13. Whenever you can come, professor, our employees will greatly enjoy your presentation.
14. At 50 per box, our std. contract forms are $9 a box, and our warranty forms are $7.95 a box.
15. We plan to establish a sales office on the west coast.

Level 2: Workplace Applications

The following items contain numerous errors in grammar, capitalization, punctuation, abbreviation, number style, word division, and vocabulary. Rewrite each sentence in the space provided, correcting all errors. Write *C* in the space after any sentence that is already correct.

1. Mc'Donalds and Sears' have partnered with the television program, "Its Showtime At The Apollo." To offer talented kids the opportunity too appear on national television.

2. Louis Vvitton, the internationally-renowned luggage maker and specialty retailer plan to open a 1000 square metre store in Edmonton, AB next year.

3. If none of the solutions seem satisfying, pick the more easier one.

4. Ken Baker, the west coast bureau chief for Macleans magazine, will be responsible for overseeing all of magazine reporting in Vancouver, conducting high profile, celebrity interviews, for identifying news stories, and assist in the generation of cover concepts.

5. With experience managing numerous enthusiast brands, including "Kawasaki" and "Skechers," Juxt Interactive are cementing their role as a leader in strategic, integrated campaigns.

6. You're message, tone, and product positioning has to be right on to be excepted and successful.

7. As I begun to put the team together, it became apparent to myself that my idea was ahead of it's time.

8. Many think that the primary market for newspapers are the readers, however advertisers generate the majority of revenues.

9. MECs new Web site, www.MEC.com, features items that are not available at MEC's physical stores, catalogue, or main website.

10. The company's C.E.O., who we had saw at the awards dinner wednesday night, was fired the next day.

11. A designer of high priced purses such as Kate Spade or Louis Vitton generally limit distribution to exclusive boutiques or high end retail stores: such as Holt Renfrew.

12. There is many indications that an economic recovery is underway, and will continue to stabilize and build however modestly.

13. We bought the equipment at a second hand store which turned out to be shoddy and defective.

14. Experts site 2 principle reasons for Webvan's failure; consumer resistance and over expansion.

15. Implementation of the over time hours guidelines will be carried out by the Human Resources Staff members.

Level 3: Document Critique

The following document may contain errors in grammar, capitalization, punctuation, abbreviation, number style, vocabulary, and spelling. You may also find problems with organization, format, and word use. Correct all errors using standard proofreading marks (see Appendix C).

Date: Thu, 25 April, 2004

From: Steve Pendergrass < spender@nait.ca>

To: Gregory Hansford < gregory.hansford@nait.ca>

CC:

BCC:

Attached:

Subject: Library Hours

Dear Mr. Hansford,

There is a favourite place in which Northern Alberta Institute of Technology students study on our campus: the library because of the quiet atmosphere excellent resources, and helpful staff. With a ajustment in library hours there assets could be taken advantage of by more students.

In an informal survey of the students in my English class, a desire for the library to be open more hours on the weekends became evident. Many students find weekends best for researching term papers: because that's when large blocks of time can be found in their schedules.

I'd like to sight several reasons for the change I am about to propose to encourage your interest and desire for my suggestion. Understandable, librarians need a day off. Perhaps students and librarians could both be accomodated if the library closed at five p.m. on Friday night. Friday night is the time most students like to relax and attend sports events or parties. The libary could then be open on Saturdays from ten a.m. until 4:30 p.m. To make this arrangement fair to librarians; perhaps their schedules could be staggered so that nobody would have to work every Saturday or those scheduled to work on Saturdays could be given Mondays or Fridays off.

Consider implementing this new schedule this Fall. Another much-appreciated service for students will be performed if you do this.

Sincerely: Steve Pendergrass, student

Workplace Skills

Business Communication Notebook

Nerves: The Secret Weapon of Polished Presenters

What do Barbra Streisand, Liza Minnelli, and Donny Osmond have in common? These professional performers and many others admit to being nervous about public speaking. If the pros can feel fear, it's no wonder beginners are sometimes scared speechless. Survey after survey has confirmed that public speaking is the number one fear in Canada and the United States—so if you're anxious about stepping in front of an audience, you're not alone.

Nervousness might make your hands tremble, your knees knock, your mouth feel dry, or your stomach churn. As bad as these symptoms can be, remember that nerves are a good indicator of your concern for the occasion, your subject, and your audience. If you didn't care, you wouldn't be anxious. A speaker who cares is more likely to seek out every method of communicating with the audience.

Remember also that you'll feel a little less nervous with every oral presentation. Once you see how the audience responds to your first attempt, you'll realize that you did better than you feared you would. People in the audience want you to succeed; they're interested in learning from you or being inspired by your words, not in straining to hear the sound of your knees knocking together.

You can harness your nerves by focusing on what you want to accomplish. In the words of actress Carol Channing, "I don't call it nervousness—I prefer to call it concentration." Like Channing, you can concentrate your efforts on making that all-important connection with your audience. But don't make the mistake of expecting perfection. Put that nervous energy into planning, preparing, and practising. Turn your negative fears into positive energy, and you'll be better equipped to face your audience the first time and every time.

You might start by listing statements that describe each of your fears: (1) the behaviour that will show your fear, (2) the effect this behaviour will have, and (3) the action you can take to change the behaviour and get rid of the fear. For example, if you're afraid that you won't be as good as you would like to be, you might say, "I'll leave out parts of my speech or act nervous (behaviour), so I won't impress the audience or get my message across (effect)." The solution is to make the speech your own before addressing your audience (action). Practise, practise, practise. Tape-record your speech or videotape yourself and look for strengths and weaknesses. Practise out loud until you've mastered the speech and it's yours. If you like your speech, your audience will like it, and you'll get your message across.

Or perhaps you're saying something like "I'll look scared (behaviour), and the audience will sense my nervousness and will snicker and make fun of me (effect)." The solution is to act confident—even if you don't feel it (action). Listeners want you to succeed, and they can't see what's happening inside you. Don't apologize for anything. If you make a mistake, don't start over; just keep going. Then enjoy the applause—your moment in the spotlight.

Applications for Success

Learn how to overcome your fear of public speaking by visiting members.shaw.ca/raestonehouse/page13g.htm and www.pe2000.com/pho-speaking.htm.

Answer the following questions:

1. Think of any lectures or presentations you've recently attended. Have you ever noticed a speaker's level of anxiety? Did any speakers succeed in overcoming this fear? Describe the ways a particular speaker visibly conquered his or her nervousness. If that speaker failed, what techniques might have helped?
2. As a member of the audience, what can you do to help a speaker overcome his or her nervousness? Briefly explain.
3. Using the "behaviour-effect-action" structure, list one of your fears and show how you plan to counter it in your next speech.

Unit 5

EMPLOYMENT MESSAGES

13 Searching for Employment and Preparing Employment Messages

From the Real World

"Experienced recruiters will spend not more than five minutes deciding who they want to consider further for pre-screening. So all the more reason to be clear, simple, and direct in your application and resumé."

–Stephanie Sykes
Practice Leader and Senior Consultant
Careers Practice
BCE Corporate Services

After studying this chapter, you will be able to

1 Discuss three results of how today's constantly changing workplace is affecting the employment-search process
2 Explain three things you can do to help you adapt to the changing workplace
3 Summarize six tasks you can do before and during your job search
4 Discuss how to choose the appropriate resumé organization, and list the advantages or disadvantages of the three options
5 List the major elements to include in a traditional resumé
6 Describe what you can do to adapt your resumé to a scannable format
7 Define the purpose of application letters, and explain how to apply the AIDA organizational approach to them

Stephanie Sykes' department at BCE Corporate Services provides recruitment and human resource planning to help Bell Canada attract and retain talented employees. Bell Canada receives more than 60 000 applications each year. "What stands out in an application," says Sykes, "is clarity and simplicity. Tell me why you want to work for Bell and what you will bring to our company. Technical skills show through easily but remember that most companies are also looking for people with leadership skills or potential."

Building Toward a Career

As Stephanie Sykes will tell you, getting the job that's right for you takes more than sending out a few resumés and application letters. Before entering the workplace, you need to learn as much as you can about your capabilities and the job marketplace.

Understanding Today's Changing Workplace

Numerous forces are changing today's workplace.

The workplace today is changing constantly.[1] The attitudes and expectations of both employers and employees are being affected not only by globalization, technology, diversity, and teams but also by deregulation, shareholder activism, corporate downsizing, mergers and acquisitions, outsourcing, and entrepreneurialism (people starting their own business or buying a franchise).[2] The results of constant change are threefold.

- **How often people look for work.** Rather than looking for lifelong employees, many employers now hire temporary workers and consultants on a project-by-project basis. Likewise, rather than staying with one employer for their entire career, growing numbers of employees are moving from company to company.
- **Where people find work.** Fewer jobs are being created by large companies. One expert predicts that soon 80 percent of the labour force will be working for firms employing fewer than 200 people. Moreover, self-employment seems to be an increasingly attractive option for many former employees.[3]
- **The type of people who find work.** Employers today are looking for people who are able and willing to adapt to diverse situations and who continue to learn throughout their careers. Companies want team players with strong work records, leaders who are versatile, and employees with diversified skills and varied job experience.[4] Plus, most employers expect employees to be sensitive to intercultural differences.[5]

Adapting to the Changing Workplace

Before you limit your employment search to a particular industry or job, do some advance preparation. Analyze what you have to offer, what you hope to get from your work, and how you can make yourself more valuable to potential employers. This preliminary analysis will help you identify employers who are likely to want you and vice versa.

Learn What You Have to Offer

When seeking employment, you must tell people about yourself, about who you are. So you need to know what talents and skills you have. You'll need to explain how these skills will benefit potential employers. Follow these guidelines:

To determine what you have to offer, carefully examine your functional skills, your education and experience, and your personality traits.

- **Jot down 10 achievements you're proud of.** Did you learn to ski, take a prize-winning photo, tutor a child, edit your school paper? Think about what skills these achievements demanded (leadership skills, speaking ability, and artistic talent may have helped you coordinate a winning presentation to your school's administration). You'll begin to recognize a pattern of skills, many of which might be valuable to potential employers.
- **Look at your educational preparation, work experience, and extracurricular activities.** What do your knowledge and experience qualify you to do? What have you learned from volunteer work or class projects that could benefit you on the job? Have you held any offices, won any awards or scholarships, mastered a second language?
- **Take stock of your personal characteristics.** Are you aggressive, a born leader? Or would you rather follow? Are you outgoing, articulate, great with people? Or do you prefer working alone? Make a list of what you believe are your four or five most important qualities. Ask a relative or friend to rate your traits as well.

Decide What You Want to Do

Knowing what you *can* do is one thing. Knowing what you *want* to do is another. Don't lose sight of your own values. Discover the things that will bring you satisfaction and happiness on the job.

When deciding what you want to do, envision your ideal day at work: your activities, independence, salary, career goals, environment, location, position, and relationships.

- **What would you like to do every day?** Talk to people in various occupations about their typical workday. You might consult relatives, local businesses, or former graduates (through your school's alumni relations office). Read about various occupations. Start with your college or university library or placement office.
- **How would you like to work?** Consider how much independence you want on the job, how much variety you like, and whether you prefer to work with products, machines, people, ideas, figures, or some combination thereof. Do you like physical work, mental work, or a mix? Constant change or a predictable role?

- **What specific compensation do you expect?** What do you hope to earn in your first year? What kind of pay increase do you expect each year? What's your ultimate earnings goal? Would you be comfortable getting paid on commission, or do you prefer a steady paycheque? Are you willing to settle for less money in order to do something you really love?

Set goals; assess your needs and preferences.

- **Can you establish some general career goals?** Consider where you'd like to start, where you'd like to go from there, and the ultimate position you'd like to attain. How soon after joining the company would you like to receive your first promotion? Your next one? What additional training or preparation will you need to achieve them?
- **What size of company would you prefer?** Do you like the idea of working for a small, entrepreneurial operation? Or would you prefer a large corporation?
- **What type of operation is appealing to you?** Do you prefer to work for a profit-making company or a non-profit organization? Are you attracted to service businesses or manufacturing operations? Do you want regular, predictable hours, or do you thrive on flexible, varied hours? Would you enjoy a seasonally varied job such as education (which may give you summers off) or retailing (with its selling cycles)?
- **What location would you like?** Would you like to work in a city, a suburb, a small town, an industrial area, or an uptown setting? Do you favour a particular part of the country? A country abroad? Do you like working indoors or outdoors?
- **What facilities do you envision?** Is it important to you to work in an attractive place, or will simple, functional quarters suffice? Do you need a quiet office to work effectively, or can you concentrate in a noisy, open setting? Is access to public transportation or freeways important?
- **What sort of corporate culture are you most comfortable with?** Would you be happy in a formal hierarchy with clear reporting relationships? Or do you prefer less structure? Are you looking for a paternalistic firm or one that fosters individualism? Do you like a competitive environment? One that rewards teamwork? What qualities do you want in a boss?

Make Yourself More Valuable to Employers

Make yourself more valuable to potential employers by tracking what you've done, broadening your experience, and constantly improving your skills.

Take positive steps toward building your career. Before you graduate from university or college or while you're seeking employment, you can do a lot. The following suggestions will help potential employers recognize the value of hiring you:

- **Keep an employment portfolio.** Keep samples that show your ability to perform (classroom or work evaluations, certificates, awards, papers you've written). Your portfolio is a great resource for writing your resumé, and it gives employers tangible evidence of your professionalism.
- **Take interim assignments.** As you search for a permanent job, consider temporary, volunteer, or freelance work. Also gain a competitive edge by participating in an internship program. These temporary assignments not only help you gain valuable experience and relevant contacts but also provide you with important references and with items for your portfolio.[6]
- **Work on polishing and updating your skills.** Whenever possible, join networks of professional colleagues and friends who can help you keep up with your occupation and industry. While waiting for responses to your resumé, take a computer course, or seek out other educational or life experiences that would be hard to get while working full-time.

Your career-building efforts don't stop after you are hired.

Even after you've been hired, continue improving your skills. Distinguish yourself from your peers and continue increasing your value to current and potential employers. Becoming a lifelong learner will help you reach your personal goals in the workplace:[7]

- Obtain as much technical knowledge as you can.
- Learn to accept and adapt to change.
- Regularly read publications such as *The Globe and Mail, Canadian Business, Maclean's,* and *Report on Business.*
- View each job as a chance to expand your knowledge, experience, and social skills.
- Take on as much responsibility as you can (listen to and learn from others while actively pursuing new or better skills).
- Stay abreast of what's going on in your organization and industry to understand the big picture.

Seeking Employment in the Changing Workplace

Look at Figure 13.1 for an idea of what an employment search entails. The first two tasks are discussed in this chapter; the rest are discussed in Chapter 14. Gather as much information as you can, narrowing it as you go until you know precisely the companies you want to approach.

The search for employment is a process.

Begin by finding out where the job opportunities are, which industries are strong, which parts of the country are booming, and which specific job categories offer the best prospects for the future. From there you can investigate individual organizations, doing your best to learn as much about them as possible. To prepare for and successfully complete your search for employment, do the following:

To learn all you can about the job opportunities available, consistently pursue six tasks.

- **Stay abreast of business and financial news.** Subscribe to a major newspaper (print or online) and scan the business pages every day. Watch some television programs that focus on business. Consult the *National Occupational Classification* (Human Resources Development Canada, in print and online at www23.hrdc-drhc.gc.ca) and Job Futures (Human Resources and Development Canada, in print and online at jobfutures.ca). View forecasts about various job titles to develop ideas for a career. In addition to the national edition of Job Futures, you can also check provincial editions. B.C. Work Futures (www.workfutures.bc.ca) provides forecasts about occupational profiles and includes links to other provinces' Work Futures sites. Alberta's Work Futures site gives you links that list the biggest companies in Alberta. Another source of detailed information about occupations and trends is

FIGURE 13.1 The Employment Search

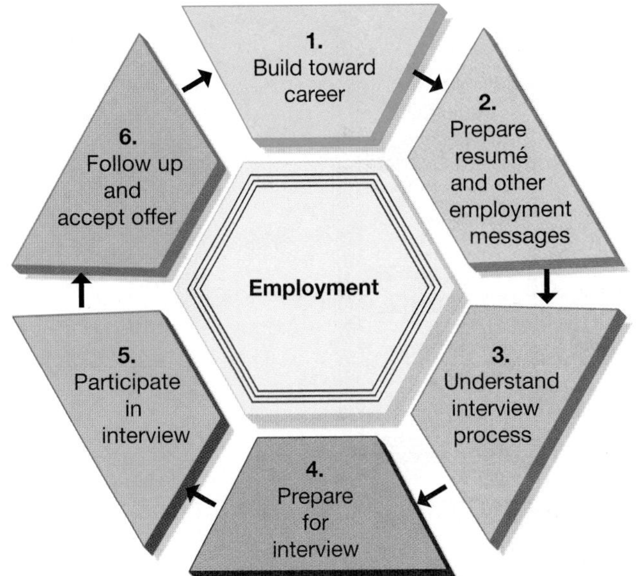

the *U.S. Occupational Outlook Handbook*, published in print and online at www.bls.gov/oco/print/ocos021.htm. Often the online versions of these materials are most up to date.

- **Research specific companies.** Compile a list of specific organizations that appeal to you (by consulting directories of employers at the library, at your career centre, or on the Web). Consult company profiles, press releases, financial information, and information on employment opportunities. Find out about a company's mission, products, annual reports, and employee benefits. Send an e-mail request for annual reports, brochures, or newsletters.
- **Look for job openings.** Check company Web sites for job openings, or find sites that list openings from multiple companies—many of which allow you to search by region, industry, job title, company, skills, or requirements (see Figure 13.2). And don't forget to look in newspapers, sign up for campus interviews, network, and find career counselling.
- **Respond to job openings.** You can respond directly to job listings by posting tailor-made resumés (that match required qualifications) and by sending e-mail resumés and focused cover letters directly to the people doing the hiring. Since companies receive thousands of electronic resumés a day, also consider a printed letter or a phone call.[8]
- **Network.** Find people in your field by participating in business organizations (such as the Canadian Marketing Association or the Canadian Institute of Management Association). Visit organizations, contact their personnel departments, and talk with key employees. On the Web, locate and communicate with potential employers using

FIGURE 13.2 Careerbuilder
Careerbuilder is just one of the many Web sites that job seekers turn to for career advice, as well as for employer information and company job postings.

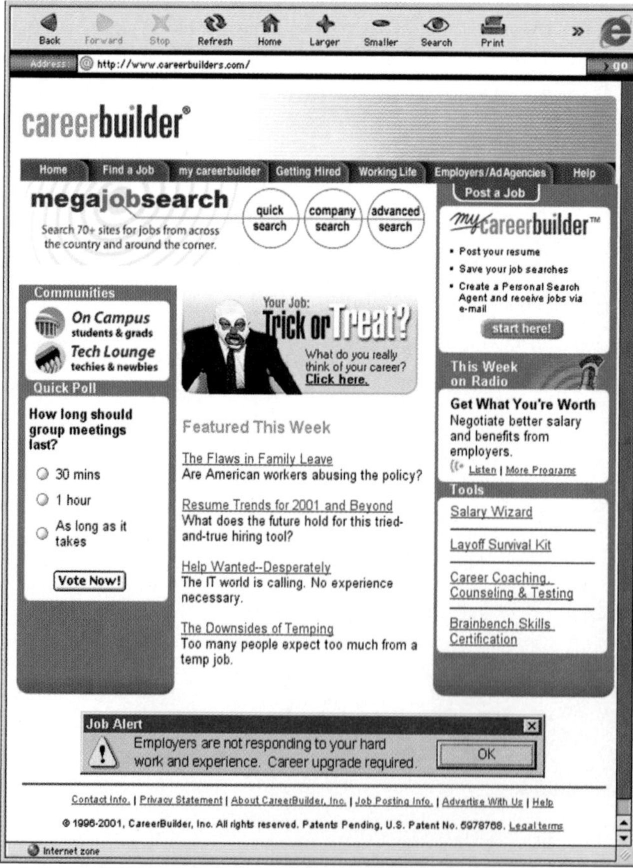

discussion groups, Usenet newsgroups (that post messages on electronic bulletin boards), and Listservs (that e-mail messages to every member). Once you locate a potential contact, send an e-mail requesting information about the company or about job openings.

- **Find career counselling.** College placement offices offer counselling, credential services, job fairs, on-campus interviews, and job listings. They provide workshops in job-search techniques, resumé preparation, interview techniques, and more.[9] College- and university-run online career centres are excellent.

Preparing Resumés

While looking for employment, you'll need to send out messages such as resumés and application letters. Whenever you send out such employment messages, you have an opportunity to showcase your communication skills—skills valued highly by the majority of employers. So write these messages carefully by following the three-step writing process (see Figure 13.3).

As with other business messages, the three-step writing process can help you plan, write, and complete your resumé and other employment messages.

Planning Your Resumé

A **resumé** is a structured, written summary of a person's education, employment background, and job qualifications. Many people have misconceptions about the value and function of resumés—see Table 13.1 on page 358. As with other business messages, planning a resumé means analyzing your purpose and audience, gathering information, and adapting the document to your purpose and audience.

Your resumé concisely summarizes your educational and employment background and shows your qualifications for a job.

- **Analyze your purpose and audience.** Your resumé must be more than a simple list of jobs you've held. It is a form of advertising intended to stimulate an employer's interest in you—in meeting you and learning more about you. With this purpose in mind, put yourself in your audience's position and tailor your resumé to satisfy audience needs.

To get an interview, analyze your audience's needs, have all the facts at your fingertips, and tailor your resumé to various audiences and situations.

FIGURE 13.3 Three-Step Writing Process for Employment Messages

Planning	Writing	Completing
Analyze the Situation Study your purpose and your audience to tailor your message for maximum effect. **Investigate the Topic** Gather relevant information about you and about the employer you're targeting. **Adapt to the Audience** Establish a good relationship by highlighting those skills and qualifications that match each employer.	**Organize the Message** Use the AIDA approach in letters and choose the most appropriate resumé format to highlight your strongest points. **Compose the Message** Make your letters friendly, businesslike, and slightly more formal than usual. For resumés, use action verbs and make your style direct, brief, and crisp.	**Revise the Message** Evaluate content, revising for both clarity and conciseness. **Produce the Message** Ensure a clean, sharp look whether your message is in print, e-mail, or online. **Proofread the Message** Look carefully for errors in spelling and mechanics that can detract from your professionalism.
1	2	3

Table 13.1 Fallacies and Facts About Resumés

Fallacy	Fact
⊗ The purpose of a resumé is to list all your skills and abilities.	☑ The purpose of a resumé is to kindle employer interest and generate an interview.
⊗ A good resumé will get you the job you want.	☑ All a resumé can do is get you in the door.
⊗ Your resumé will be read carefully and thoroughly by an interested employer.	☑ Your resumé probably has less than 45 seconds to make an impression.
⊗ The more good information you present about yourself in your resumé, the better.	☑ Too much information on a resumé may actually kill the reader's appetite to know more.
⊗ If you want a really good resumé, have it prepared by a resumé service.	☑ Prepare your own resumé—unless the position is especially high-level or specialized. Even then, you should check carefully before using a service.
⊗ Using a Word template will make a professional impression.	☑ Design your own resumé to be distinct and show your communication skills.

- **Investigate pertinent information.** Gather every scrap of pertinent personal history you can and have it at your fingertips: all details of previous jobs (dates, duties, accomplishments), all relevant educational experience (formal degrees, skill certificates, academic or civic awards), all relevant information about personal endeavours (dates of membership in an association, offices you held in a club or organization, presentations you made to a community group).
- **Adapt your resumé to your audience.** Your resumé must make an impression quickly. Focus on your audience. Ask yourself what key qualifications this employer will be looking for. Decide which qualifications are your greatest strengths. Choose three or four of your most relevant accomplishments and what resulted from these accomplishments. A good resumé is flexible and can be customized for various situations and employers.

Don't exaggerate, and don't alter the past or claim skills you don't have. However, don't dwell on negatives, either. By knowing yourself and your audience, you'll focus successfully on the strengths needed by potential employers.

Writing Your Resumé

To write a successful resumé, you need to convey seven qualities that employers seek. You want to show that you

- think in terms of results
- know how to get things done
- are well rounded
- show signs of progress
- have personal standards of excellence
- are flexible and willing to try new things
- possess strong communication skills

As you organize and compose your resumé, think about how you can convey those seven qualities.

Organize Your Resumé Around Your Strengths

Although you may want to include a little information in all categories, emphasize the information that has a bearing on your career objective, and minimize or exclude any that is irrelevant or counterproductive. Call attention to your best features and downplay your weaknesses—but be sure you do so without distorting or misrepresenting the facts.[10] To focus attention on your strongest points, adopt the appropriate organizational approach—make your resumé chronological, functional, or a combination of the two. The "right" choice depends on your background and your goals.

Select an organizational pattern that focuses attention on your strengths.

The Chronological Resumé In a **chronological resumé,** the "Work Experience" section dominates and is placed immediately after the name and address and the objective. You list your jobs sequentially in reverse order, beginning with the most recent position and working backwards toward earlier jobs. Under each job listing, describe your responsibilities and accomplishments, giving the most space to the most recent positions. If you're just starting your career, you can vary this chronological approach by putting your educational qualifications before your experience, thereby focusing attention on your training and academic credentials.

The chronological approach is the most common way to organize a resumé, and many employers prefer it. This approach has three key advantages: (1) employers are familiar with it and can easily find information, (2) it highlights growth and career progression, and (3) it highlights employment continuity and stability.[11] The chronological approach is especially appropriate if you have a strong employment history and are aiming for a job that builds on your current career path. This is the case for Lareine Chan. Compare the ineffective and effective versions of Chan's resumé in Figures 13.4 (on page 360) and 13.5 (on page 361).

Most recruiters prefer the chronological plan: a historical summary of your education and work experience.

The Functional Resumé A **functional resumé** emphasizes a list of skills and accomplishments, identifying employers and academic experience in subordinate sections. This pattern stresses individual areas of competence, so it's useful for people who are just entering the job market, who want to redirect their careers, or who have little continuous career-related experience. The functional approach also has three advantages: (1) without having to read through job descriptions, employers can see what you can do for them, (2) you can emphasize earlier job experience, and (3) you can de-emphasize any lack of career progress or lengthy unemployment.

A functional resumé focuses attention on your areas of competence.

Figure 13.6 on page 362 illustrates how Glenda Johns uses the functional approach to showcase her qualifications for a career in retail. Although she has not held any paid, full-time positions in retail sales, Johns has participated in work-experience programs, and she knows a good deal about the profession from research and from talking with people in the industry. She organized her resumé in a way that demonstrates her ability to handle such a position. Bear in mind, however, that many employment professionals assume that candidates who use this organization are trying to hide something.[12]

The Combination Resumé A **combination resumé** includes the best features of the chronological and functional approaches. Nevertheless, it is not commonly used, and it has two major disadvantages: (1) it tends to be longer, and (2) it can be repetitious if you have to list your accomplishments and skills in both the functional section and the chronological job descriptions.[13] When Erica Vorkamp developed her resumé, she chose not to use a chronological pattern, which would focus attention on her lack of recent work experience. As Figure 13.7 on page 363 shows, she used a combination approach to emphasize her abilities, skills, and accomplishments while also including a complete job history.

A combination resumé is a hybrid of the chronological and functional resumés.

Compose Your Resumé to Impress

To save your readers time and to state your information as forcefully as possible, write your resumé using a simple and direct style. Use short, crisp phrases instead of whole sentences, and focus on what your reader needs to know. Avoid using the word *I*. Instead, start your phrases with impressive action verbs such as the ones listed in Table 13.2 on page 360. For instance, you might say, "Coached a Little League team to the regional playoffs" or

To capture attention quickly, leave out the word *I*, and begin your phrases with strong, action verbs.

FIGURE 13.4 Ineffective Chronological Resumé

Fails to combine accounting expertise with international experience in the minds of employers by stating it in an overall objective

Uses bulleted lists ineffectively:

- Lacks parallelism
- Lacks logical organization
- Often highlights wrong information
- Uses the word "I" too often
- Uses too many unnecessary words (such as "I was responsible for")
- Fails to highlight important skills by breaking them out into a separate list

Includes too many words in educational information and lacks parallelism

Lareine Chan

5687 Crosswoods Drive, Richmond, BC V59 2T1
Home: (604) 273-0086 Office: (604) 273-6624

I have been staff accountant/financial analyst at Inter-Asian Imports in Vancouver, BC, from March 2001 to present.

- I have negotiated with major suppliers.
- I speak both Cantonese and Mandarin fluently, and I was recently encouraged to implement an electronic funds transfer for vendor disbursements.
- In my current position, I am responsible for preparing accounting reports.
- I have audited financial transactions.
- I have also been involved in the design of a computerized model to adjust accounts for fluctuations in currency exchange rates.
- I am skilled in the use of Excel, Access, HTML, and Visual Basic.

Was staff accountant with Monsanto Agricultural Chemicals in Shanghai, China (October 1997 to March 2001).

- While with Monsanto in Shanghai, I was responsible for budgeting and billing.
- I was responsible for credit-processing functions.
- I was also responsible for auditing the travel and entertainment expenses for the sales department.
- I launched an online computer system to automate all accounting functions.
- Also during this time, I was able to travel extensively in Asia.

I have my Master of Business Administration with emphasis on international business, which I earned while attending University of British Columbia in Vancouver, B.C., from 1995 to 1997.

Bachelor of Business Administration (1992–1995), earned while attending Memorial University in St. John's, Newfoundland and Labrador.

Organizes information chronologically but hides that fact with awkward format

Fails to draw reader's attention to important points:

- Fails to provide the sort of specific information on duties and accomplishments that catches an employer's eye
- Fails to use active language consistently to describe duties

Lacks informative headings throughout, making it difficult for potential employers to find work-related, educational, or skills information easily

Table 13.2 Action Verbs to Use in Resumés

accomplished	coordinated	initiated	participated	set up
achieved	created	installed	performed	simplified
administered	demonstrated	introduced	planned	sparked
approved	developed	investigated	presented	streamlined
arranged	directed	joined	proposed	strengthened
assisted	established	launched	raised	succeeded
assumed	explored	maintained	recommended	supervised
budgeted	forecasted	managed	reduced	systematized
chaired	generated	motivated	reorganized	targeted
changed	identified	operated	resolved	trained
compiled	implemented	organized	saved	transformed
completed	improved	oversaw	served	upgraded

Planning

Analyze the Situation
Decide how best to combine accounting expertise with international experience.

Investigate the Topic
Gather data from contacts and research.

Adapt to the Audience
Point out specific achievements to interest potential employers.

1

Writing

Organize the Message
A chronological resumé will best emphasize years of work experience.

Compose the Message
The style is direct, brief, and crisp, using action verbs to focus on employment history, professional achievements, and international abilities.

2

Completing

Revise the Message
Make content clear and concise.

Produce the Message
Give traditional resumé a clean, sharp look with dates set off in margin.

Proofread the Message
Review for spelling and mechanical errors.

3

FIGURE 13.5 Effective Chronological Resumé

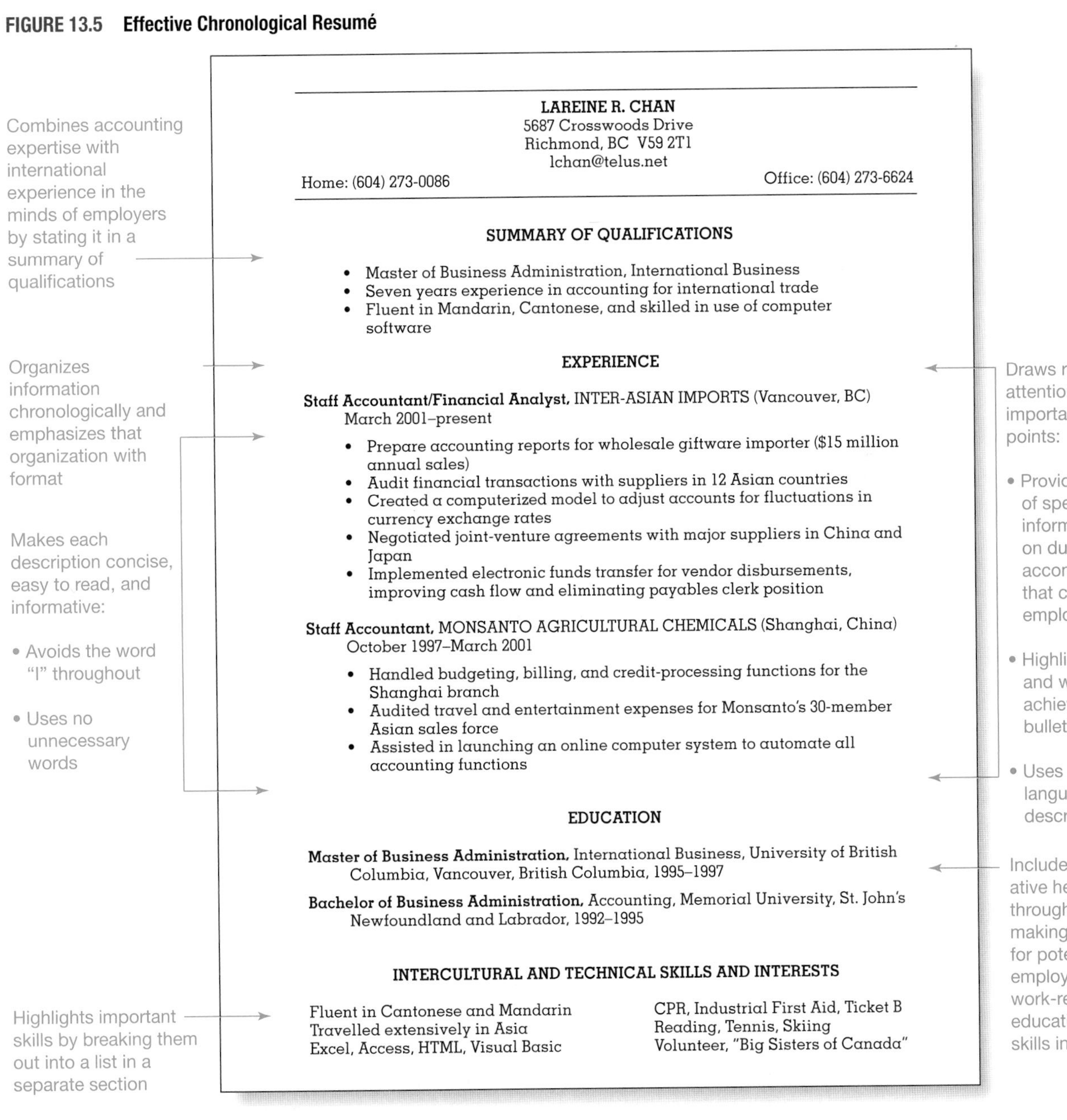

LAREINE R. CHAN
5687 Crosswoods Drive
Richmond, BC V59 2T1
lchan@telus.net
Home: (604) 273-0086 Office: (604) 273-6624

SUMMARY OF QUALIFICATIONS

- Master of Business Administration, International Business
- Seven years experience in accounting for international trade
- Fluent in Mandarin, Cantonese, and skilled in use of computer software

EXPERIENCE

Staff Accountant/Financial Analyst, INTER-ASIAN IMPORTS (Vancouver, BC)
March 2001–present

- Prepare accounting reports for wholesale giftware importer ($15 million annual sales)
- Audit financial transactions with suppliers in 12 Asian countries
- Created a computerized model to adjust accounts for fluctuations in currency exchange rates
- Negotiated joint-venture agreements with major suppliers in China and Japan
- Implemented electronic funds transfer for vendor disbursements, improving cash flow and eliminating payables clerk position

Staff Accountant, MONSANTO AGRICULTURAL CHEMICALS (Shanghai, China)
October 1997–March 2001

- Handled budgeting, billing, and credit-processing functions for the Shanghai branch
- Audited travel and entertainment expenses for Monsanto's 30-member Asian sales force
- Assisted in launching an online computer system to automate all accounting functions

EDUCATION

Master of Business Administration, International Business, University of British Columbia, Vancouver, British Columbia, 1995–1997

Bachelor of Business Administration, Accounting, Memorial University, St. John's Newfoundland and Labrador, 1992–1995

INTERCULTURAL AND TECHNICAL SKILLS AND INTERESTS

Fluent in Cantonese and Mandarin
Travelled extensively in Asia
Excel, Access, HTML, Visual Basic
CPR, Industrial First Aid, Ticket B
Reading, Tennis, Skiing
Volunteer, "Big Sisters of Canada"

Combines accounting expertise with international experience in the minds of employers by stating it in a summary of qualifications
Organizes information chronologically and emphasizes that organization with format
Makes each description concise, easy to read, and informative:
• Avoids the word "I" throughout
• Uses no unnecessary words
Highlights important skills by breaking them out into a list in a separate section
Draws reader's attention to important points:
• Provides the sort of specific information on duties and accomplishments that catches an employer's eye
• Highlights duties and work achievements in bulleted lists
• Uses active language to describe duties
Includes informative headings throughout, making it easy for potential employers to find work-related, educational, or skills information

FIGURE 13.6 Functional Resumé

Glenda S. Johns

Home: 457 Mountain View Road
Clear Lake, Manitoba R2H 0J9
(204) 733-5971

College: 1254 Main Street
Brandon, Manitoba R5Y 2P5
(204) 438-5254

OBJECTIVE: Retailing position

RELEVANT SKILLS

Describes relevant skills first because Johns is a recent graduate

- **Personal Selling/Retailing**
  - Led housewares department in employee sales for spring 2004
  - Created end-cap and shelf displays for special promotions
  - Sold the most benefit tickets during college fundraising drive for local community centre
- **Public Interaction**
  - Commended by housewares manager for resolving customer complaints amicably
  - Performed in summer theatre productions in Clear Lake, MB
- **Managing**
  - Trained part-time employees in cash register operation and customer service
  - Reworked employee schedules as assistant manager
  - Organized summer activities for children 6–12 years old for town of Clear Lake, MB—including reading programs, sports activities, and field trips

Uses action verbs to enhance resumé effectiveness

EDUCATION

- Diploma in Business Administration (E-Business) (3.81 GPA /4.0 scale), Red River Community College, June 2005
- Courses included marketing, accounting, retail management, Web site design, e-marketing, and consumer behaviour

WORK EXPERIENCE

Describes but does not emphasize Johns' sketchy work history

- **Assistant Manager**, housewares, at Jefferson's Department Store during off-campus work experience program, Brandon, MB (fall 2004–spring 2005)
- **Sales Clerk**, housewares, at Jefferson's Department Store during off-campus work experience program, Brandon, MB (fall 2003–spring 2004)
- **Assistant Director**, Summer Recreation Program, Clear Lake, MB (summer 2003)
- **Actress**, Cobblestone Players, Clear Lake, MB (summer 2002)

LEADERSHIP EXPERIENCE

- Student Co-Chair for Clear Lake Women's Club Fashion Show, 2005 (raised $45 000)
- President of Student Housing Society, 2004
- Student representative (high school) to Clear Lake Chamber of Commerce (2 years)

Calls attention to leadership abilities and experience by listing her leadership positions in a separate section

"Managed a fast-food restaurant and four employees." Here are some additional examples of how to phrase your accomplishments using active statements that show results:

Avoid Weak Statements	Use Active Statements That Show Results
Responsible for developing a new filing system	Developed a new filing system that reduced paperwork by 50 percent
I was in charge of customer complaints and all ordering problems	Handled all customer complaints and resolved all product order discrepancies
Won a trip to Europe for opening the most new customer accounts in my department	Generated the highest number of new customer accounts in my department

FIGURE 13.7 Combination Resumé

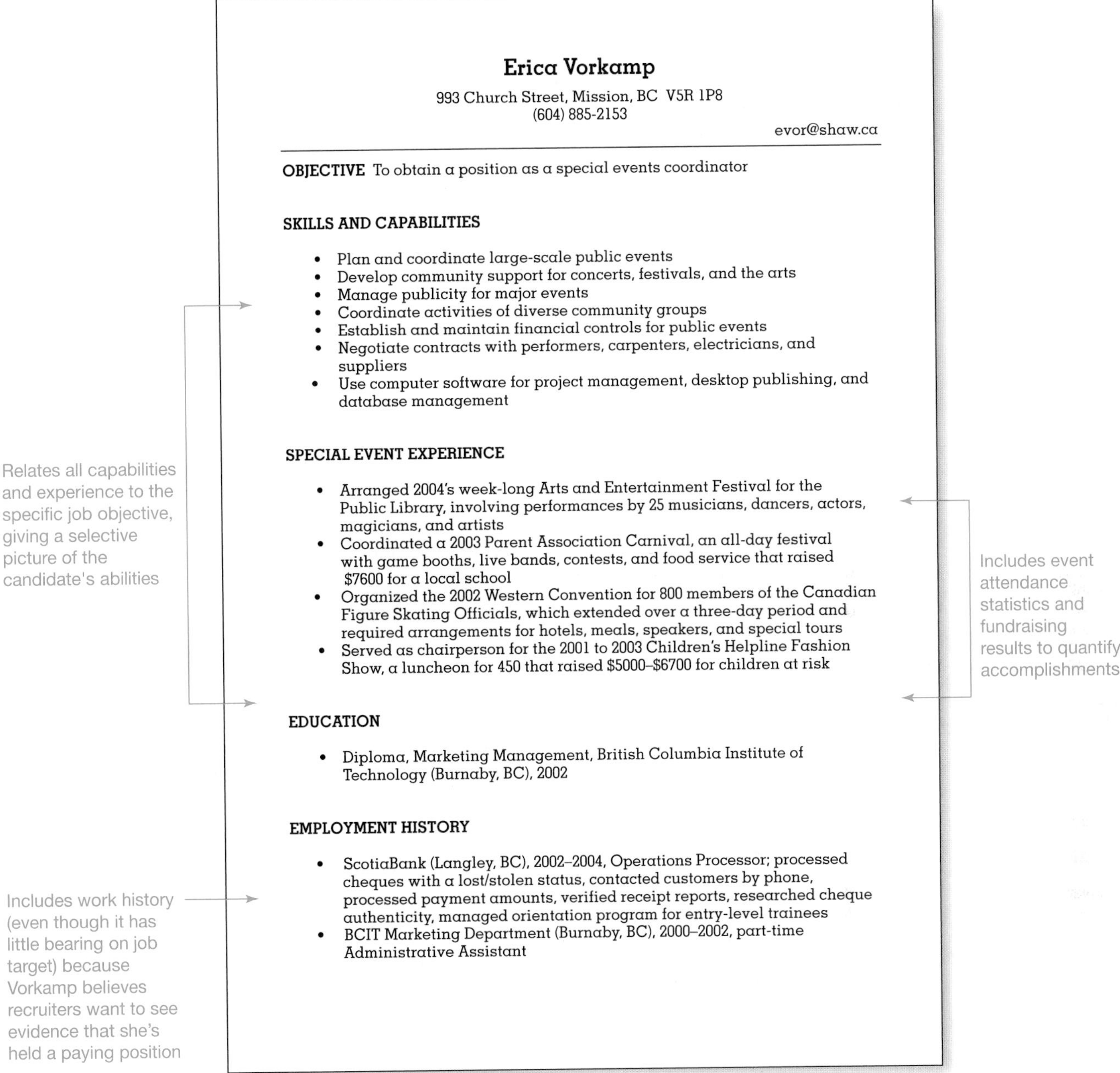

Erica Vorkamp

993 Church Street, Mission, BC V5R 1P8
(604) 885-2153
evor@shaw.ca

OBJECTIVE To obtain a position as a special events coordinator

SKILLS AND CAPABILITIES

- Plan and coordinate large-scale public events
- Develop community support for concerts, festivals, and the arts
- Manage publicity for major events
- Coordinate activities of diverse community groups
- Establish and maintain financial controls for public events
- Negotiate contracts with performers, carpenters, electricians, and suppliers
- Use computer software for project management, desktop publishing, and database management

SPECIAL EVENT EXPERIENCE

- Arranged 2004's week-long Arts and Entertainment Festival for the Public Library, involving performances by 25 musicians, dancers, actors, magicians, and artists
- Coordinated a 2003 Parent Association Carnival, an all-day festival with game booths, live bands, contests, and food service that raised $7600 for a local school
- Organized the 2002 Western Convention for 800 members of the Canadian Figure Skating Officials, which extended over a three-day period and required arrangements for hotels, meals, speakers, and special tours
- Served as chairperson for the 2001 to 2003 Children's Helpline Fashion Show, a luncheon for 450 that raised $5000–$6700 for children at risk

EDUCATION

- Diploma, Marketing Management, British Columbia Institute of Technology (Burnaby, BC), 2002

EMPLOYMENT HISTORY

- ScotiaBank (Langley, BC), 2002–2004, Operations Processor; processed cheques with a lost/stolen status, contacted customers by phone, processed payment amounts, verified receipt reports, researched cheque authenticity, managed orientation program for entry-level trainees
- BCIT Marketing Department (Burnaby, BC), 2000–2002, part-time Administrative Assistant

Relates all capabilities and experience to the specific job objective, giving a selective picture of the candidate's abilities
Includes event attendance statistics and fundraising results to quantify accomplishments
Includes work history (even though it has little bearing on job target) because Vorkamp believes recruiters want to see evidence that she's held a paying position

Avoid Weak Statements	Use Active Statements That Show Results
Member of special campus task force to resolve student problems with existing cafeteria assignments	Assisted in implementing new campus dining program allowing students to eat at any college dorm

Elements to include in your resumé are your name and address, academic credentials, employment history, activities and achievements, and relevant personal data.

Name and Address The first thing an employer needs to know is who you are and where you can be reached: your name, address, phone number, and e-mail address (or URL, if you have one). If you have contact information at school and at home, you can include both. Similarly, if you have a work phone and a home phone, list both and indicate which

The opening section shows at a glance

- Who you are
- How to reach you

Include your e-mail address.

is which. Many resumé headings are nothing more than the name and address centred at the top of the page. You don't really need to include the word *resumé*. Just make sure the reader can tell in an instant who you are and how to communicate with you.

Stating your objective helps the recruiter categorize you.

Career Objective Experts disagree about the need to state a career objective on your resumé. Some argue that your objective is obvious from your qualifications. Some also maintain that such a statement only limits you as a candidate (especially if you want to be considered for a variety of openings) because it labels you as being interested in only one thing. Other experts argue that employers will try to categorize you anyway, so you might as well make sure they attach the right label. Remember, your goal is to generate interest immediately. If you decide to state your objective, make it effective by being as specific as possible about what you want:

A software sales position in a growing company requiring international experience

Advertising assistance with print media emphasis requiring strong customer-contact skills

If you have different types of qualifications (such as a certificate in secretarial science and two years' experience in retail sales), prepare separate resumés, each with a different objective. If your immediate objective differs from your ultimate one, combine the two in a single statement:

A marketing position with an opportunity for eventual managerial status

Proposal writer, with the ultimate goal of becoming a contracts administrator

Use a summary of qualifications instead of an objective if you have several key qualifications to highlight.

Summary of Qualifications Instead of stating your objective, you might summarize your qualifications in a brief statement that highlights your strongest points, particularly if you have had a good deal of varied experience. Use a short, simple phrase:

Summary of qualifications: Ten years of experience in commission selling with track record of generating new customer leads through creative advertising and community leadership positions

Or, you could put a heading at the beginning of your resumé, "Summary of Qualifications," and under it list three or four points summarizing the main reasons that the company should hire you. You may want to add together the months of experience you have had in short, part-time jobs to get a total and express how that experience is transferable to the professional environment you are entering. For example, if you had a number of part-time jobs in restaurants and retail each lasting several months, you might say "three years of experience in the hospitality industry" and highlight it in the summary as follows:

Summary of Qualifications
- Bachelor of Commerce, University of British Columbia
- *Three years of experience in customer service*
- Bilingual (French/English)
- Skilled in office and accounting software

The career objective or summary may be the only section read fully by the employer, so if you include either one, make it strong, concise, and convincing.

If education is your strongest selling point, discuss it thoroughly and highlight it visually.

Education If you're still in school, education is probably your strongest selling point, so present your educational background in depth, choosing facts that match the position you are seeking. Give this section a heading such as "Education" or "Professional Training." Then, starting with the school you most recently attended, list the name and location of each one, the term of your enrolment (in months and years), your major and minor fields of study, significant skills and abilities you've developed in your course work, and the degrees, diplomas, or certificates you've earned. If you're working on an uncompleted degree or diploma, include in parentheses the expected date of completion. Showcase your qualifications by listing skills courses that have directly equipped you for the job you are seeking, and indicate any scholarships, awards, or academic honours you've received.

The education section also includes off-campus training sponsored by business or government. Include any relevant seminars or workshops you've attended, as well as the certificates or other documents you've received. Whether you list your grades depends on the job you want and the quality of your grades. If you choose to show a grade-point average, be sure to mention the scale, especially if a five-point scale is used instead of a four-point scale.

Education is usually given less emphasis in a resumé after you've worked in your chosen field for a year or more. If work experience is your strongest qualification, save the section on education for later in the resumé and provide less detail.

Work Experience, Skills, and Accomplishments Like the education section, the work-experience section focuses on your overall theme. Tailor your description to highlight the relationship between your previous responsibilities and your target field. Call attention to skills you've developed and your progression from jobs of lesser to greater responsibility.

The work experience section lists all the related jobs you've had:

- Name and location of employer
- What the organization does (if not clear from its name)
- Your functional title
- How long you worked there
- Your duties and responsibilities
- Your significant achievements or contributions

When describing your work experience, list your jobs in chronological order, with the current or last one first. Include any part-time, summer, or intern positions, even if unrelated to your current career objective. Employers will see that you have the ability to get and hold a job—an important qualification in itself. If you have worked your way through school, say so. Employers interpret this behaviour as a sign of character.

Each listing includes the name, city, and province of the employer. If readers are unlikely to recognize the organization, briefly describe what it does. When you want to keep the name of your current employer confidential, identify the firm by industry only ("a large film-processing laboratory") or use the name but request confidentiality in the application letter or in an underlined note ("Resumé submitted in confidence") at the top or bottom of the resumé. If an organization's name or location has since changed, state the current name and location and then "formerly . . . "

Before each job listing, state your functional title, such as "clerk typist" or "salesperson." If you were a dishwasher, say so. Don't try to make your role seem more important by glamorizing your job title, functions, or achievements. Employers are checking on candidates' backgrounds more than they used to, so inaccuracies are likely to be exposed sooner or later. Also state how long you worked on each job, from month/year to month/year. Use the phrase "to present" to denote current employment. If a job was part-time, say so.

Devote the most space to the jobs that are related to your target position. If you were personally responsible for something significant, be sure to mention it ("Devised a new collection system that accelerated payment of overdue receivables"). Facts about your skills and accomplishments are the most important information you can give a prospective employer, so quantify them whenever possible:

Quantify your accomplishments whenever possible.

Designed a new ad that increased sales by 9 percent

Raised $2500 in 15 days for cancer research

You may also include a section describing other aspects of your background that pertain to your career objective. If you were applying for a position with a multinational organization, you would mention your command of another language or your travel experience. Other skills you might mention include the ability to operate a computer, word processor, or other specialized equipment. You might title a special section "Computer Skills" or "Language Skills" and place it near your "Education" or "Work Experience" section. If samples of your work might increase your chances of getting the job, insert a line at the end of your resumé offering to supply a portfolio of them on request.

Include facts that are related to your career objective:

- Command of other languages
- Computer expertise
- Date you can start working

Draw attention to key qualifications by making them section titles, for example, "Language Skills."

References Experts debate the value of putting references in a resumé. Some say that putting them in is unnecessary and takes up valuable space since they are not used until after the interview. In this case, bring reference information from past employment and education to the interview. Ensure that you have the reference's name, job title, company name and address, telephone number, and e-mail address. Also have the person's permission. Talk to references about what they will say about you.

Others say that having references in the resumé shows you are organized and it may make it easy for the recruiter to call references without any further communication with you. Also, it may be possible to create a positive impression of the applicant if the reference named is impressive. If you do decide to put references in, since you are limited in space, consider putting in two: one from work and one from education. Personal references are not as persuasive.

Nonpaid activities may provide evidence of work-related skills.

Activities and Achievements Your resumé should also describe any volunteer activities that demonstrate your abilities. Include the category "Volunteer Experience." List projects that require leadership, organization, teamwork, and cooperation. Emphasize career-related activities, such as "member of the Student Marketing Association." List skills you learned in these activities, and explain how these skills are related to the job you're applying for. Include speaking, writing, or tutoring experience; participation in athletics or creative projects; fundraising or community-service activities; and offices held in academic or professional organizations. (However, mention of political or religious organizations may be a red flag to someone with differing views, so use your judgment.)

Note any awards you've received. Again, quantify your achievements whenever possible. Instead of saying that you addressed various student groups, state how many and the approximate audience sizes. If your activities have been extensive, you may want to group them into divisions such as "College Activities," "Community Service," "Professional Associations," "Seminars and Workshops," and "Speaking Activities." An alternative is to divide them into two categories: "Service Activities" and "Achievements, Awards, and Honours."

Provide only the personal data that will help you get the job.

Interests Including interests can enhance the employer's understanding of how you would fit in the company.[14] For instance, candidates applying for a bodyguard position with Pinkerton's security division may want to list martial arts achievements among their personal interests. Someone applying to Mountain Equipment Co-op may want to list outdoor activities. Such information helps show how a candidate will fit in with the organization's culture.

Some information is best excluded from your resumé. Federal human rights laws prohibit employers from discriminating on the basis of gender, marital or family status, age, race, religion, national origin, and physical or mental disability. So be sure to exclude any items that could encourage discrimination. Experts also recommend excluding from resumés salary information, reasons for leaving jobs, names of previous supervisors, your social insurance number, and other identification codes. Save these items for the interview, and offer them only if the employer specifically requests them.

Avoid Resumé Deception

In an effort to put your best foot forward, you may be tempted to avoid a few points that could raise questions about your resumé. Although statistics on the prevalence of resumé inflation are difficult to gather, the majority of recruiters agree that distortion is common. Avoid the most frequent forms of deception:

Do not misrepresent your background or qualifications.

- **Do not claim educational credits you don't have.** Candidates may state (or imply) that they earned a degree when, in fact, they never attended the school or attended but did not complete the regular program. A typical claim might read, "Majored in commerce at Queen's University."
- **Do not inflate your grade-point average.** Students who feel pressured to impress employers with their academic performance may claim a higher GPA than they actually achieved.
- **Do not stretch dates of employment to cover gaps.** Many candidates try to camouflage gaps in their work history by giving vague dates of employment. For example, a

candidate who left a company in January 1994 and joined another in December 1995 might cover up by showing that the first job ended in 1994 and the next began in 1995.

- **Do not claim to be self-employed if you were not.** Another common way people cover a period of unemployment is by saying that they were "self-employed" or a "consultant." Only include this experience if you were operating an independent business.
- **Do not claim to have worked for companies that are out of business.** Candidates who need to fill a gap in their work record sometimes say they worked for a firm that has gone out of business. Checking such claims is difficult because the people who were involved in the disbanded business are hard to track down.
- **Do not omit jobs that might cause embarrassment.** Being laid off from one or two jobs is understandable when corporate mergers and downsizing are commonplace. However, a candidate who has lost several jobs in quick succession may seem a poor employee to recruiters.
- **Do not exaggerate expertise or experience.** Candidates often inflate their accomplishments by using verbs somewhat loosely. Words such as *supervised, managed, increased, improved,* and *created* imply that the candidate was personally responsible for results that, in reality, were the outcome of a group effort.

If you misrepresent your background and your resumé raises suspicion, you will probably get caught, and your reputation will be damaged. A deceptive resumé can seriously affect your ability to get hired and pursue your career (see Table 13.3).

Completing Your Resumé

The last step in the three-step writing process for resumés is no less important than the other two. As with any other business message, you need to revise your resumé, produce it in an appropriate form, and proofread it for any errors.

Revise Your Resumé

The key to writing a successful resumé is to adopt the "you" attitude and focus on your audience. Think about what the prospective employer needs, and then tailor your resumé accordingly. Employers read thousands of resumés every year, and they complain about common problems.

Table 13.3 How Far Can You Go to Make Your Resumé Strong and Positive?

Do	Don't
☑ **Tell the truth.** If you lie, you will almost certainly get caught, and the damage to your career could be significant.	⊗ **Fabricate.** Fake academic degrees and nonexistent jobs are checked first and will cost you the job, before or after you're hired.
☑ **Make your story positive.** Most blemishes on your record can be framed in a positive way.	⊗ **Make blatant omissions.** Failing to disclose a job that didn't work out is almost as bad as making one up.
☑ **Sanitize your record.** Clear up unresolved issues such as tax liens and lawsuits.	⊗ **Exaggerate successes.** Be ready to prove any claim about your accomplishments.
☑ **Think small.** Candidates with criminal histories or other career impediments should focus on smaller companies, which are less likely to conduct background checks.	⊗ **Go overboard.** There's usually no need to disclose career or personal history that's more than 15 years old. If asked directly, answer truthfully—but with a minimum of elaboration.

Do not submit a resumé that is

Avoid common resumé problems.

- **Too long.** One or two pages is a good length. The resumé should be concise, relevant, and to the point.
- **Too short or sketchy.** The resumé should give enough information for a proper evaluation of the applicant.
- **Hard to read.** A lack of "white space" and of devices such as indentions and boldfacing makes the reader's job more difficult.
- **Wordy.** Descriptions are verbose, with numerous words used for what could be said more simply.
- **Too slick.** The resumé will appear to have been written by someone other than the applicant, which raises the question of whether the qualifications have been exaggerated.
- **Misspelled and ungrammatical throughout.** Recruiters conclude that candidates who make spelling and grammar mistakes lack good verbal skills, which are important on the job.
- **Boastful.** The overconfident tone makes the reader wonder whether the applicant's self-evaluation is realistic.
- **Dishonest.** The applicant claims to have expertise or work experience that he or she does not possess.

Make Your Traditional Resumé Easy for People to Scan

Check what stands out. Have you highlighted key selling points?

With less than a minute to make a good impression, your resumé needs to look sharp and grab a recruiter's interest in the first few lines. A typical recruiter devotes 45 seconds to each resumé before tossing it into either the "maybe" or the "reject" pile.[15] Most recruiters **scan** through a resumé rather than read it from top to bottom. If the content in your resumé doesn't stand out, chances are the recruiter won't look at it long enough to judge your qualifications at a glance.

The key characteristics of a good resumé are

- Neatness
- Simplicity
- Accuracy
- Honesty
- Scannability

To give your printed resumé the best appearance possible, use a clean typeface on high-grade, letter-sized bond paper (in white or some light earth tone). Your stationery and envelope should match. Leave ample margins all around, and make sure that any corrections are unnoticeable. Avoid italic typefaces, which are difficult to read, and use a quality printer.

Keep your resumé to one or two pages. If you have a great deal of experience and are applying for a higher-level position, you may need to prepare a somewhat longer resumé.

Lay out your resumé to make important information easy to spot at a glance.[16] Break up the text with headings that call attention to various aspects of your background, such as work experience and education. Underline or capitalize key points, or set them off in the left margin. Use lists to itemize your most important qualifications, and leave plenty of white space, even if doing so forces you to use two pages rather than one. Use boldface or visual elements to draw the eye to important qualifications.

Convert Your Traditional Resumé to a Computer-Scannable Format

Reformatting your traditional resumé is helpful if it will be scanned or if you will be posting it on the Internet or submitting it via e-mail.

You need to format your resumé in at least two and maybe three ways: (1) as a traditional printed document such as the one just discussed, (2) as a plain-text (or ASCII) document that can be scanned from a hard copy or submitted electronically, and (3) as an HTML-coded document that can be uploaded to the Internet to post on a Web page (should you choose to).

Overwhelmed by the number of resumés they receive, many large organizations such as banks encourage applicants to submit electronic (scannable) resumés. By scanning these resumés into their electronic database, companies can quickly narrow the field of applicants. However, good scanning systems cost up to $100 000, so companies with fewer than 100 employees seldom use them.[17] If you're unsure whether an employer accepts scannable resumés, call and ask, or visit the company's Web site.

Electronically scannable resumés should convey the same information as traditional resumés, but the format and style must be changed to be computer friendly. Electronically scannable resumés are not intended to be read by humans. To understand why the format is different for scannable resumés, here's a closer look at how resumé scanning works.

A system with special software and hardware reads your scannable resumé and stores it in a database that can be searched by employers.

During the computer scanning process, special hardware and software are used to convert a paper resumé into an image on the employer's computer. Optical character recognition (OCR) software creates an electronic text document from the original and downloads it into a company database, which can be searched and sorted by keywords or criteria (see Figure 13.8). For example, a manager may want to hire a sales representative who is fluent in French, has five years' sales experience, and is experienced in cold calling. The employer enters these keywords (plus others) into the database program and performs a sort function on all the resumés in the database. The computer then provides a list of candidates whose resumés include these keywords. Next to the candidate's name is a percentage indicating how closely the resumé reflects the employer's requirements.[18]

To make your traditional resumé a computer-scannable one, format it as a plain text (ASCII) document, improve its look, and modify its content slightly by providing a list of keywords and by balancing common language with current jargon.[19]

ASCII is a plain-text language that can be read by any computer, regardless of the word-processing software.

Preparing Your Resumé in ASCII Format ASCII is a common plain-text language that allows your resumé to be read by any scanner and accessed by any computer, regardless of the word-processing software you used to prepare the document. All word-processing programs allow you to save files as plain text.

FIGURE 13.8 Understanding the Scanning Process

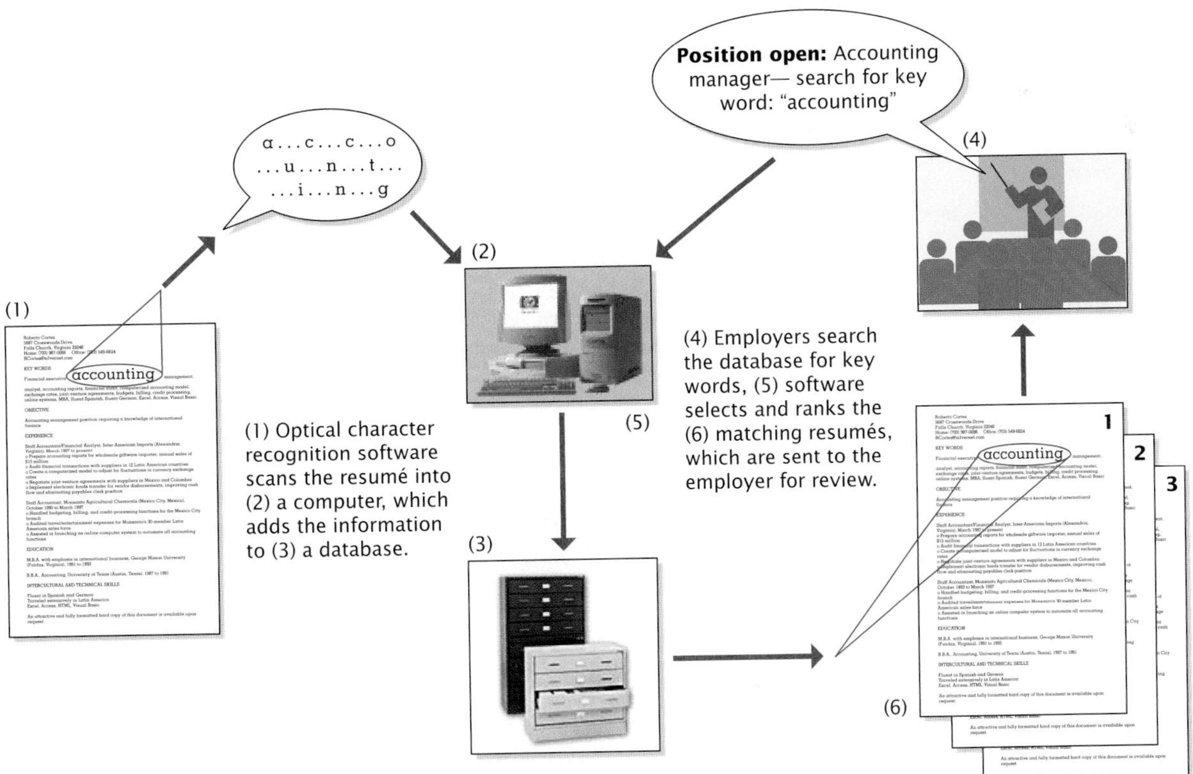

To convert your resumé to an ASCII plain-text file, do the following:

- Remove all formatting (boldfacing, underlining, italics, centring, bullets, graphic lines, etc.) and all formatting codes such as tab settings or tables.
- Remove shadows and reverse print (white letters on black background).
- Remove graphics and boxes.
- Use scannable typefaces (such as Helvetica, Futura, Optima, Univers, Times New Roman, Palatino, New Century Schoolbook, and Courier).
- Use a font size of 10 to 14 points.
- Remove multi-column formats that resemble newspapers or newsletters.
- Save your document under a different name by using your word processor's "save as" option and selecting "text only with line breaks."

Improving the Look of Your Computer-Scannable Resumé Resumés in ASCII format look ugly in comparison to traditional resumés. The following formatting techniques are acceptable for scannable resumés and will enhance your resumé's overall look and effectiveness:[20]

Simple formatting improves the appearance of ASCII documents.

- Align text by adding some blank spaces (rather than tabs).
- Create headings and separate paragraphs by adding a few blank lines.
- Indicate bullets with an asterisk or the lower case letter *o*.
- Use white space so that scanners and computers can tell when one topic ends and another begins.
- Do not condense the spacing between letters.
- Use all-capital letters for section headings as long as the letters do not touch each other.
- Put your name at the top of each page on its own line (with no text appearing above or beside your name).
- Use the standard address format below your name.
- List each phone number on its own line.
- Use white or light-coloured 8½-by-11-inch paper, printing on one side only.

Keep in mind that scannable resumés are read by computers, so it's fine to submit multiple pages, as long as you don't get carried away. To increase your chances of a quality scan, do not fold or staple the resumé and do not send a photocopy. Provide a printed original, if possible.

Keywords help potential employers sort through an entire database of resumés.

Providing a List of Keywords When converting your resumé to a scannable format, emphasize certain keywords to help potential employers select your resumé from the thousands they scan. Employers generally search for nouns (since verbs tend to be generic rather than specific to a particular position or skill). To maximize the number of matches (or hits) include a keyword summary of 20 to 30 words and phrases that define your skills, experience, education, professional affiliations, and so on. Place this list right after your name and address. Shown next is an example of a possible keyword summary for an accountant.

Keyword Summary

Accountant, Corporate Controller, Receivables, Payables, Inventory, Cash Flow, Financial Analysis, Payroll Experience, Corporate Taxes, Activity-Based Accounting, Problem Solving, Computer Skills, Excel, Access, Networks, HTML, HMML, Quick Books, BA Memorial University--Accounting, CPA, Dean's List, Articulate, Team Player, Flexible, Willing to Travel, Fluent French

One way to identify which keywords to include in your electronic summary is to underline all the skills listed in ads for the types of jobs you're interested in. Make sure these ads match your qualifications and experience. Include *interpersonal keywords* that tell what kind of person you are (see Table 13.4).

Use words your employer will understand by including some jargon specific to your field.

Balancing Common Language with Current Jargon Another way to maximize hits on your resumé is to use words that potential employers will understand (for example, say *keyboard,* not *input device*). Also, use abbreviations sparingly (except for common ones such as BA or MBA). At the same time, learn and use the important buzzwords in your

Table 13.4 Interpersonal Keywords

ability to delegate	communication skills	follow instructions	open minded	self-accountable
ability to implement	competitive	follow through	oral communication	self-managing
ability to plan	conceptual ability	follow up	organizational skills	sensitive
ability to train	creative	high energy	persuasive	setting priorities
accurate	customer oriented	industrious	problem solving	supportive
adaptable	detail minded	innovative	public speaking	takes initiative
aggressive work	empowering others	leadership	results oriented	team player
analytical ability	ethic	multi-tasking	risk taking	tenacious
assertive	flexible	open communication	safety conscious	willing to travel

field. Look for current jargon in the want ads of major newspapers such as *The Globe and Mail* and in other resumés in your field that are posted online. Be careful to check and recheck the spelling, capitalization, and punctuation of any jargon you include, and use only those words you see most often.

Lareine Chan created an electronic resumé by changing her formatting and adding a list of keywords. However, the information remains essentially the same and appears in the same order, as you can see in Figure 13.9 on page 372. Now her target employers can scan her resumé into a database, and Chan can submit her resumé via e-mail or post it on the Internet.

Submitting Your Scannable Resumé If an employer gives you an option of submitting a scannable resumé by mail, by fax, or by e-mail, choose e-mail. E-mail puts your resumé directly into the employer's database, bypassing the scanning process. If you send your resumé in a paper format by regular mail or by fax, you run the risk that an OCR scanning program will create an error when reading it. In fact, increasing numbers of job applicants are submitting both a traditional and a scannable resumé, explaining in their cover letter that the scannable resumé is for downloading into a database if the company desires.[21]

E-mail is the best way to transmit your plain-text resumé.

When submitting your resumé by e-mail, don't attach it as a separate document. Most human resources departments won't accept attached files (they're concerned about computer viruses). Instead, paste your resumé into the body of your e-mail message. Whenever you know a reference number or a job ad number, include it in your e-mail subject line.

Paste your resumé into the body of your e-mail message if submitting it by e-mail.

If you're posting your scannable resumé to an employer's online resumé builder, copy and paste the appropriate sections from your electronic file directly into the employer's form. This method avoids rekeying and eliminates errors.

If you fax your scannable resumé, set your machine to "fine" mode (to ensure a high-quality printout on the receiving end). If you're mailing your resumé, you may want to send both a well-designed traditional resumé and a scannable one. Simply attach sticky notes, labelling one "visual resumé" and the other "scannable resumé."

Build an Online Resumé

If you wish to post your resumé on your Web page, provide employers with your URL; most recruiters won't take the time to use search engines to find your site.[22] As you design your Web site resumé, think of important keywords to use as hyperlinks—words that will grab an employer's attention and make the recruiter want to click on that hyperlink to learn more about you. You can make links to papers you've written, recommendations, and sound or video clips. Don't distract potential employers from your credentials by using hyperlinks to organizations or other Web sites.

One advantage of posting your resumé on your Web site is the opportunity to use hyperlinks.

To post your resumé with an index service, you must convert it to an electronic format (see Figure 13.9). Transmit it by mail, fax, modem, or e-mail. Once your resumé is in the service's database, it is sent to employers who match the keywords you've listed.

FIGURE 13.9 Electronic Resumé Designed for Computer Scanning

Removes all boldfacing, rules, bullets, and two-column formatting
Includes carefully selected keywords that describe Chan's skills and accomplishments
Uses a lower case letter *o* in bulleted lists
Singles Chan out from the crowd by including in the keyword section specific attributes such as "fluent Mandarin" and "willing to travel"
Uses ample white space to make her plain-text resumé easier to scan

Lareine Chan
5687 Crosswoods Drive
Richmond, BC V5R 2T1
Home: (604) 273-0086 Office: (604) 273-6624
RChan@telus.net

KEYWORDS

Financial executive, accounting management, international finance, financial analyst, accounting reports, financial audit, computerized accounting model, exchange rates, joint-venture agreements, budgets, billing, credit processing, online systems, MBA, fluent Cantonese, fluent Mandarin, Excel, Access, Visual Basic, team player, willing to travel

OBJECTIVE

Accounting management position requiring a knowledge of international finance

EXPERIENCE

Staff Accountant/Financial Analyst, Inter-Asian Imports (Vancouver, BC), March 2001 to present
o Prepare accounting reports for wholesale giftware importer, annual sales of $15 million
o Audit financial transactions with suppliers in 12 Asian countries
o Created a computerized model to adjust for fluctuations in currency exchange rates
o Negotiated joint-venture agreements with suppliers in Hong Kong and Taiwan
o Implemented electronic funds transfer for vendor disbursements, improving cash flow and eliminating payables clerk position

Staff Accountant, Monsanto Agricultural Chemicals (Shanghai, China), October 1997 to March 2001
o Handled budgeting, billing, and credit-processing functions for the Shanghai branch
o Audited travel/entertainment expenses for Monsanto's 30-member Asian sales force
o Assisted in launching an online computer system to automate accounting

EDUCATION

Master of Business Administration with emphasis in international business, University of British Columbia (Vancouver, BC), 1995–1997

Bachelor of Business Administration, Accounting, Memorial University (St. John's, NL), 1992–1995

INTERCULTURAL AND TECHNICAL SKILLS

Fluent in Cantonese and Mandarin
Travelled extensively in Asia
Excel, Access, HTML, Visual Basic

An attractive and fully formatted hard copy of this document is available upon request.

Do not use photos, and avoid providing information that reveals your age, gender, race, marital status, or religion. Because a Web site is a public access area, you should also leave out the names of references and previous employers. Either mention that references are available on request, or say nothing. Also, instead of naming companies, simply refer to "a large accounting firm" or "a wholesale giftware importer." Finally, include an ASCII version of your resumé on your Web page so that prospective employers can download it into their company's database.

Proofread Your Resumé

Your resumé is a concrete example of how you will prepare material on the job. So in every format, remember to pay close attention to mechanics and details. Check all headings and lists for parallelism, and be sure that your grammar, spelling, and punctuation are correct.

Once your resumé is complete, update it continually. As already mentioned, employment is becoming much more flexible these days, so it's likely you'll want to change employers. Besides, you'll also need your resumé to apply for membership in professional organizations and to work toward a promotion. Keeping your resumé updated is a good idea.

Keep your resumé up to date.

Preparing Other Types of Employment Messages

Although your resumé will take the greatest amount of time and effort, you'll also need to prepare other employment messages, including application letters, application forms, and follow-up notes.

Application Letters

Whenever you submit your resumé, accompany it with a cover, or application letter to let readers know what you're sending, why you're sending it, and how they can benefit from reading it. Because your application letter is in your own style (rather than the choppy, shorthand style of your resumé), it gives you a chance to show your communication skills and some personality.

Always send your resumé and application letter together, because each has a unique job to perform. The purpose of your resumé is to get employers interested enough to contact you for an interview. The purpose of your application letter is to get employers interested enough to read your resumé.

Application letters are intended to interest readers enough to read your resumé.

Show You Know the Company

Before drafting a letter, learn something about the organization you're applying to; then focus on your audience so that you can show you've done your homework. Imagine yourself in the recruiter's situation, and show how your background and talents will solve a particular problem or fill a specific need the company has. The more you can learn about the organization, the better you'll be able to capture the reader's attention and convey your interest in the company.[23] During your research, find out the name, title, and department of the person you're writing to. Reaching and addressing the right person is the most effective way to gain attention. Avoid phrases such as "To Whom It May Concern" and "Dear Sir or Madam."

Research the company so you can show specifically how you "fit" into their workplace.

Keep It Short

When putting yourself in your reader's shoes, remember that this person's in-box is probably overflowing with resumés and cover letters. So respect your reader's time. A good application letter should be no longer than one page. It should maintain a friendly, conversational tone. Highlight the specific points the company is looking for. Show that you know the job.

If you're sending a **solicited application letter**—in response to an announced job opening—you'll usually know what qualifications the organization is seeking. You'll also have more competition because hundreds of other job seekers will have seen the listing and may be sending applications too. The letter in Figure 13.10 was written in response to a help-wanted ad. Nick Caruso highlights his chief qualifications and mirrors the requirements specified in the ad.

You write a solicited application letter in response to an announced job opening.

In some respects, an **unsolicited letter**—sent to an organization that has not announced an opening—stands a better chance of being read and receiving individualized attention. In her unsolicited application letter in Figure 13.11, Glenda Johns manages to give a snapshot of her qualifications and skills. She gains attention by focusing on the needs of the employer.

You write an unsolicited application letter to an organization that has not announced a job opening.

Both solicited and unsolicited letters present your qualifications similarly. The main difference is in the opening paragraph. In a solicited letter, you need no special attention-getter because you have been invited to apply. In an unsolicited letter, you need to start by capturing the reader's attention and interest.

Getting Attention

Follow the AIDA approach when writing your application letter: attention, interest, desire, action.

The opening of an application letter captures attention, gives the reason you're writing, and states which job you're applying for.

Like your resumé, your application letter is a form of advertising, so organize it as you would a sales letter: Use the AIDA approach, focus on your audience, and emphasize reader benefits (as discussed in Chapter 9). Make sure your style projects confidence. To sell a potential employer on your merits, you must believe in them and sound as though you do.

The opening paragraph of your application letter must also state your reason for writing and the position you are applying for. Table 13.5 on page 377 highlights some important ways to spark interest and grab attention in your opening paragraph. All these openings demonstrate the "you" attitude, and many indicate how the applicant can serve the employer. You can give your reason for writing by saying something like the following examples:

FIGURE 13.10 Sample Solicited Application Letter

2893 Jack Pine Road
Hamilton, ON L2H 8Y7

February 3, 2003

Ms. Angela Clair
Director of Administration
Cummings and Welbane, Inc.
770 Campus Point Drive
Hamilton, ON L8N 3T2

Dear Ms. Clair:

WORKING WITH YOU

States the reason for writing and links the writer's experience to stated qualifications

Please consider me for the office assistant position you advertised in the January 31 issue of the *Toronto Star*. In addition to experience in a variety of office settings, I am familiar with the computer software used in your office.

I recently completed a three-course sequence at Hamilton College on Microsoft Word and PowerPoint. I learned how to apply those programs to speed up letter- and report-writing tasks. A workshop on "Writing and Editing with the Unix Processor" gave me experience with other valuable applications such as composing and formatting sales letters, financial reports, and presentation slides.

Discusses how specific skills apply to the job sought, showing that Caruso understands the job's responsibilities

Explains an achievement mentioned in the resumé and refers the reader to the enclosure

These skills have been invaluable to me as assistant to the chief nutritionist at our campus cafeteria (please refer to my resumé). The order-confirmation system I designed has sharply reduced the problems of late shipments and depleted inventories.

I would appreciate an interview with you. Please telephone me any afternoon between 3 and 5 p.m. at (905) 220-6139 to let me know the day and time most convenient for you.

Asks for an interview and facilitates action

Sincerely,

Nick Caruso

Nick Caruso

Enclosure: Resumé

Please consider my application for an entry-level position in technical writing.

Your firm advertised a fleet sales position (on September 23, 2005, in the *Edmonton Sun*).

Another way to state your reason for writing is to use a subject line in the opening of your letter:

Subject: Application for bookkeeper position

Building Interest and Increasing Desire

The middle section of your application letter presents your strongest selling points in terms of their potential benefit to the organization, thereby building interest in you and creating a desire to interview you. If you already mentioned your selling points in the opening, don't repeat them. Simply give supporting evidence. Be careful not to repeat the facts presented in your resumé; instead, interpret those facts for the reader. Spell out a few

The middle section of an application letter

- Summarizes your relevant qualifications
- Emphasizes your accomplishments
- Suggests desirable personal qualities
- Justifies salary requirements
- Refers to your resumé

FIGURE 13.11 Sample Unsolicited Application Letter

1254 Main Street
Summerside, PE C1N 3C4

June 16, 2005

Ms. Patricia Downings, Store Manager
Wal-Mart
840 South Oak
Charlottetown, PE C2R 5H6

Dear Ms. Downings:

APPLICATION FOR MANAGERIAL POSITION

Gains attention in the first paragraph →

Do you want retail clerks and managers who are accurate, enthusiastic, and experienced. Do you look for someone who cares about customer service, who understands merchandising, and who can work with others to get the job done? When you next need a manager trainee or a clerk who is willing to work toward promotion, please consider me for the job.

Working as a clerk and then as an assistant department manager in a large department store has taught me how challenging a career in retailing can be. Moreover, my diploma in retailing (including work in such courses as retailing, marketing, and business information systems) will provide your store with a well-rounded associate. Most important, I can offer your store more than my two years of study and field experience. You'll find that I'm interested in every facet of retailing, eager to take on responsibility, and willing to continue learning throughout my career. Please look over my resumé to see how my skills can benefit your store.

← Points out personal qualities that aren't specifically stated in her resumé

Interests reader with knowledge of the company's policy toward promotion →

I understand that Wal-Mart prefers to promote its managers from within the company, and I would be pleased to start out with an entry-level position until I gain the necessary experience. Do you have any associate positions opening up soon? Could we discuss my qualifications? I will phone you early next Wednesday to arrange a meeting at your convenience, or please call me at (204) 733-5981.

← Focuses on the audience and displays the "you" attitude, even though the last paragraph uses the word "I"

Sincerely,

Glenda Johns

Glenda Johns

Enclosure

of your key qualifications, and back up your assertions with some convincing evidence of your ability to perform:

Poor: I completed three college courses in business communication, earning an A in each course, and have worked for the past year at Imperial Construction.

Improved: Using the skills gained from three semesters of training in business communication, I developed a collection system for Imperial Construction that reduced its 2005 bad-debt losses by 3.7 percent, or $9902, over those of 2004. Instead of using timeworn terminology, the new system's collection letters offered discount incentives for speedy payment.

Improved: Experience in customer relations and courses in public relations have taught me how to handle the problem-solving tasks that arise in a leading retail clothing firm like yours. Such important tasks include identifying and resolving customer complaints, writing letters that build good customer relations, and above all, promoting the organization's positive image.

When writing a solicited letter responding to an advertisement, be sure to discuss each requirement specified in the ad.

The middle of your application letter also demonstrates a few significant job-related qualities, such as your diligence or your ability to work hard, learn quickly, handle responsibility, or get along with people:

> While attending university full-time, I trained three hours a day with the track team. In addition, I worked part-time during the school year and up to 60 hours a week each summer in order to be totally self-supporting while in university. I can offer your organization the same level of effort and perseverance.

Toward the end of this section, refer the reader to your resumé by citing a specific fact or general point covered there:

> As you can see in the attached resumé, I've been working part-time with a local publisher since my second year of college, and during that time, I have successfully resolved more than a few "client crises."

Motivating Action

Close by asking for an interview and making the interview easy to arrange.

The final paragraph of your application letter has two important functions: to ask the reader for a specific action and to make a reply easy. In almost all cases, the action you request is an interview. Don't demand it, however; try to sound natural and appreciative. Offer to come to the employer's office at a convenient time or, if the firm is some distance away, to meet with its nearest representative. Make the request easy to fulfil by stating your phone number and the best time to reach you—or, if you wish to be in control, by mentioning that you will follow up with a phone call in a few days.

> After you have reviewed my qualifications, could we discuss the possibility of putting my marketing skills to work for your company? Because I will be on spring break the week of March 8, I would like to arrange a time to talk then. I will call in late February to schedule a convenient time when we could discuss employment opportunities at your company.

Once you have edited and proofread your application letter, mail it and your resumé promptly, especially if they have been solicited.

Table 13.5 Tips for Getting Attention in Application Letters

Tip	Example
Unsolicited Application Letters	
• Show how your strongest skills will benefit the organization. A 20-year-old in her third year of college might begin like this:	When you need a secretary in your export division who can take shorthand at 125 words a minute and transcribe notes at 70—in English, French, or Spanish—call me.
• Describe your understanding of the job's requirements and then show how well your qualifications fit them	Your annual report states that Husky Oil runs employee-training programs about workforce diversity. The difficulties involved in running such programs can be significant, as I learned while tutoring inner-city high-school students last summer. My 12 pupils were enrolled in vocational training programs and came from diverse ethnic and racial backgrounds. The one thing they had in common was a lack of familiarity with the typical employer's expectations. To help them learn the "rules of the game," I developed exercises that cast them in various roles: boss, customer, new recruit, and co-worker. Of the 12 students, 10 subsequently found full-time jobs and have called or written to tell me how much they gained from the workshop.
• Mention the name of a person known to and highly regarded by the reader	When Janice McHugh of your franchise sales division spoke to our business communication class last week, she said you often need promising new marketing graduates at this time of year.
• Refer to publicized company activities, achievements, changes, or new procedures	Today's issue of the *Examiner* reports that you may need the expertise of computer programmers versed in robotics when your Windsor tire plant automates this spring.
• Use a catchphrase opening if the job requires ingenuity and imagination	*Haut monde*—whether said in French, Italian, or Arabic, it still means "high society." As an interior designer for your Westmount showroom, not only could I serve and sell to your distinguished clientele, but I could do it in all these languages. I speak, read, and write them fluently.
Solicited Application Letters	
• Identify the publication in which the ad ran; then describe what you have to offer	Your ad in the April issue of *Travel & Leisure* for a cruise-line social director caught my eye. My eight years of experience as a social director in the travel industry in the Maritimes would allow me to serve your new Atlantic cruise division well.

Adapting Style and Approach to Culture

The AIDA approach isn't appropriate for job seekers in every culture. If you're applying for a job abroad or want to work with a subsidiary of an organization that is based in another country, you may need to adjust your tone. Blatant self-promotion is considered bad form in some cultures. Other cultures stress group performance over individual contributions. As for format, recruiters in some countries (including France) prefer handwritten letters to printed or typed ones—another good reason to research a company carefully before drafting your application letter. For Canadian and U.S. companies, let your letter reflect your personal style. Be yourself, but be businesslike too; avoid sounding cute. Don't use slang or a gimmicky layout.

You may need to vary your approach according to your reader's culture.

Application Forms

Before considering you for a position, some organizations require you to fill out and submit an **application form,** a standardized data sheet that simplifies the comparison of applicants' qualifications. Organizations will use your application form as a convenient

An application form, is a standardized data sheet that simplifies comparison of applicants' credentials.

one-page source of information about your qualifications, so try to be thorough and accurate when filling it out. Have your resumé with you to remind you of important information, and if you can't remember something and have no record of it, provide the closest estimate possible.

Application Follow-Ups

Use a follow-up letter to let the employer know you're still interested in the job.

If your application letter and resumé do not bring a response within a month or so, follow up with a second letter to keep your file active. This follow-up letter also gives you a chance to update your original application with any recent job-related information:

> Since applying to you on May 3 for an executive secretary position, I have completed a course in office management at Red River Community College. I achieved a first-class standing in the course. I now am a proficient user of MS Word, including macros and other complex functions.
>
> Please keep my application in your active file, and let me know when you need a skilled executive secretary.

Even if you've received a letter acknowledging your application and saying that it will be kept on file, send a follow-up letter three months later to show that you are still interested:

> Three months ago I applied for an underwriting position, and I want to let you know that I am still very interested in joining your company.
>
> I recently completed a four-week temporary work assignment at a large local insurance agency. I learned several new verification techniques and gained experience in using the online computer system. This experience could increase my value to your underwriting department.
>
> Please keep my application in your active file, and let me know when a position opens for a capable underwriter.

A follow-up letter can demonstrate that you're sincerely interested in working for the organization, that you're persistent in pursuing your goals, and that you're upgrading your skills to make yourself a better employee. And it might just get you an interview.

Reviewing Key Points

In this chapter you learned about searching for employment and preparing resumés and letters of application. You learned how to research career and job prospects by checking forecasts in occupational handbooks and how to organize resumés. You can choose to show your work history in reverse chronological order or by categorizing your skills in a functional resumé. Whichever way you decide to organize your resumé, you should

- Keep the length to one or two pages
- Summarize and select key information according to job requirements
- Use headings and lists to highlight important information
- Include education, work and volunteer experience, market-related skills, and interests
- Be accurate, concise, clear, and use parallel structure
- Use verbs to create a dynamic style
- Make the resumé easy to skim by using layout, white space, indentation, headings, boldface, and visual features for emphasis

If the company of interest uses computer software to scan applicant's resumés, you will need to convert your resumé for electronic scanning by removing indentation, boldface, and visual features and by aligning the points on the left margin.

In letters of application

- Write the letter as you would a "sales" letter and use AIDA
- Open with the job request
- Use research to show how you "fit" the company
- Emphasize the skills you can contribute
- Ask for an interview in the last paragraph and "make the action easy"
- Keep it to one page
- Follow up if the company has not responded

Test Your Knowledge

1. In what three ways is the employment search affected by the results of today's changing workplace?

2. What three things can you do to make yourself more valuable to an employer?

3. What is a resumé, and why is it important to adopt a "you" attitude when preparing one?

4. How does a chronological resumé differ from a functional resumé, and when is each appropriate?

5. What elements are commonly included in a resumé?

6. What are some of the most common problems with resumés?

7. Why is it important to provide a keyword summary in a scannable or electronic resumé?

8. What advantages do resumés sent by e-mail have over resumés sent by fax or by mail?

9. How does a solicited application letter differ from an unsolicited letter?

10. How does the AIDA approach apply to an application letter?

Apply Your Knowledge

1. According to experts in the job-placement field, the average job seeker relies too heavily on the resumé and not enough on other elements of the job search. Which elements do you think are most important? Please explain.

2. One of the disadvantages of resumé scanning is that some qualified applicants will be missed because the technology isn't perfect. However, more companies are using this approach. Do you think that resumé scanning is a good idea? Please explain.

3. Stating your career objective on a resumé or application might limit your opportunities by labelling you too narrowly. Not stating your objective, however, might lead an employer to categorize you incorrectly. Which outcome is riskier? Do summaries of qualifications overcome such drawbacks? If so, how? Explain briefly.

4. When writing a solicited application letter and describing the skills requested in the employer's ad, how can you avoid using *I* too often? Explain and give examples.

5. **Ethical Choices** Between your second and third year, you quit school for a year to earn the money to finish university. You worked as a clerk in a finance company, checking references on loan applications, typing, and filing. Your manager made a lot of the fact that he had never attended university. He seemed to resent you for pursuing your education, but he never criticized your work, so you thought you were doing okay. After you'd been working there for six months, he fired you, saying that you failed to be thorough enough in your credit checks. You were actually glad to leave, and you found another job right away at a bank doing similar duties. Now that you've graduated from university, you're writing your resumé. Will you include the finance company job in your work history? Please explain. What other ethical issue could you be concerned about?

Practise Your Knowledge

Activities

For live links to all Web sites discussed in this chapter, visit this text's Web site at www.pearsoned.ca/bovee. Just log on and select Chapter 13, and click on "Student Resources." Locate the page or the URL related to the material in the text. For "Exploring the Best of the Web" exercises, you'll also find navigational directions. Click on the live link to the site.

1. **Analyze This Document** Read the following resumé; then (1) analyze its strengths and weaknesses and (2) revise the document so that it follows the guidelines presented in this chapter.

   Sylvia Manchester

   765 Belle Fleur Blvd.

   St-Laurent, QC H4L 3X9

   (514) 312-9504

   smanchester@bce.net

   PERSONAL: Single, excellent health, 5′8″, 116 lb.; hobbies include cooking, dancing, and reading.

   JOB OBJECTIVE: To obtain a responsible position in marketing or sales with a good company.

   Education: BSc degree in biology, Dalhousie University. Graduated with a 3.0 average. Member of the varsity volleyball team. President of Dalhousie Chess Club.

WORK EXPERIENCE

Fisher Scientific Instruments, 2003 to present, field sales representative. Responsible for calling on customers and explaining the features of Fisher's line of laboratory instruments. Also responsible for writing sales letters, attending trade shows, and preparing weekly sales reports.

Fisher Scientific Instruments, 1999–2001, customer service representative. Was responsible for handling incoming phone calls from customers who had questions about delivery, quality, or operation of Fisher's line of laboratory instruments. Also handled miscellaneous correspondence with customers.

Medical Electronics, Inc. 1997–1999, administrative assistant to the vice-president of marketing. In addition to handling typical secretarial chores for the vice-president of marketing, I was in charge of compiling the monthly sales reports, using figures provided by members of the field sales force. I also was given responsibility for doing various market research activities.

Ottawa Convention and Visitors Bureau. 1995–97, summers, tour guide. During the summers of my university years, I led tours of Ottawa for tourists visiting the city. My duties included greeting conventioneers and their spouses at hotels, explaining the history and features of the city during an all-day sightseeing tour, and answering questions about Ottawa and its attractions. During my fourth summer with the bureau, I was asked to help train the new tour guides. I prepared a handbook that provided interesting facts about the various tourist attractions, as well as answers to the most commonly asked tourist questions. The bureau was so impressed with the handbook they had it printed up so that it could be given as a gift to visitors.

Dalhousie University. 1995–97, part-time clerk in admissions office. While I was a student in university, I worked 15 hours a week in the admissions office. My duties included filing, processing applications, and handling correspondence from high-school students and administrators.

2. **Analyze This Document** Read the following letter; then (1) analyze its strengths and weaknesses and (2) revise the letter so that it follows the guidelines presented in this chapter.

I'm writing to let you know about my availability for the brand manager job you advertised. As you can see from my enclosed resumé, my background is perfect for the position. Even though I don't have any real job experience, my grades have been outstanding considering that I went to a top-ranked business school.

I did many things during my undergraduate years to prepare me for this job:

- Earned a 3.4 out of a 4.0 with a 3.8 in my business courses
- Elected representative to the student governing association
- Selected to receive the Terry Fox Award
- Worked to earn a portion of my tuition

I am sending my resumé to all the top firms, but I like yours better than any of the rest. Your reputation is tops in the industry, and I want to be associated with a business that can pridefully say it's the best.

If you wish for me to come in for an interview, I can come on a Friday afternoon or anytime on weekends when I don't have classes. Again, thanks for considering me for your brand manager position.

3. **Analyze This Document** Read the following letter; then (1) analyze its strengths and weaknesses and (2) revise the letter so that it follows the guidelines presented in this chapter.

Did you receive my resumé? I sent it to you at least two months ago and haven't heard anything. I know you keep resumés on file, but I just want to be sure that you keep me in mind. I heard you are hiring health-care managers and certainly would like to be considered for one of those positions.

Since I last wrote you, I've worked in a variety of positions that have helped prepare me for management. To wit, I've become lunch manager at the restaurant where I work, which involved a raise in pay. I now manage a wait staff of 12 girls and take the lunch receipts to the bank every day.

Of course, I'd much rather be working at a real job, and that's why I'm writing again. Is there anything else you would like to know about me or my background? I would really like to know more about your company. Is there any literature you could send me? If so, I would really appreciate it.

I think one reason I haven't been hired yet is that I don't want to leave Winnipeg. So I hope when you think of me, it's for a position that wouldn't require moving. Thanks again for considering my application.

4. **Work-Related Preferences: Self-Assessment** What work-related activities and situations do you prefer? Evaluate your preferences in each of the following areas. Use the results as a good start for guiding your job search.

Activity or Situation	Strongly Agree	Agree	Disagree	No Preference
1. I want to work independently.	_____	_____	_____	_____
2. I want variety in my work.	_____	_____	_____	_____
3. I want to work with people.	_____	_____	_____	_____
4. I want to work with products or machines.	_____	_____	_____	_____
5. I want physical work.	_____	_____	_____	_____
6. I want mental work.	_____	_____	_____	_____
7. I want to work for a large organization.	_____	_____	_____	_____
8. I want to work for a non-profit organization.	_____	_____	_____	_____
9. I want to work for a small family business.	_____	_____	_____	_____
10. I want to work for a service business.	_____	_____	_____	_____
11. I want regular, predictable work hours.	_____	_____	_____	_____
12. I want to work in a city location.	_____	_____	_____	_____
13. I want to work in a small town or suburb.	_____	_____	_____	_____
14. I want to work in another country.	_____	_____	_____	_____
15. I want to work outdoors.	_____	_____	_____	_____
16. I want to work in a structured environment.	_____	_____	_____	_____

5. **Teamwork** Working with another student, change the following statements to make them more effective for a traditional resumé by using action verbs.

   a. Have some experience with database design
   b. Assigned to a project to analyze the cost accounting methods for a large manufacturer
   c. I was part of a team that developed a new inventory control system.
   d. Am responsible for preparing the quarterly department budget
   e. Was a manager of a department with seven employees working for me
   f. Was responsible for developing a spreadsheet to analyze monthly sales by department
   g. Put in place a new program for ordering supplies

6. **Resumé Preparation: Work Accomplishments** Using your team's answers to Activity 5, make the statements stronger by quantifying them (make up any numbers you need).

7. **Ethical Choices** Assume that you achieved all the tasks shown in Activity 5 not as an individual employee, but as part of a work team. In your resumé, must you mention other team members? Explain your answer.

8. **Resumé Preparation: Electronic Version** Using your revised version of the resumé in Activity 1, prepare a fully formatted print resumé. What formatting changes would Sylvia Manchester need to make if she were sending her resumé electronically? Develop a keyword summary and make all the changes needed to complete this electronic resumé.

Expand Your Knowledge

Best of the Web

Post an Online Resumé At Careerbuilder, you'll find sample resumés, tips on preparing different types of resumés (including scannable ones), links to additional articles, and expert advice on creating resumés that bring positive results. After you've polished your resumé-writing skills, you can search for jobs online using the site's numerous links to national and international industry-specific Web sites. You can access the information at Monster.ca to develop your resumé and then post it with prospective employers—all free. Take advantage of what this site offers, and get ideas for writing or improving a new resumé.

www.monster.ca

Exercises

1. Before writing a new resumé, make a list of action verbs that describe your skills and experience.
2. Describe the advantages and disadvantages of chronological and functional resumé formats. Do you think a combination resumé would be an appropriate format for your new resumé? Explain why or why not.
3. List some of the tips you learned for preparing an electronic resumé.

Exploring the Web on Your Own

Review these chapter-related Web sites on your own to learn more about writing resumés and cover letters.

1. Find out what happens when resumés are scanned at Proven Resumés, www.provenresumes.com/reswkshps/electronic/scnres.html.
2. Learn how to produce cover letters with brilliance, flair, and speed at So You Wanna Write a Cover Letter?, www.soyouwanna.com/site/syws/coverletter/coverletter.html.
3. For expert advice on writing resumés and cover letters, go to www.wetfeet.com.

Learn Interactively

Interactive Study Guide

Visit the Companion Website at www.pearsoned.ca/bovee. For Chapter 13, take advantage of the interactive "Study Guide" to test your chapter knowledge. Get instant feedback on whether you need additional studying.

This site offers a variety of additional resources: The "Research Area" helps you locate a wealth of information to use in course assignments. The "Study Hall" helps you succeed in this course by offering support with writing and study skills, time management, and career skills, as well as numerous other resources.

Peak Performance Grammar and Mechanics

Use the Peak Performance Grammar and Mechanics CD to test your skill with capitalization, numbers, and other mechanics of writing. In the "Mechanics" section, take the Pretest to determine whether you have any weak areas. Then review those areas in the Refresher Course. Take the Follow-Up Test to check your grasp of punctuation. For an extra challenge or advanced practice, take the Advanced Test.

Cases

Apply each step in Figure 13.3 to the following cases, as assigned by your instructor.

Building Toward a Career

1. Taking stock and taking aim: Application package for the right job

Think about yourself. What are some things that come easily to you? What do you enjoy doing? In what part of the country would you like to live? Do you like to work indoors? Outdoors? A combination of the two? How much do you like to travel? Would you like to spend considerable time on the road? Do you like to work closely with others or more independently? What conditions make a job unpleasant? Do you delegate responsibility easily, or do you like to do things yourself? Are you better with words or numbers? Better at speaking or writing? Do you like to work under fixed deadlines? How important is job security to you? Do you want your supervisor to state clearly what is expected of you, or do you like the freedom to make many of your own decisions?

Your Task After answering these questions, gather information about possible jobs that suit your profile by consulting reference materials (from your university or college library or placement centre) and by searching the Internet (using some of the search strategies discussed in Chapter 10). Next, choose a location, a company, and a job that interests you. With guidance from your instructor, decide whether to apply for a job you're qualified for now or one you'll be qualified for with additional education. Then, as directed by your instructor, write one or more of the following: (a) a job-inquiry letter, (b) a resumé, (c) a letter of application, (d) a follow-up letter to your application letter.

WEB SKILLS 2. Scanning the possibilities: Resumé for the Internet

In your search for a position, you discover Career Magazine, a Web site that lists hundreds of companies advertising on the Internet. Your chances of getting an interview with a leading company will be enhanced if you submit your resumé and cover letter electronically. On the Web, explore www.careermag.com.

Your Task Prepare a scannable résumé that could be submitted to one of the companies advertising at the Career Magazine Web site. Print out the resumé for your instructor.

WEB SKILLS 3. Online application: Electronic cover letter introducing a resumé

Motley Fool (www.fool.com) is a "Generation X" online magazine accessed via the Web. Although its founders and writers are extremely creative and motivated, they lack business experience and need a fellow "X'er" to help them manage the business. Among articles in a recent edition was one titled "The Soul of the Dead," about the influence of the Grateful Dead on more than one generation of concertgoers. Other articles deal with lifestyle issues, pop movies, music, and "trends for an old-young generation."

Your Task Write an e-mail message that will serve as your cover letter and address your message to Louis Corrigan, managing editor. Try to limit your message to one screen (about 23 lines). You'll need a creative "hook" and a reassuring approach that identifies you as the right person to help Motley Fool become financially viable.

Writing a Resumé and an Application Letter

4. "Help wanted": Application for a job listed in the classified section

Among the jobs listed in today's *Vancouver Sun* (435 Redwood Avenue, Vancouver, BC V6T 1F7) are the following:

ACCOUNTING ASSISTANT
Established leader in the vacation ownership industry has immediate opening in its Northbrook corp. accounting dept. for an accounting assistant. Responsibilities include bank reconciliation, preparation of deposits, AP, and cash receipt posting. Join our fast-growing company and enjoy our great benefits package. Flex work hours, medical, dental insurance. Fax resumé to Lisa: 604-564-3876.

ADMINISTRATIVE ASSISTANT
Fast-paced Mill Woods office seeks professional with strong computer skills. Proficient in MS Word & Excel, PowerPoint a plus. Must be detail oriented, able to handle multiple tasks, and possess strong communication skills. Excellent benefits, salary, and work environment. Fax resumé to 604-350-8649.

CUSTOMER SERVICE
A nationally known computer software developer has an exciting opportunity in customer service and inside sales support in its fast-paced downtown Burnaby office. You'll help resolve customer problems over the phone, provide information, assist in account management, and administer orders. If you're friendly, self-motivated, energetic, and have two years of experience, excellent problem-solving skills, organizational, communication, and PC skills, and communicate well over the phone, send resumé to J. Haber, 233 North Lake Shore Drive, Burnaby, BC V1H 5N1.

SALES-ACCOUNT MANAGER
Aqua Springs Water Company is seeking an Account Manager to sell and coordinate our programs to major accounts in the Alberta market. The candidate should possess strong analytical and selling skills and demonstrate computer proficiency. Previous sales experience with major account level assignment desired. A degree in business or equivalent experience preferred. For confidential consideration please mail resumé to Steven Crane, Director of Sales, Aqua Springs Water Company, 133 N. Railroad Avenue, Langley, BC V5J 4S2

Your Task Send a resumé and an application letter to one of these potential employers.

Writing Other Types of Employment Messages

5. Crashing the last frontier: Letter of inquiry about jobs in Inuvik

Your friend can't understand why you would want to move to the Arctic. So you explain: "What really decided it for me was that I'd never seen the Northern Lights."

"But what about the bears? The 60-degree-below winters? The permafrost?" asks your friend.

"No problem. Anyhow, I want to live in the North. Inuvik has lots of small businesses, like a frontier town in the West about 150 years ago. I think it still has homesteading tracts for people who want to do their own building and are willing to stay for a certain number of years."

"Your plans seem a little hasty," your friend warns. "Maybe you should write for information before you just take off. How do you know you could get a job?"

Your Task Take your friend's advice and write to the Chamber of Commerce, Inuvik, NT Y0X 2YR Ask what types of employment are available to someone with your education and experience, and ask who specifically is hiring year-round employees.

Improve Your Grammar, Mechanics, and Usage

Level 1: Self-Assessment—Numbers

Review Section 3.3 in the Handbook of Grammar, Mechanics, and Usage, and then look at the following 15 items.

For items 1–15, correct number style wherever necessary:

1. We need to hire one office manager, four bookkeepers, and twelve clerk-typists.
2. The market for this product is nearly six million people in our region alone.
3. Make sure that all 1835 pages are on my desk no later than nine o'clock a.m.
4. 2002 was the year that Jasminder Bohal sold more than $50 thousand dollars worth of stock.
5. Our deadline is 4/7, but we won't be ready before 4/11.
6. 95 percent of our customers are men.
7. More than ½ the Canadian population is female.
8. Cecile Simmons, thirty-eight, is the first woman in this company to be promoted to management.

9. Last year, I wrote 20 15-page reports, and Michelle wrote 24 three-page reports.
10. Of the 15 applicants, seven are qualified.
11. Our blinds should measure 90 cm wide by one and one half metres long by 4 cm deep.
12. Deliver the couch to seven eighty-three Fountain Rd., Suite three, Drayton Valley, AB, TYN 5H5.
13. Here are the corrected figures: 42.7% agree, 23.25% disagree, 34% are undecided, and the error is .05%.
14. You have to agree that 5 000 000 Canadian citizens cannot be wrong.
15. We need a set of shelves 1 metre, four centimetres long.

Level 2: Workplace Applications

The following items contain numerous errors in grammar, capitalization, punctuation, abbreviation, number style, word division, and vocabulary. Rewrite each sentence in the space provided, correcting all errors. Write *C* in the space after any sentence that is already correct.

1. Speaking at a recent software conference Alan Nichols; ceo of Tekco Systems; said the companys' goal is to reduce response time to 2 to 4 hrs., using software as an enabler.
2. Selling stocks short are the latest rage on wall street, where lately things have just gone from bad to worst.
3. As Electronic Commerce grows people are trying to find new ways to make money off of it.
4. We give a notification not only to the customer but also our salespeople that the product has been shipped because they will want to follow up.
5. When deciding between these various suppliers, we found that each of them offer both advantages and also disadvantages.

6. I found the book, "Marketing is Easy, Selling is Hard," for three different prices on the Internet: $14, $13.25, and $12.00.

7. United Agra Products, a distributor of fertilizers and seeds, in transmission of customer orders over it's private network faced the possibility of serious bottlenecks.

8. The answers you receive on your questionnaire, are influenced by the types of question you ask, the way they are asked, and your subjects cultural and language background.

9. The creation of hazardous by products, like silver in film processing, require us to collect our used chemicals for disposal at a hazardous-waste-facility.

10. As a source of ingredients for our products, we try to establish relationships with small cooperative or farming communities - often in developing countries – because, we believe that the best way to improve peoples' lives is to give them a chance at self reliance.

11. A entrepreneur really should never be in any organization that get's so big that it looses intimacy.

12. Racecar Driver Eddie Cheever, is founder of Aleanza Marketing Group, a seven-person company that handles $10 million dollars in sponsorship campaigns for Cheevers' team Red Bull Cheever Racing.

13. Over the last six years, Business Cluster Development have started 13 technology related incubators, that they call 'business clusters.'

14. In an interview, Gary Hoover said "When I dreamed up Bookstop, we asked people, "If there was a bookstore that carried a huge selection of books and had them all at discount prices, would you go there"? and we got a lot of yawns".

15. The chief attraction of vending machines are their convenience, they are open 24 hours a day, on the other hand, vending machine prices are no bargain.

Level 3: Document Critique

The following document may contain errors in grammar, capitalization, punctuation, abbreviation, number style, vocabulary, and spelling. You may also find problems with word use and format. Correct all errors using standard proofreading marks (see Appendix C).

The Executve Summary (Excerpt)

Purpose of the Proposal

This document will acquaint the reader with 3 principle topics by

- Showing what the Queen's University (QU) *Suntrakker* project is
- Showing that the team-oriented, inerdepartmental diciplines at QU possesses the tenacity and knowhow to build and race a solar-powered vehical in the World solar Challenge Race in Austrailia in 2004;
- Define and articulate how this business team expect to promote and generate the neccesary support; funds, and materials from the student body, alumni, community and local businesses to sieze and executive this opportunity;

Project Profile

The *Suntrakker* Solar Car project was conceived in July; 2002, when a small group of Queen's university mechanical engineering students motivated by the successof of the General motors "Sunrayce," committed itself to designing and building a superior solar-powered vehicle to compete in the world Solar Challenge.

From modest Beginnings, the *Suntrakker* project quickly revolved into a cross-disciplinary educational effort encompassing students from many departments of Queen's University. The project has provides students participants and volunteers with valuable real life experiences and has brought them together in an effort that benefits not only the students and the university but also the environment.

Sponsors of this project are not only contributing to the successful achievment of the overall *Suntrakker* project but will also enhance their goodwill, advertising, and name promotion by association with the project. In addition, the *Suntrakker* offers a unique opportunity for the companies who can donate parts and accessories to showcase their name and test field their products in public in this highly publicized international contest.

Technology

Business Communication Notebook

Netting a Job on the Web

Can the Web provide the answer to all your employment dreams? Perhaps . . . or perhaps not. As the Web grows, the employment information it provides is constantly expanding. And you're fortunate because you don't have to start from scratch like some intrepid adventurer. For helpful hints and useful Web addresses, you can turn to books such as *What Color Is Your Parachute?* by Richard Nelson Bolles. Other places to check out online include the following:*

- **National Job Bank** (jb-ge.hrdc-drhc.gc.ca). Human Resources Development Canada hosts a site that posts thousands of jobs and offers helpful resumé and application tips. It includes links to provincial job opportunities, labour market information, and other job-hunting services. Follow related links to sites such as N.B. Jobs, which posts opportunities in the province of New Brunswick, or to the Electronic Labour Exchange site.
- **WORKink** (www.workink.com) The Canadian Council on Rehabilitation and Work hosts a "virtual employment resource centre" with support from HRDC. It is administered with provincial and territorial partners. Although WORKink's mission is to facilitate and enhance resources available for employment of people with disabilities, its service is useful for any job seeker.
- **The Monster Board** (www.monster.ca). Posts openings and resumés. Heavily marketed, it brings a flood of employers (many with fewer than 500 employees).
- **HotJobs.Com** (www.hotjobs.com). A member-based site that charges companies a hefty fee to post openings or search through resumés. Job seekers can create a personal page to manage their search and collect statistics on how many companies have retrieved their resumé. The site has a "HotJobs Canada" link (ca.hotjobs.yahoo.com/).
- **4Work** (www.4work.ca). One of the few sites that includes listings of internships and volunteer opportunities.
- **Net-Temps** (www.net-temps.com). Maintained by career consultants; offers several thousand updated listings and real-time seminars. Network forums help you develop new contacts and job leads. Includes chat room for online interviews. Check the link to "Canada" under "Search Jobs by Career Channel."
- **Careerbuilder** (www.careerbuilder.ca). Offers a network of career services, job-search information, and tips on how to succeed once you're hired. Includes a database of 20 000 openings and a Canadian site link.
- **MonsterTrak** (www.monstertrak.com). Has formed partnerships with campuses and serves as a virtual career centre for students and alumni. Many entry-level postings.
- **Yahoo! Classifieds** (classifieds.yahoo.com). Offers extensive listing of companies by city, in addition to a wealth of job-related information at the parent Web site, www.yahoo.com. Click on Business & Economy/Jobs/Company Job Listings.

*Direct links to these Web sites can be accessed at the Riley Guide (www.rileyguide.com).

Applications for Success

1. Surfing the Web can chew up a disproportionate amount of your job-seeking time. Explain how you can limit the amount of time you spend on the Web and still make it work for you.
2. When posting your resumé on the Web, you're revealing a lot of information about yourself that could be used by people other than employers (salespeople, people competing for similar positions, con artists). What sort of information might you leave off your Web resumé that would certainly appear on a traditional resumé?
3. Visit at least two of these online indexes, and check out features such as job searches, career centres, and tips for finding employment. Compare the features of the indexes and choose the one you find the most convenient and helpful. Explain your choice in a one-page e-mail to your instructor.

14 Interviewing for Employment and Following Up

From the Real World

"Given the impact of the Internet and the ease with which information can now be gained, the expectation around preparation for interviews has escalated. Every candidate should have done significant research prior to an interview. Candidates need to appear knowledgeable, interested, and be able to both answer general questions or ask informed, direct questions about the industry, the environment, and the company."

–Caroline Jellinck
Partner, Ray & Berndtson, Tanton Mitchell

After studying this chapter, you will be able to

1. Define *employment interview* and explain its dual purpose
2. Discuss the three stages in a typical sequence of interviews
3. Identify and briefly describe six types of employment interviews
4. List six tasks you need to complete to prepare for a successful job interview
5. Explain the three stages of a successful employment interview
6. Describe four ways you can respond to unethical or illegal questions during an interview
7. Name three common employment messages that follow an interview and state briefly when you would use each one

In her job at Ray & Berndtson,Tanton Mitchell, an international executive search firm, Caroline Jellinck interviews more than 100 people each year. When evaluating candidates, she looks for people who are confident without being arrogant and who can be specific, yet succinct in their replies. "The only way to judge if someone is going to be successful in the future," says Jellinck, "is to know where they have been successful in the past. Realistic, honest stories about past achievements can give interviewers a picture of future potential."

Understanding the Interviewing Process

Interviewers are not trying to intimidate or scare people; employers want to find out as much as they can. Employment interviews have a dual purpose:

An interview helps both the interviewer and the applicant achieve their goals.

- **Organization's main objective.** To find the best person available for the job
- **Applicant's main objective.** To find the job best suited to his or her goals and capabilities

While recruiters are trying to decide whether you are right for them, you must decide whether the company is right for you.

An **employment interview** is a formal meeting during which both employer and applicant ask questions and exchange information to see whether the applicant and the organization are a good match. Because interviewing takes time, you'll want to begin seeking jobs well in advance of the date you want to start work. Some students begin

In a typical job search, you can expect to have many interviews before you accept a job offer.

their job search as much as nine months before graduation. It takes an average of 10 interviews to get one job offer, so if you hope to have several offers to choose from, expect to go through 20 or 30 interviews during your job search.[1] Also, in one company you may face a series of interviews, each with a different purpose.

The Typical Sequence of Interviews

Not all organizations interview potential candidates the same way. However, many employers interview an applicant two or three times before deciding to make a job offer.

The Screening Stage

The preliminary *screening stage* can be held on campus to help employers screen out unqualified applicants. These interviews are fairly structured: Applicants are often asked roughly the same questions so that all the candidates will be measured against the same criteria. In some cases, technology has transformed the initial, get-to-know-you interview, allowing employers to screen candidates by phone, video, or computer.[2]

Your best approach to the screening stage is to follow the interviewer's lead. Keep your responses short and to the point. Time is limited, so talking too much can be a big mistake. However, try to differentiate yourself from other candidates. Without resorting to gimmicks, call attention to one key aspect of your background. Then the recruiter can say, "Oh yes, I remember Scott—the one who sold used Toyotas in Edmonton." Just be sure the trait you accentuate is relevant to the job in question. Also be ready to demonstrate a particular skill (perhaps problem solving) if asked to do so. Candidates who meet the company's requirements are invited to visit company offices for further evaluation.

During the screening stage of interviews, try to differentiate yourself from other candidates.

The Selection Stage

The next stage of interviews helps the organization narrow the field a little further. Typically, if you're invited to visit a company, you'll talk with several people: a member of the human resources department, one or two potential colleagues, and your potential supervisor. You might face a panel of several interviewers who ask you questions during a single session. By noting how you listen, think, and express yourself, they can decide how likely you are to get along with colleagues.

Show interest in the job. Relate your skills and experience to the organization's needs. Touch briefly on all your strengths, but explain three or four of your best qualifications in depth. At the same time, probe for information that will help you evaluate the position objectively. As important as it is to get an offer, it's also important to learn whether the job is right for you. Also, be sure to listen attentively, ask insightful questions, and display enthusiasm. If the interviewers agree that you're a good candidate, you may receive a job offer, either on the spot or a few days later by phone or mail.

During the selection stage of interviews, cover all your strengths and relate them to the organization's needs.

The Final Stage

You may be invited back for a final evaluation by a higher-ranking executive with the authority to make an offer and negotiate terms. This person may already have concluded that your background is right and may be more concerned with sizing up your personality. You both need to see whether there is a good psychological fit, so be honest about your motivations and values. An underlying objective of the *final stage* is often to sell you on the advantages of joining the organization.

During the final stage, emphasize your personality, describing your motivations and values honestly.

Types of Interviews

Organizations use various types of interviews to discover as much as possible about applicants.

Interviews vary from employer to employer.

- **Structured interviews.** Generally used in the screening stage, structured interviews are controlled by the employer, who asks a series of prepared questions in a set order. All answers are noted. Although useful in gathering facts, the structured interview is generally a poor measure of an applicant's personal qualities. Nevertheless, some companies use structured interviews to create uniformity in their hiring process.[3]

- **Open-ended interviews.** Less formal and unstructured, these interviews often have a relaxed format. The interviewer asks broad, open-ended questions, encouraging applicants to talk freely. Such interviews bring out an applicant's personality and test professional judgment. However, some candidates reveal too much, rambling on about personal or family problems, so strike a balance between being friendly and remembering that you're in a business situation.
- **Group interviews.** To judge interpersonal skills, some employers meet with several candidates simultaneously to see how they interact. For example, the Walt Disney Company uses group interviews when hiring people for its theme parks. During a 45-minute session, the Disney recruiter watches how three candidates relate to one another. Do they smile? Are they supportive of one another's comments? Do they try to score points at each other's expense?[4]
- **Stress interviews.** Perhaps the most unnerving, stress interviews are set up to see how well a candidate handles stressful situations (an important qualification for certain jobs). You might be asked pointed questions designed to irk or unsettle you. You might be subjected to long periods of silence, criticisms of your appearance, deliberate interruptions, and abrupt or even hostile reactions by the interviewer.
- **Video interviews.** To cut travel costs, many large companies use videoconferencing systems. You need to prepare a bit differently for a video interview by (1) requesting a preliminary phone conversation to establish rapport with the interviewer, (2) arriving early enough to get used to the equipment and setting, (3) speaking clearly but no more slowly than normal, (4) sitting straight and looking up but not down, and (5) showing some animation (but not too much since it will appear blurry to the interviewer).[5]
- **Situational interviews.** Many companies claim that interviewing is about the job, not about a candidate's five-year goals, weaknesses or strengths, challenging experiences, or greatest accomplishments. An interviewer describes a situation and asks, "How would you handle this?" So the situational interview is a hands-on, at-work meeting between an employer who needs a job done and a worker who must be fully prepared to do the work.[6]

Regardless of the type of interview you may face, a personal interview is vital because your resumé can't show whether you're lively and outgoing or subdued and low-key, able to take direction or able to take charge. Each job requires a different mix of personality traits. The interviewer's task is to find out whether you will be effective on the job.

Preparing for a Job Interview

Just as written messages need planning, employment interviews need preparation.

It's perfectly normal to feel a little anxious before an interview. But good preparation will help you perform well. Be sure to consider any cultural differences when preparing for interviews, and base your approach on what your audience expects. The advice in this chapter is most appropriate for companies and employers in Canada and the United States. Before the interview, do some more research, think ahead about questions, bolster your confidence, polish your interview style, plan to look good, and be ready when you arrive.

Do Some Additional Research

Be prepared to relate your qualifications to the organization's needs.

You will already have researched the companies you sent your resumé to. But now that you've been invited for an interview, you'll want to fine-tune your research and brush up on the facts you've collected (see Table 14.1). Learning about the organization and the job enables you to show the interviewer just how you will meet the organization's particular needs.

Table 14.1 Finding Out About the Organization and the Job

Where to Look for Information	
• *Annual report*	Summarizes operations; describes products, lists events, names key personnel
• *In-house magazine or newspaper*	Reveals information about company operations, events, personnel
• *Product brochure or publicity release*	Gives insight into firm's operations and values (obtain from public relations office)
• *Stock research report*	Helps assess stability and growth prospects (obtain online or from stockbroker)
• *Newspaper's business or financial pages*	Contain news items about organizations, current performance figures
• *Periodicals indexes*	Contain descriptive listings of magazine/newspaper articles about firms (obtain from library)
• *Better Business Bureau and Chamber of Commerce*	Distribute information about some local organizations
• *Former and current employees*	Have insight into job and work environment
• *College placement office*	Collects information on organizations that recruit and on job qualifications and salaries
What to Find Out About the Organization	
• *Full name*	How the firm is officially known (e.g., CIBC is Canadian Imperial Bank of Commerce)
• *Location*	Where the organization's headquarters, branch offices, and plants are
• *Age*	How long the organization has been in business
• *Products*	What goods and services the organization produces and sells
• *Industry position*	What the organization's current market share, financial position, and profit picture are
• *Earnings*	What the trends in the firm's stock prices and dividends are (if firm is publicly held)
• *Growth*	How the firm's earnings/holdings have changed in recent years and prospects for expansion
• *Organization*	What subsidiaries, divisions, and departments make up the whole
What to Find Out About the Job	
• *Job title*	What you will be called
• *Job functions*	What the main tasks of the job are
• *Job qualifications*	What knowledge and skills the job requires
• *Career path*	What chances for ready advancement exist
• *Salary range*	What the firm typically offers and what is reasonable in this industry and geographic area
• *Travel opportunities*	How often, long, and far you'll be allowed (or required) to travel
• *Relocation opportunities*	Where you might be allowed (or required) to move and how often

Think Ahead About Questions

Planning ahead for the interviewer's questions will help you handle them more confidently and intelligently. Moreover, you will want to prepare intelligent questions of your own.

Planning for the Employer's Questions

Employers usually gear their interview questions to specific organizational needs. You can expect to be asked about your skills, achievements, and goals, as well as about your attitude toward work and school, your relationships with others (work supervisors, colleagues, and fellow students), and occasionally your hobbies and interests. For a look at the types of questions often asked, see Table 14.2 on page 396. Jot down a brief answer to each one. Then read over the answers until you feel comfortable with each of them.

Table 14.2 Twenty-Five Common Interview Questions

Questions About College or University

1. What courses did you like most? Least? Why?
2. Do you think your extracurricular activities were worth the time you spent on them? Why or why not?
3. When did you choose your major? Did you ever change your major? If so, why?
4. Do you feel you did the best scholastic work you are capable of?
5. Which of your college or university years was the toughest? Why?

Questions About Employers and Jobs

6. What jobs have you held? Why did you leave?
7. What percentage of your post-secondary expenses did you earn? How?
8. Why did you choose your particular field of work?
9. What are the disadvantages of your chosen field?
10. Why do you want to work for this company?
11. What do you think about how this industry operates today?
12. Why do you think you would like this particular type of job?

Questions About Personal Attitudes and Preferences

13. Do you prefer to work in any specific geographic location? If so, why?
14. How much money do you hope to be earning in 5 years? In 10 years?
15. What do you think determines a person's progress in a good organization?
16. What personal characteristics do you feel are necessary for success in your chosen field?
17. Tell me a story.
18. Do you like to travel?
19. Do you think grades should be considered by employers? Why or why not?

Questions About Work Habits

20. Do you prefer working with others or by yourself?
21. What type of boss do you prefer?
22. Have you ever had any difficulty getting along with colleagues or supervisors? With instructors? With other students?
23. Would you prefer to work in a large or a small organization? Why?
24. How do you feel about overtime work?
25. What have you done that shows initiative and willingness to work?

Practise answering interview questions.

Although practising your answers will help you feel prepared and confident, you don't want to memorize responses or sound over-rehearsed. Try giving a list of interview questions to a friend or relative and have that person ask you various questions at random. Such practice helps you learn to articulate answers and to look at the person as you answer.

Planning Questions of Your Own

You are responsible for deciding whether the work and the organization are compatible with your goals and values.

The questions you ask in an interview are just as important as the answers you provide. By asking intelligent questions, you demonstrate your understanding of the organization, and you can steer the discussion into those areas that allow you to present your qualifications to best advantage. Before the interview, prepare a list of questions you need answered in order to evaluate the organization and the job. Here's a list of some things you might want to find out:

- **Are these my kind of people?** Observe the interviewer, and if you can, arrange to talk with other employees.

- **Can I do this work?** Compare your qualifications with the requirements described by the interviewer.
- **Will I enjoy the work?** Know yourself and what's important to you. Will you find the work challenging? Will it give you feelings of accomplishment, of satisfaction, and of making a real contribution?
- **Is the job what I want?** You may never find a job that fulfils all your wants, but the position you accept should satisfy at least your primary ones. Will it make use of your best capabilities? Does it offer a career path to the long-term goals you've set?
- **Does the job pay what I'm worth?** By comparing jobs and salaries before you're interviewed, you'll know what's reasonable for someone with your skills in your industry.
- **What kind of person would I be working for?** If the interviewer is your prospective boss, watch how others interact with that person, tactfully query other employees, or pose a careful question or two during the interview. If your prospective boss is someone else, ask for that person's name, job title, and responsibilities. Try to learn all you can.
- **What sort of future can I expect with this organization?** How healthy is the organization? Can you look forward to advancement? Does the organization offer insurance, pension, vacation, or other benefits?

Assess whether the job satisfies your needs.

Rather than bombarding the interviewer with these questions the minute you walk in the room, use a mix of formats to elicit this information. Start with a warm-up question to help break the ice. You might ask, "What departments usually hire new graduates?" After that, you might build rapport by asking an open-ended question that draws out the interviewer's opinion ("How do you think Internet sales will affect the company's continued growth?"). Indirect questions can elicit useful information and show that you've prepared for the interview ("I'd really like to know more about the company's plans for expanding its corporate presence on the Web" or "That recent *Toronto Star* article about the company was very interesting"). Any questions you ask should be in your own words so that you don't sound like every other candidate. For a list of other good questions you might use as a starting point, see Table 14.3.

Types of questions to ask during an interview:

- Warm-up
- Open-ended
- Indirect

Take your list of word-processed questions to the interview. If you need to, jot down brief notes during the meeting, and be sure to record answers in more detail afterwards. Having a list of questions should impress the interviewer with your organization and thoroughness. It will also show that you're there to evaluate the organization and the job as well as to sell yourself.

Table 14.3 Fifteen Questions to Ask the Interviewer

Questions About the Job	Questions About the Organization
What are the job's major responsibilities?	What are the organization's major strengths? Weaknesses?
What qualities do you want in the person who fills this position?	Who are your organization's major competitors, and what are their strengths and weaknesses?
Do you want to know more about my related training?	What makes your organization different from others in the industry?
What is the first problem that needs the attention of the person you hire?	What are your organization's major markets?
Would relocation be required now or in the future?	Does the organization have any plans for new products? Acquisitions?
Why is this job now vacant?	How would you define your organization's managerial philosophy?
What can you tell me about the person I would report to?	What additional training does your organization provide?
	Do employees have an opportunity to continue their education with help from the organization?

Bolster Your Confidence

Building your confidence helps you make a better impression. The best way to counteract any apprehension is to remove its source. You may feel shy or self-conscious because you think you have some flaw that will prompt others to reject you. But you're much more conscious of your limitations than other people are.

If some aspect of your appearance or background makes you uneasy, correct it or offset it by exercising positive traits such as warmth, wit, intelligence, or charm. Instead of dwelling on your weaknesses, focus on your strengths so that you can emphasize them to an interviewer. Make a list of your good points and compare them with what you see as your shortcomings. Remember that you're not alone. All the other candidates for the job are just as nervous as you are. Even the interviewer may be nervous.

If you feel shy or self-conscious, remember that recruiters are human too.

Polish Your Interview Style

Confidence helps you walk into an interview, but once you're there, you want to give the interviewer an impression of poise, good manners, and good judgment. You can develop an adept style by staging mock interviews with a friend. After each practice session, try to identify opportunities for improvement. Have your friend critique your performance, using the list of interview faults shown in Figure 14.1. You can tape-record or videotape these mock interviews and then evaluate them yourself.

Staging mock interviews with a friend is a good way to hone your style.

As you stage your mock interviews, pay particular attention to your nonverbal behaviour. In Canada, you are more likely to have a successful interview if you maintain eye contact, smile frequently, sit in an attentive position, and use frequent hand gestures. These nonverbal signals convince the interviewer that you're alert, assertive, dependable, confident, responsible, and energetic.[7] Some companies based in Canada are owned and managed by people from other cultures, so during your research, find out about the company's cultural background and preferences regarding nonverbal behaviour.

Nonverbal behaviour has a significant effect on the interviewer's opinion of you.

The sound of your voice can also have a major impact on your success in a job interview.[8] You can work with a tape recorder to overcome voice problems. If you tend to speak too rapidly, practise speaking more slowly. If your voice sounds too loud or too soft, practise adjusting it. Work on eliminating speech mannerisms such as *you know, like,* and *um,* which might make you sound inarticulate.

Plan to Look Good

"Looks count," says Jellinck, "not in your physical features, but in the way you present yourself. Candidates need to be well turned out and professional." When it comes to clothing, the best policy is to dress conservatively. Wear the best-quality businesslike clothing you can, preferably in a dark, solid colour. Avoid flamboyant styles, colours, and prints. Even in companies where interviewers may dress casually, it's important to show good judgment by dressing (and acting) in a professional manner. Good grooming makes any style of clothing look better. Make sure your clothes are clean and unwrinkled, your shoes unscuffed and well shined, your hair neatly styled and combed, your fingernails clean, and your breath fresh.

To look like a winner

- Dress conservatively
- Be well groomed
- Smile when appropriate

Be Ready When You Arrive

Plan to take a small notebook, a pen, a list of the questions you want to ask, two copies of your resumé (protected in a folder), a list of references, an outline of what you have learned about the organization, and any past correspondence about the position. You may also want to take a small calendar, a transcript of your grades, and a portfolio containing samples of your work, performance reviews, and certificates of achievement. In an era when many people exaggerate their qualifications, visible proof of your abilities carries a lot of weight.[9]

Be prepared for the interview by

- Taking proof of your accomplishments
- Arriving on time
- Waiting graciously

FIGURE 14.1 Marks Against Applicants (in General Order of Importance)

WHAT EMPLOYERS DON'T LIKE TO SEE IN CANDIDATES

- Poor personal appearance
- Overbearing, overaggressive, conceited demeanour; a "superiority complex"; a know-it-all attitude
- Inability to express ideas clearly; poor voice, diction, grammar
- Lack of knowledge or experience
- Poor preparation for the interview
- Lack of interest in the job
- Lack of planning for career; lack of purpose, goals
- Lack of enthusiasm; passive and indifferent demeanour; lack of vitality
- Lack of confidence and poise; appearance of being nervous and ill at ease
- Insufficient evidence of achievement
- Failure to participate in extracurricular activities
- Overemphasis on money; interest only in the best dollar offer
- Poor scholastic record; just got by
- Unwillingness to start at the bottom; expecting too much too soon
- Tendency to make excuses
- Evasive answers; hedges on unfavourable factors in record
- Lack of tact, maturity, courtesy
- Poor listening skills
- Condemnation of past employers
- Lack of social skills
- Marked dislike for schoolwork
- Failure to look interviewer in the eye
- Limp, weak handshake

Be sure you know when and where the interview will be held. The worst way to start any interview is to be late. Allow a little extra time in case you run into a problem on the way.

Once you arrive, relax. Be polite to the interviewer's assistant. If the opportunity presents itself, ask a few questions about the organization or express enthusiasm for the job. Refrain from smoking before the interview, and avoid chewing gum in the waiting room.

Interviewing for Success

As discussed earlier, how you handle a particular interview depends on where you stand in the sequence of interviews. Is this your first interview in the screening process? Have you made it to the selection interview or even the final interview? Regardless of where you are in the process, every interview will proceed through three stages: the warm-up, the question-and-answer session, and the close.

The Warm-Up

Of the three stages, the warm-up is the most important, even though it may account for only a small fraction of the time you spend in the interview. Psychologists say that 50 percent of an interviewer's decision is made within the first 30 to 60 seconds, and another 25 percent is made within 15 minutes. If you get off to a bad start, it's extremely difficult to turn the interview around.[10]

The first minute of the interview is crucial.

Body language is important at this point. Because you won't have time to say much in the first minute or two, you must sell yourself nonverbally. Begin by using the interviewer's name if you're sure you can pronounce it correctly. If the interviewer extends a hand, respond with a firm but gentle handshake, and wait until you're asked to be seated. Let the interviewer start the discussion, and listen for cues that tell you what he or she is interested in knowing about you as a potential employee.

The Question-and-Answer Stage

Questions and answers will consume the greatest part of the interview. The interviewer will ask you about your qualifications and discuss many of the points mentioned in your resumé. You'll also be asking questions of your own.

Handling Questions

Tailor your answers to emphasize your strengths.

Let the interviewer lead the conversation, and never answer a question before he or she has finished asking it. Surprisingly, the last few words of the question might alter how you respond. As questions are asked, tailor your answers to make a favourable impression. Don't limit yourself to yes-or-no answers. If you're asked a difficult question, be sure you pause to think before responding.

If you periodically ask a question or two from the list you've prepared, you'll not only learn something but also demonstrate your interest. Probe for what the company is looking for in its new employees so that you can show how you meet the firm's needs. Also try to zero in on any reservations the interviewer might have about you so that you can dispel them.

Listening to the Interviewer

Paying attention to both verbal and nonverbal messages can help you turn the question-and-answer stage to your advantage.

Paying attention when the interviewer speaks can be as important as giving good answers or asking good questions. Listening should make up about half the time you spend in an interview. For tips on becoming a better listener, see Chapter 2.

The interviewer's facial expressions, eye movements, gestures, and posture may tell you the real meaning of what is being said. Be especially aware of how your comments are received. Does the interviewer nod in agreement or smile to show approval? If so, you're making progress. If not, you might want to introduce another topic or modify your approach.

Fielding Discriminatory Questions

Some questions should not be asked by interviewers.

Employers cannot legally discriminate against a job candidate on the basis of race, colour, gender, age (from 40 to 70), marital status, religion, national origin, or disability. In general, the following topics should not be directly or indirectly introduced by an interviewer:[11]

- Your religious affiliation or organizations and lodges you belong to
- Your national origin, age, marital status, or former name
- Your spouse, spouse's employment or salary, dependants, children, or child-care arrangements
- Your height, weight, gender, pregnancy, or any health conditions or disabilities that are not reasonably related to job performance
- Arrests or criminal convictions that are not related to job performance

Table 14.4 compares specific questions that may and may not be asked during an employment interview.

Think in advance about how you might respond to unlawful interview questions.

How to Respond If your interviewer asks these personal questions, how you respond depends on how badly you want the job, how you feel about revealing the information asked for, what you think the interviewer will do with the information, and whether you want to work for a company that asks such questions. If you don't want the job, you

Table 14.4 Interview Questions That May and May Not Be Asked

You may ask this . . .	But not this
What is your name?	What was your maiden name?
Are you over 18?	When were you born?
Did you graduate from high school?	When did you graduate from high school?
[No questions about race are allowed.]	What is your race?
Can you perform [specific tasks]?	Do you have physical or mental disabilities?
	Do you have a drug or alcohol problem?
	Are you taking any prescription drugs?
Would you be able to meet the job's requirement to frequently work weekends?	Would working on weekends conflict with your religion?
Do you have the legal right to work in Canada?	What country are you a citizen of?
Have you ever been convicted of a crime?	Have you ever been arrested?
This job requires that you speak French. Do you?	What language did you speak in your home when you were growing up?

can tell the interviewer that you think a particular question is unethical or simply refuse to answer—responses that will leave an unfavourable impression.[12] If you do want the job, you might (1) ask how the question is related to your qualifications, (2) explain that the information is personal, (3) respond to what you think is the interviewer's real concern, or (4) answer both the question and the concern. If you answer an unethical or unlawful question, you run the risk that your answer may hurt your chances, so think carefully before answering.[13]

The Close

Like the opening, the end of the interview is more important than its duration would indicate. In the last few minutes, you need to evaluate how well you've done. You also need to correct any misconceptions the interviewer might have.

Concluding Gracefully

Conclude the interview with courtesy and enthusiasm.

You can generally tell when the interviewer is trying to conclude the session. He or she may ask whether you have any more questions, sum up the discussion, change position, or indicate with a gesture that the interview is over. When you get the signal, respond promptly, but don't rush. Be sure to thank the interviewer for the opportunity and express an interest in the organization. If you can do so comfortably, try to pin down what will happen next, but don't press for an immediate decision.

If this is your second or third visit to the organization, the interview may culminate with an offer of employment. You have two options: Accept it or request time to think it over. The best course is usually to wait. If no job offer is made, the interviewer may not have reached a decision yet, but you may tactfully ask when you can expect to know the decision.

Discussing Salary

Be realistic in your salary expectations and diplomatic in your negotiations.

If you do receive an offer during the interview, you'll naturally want to discuss salary. However, let the interviewer raise the subject. If asked your salary requirements, say that you would expect to receive the standard salary for the job in question. If you have added qualifications, point them out: "With my 18 months of experience in the field, I would expect to start in the middle of the normal salary range." Some applicants find the Internet a terrific resource for salary information.

When to Negotiate If you don't like the offer, you might try to negotiate, provided you're in a good bargaining position and the organization has the flexibility to accommodate you. You'll be in a fairly strong position if your skills are in short supply and you have several other offers. It also helps if you're the favourite candidate and the organization is booming. Even though many organizations are relatively rigid in their salary practices, particularly at the entry level, in Canada and the United States and in some European countries, it is perfectly acceptable to ask, "Is there any room for negotiation?"

What to Negotiate Even if you can't bargain for more money, you may be able to win some concessions on benefits and perquisites. The value of negotiating can be significant because benefits often cost the employer 25 percent to 45 percent of your salary. Don't inquire about benefits, however, until you know you have a job offer.

Interview Notes

Keep a written record of your job interviews.

If yours is a typical job search, you'll have many interviews before you accept an offer. For that reason, keep a notebook. As soon as the interview ends, jot down the names and titles of the people you met. Briefly summarize the interviewer's answers to your questions. Then quickly evaluate your performance during the interview.[14] In addition to improving your performance during interviews, interview notes will help you keep track of any follow-up messages you'll need to send.

Following up After the Interview

Touching base with the prospective employer after the interview, either by phone or in writing, shows that you really want the job and are determined to get it. Following up brings your name to the interviewer's attention once again and reminds him or her that you're waiting for the decision.

Two types of follow-up messages:

- Thank-you message
- Inquiry

The two most common forms of follow-up are the thank-you message and the inquiry. These messages are often handled by letter, but an e-mail or a phone call can be just as effective, particularly if the employer seems to favour a casual, personal style.

Thank-You Message

Express your thanks within two days after the interview, even if you feel you have little chance for the job. Acknowledge the interviewer's time and courtesy, and be sure to restate the specific job you're applying for. Convey your continued interest, then ask politely for a decision.

A note or phone call thanking the interviewer

- Is organized like a routine message
- Closes with a request for a decision or future consideration

Keep your thank-you message brief (less than five minutes for a phone call or only one page for a letter), and organize it like a routine message. Demonstrate the "you" attitude, and sound positive without sounding overconfident. The following sample thank-you letter shows how to achieve all this in three brief paragraphs:

Reminds the interviewer of the reasons for meeting and graciously acknowledges the consideration shown to the applicant →

After talking with you yesterday, touring your sets, and watching the television commercials being filmed, I remain very enthusiastic about the possibility of joining your staff as a television/film production assistant. Thanks for taking so much time to show me around.

During our meeting, I said that I would prefer not to relocate, but I've reconsidered the matter. I would be pleased to relocate wherever you need my skills in set decoration and prop design.

← Indicates the writer's flexibility and commitment to the job if hired

Now that you've explained the details of your operation, I feel quite strongly that I can make a contribution to the sorts of productions you're lining up. You can also count on me to be an energetic employee and a positive addition to your crew. Please let me know your decision as soon as possible.

← Reminds the recruiter of special qualifications

← Closes on a confident, "you"-oriented note

Ends with a request for a decision →

Even if the interviewer has said that you're unqualified for the job, a thank-you message may keep the door open. Riley Mullins followed up a recent job interview with a thank-you message sent by e-mail the same day (see Figure 14.2).

Letter of Inquiry

If you're not advised of the interviewer's decision by the promised date or within two weeks, you might make an inquiry. A letter of inquiry is particularly appropriate if you've received a job offer from a second firm and don't want to accept it before you have an answer from the first. The following letter illustrates the general plan for a direct request; the writer assumes that a simple oversight, and not outright rejection, is the reason for the delay:

An inquiry about a hiring decision follows the plan for a direct request.

Identifies the position and introduces the main idea → When we talked on April 7 about the fashion coordinator position in your Park Drive showroom, you said you would be making your decision before May 1. I would still like the position very much, so I'm eager to know what conclusion you've reached.

Places the reason for the request second → To complicate matters, another firm has now offered me a position and has asked that I reply within the next two weeks.

Because your company seems to offer a greater challenge, I would appreciate knowing about your decision by Thursday, May 12. If you need more information before then, please let me know. ← Makes a courteous request for specific action last, while clearly stating a preference for this organization

FIGURE 14.2 Thank-You by E-mail

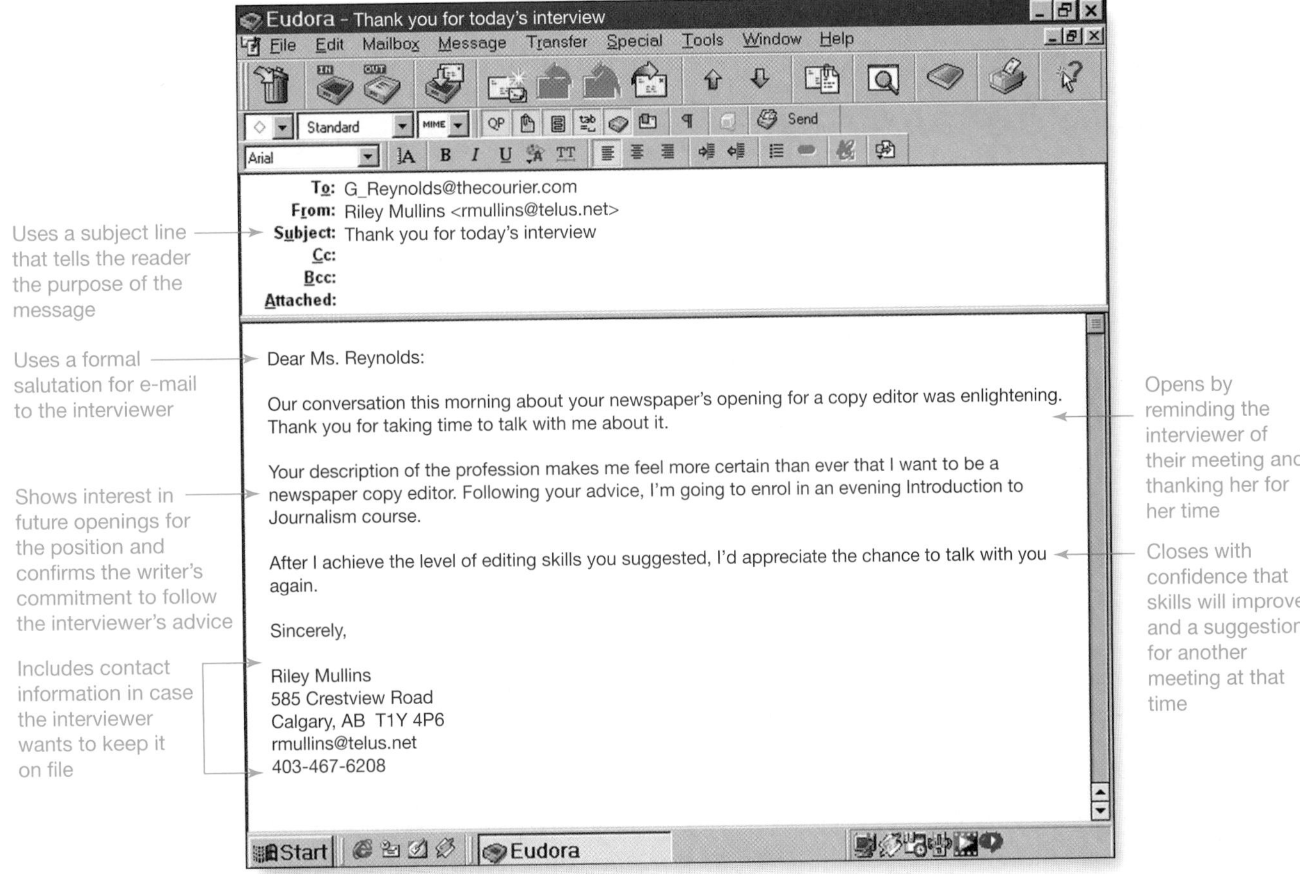

Reviewing Key Points

This chapter discussed interviewing for employment and following up. Companies often conduct three interviews to screen, select, and approve a candidate. Each interview type has stages. In the warm-up stage you hope to make a positive impression through nonverbal communication and through a warm, friendly, and professional approach. In the question-and-answer stage you give specific examples, showing you know the company and what you can contribute. In the closing stage, you recap your main strengths. When you get an interview, you should

- Research the company, so that you can ask good questions, show how you would fit and contribute, and determine how to dress appropriately
- Be early, well groomed, and well prepared for questions
- Listen carefully, answer succinctly, and do not interrupt
- Give examples of skills and traits needed for the job
- Follow up after the interview with a specific thank-you note or call

If you haven't heard back from the company in a reasonable period, follow up with a letter expressing your continued interest.

Test Your Knowledge

1. What should your objective be during a selection interview?

2. How does a structured interview differ from an open-ended interview and a situational interview?

3. What typically occurs during a stress interview?

4. Why are the questions you ask during an interview as important as the answers you give to the interviewer's questions?

5. What is the best way to polish your interview style?

6. What are the three stages of every interview, and which is the most important?

7. How should you respond if an interviewer at a company where you want to work asks you a question that seems too personal or unethical?

8. What should you include in your interview notes?

9. What should you say in a thank-you message after an interview?

10. What is the purpose of sending a letter of inquiry after an interview?

Apply Your Knowledge

1. How can you distinguish yourself from other candidates in a screening interview and still keep your responses short and to the point? Explain.

2. What can you do to make a favourable impression when you discover that an open-ended interview has turned into a stress interview? Briefly explain your answer.

3. If you want to switch jobs because you can't work with your supervisor, how can you explain this situation to a prospective employer? Give an example.

4. During a group interview you notice that one of the other candidates is trying to monopolize the conversation. He's always the first to answer, his answer is the longest, and he even interrupts the other candidates while they are talking. The interviewer doesn't seem to be concerned about his behaviour, but you are. You would like to have more time to speak so that the interviewer could get to know you better. What should you do?

5. **Ethical Choices** Why is it important to distinguish unethical or illegal interview questions from acceptable questions? Explain.

Practise Your Knowledge

Activities

For live links to all Web sites discussed in this chapter, visit this text's Web site at www.pearsoned.ca/bovee. Just log on and select Chapter 14, and click on "Student Resources." Locate the page or the URL related to the material in the text. For "Exploring the Best of the Web" exercises, you'll also find navigational directions. Click on the live link to the site.

1. **Analyze This Document** Read the following document; then (1) analyze its strengths and weaknesses and (2) revise the document so that it follows this chapter's guidelines.

   Thank you for the really marvellous opportunity to meet you and your colleagues at Epcor Utilities. I really enjoyed touring your facilities and talking with all the people there. You have quite a crew! Some of the other companies I have visited have been so rigid and uptight that I can't imagine how I would fit in. It's a relief to run into a group of people who seem to enjoy their work as much as all of you do.

   I know that you must be looking at many other candidates for this job, and I know that some of them will probably be more experienced than I am. But I do want to emphasize that my two-year hitch in the Navy involved a good deal of engineering work. I don't think I mentioned all my shipboard responsibilities during the interview.

   Please give me a call within the next week to let me know your decision. You can usually find me at my residence in the evening after dinner (phone: 877-9080).

2. **Analyze This Document** Read the following document; then (1) analyze its strengths and weaknesses and (2) revise the document so that it follows this chapter's guidelines.

   I have recently received a very attractive job offer from the Warrington Company. But before I let them know one way or another, I would like to consider any offer that your firm may extend. I was quite impressed with your company during my recent interview, and I am still very interested in a career there.

   I don't mean to pressure you, but Warrington has asked for my decision within 10 days. Could you let me know by Tuesday whether you plan to offer me a position? That would give me enough time to compare the two offers.

3. **Analyze This Document** Read the following document; then (1) analyze its strengths and weaknesses and (2) revise the document so that it follows this chapter's guidelines.

   I'm writing to say that I must decline your job offer. Another company has made me a more generous offer, and I have decided to accept. However, if things don't work out for me there, I will let you know. I sincerely appreciate your interest in me.

4. **Teamwork** Divide the class into two groups. Half the class will be recruiters for a large chain of national department stores looking to fill manager trainee positions (there are 15 openings). The other half of the class will be candidates for the job. The company is specifically looking for candidates who demonstrate these three qualities: initiative, dependability, and willingness to assume responsibility.

   a. Have each recruiter select and interview an applicant for 10 minutes.
   b. Have all the recruiters discuss how they assessed the applicant against each of the three desired qualities. What questions did they ask or what did they use as an indicator to determine whether the candidate possessed the quality?
   c. Have all the applicants discuss what they said to convince the recruiters that they possessed each of these qualities.

5. **Internet** Select a large company (one that you can easily find information about) where you might like to work. Use Internet sources to gather some preliminary research on the company.

   a. What did you learn about this organization that would help you during an interview there?
   b. What Internet sources did you use to obtain this information?
   c. Armed with this information, what aspects of your background do you think might appeal to this company's recruiters?
   d. If you choose to apply for a job with this company, what keywords would you include on your resumé, and why?

6. **Interviews: Being Prepared** Prepare written answers to 10 of the questions listed in Table 14.2, "Twenty-Five Common Interview Questions."

7. **Interviews: Understanding Qualifications** Write a short memo to your instructor discussing what you believe are your greatest employment strengths and weaknesses. Next, explain how these strengths and weaknesses would be viewed by interviewers evaluating your qualifications.

Expand Your Knowledge

Best of the Web

Planning for a Successful Job Interview How can you practise for a job interview? What are some questions that you might be asked, and how should you respond? What questions are you not obligated to answer? *Job-interview.net* provides mock interviews based on actual job openings. It provides job descriptions, questions and answers for specific careers and jobs, and links to company guides and annual reports. You'll find a step-by-step plan that outlines key job requirements, lists practice interview questions, and helps you put together practice interviews. The site offers tips on the keywords to look for in a job description that will help you narrow your search and anticipate the questions you might be asked on your first or next job interview.

www.job-interview.net

Exercises

1. What are some problem questions you might be asked during a job interview? How would you handle these questions?

2. Choose a job title from the list, and read more about it. What did you learn that could help during an actual interview for the job you selected?

3. Developing an "interview game plan" ahead of time helps you make a strong, positive impression during an interview. What are some of the things you can practise to help make everything you do during an interview seem to come naturally?

Exploring the Web on Your Own

Review these chapter-related Web sites on your own to learn more about interviewing for jobs.

1. Get more than 2000 pages of career advice at Monster.ca, www.monster.ca, and talk to career experts in your choice of industry or profession.
2. Learn how to prepare for and handle yourself with care during a job interview at SoYouWannaAceAJob Interview, www.soyouwanna.com/site/syws/aceinterview/aceinterview.html.
3. Follow the steps at www.job-interview.net, and be prepared for your next job interview.

Learn Interactively

Interactive Study Guide

Visit the Companion Website at www.pearsoned.ca/bovee. For Chapter 14, take advantage of the interactive "Study Guide" to test your chapter knowledge. Get instant feedback on whether you need additional studying.

This site offers a variety of additional resources: The "Research Area" helps you locate a wealth of information to use in course assignments. The "Study Hall" helps you succeed in this course by offering support with writing and study skills, time management, and career skills, as well as numerous other resources.

Peak Performance Grammar and Mechanics

PEAK Use the Peak Performance Grammar and Mechanics CD to test your skill with vocabulary and usage. In the "Vocabulary" sections, take the Pretest to determine whether you have any weak areas. Then review those areas in the Refresher Course. Take the Pretest to check your grasp of punctuation. For an extra challenge or advanced practice, take the Advanced Test.

Interviewing with Potential Employers

1. Interviewers and interviewees: Classroom exercise in interviewing

Interviewing is clearly an interactive process involving at least two people. The best way to practise for interviews is to work with others.

Your Task You and all other members of your class are to write letters of application for an entry-level or management-trainee position requiring a pleasant personality and intelligence but a minimum of specialized education or experience. Sign your letter with a fictitious name that conceals your identity. Next polish (or prepare) a resumé that accurately identifies you and your educational and professional accomplishments.

Now, three members of the class who volunteer as interviewers divide among themselves all the anonymously written application letters. Then each interviewer selects a candidate who seems the most pleasant and convincing in his or her letter. At this time the selected candidates identify themselves and give the interviewers their resumés.

Each interviewer then interviews his or her chosen candidate in front of the class, seeking to understand how the items on the resumé qualify the candidate for the job. At the end of the interviews, the class may decide who gets the job and discuss why this candidate was successful. Afterwards, retrieve your letter, sign it with the right name, and submit it to the instructor for credit.

WEB SKILLS 2. Internet interview: Exercise in interviewing

Using the Work Futures site for your province, locate the home page of a company you would like to work for (use the links to other provinces on www.bcworkfutures.ca to find your province's site). Then identify a position within the company for which you would like to apply. Study the company using any online business resources you choose, and prepare for an interview with that company.

Your Task Working with a classmate, take turns interviewing each other for your chosen positions. Interviewers should take notes during the interview. Once the interview is complete, critique each other's performance (interviewers should critique how well candidates prepared for the interview and answered the questions; interviewees should critique the quality of the questions asked). Write a follow-up letter thanking your interviewer, and submit the letter to your instructor.

Following up After the Interview

3. A slight error in timing: Letter asking for delay of an employment decision

You botched your timing and applied for your third-choice job before going after what you really wanted. What you want to do is work in retail at Holt Renfrew in Toronto; what you have been offered is a retail job with Longhorn Leather and Lumber, 40 km away in Etobicoke.

You review your notes. Your Longhorn interview was three weeks ago with the human resources manager, R. P. Bronson, a congenial person who has just written to offer you the position. The store's address is 27 Flanigan Drive, Etobicoke, ON M6H 2L1. Mr. Bronson notes that he can hold the position open for 10 days. You have an interview scheduled with Holt's next week, but it is unlikely that you will know the store's decision within this 10-day period.

Your Task Write to R. P. Bronson, requesting a reasonable delay in your consideration of his job offer.

4. Job hunt: Set of employment-related letters to a single company

Where would you like to work? Pick a real or an imagined company, and assume that a month ago you sent your resumé and application letter. Not long afterwards, you were invited to come for an interview, which seemed to go very well.

Your Task Use your imagination to write the following: (a) a thank-you letter for the interview, and (b) a note of inquiry.

Improve Your Grammar, Mechanics, and Usage

Level 1: Self-Assessment—Vocabulary

Review Sections 4.1, 4.2, and 4.3 in the Handbook of Grammar, Mechanics, and Usage, and then look at the following 15 items.

In items 1–7, write the correct word in the space provided:

1. Everyone (*accept/except*) __________ Barbara King has registered for the company competition.
2. We need to find a new security (*device/devise*) __________ .
3. The Jennings are (*loath/loathe*) __________ to admit that they are wrong.
4. The judge has ruled that this town cannot enforce such a local (*ordinance/ ordnance*) __________ .
5. To stay on schedule, we must give (*precedence/precedents*) __________ to the Marley project.
6. This month's balance is greater (*than/then*) __________ last month's.
7. That decision lies with the director, (*who's/whose*) __________ in charge of this department.

In items 8–15, underline errors and write corrections in the space provided:

8. __________ In this department, we see alot of mistakes like that.
9. __________ In my judgement, you'll need to redo the cover.
10. __________ He decided to reveal the information, irregardless of the consequences.
11. __________ Why not go along when it is so easy to accomodate his demands?
12. __________ When you say that, do you mean to infer that I'm being unfair?
13. __________ She says that she finds this sort of ceremony embarassing.
14. __________ All we have to do is try and get along with him for a few more days.
15. __________ A friendly handshake should always preceed negotiations.

Level 2: Workplace Applications

The following items contain numerous errors in grammar, capitalization, punctuation, abbreviation, number style, word division, and vocabulary. Rewrite each sentence in the space provided, correcting all errors. Write *C* in the space after any sentence that is already correct.

1. An entrepreneur and their business, are so closely tied together that a bank will want to see how they handle their personal affairs, before granting a small business line of credit.

2. The companys' annual meeting will be held from 2-4 PM on May 3d in the Grand room at the Delta hotel.

3. Hundreds of outstanding students from coast-to-coast, have realized their dreams of a college or university education thanks to union-funded scholarship programs.

4. If you're home is you're principle place of business you can deduct generally the cost of travelling from you're home, to any business destination.

5. Companies like Fido sprung into being in the 1990's to provide mobile phone services to small- and medium-size businesses in competition with the established telecoms.

6. Some question whether a 'new economy' exists and if so how it differs from the old economy?

7. When the music industry claimed by stealing intellectual property Napster were committing piracy - Napster argued that it was'nt doing anything illegal or un-ethical.

8. The World Bank plays an important roll in todays fast changing closely-meshed global economy.

9. When it comes to consumer rights Health Canada, Agriculture Canada and local health departments are concerned not only with safety but also accurate information.

10. Fujitsu, a $50 billion company with 190 000 employees, dominates the Japanese computer industry.

11. The fortune 500 ranks not only corporations by size but also offers brief company descriptions; along with industry statistics, and additional measures of corporate performance.

12. Having bought 55 companies over the past decade, plans to make ten to 15 new acquisitions each year are being made by Cisco Systems.

13. In 1984 Michael Dell decided to sell P.C.'s direct and built to order, now everybody in the industry are trying to imitate Dells' strategy.

14. Resulting in large cost savings for the company, American Express have reduced the number of field office's from 85 to 7 by using virtual teams.

15. In Europe and Asia, people are using mobile phones to send text messages to other users; exchange e-mail; read the morning news; surfing certain Web sites; and to make purchases such as movie tickets and charge it to they're monthly phone bill.

Level 3: Document Critique

The following document may contain errors in grammar, capitalization, punctuation, abbreviation, number style, vocabulary, and spelling. Based on what you've learned in this chapter, you may also find problems with organization, usage, and word choice. Correct all errors using standard proofreading marks (see Appendix C).

MORGAN McLEOD

2397 Glencrest ridge, Ottawa, ON K1K 4R3

(613/ 226-1804

February 2 2004:

Norton Acctg. Group

Ms Nancy Remington, Human Resources

3778 Parkway North

Ottawa, ON K1K 5P8

Dear Ms. Remington—

With your companys' reputation for quality, customer service, employee empowerment, you'll will want to hire someone who is not only accurrate and efficient but also self motivated and results-oriented—someone who is able to make decisions as well as coperate with team members and clients. The ad you placed in the February 1st issue of *The National Post* for someone to fill a financial management position really has me very excited and eager.

During my 3 years at EnCana corporation -see attached resumé- I've conducted internal auditing for accounts valued at $450 million dollars. Some of my many, countless accomplishments include

- Increasing both internal and client support for the auditing process
- I save the company over 2.5 million dollars when I discovered billing errors
- Suggest ways accounts receivable processes could be streamlined

In addition it might be that Norton Accounting may appreciate my ability to complete projects on time as well as keeping them under budget. One of my priorities is a position in which my expereince will be broaden: so any opportunity to travel would be welcomed by me!

I'll be in your area during the weak of February 20; I'll call your office on Feb. 8 to see whether we can arrange to meet. I hope you'll give me a chance, please.

Sincerely,

Morgan McLeod,

Applicant

Interview Strategies: Answering the 16 Toughest Questions

The answers to challenging interview questions can reveal a lot about a candidate. You can expect to face several such questions during every interview. If you're prepared with thoughtful answers that are related to your specific situation, you're bound to make a good impression. Here are 16 tough questions and guidelines for planning answers that put your qualities in the best light.

1. **What was the toughest decision you ever had to make?** Be prepared with a good example, explaining why the decision was difficult and how you decided.
2. **Why do you want to work for this organization?** Show that you've done your homework, and cite some things going on in the company that appeal to you.
3. **Why should we employ you?** Emphasize your academic strengths, job skills, and enthusiasm for the firm. Tie specific skills to the employer's needs, and give examples of how you can learn and become productive quickly. Cite past activities to prove you can work with others as part of a team.
4. **If we hire you, what changes would you make?** No one can know what to change in a position before settling in and learning about the job and company operations. State that you would take a good hard look at everything the company is doing before making recommendations.
5. **Can we offer you a career path?** Reply that you believe so, but you need to know more about the normal progression within the organization.
6. **What are your greatest strengths?** Answer sincerely by summarizing your strong points: "I can see what must be done and then do it," or "I'm willing to make decisions," or "I work well with others."
7. **What are your greatest weaknesses?** Describe a weakness so that it sounds like a virtue—honestly revealing something about yourself while showing how it works to an employer's advantage. If you sometimes drive yourself too hard, explain that it has helped when you've had to meet deadlines.
8. **What didn't you like about previous jobs you've held?** State what you didn't like and discuss what the experience taught you. Avoid making slighting references to former employers.
9. **How do you spend your leisure time?** Rather than focusing on just one, mention a cross-section of interests—active and quiet, social and solitary.
10. **Are there any weaknesses in your education or experience?** Take stock of your weaknesses before the interview, and practise discussing them in a positive light. You'll see they're minor when discussed along with the positive qualities you have to offer.
11. **Where do you want to be five years from now?** This question tests (1) whether you're merely using this job as a stopover until something better comes along and (2) whether you've given thought to your long-term goals. Saying that you'd like to be company president is unrealistic, and yet few employers want people who are content to sit still. Your answer should reflect your long-term goals and the organization's advancement opportunities.
12. **What are your salary expectations?** If you're asked this at the outset, say, "Why don't we discuss salary after you decide whether I'm right for the job?" If the interviewer asks this after showing real interest in you, speak up. Do your homework, but if you need a clue about salary levels, say, "Can you discuss the salary range with me?"
13. **What would you do if . . .** This question tests your resourcefulness. For example: "What would you do if your computer broke down during an audit?" Your answer is less important than your approach to the problem—and a calm approach is best.
14. **What type of position are you interested in?** Job titles and responsibilities vary from firm to firm. So state your skills ("I'm good with numbers") and the positions that require those skills ("accounts payable").
15. **Tell me something about yourself.** Answer that you'll be happy to talk about yourself, and ask what the interviewer wants to know. If this point is clarified, respond. If it isn't, explain how your skills can contribute to the job and the organization. This is a great chance to sell yourself.

16. **Do you have any questions about the organization or the job?** Employers like candidates who are interested in the organization. Convey your interest and enthusiasm. Be sure that your answers are sincere, truthful, and positive. Take a moment to compose your thoughts before responding, so that your answers are to the point.

Applications for Success

Improve your interviewing skills by visiting the "Interview" section at Hotjobs (www.hotjobs.ca/htdocs/tools/interviews/index-ca.html).

Answer the following questions:

1. When an interviewer asks you a question, what makes one answer more effective than another? Consider some of the ways answers can vary: specific versus general, assertive versus passive, informal versus formal.
2. Think of four additional questions that pertain specifically to your resumé. Practise your answers.
3. Which of the 16 questions seems the toughest to you? In no more than two paragraphs, write out your answer to the question that you think is the toughest of all. Then submit your work to your instructor.

Appendix A

Format and Layout of Business Documents

The format and layout of business documents vary from country to country; they even vary within Canada. In addition, many organizations develop their own variations of standard styles, adapting documents to the types of messages they send and the kinds of audiences they communicate with. The formats described here are more common than others.

First Impressions

Your documents tell readers a lot about you and about your company's professionalism. So all your documents must look neat, present a professional image, and be easy to read. Your audience's first impression of a document comes from the quality of its paper, the way it is customized, and its general appearance.

Paper

To give a quality impression, business people consider carefully the paper they use. Several aspects of paper contribute to the overall impression:

- **Weight.** Paper quality is judged by weight. The weight most commonly used by Canadian businesses is 20-pound paper, but 16- and 24-pound versions are also used.
- **Cotton content.** Paper quality is also judged by the percentage of cotton in the paper. Cotton doesn't yellow over time the way wood pulp does, plus it's both strong and soft. For letters and outside reports, use paper with a 25 percent cotton content. For memos and other internal documents, you can use a lighter-weight paper with lower cotton content. Airmail-weight paper may save money for international correspondence, but make sure it isn't too flimsy.[1]
- **Size.** In Canada, the standard paper size for business documents is 8½ by 11 inches. Standard legal documents are 8½ by 14 inches. Executives sometimes have heavier 7-by-10-inch paper on hand (with matching envelopes) for personal messages such as congratulations and recommendations.[2] They may also have a box of note cards imprinted with their initials and a box of plain folded notes for condolences or for acknowledging formal invitations.
- **Colour.** White is the standard colour for business purposes, although neutral colours such as grey and ivory are sometimes used. Memos can be produced on pastel-coloured paper to distinguish them from external correspondence. In addition, memos are sometimes produced on various colours of paper for routing to separate departments. Light-coloured papers are appropriate, but bright or dark colours make reading difficult and may appear too frivolous.

Customization

For letters to outsiders, Canadian businesses commonly use letterhead stationery, which may be either professionally printed or designed in-house using word-processing templates and graphics. The letterhead includes the company's name and address, usually at the top of the page but sometimes along the left side or even at the bottom. Other information may be included in the letterhead as well: the company's telephone number, fax number, cable address, Website address, product lines, date of establishment, officers and directors, slogan, and symbol (logo). Well-designed letterhead gives readers[3]

- Pertinent reference data
- A favourable image of the company
- A good idea of what the company does

For as much as it's meant to accomplish, the letterhead should be as simple as possible. Too much information makes the page look cluttered, occupies space needed for the message, and might become outdated before all the stationery can be used. If you correspond frequently with people abroad, your letterhead must be intelligible to foreigners. It must include the name of your country in addition to your cable, telex, e-mail, or fax information.

In Canada, businesses always use letterhead for the first page of a letter. Successive pages are usually plain sheets of paper that match the letterhead in colour and quality. Some companies use a specially printed second-page letterhead that bears only the company's name. Other countries have other conventions.

Many companies also design and print standardized forms for memos and frequently written reports that always require the same sort of information (such as sales reports and expense reports). These forms may be printed in sets for use with carbon paper or in carbonless-copy sets that produce multiple copies automatically. More and more organizations use computers to generate their standardized forms, which can save them both money and time.[4]

Appearance

Produce almost all of your business documents using either a printer (letter-quality, not a dot matrix) or a typewriter. Certain documents, however, should be handwritten (such as a short informal memo or a note of condolence). Be sure to handwrite, print, or type the envelope to match the document. However, even a letter on the best-quality paper with the best-designed letterhead may look unprofessional if it's poorly produced. So pay close attention to all the factors affecting appearance, including the following:

- **Margins.** Companies in Canada make sure that documents (especially external ones) are centred on the page, with margins of at least 2.5 cm all around. Using word-processing software, you can achieve this balance simply by defining the format parameters.
- **Line length.** Lines are rarely right-hand justified, because the resulting text looks too much like a form letter and can be hard to read (even with proportional spacing). Varying line length makes the document look more personal and interesting.
- **Line spacing.** You can adjust the number of blank lines between elements (such as between the date and the inside address) to ensure that a short document fills the page vertically or that a longer document extends at least two lines of the body onto the last page.
- **Character spacing.** Use proper spacing between characters and after punctuation. For example, Canadian conventions include leaving one space after commas, semicolons, colons, and sentence-ending periods. Each letter in a person's initials is followed by a period and a single space. However, abbreviations such as U.S.A. or MBA may or may not have periods, but they never have internal spaces.
- **Special symbols.** When using a computer, use appropriate symbols to give your document a professional look (see Table A.1 for examples).
- **Corrections.** Messy corrections are obvious and unacceptable in business documents. Reprint or retype any letter, report, or memo requiring a lot of corrections.

Table A.1 Special Symbols on Computer

	Computer symbol	Typed symbol
Case fractions	½	1/2
Copyright	©	(c)
Registered trademark	®	(R)
Cents	¢	None
British pound	£	None
Paragraph	¶	None
Bullets	●, ◆, ■, □, ✓, ☑, ⊗	*, #, 0
Em dash	—	-- (two hyphens)
En dash	–	- (one hyphen)

Letters

All business letters have certain elements in common. Several of these elements appear in every letter; others appear only when desirable or appropriate. In addition, these letter parts are usually arranged in one of three basic formats.

Standard Letter Parts

The letter in Figure A.1 shows the placement of standard letter parts. The writer of this business letter had no letterhead available but correctly included a heading. All business letters typically include these eight elements.

Heading

Letterhead (the usual heading) shows the organization's name, full address, telephone number (almost always), and e-mail address (often). Computers allow you to design your own letterhead (either one to use for all correspondence or a new one for each piece of correspondence). If letterhead stationery is not available, the heading includes a return address (but no name) and starts 13 lines from the top of the page, which leaves a 5-cm top margin.

Date

If you're using letterhead, place the date at least one blank line beneath the lowest part of the letterhead. Without letterhead, place the date immediately below the return address. The ususal method of writing the date in Canada uses the full name of the month (no abbreviations), followed by the day (in numerals, without *st, nd, rd,* or *th*), a comma, and then the year: July 14, 2004 (7/14/04). Some organizations follow other conventions (see Table A.2). To maintain the utmost clarity in international correspondence, always spell out the name of the month in dates.[5]

When communicating internationally, you may also experience some confusion over time. Some companies in Canada refer to morning (A.M.) and afternoon (P.M.), dividing a 24-hour day into 12-hour blocks so that they refer to four o'clock in the morning (4:00 A.M.) or four o'clock in the afternoon (4:00 P.M.). European companies refer to one 24-hour period so that 0400 hours (4:00 A.M.) is always in the morning and 1600 hours (4:00 P.M.) is always in the afternoon.[6] Make sure your references to time are as clear as possible, and be sure you clearly understand your audience's time references.

FIGURE A.1 Standard Letter Parts

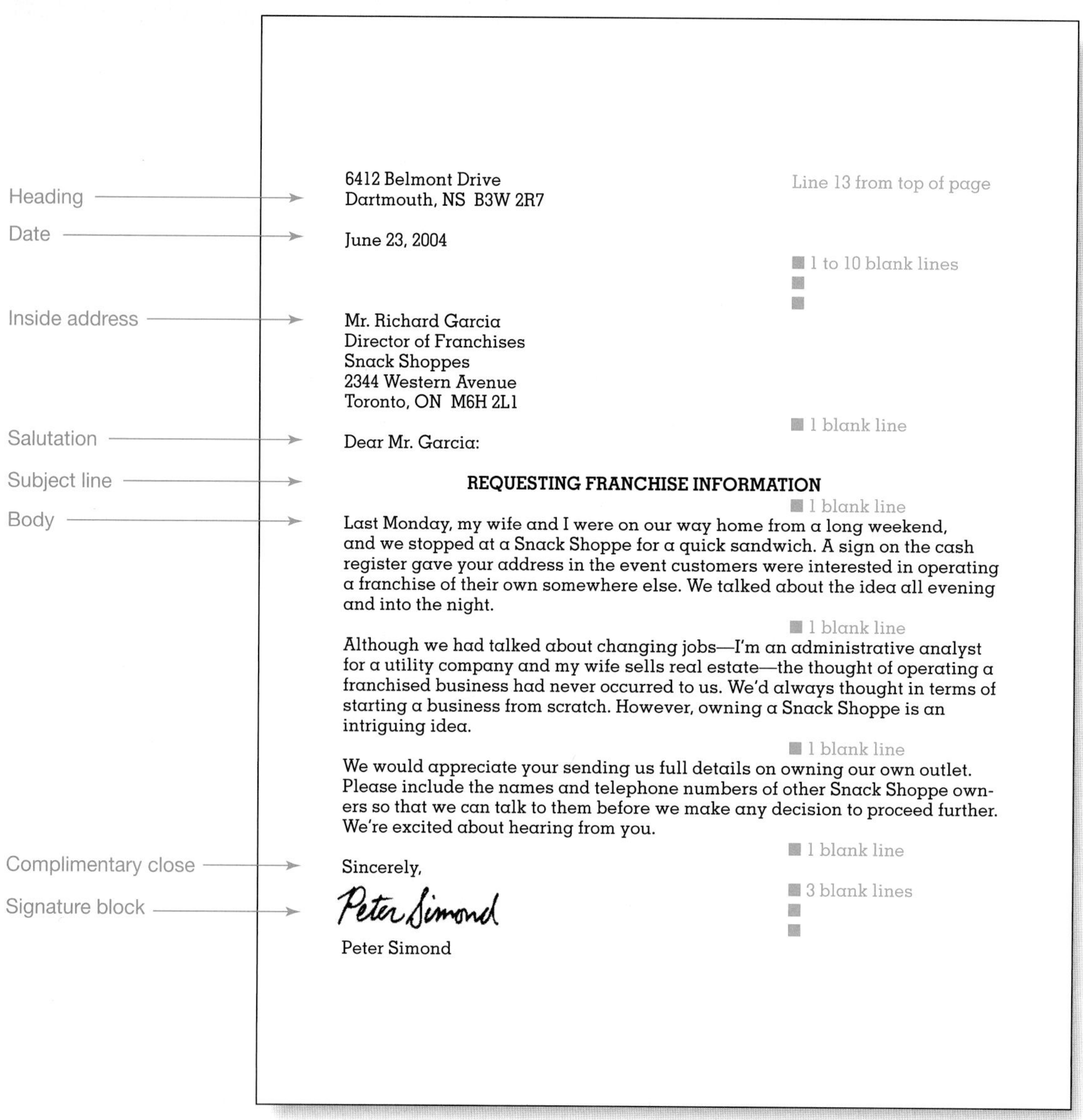

Inside Address

The inside address identifies the recipient of the letter. For Canadian correspondence, begin the inside address at least one line below the date. Precede the addressee's name with a courtesy title, such as *Dr., Mr.,* or *Ms.* The accepted courtesy title for women in business is *Ms.*, although a woman known to prefer the title *Miss* or *Mrs.* is always accommodated. If you don't know whether a person is a man or a woman (and you

Table A.2 Common Date Forms

Convention	Description	Date—Mixed	Date—All Numerals
Canadian and U.S. standard	Month (spelled out) day, year	July 14, 2004	7/14/04
Alternative	Day (in numerals) month (spelled out) year	14 July 2004	14/7/04
European	Replace diagonal line with periods	14 July 2004	14.7.2004
International standard	Year month day	2004 July 14	2004,7,14

Table A.3 Forms of Address

Person	In Address	In Salutation
Personal Titles		
Man	Mr. [first & last name]	Dear Mr. [last name]:
Woman (marital status unknown)	Ms. [first & last name]	Dear Ms. [last name]:
Woman (single)	Ms. or Miss [first & last name]	Dear Ms. *or* Miss [last name]:
Woman (married)	Ms. or Mrs. [wife's first & last name] or Mrs. [husband's first & last name]	Dear Ms. *or* Mrs. [last name]:
Woman (widowed)	Ms. or Mrs. [wife's first name & last name]	Dear Ms. *or* Mrs. [last name]:
Woman (separated or divorced)	Ms. or Mrs. [first & last name]	Dear Ms. *or* Mrs. [last name]:
Two men (or more)	Mr. [first & last name] and Mr. [first & last name]	Dear Mr. [last name] and Mr. [last name] *or* Messrs. [last name] and [last name]:
Two women (or more)	Ms. [first & last name] and Ms. [first & last name]	Dear Ms. [last name] and Ms. [last name] *or* Mses. [last name] and [last name]:
	or Mrs. [first & last name] and Mrs. [first & last name]	Dear Mrs. [last name] and Mrs. [last name]: *or* Dear Mesdames [last name] and [last name] *or* Mesdames:
	Miss [first & last name] Mrs. [first & last name]	Dear Miss [last name] and Mrs. [last name]:
One woman and one man	Ms. [first & last name] and Mr. [first & last name]	Dear Ms. [last name] and Mr. [last name]:
Couple (married)	Mr. and Mrs. [husband's first & last name]	Dear Mr. and Mrs. [last name]:
Couple (married with different last names)	[title] [first & last name of husband] [title] [first & last name of wife]	Dear [title] [husband's last name] and [title] [wife's first & last name]:
Couple (married professionals with same title and same last name)	[title in plural form] [husband's first name] and [wife's first & last name]	Dear [title in plural form] [last name]:
Couple (married professionals with different titles and same last name)	[title] [first & last name of husband] and [title] [first & last name of wife]	Dear [title] and [title] [last name]:

(continued)

have no way of finding out), omit the courtesy title. For example, *Terry Smith* could be either a man or a woman. The first line of the inside address would be just *Terry Smith,* and the salutation would be *Dear Terry Smith.* The same is true if you know only a person's initials, as in *S. J. Adams.*

Spell out and capitalize titles that precede a person's name, such as *Professor* or *General* (see Table A.3 for the proper forms of address). The person's organizational title, such as *Director,* may be included on this first line (if it is short) or on the line below; the name of a department may follow. In addresses and signature lines, don't forget to capitalize any professional title that follows a person's name:

> Mr. Ray Johnson, Dean
>
> Ms. Patricia T. Higgins
> Assistant Vice-President

However, professional titles not appearing in an address or signature line are capitalized only when they directly precede the name.

> President Kenneth Johanson will deliver the speech.
>
> Maria La Mothe, president of ABC Enterprises, will deliver the speech.

Table A.3 Continued

Person	In Address	In Salutation
Professional Titles		
President of a college or university (doctor)	Dr. [first & last name], President	Dear Dr. [last name]:
Dean of a school of college or university	Dean [first & last name] *or* [title] Miss [first & last name] Dean of [school]	Dear Dean [last name]: Dear [title] [last name] Miss [last name]:
Professor	Professor [first & last name]	Dear Professor [last name]:
Physician	[first & last name], M.D.	Dear Dr. [last name]:
Governmental Titles		
Prime Minister of Canada	The Prime Minister	Dear Mr. *or* Madam Prime Minister:
Member of Parliament	Honourable [first & last name]	Dear Honourable Member of Parliament [last name]:
Mayor	Honourable [first & last name] Mayor of [name of city]	Dear Mayor [last name]:
Judge	The Honourable [name]	Dear Judge [last name]:
Religious Titles		
Priest	The Reverend [first & last name], [initials of order, if any]	Reverend Sir: (formal) *or* Dear Father [last name]: (informal)
Rabbi	Rabbi [first & last name]	Dear Rabbi [last name]:
Minister	The Reverend [first & last name], [title, if any]	Dear Reverend [last name]:

The Honourable Helen Masters, member of Parliament from Nepean, will deliver the speech.

If the name of a specific person is unavailable, you may address the letter to the department or to a specific position within the department. Also, be sure to spell out company names in full, unless the company itself uses abbreviations in its official name.

Other address information includes the treatment of buildings, house numbers, and compass directions (see Table A.4 on page A-6). The following example shows all the information that may be included in the inside address and its proper order for Canadian correspondence:

Dr. H. C. Armstrong
Research and Development
Commonwealth Mining Consortium
The Chelton Building, Suite 301
585 Second Street SW
Calgary, Alberta T2P 2P5

The order and layout of address information vary from country to country. So when addressing correspondence for other countries, carefully follow the format and information that appear in the company's letterhead. However, when you're sending mail from Canada, be sure that the name of the destination country appears on the last line of the address in capital letters. Use the English version of the country name so that your mail is routed to the right country. Then, to be sure your mail is routed correctly within the destination country, use the foreign spelling of the city name (using the characters and diacritical marks that would be commonly used in the region).

For example, the following address uses *Köln* instead of *Cologne*:

H. R. Veith, Director	Addressee
Eisfieren Glaswerk	Company name
Blaubachstrabe 13	Street address
Postfach 10 80 07	Post office box
D-5000 Köln I	District, city
GERMANY	Country

Table A.4 Inside Address Information

Description	Example
Capitalize building names.	Welland Building
Capitalize locations within buildings (apartments, suites, rooms).	Suite 1073
Use numerals for all house or building numbers, except the number *one.*	One Trinity Lane 637 Adams Avenue, Apt. 7
Spell out compass directions that fall within a street address	1074 West Connover Street
Abbreviate compass directions that follow the street address	783 Main Street, N.E., Apt. 27

For additional examples of international addresses, refer to the table on the Companion Website at www.pearsoned.ca/bovee.

Be sure to use organizational titles correctly when addressing international correspondence. Job designations vary around the world. In England, for example, a managing director is often what a Canadian company would call its chief executive officer or president, and a British deputy is the equivalent of a vice-president. In France, responsibilities are assigned to individuals without regard to title or organizational structure, and in China the title *project manager* has meaning, but the title *sales manager* may not.

To make matters worse, business people in some countries sign correspondence without their names typed below. In Germany, for example, the belief is that employees represent the company, so it's inappropriate to emphasize personal names.[7]

Salutation

In the salutation of your letter, follow the style of the first line of the inside address. If the first line is a person's name, the salutation is *Dear Mr.* or *Ms. Name.* The formality of the salutation depends on your relationship with the addressee. If in conversation you would say "Mary," your letter's salutation should be *Dear Mary,* followed by a colon. Otherwise, include the courtesy title and last name, followed by a colon. Presuming to write *Dear Lewis* instead of *Dear Professor Chang* demonstrates a disrespectful familiarity that the recipient will probably resent.

If the first line of the inside address is a position title such as *Director of Personnel,* then use *Dear Director*. If the addressee is unknown, use a polite description, such as *Dear Alumnus, Dear SPCA Supporter,* or *Dear Voter.* If the first line is plural (a department or company), then use *Ladies and Gentlemen* (look again at Table A.3).

Subject Line

The subject line tells recipients at a glance what the document is about (and indicates where to file the letter for future reference). It usually appears below the salutation, either against the left margin, indented (as a paragraph in the body), or centred. It can be placed above the salutation or at the very top of the page, and it can be underscored. Some businesses omit the word *Subject.* The subject line may take a variety of forms, including the following:

Subject: RainMaster Sprinklers

FALL 1998 SALES MEETING

Reference Order No. 27920

Body

The body of the letter is your message. Almost all letters are single-spaced, with one blank line before and after the salutation or opening, between paragraphs, and before the complimentary close. The body may include indented lists, entire paragraphs indented for emphasis, and even subheadings. If it does, all similar elements should be treated in the same way. Your department or company may select a format to use for all letters.

Complimentary Close

The complimentary close begins on the second line below the body of the letter. Alternatives for wording are available, but currently the trend seems to be toward using one-word closes, such as *Sincerely.* In any case, the complimentary close reflects the relationship between you and the person you're writing to. Avoid cute closes, such as *Yours for bigger profits.* If your audience doesn't know you well, your sense of humour may be misunderstood.

Signature Block

Leave three blank lines for a written signature below the complimentary close, and then include the sender's name (unless it appears in the letterhead). The person's title may appear on the same line as the name or on the line below:

Yours truly,

Raymond Dunnigan

Director of Human Resources

Your letterhead indicates that you're representing your company. However, if your letter is on plain paper or runs to a second page, you may want to emphasize that you're speaking legally for the company. The accepted way of doing that is to place the company's name in capital letters a double space below the complimentary close and then include the sender's name and title four lines below that:

Sincerely,

WENTWORTH INDUSTRIES

(Mrs.) Helen B. Taylor
President

If your name could be taken for either a man's or a woman's, a courtesy title indicating gender should be included, with or without parentheses. Also, women who prefer a particular courtesy title should include it:

Mrs. Nancy Winters
(Miss) Celine Dufour
Ms. Pat Li
(Mr.) Jamie Saunders

Additional Letter Parts

Letters vary greatly in subject matter and thus in the identifying information they need and the format they adopt. The letter in Figure A.2 on page A-8 shows how these additional parts should be arranged. The following elements may be used in any combination, depending on the requirements of the particular letter:

- **Addressee notation.** Letters that have a restricted readership or that must be handled in a special way should include such addressee notations as *Personal, Confidential,* or *Please Forward.* This sort of notation appears a double space above the inside address, in all-capital letters.
- **Attention line.** Although not commonly used today, an attention line can be used if you know only the last name of the person you're writing to. It can also direct a letter to a position title or department. Place the attention line on the first line of the inside address and put the company name on the second.[8] An attention line may take any of the following forms or variants of them:

  Attention Dr. McHenry
  Attention Director of Marketing
  Attention Marketing Department

- **Second-page heading.** Use a second-page heading whenever an additional page is required. Some companies have second-page letterhead (with the company name and address on one line and in a smaller typeface). The heading bears the name (person or organization) from the first line of the inside address, the page number, the date, and perhaps a reference number. Leave two blank lines before the body. Make sure that at least two lines of a continued paragraph appear on the first and second pages. Never allow the closing lines to appear alone on a continued page. Precede the complimentary close or signature lines with at least two lines of the body. Also, don't hyphenate the last word on a page. All the following are acceptable forms for second-page headings:

  Ms. Melissa Baker
  May 10, 2004
  Page 2

  Ms. Melissa Baker, May 10, 2004, Page 2

  Ms. Melissa Baker -2- May 10, 2004

- **Company name.** If you include the company's name in the signature block, put it all in capital letters a double space below the complimentary close. You usually include the company's name in the signature block only when the writer is serving as the company's official spokesperson or when letterhead has not been used.
- **Reference initials.** When business people keyboard their own letters, reference initials are unnecessary, so they are becoming rare. When one person dictates a letter and another person produces it, reference initials show who helped prepare it. Place initials at the left margin, a double space below the signature block. When the signature block includes the writer's name, use only the preparer's initials. If the signature block includes only the department, use both sets of initials, usually in one of the following forms: *RSR/sm, RSR:sm,* or *RSR:SM* (writer/preparer). When the writer and the signer are different people, at least the file copy should bear both their initials as well as the typist's: *JFS/RSR/sm* (signer/writer/preparer).
- **Enclosure notation.** Enclosure notations appear at the bottom of a letter, one or two lines below the reference initials. Some common forms include the following:

  Enclosure
  Enclosures (2)
  Enclosures: Resumé
  Photograph
  Attachment

- **Copy notation.** Copy notations may follow reference initials or enclosure notations. They indicate who's receiving a *courtesy copy* (*cc*) or they simply use *copy* (*c*). Recipients are listed in order of rank or (rank being equal) in alphabetical order. Among the forms used are the following:

  cc: David Wentworth, Vice-President
  c: Dr. Martha Littlefield
  Copy to Hans Vogel
  748 Chesterton Road
  Kitimat, BC V8C 5V1

When sending copies to readers other than the person receiving the original letter, place *bc, bcc,* or *bpc* ("blind copy," "blind courtesy copy," or "blind photocopy") along with the name and any other information only on the copy, not on the original.

FIGURE A.2 Additional Letter Parts

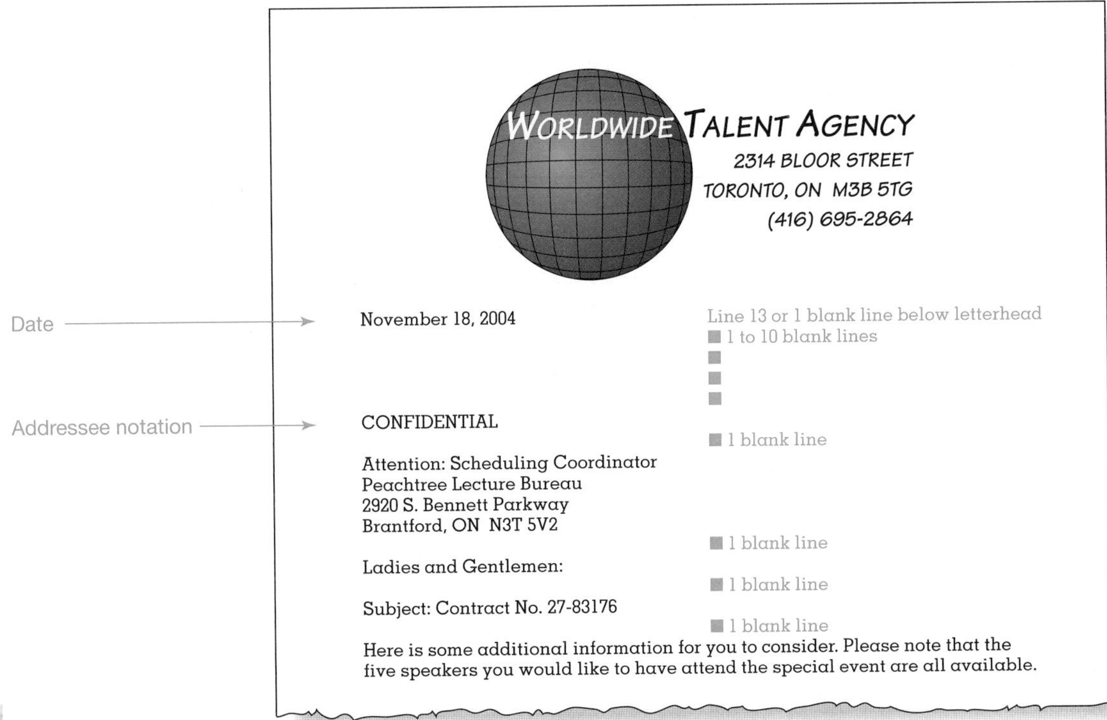

WORLDWIDE TALENT AGENCY
2314 BLOOR STREET
TORONTO, ON M3B 5TG
(416) 695-2864
Date
November 18, 2004
Line 13 or 1 blank line below letterhead
1 to 10 blank lines
Addressee notation
CONFIDENTIAL
1 blank line
Attention: Scheduling Coordinator
Peachtree Lecture Bureau
2920 S. Bennett Parkway
Brantford, ON N3T 5V2
1 blank line
Ladies and Gentlemen:
1 blank line
Subject: Contract No. 27-83176
1 blank line
Here is some additional information for you to consider. Please note that the five speakers you would like to have attend the special event are all available.

- **Mailing notation.** You may place a mailing notation (such as *Special Delivery* or *Registered Mail*) at the bottom of the letter, after reference initials or enclosure notations (whichever one is last) and before copy notations. Or you may place it at the top of the letter, either above the inside address on the left-hand side or just below the date on the right-hand side. For greater visibility, mailing notations may appear in capital letters.
- **Postscript.** A postscript is an afterthought to the letter, a message that requires emphasis, or a personal note. It is usually the last thing on any letter and may be preceded by *P.S.*, *PS.*, *PS:*, or nothing at all. A second afterthought would be designated *P.P.S.* (post postscript). Since postscripts usually indicate poor planning, generally avoid them. However, they're common in sales letters as a punch line to remind readers of a benefit for taking advantage of the offer.

Letter Formats

A letter format is the way of arranging all the basic letter parts. Sometimes a company adopts a certain format as its policy; sometimes the individual letter writer or preparer is allowed to choose the most appropriate format. In Canada, three major letter formats are commonly used:

- **Block format.** Each letter part begins at the left margin. The main advantage is quick and efficient preparation (see Figure A.3 on page A-10).
- **Modified block format.** Same as block format, except that the date, complimentary close, and signature block start near the centre of the page (see Figure A.4 on page A-11). The modified block format does permit indentions as an option. This format mixes preparation speed with traditional placement of some letter parts. It also looks more balanced on the page than the block format does.
- **Simplified format.** Instead of using a salutation, this format often weaves the reader's name into the first line or two of the body and often includes a subject line in capital letters (see Figure A.5 on page A-12). With no complimentary close, your signature appears after the body, followed by your printed (or typewritten) name (usually in all capital letters). This format is convenient when you don't know the reader's name; however, some people object to it as mechanical and impersonal (a drawback you can overcome with a warm writing style). Because certain letter parts are eliminated, some line spacing is changed.

The most common formats for intercultural business letters are the block style and the modified block style.

In addition to these three letter formats, letters may also be classified according to their style of punctuation. *Standard,* or *mixed, punctuation* uses a colon after the salutation (a comma if the letter is social or personal) and a comma after the complimentary close. *Open punctuation* uses no colon or comma after the salutation or the complimentary close. Although the most popular style in business communication is mixed punctuation, either style of punctuation may be used with block or modified block letter formats. Because the simplified letter format has no salutation or complimentary close, the style of punctuation is irrelevant.

FIGURE A.2 Continued

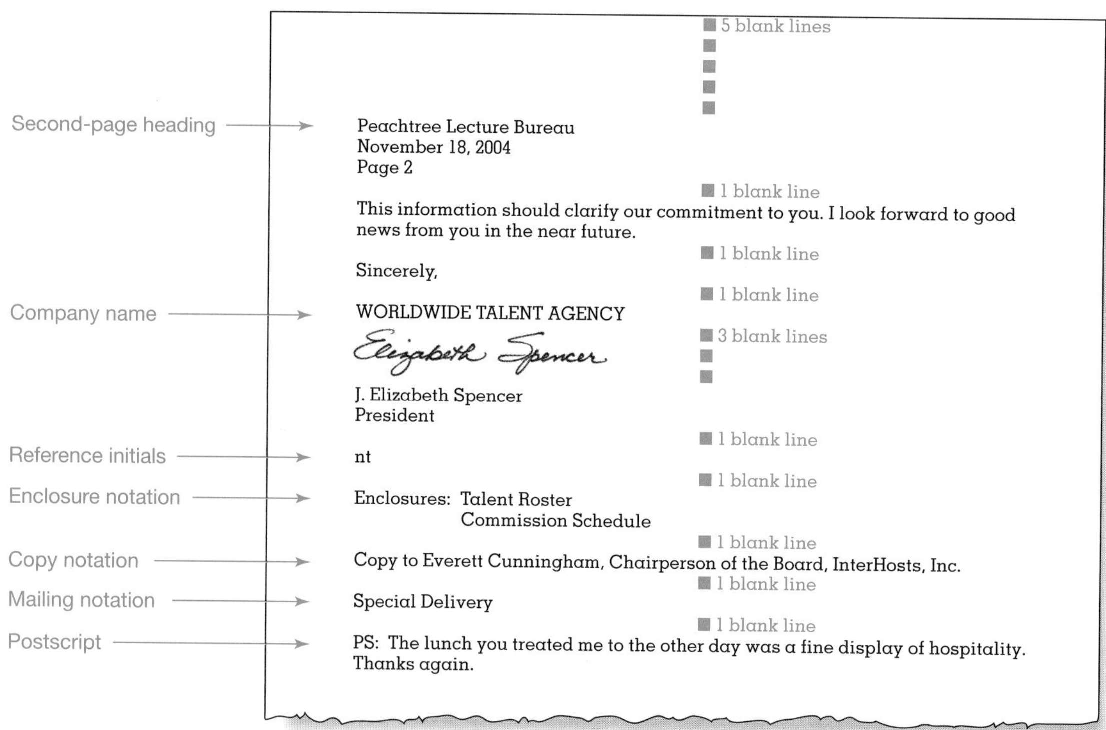

5 blank lines
Second-page heading
Peachtree Lecture Bureau
November 18, 2004
Page 2
1 blank line
This information should clarify our commitment to you. I look forward to good news from you in the near future.
1 blank line
Sincerely,
1 blank line
Company name
WORLDWIDE TALENT AGENCY
3 blank lines
J. Elizabeth Spencer
President
1 blank line
Reference initials
nt
1 blank line
Enclosure notation
Enclosures: Talent Roster
Commission Schedule
1 blank line
Copy notation
Copy to Everett Cunningham, Chairperson of the Board, InterHosts, Inc.
1 blank line
Mailing notation
Special Delivery
1 blank line
Postscript
PS: The lunch you treated me to the other day was a fine display of hospitality. Thanks again.

Envelopes

For a first impression, the quality of the envelope is just as important as the quality of the stationery. Letterhead and envelopes should be of the same paper stock, have the same colour ink, and be imprinted with the same address and logo. Most envelopes used by Canadian businesses are No. 10 envelopes (9½ inches long), which are sized for an 8½-by-11-inch piece of paper folded in thirds. Some occasions call for a smaller, No. 6¾, envelope or for envelopes proportioned to fit special stationery. Figure A.6 on page A-13 shows the two most common sizes.

Addressing the Envelope

No matter what size the envelope, the address is always single-spaced with all lines aligned on the left. The address on the envelope is in the same style as the inside address and presents the same information. The order to follow is from the smallest division to the largest:

1. Name and title of recipient
2. Name of department or subgroup
3. Name of organization
4. Name of building
5. Street address and suite number, or post office box number
6. City, province, and postal code
7. Name of country (if the letter is being sent abroad)

Because Canada Post uses optical scanners to sort mail, envelopes for quantity mailings, in particular, should be addressed in the prescribed format. No punctuation is included, and all mailing instructions of interest to the post office are placed above the address area (see Figure A.6). Canada Post requires that the city is all in capitals, and the postal code is placed on the line below the name of the city. The post office scanners read addresses from the bottom up, so if a letter is to be sent to a post office box rather than to a street address, the street address should appear on the line above the box number. Figure A.6 also shows the proper spacing for addresses and return addresses.

Canada Post Corporation and the U.S. Postal Service have published lists of two-letter mailing abbreviations for provinces, territories, and states (see Table A.5 on page A-14). Postal authorities prefer no punctuation with these abbreviations, but some executives prefer to have province and state names spelled out in full and set off from city names by a comma. The issue is unresolved, although the comma is most often included. For all out-of-office correspondence, use postal codes that have been assigned to speed mail delivery. Canadian postal codes are alphanumeric, with a three-character "area code" and a three-character "local code" separated by a single space (K2P 5A5). Canadian postal codes may be separated from the province by one space or put in the bottom line of the address all by itself.

FIGURE A.3 Block Letter Format

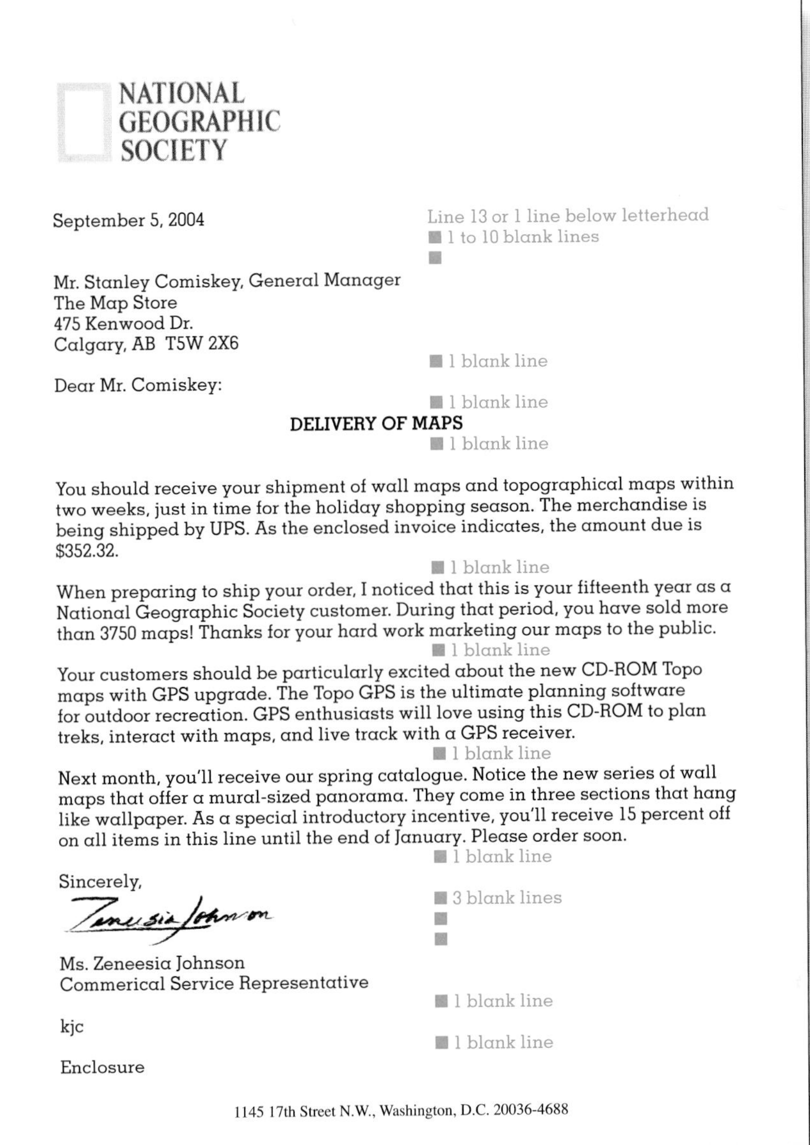
NATIONAL GEOGRAPHIC SOCIETY

September 5, 2004

Line 13 or 1 line below letterhead
1 to 10 blank lines

Mr. Stanley Comiskey, General Manager
The Map Store
475 Kenwood Dr.
Calgary, AB T5W 2X6

1 blank line

Dear Mr. Comiskey:

1 blank line

DELIVERY OF MAPS

1 blank line

You should receive your shipment of wall maps and topographical maps within two weeks, just in time for the holiday shopping season. The merchandise is being shipped by UPS. As the enclosed invoice indicates, the amount due is $352.32.

1 blank line

When preparing to ship your order, I noticed that this is your fifteenth year as a National Geographic Society customer. During that period, you have sold more than 3750 maps! Thanks for your hard work marketing our maps to the public.

1 blank line

Your customers should be particularly excited about the new CD-ROM Topo maps with GPS upgrade. The Topo GPS is the ultimate planning software for outdoor recreation. GPS enthusiasts will love using this CD-ROM to plan treks, interact with maps, and live track with a GPS receiver.

1 blank line

Next month, you'll receive our spring catalogue. Notice the new series of wall maps that offer a mural-sized panorama. They come in three sections that hang like wallpaper. As a special introductory incentive, you'll receive 15 percent off on all items in this line until the end of January. Please order soon.

1 blank line

Sincerely,

3 blank lines

Ms. Zeneesia Johnson
Commerical Service Representative

1 blank line

kjc

1 blank line

Enclosure

1145 17th Street N.W., Washington, D.C. 20036-4688

Folding to Fit

The way a letter is folded also contributes to the recipient's overall impression of your organization's professionalism. When sending a standard-size piece of paper in a No. 10 envelope, fold it in thirds, with the bottom folded up first and the top folded down over it (see Figure A.7 on page A-15); the open end should be at the top of the envelope and facing out. Fit smaller stationery neatly into the appropriate envelope simply by folding it in half or in thirds. When sending a standard-size letterhead in a No. 6¾ envelope, fold it in half from top to bottom and then in thirds from side to side.

International Mail

Postal service differs from country to country. For example, street addresses are uncommon in India, and the mail there is unreliable.[9] It's usually a good idea to send international correspondence by airmail and to ask that responses be sent that way as well.

Memos

Many organizations have memo forms preprinted, with labelled spaces for the recipient's name (or sometimes a checklist of all departments in an organization or all persons in a department), the sender's name, the date, and the subject (see Figure A.8 on page A-15). If such forms don't exist, you can use a memo template (which comes with word-processing software and provides margin settings, headings, and special formats), or you can use plain paper.

On your document, include a title such as *MEMO* or *INTEROFFICE CORRESPONDENCE* (all in capitals) centred at the top of the page or aligned with the left margin.

FIGURE A.4 Modified Block Letter Format

Greyhound Canada
P.O. Box 850•Calgary, AB T2E 4S7

■ line 13 from top of page November 3, 2004
■ 1 to 10 blank lines
■

Mrs. Eugenia Preston, President
Drayton Valley High School PAC
P.O. Box 335
Drayton Valley, AB T7A 1T9
■ 1 blank line
Dear Mrs. Preston:
■ 1 blank line
TRAVELLING TO EDMONTON
■ 1 blank line
Thank you for inviting us to participate in your "Government Experience" program. So that your honours students can experience government firsthand, we will be delighted to provide one of our motor coaches next May at a 15% discount to transport up to 40 students and 7 teachers from Drayton Valley to Edmonton and back.
■ 1 blank line
Our buses seat 47 passengers, are fully equipped with restrooms and reclining seats, and are climate controlled for year-round comfort. You can rely on us for your charter transportation needs:
■ 1 blank line

- Our intensive, ongoing driver-training program ensures your safety and satisfaction.
- Our competitive pricing allows us to compete both locally and nationwide.
- Our state-of-the-art maintenance facilities are located in all major Canadian cities to ensure quality, reliability, and excellent service.

■ 1 blank line
Please give me a call at (403) 997-4646 to discuss the specific date of your event, departure times, and the discounted price for your trip. Together, we'll make sure your students have a day that's not only fun and educational but safe and secure. I look forward to hearing from you.
■ 1 blank line
Yours truly,
■ 3 blank lines
■
■
Ronald Struthers
Ronald Struthers
Vice-President, Public Relations
■ 1 blank line
pf
■ 1 blank line
Enclosure

Also at the top, include the words *To, From, Date,* and *Subject*—followed by the appropriate information—with a blank line between, as shown here:

MEMO

TO:

FROM:

DATE:

SUBJECT:

Sometimes the heading is organized like this:

MEMO

TO:	DATE:
FROM:	SUBJECT:

You can arrange these four pieces of information in almost any order. The date sometimes appears without the heading *Date.* The subject may be presented with the letters *Re:* (in place of *SUBJECT:*) or without any heading (but in capital letters so that it stands out clearly). You may want to include a file or reference number, introduced by the word *File.*

The following guidelines will help you effectively format specific memo elements:

- **Addressees.** When sending a memo to a long list of people, include the notation *See distribution list* or *See below* in the *To* position at the top; then list the names at the end of the memo. Arrange this list alphabetically, except when high-ranking officials deserve more prominent placement. You can also address memos to groups of people—*All Sales Representatives, Production Group, New Product Team.*

FIGURE A.5 Simplified Letter Format

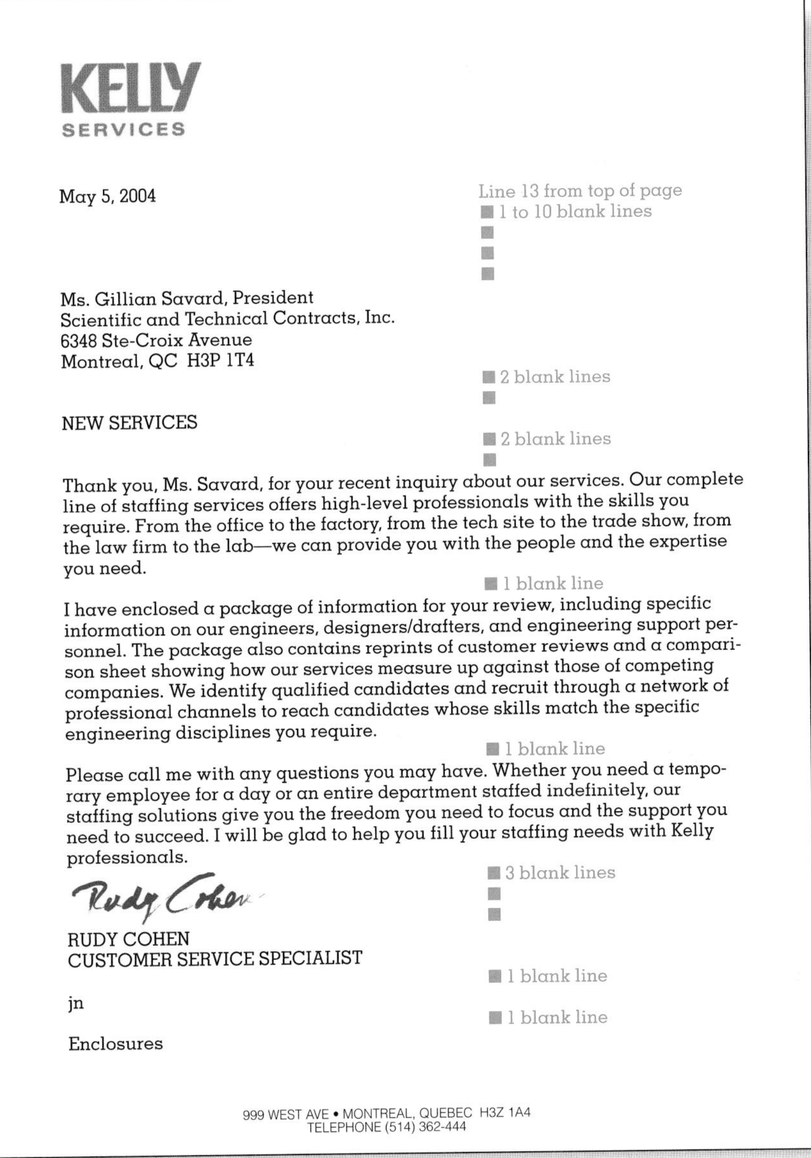
KELLY
SERVICES

May 5, 2004

Ms. Gillian Savard, President
Scientific and Technical Contracts, Inc.
6348 Ste-Croix Avenue
Montreal, QC H3P 1T4

NEW SERVICES

Thank you, Ms. Savard, for your recent inquiry about our services. Our complete line of staffing services offers high-level professionals with the skills you require. From the office to the factory, from the tech site to the trade show, from the law firm to the lab—we can provide you with the people and the expertise you need.

I have enclosed a package of information for your review, including specific information on our engineers, designers/drafters, and engineering support personnel. The package also contains reprints of customer reviews and a comparison sheet showing how our services measure up against those of competing companies. We identify qualified candidates and recruit through a network of professional channels to reach candidates whose skills match the specific engineering disciplines you require.

Please call me with any questions you may have. Whether you need a temporary employee for a day or an entire department staffed indefinitely, our staffing solutions give you the freedom you need to focus and the support you need to succeed. I will be glad to help you fill your staffing needs with Kelly professionals.

Rudy Cohen

RUDY COHEN
CUSTOMER SERVICE SPECIALIST

jn

Enclosures

999 WEST AVE • MONTREAL, QUEBEC H3Z 1A4
TELEPHONE (514) 362-444

- **Subject line.** The subject line of a memo helps busy colleagues quickly find out what your memo is about. Although the subject "line" may overflow onto a second line, it's most helpful when it's short (but still informative).
- **Body.** Start the body of the memo on the second or third line below the heading. Like the body of a letter, it's usually single-spaced with blank lines between paragraphs. Indenting paragraphs is optional. Handle lists, important passages, and subheadings as you do in letters.
- **Second page.** If the memo carries over to a second page, head the second page just as you head the second page of a letter.
- **Writer's initials.** Unlike a letter, a memo doesn't require a complimentary close or a signature, because your name is already prominent at the top. However, you may initial the memo—either beside the name appearing at the top of the memo or at the bottom of the memo—or you may even sign your name at the bottom, particularly if the memo deals with money or confidential matters.
- **Other elements.** Treat elements such as reference initials, enclosure notations, and copy notations just as you would in a letter.

Informal, routine, or brief reports for distribution within a company are often presented in memo form (see Chapter 10). Don't include report parts such as a table of contents and appendices.

E-mail

Because e-mail messages can act both as memos (carrying information within your company) and as letters (carrying information outside your company and around the world), their format depends on your audience and pur-

FIGURE A.6 Prescribed Envelope Format

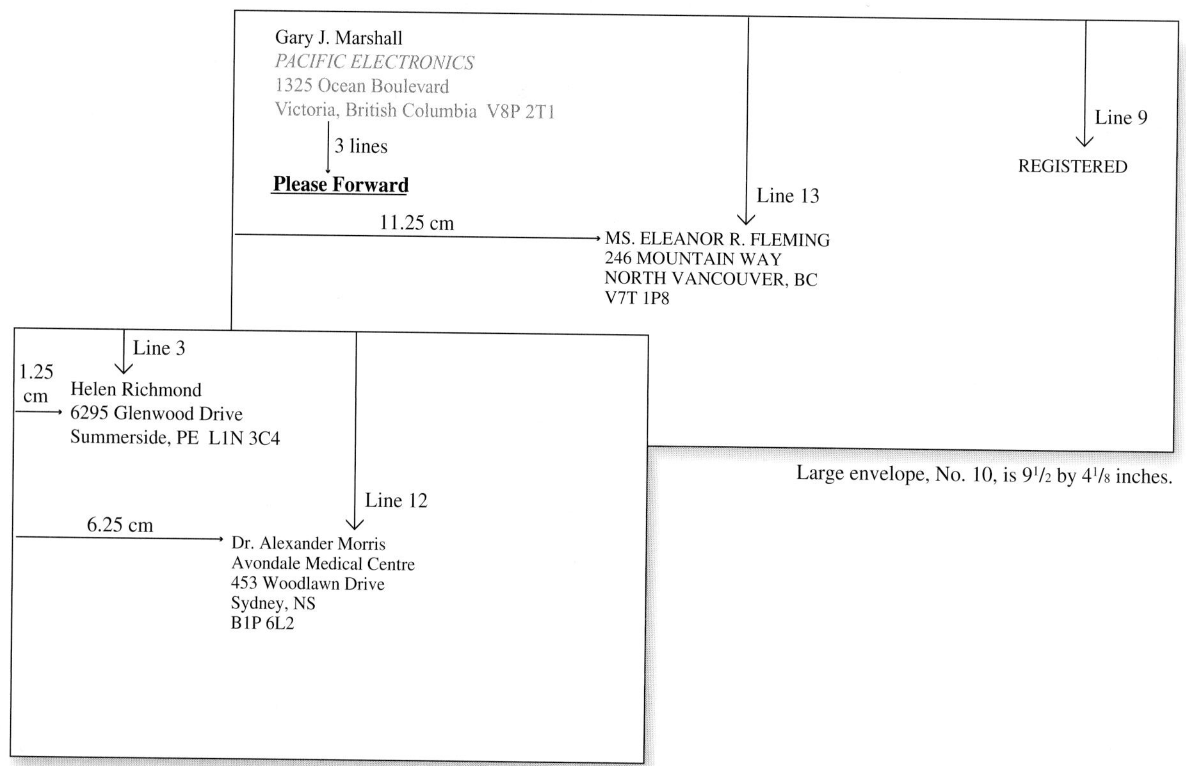

Large envelope, No. 10, is 9½ by 4⅛ inches.

Small envelope, No. 6¾, is 6½ by 3⅝ inches.

pose. You may choose to have your e-mail resemble a letter or you may decide to keep things as simple as an interoffice memo. A modified memo format is appropriate for most e-mail messages.[10] All e-mail programs include two major elements: the header and the body (see Figure A.9 on page A-16).

Header

The e-mail header depends on the particular program you use. Some programs even allow you to choose between a shorter and a longer version. However, most headers contain similar information.

- **To:** Contains the name of the receiver and/or audience's e-mail address (see Figure A.10 on page A-17). Most e-mail programs also allow you to send mail to an entire group of people all at once. First, you create a distribution list. Then you type the name of the list in the To: line instead of typing the addresses of every person in the group.[11]
- **From:** Contains your e-mail address.
- **Date:** Contains the day of the week, date (day, month, year), time, and time zone.
- **Subject:** Describes the content of the message and presents an opportunity for you to build interest in your message.
- **Cc:** Allows you to send copies of a message to more than one person at a time. It also allows everyone on the list to see who else received the same message.
- **Bcc:** Lets you send copies to people without the other recipients knowing—a practice considered unethical by some.[12]
- **Attachments:** Contains the name(s) of the file(s) you attach to your e-mail message. The file can be a word-processing document, a digital image, an audio or video message, a spreadsheet, or a software program.[13]

Body

The rest of the space below the header is for the body of your message. In the *To:* and *From:* lines, some headers actually print out the names of the sender and receiver (in addition to their e-mail addresses). Other headers do not. If your mail program includes only the e-mail addresses, you might consider including your own memo-type header in the body of your message, as in Figure A.9. The writer even included a second, more specific subject line in his memo-type header. Some recipients may applaud the clarity of such second headers; however, others will criticize the space it takes. Your decision depends on how formal you want to be.

Do include a greeting in your e-mail. As pointed out in Chapter 6, greetings personalize your message. Leave one line space above and below your greeting to set it off from the rest of your message. You may end your greeting with a colon (formal), a comma (conversational), or even two hyphens (informal)—depending on the level of formality you want.

Your message begins one blank line space below your greeting. Just as in memos and letters, skip one line space between paragraphs and include headings, numbered lists, bulleted lists, and embedded lists when appropriate. Limit your line lengths to a maximum of 80 characters by inserting a hard return at the end of each line.

Table A.5 Two-Letter Mailing Abbreviations for Canada and the United States

Province/ Territory or State	Abbreviation	Province/ Territory or State	Abbreviation	Province/ Territory or State	Abbreviation
Canada		Delaware	DE	New Jersey	NJ
Alberta	AB	District of Columbia	DC	New Mexico	NM
British Columbia	BC	Florida	FL	New York	NY
Manitoba	MB	Georgia	GA	North Carolina	NC
New Brunswick	NB	Hawaii	HI	North Dakota	ND
Newfoundland and Labrador	NL	Idaho	ID	Ohio	OH
Northwest Territories	NT	Illinois	IL	Oklahoma	OK
Nova Scotia	NS	Indiana	IN	Oregon	OR
Nunavut	NU	Iowa	IA	Pennsylvania	PA
Ontario	ON	Kansas	KS	Puerto Rico	PR
Prince Edward Island	PE	Kentucky	KY	Rhode Island	RI
Quebec	QC	Louisiana	LA	South Carolina	SC
Saskatchewan	SK	Maine	ME	South Dakota	SD
Yukon Territory	YT	Maryland	MD	Tennessee	TN
United States		Massachusetts	MA	Texas	TX
Alabama	AL	Michigan	MI	Utah	UT
Alaska	AK	Minnesota	MN	Vermont	VT
American Samoa	AS	Mississippi	MS	Virginia	VA
Arizona	AZ	Missouri	MO	Virgin Islands	VI
Arkansas	AR	Montana	MT	Washington	WA
California	CA	Nebraska	NE	West Virginia	WV
Colorado	CO	Nevada	NV	Wisconsin	WI
Connecticut	CT	New Hampshire	NH	Wyoming	WY

One blank line space below your message, include a simple closing, often just one word. A blank line space below that, include your signature. Whether you type your name or use a signature file, including your signature personalizes your message.

Time-Saving Messages

Telephone and e-mail systems are quick, as are mailgrams, telegrams, faxes, and the like. Organizations have developed special formats to reduce the amount of time spent writing and typing short messages:

- **Fax cover sheets.** When faxing messages, you may use a fax cover sheet, which includes the recipient's name, company, fax number, and city; the sender's name, complete address, fax number, and telephone number; the number of pages being sent; a phone number to call if the faxed transmission isn't successful; and enough space for any brief message.[14] The format for this information varies widely. When a document is self-explanatory, a cover sheet may be unnecessary, so be sure not to waste paper or transmission time.
- **Short-note reply technique.** Popular in many organizations, this technique can be used even without a special form. The recipient of a memo (or sometimes a letter) simply handwrites a response on the original document, makes a copy for the files, and sends the annotated original back to the person who wrote it.

FIGURE A.7 Folding Standard-Size Letterhead

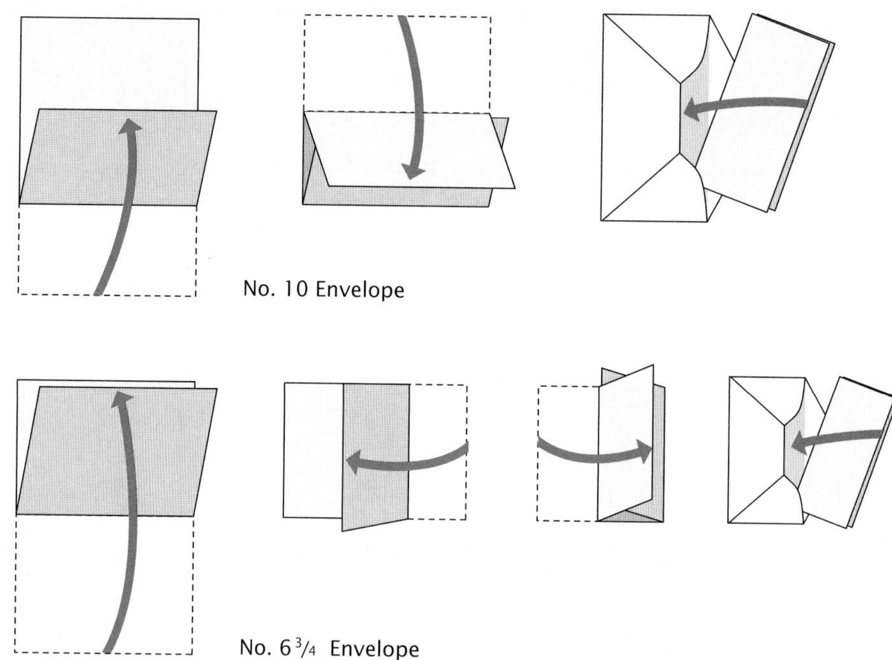

Reports

Enhance your report's effectiveness by paying careful attention to its appearance and layout. Follow whatever guidelines your organization prefers, always being neat and consistent throughout. If it's up to you to decide formatting questions, the following conventions may help you decide how to handle margins, headings, spacing and indention, and page numbers.

Margins

All margins on a report page are at least 2.5 cm wide. For double-spaced pages, use 2.5-cm margins; for single-spaced pages, set margins between 3-cm and 3.75 cm. The top, left, and right margins are usually the same, but the bottom margins can be one and a half times deeper. Some special pages also have deeper top margins. Set top margins as deep as 5 cm for pages that contain major titles: prefatory parts (such as the table of contents or the executive summary), supplementary parts (such as the reference notes or bibliography), and textual parts (such as the first page of the text or the first page of each chapter).

If you're going to bind your report at the left or at the top, add 1.25 cm to the margin on the bound edge (see Figure A.11 on page A-17). The space taken by the binding on left-bound reports makes the centre point of the text 0.5 cm to the right of the centre of the paper. Be sure to centre headings between the margins, not between the edges of the paper. Computers can do this for you automatically. Other guidelines for report formats are in the Chapter 11 sample.

Headings

Headings of various levels provide visual clues to a report's organization. Chapter 11's Figure 11.9 illustrates one good system for showing these levels, but many variations exist. No matter which system you use, be sure to be consistent.

FIGURE A.8 Preprinted Memo Form

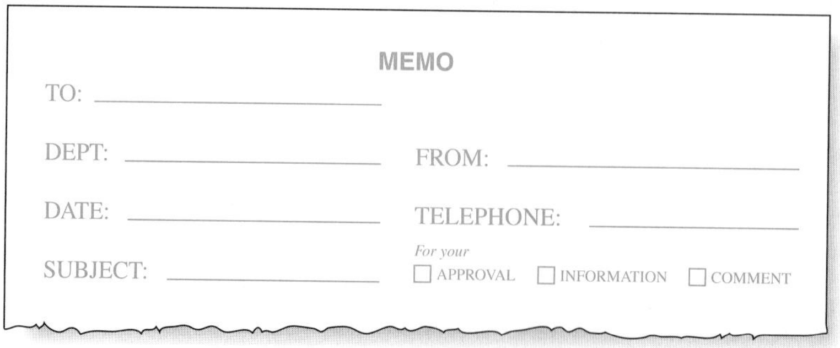

MEMO

TO: ____________________

DEPT: ____________________ FROM: ____________________

DATE: ____________________ TELEPHONE: ____________________

SUBJECT: ____________________ *For your* ☐ APPROVAL ☐ INFORMATION ☐ COMMENT

Spacing and Indentions

If your report is double-spaced (perhaps to ease comprehension of technical material), indent all paragraphs five character spaces (or about 1.25 cm). In single-spaced reports, block the paragraphs (no indentions) and leave one blank line between them.

Make sure the material on the title page is centred and well balanced, as on the title page of the sample report in Chapter 11.

Page Numbers

Remember that every page in the report is counted; however, not all pages show numbers. The first page of the report, normally the title page, is unnumbered. All other pages in the prefatory section are numbered with a lower case roman numeral, beginning with *ii* and continuing with *iii, iv, v,* and so on. The unadorned (no dashes, no period) page number is centred at the bottom margin.

Number the first page of the text of the report with the unadorned arabic numeral 1, centred at the bottom margin (double- or triple-spaced below the text). In left-bound reports, number the following pages (including the supplementary parts) consecutively with unadorned arabic numerals (2, 3, and so on), placed at the top right-hand margin (double- or triple-spaced above the text). For top-bound reports and for special pages having 5-cm top margins, centre the page numbers at the bottom margin (Figure A.11).

FIGURE A.9 A Typical E-mail Message

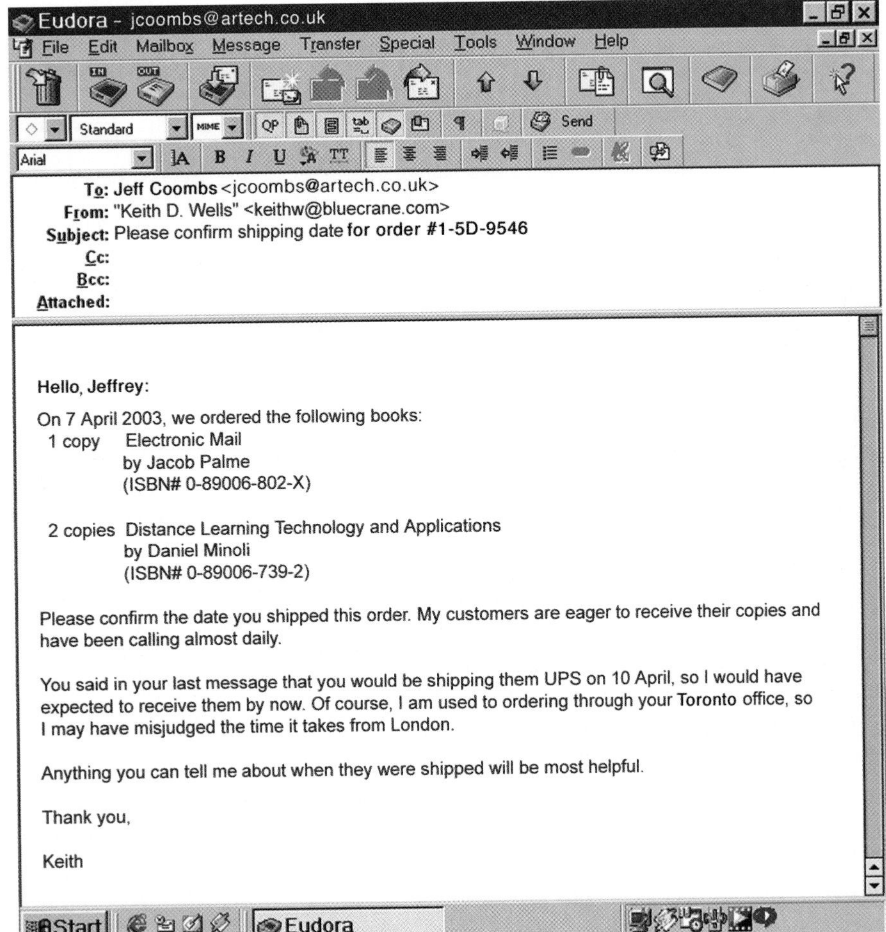

Eudora - jcoombs@artech.co.uk

File Edit Mailbox Message Transfer Special Tools Window Help

To: Jeff Coombs <jcoombs@artech.co.uk>
From: "Keith D. Wells" <keithw@bluecrane.com>
Subject: Please confirm shipping date for order #1-5D-9546
Cc:
Bcc:
Attached:

Hello, Jeffrey:

On 7 April 2003, we ordered the following books:
1 copy Electronic Mail
by Jacob Palme
(ISBN# 0-89006-802-X)

2 copies Distance Learning Technology and Applications
by Daniel Minoli
(ISBN# 0-89006-739-2)

Please confirm the date you shipped this order. My customers are eager to receive their copies and have been calling almost daily.

You said in your last message that you would be shipping them UPS on 10 April, so I would have expected to receive them by now. Of course, I am used to ordering through your Toronto office, so I may have misjudged the time it takes from London.

Anything you can tell me about when they were shipped will be most helpful.

Thank you,

Keith

Start Eudora

FIGURE A.10 Anatomy of an E-Mail Address

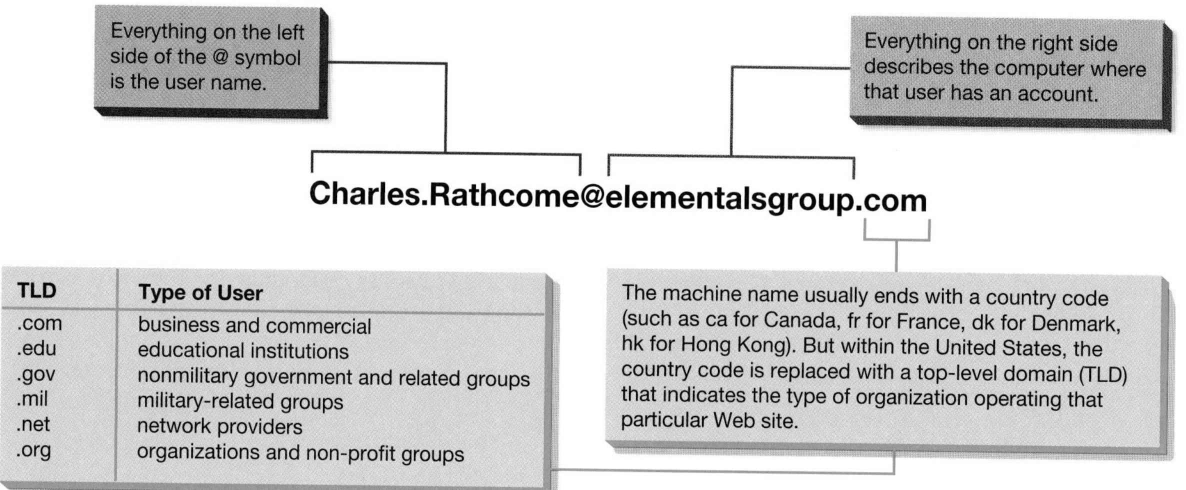

FIGURE A.11 Margins for Formal Reports

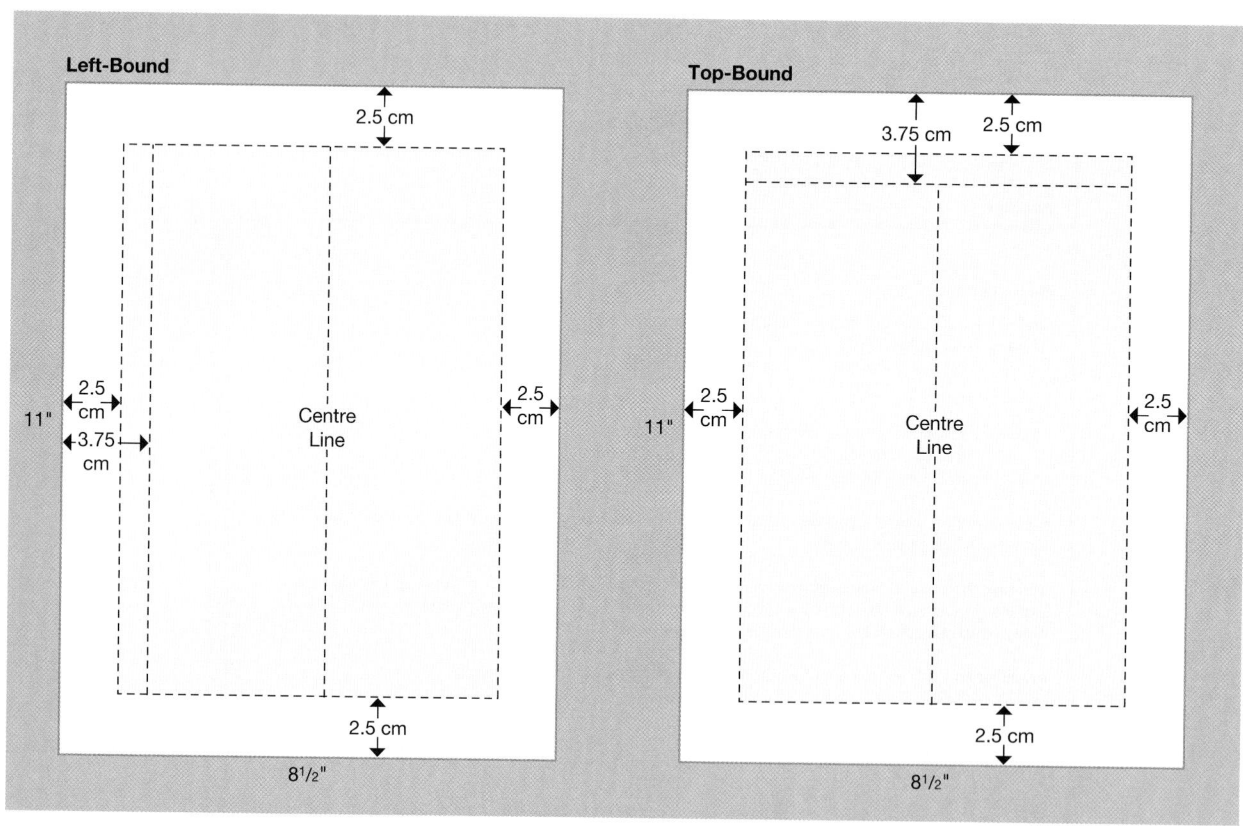

Appendix B

Documentation of Report Sources

Documenting a report is too important a task to undertake haphazardly. By providing information about your sources, you improve your own credibility as well as the credibility of the facts and opinions you present. Documentation gives readers the means for checking your findings and pursuing the subject further. Also, documenting your report is the accepted way to give credit to the people whose work you have drawn from.

Experts recommend various forms, depending on your field or discipline. Business writers do not all use the same style. Whatever style you choose, be consistent within any given report, using the same order, punctuation, and format from one reference citation or bibliography entry to the next.

A wide variety of style manuals provide detailed information on documentation. Here is a brief annotated list:

- American Psychological Association, *Publication Manual of the American Psychological Association,* 5th ed. (Washington, DC: American Psychological Association, 2001). Details the author-date system, which is preferred in the social sciences and often in business as well.
- *The Chicago Manual of Style,* 14th ed. (Chicago: University of Chicago Press, 1993). Often referred to only as *Chicago* and widely used in the publishing industry; provides detailed treatment of documentation in Chapters 15 and 16.
- Joseph Gibaldi, *MLA Style Manual and Guide to Scholarly Publishing,* 2d ed. (New York: Modern Language Association, 1998). Serves as the basis for the note and bibliography style used in much academic writing and is recommended in many university and college textbooks on writing term papers; provides a lot of examples in the humanities.
- Andrew Harnack and Eugene Kleppinger, *Online! A Reference Guide to Using Internet Sources—2000* (New York: St. Martin's Press, 2000). Offers an approach to style for citing online references.

Although many schemes have been proposed for organizing the information in source notes, all of them break the information into parts: (1) information about the author (name), (2) information about the work (title, edition, volume number), (3) information about the publication (place, publisher), (4) information about the date, and (5) information on relevant page ranges.

In the following sections, we summarize the major conventions for documenting sources in three styles: the *Publication Manual of the American Psychological Association* (APA), *The Chicago Manual of Style* (Chicago), and the *MLA Style Manual* (MLA).

APA Style

The American Psychological Association (APA) recommends the author-date system of documentation, which is popular in the physical, natural, and social sciences, and in business. When using this system, you simply insert the author's last name and the year of publication within parentheses following the text discussion of the material cited. Include a page number if you use a direct quote. This approach briefly identifies the source so that readers can locate complete information in the alphabetical reference list at the end of the report. The author-date system is both brief and clear, saving readers time and effort.

In-Text Citation—APA Style

To document report sources in text using APA style, insert the author's surname and the date of publication at the end of a statement. Enclose this information in parentheses. If the author's name is referred to in the text itself, then the name can be omitted from parenthetical material.

> Some experts recommend both translation and back-translation when dealing with any non-English-speaking culture (Assira, 2003).

> Toller and Fielding (2004) make a strong case for small companies succeeding in global business.

Personal communications and interviews conducted by the author would not be listed in the reference list at all. Such citations would appear in the text only.

> Increasing the role of cable companies is high on the list of Georgia Stainer, general manager at Day Cable and Communications (personal communication, March 2, 2004).

List of References—APA Style

For APA style, list only those works actually cited in the text (so you would not include works for background or for further reading). Report writers must choose their references judiciously. Following are the major conventions for developing a reference list according to APA style (see Figure B.1):

- Format entries as hanging indents.
- List all author names in reversed order (last name first), and use only initials for the first and middle names.
- Arrange entries in the following general order: (1) author name, (2) date, (3) title information, (4) publication information, (5) periodical page range.
- Follow the author name with the date of publication in parentheses.
- List titles of articles from magazines, newspapers, and journals without underlines or quotation marks. Capitalize only the first word of the title, any proper nouns, and the first word to follow an internal colon.
- Italicize titles of books, capitalizing only the first word, any proper nouns, and the first word to follow a colon.
- Italicize names of magazines, newspapers, journals, and other complete publications—capitalizing all the important words.
- For journal articles, include the volume number (in italics) and, if necessary, the issue number (in parentheses). Finally, include the page range of the article: *Journal of Business Communication, 36*(4), 72. (In this example, the volume is 36, the number is 4, and the page number is 72.)
- Include personal communications (such as letters, memos, e-mail, and conversations) only in text, not in reference lists.
- Electronic references include author, date of publication, title of article, name of publication (if one), volume, date of retrieval (month, day, year), and the source.
- For electronic references, indicate the actual year of publication, and the exact date of retrieval.
- For electronic references, specify the URL, leave periods off the ends of URLs.

Chicago Humanities Style

The Chicago Manual of Style recommends two types of documentation systems. The *documentary-note*, or *humanities*, style gives bibliographic citations in notes—either footnotes (when printed at the bottom of a page) or endnotes (when printed at the end of the report). The humanities system is often used in literature, history, and the arts. The other system strongly recommended by Chicago is the *author-date* system, which cites the author's last name and the date of publication in the text, usually in parentheses, reserving full documentation for the reference list (or bibliography). For the purpose of comparing styles, we will concentrate on the humanities system, which is described in detail in Chicago.

In-Text Citation—Chicago Humanities Style

To document report sources in text, the humanities system relies on superscripts—arabic numerals placed just above the line of type at the end of the reference:

> Toward the end of his speech, Myers sounded a note of caution, saying that even though the economy is expected to grow, it could easily slow a bit.[10]

The superscript lets the reader know how to look for source information in either a footnote or an endnote (see Figure B.2 on page A-22). Some readers prefer footnotes so that they can simply glance at the bottom of the page for information. Others prefer endnotes so that they can read the text without a clutter of notes on the page. Also, endnotes relieve the writer from worrying about how long each note will be and how much space it will take away from the page. Both footnotes and endnotes are handled automatically by today's word-processing software.

For the reader's convenience, you can use footnotes for **content notes** (which may supplement your main text with asides about a particular issue or event, provide a cross-reference to another section of your report, or direct the reader to a related source). Then you can use endnotes for **source notes** (which document direct quotations, paraphrased passages, and visual aids). Consider which type of note is most common in your report, and then choose whether to present these notes all as endnotes or all as footnotes. Regardless of the method you choose for referencing textual information in your report, notes for visual aids (both content notes and source notes) are placed on the same page as the visual.

Bibliography—Chicago Humanities Style

The humanities system may or may not be accompanied by a bibliography (because the notes give all the necessary bibliographic information). However, endnotes are arranged in order of appearance in the text, so an alphabetical bibliography can be valuable to your readers. The bibliography may be titled *Bibliography, Reference List, Sources, Works Cited* (if you include only those sources you actually cited in your report), or *Works Consulted* (if you include uncited sources as well). This list of sources may also serve as a reading list for those who want to pursue the subject of your report further, so you may want to annotate each entry—that is, comment on the subject matter and viewpoint of the source, as well as on its usefulness to readers. Annotations may be written in either complete or incomplete sentences. (See the annotated list of style manuals early in this appendix.) A bibliography may also be more manageable if you subdivide it into categories (a classified bibliography), either by type of reference (such as books, articles, and unpublished material) or by subject matter (such as government regulation, market forces, and so on). Following are the major conventions for developing a bibliography according to Chicago style (see Figure B.3 on page A-23):

- Exclude any page numbers that may be cited in source notes, except for journals, periodicals, and newspapers.

FIGURE B.1 Sample References—APA Style

	REFERENCES
Journal article with volume and issue numbers	Assira, J. (2003). Are they speaking English in Japan? *Journal of Business Communication, 36*(4), 72.
Brochure	BestTemp Staffing Services. (2002). *An employer's guide to staffing services* (2nd ed.) [Brochure]. Denver: BestTemp Information Center.
Newspaper article, no author	Buying Asian supplies on the net. (2003, February 12). *The Globe and Mail*, p. D3.
Annual report	Eurotec. (2000). *2000 annual report*. New York: Eurotec.
Magazine article	Graves, H. (2003, November 17). Prospecting online. *Report on Business*, 43–45.
Television broadcast	Han, D. (2002, March 5). Trade wars heating up around the globe. *CNN Headline News*. [Television broadcast]. Atlanta, GA: CNN.
Internet, World Wide Web	Hoover's Online. (2003). *Intel—Company Capsule*. Retrieved March 8, 2003, from http://www.hoovers.com/capsules/13787.html
Book, component parts	Kuntz, S. (2004). Moving beyond benefits. In Randolph Jacobson (Ed.), *Our changing workforce* (pp. 213–227). New York: Citadel Press.
Unpublished dissertation or thesis	Morales, G. H. (2003). *The economic pressures on industrialized nations in a global economy*. Unpublished doctoral dissertation, University of San Diego.
Paper presented at a meeting	Myers, C. (2004, August). *HMOs in today's environment*. Paper presented at the Conference on Medical Insurance Solutions, Chicago, IL.
Online magazine article	Norwalk, P. (2003, July 17). Training managers to help employees accept change. *Business Line*. Retrieved March 8, 2003, from http://www.busline.com/news
CD-ROM encyclopedia article, one author	Parkings, R. (2004). George Eastman. On *The concise Columbia encyclopedia*. [CD-ROM]. New York: Columbia University Press.
Interview	*Cited in text only, not in the list of references.*
Newspaper article, one author	Standish, E. (2002, January 19). Global market crushes OPEC's delicate balance of interests. *Wall Street Journal*, p. A1.
Book, two authors	Toller, M., & Fielding, J. (2004). *Global business for smaller companies*. Rocklin, CA: Prima Publishing.
Government publication	U.S. Department of Defense. (2004). *Stretching research dollars: Survival advice for universities and government labs*. Washington, DC: U.S. Government Printing Office.

- Alphabetize entries by the last name of the lead author (listing last name first). The names of second and succeeding authors are listed in normal order. Entries without an author name are alphabetized by the first important word in the title.
- Format entries as hanging indents (indent second and succeeding lines three to five spaces).
- Arrange entries in the following general order: (1) author name, (2) title information, (3) publication information, (4) date, (5) periodical page range.
- Use quotation marks around the titles of articles from magazines, newspapers, and journals—capitalizing the first and last words, as well as all other important words (except prepositions, articles, and coordinating conjunctions).
- Use italics to set off the names of books, newspapers, journals, and other complete publications—capitalizing the first and last words, as well as all other important words.
- For journal articles, include the volume number and the issue number (if necessary). Include the year of publication inside parentheses and follow with a colon and the page range of the article: *Journal of Business Communication* 36, no. 4 (2004): 72. (In this source, the volume is 36, the number is 4, and the page is 72.)
- Use brackets to identify all electronic references: [Online database] or [CD-ROM].
- Explain how electronic references can be reached: Available from www.spaceless.com/WWWVL.
- Give the citation date for online references: Cited 23 August 2004.

FIGURE B.2 Sample Endnotes—Chicago Humanities Style

NOTES

Journal article with volume and issue numbers	1. James Assira, "Are They Speaking English in Japan?" *Journal of Business Communication* 36, no. 4 (Fall 2003): 72.
Brochure	2. BestTemp Staffing Services, *An Employer's Guide to Staffing Services,* 2d ed. (Denver: BestTemp Information Center, 2002), 31.
Newspaper article, no author	3. "Buying Asian Supplies on the Net," *The Globe and Mail,* 12 February 2003, sec. D, p. 3.
Annual report	4. Eurotec, *2000 Annual Report* (New York: Eurotec, Inc., 2000), 48.
Magazine article	5. Holly Graves, "Prospecting Online," *Report on Business,* 17 November 2002, 43–5.
Television broadcast	6. Daniel Han, "Trade Wars Heating Up Around the Globe," *CNN Headline News* (Atlanta: CNN, 5 March 2002).
Internet, World Wide Web	7. "Intel—Company Capsule," Hoover's Online [cited 8 March 2003], 3 screens; available from www.hoovers.com/capsules/13787.html.
Book, component parts	8. Sonja Kuntz, "Moving Beyond Benefits," in *Our Changing Workforce,* ed. Randolf Jacobson (New York: Citadel Press, 2004), 213–27.
Unplublished dissertation or thesis	9. George H. Morales, "The Economic Pressures on Industrialized Nations in a Global Economy" (Ph.D. diss., University of San Diego, 2003), 32–47.
Paper presented at a meeting	10. Charles Myers, "HMOs in Today's Environment" (paper presented at the Conference on Medical Insurance Solutions, Chicago, Ill., August 2004), 16–17.
Online magazine article	11. Preston Norwalk, "Training Managers to Help Employees Accept Change," in Business Line [online] (San Francisco, 2001 [updated 17 September 2003; cited 3 October 2003]); available from www.busline.com/news.
CD-ROM encyclopedia article, one author	12. Robert Parkings, "George Eastman," *The Concise Columbia Encyclopedia* (New York: Columbia University Press, 2004) [CD-ROM].
Interview	13. Georgia Stainer, general manager, Day Cable and Communications, interview by author, Topeka, Kan., 2 March 2003.
Newspaper article, one author	14. Evelyn Standish, "Global Market Crushes OPEC's Delicate Balance of Interests," Wall Street Journal, 19 January 2002, sec. A, p. 1.
Book, two authors	15. Miriam Toller and Jay Fielding, *Global Business for Smaller Companies* (Rocklin, Calif.: Prima Publishing, 2004), 102–3.
Government publication	16. U.S. Department of Defense, *Stretching Research Dollars: Survival Advice for Universities and Government Labs* (Washington, D.C.: GPO, 2004), 126.

MLA Style

The style recommended by the Modern Language Association of America is used widely in the humanities, especially in the study of language and literature. Like APA style, MLA style uses brief parenthetical citations in the text. However, instead of including author name and year, MLA citations include author name and page reference.

In-Text Citation—MLA Style

To document report sources in text using MLA style, insert the author's last name and a page reference inside parentheses following the cited material: (Matthews 63). If the author's name is mentioned in the text reference, the name can be omitted from the parenthetical citation: (63). The citation indicates that the reference came from page 63 of a work by Matthews. With the author's name, readers can find complete publication information in the alphabetically arranged list of works cited that comes at the end of the report.

> Some experts recommend both translation and back-translation when dealing with any non-English-speaking culture (Assira 72).

> Toller and Fielding make a strong case for small companies succeeding in global business (102–03).

FIGURE B.3 Sample Bibliography—Chicago Humanities Style

BIBLIOGRAPHY

Journal article with volume and issue numbers	Assira, James. "Are They Speaking English in Japan?" *Journal of Business Communication* 36, no. 4 (Fall 2003): 72.
Brochure	BestTemp Staffing Services. *An Employer's Guide to Staffing Services.* 2d ed. Denver: BestTemp Information Center, 1999.
Newspaper article, no author	"Buying Asian Supplies on the Net." *The Globe and Mail,* 12 February 2003, sec. D, p. 3.
Annual report	Eurotec. *2000 Annual Report.* New York: Eurotec, Inc., 2000.
Magazine article	Graves, Holly. "Prospecting Online." *Report on Business,* 17 November 2002, 43–5.
Television broadcast	Han, Daniel. "Trade Wars Heating Up Around the Globe." *CNN Headline News.* Atlanta: CNN, 5 March 2002.
Internet, World Wide Web	"Intel—Company Capsule." *Hoover's Online* [cited 8 March 2003]. 3 screens; Available from www.hoovers.com/capsules/13787.html.
Book, component parts	Kuntz, Sonja. "Moving Beyond Benefits." In Our Changing Workforce, edited by Randolf Jacobson. New York: Citadel Press, 2004.
Unpublished dissertation or thesis	Morales, George H. "The Economic Pressures on Industrialized Nations in a Global Economy." Ph.D. diss., University of San Diego, 2003.
Paper presented at a meeting	Myers, Charles. "HMOs in Today's Environment." Paper presented at the Conference on Medical Insurance Solutions, Chicago, Ill., August 2004.
Online magazine article	Norwalk, Preston. "Training Managers to Help Employees Accept Change." In *Business Line* [online]. San Francisco, 2001 [updated 17 September 2003; cited 3 October 2003]. Available from www.busline.com/news.
CD-ROM encyclopedia article, one author	Parkings, Robert. "George Eastman." *The Concise Columbia Encyclopedia.* New York: Columbia University Press, 2004. [CD-ROM].
Interview	Stainer, Georgia, general manager, Day Cable and Communications. Interview by author. Topeka, Kan., 2 March 2003.
Newspaper article, one author	Standish, Evelyn. "Global Market Crushes OPEC's Delicate Balance of Interests." *Wall Street Journal,* 19 January 2002, sec. A, p. 1.
Book, two authors	Toller, Miriam, and Jay Fielding. *Global Business for Smaller Companies.* Rocklin, Calif.: Prima Publishing, 2004.
Government publication	U.S. Department of Defense. *Stretching Research Dollars: Survival Advice for Universities and Government Labs.* Washington, D.C.: GPO, 2004.

List of Works Cited—MLA Style

The *MLA Style Manual* recommends preparing the list of works cited first so that you will know what information to give in the parenthetical citation (for example, whether to add a short title if you're citing more than one work by the same author, or whether to give an initial or first name if you're citing two authors who have the same last name). The list of works cited appears at the end of your report, contains all the works that you cite in your text, and lists them in alphabetical order. Following are the major conventions for developing a reference list according to MLA style (see Figure B.4 on page A-24):

- Format entries as hanging indents.
- Arrange entries in the following general order: (1) author name, (2) title information, (3) publication information, (4) date, (5) periodical page range.
- List the lead author's name in reverse order (last name first), using either full first names or initials. List second and succeeding author names in normal order.
- Use quotation marks around the titles of articles from magazines, newspapers, and journals—capitalize all important words.
- Italicize the names of books, newspapers, journals and other complete publications, capitalizing all main words in the title.

FIGURE B.4 Sample Works Cited—MLA Style

WORKS CITED

Journal article with volume and issue numbers	Assira, James. "Are They Speaking English in Japan?" *Journal of Business Communication* 36.4 (2003): 72.
Brochure	BestTemp Staffing Services. *An Employer's Guide to Staffing Services.* 2d ed. Denver: BestTemp Information Center, 2002.
Newspaper article, no author	"Buying Asian Supplies on the Net." *The Globe and Mail* 12 Feb. 2003: D3.
Annual report	Eurotec. *2000 Annual Report.* New York: Eurotec, Inc., 2000.
Magazine article	Graves, Holly. "Prospecting Online." *Report on Business* 17 Nov. 2002: 43–45.
Television broadcast	Han, Daniel. "Trade Wars Heating Up Around the Globe." *CNN Headline News.* CNN, Atlanta. 5 Mar. 2002.
Internet, World Wide Web	"Intel—Company Capsule." *Hoover's Online.* 2003. Hoover's Company Information. 8 Mar. 2003 <http://www.hoovers.com/capsules/13787.html>.
Book, component parts	Kuntz, Sonja. "Moving Beyond Benefits." *Our Changing Workforce.* Ed. Randolf Jacobson. New York: Citadel Press, 2004. 213–27.
Unpublished dissertation or thesis	Morales, George H. "The Economic Pressures on Industrialized Nations in a Global Economy." Diss. U of San Diego, 2004.
Paper presented at a meeting	Myers, Charles. "HMOs in Today's Environment." Conference on Medical Insurance Solutions. Chicago. 13 Aug. 2000.
Online magazine article	Norwalk, Preston. "Training Managers to Help Employees Accept Change." *Business Line* 17 July 2001. 8 Mar. 2003 <http://www.busline.com/news>.
CD-ROM encyclopedia article, one author	Parkings, Robert. "George Eastman." *The Concise Columbia Encyclopedia.* CD-ROM. New York: Columbia UP, 2004.
Interview	Stainer, Georgia, general manager, Day Cable and Communications. Telephone interview. 2 Mar. 2004.
Newspaper article, one author	Standish, Evelyn. "Global Market Crushes OPEC's Delicate Balance of Interests." *Wall Street Journal* 19 Jan. 2002: A1.
Book, two authors	Toller, Miriam, and Jay Fielding. *Global Business for Smaller Companies.* Rocklin, CA: Prima Publishing, 2004.
Government publication	United States. Department of Defense. *Stretching Research Dollars: Survival Advice for Universities and Government Labs.* Washington: GPO, 2004.

- For journal articles, include the volume number and the issue number (if necessary). Include the year of publication inside parentheses and follow with a colon and the page range of the article: *Journal of Business Communication* 36.4 (2004): 72. (In this source, the volume is 36, the number is 4, and the page is 72.)
- Electronic sources are less fixed than print sources, and they may not be readily accessible to readers. So citations for electronic sources must provide more information. Always try to be as comprehensive as possible, citing whatever information is available.
- The date for electronic sources should contain both the date assigned in the source and the date accessed by the researcher.
- The URL for electronic sources must be as accurate and complete as possible, from access-mode identifier (http, ftp, gopher, telnet) to all relevant directory and file names. Be sure to enclose this path inside angle brackets: <http://www.hoovers.com/capsules/13787.html>.

Appendix C

Correction Symbols

Instructors often use these short, easy-to-remember correction symbols and abbreviations when evaluating students' writing. You can use them too, to understand your instructor's suggestions and to revise and proofread your own letters, memos, and reports. Refer to the Handbook of Grammar, Mechanics, and Usage (pp. H-1–H-29) for further information.

Content and Style

Acc	Accuracy. Check to be sure information is correct.
ACE	Avoid copying examples.
ACP	Avoid copying problems.
Adp	Adapt. Tailor message to reader.
App	Approach. Follow proper organizational approach. (Refer to Chapter 4.)
Assign	Assignment. Review instructions for assignment.
AV	Active verb. Substitute active for passive.
Awk	Awkward phrasing. Rewrite.
BC	Be consistent.
BMS	Be more sincere.
Chop	Choppy sentences. Use longer sentences and more transitional phrases.
Con	Condense. Use fewer words.
CT	Conversational tone. Avoid using overly formal language.
Depers	Depersonalize. Avoid attributing credit or blame to any individual or group.
Dev	Develop. Provide greater detail.
Dir	Direct. Use direct approach; get to the point.
Emph	Emphasize. Develop this point more fully.
EW	Explanation weak. Check logic; provide more proof.
Fl	Flattery. Avoid compliments that are insincere.
FS	Figure of speech. Find a more accurate expression.
GNF	Good news first. Use direct order.
GRF	Give reasons first. Use indirect order.
GW	Goodwill. Put more emphasis on expressions of goodwill.
H/E	Honesty/ethics. Revise statement to reflect good business practices.
Imp	Imply. Avoid being direct.
Inc	Incomplete. Develop further.
Jar	Jargon. Use less specialized language.
Log	Logic. Check development of argument.
Neg	Negative. Use more positive approach or expression.
Obv	Obvious. Do not state point in such detail.
OC	Overconfident. Adopt humbler language.
OM	Omission.
Org	Organization. Strengthen outline.
OS	Off the subject. Close with point on main subject.
Par	Parallel. Use same structure.
Pom	Pompous. Rephrase in down-to-earth terms.
PV	Point of view. Make statement from reader's perspective rather than your own.
RB	Reader benefit. Explain what reader stands to gain.
Red	Redundant. Reduce number of times this point is made.
Ref	Reference. Cite source of information.
Rep	Repetitive. Provide different expression.
RS	Resale. Reassure reader that he or she has made a good choice.
SA	Service attitude. Put more emphasis on helping reader.
Sin	Sincerity. Avoid sounding glib or uncaring.
SL	Stereotyped language. Focus on individual's characteristics instead of on false generalizations.

Spec	Specific. Provide more specific statement.
SPM	Sales promotion material. Tell reader about related goods or services.
Stet	Let stand in original form.
Sub	Subordinate. Make this point less important.
SX	Sexist. Avoid language that contributes to gender stereotypes.
Tone	Tone needs improvement.
Trans	Transition. Show connection between points.
UAE	Use action ending. Close by stating what reader should do next.
UAS	Use appropriate salutation.
UAV	Use active voice.
Unc	Unclear. Rewrite to clarify meaning.
UPV	Use passive voice.
USS	Use shorter sentences.
V	Variety. Use different expression or sentence pattern.
W	Wordy. Eliminate unnecessary words.
WC	Word choice. Find a more appropriate word.
YA	"You" attitude. Rewrite to emphasize reader's needs.

Grammar, Mechanics, and Usage

Ab	Abbreviation. Avoid abbreviations in most cases; use correct abbreviation.
Adj	Adjective. Use adjective instead.
Adv	Adverb. Use adverb instead.
Agr	Agreement. Make subject and verb or noun and pronoun agree.
Ap	Appearance. Improve appearance.
Apos	Apostrophe. Check use of apostrophe.
Art	Article. Use correct article.
BC	Be consistent.
Cap	Capitalize.
Case	Use cases correctly.
CoAdj	Coordinate adjective. Insert comma between coordinate adjectives; delete comma between adjective and compound noun.
CS	Comma splice. Use period or semicolon to separate clauses.
DM	Dangling modifier. Rewrite so that modifier clearly relates to subject of sentence.
Exp	Expletive. Avoid expletive beginnings, such as *it is, there are, there is, this is,* and *these are.*
F	Format. Improve layout of document.
Frag	Fragment. Rewrite as complete sentence.
Gram	Grammar. Correct grammatical error.
HCA	Hyphenate compound adjective.
lc	Lower case. Do not use capital letter.
M	Margins. Improve frame around document.
MM	Misplaced modifier. Place modifier close to word it modifies.
NRC	Nonrestrictive clause (or phrase). Separate from rest of sentence with commas.
P	Punctuation. Use correct punctuation.
Par	Parallel. Use same structure.
PH	Place higher. Move document up on page.
PL	Place lower. Move document down on page.
Prep	Preposition. Use correct preposition.
RC	Restrictive clause (or phrase). Remove commas that separate clause from rest of sentence.
RO	Run-on sentence. Separate two sentences with comma and coordinating conjunction or with semicolon.
SC	Series comma. Add comma before *and.*
SI	Split infinitive. Do not separate *to* from rest of verb.
Sp	Spelling error. Consult dictionary.
S-V	Subject-verb pair. Do not separate with comma.
Syl	Syllabification. Divide word between syllables.
WD	Word division. Check dictionary for proper end-of-line hyphenation.
WW	Wrong word. Replace with another word.

Proofreading Marks

Symbol	Meaning	Symbol Used in Context	Corrected Copy
	Align horizontally	meaningful result	meaningful result
	Align vertically	1. Power cable 2. Keyboard	1. Power cable 2. Keyboard
	Capitalize	Pepsico, Inc.	PepsiCo, Inc.
	Centre	Awards Banquet	Awards Banquet
	Close up space	self- confidence	self-confidence
	Delete	harrassment and abuse	harassment
ds	Double-space	text in first line text in second line ds	text in first line text in second line
	Insert	u and white tirquoise shirts	turquoise and white shirts
	Insert apostrophe	our teams goals	our team's goals
	Insert comma	a, b and c	a, b, and c
	Insert hyphen	third quarter sales	third-quarter sales
	Insert period	Harrigan et al	Harrigan et al.
	Insert quotation marks	This team isn't cooperating.	This "team" isn't cooperating.
#	Insert space	# # realestate testcase	real estate test case
	Lower case	TULSA, South of here	Tulsa, south of here
	Move down	Sincerely,	Sincerely,
	Move left	Attention: Security	Attention: Security
	Move right	February 2, 2004	February 2, 2004
	Move up	THIRD-QUARTER SALES	THIRD-QUARTER SALES
STET	Restore	staff talked openly and frankly STET	staff talked openly
	Run lines together	Manager, Distribution	Manager, Distribution
ss	Single space	ss text in first line text in second line	text in first line text in second line
	Spell out	COD	cash on delivery
sp	Spell out	sp Assn. of Biochem. Engrs.	Association of Biochemical Engineers
	Start new line	Marla Fenton, Manager, Distri-bution	Marla Fenton, Manager, Distribution
¶	Start new paragraph	¶ The solution is easy to determine but difficult to implement in a competitive environment like the one we now face.	The solution is easy to determine but difficult to implement in a competitive environment like the one we now face.
	Transpose	airy, light, casaul tone	light, airy, casual tone
bf	Use boldface	Recommendations bf	**Recommendations**
ital	Use italics	Quarterly Report ital	*Quarterly Report*

Handbook of Grammar, Mechanics, and Usage

Grammar and mechanics are nothing more than the way words are combined into sentences. Usage is the way words are used by a network of people—in this case, the community of business people who use English. You'll find it easier to get along in this community if you know the accepted standards of grammar, mechanics, and usage. This handbook offers you valuable opportunities in three sections:

- **Diagnostic Test of English Skills.** Testing your current knowledge of grammar, mechanics, and usage helps you find out where your strengths and weaknesses lie. This test offers 60 items taken from the topics included in this Handbook.
- **Assessment of English Skills.** After completing the diagnostic test, use the assessment form to highlight those areas you most need to review.
- **Essentials of Grammar, Mechanics, and Usage with Practice Sessions.** This section helps you quickly review the basics. You can study the things you've probably already learned but may have forgotten about grammar, punctuation, capitalization, mechanics (including capitalization, abbreviation, number style, and word division), and vocabulary (including frequently confused words, frequently misused words, frequently misspelled words, and transitional words and phrases). Practice sessions throughout this section help you test yourself and reinforce what you learn. Use this essential review not only to study and improve your English skills but also as a reference for any questions you may have during this course.

Without a firm grasp of the basics of grammar, punctuation, mechanics, and vocabulary, you risk being misunderstood, damaging your company's image, losing money for your company, and possibly even losing your job. However, once you develop strong English skills, you will create clear and concise messages, you will enhance your company's image as well as your own, and you will not only increase your company's profits but expand your own chances of success.

Diagnostic Test of English Skills

Use this test to help you determine whether you need more practice with grammar, punctuation, mechanics, or vocabulary. When you've answered all the questions, ask your instructor for an answer sheet so that you can score the test. On the Assessment of English Skills form (page H-3), record the number of questions you answered correctly in each section.

The following choices apply to items 1–10. In each blank, write the letter of the choice that best describes the problem with each sentence.

A. sentence incomplete
B. too many phrases/clauses strung together
C. modifying elements misplaced (dangling)
D. structure not parallel
E. nothing wrong

____ **1.** Stop here.
____ **2.** Your duties are interviewing, hiring, and also to fire employees.
____ **3.** After their presentation, I was still undecided.
____ **4.** Speaking freely, the stock was considered a bargain.
____ **5.** Margaret, pressed for time, turned in unusually sloppy work.
____ **6.** Typing and filing, routine office chores.
____ **7.** With care, edit the report.
____ **8.** When Paul came to work here, he brought some outmoded ideas, now he has accepted our modern methods.
____ **9.** To plan is better than improvising.
____ **10.** Hoping to improve performance, practice is advisable.

The following choices apply to items 11–20. In each blank, write the letter of the choice that identifies the underlined word(s) in each sentence.

A. subject
B. predicate (verb)
C. object
D. modifier
E. conjunction/preposition

____ **11.** Take his <u>memo</u> upstairs.
____ **12.** Before leaving, he <u>repaired</u> the photocopier.
____ **13.** <u>Velnor, Inc.</u>, will soon introduce a new product line.
____ **14.** We must hire only <u>qualified</u>, ambitious graduates.
____ **15.** They <u>are having</u> trouble with their quality control systems.
____ **16.** <u>After</u> she wrote the report, Jill waited eagerly for a response.
____ **17.** The route to the plant isn't paved <u>yet</u>.
____ **18.** See <u>me</u> after the meeting.

____ **19.** Your new <u>home</u> is ready and waiting.
____ **20.** BFL is large <u>but</u> caring.

In the blanks for items 21–30, write the letter of the word that best completes each sentence.

____ **21.** Starbucks (A. is, B. are) opening five new stores in British Columbia in the next year.
____ **22.** There (A. is, B. are) 50 applicants for the job opening.
____ **23.** Anyone who wants to be (A. their, B. his or her) own boss should think about owning a franchise.
____ **24.** Neither of us (A. was, B. were) prepared for the meeting.
____ **25.** Another characteristic of a small business is that (A. they tend, B. it tends) to be more innovative than larger firms.
____ **26.** After he had (A. saw, B. seen) the revised budget, Raymond knew he wouldn't be getting a new desk.
____ **27.** The number of women-owned small businesses (A. has, B. have) increased sharply in the past two decades.
____ **28.** If I (A. was, B. were) you, I'd stop sending personal e-mails at work.
____ **29.** Eugene (A. lay, B. laid) the files on the desk.
____ **30.** Either FedEx or UPS (A. has, B. have) been chosen as our preferred shipping service.

The following choices apply to items 31–40. In each blank, write the letter of the choice that best describes each sentence.

A. all punctuation used correctly
B. some punctuation used incorrectly or incorrectly omitted

____ **31.** The president who rarely gave interviews, agreed to write an article for the company newsletter.
____ **32.** Give the assignment to Karen Schiff, the new technical writer.
____ **33.** Could you please send a replacement for Item No. 3-303.
____ **34.** Debbie said that, "technicians must have technical degrees."
____ **35.** We'll have branches in Dartmouth, Nova Scotia, Moncton, New Brunswick, and Charlottetown, Prince Edward Island.
____ **36.** Before leaving her secretary finished typing the memo.
____ **37.** How many of you consider yourselves "computer literate?"
____ **38.** This, then, is our goal: to increase market share by 50 percent.
____ **39.** They plan to move soon, however, they still should be invited.
____ **40.** Health, wealth, and happiness—those are my personal goals.

The following choices apply to items 41–50. In each blank, write the letter of the choice that best describes the problem with each sentence.

A. error in punctuation
B. error in use of abbreviations or symbols
C. error in use of numbers
D. error in capitalization
E. no errors

____ **41.** Most of last year's sales came from the midwest.
____ **42.** We can provide the items you are looking for @ $2 each.
____ **43.** Alex noted: "few of our competitors have tried this approach."
____ **44.** Address the letter to professor Elliott Barker, Psychology Department, Queen's University.
____ **45.** They've recorded 22 complaints since yesterday, all of them from long-time employees.
____ **46.** Leslie's presentation—"New Markets for the Nineties"—was well organized.
____ **47.** We're having a sale in the childrens' department, beginning Wednesday, August 15.
____ **48.** About 50 of the newly inducted members will be present.
____ **49.** Mister Spencer has asked me to find 10 volunteers.
____ **50.** Let's meet in Beth and Larry's office at one o'clock.

In the blanks for items 51–60, write the letter of the word that best completes each sentence.

____ **51.** Will having a degree (A. affect, B. effect) my chances for promotion?
____ **52.** Place the latest drawings (A. beside, B. besides) the others.
____ **53.** Try not to (A. loose, B. lose) this key; we will charge you a fee to replace it.
____ **54.** Let us help you choose the right tie to (A. complement, B. compliment) your look.
____ **55.** The five interviewers should discuss the candidates' qualifications (A. among, B. between) themselves.
____ **56.** New employees spend their time looking for (A. perspective, B. prospective) clients.
____ **57.** Are the goods you received different (A. from, B. than) the goods you ordered?
____ **58.** He took those courses to (A. farther, B. further) his career.
____ **59.** We are (A. anxious, B. eager) to see you next Thursday.
____ **60.** All commissions will be (A. disbursed, B. dispensed, C. dispersed) on the second Friday of every month.

Assessment of English Skills

In the space provided below, record the number of questions you answered correctly.

Questions	Number You Got Correct	Skill Area
1–10	______	Sentence structure
11–20	______	Grammar: Parts of speech
21–30	______	Grammar: Verbs and agreement
31–40	______	Punctuation
41–50	______	Punctuation and mechanics
51–60	______	Vocabulary

If you scored 8 or lower in any of the skill areas, focus on those areas in the appropriate sections of this Handbook.

Essentials of Grammar, Mechanics, and Usage

The sentence below looks innocent, but is it really?

> We sell tuxedos as well as rent.

You might sell rent, but it's highly unlikely. Whatever you're selling, some people will ignore your message because of a blunder like this. The following sentence has a similar problem:

> Vice-President Eldon Neale told his chief engineer that he would no longer be with Avix, Inc., as of June 30.

Is Eldon or the engineer leaving? No matter which side the facts are on, the sentence can be read the other way. Now look at this sentence:

> The year before we budgeted more for advertising sales were up.

Confused? Perhaps this is what you meant:

> The year before, we budgeted more for advertising. Sales were up.

Maybe you meant this:

> The year before we budgeted more for advertising, sales were up.

The meaning of language falls into bundles called sentences. A listener or reader can take only so much meaning before filing a sentence away and getting ready for the next one. So, as a business writer, you have to know what a sentence is. You need to know where one ends and the next one begins.

If you want to know what a sentence is, you have to find out what goes into it, what its ingredients are. Luckily, the basic ingredients of an English sentence are simple: The parts of speech combine with punctuation, mechanics, and vocabulary to convey meaning.

1.0 Grammar

Grammar is the study of how words come together to form sentences. Categorized by meaning, form, and function, English words fall into various parts of speech: nouns, pronouns, verbs, adjectives, adverbs, prepositions, conjunctions, articles, and interjections. You will communicate more clearly if you understand how each of these parts of speech operates in a sentence.

1.1 Nouns

A noun names a person, place, or thing. Anything you can see or detect with one of your other senses has a noun to name it. Some things you can't see or sense are also nouns—ions, for example, or space. So are things that exist as ideas, such as accuracy and height. (You can see that something is accurate or that a building is tall, but you can't see the idea of accuracy or the idea of height.) These names for ideas are known as abstract nouns. The simplest nouns are the names of things you can see or touch: car, building, cloud, brick.

1.1.1 Proper Nouns and Common Nouns

So far, all the examples of nouns have been common nouns, referring to general classes of things. The word *building* refers to a whole class of structures. Common nouns such as *building* are not capitalized.

If you want to talk about one particular building, however, you might refer to the Glazier Building. The name is capitalized, indicating that *Glazier Building* is a proper noun.

Here are three sets of common and proper nouns for comparison:

Common	Proper
city	Langley City
company	Blaisden Company
store	Books Galore

1.1.2 Nouns as Subject and Object

Nouns may be used in sentences as subjects or objects. That is, the person, place, idea, or thing that is being or doing (subject) is represented by a noun. So is the person, place, idea, or thing that is being acted on (object). In the following sentence, the nouns are underlined.

> The <u>secretary</u> keyboarded the <u>report</u>.

The secretary (subject) is acting in a way that affects the report (object). The following sentence is more complicated:

> The <u>installer</u> delivered the <u>carpeting</u> to the <u>customer</u>.

Installer is the subject. *Carpeting* is the object of the main part of the sentence (acted on by the installer), whereas *customer* is the object of the phrase *to the customer.* Nevertheless, both *carpeting* and *customer* are objects.

1.1.3 Plural Nouns

Nouns can be either singular or plural. The usual way to make a plural noun is to add *s* to the singular form of the word:

Singular	Plural
rock	rocks
picture	pictures
song	songs

Many nouns have other ways of forming the plural. Letters, numbers, and words used as words are sometimes made plural by adding an apostrophe and an *s*. Very often, *'s* is used with abbreviations that have periods, lower case letters that stand alone, and capital letters that might be confused with words when made into plurals:

> Spell out all *St.*'s and *Ave.*'s.
>
> He divided the page with a row of *x*'s.
>
> Sarah will register the *A*'s through the *G*'s at the convention.

In other cases, however, the apostrophe may be left out:

> They'll review their ABCs.
>
> The stock market climbed through most of the 1980s.
>
> Circle all *the*s in the paragraph.

In some of these examples, the letters used as letters and words used as words are *italicized* (a mechanics issue that is discussed later).

Other nouns, such as those below, are so-called irregular nouns; they form the plural in some way other than simply adding *s:*

Singular	Plural
tax	taxes
specialty	specialties
cargo	cargoes
shelf	shelves
child	children
woman	women
tooth	teeth
mouse	mice
parenthesis	parentheses
son-in-law	sons-in-law
editor-in-chief	editors-in-chief

Rather than memorize a lot of rules about forming plurals, use a dictionary. If the dictionary says nothing about the plural of a word, it's formed the usual way: by adding *s*. If the plural is formed in some irregular way, the dictionary often shows the plural spelling.

1.1.4 Possessive Nouns

A noun becomes possessive when it's used to show the ownership of something. Then you add *'s* to the word:

> the man's car   the woman's apartment

However, ownership does not need to be legal:

> the secretary's desk   the company's assets

Also, ownership may be nothing more than an automatic association:

> a day's work   the job's prestige

An exception to the rule about adding *'s* to make a noun possessive occurs when the word is singular and already has two "s" sounds at the end. In cases like the following, an apostrophe is all that's needed:

> crisis' dimensions   Mr. Moses' application

When the noun has only one "s" sound at the end, however, retain the *'s:*

> Chris's book   Carolyn Nuss's office

With hyphenated nouns (compound nouns), add *'s* to the last word:

Hyphenated Noun	Possessive Noun
mother-in-law	mother-in-law's
mayor-elect	mayor-elect's

To form the possessive of plural nouns, just begin by following the same rule as with singular nouns: add *'s*. However, if the plural noun already ends in an *s* (as most do), drop the one you've added, leaving only the apostrophe:

> the clients' complaints   employees' benefits

Practice Session: Nouns

Underline the preferred choice within each set of parentheses in the following sentences.

1. We are moving company headquarters to New York (*City, city*).
2. The historic Taylor (*Building, building*) is the site of the press conference; the (*Building, building*) is located in downtown Toronto.
3. During the conference, our staff will be staying at the Hyatt, Fairmont, and Marriott (*Hotels, hotels*).
4. Accuracy requires that you cross your (*ts, t's*) and dot your (*is, i's*).

5. The industry has been on a downward spiral since the early (*1990's, 1990s*).
6. The new (*shelfs, shelves*) will be installed on Friday.
7. Our (*specialtys, specialties*) are unparalleled service and premium brands.
8. As a result of several Internet-related (*cases, case's*), the copyright laws are under scrutiny.
9. Before a job interview, you should learn about the (*company's, companies'*) mission statement.
10. Sending the newsletter to the printer is the (*editor's-in-chief, editor-in-chief's*) responsibility.
11. All the downtown (*business', businesses', businesses's*) signs must be repainted.
12. Because the (*passenger's, passengers'*) luggage had been damaged, they had to file claims with the airline.
13. Dealing with angry customers is all in a (*days, day's, days'*) work for Mr. Jemas.
14. Its large airport is one of (*Dallases, Dallas', Dallas's*) main appeals for industrial firms.
15. We were sceptical of (*Jone's, Jones', Jones's*) plan.

Answers: 1. City 2. Building / building 3. hotels 4. *t*'s / *i*'s 5. 1990s 6. shelves 7. specialties 8. cases 9. company's 10. editor-in-chief's 11. businesses' 12. passengers' 13. day's 14. Dallas's 15. Jones's

1.2 Pronouns

A pronoun is a word that stands for a noun; it saves repeating the noun:

> Drivers have some choice of weeks for vacation, but *they* must notify this office of *their* preference by March 1.

The pronouns *they* and *their* stand in for the noun *drivers*. The noun that a pronoun stands for is called the antecedent of the pronoun; *drivers* is the antecedent of *they* and *their*.

When the antecedent is plural, the pronoun that stands in for it has to be plural; *they* and *their* are plural pronouns because *drivers* is plural. Likewise, when the antecedent is singular, the pronoun has to be singular:

> We thought the *contract* had expired, but we soon learned that *it* had not.

1.2.1 Multiple Antecedents

Sometimes a pronoun has a double (or even a triple) antecedent:

> *Kathryn Boettcher* and *Luis Gutierrez* went beyond *their* sales quotas for January.

If taken alone, *Kathryn Boettcher* is a singular antecedent. So is *Luis Gutierrez*. However, when together they are the plural antecedent of a pronoun, so the pronoun has to be plural. Thus the pronoun is *their* instead of *her* or *his*.

1.2.2 Unclear Antecedents

In some sentences the pronoun's antecedent is unclear:

> Sandy Wright sent Jane Brougham *her* production figures for the previous year. *She* thought they were too low.

To which person does the pronoun *her* refer? Someone who knew Sandy and Jane and knew their business relationship might be able to figure out the antecedent for *her*. Even with such an advantage, however, a reader might receive the wrong meaning. Also, it would be nearly impossible for any reader to know which name is the antecedent of *she*.

The best way to clarify an ambiguous pronoun is usually to rewrite the sentence, repeating nouns when needed for clarity:

> Sandy Wright sent her production figures for the previous year to Jane Brougham. *Jane* thought they were too low.

The noun needs to be repeated only when the antecedent is unclear.

1.2.3 Gender-Neutral Pronouns

The pronouns that stand for males are *he, his,* and *him*. The pronouns that stand for females are *she, hers,* and *her*. However, you'll often be faced with the problem of choosing a pronoun for a noun that refers to both females and males:

> Each manager must make up (his, her, his or her, its, their) own mind about stocking this item and about the quantity that (he, she, he or she, it, they) can sell.

This sentence calls for a pronoun that's neither masculine nor feminine. The issue of gender-neutral pronouns responds to efforts to treat females and males evenhandedly. Here are some possible ways to deal with this issue:

> Each manager must make up *his* . . .
>
> (Not all managers are men.)

> Each manager must make up *her* . . .
>
> (Not all managers are women.)

> Each manager must make up *his* or *her* . . .
>
> (This solution is acceptable but becomes awkward when repeated more than once or twice in a document.)

> Each manager must make up *her* . . . Every manager will receive *his* . . . A manager may send *her* . . .
>
> (A manager's gender does not alternate like a windshield wiper!)

> Each manager must make up *their* . . .
>
> (The pronoun can't be plural when the antecedent is singular.)

Each manager must make up *its* . . .

(*It* never refers to people.)

The best solution is to make the noun plural or to revise the passage altogether:

Managers must make up *their* minds . . .

Each manager must decide whether . . .

Be careful not to change the original meaning.

1.2.4 Case of Pronouns

The case of a pronoun tells whether it's acting or acted upon:

She sells an average of five packages each week.

In this sentence, *she* is doing the selling. Because *she* is acting, *she* is said to be in the nominative case. Now consider what happens when the pronoun is acted upon:

After six months, Ms. Browning promoted *her.*

In this sentence, the pronoun *her* is acted upon. The pronoun *her* is thus said to be in the objective case.

Contrast the nominative and objective pronouns in this list:

Nominative	Objective
I	me
we	us
he	him
she	her
they	them
who	whom
whoever	whomever

Objective pronouns may be used as either the object of a verb (such as *promoted*) or the object of a preposition (such as *with*):

Rob worked with *them* until the order was filled.

In this example, *them* is the object of the preposition *with* because Rob acted upon—worked with—them. Here's a sentence with three pronouns, the first one nominative, the second the object of a verb, and the third the object of a preposition:

He paid *us* as soon as the cheque came from *them.*

He is nominative; *us* is objective because it's the object of the verb *paid; them* is objective because it's the object of the preposition *from.*

Every writer sometimes wonders whether to use *who* or *whom:*

(Who, Whom) will you hire?

Because this sentence is a question, it's difficult to see that *whom* is the object of the verb *hire.* You can figure out which pronoun to use if you rearrange the question and temporarily try *she* and *her* in place of *who* and *whom:* "Will you hire *she?*" or "Will you hire *her?*" *Her* and *whom* are both objective, so the correct choice is "*Whom* will you hire?" Here's a different example:

(Who, Whom) logged so much travel time?

Turning the question into a statement, you get:

He logged so much travel time.

Therefore, the correct statement is:

Who logged so much travel time?

1.2.5 Possessive Pronouns

Possessive pronouns work like possessive nouns: They show ownership or automatic association.

her job	their preferences
his account	its equipment

However, possessive pronouns are different from possessive nouns in the way they are written. That is, possessive pronouns never have an apostrophe.

Possessive Noun	Possessive Pronoun
the woman's estate	her estate
Roger Franklin's plans	his plans
the shareholders' feelings	their feelings
the vacuum cleaner's attachments	its attachments

The word *its* is the possessive of *it.* Like all other possessive pronouns, its has no apostrophe. Some people confuse *its* with *it's,* the contraction of *it is.* Contractions are discussed later.

Practice Session: Pronouns

Underline the preferred choice within each set of parentheses in the following sentences.

1. Just between you and (*I, me*), I don't think we will make the deadline.
2. The final speaker at the luncheon was (*she, her*).
3. When you are finished, give the report to (*he, him*).
4. (*We, Us*) telemarketers have a tarnished reputation.
5. The company is sending the marketing communications staff—Mary-Ann, Alan, and (*I, me, myself*)—to the conference.
6. The company will issue (*their, its*) annual report next month.
7. Anyone who hasn't yet turned in (*their, his or her*) questionnaire should do so by tomorrow.
8. (*Who, Whom*) shall I say called?

9. To (*who, whom*) should I address the letter?
10. (*Who, Whom*) will they hire?
11. We need more people in our department like (*she, her*).
12. When dealing with an angry customer, try to calm (*him, him or her, them*) down.
13. It was either Sarah or Charlene who left (*her, their*) briefcase on the train.
14. The company needs to update (*its, it's*) Web site.
15. (*Who, Whom*) do you think will be given the promotion?
16. Be sure to include (*your, you're*) e-mail address on the form.
17. Each brand should have (*its, their*) own trademark.
18. The "dynamic duo"—Bruce and (*I, me*)—are in charge of next week's office party.
19. The supervisor thanked the team members for (*their, they're*) support.
20. The pharmaceutical giant agreed to take (*their, its*) diet drug off the market.

Answers: 1. me 2. she 3. him 4. We 5. me 6. its 7. his or her 8. Who 9. whom 10. Whom 11. her 12. him or her 13. her 14. its 15. Who 16. your 17. its 18. I 19. their 20. its

1.3 Verbs

A verb describes an action:

They all *quit* in disgust.

It may also describe a state of being:

Working conditions *were* substandard.

The English language is full of action verbs. Here are a few you'll often run across in the business world:

verify	perform	fulfil
hire	succeed	send
leave	improve	receive
accept	develop	pay

You could undoubtedly list many more.

The most common verb describing a state of being instead of an action is *to be* and all its forms:

I *am, was,* or *will be;* you *are, were,* or *will be*

Other verbs also describe a state of being:

It *seemed* a good plan at the time.

She *sounds* impressive at a meeting.

These verbs link what comes before them in the sentence with what comes after; no action is involved. (See Section 1.7.5 for a fuller discussion of linking verbs.)

1.3.1 Verb Tenses

English has three simple verb tenses: present, past, and future.

Present: Our branches in Whitehorse *stock* other items.

Past: We *stocked* Purquil pens for a short time.

Future: Rotex Tire Stores *will stock* your line of tires when you begin a program of effective national advertising.

With most verbs (the regular ones), the past tense ends in *ed,* and the future tense always has *will* or *shall* in front of it. But the present tense is more complex, depending on the subject:

	First Person	Second Person	Third Person
Singular	I stock	you stock	he/she/it stocks
Plural	we stock	you stock	they stock

The basic form, *stock,* takes an additional *s* when *he, she,* or *it* precedes it. (See section 1.3.4 for more on subject-verb agreement.)

In addition to the three simple tenses, there are three perfect tenses using forms of the helping verb *have.* The present perfect tense uses the past participle (regularly the past tense) of the main verb, *stocked,* and adds the present-tense *have* or *has* to the front of it:

(I, we, you, they) *have stocked.*

(He, she, it) *has stocked.*

The past perfect tense uses the past participle of the main verb, *stocked,* and adds the past-tense *had* to the front of it:

(I, you, he, she, it, we, they) *had stocked.*

The future perfect tense also uses the past participle of the main verb, *stocked,* but adds the future-tense *will have:*

(I, you, he, she, it, we, they) *will have stocked.*

Keep verbs in the same tense when the actions occur at the same time:

When the payroll cheques *came* in, everyone *showed* up for work.

We *have found* that everyone *has pitched* in to help.

When the actions occur at different times, you may change tense accordingly:

The shipment *came* last Wednesday, so if another one *comes* in today, please *return* it.

The new employee *had been* ill at ease, but now she *has become* a full-fledged member of the team.

1.3.2 Irregular Verbs

Many verbs don't follow in every detail the patterns already described. The most irregular of these verbs is *to be:*

Tense	Singular	Plural
Present:	I *am*	we *are*
	you *are*	you *are*
	he, she, it *is*	they *are*
Past:	I *was*	we *were*
	you *were*	you *were*
	he, she, it *was*	they *were*

The future tense of *to be* is formed in the same way that the future tense of a regular verb is formed.

The perfect tenses of *to be* are also formed as they would be for a regular verb, except that the past participle is a special form, *been,* instead of just the past tense:

Present perfect:	you have been
Past perfect:	you had been
Future perfect:	you will have been

Here's a sampling of other irregular verbs:

Present	Past	Past Participle
begin	began	begun
shrink	shrank	shrunk
know	knew	known
rise	rose	risen
become	became	become
go	went	gone
do	did	done

Dictionaries list the various forms of other irregular verbs.

1.3.3 Transitive and Intransitive Verbs

Many people are confused by three particular sets of verbs:

lie/lay sit/set rise/raise

Using these verbs correctly is much easier when you learn the difference between transitive and intransitive verbs.

Transitive verbs convey their action to an object; they "transfer" their action to an object. Intransitive verbs do not. Here are some sample uses of transitive and intransitive verbs:

Intransitive	Transitive
We should include in our new offices a place to *lie* down for a nap.	The workers will be here on Monday to *lay* new carpeting.
Even the way an interviewee *sits* is important.	That crate is full of stemware, so *set* it down carefully.
Salaries at Compu-Link, Inc., *rise* swiftly.	They *raise* their level of production every year.

The workers *lay* carpeting, you *set* down the crate, they *raise* production; each action is transferred to something. In the intransitive sentences, one *lies* down, an interviewee *sits,* and salaries *rise* without (at least grammatically) affecting anything else. Intransitive sentences are complete with only a subject and a verb; transitive sentences are not complete unless they also include an object, or something to transfer the action to.

Tenses are a confusing element of the *lie/lay* problem:

Present	Past	Past Participle
I lie	I lay	I have lain
I lay (something down)	I laid (something down)	I have laid (something down)

The past tense of *lie* and the present tense of *lay* look and sound alike, even though they're different verbs.

1.3.4 Subject-Verb Agreement

Whether regular or irregular, every verb must agree with its subject, both in person (first, second, or third) and in number (single or plural).

In a simple sentence, making a verb agree with its subject is a straightforward task:

	First Person	Second Person	Third Person
Singular	I *am;* I *write*	you *are;* you *write*	he/she/it *is;* he/she/it *writes*
Plural	we *are;* we *write*	you *are;* you *write*	they *are;* they *write*

David Lee *is* a strong competitor. (third-person singular)

We *write* to you every month. (first-person plural)

Confusion sometimes arises when sentences are a bit more complicated. For example, be sure to avoid agreement problems when words come between the subject and verb. In the following examples, the verb appears in italics, and its subject is underlined:

The analysis of existing documents *takes* a full week.

Even though *documents* is a plural, the verb is in the singular form. That's because the subject of the sentence is *analysis,* a singular noun. The phrase *of existing documents* can be disregarded. Here is another example:

The answers for this exercise *are* in the study guide.

Take away the phrase *for this exercise* and you are left with the plural subject *answers.* Therefore, the verb takes the plural form.

Verb agreement is also complicated when the subject is not a specific noun or pronoun and when the subject may be considered either singular or plural. In such cases, you have to analyze the surrounding sentence to determine which verb form to use.

> The staff *is* quartered in the warehouse.
>
> The staff *are* at their desks in the warehouse.
>
> The computers and the staff *are* in the warehouse.
>
> Neither the staff nor the computers *are* in the warehouse.
>
> Every computer *is* in the warehouse.
>
> Many a computer *is* in the warehouse.

Did you notice that words such as *every* use the singular verb form? In addition, when an *either/or* or a *neither/nor* phrase combines singular and plural nouns, the verb takes the form that matches the noun closest to it.

In the business world, some subjects require extra attention. Company names, for example, are considered singular and therefore take a singular verb in most cases—even if they contain plural words:

> Yong Brothers *offers* convenient grocery shopping.

In addition, quantities are sometimes considered singular and sometimes plural. If a quantity refers to a total amount, it takes a singular verb; if a quantity refers to individual, countable units, it takes a plural verb:

> Three hours *is* a long time.
>
> The eight dollars we collected for the fund *are* tacked on the bulletin board.

Fractions may also be singular or plural, depending on the noun that accompanies them:

> One-third of the warehouse *is* devoted to this product line.
>
> One-third of the products *are* defective.

For a related discussion, see Section 1.7.2, "Longer Sentences," later in this Handbook.

1.3.5 Voice of Verbs

Verbs have two voices, active and passive. When the subject comes first, the voice is active. When the object comes first, the voice is passive:

Active:	The buyer paid a large amount.
Passive:	A large amount was paid by the buyer.

The passive voice uses a form of the verb *to be*, which adds words to a sentence. In the example, the passive-voice sentence uses eight words, whereas the active-voice sentence uses only six to say the same thing. The words *was* and *by* are unnecessary to convey the meaning of the sentence. In fact, extra words usually clog meaning. So be sure to opt for the active voice when you have a choice.

At times, however, you have no choice:

> Several items *have been taken*, but so far we don't know who took them.

The passive voice becomes necessary when you don't know (or don't want to say) who performed the action; the active voice is bolder and more direct.

1.3.6 Mood of Verbs

You have three moods to choose from, depending on your intentions. Most of the time you use the indicative mood to make a statement or to ask a question:

> The secretary *mailed* a letter to each supplier.
>
> Did the secretary *mail* a letter to each supplier?

When you wish to command or request, use the imperative mood:

> Please *mail* a letter to each supplier.

Sometimes, especially in business, a courteous request is stated like a question; in that case, however, no question mark is required:

> Would you *mail* a letter to each supplier.

The subjunctive mood, most often used in formal writing or in presenting bad news, expresses a possibility or a recommendation. The subjunctive is usually signalled by a word such as *if* or *that*. In these examples, the subjunctive mood uses special verb forms:

> If the secretary *were to mail* a letter to each supplier, we might save some money.
>
> I suggested that the secretary *mail* a letter to each supplier.

Although the subjunctive mood is not used as often as it once was, it's still found in such expressions as *Come what may* and *If I were you.* In general, it is used to convey an idea that is contrary to fact: If iron *were* lighter than air.

Practice Session: Verbs

Underline the preferred choice within each set of parentheses in the following sentences.

1. When Hastings (*come, comes, came*) in, tell him I (*want, wanted*) to see him.
2. Even though Sheila (*knowed, knew*) the right password, she typed it incorrectly.
3. The presentation had not yet (*began, begun*) when Charles arrived.
4. What I always say is, let sleeping dogs (*lay, lie*).
5. The workers (*lay, laid*) the tile in the executive bathroom yesterday.
6. This is where the president of the board (*sits, sets*) during meetings.

7. Just (*sit, set*) the boxes down over there.
8. Do you think management will (*raise, rise*) prices across the board next week?
9. A list of promotions (*was, were*) posted on the company intranet.
10. The supervisor of the assembly-line workers (*is, are*) being replaced.
11. The committee (*is, are*) considering the proposal today.
12. The board and the committee (*is, are*) having a joint meeting on June 25.
13. Neither the board nor the committee (*is, are*) expected to approve the proposal.
14. Every member of the board (*is, are*) going to make a statement.
15. Katten and Associates (*represent, represents*) clients in the entertainment industry.
16. Five hours (*is, are*) all I can give you to get the project done.
17. Half of the vacant lots (*is, are*) already sold.
18. Half of the hall (*is, are*) reserved for the luncheon.
19. Mario suggested that the public relations department (*send, sends*) out a news release about the merger.
20. If I (*was, were*) CEO, I'd fire the whole accounting staff.

Answers: 1. comes, want 2. knew 3. begun 4. lie 5. laid 6. sits 7. set 8. raise 9. was 10. is 11. is 12. are 13. is 14. is 15. represents 16. is 17. are 18. is 19. send 20. were

1.4 Adjectives

An adjective modifies (tells something about) a noun or pronoun. Each of the following phrases says more about the noun or pronoun than the noun or pronoun would say alone.

an *efficient* staff	a *heavy* price
brisk trade	*poor* you

Adjectives always tell us something that we wouldn't know without them. So you don't need to use adjectives when the noun alone, or a different noun, will give the meaning:

a *company* employee

(An employee ordinarily works for a company.)

a *crate-type* container

(*Crate* gives the entire meaning.)

Verbs in the *ing* (present participle) form can be used as adjectives:

A *boring* job can sometimes turn into a *fascinating* career.

So can the past participle of verbs:

A freshly *painted* house is a *sold* house.

Adjectives modify nouns more often than they modify pronouns. When adjectives do modify pronouns, however, the sentence usually has a linking verb:

They were *attentive.*	It looked *appropriate.*
He seems *interested.*	You are *skilful.*

At times, a series of adjectives precedes a noun:

It was a *long* and *active* workday.

Such strings of adjectives are acceptable as long as they all convey a different part of the phrase's meaning. However, adjectives often pile up in front of a noun, like this:

The *superficial, obvious* answer was the one she gave.

The most valuable animal on the ranch is a *small black* horse.

The question is whether a comma should be used to separate the adjectives. The answer is to use a comma when the two adjectives independently modify the noun; do not use a comma when one of the adjectives is closely identified with the noun. In the first example above, the answer was both superficial and obvious. But in the second example, the black horse is small.

Another way to think about this is to use the word *and* as a replacement for the comma. Study the following example:

We recommend a diet of leafy green vegetables.

We recommend a diet of green, leafy vegetables.

Because some green vegetables are not leafy (cucumbers and zucchini, for example), it is correct to leave out the comma in the first example so that you know which kind of green vegetables are being discussed. But because all leafy vegetables are also green (green and leafy), the comma must be included in the second example.

You might also try switching the adjectives. If the order of the adjectives can be reversed without changing the meaning of the phrase, you should use a comma. If the order cannot be reversed, you should not use a comma. Consider these examples:

Here's our *simplified credit* application.

Here's our *simplified, easy-to-complete* application.

Here's our *easy-to-complete, simplified* application.

A credit application may be simple or complex; however, you cannot talk about a credit, simplified application; therefore, leave the comma out of the first example. The application in the second and third examples is both simplified and easy to complete, no matter how you arrange the words, so include the comma in these examples.

1.4.1 Comparative Degree

Most adjectives can take three forms: simple, comparative, and superlative. The simple form modifies a single noun or pronoun. Use the comparative form when comparing two items. When comparing three or more items, use the superlative form.

Simple	Comparative	Superlative
hard	harder	hardest
safe	safer	safest
dry	drier	driest

The comparative form adds *er* to the simple form, and the superlative form adds *est.* (The *y* at the end of a word changes to *i* before the *er* or *est* is added.)

A small number of adjectives are irregular, including these:

Simple	Comparative	Superlative
good	better	best
bad	worse	worst
little	less	least

When the simple form of an adjective is two or more syllables, you usually add *more* to form the comparative and *most* to form the superlative:

Simple	Comparative	Superlative
useful	more useful	most useful
exhausting	more exhausting	most exhausting
expensive	more expensive	most expensive

The most common exceptions are two-syllable adjectives that end in *y:*

Simple	Comparative	Superlative
happy	happier	happiest
costly	costlier	costliest

If you choose this option, change the *y* to *i,* and tack *er* or *est* onto the end.

Some adjectives cannot be used to make comparisons because they themselves indicate the extreme. For example, if something is perfect, nothing can be more perfect. If something is unique or ultimate, nothing can be more unique or more ultimate.

1.4.2 Hyphenated Adjectives

Many adjectives used in the business world are actually combinations of words: *up-to-date* report, *last-minute* effort, *fifth-floor* suite, *well-built* engine. As you can see, they are hyphenated when they come before the noun they modify. However, when they come after the noun they modify, they are not hyphenated. In the following example, the adjectives appear in italics and the nouns they modify are underlined:

> The <u>report</u> is *up to date* because of our team's *last-minute* <u>efforts</u>.

Hyphens are not used when part of the combination is a word ending in *ly* (because that word is usually not an adjective). Hyphens are also omitted from word combinations that are used frequently.

> We live in a *rapidly shrinking* world.
>
> Our *highly motivated* employees will be well paid.
>
> Please consider renewing your *credit card* account.
>
> Send those figures to our *data processing* department.
>
> Our new intern is a *high school* student.

1.5 Adverbs

An adverb modifies a verb, an adjective, or another adverb:

Modifying a verb:	Our marketing department works *efficiently.*
Modifying an adjective:	She was not dependable, although she was *highly* intelligent.
Modifying another adverb:	His territory was *too* broadly diversified, so he moved *extremely* cautiously.

Most of the adverbs mentioned are adjectives turned into adverbs by adding *ly,* which is how many adverbs are formed:

Adjective	Adverb
efficient	efficiently
extreme	extremely
high	highly
official	officially
separate	separately
special	specially

Some adverbs are made by dropping or changing the final letter of the adjective and then adding *ly:*

Adjective	Adverb
due	duly
busy	busily

Other adverbs don't end in *ly* at all. Here are a few examples of this type:

often	fast	too
soon	very	so

Some adverbs are difficult to distinguish from adjectives. For example, in the following sentences, is the underlined word an adverb or an adjective?

> They worked <u>well</u>.
>
> The baby is <u>well</u>.

In the first sentence, *well* is an adverb modifying the verb worked. In the second sentence, *well* is an adjective modifying the noun *baby*. To choose correctly between adverbs and adjectives, remember that verbs of being link a noun to an adjective describing the noun. In contrast, you would use an adverb to describe an action verb.

Adjective	Adverb
He is a *good* worker. (What kind of worker is he?)	He works *well*. (How does he work?)
It is a *real* computer. (What kind of computer is it?)	It *really* is a computer. (To what extent is it a computer?)
The traffic is *slow*. (What quality does the traffic have?)	The traffic moves *slowly*. (How does the traffic move?)

1.5.1 Negative Adverbs

Negative adverbs (such as *neither, no, not, scarcely,* and *seldom*) are powerful words and therefore do not need any help in conveying a negative thought. In fact, using double negatives gives a strong impression of illiteracy, so avoid sentences like these:

> I don't want no mistakes.
> (Correct: "I don't want any mistakes," or "I want no mistakes.")
>
> They couldn't hardly read the report.
> (Correct: "They could hardly read the report," or "They couldn't read the report.")
>
> They scarcely noticed neither one.
> (Correct: "They scarcely noticed either one," or "They noticed neither one.")

1.5.2 Comparative Degree

Like adjectives, adverbs can be used to compare items. Generally, the basic adverb is combined with *more* or *most,* just as long adjectives are. However, some adverbs have one-word comparative forms:

One Item	Two Items	Three Items
quickly	more quickly	most quickly
sincerely	less sincerely	least sincerely
fast	faster	fastest
well	better	best

Practice Session: Adjectives and Adverbs

Underline the preferred choice within each set of parentheses in the following sentences.

1. I always choose the (*less, least*) expensive brand.
2. Which would be (*better, best*), the store brand or the generic brand?
3. This audit couldn't have come at a (*worse, worst*) time.
4. When it comes to data analysis, Claire is (*more competent, competenter*) than Alexander.
5. The ad agency's campaign for our new vitamin supplement is (*unique, very unique, most unique*), to say the least.
6. A corporation can benefit from a (*well written, well-written*) annual report.
7. The chairman's introductory message to the annual report was (*well written, well-written*).
8. Even a (*beautifully written, beautifully-written*) report can be hampered by poor design and production.
9. According to Bank of Montreal, the number of (*credit-card, credit card*) applications has tripled in the past year.
10. Angela wasn't feeling (*good, well*), so she went home early.
11. Harrison and Martinez work (*good, well*) together.
12. We are (*real, really*) excited about next week's product launch.
13. Could this project be moving any more (*slow, slowly*) through the bureaucratic system?
14. We (*could hardly, couldn't hardly*) wait to see how the brochure had turned out.
15. Today TeKTech is (*more heavy, more heavily, most heavily*) involved in nanotechnology, compared to five years ago.

Answers: 1. least 2. better 3. worse 4. more competent 5. unique 6. well-written 7. well written 8. beautifully written 9. credit card 10. well 11. well 12. really 13. slowly 14. could hardly 15. more heavily

1.6 Other Parts of Speech

Nouns, pronouns, verbs, adjectives, and adverbs carry most of the meaning in a sentence. Four other parts of speech link them together in sentences: prepositions, conjunctions, articles, and interjections.

1.6.1 Prepositions

Prepositions are words like these:

of	to	for	with
at	by	from	about

Some prepositions consist of more than one word—like these:

because of   in addition to   out of   except for

And some prepositions are closely linked with a verb. When using phrases such as *look up* and *wipe out,* keep the phrase intact and do not insert anything between the verb and the preposition.

Prepositions most often begin prepositional phrases, which function like adjectives and adverbs by telling more about a pronoun, noun, or verb:

of a type	*by* Friday
to the point	*with* characteristic flair

To prevent misreading, prepositional phrases should be placed near the element they modify:

Of all our technicians, she is the best trained.

They couldn't see the merit *in my proposal.*

Someone left a folder *on my desk.*

It was once considered totally unacceptable to put a preposition at the end of a sentence. Now you may:

I couldn't tell what they were interested in.

What did she attribute it to?

However, be careful not to place prepositions at the end of sentences when doing so is unnecessary. In fact, avoid using any unnecessary preposition. In the following examples, the prepositions in parentheses should be omitted:

All (of) the staff members were present.

I almost fell off (of) my chair with surprise.

Where was Mr. Steuben going (to)?

They couldn't help (from) wondering.

The opposite problem is failing to include a preposition when you should. Consider the two sentences that follow:

Sales were more than $100 000 for Linda and Bill.

Sales were more than $100 000 for Linda and for Bill.

The first sentence indicates that Linda and Bill had combined sales over $100 000; the second, that Linda and Bill each had sales over $100 000, for a combined total in excess of $200 000. The preposition *for* is critical here.

Prepositions are also required in sentences like this one:

Which type of personal computer do you prefer?

Certain prepositions are used with certain words. When the same preposition can be used for two or more words in a sentence without affecting the meaning, only the last preposition is required:

We are familiar (*with*) and satisfied *with* your company's products.

But when different prepositions are normally used with the words, all the prepositions must be included:

We are familiar *with* and interested *in* your company's products.

Here is an incomplete list of prepositions that are used in a particular way with particular words:

among/between: *Among* is used to refer to three or more (*Circulate the memo among the staff*); *between* is used to refer to two (*Put the copy machine between Judy and Dan*).

as if/like: *As if* is used before a clause (*It seems as if we should be doing something*); *like* is used before a noun or pronoun (*He seems like a nice guy*).

have/of: *Have* is a verb used in verb phrases (*They should have checked first*); *of* is a preposition and is never used in such cases.

in/into: *In* is used to refer to a static position (*The file is in the cabinet*); *into* is used to refer to movement toward a position (*Put the file into the cabinet*).

And here is an incomplete list of some prepositions that have come to be used with certain words:

according to	different from	prior to
agree to (a proposal)	get from (receive)	reason with
agree with (a person)	get off (dismount)	responsible for
buy from	in accordance with	similar to
capable of	in search of	talk to (without interaction)
comply with	independent of	talk with (with interaction)
conform to	interior to	wait for (person or thing)
differ from (things)	plan to	wait on (like a waiter)
differ with (person)	prefer to	

1.6.2 Conjunctions

Conjunctions connect the parts of a sentence: words, phrases, and clauses. You are probably most familiar with coordinating conjunctions such as the following:

and	for	or	yet
but	nor	so	

Conjunctions may be used to connect clauses (which have both a subject and a predicate) with other clauses, to connect clauses with phrases (which do not have both a subject and a predicate), and to connect words with words:

We sell designer clothing *and* linens.
(Words with words)

Their products are expensive *but* still appeal to value-conscious consumers.
(Clauses with phrases)

I will call her on the phone today, *or* I will visit her office tomorrow.
(Clauses with clauses)

Some conjunctions are used in pairs:

both . . . and	neither . . . nor	whether . . . or
either . . . or	not only . . . but also	

With paired conjunctions, you must be careful to construct each phrase in the same way.

They *not only* are out of racquets *but also* are out of balls.

They are *not only* out of racquets *but also* out of balls.

They are out of *not only* racquets *but also* balls.

In other words, the construction that follows each part of the pair must be parallel, containing the same verbs, prepositions, and so on. The same need for parallelism exists when using conjunctions to join the other parts of speech:

He is listed in *either* your roster *or* my roster.

He is listed *neither* in your roster *nor* on the master list.

They *both* gave *and* received notice.

A certain type of conjunction is used to join clauses that are unequal—that is, to join a main clause to one that is subordinate or dependent. Here is a partial list of conjunctions used to introduce dependent clauses:

although	before	once	unless
as soon as	even though	so that	until
because	if	that	when

Using conjunctions is also discussed in sections 1.7.3 and 1.7.4.

1.6.3 Articles and Interjections

Only three articles exist in English: *the, a,* and *an.* These words are used, like adjectives, to specify which item you are talking about.

Interjections are words that express no solid information, only emotion:

Wow!	Well, well!
Oh, no!	Good!

Such purely emotional language has its place in private life and advertising copy, but it only weakens the effect of most business writing.

Practice Session: Prepositions, Conjunctions, and Articles

Circle the letter of the preferred choice in each pair of sentences.

1. **a.** If we want to have the project done next week, we'll need those balance sheets by Wednesday.
   b. If we want to have the project done next week, by Wednesday we'll need those balance sheets.
2. **a.** From where did that information come?
   b. Where did that information come from?
3. **a.** Please look up the shipping rates for packages to France.
   b. Please look the shipping rates up for packages to France.
4. **a.** You need to indicate the type job you're seeking.
   b. You need to indicate the type of job you're seeking.
5. **a.** Michael got the actuarial data off of the Internet.
   b. Michael got the actuarial data off the Internet.
6. **a.** When the meeting is over, Michelle will prepare the minutes.
   b. When the meeting is over with, Michelle will prepare the minutes.
7. **a.** Sharon is familiar and knowledgeable about HTML coding.
   b. Sharon is familiar with and knowledgeable about HTML coding.
8. **a.** We'll be deciding among the four applicants this afternoon.
   b. We'll be deciding between the four applicants this afternoon.
9. **a.** Since Marshall isn't here, it looks like the conference call will have to be cancelled.
   b. Since Marshall isn't here, it looks as if the conference call will have to be cancelled.
10. **a.** I would have had the memo done sooner, but my computer crashed.
    b. I would of had the memo done sooner, but my computer crashed.
11. **a.** Once we have the survey results, we can put them in the report.
    b. Once we have the survey results, we can put them into the report.
12. **a.** If you agree with the settlement, I can prepare the final papers.
    b. If you agree to the settlement, I can prepare the final papers.
13. **a.** It is important that you provide not only your name but also your address and telephone number.
    b. It is important that you provide not only your name but also address and telephone number.
14. **a.** The conference will be held in either March or July.
    b. The conference will be held either in March or July.
15. **a.** Please prepare an RFP for the construction job.
    b. Please prepare a RFP for the construction job.

Answers: 1. a 2. b 3. a 4. b 5. b 6. a 7. b 8. a 9. b 10. a 11. b 12. b 13. a 14. a 15. a

1.7 Sentences

Sentences are constructed with the major building blocks, the parts of speech.

> Money talks.

This two-word sentence consists of a noun (*money*) and a verb (*talks*). When used in this way, the noun works as the first requirement for a sentence, the subject, and the verb works as the second requirement, the predicate. Now look at this sentence:

> They merged.

The subject in this case is a pronoun (*they*), and the predicate is a verb (*merged*). This is a sentence because it has a subject and a predicate. Here is yet another kind of sentence:

> The plans are ready.

This sentence has a more complicated subject, the noun *plans* and the article *the;* the complete predicate is a state-of-being verb (*are*) and an adjective (*ready*).

Without a subject (who or what does something) and a predicate (the doing of it), you have merely a collection of words, not a sentence.

1.7.1 Commands

In commands, the subject (always *you*) is only understood, not stated:

> (You) Move your desk to the better office.
>
> (You) Please try to finish by six o'clock.

1.7.2 Longer Sentences

More complicated sentences have more complicated subjects and predicates, but they still have a simple subject and a predicate verb. In the following examples, the subject is underlined once, the predicate verb twice:

> Marex and Contron enjoy higher earnings each quarter.
>
> (*Marex* [and] *Contron* do something; *enjoy* is what they do.)
>
> My interview, coming minutes after my freeway accident, did not impress or move anyone.
>
> (*Interview* is what did something. What did it do? It *did* [not] *impress* [or] *move*.)
>
> In terms of usable space, a steel warehouse, with its extremely long span of roof unsupported by pillars, makes more sense.
>
> (*Warehouse* is what *makes*.)

These three sentences demonstrate several things. First, in all three sentences, the simple subject and predicate verb are the "bare bones" of the sentence, the parts that carry the core idea of the sentence. When trying to find the subject and predicate verb, disregard all prepositional phrases, modifiers, conjunctions, and articles.

Second, in the third sentence the verb is singular (*makes*) because the subject is singular (*warehouse*). Even though the plural noun *pillars* is closer to the verb, *warehouse* is the subject. So *warehouse* determines whether the verb is singular or plural. Subject and predicate must agree.

Third, the subject in the first sentence is compound (*Marex* [and] *Contron*). A compound subject, when connected by *and,* requires a plural verb (*enjoy*). Also in the second sentence, compound predicates are possible (*did* [not] *impress* [or] *move*).

Fourth, the second sentence incorporates a group of words—*coming minutes after my freeway accident*—containing a form of a verb (*coming*) and a noun (*accident*). Yet this group of words is not a complete sentence for two reasons:

- Not all nouns are subjects: *Accident* is not the subject of *coming.*
- Not all verbs are predicates: A verb that ends in *ing* can never be the predicate of a sentence (unless preceded by a form of *to be,* as in *was coming*).

Because they don't contain a subject and a predicate, the words *coming minutes after my freeway accident* (called a phrase) can't be written as a sentence. That is, the phrase cannot stand alone; it cannot begin with a capital letter and end with a period. So a phrase must always be just one part of a sentence.

Sometimes a sentence incorporates two or more groups of words that do contain a subject and a predicate; these word groups are called clauses:

> My *interview,* because it came minutes after my freeway accident, did not impress or move anyone.

The independent clause is the portion of the sentence that could stand alone without revision:

> My interview did not impress or move anyone.

The other part of the sentence could stand alone only by removing *because:*

> (because) It came minutes after my freeway accident.

This part of the sentence is known as a dependent clause; although it has a subject and a predicate (just as an independent clause does), it's linked to the main part of the sentence by a word (*because*) showing its dependence.

In summary, the two types of clauses—dependent and independent—both have a subject and a predicate. Dependent clauses, however, do not bear the main meaning of the sentence and are therefore linked to an independent clause. Nor can phrases stand alone, because they lack both a subject and a predicate. Only independent clauses can be written as sentences without revision.

1.7.3 Sentence Fragments

An incomplete sentence (a phrase or a dependent clause) that is written as though it were a complete sentence is called a fragment. Consider the following sentence fragments:

> Marilyn Sanders, having had pilferage problems in her store for the past year. Refuses to accept the results of our investigation.

This serious error can easily be corrected by putting the two fragments together:

> Marilyn Sanders, having had pilferage problems in her store for the past year, refuses to accept the results of our investigation.

Not all fragments can be corrected so easily. Here's more information on Sanders's pilferage problem.

> Employees a part of it. No authority or discipline.

Only the writer knows the intended meaning of those two phrases. Perhaps the employees are taking part in the pilferage. If so, the sentence should read:

> Some employees are part of the pilferage problem.

On the other hand, it's possible that some employees are helping with the investigation. Then the sentence would read:

> Some employees are taking part in our investigation.

It's just as likely, however, that the employees are not only taking part in the pilferage but are also being analyzed:

> Those employees who are part of the pilferage problem will accept no authority or discipline.

Even more meanings could be read into these fragments. Because fragments can mean so many things, they mean nothing. No well-written memo, letter, or report ever demands the reader to be an imaginative genius.

One more type of fragment exists, the kind represented by a dependent clause. Note what *because* does to change what was once a unified sentence:

> Our stock of sprinklers is depleted.
>
> Because our stock of sprinklers is depleted.

Although the second version contains a subject and a predicate, adding *because* makes it a fragment. Words such as *because* form a special group of words called subordinating conjunctions. Here's a partial list:

after	if	unless
although	since	whenever
even if	though	while

When a word of this type begins a clause, the clause is dependent and cannot stand alone as a sentence. However, if a dependent clause is combined with an independent clause, it can convey a complete meaning. The independent clause may come before or after the dependent clause:

> We are unable to fill your order because our stock of sprinklers is depleted.
>
> Because our stock of sprinklers is depleted, we are unable to fill your order.

Also, to fix a fragment that is a dependent clause, remove the subordinating conjunction. Doing so leaves a simple but complete sentence:

> Our stock of sprinklers is depleted.

The actual details of a situation will determine the best way for you to remedy a fragment problem.

The ban on fragments has one exception. Some advertising copy contains sentence fragments, written knowingly to convey a certain rhythm. However, advertising is the only area of business in which fragments are acceptable.

1.7.4 Fused Sentences and Comma Splices

Just as there can be too little in a group of words to make it a sentence, there can also be too much:

> All our mail is run through a postage meter every afternoon someone picks it up.

This example contains two sentences, not one, but the two have been blended so that it's hard to tell where one ends and the next begins. Is the mail run through a meter every afternoon? If so, the sentences should read:

> All our mail is run through a postage meter every afternoon. Someone picks it up.

Perhaps the mail is run through a meter at some other time (morning, for example) and is picked up every afternoon:

> All our mail is run through a postage meter. Every afternoon someone picks it up.

The order of words is the same in all three cases; sentence division makes all the difference. Either of the last two cases is grammatically correct. The choice depends on the facts of the situation.

Sometimes these so-called fused sentences have a more obvious point of separation:

> Several large orders arrived within a few days of one another, too many came in for us to process by the end of the month.

Here the comma has been put between two independent clauses in an attempt to link them. When a lowly comma separates two complete sentences, the result is called a comma splice. A comma splice can be remedied in one of three ways:

- Replace the comma with a period and capitalize the next word: ". . . one another. Too many . . ."
- Replace the comma with a semicolon and do not capitalize the next word: ". . . one another; too many . . ." This remedy works only when the two sentences have closely related meanings.
- Change one of the sentences so that it becomes a phrase or a dependent clause. This remedy often produces the best writing, but it takes more work.

The third alternative can be carried out in several ways. One is to begin the blended sentence with a subordinating conjunction:

> Whenever several large orders arrived within a few days of one another, too many came in for us to process by the end of the month.

Another way is to remove part of the subject or the predicate verb from one of the independent clauses, thereby creating a phrase:

> Several large orders arrived within a few days of one another, too many for us to process by the end of the month.

Finally, you can change one of the predicate verbs to its *ing* form:

> Several large orders arrived within a few days of one another, too many coming in for us to process by the end of the month.

At other times a simple coordinating conjunction (such as *or, and,* or *but*) can separate fused sentences:

> You can fire them, or you can make better use of their abilities.
>
> Margaret drew up the designs, and Matt carried them out.
>
> We will have three strong months, but after that sales will taper off.

Be careful using coordinating conjunctions: Use them only to join simple sentences that express similar ideas.

Also, because they say relatively little about the relationship between the two clauses they join, avoid using coordinating conjunctions too often: *and* is merely an addition sign; *but* is just a turn signal; *or* only points to an alternative. Subordinating conjunctions such as *because* and *whenever* tell the reader a lot more.

1.7.5 Sentences with Linking Verbs

Linking verbs were discussed briefly in the section on verbs (Section 1.3). Here you can see more fully the way they function in a sentence. The following is a model of any sentence with a linking verb:

> A (*verb*) B.

Although words such as *seems* and *feels* can also be linking verbs, let's assume that the verb is a form of *to be:*

> A *is* B.

In such a sentence, A and B are always nouns, pronouns, or adjectives. When one is a noun and the other is a pronoun, or when both are nouns, the sentence says that one is the same as the other:

> She is president.
>
> Rachel is president.

When one is an adjective, it modifies or describes the other:

> She is forceful.

Remember that when one is an adjective, it modifies the other as any adjective modifies a noun or pronoun, except that a linking verb stands between the adjective and the word it modifies.

1.7.6 Misplaced Modifiers

The position of a modifier in a sentence is important. The movement of *only* changes the meaning in the following sentences:

> Only we are obliged to supply those items specified in your contract.
>
> We are obliged only to supply those items specified in your contract.
>
> We are obliged to supply only those items specified in your contract.
>
> We are obliged to supply those items specified only in your contract.

In any particular set of circumstances, only one of those sentences would be accurate. The others would very likely cause problems. To prevent misunderstanding, place such modifiers as close as possible to the noun or verb they modify.

For similar reasons, whole phrases that are modifiers must be placed near the right noun or verb. Mistakes in placement create ludicrous meanings.

> Antia Information Systems has bought new computer chairs for the programmers *with more comfortable seats.*

The anatomy of programmers is not normally a concern of business writers. Obviously, the comfort of the chairs was the issue:

Antia Information Systems has bought new computer chairs *with more comfortable seats* for the programmers.

Here is another example:

I asked him to file all the letters in the cabinet that had been answered.

In this ridiculous sentence the cabinet has been answered, even though no cabinet in history is known to have asked a question.

That had been answered is too far from *letters* and too close to *cabinet.* Here's an improvement:

I asked him to file in the cabinet all the letters that had been answered.

In some cases, instead of moving the modifying phrase closer to the word it modifies, the best solution is to move the word closer to the modifying phrase.

Practice Session: Sentences

Circle the letter of the preferred choice in each group of sentences.

1. **a.** Cyberterrorism—orchestrated attacks on a company's information systems for political or economic purposes—is a very real threat.
   b. Cyberterrorism—orchestrated attacks on a company's information systems for political or economic purposes—are a very real threat.

2. **a.** E-mail, phone calls, and faxes, each one a distraction, interrupts employees when they work.
   b. E-mail, phone calls, and faxes, each one a distraction, interrupt employees when they work.

3. **a.** About 35 percent of major Canadian companies keep tabs on workers. Because they want to protect valuable company information.
   b. About 35 percent of major Canadian companies keep tabs on workers, because they want to protect valuable company information.
   c. About 35 percent of major Canadian companies keep tabs on workers; because they want to protect valuable company information.

4. **a.** Despite its small size and relative isolation in the Arctic Circle. Finland leads the pack in mobile phone technology and its applications.
   b. Despite its small size and relative isolation in the Arctic Circle; Finland leads the pack in mobile phone technology and its applications.
   c. Despite its small size and relative isolation in the Arctic Circle, Finland leads the pack in mobile phone technology and its applications.

5. **a.** Many employees erroneously believe that their e-mail and voice mail messages are private they're surprised when e-mail ends up in places where they did not intend it to go.
   b. Many employees erroneously believe that their e-mail and voice mail messages are private, they're surprised when e-mail ends up in places where they did not intend it to go.
   c. Many employees erroneously believe that their e-mail and voice mail messages are private, so they're surprised when e-mail ends up in places where they did not intend it to go.

6. **a.** Each day people in the United States treat themselves to more than 3 million Krispy Kreme doughnuts, they buy more than 11 000 dozen of those doughnuts every hour.
   b. Each day people in the United States treat themselves to more than 3 million Krispy Kreme doughnuts, buying more than 11 000 dozen of those doughnuts every hour.

7. **a.** The procedure for making Krispy Kreme doughnuts takes about an hour, the manufacturing process begins long before local stores crank up their production lines.
   b. The procedure for making Krispy Kreme doughnuts takes about an hour; the manufacturing process begins long before local stores crank up their production lines.
   c. The procedure for making Krispy Kreme doughnuts takes about an hour. But the manufacturing process begins long before local stores crank up their production lines.

8. **a.** After blending the ingredients, the doughnut mix is stored in Krispy Kreme's warehouse for a week.
   b. After blending the ingredients, Krispy Kreme's warehouse is used to store the doughnut mix for a week.
   c. After the ingredients have been blended, the doughnut mix is stored in Krispy Kreme's warehouse for a week.

9. **a.** All the company's bikes are custom-made by Rocky Mountain Cycles to meet the rider's size and component preferences.
   b. All the company's bikes are custom-made to meet the rider's size and component preferences by Rocky Mountain Cycles.

10. **a.** Catering to its customers, about 2000 bikes are built annually by Rocky Mountain Cycles.
    b. Catering to its customers, about 2000 bikes are built by Rocky Mountain Cycles annually.
    c. Catering to its customers, Rocky Mountain Cycles builds about 2000 bikes annually.

Answers: 1. a 2. b 3. b 4. c 5. c 6. b 7. c 8. c 9. a 10. c

2.0 Punctuation

On the highway, signs tell you when to slow down or stop, where to turn, when to merge. In similar fashion, punctuation helps readers negotiate your prose. The proper use of punctuation keeps readers from losing track of your meaning.

2.1 Periods

Use a period (1) to end any sentence that is not a question, (2) with certain abbreviations, and (3) between dollars and cents in an amount of money.

2.2 Question Marks

Use a question mark after any direct question that requests an answer:

> Are you planning to enclose a cheque, or shall we bill you?

Don't use a question mark with commands phrased as questions for the sake of politeness:

> Will you send us a cheque today.

2.3 Exclamation Points

Use exclamation points after highly emotional language. Because business writing almost never calls for emotional language, you will seldom use exclamation points.

2.4 Semicolons

Semicolons have three main uses. One is to separate two closely related independent clauses:

> The outline for the report is due within a week; the report itself is due at the end of the month.

A semicolon should also be used instead of a comma when the items in a series have commas within them:

> Our previous meetings were on November 11, 1998; February 20, 1999; and April 28, 2000.

Finally, a semicolon should be used to separate independent clauses when the second one begins with a word such as *however, therefore,* or *nevertheless* or a phrase such as *for example* or *in that case:*

> Our supplier has been out of part D712 for 10 weeks; however, we have found another source that can ship the part right away.
>
> His test scores were quite low; on the other hand, he has a lot of relevant experience.

Section 4.4 has more information on using transitional words and phrases.

2.5 Colons

Use a colon after the salutation in a business letter. You also use a colon at the end of a sentence or phrase introducing a list or (sometimes) a quotation:

> Our study included the three most critical problems: insufficient capital, incompetent management, and inappropriate location.

In some introductory sentences, phrases such as *the following* or *that is* are implied by using a colon.

A colon should not be used when the list, quotation, or idea is a direct object or part of the introductory sentence:

> We are able to supply
> staples
> wood screws
> nails
> toggle bolts
>
> This shipment includes 9 videotapes, 12 CDs, and 14 cassette tapes.

Another way you can use a colon is to separate the main clause and another sentence element when the second explains, illustrates, or amplifies the first:

> Management was unprepared for the union representatives' demands: this fact alone accounts for their arguing well into the night.

However, in contemporary usage, such clauses are frequently separated by a semicolon.

Practice Session: Punctuation 1

Circle the letter of the preferred choice in the following groups of sentences.

1. **a.** She asked me whether we should increase our insurance coverage?
   b. She asked me whether we should increase our insurance coverage.

2. **a.** Would you please let me know when the copier is free.
   b. Would you please let me know when the copier is free?

3. **a.** You won't want to miss this exciting seminar!
   b. You won't want to miss this exciting seminar.

4. **a.** The officers of the board of directors are John Rogers, president, Robin Doug Donlan, vice-president for programming, Bill Pittman, vice-president for operations, and Mary Sturhann, secretary.
   b. The officers of the board of directors are John Rogers, president; Robin Doug Donlan, vice-president for programming; Bill Pittman, vice-president for operations; and Mary Sturhann, secretary.
   c. The officers of the board of directors are John Rogers, president; Robin Doug Donlan, vice-president for programming; Bill Pittman, vice-president for operations, and Mary Sturhann, secretary.

5. a. Cancorps is the best brokerage house in Canada; it's got more offices than any other brokerage house.
   b. Cancorps is the best brokerage house in Canada, it's got more offices than any other brokerage house.

6. a. One of the VSE's top priorities is to crack down on insider trading, however it readily admits that it has not been very successful to date.
   b. One of the VSE's top priorities is to crack down on insider trading; however, it readily admits that it has not been very successful to date.

7. a. To keep on top of financial news, you should consult newspapers aimed specifically at investors, such as *The Globe and Mail* and *Report on Business.*
   b. To keep on top of financial news, you should consult newspapers aimed specifically at investors; such as, *The Globe and Mail* and *Report on Business.*
   c. To keep on top of financial news, you should consult newspapers aimed specifically at investors; such as *The Globe and Mail* and *Report on Business.*

8. a. Dear Dr. Schatzman,
   b. Dear Dr. Schatzman:

9. a. The three basic concepts that guide accountants are: the fundamental accounting equation, double-entry bookkeeping, and the matching principle.
   b. The three basic concepts that guide accountants are the fundamental accounting equation, double-entry bookkeeping, and the matching principle.
   c. The three basic concepts that guide accountants are the fundamental accounting equation; double-entry bookkeeping; and the matching principle.

10. a. Accountants are guided by three basic concepts, the fundamental accounting equation, double-entry bookkeeping, and the matching principle.
    b. Accountants are guided by three basic concepts: the fundamental accounting equation; double-entry bookkeeping; and the matching principle.
    c. Accountants are guided by three basic concepts: the fundamental accounting equation, double-entry bookkeeping, and the matching principle.

Answers: 1. b 2. a 3. b 4. b 5. a 6. b 7. a 8. b 9. b 10. c

2.6 Commas

Commas have many uses; the most common is to separate items in a series:

> He took the job, learned it well, worked hard, and succeeded.
>
> Put paper, pencils, and paper clips on the requisition list.

Company style often dictates omitting the final comma in a series. However, if you have a choice, use the final comma; it's often necessary to prevent misunderstanding.

A second place to use a comma is between independent clauses that are joined by a coordinating conjunction (*and, but,* or *or*) unless one or both are very short:

> She spoke to the sales staff, and he spoke to the production staff.
>
> I was advised to proceed and I did.

A third use for the comma is to separate a dependent clause at the beginning of a sentence from an independent clause:

> Because of our lead in the market, we may be able to risk introducing a new product.

However, a dependent clause at the end of a sentence is separated from the independent clause by a comma only when the dependent clause is unnecessary to the main meaning of the sentence:

> We may be able to introduce a new product, although it may involve some risk.

A fourth use for the comma is after an introductory phrase or word:

> Starting with this amount of capital, we can survive in the red for one year.
>
> Through more careful planning, we may be able to serve more people.
>
> Yes, you may proceed as originally planned.

However, with short introductory prepositional phrases and some one-syllable words (such as *hence* and *thus*), the comma is often omitted:

> Before January 1 we must complete the inventory.
>
> Thus we may not need to hire anyone.
>
> In short the move to Winnipeg was a good idea.

Fifth, commas are used to surround nonrestrictive phrases or words (expressions that can be removed from the sentence without changing the meaning):

> The new owners, the Kowacks, are pleased with their purchase.

Sixth, commas are used between adjectives modifying the same noun (coordinate adjectives):

> She left Monday for a long, difficult recruiting trip.

To test the appropriateness of such a comma, try reversing the order of the adjectives: *a difficult, long recruiting trip.* If the order cannot be reversed, leave out the comma (*a good old friend* isn't the same as *an old good friend*). A comma is also not used when one of the adjectives is part of the noun. Compare these two phrases:

> a distinguished, well-known figure

a distinguished public figure

The adjective-noun combination of *public* and *figure* has been used together so often that it has come to be considered a single thing: *public figure.* So no comma is required.

Seventh, commas are used both before and after the year in sentences that include month, day, and year:

It will be sent by December 15, 2004, from our Windsor plant.

Some companies write dates in another form: 15 December 2004. No commas should be used in that case. Nor is a comma needed when only the month and year are present (December 2004).

Eighth, commas are used to set off a variety of parenthetical words and phrases within sentences, including province names, dates, abbreviations, transitional expressions, and contrasted elements:

They were, in fact, prepared to submit a bid.

Our best programmer is Ken, who joined the company just a month ago.

Habermacher, Inc., went public in 2002.

Our goal was increased profits, not increased market share.

Service, then, is our main concern.

The factory was completed in Fredericton, New Brunswick, just three weeks ago.

Joanne Dubiik, M.D., has applied for a loan from RBC.

I started work here on March 1, 2001, and soon received my first promotion.

Ninth, a comma is used to separate a quotation from the rest of the sentence:

Your warranty reads, "These conditions remain in effect for one year from date of purchase."

However, the comma is left out when the quotation as a whole is built into the structure of the sentence:

He hurried off with an angry "Look where you're going."

Finally, a comma should be used whenever it's needed to avoid confusion or an unintended meaning. Compare the following:

Ever since they have planned new ventures more carefully.

Ever since, they have planned new ventures more carefully.

2.7 Dashes

Use a dash to surround a comment that is a sudden turn in thought:

Membership in the ITVA—it's expensive but worth it—may be obtained by applying to our Vancouver office.

A dash can also be used to emphasize a parenthetical word or phrase:

Third-quarter profits—in excess of $2 million—are up sharply.

Finally, use dashes to set off a phrase that contains commas:

All our offices—Calgary, Mississauga, and Moncton—have sent representatives.

Don't confuse a dash with a hyphen. A dash separates and emphasizes words, phrases, and clauses more strongly than a comma or parentheses can; a hyphen ties two words so tightly that they almost become one word.

On computer, use the em dash symbol. When typing a dash in e-mail or on a typewriter, type two hyphens with no space before, between, or after.

2.8 Hyphens

Hyphens are mainly used in three ways. The first is to separate the parts of compound words beginning with such prefixes as *self-*, *ex-*, *quasi-*, and *all-:*

self-assured quasi-official
ex-wife all-important

However, omit hyphens from and close up those words that have prefixes such as *pro, anti, non, re, pre, un, inter,* and *extra:*

prolabour nonunion
antifascist interdepartmental

Exceptions occur when (1) the prefix occurs before a proper noun or (2) the vowel at the end of the prefix is the same as the first letter of the root word:

pro-Parti Québécois anti-American
anti-inflammatory extra-atmospheric

When in doubt, consult your dictionary.

Hyphens are also used in some compound adjectives, which are adjectives made up of two or more words. Specifically, you should use hyphens in compound adjectives that come before the noun:

an interest-bearing account well-informed executives

However, you need not hyphenate when the adjective follows a linking verb:

This account is interest bearing.

Their executives are well informed.

You can shorten sentences that list similar hyphenated words by dropping the common part from all but the last word:

> Check the costs of first-, second-, and third-class postage.

Finally, hyphens may be used to divide words at the end of a typed line. Such hyphenation is best avoided, but when you have to divide words at the end of a line, do so correctly (see Section 3.4). A dictionary will show how words are divided into syllables.

2.9 Apostrophes

Use an apostrophe in the possessive form of a noun (but not in a pronoun):

> On *his* desk was a reply to Bette *Ainsley's* application for the *manager's* position.

Apostrophes are also used in place of the missing letter(s) of a contraction:

Whole Words	Contraction
we will	we'll
do not	don't
they are	they're

2.10 Quotation Marks

Use quotation marks to surround words that are repeated exactly as they were said or written:

> The collection letter ended by saying, "This is your third and final notice."

Remember: (1) When the quoted material is a complete sentence, the first word is capitalized. (2) The final comma or period goes inside the closing quotation marks.

Quotation marks are also used to set off the title of a newspaper story, magazine article, or book chapter:

> You should read "Legal Aspects of the Collection Letter" in *Today's Credit.*

The book title is shown here in italics. When typewritten, the title is underlined. The same treatment is proper for newspaper and magazine titles. (Appendix B explains documentation style in more detail.)

Quotation marks may also be used to indicate special treatment for words or phrases, such as terms that you're using in an unusual or ironic way:

> Our management "team" spends more time squabbling than working to solve company problems.

When you are defining a word, put the definition in quotation marks:

> The abbreviation *etc.* means "and so forth."

When using quotation marks, take care to insert the closing marks as well as the opening ones.

Although periods and commas go inside any quotation marks, colons and semicolons go outside them. A question mark goes inside the quotation marks only if the quotation is a question:

> All that day we wondered, "Is he with us?"

If the quotation is not a question but the entire sentence is, the question mark goes outside:

> What did she mean by "You will hear from me"?

2.11 Parentheses

Use parentheses to surround comments that are entirely incidental:

> Our figures do not match yours, although (if my calculations are correct) they are closer than we thought.

Parentheses are also used in legal documents to surround figures in arabic numerals that follow the same amount in words:

> Remittance will be One Thousand Two Hundred Dollars ($1200).

Be careful to put punctuation (period, comma, and so on) outside the parentheses unless it is part of the statement in parentheses.

2.12 Ellipses

Use ellipsis points, or dots, to indicate that material has been left out of a direct quotation. Use them only in direct quotations and only at the point where material was left out. In the following example, the first sentence is quoted in the second:

> The Dow Jones Industrial Average, which skidded 38.17 points in the previous five sessions, gained 4.61 to end at 2213.84.
>
> According to the Montreal *Gazette,* "The Dow Jones Industrial Average . . . gained 4.61" on June 10.

The number of dots in ellipses is not optional; always use three. Occasionally, the points of ellipsis come at the end of a sentence, where they seem to grow a fourth dot. Don't be fooled: One of the dots is a period.

2.13 Underscores and Italics

Usually a line typed underneath a word or phrase either provides emphasis or indicates the title of a book, magazine, or newspaper. If possible, use italics instead of an underscore. Italics (or underlining) should also be used for defining terms and for discussing words as words:

> In this report *net sales* refers to after-tax sales dollars.

The word *building* is a common noun and should not be capitalized.

Practice Session: Punctuation 2

Circle the letter of the preferred choice in each group of sentences.

1. **a.** Capital One uses data mining to predict what customers might buy, and how the company can sell those products to them.
   b. Capital One uses data mining to predict what customers might buy and how the company can sell those products to them.

2. **a.** During the three-year lawsuit, pressure built to settle out of court.
   b. During the three-year lawsuit pressure built to settle out of court.

3. **a.** The music store, which had been in the Harper family for three generations, was finally sold to a conglomerate.
   b. The music store which had been in the Harper family for three generations was finally sold to a conglomerate.

4. **a.** After the fire, Hanson resolved to build a bigger better bottling plant.
   b. After the fire, Hanson resolved to build a bigger, better bottling plant.

5. **a.** Wild Oats, a chain of natural food grocery stores, uses kiosks to deliver nutrition information to customers.
   b. Wild Oats; a chain of natural food grocery stores; uses kiosks to deliver nutrition information to customers.

6. **a.** Management consultant Peter Drucker said "The aim of marketing is to know the customer so well that the product or service sells itself.
   b. Management consultant Peter Drucker said, "The aim of marketing is to know the customer so well that the product or service sells itself."

7. **a.** Companies use a wide variety of techniques - contests, displays, and giveaways, to name a few - to sell you things.
   b. Companies use a wide variety of techniques—contests, displays, and giveaways, to name a few—to sell you things.
   c. Companies use a wide variety of techniques—contests, displays, and giveaways to name a few—to sell you things.

8. **a.** Self-insurance plans are not subject to provincial regulation or premium taxes.
   b. Self insurance plans are not subject to provincial regulation or premium taxes.
   c. Selfinsurance plans are not subject to provincial regulation or premium taxes.

9. **a.** Because ours is a non-profit corporation, we don't pay federal taxes.
   b. Because ours is a nonprofit corporation, we don't pay federal taxes.

10. **a.** The decision-making process depends on a buyer's culture, social class, and self-image.
    b. The decision-making process depends on a buyer's culture, social class, and self image.
    c. The decision making process depends on a buyer's culture, social class, and self-image.

11. **a.** Situation factors also play a role in consumer decision-making.
    b. Situation factors also play a role in consumer decision making.

12. **a.** Joel told me, "I can't stop humming this song in my head, 'There's a Moon Out Tonight."
    b. Joel told me, "I can't stop humming this song in my head, 'There's a Moon Out Tonight'."
    c. Joel told me, "I can't stop humming this song in my head, 'There's a Moon Out Tonight.'"

13. **a.** An insider at Arthur Andersen said that "the fall of the accounting giant stemmed from a series of poor management decisions made over decades.""
    b. An insider at Arthur Andersen said that, "The fall of the accounting giant stemmed from a series of poor management decisions made over decades.""

14. **a.** Have you read Jason Zein's article "Measuring the Internet?"
    b. Have you read Jason Zein's article "Measuring the Internet"?

15. **a.** According to Jamba Juice founder Kirk Peron, "jamba" is a West African word meaning *to celebrate.*
    b. According to Jamba Juice founder Kirk Peron, *jamba* is a West African word meaning "to celebrate."
    c. According to Jamba Juice founder Kirk Peron, "jamba" is a West African word meaning to celebrate.

Answers: 1. b 2. a 3. a 4. b 5. a 6. b 7. b 8. a 9. b 10. a 11. b 12. c 13. a 14. b 15. b

3.0 Mechanics

The most obvious and least tolerable mistakes that a business writer makes are probably those related to grammar and punctuation. However, a number of small details, known as writing mechanics, demonstrate the writer's polish and reflect on the company's professionalism.

3.1 Capitals

Capitals are used at the beginning of certain word groups:

- **Complete sentence:**
  Before hanging up, he said, "*We'll* meet here on Wednesday at noon."

- **Formal statement following a colon:**
  She has a favourite motto: Where there's a will, there's a way.
  (Otherwise, the first word after a colon should not be capitalized—see Section 2.5.)
- **Phrase used as sentence:**
  Absolutely not!
- **Quoted sentence embedded in another sentence:**
  Scot said, "Nobody was here during lunch hour except me."
- **List of items set off from text:**
  Three preliminary steps are involved:
  Design review
  Budgeting
  Scheduling

Capitalize proper adjectives and proper nouns (the names of particular persons, places, and things):

George Bowering lived in a Victorian mansion.

We sent Ms. Larson an application form, informing her that not all applicants are interviewed.

Let's consider opening a branch in the West, perhaps at the west end of Calgary, Alberta.

As office buildings go, the Kinney Building is a pleasant setting for TDG Office Equipment.

Ms. Larson's name is capitalized because she is a particular applicant, whereas the general term *applicant* is left uncapitalized. Likewise, *West* is capitalized when it refers to a particular place but not when it means a direction. In the same way, *office* and *building* are not capitalized when they are general terms (common nouns), but they are capitalized when they are part of the title of a particular office or building (proper nouns).

Titles within families, governments, or companies may also be capitalized:

I turned down Uncle David when he offered me a job, since I wouldn't be comfortable working for one of my relatives.

We've never had a president quite like President Sweeney.

People's titles are capitalized when they are used in addressing a person, especially in a formal context. They are not usually capitalized, however, when they are used merely to identify the person:

Address the letter to Chairperson Anna Palmer.

I wish to thank Chairperson Anna Palmer for her assistance.

Please deliver these documents to board chairperson Anna Palmer.

Anna Palmer, chairperson of the board, took the podium.

Also capitalize titles if they are used by themselves in addressing a person:

Thank you, Doctor, for your donation.

Titles used to identify a person of very high rank are capitalized regardless of where they fall or how much of the name is included:

the Prime Minister of Canada

the Pope

In addresses, salutations, signature blocks, and some formal writing (such as acknowledgements), all titles are capitalized whether they come before or after the name. In addition, always capitalize the first word of the salutation and complimentary close of a letter:

Dear Mr. Andrews: *Yours* very truly,

The names of organizations are capitalized, of course; so are the official names of their departments and divisions. However, do not use capitals when referring in general terms to a department or division, especially one in another organization:

Route this memo to Personnel.

Larry Tien was transferred to the Microchip Division

Will you be enrolled in the Psychology Department?

Someone from the engineering department at EnerTech stopped by the booth.

Our production department has reorganized for efficiency.

Send a copy to their school of business administration.

Capitalization is unnecessary when using a word like *company, corporation,* or *university* alone:

The corporation plans to issue 50 000 shares of common stock.

Likewise, the names of specific products are capitalized, although the names of general product types are not:

Compaq computer   Tide laundry detergent

One problem that often arises in writing about places is the treatment of two or more proper nouns of the same type. When the common word comes before the specific names, it is capitalized; when it comes after the specific names, it is not:

Lakes Ontario and Huron

Bow and Assinaboine rivers

The names of languages, races, and ethnic groups are capitalized: *Japanese, Caucasian, Chinese.* But racial terms that denote only skin colour are not capitalized: *black, white.*

When referring to the titles of books, articles, magazines, newspapers, reports, movies, and so on, you should capitalize the first and last words and all nouns, pronouns, adjectives, verbs, adverbs, and prepositions and conjunctions with five letters or more. Except for the first and last words, do not capitalize articles:

Economics During the Great War

"An Investigation into the Market for Long-Distance Services"

"What Successes Are Made Of"

When *the* is part of the official name of a newspaper or magazine, it should be treated this way too: *The Globe and Mail.*

References to specific pages, paragraphs, lines, and the like are not capitalized: *page 73, line 3.* However, in most other numbered or lettered references, the identifying term is capitalized: *Chapter 4, Serial No. 382-2203, Item B-11.*

Finally, the names of academic degrees are capitalized when they follow a person's name but are not capitalized when used in a general sense:

I received a bachelor of science degree.

Thomas Whitelaw, Doctor of Philosophy, will attend.

Similarly, general courses of study are not capitalized, but the names of specific classes are:

She studied accounting as an undergraduate.

She is enrolled in Accounting 201.

3.2 Abbreviations

Abbreviations are used heavily in tables, charts, lists, and forms. They're used sparingly in prose paragraphs, however. Here are some abbreviations often used in business writing:

Abbreviation	Full Term
b/l	bill of lading
ca.	circa (about)
dol., dols.	dollar, dollars
etc.	et cetera (and so on)
Inc.	Incorporated
L.f.	Ledger folio
Ltd.	Limited
mgr.	manager
NSF or N/S	not sufficient funds
P&L or P/L	profit and loss
reg.	regular
whsle.	wholesale

One way to handle an abbreviation that you want to use throughout a document is to spell it out the first time you use it, follow it with the abbreviation in parentheses, and then use the abbreviation in the remainder of the document.

Because *etc.* contains a word meaning "and," never write *and etc.* In fact, try to limit your use of such abbreviations to tables and parenthetical material.

3.3 Numbers

Numbers may be correctly handled many ways in business writing, so follow company style. In the absence of a set style, however, generally spell out all numbers from one to nine and use arabic numerals for the rest.

There are some exceptions to this general rule. For example, never begin a sentence with a numeral:

Twenty of us produced *641* units per week in the first *12* weeks of the year.

Use numerals for the numbers one through ten if they're in the same list as larger numbers:

Our weekly quota rose from *9* to *15* to *27.*

Use numerals for percentages, time of day (except with *o'clock*), dates, and (in general) dollar amounts.

Our division is responsible for *7* percent of total sales.

The meeting is scheduled for *8:30* A.M. on August *2.*

Add *$3* for postage and handling.

Use a space in numbers expressing thousands (*12 257*), unless your company specifies another style. In four-digit numbers the space is optional (1257). Use a comma in the accounting profession. When dealing with numbers in the millions and billions, combine words and figures: *7.3 million, 2 billion.*

When writing dollar amounts, use a decimal point only if cents are included. In lists of two or more dollar amounts, use the decimal point either for all or for none:

He sent two cheques, one for *$67.92* and one for *$90.00.*

When two numbers fall next to each other in a sentence, use figures for the number that is largest, most difficult to spell, or part of a physical measurement; use words for the other:

I have learned to manage a classroom of 30 twelve-year-olds.

She's won a bonus for selling 24 thirty-volume sets.

You'll need twenty 3-cm bolts.

In addresses, all street numbers except *One* are in figures. So are suite and room numbers and postal codes. For street names that are numbered, practice varies so widely that you should use the form specified on an organization's letterhead or in a reliable directory. All of the following examples are correct:

One Fifth Avenue	297 Ninth Street
1839 44th Street	11026 West 78 Place

Telephone numbers are always expressed in figures. Parentheses may separate the area code from the rest of the number, but a slash or a dash may be used instead, especially if the entire phone number is enclosed in parentheses:

382-8329 (602/382-8329) (602) 382-8329

Percentages are always expressed in figures. The word *percent* is used in most cases, but % may be used in tables, forms, and statistical writing.

Physical measurements such as distance, weight, and volume are also often expressed in figures: *9 km, 8.25 m, 4.7 kg.*

Ages are usually expressed in words—except when a parenthetical reference to age follows someone's name:

Mrs. Margaret Sanderson is seventy-two.

Mrs. Margaret Sanderson, 72, swims daily.

Also, ages expressed in years and months are treated like physical measurements that combine two units of measure: *5 years 6 months.*

Decimal numbers are always written in figures. In most cases, add a zero to the left of the decimal point if the number is less than one and does not already start with a zero:

1.38 .07 0.2

In a series of related decimal numbers with at least one number greater than one, make sure that all numbers smaller than one have a zero to the left of the decimal point: *1.20, 0.21, 0.09.* Also, express all decimal numbers in a series to the same number of places by adding zeroes at the end:

The responses were Yes, 37.2 percent; No, 51.0; Not Sure, 11.8.

Simple fractions are written in words, but more complicated fractions are expressed in figures or, if easier to read, in figures and words:

two-thirds 9/32 2 hundredths

A combination of whole numbers and a fraction should always be written in figures. Note that a hyphen is used to separate the fraction from the whole number when a slash is used for the fraction: *2-11/16.*

3.4 Word Division

In general, avoid dividing words at the ends of lines. When you must do so, follow these rules:

- Don't divide one-syllable words (such as *since, walked,* and *thought*); abbreviations (*mgr.*); contractions (*isn't*); or numbers expressed in numerals (*117 500*).
- Divide words between syllables, as specified in a dictionary or word-division manual.
- Make sure that at least three letters of the divided word are moved to the second line: *sin-cerely* instead of *sincere-ly.*
- Do not end a page or more than three consecutive lines with hyphens.
- Leave syllables consisting of a single vowel at the end of the first line (*impedi-ment* instead of *imped-iment*), except when the single vowel is part of a suffix such as *-able, -ible, -ical,* or *-ity* (*re-spons-ible* instead of *re-sponsi-ble*).
- Divide between double letters (*tomor-row*), except when the root word ends in double letters (*call-ing* instead of *cal-ling*).
- Wherever possible, divide hyphenated words at the hyphen only: instead of *anti-inde-pendence,* use *anti-independence.*

Practice Session: Mechanics

Circle the letter of the preferred choice in each of the following groups of sentences.

1. **a.** When you are in Vancouver for the sales meeting, be sure to visit the art deco Marine Building.
   b. When you are in Vancouver for the sales meeting, be sure to visit the Art Deco Marine building.
   c. When you are in Vancouver for the sales meeting, be sure to visit the Art Deco Marine Building.

2. **a.** We plan to expand our national operations to the west, as well as the east.
   b. We plan to expand our national operations to the West, as well as the East.
   c. We plan to expand our national operations to the west, as well as the East.

3. **a.** Lee Marrs, who is President of Lee Marrs Designs, has been chosen to revamp our Web site.
   b. Lee Marrs, who is president of Lee Marrs Designs, has been chosen to revamp our Web site.
   c. Lee Marrs, who is President of Lee Marrs Designs, has been chosen to revamp our Web site.

4. **a.** There's one thing we know for sure: Having a good idea doesn't guarantee success.
   b. There's one thing we know for sure: having a good idea doesn't guarantee success.

5. **a.** Be sure to order manila envelopes in all sizes: 9″ × 12″, 11″, 14″, etc.
   b. Be sure to order manila envelopes in all sizes: 9″ × 12″, 11″, 14″ and etc.

6. **a.** The traditional trading period for Canadian stock exchanges is 9:30 A.M. to 4 o'clock P.M.
   b. The traditional trading period for Canadian stock exchanges is 9:30 A.M. to 4 P.M.
   c. The traditional trading period for Canadian stock exchanges is 9:30 A.M. to 4:00 P.M.

7. **a.** The number of members on the board of directors has been reduced from 13 to nine.
   b. The number of members on the board of directors has been reduced from 13 to 9.

8. **a.** The CDs are priced at $15, $12.95, and $11.00.
   b. The CDs are priced at $15.00, $12.95, and $11.00.